Belongs
to ...
Kaya♡

PRACTICAL COOKERY

FOR LEVEL 2 NVQS AND APPRENTICESHIPS

13TH EDITION

DAVID FOSKETT

NEIL RIPPINGTON

PATRICIA PASKINS

STEVE THORPE

Orders: please contact Bookpoint Ltd, 130 Milton Park, Abingdon, Oxon OX14 4SB. Telephone: (44) 01235 827720. Fax: (44) 01235 400454. Lines are open from 9 a.m. to 5 p.m., Monday to Saturday, with a 24-hour message answering service. You can also order through our website: www.hoddereducation.co.uk

If you have any comments to make about this, or any of our other titles, please send them to educationenquiries@hodder.co.uk

British Library Cataloguing in Publication Data

A catalogue record for this title is available from the British Library

ISBN: 978 1 471 83957 3

ISBN (HELPE): 978 1 471 83958 0

First published 1962
Second edition 1967
Third edition 1972
Fourth edition 1974
Fifth edition 1981
Sixth edition 1987
Seventh edition 1990
Eighth edition 1995
Ninth edition 2000
Tenth edition 2004
Eleventh edition 2008
Twelfth edition 2012
This edition published 2015.

Impression number   10 9 8 7 6 5 4 3 2 1

Year   2015, 2016, 2017, 2018

Hachette UK's policy is to use papers that are natural, renewable and recyclable products and made from wood grown in sustainable forests. The logging and manufacturing processes are expected to conform to the environmental regulations of the country of origin.

Typeset by DC Graphic Design Limited, Swanley Village, Kent.

Printed in India for Hodder Education, an Hachette UK Company, 338 Euston Road, London NW1 3BH.

Contents

Accessing the videos

There are free videos on the website. Look out for the QR codes throughout the book.

To view the videos, you will need a QR code reader for your smartphone/tablet. There are many free readers available, depending on the smartphone/tablet you are using.

Once you have downloaded a QR code reader, simply open the reader app and use it to take a photo of the code. The file will then load on your smartphone/tablet.

If you cannot read the QR code or you are using a computer, the web link next to the code will take you directly to the same place.

How to use this book

At the start of each chapter is a list telling you which NVQ units are covered in the chapter. Each chapter includes some underpinning knowledge and theory.

If the chapter topic is a food commodity, there is also a list of the recipes on the first page of the chapter. There is also a complete index of recipes at the back of the book.

Test yourself questions in each chapter help you to test your knowledge and prepare for short-answer and multiple-choice tests.

Refer to the 'Preparing for assessment' section on page viii for more guidance on assessment and how this book can help you to prepare.

In the recipes, the main methods of cookery are shown by icons. So if you want to practise shallow frying for example, look for the relevant icon. They look like this:

Baking   Boiling   Stewing

Deep frying   Shallow frying

Grilling   Poaching   Roasting

Steaming   Braising

Recipes also include the following features:

- **Ingredients lists** are provided for making smaller and larger quantities.
- **Nutritional data** is included for most recipes to help you make informed choices about what to cook and eat.
- **Professional tips** help you to understand the dish and produce it successfully.
- **Healthy eating tips** provide suggestions on how recipes can be adapted to make them healthier.
- **Variation boxes** suggest alternative ingredients, cooking methods or presentation, finishing and serving styles that could be used.

Foreword

I'm delighted to be asked to write this foreword to the thirteenth edition of *Practical Cookery*. There's no doubt that training to be a professional chef takes hard work and dedication, but for me nothing beats working with food – experimenting, exploring new techniques and discovering new flavours. I've spent years cooking the same dishes over and over, perfecting the techniques and seeking out the best ways to harness flavour. *Practical Cookery* will help you as you embark on this process: it provides you with all of the classic recipes, as well the basic skills, techniques and knowledge you'll need when working in the professional kitchen. It will be a point of reference for you to return to time and again throughout your career as you hone your skills.

My approach has also been to question and test culinary ideas, and to combine this with more traditional kitchen skills. While learning the foundations is important, so too is a natural curiosity and a desire to learn about every aspect of gastronomy, including exploring the latest principles and techniques. It is this combination of the traditional with the modern that is at the heart of the *Practical Cookery* approach.

I wish you every success with your course, and with your career in the professional kitchen.

Heston Blumenthal

Preparing for assessment

Chefs are assessed regularly in many different ways: each meal that is served is evaluated by the customer, who will consider many things about their meal experience and often provide feedback.

To continue to develop skills and knowledge, a programme of training and development should be set up to meet the requirements of the individual as well as to support the organisation in which they work; this can be scheduled for both 'on the job' and/or 'off the job'.

On-the-job training

On-the-job training is development that takes place within the normal workplace and covers things like an induction phase, health and safety information about the use of equipment, or skills development to enable chefs to produce dishes on the menu. It could include a short time shadowing or working alongside another chef to learn a skill.

Off-the-job training

Off-the-job training is a development programme of training, which could be a single day, one day a week for a period of time, or even block release. This type of training may lead to a recognised qualification or certificate of completion. Examples of off-the-job programmes include:

- Food hygiene or health and safety qualifications
- Certificate in the Principles for Catering
- Qualifications in maths and English
- Work experience or placement within a different kitchen.

This book has been designed to support chefs working in a range of professional cookery training and development programmes, but is specifically designed for those completing the Level 2 NVQ Diploma in Food Production and Cooking or the Level 2 NVQ Diploma in Professional Cookery, and those working towards Intermediate Level Apprenticeships.

Apprenticeships

The apprenticeship programme is a prestigious learning and development programme, valued by employers, trade associations and professional bodies in the industry. Intermediate Level Apprentices will train as Kitchen Assistants, Cooks and Chefs in large-volume, fine or casual dining settings or in a range of cuisines, including Craft, Asian and Oriental cuisine. Advanced Level Apprentices will train as Sous/Senior Chefs, working in fine or casual dining settings, as Pastry Chefs or as Sous/Senior Chefs in Craft Cuisine.

Defining apprenticeships

An apprenticeship:
- is a job in a skilled occupation
- requires substantial and sustained training, lasting a minimum of 12 months (with no exemption for prior learning) and should include at least 20 per cent off-the-job training (with the expectation that this will be delivered away from the workplace)
- leads to full competency in a role, which achieving an employer-defined apprenticeship standard will demonstrate
- develops transferable skills, including English and maths, to progress careers (with the intention for apprentices to work towards at least Level 2 standard).

Initial assessment

Prior to starting an apprenticeship it is normal to complete an initial assessment to identify the following:

- Specific training needs, support or guidance that may be required while working towards final qualification and recognition of the apprenticeship.
- Any prior recognised qualifications that may be relevant to the apprenticeship, including English and maths (for example, GCSEs completed at school or college, although these only remain valid for five years).

Training and development

For apprentices, training takes place at various times and is measured through regular reviews and discussions, which may cover a number of different tasks and assessments. These are set by the awarding organisation and the training provider offering the programme, and may involve some of the methods of assessment and testing described below.

Knowledge assessment (knowledge and understanding – 'do you know it')

Knowledge assessment involves the completion of set exercises, through written or oral questioning, that enable the candidate to show their individual understanding of a given subject area. Subjects may include the current legislation about providing food for sale, the techniques and methods used to produce dishes to meet customer requirements, product knowledge and an understanding of traditional and contemporary cooking methods, linked to the subject specifications.

Skills assessment for competency ('can you show it')

Skills assessment involves a set of practical tasks that cover all areas of the qualification; these normally cover complete dishes that may be on the menu at the time. Assessors or mentors use this process to evaluate the apprentice's progress and the assessments are part of a development programme for individual chefs. These could also be set in the workplace to cover the introduction of new dishes onto the menu to ensure that all in the team can produce to the required specification for continuity.

Skills test (basket of goods) (behaviours – 'do you live it')

As part of employment and application processes, many employers use skills assessment. This could be a simple stage in the kitchen or a complete mystery basket test. The test assesses practical skills as well as working practices and behaviours prior to offering employment to an individual.

There are also other times which could be considered as an assessment opportunity or a review of knowledge and skills of a chef, such as completing a college course or entering a competition.

Qualifications that provide evidence of training and development

Throughout your apprenticeship you will be given the opportunity to develop wider craft and transferable skills that will enhance your knowledge and understanding of the sector and your role within it. This will be assessed and confirmed through a number of achievements and supporting evidence leading to the following qualifications prior to confirmation of your apprenticeship:

- Level 2 Certificate in Hospitality and Catering Principles (Professional Cookery)
- Level 2 NVQ Diploma in Professional Cookery
- GCSE Maths and English at grade C or Functional Skills at Level 1.

As part of Government reforms, new apprenticeship standards for relevant occupations within the industry are in the process of being developed. The focus will shift from a number of different inputs (qualifications) to an outcome-based approach that needs to be achieved for someone to complete an apprenticeship through a training and development programme lasting around 12 to 24 months. The proposed future model is that two-thirds of the assessment will be delivered as an end test or assessment. These will be completed by a separate organisation, not the employer or provider who delivers the training, who will manage the process. This section will be updated accordingly when the new standards come into force.

How you can prepare for assessment

Regardless of the programme you are completing, prior planning and preparation is most important to enable you to achieve the maximum from any assessment. You cannot beat the feeling of receiving the highest mark possible or gaining praise from a customer. To do that you will have to work in a methodical manner, be prepared to practise and listen to feedback, as well as personally reflecting on what you have completed.

1 Read the instructions or brief that is given to you; make sure you understand what you have to do. This includes the criteria you will judged or assessed on, which could include use of equipment, professional standards, use of materials, skills and techniques to be covered, time allowed, and any preparations that can be completed before the test starts.

2 Carry out any research, find or develop your recipes and consider which ingredients and skills you will need to include within the test.

3 Prepare and plan your time; this could include some practice time for competitions, as well as a time plan for the actual assessment. This plan isn't only for the day itself but includes how you may prepare before the test date.

4 Prepare a list of equipment you will require to complete the task; make sure you have what you need. It may be helpful to check whether there is time to set out your work station before the assessment takes place.

On the day of assessment you should arrive at the assessment centre in plenty of time.

Use this book to help develop your knowledge and experience.

Professional practice

'Professional practice' covers what you do while producing your dishes. Whether for a practical test or an assessment, the mentors or assessors will be looking at how you conduct yourself in the kitchen area. Things to consider:

● Personal hygiene and turnout – this includes your dress. Make sure your whites are clean and pressed. Personal hygiene standards cover things like jewellery, hair and nails. Make sure that you are seen washing your hands as required.

● Correct craft skills – these should be appropriate for the dish. You will be assessed on your knife skills, the ease of the technique used and the consistency of skills shown.

● Correct use of equipment – use the correct tools or equipment safely and correctly to complete tasks. This will include the use of pans and could include energy. Do you really need to have the grill on 120 minutes before you glaze a fish dish?

● Work methods – ensure you work in a logical and organised manner, using appropriate time and temperature controls for food items. 'Clean as You Go' is the mantra used across kitchens. Be aware of cross-contamination threats to your dishes.

Culinary practice and finished dishes

'Culinary practice' covers the selection of ingredients, choice of cooking methods and techniques, and application of knowledge and skills to an appropriate level for the assessment. The checking of the finished dish will cover presentation, portioning, flavour, texture, seasoning and of course cooking. Things to consider:

● Use of food items – have you selected ingredients that balance in terms of texture, colour and flavours within the overall dish? In some settings, you may also be asked to consider seasonality as part of the assessment.

● Techniques or skills – preparation of ingredients should be completed in a logical sequence and with an understanding and awareness of portion sizes or waste from trimming and peeling.

● Cooking methods – the correct use of these for the dish requirements and ingredients will be assessed. You will need to consider the use of time and temperature to ensure that dishes are cooked correctly and ready for the target service time.

● Monitoring cooking process – this includes tasting and evaluating elements of the dish prior to finishing; this will cover consistency and will enable you to correct the balance of the dish through the process.

● Presentation – the final stage of any practical assessment is how the dish is finished to present to the potential customer; this is an opportunity to show final flair and creativity as a chef, and includes how you garnish and finish the dish. Make sure you don't allow the food to go cold while trying to get it on the plate.

Acknowledgements

Photography

Most of the photos in this book are by Andrew Callaghan of Callaghan Studios. The photography work could not have been completed without the generous help of the authors and their colleagues and students at the University of West London (UWL) and University College Birmingham (UCB). The publishers would particularly like to acknowledge the following for their work.

Gary Farrelly and Ketharanathan Vasanthan organised the cookery at UWL. They were assisted in the kitchen by:

- Josephine Barone
- Khloe Best
- Jonathon Bowers
- Livio Capillera
- James Cher
- Tia-Louise Hudson Halsey
- Freya Massingham
- Violeta Saninta
- Grimaldy Cassidy Dos Santos
- Rachel Shelly
- Amilda Venancio.

Neil Rippington organised the photography at UCB. He was assisted in the kitchen by Richard Taylor.

The authors and publishers are grateful to everyone involved for their hard work.

We are also very grateful to Watts Farms for providing much of the fruit and vegetables shown in the photographs. Watts Farms is a family-run fresh produce business specialising in the growing, packing and supply of a wide range of seasonal produce from spinach, baby leaf salads, herbs and legumes to fruit, chillies, asparagus, brassicas and specialist interest crops.

Picture credits

Every effort has been made to trace the copyright holders of material reproduced here. The authors and publishers would like to thank the following for permission to reproduce copyright illustrations:

Page vii courtesy of Heston Blumenthal; page 12 © Getty Images/iStockphoto/Thinkstock; page 13 © Bananastock/Photolibrary Group Ltd/Getty Images; pages 32, 33 and 42 Russums; page 121 (bottom) © woyzzeck – Fotolia; page 137 top left © Constantinos – Fotolia, top middle © Denisa V – Fotolia, top right © spinetta – Fotolia; page 219 (top and middle), 220 (bottom), 223 (top left and right) and 227 (top) © EBLEX; page 229 and 231 (right) © BPEX; page 233 © EBLEX; page 246 (bottom) and 316 (top) © Sarah Bailey/Hodder Education; page 348 Potato Council; page 564 Crown copyright; page 573 © Food and Drink/REX Features.

The photos on pages 60, 65, 110 (bottom), 128–131, 159, 155, 162 (bottom), 164, 172, 176 (top), 205, 209, 220 (top), 227 (bottom), 256 (top), 274 (top), 302, 314, 318, 324 (bottom), 328, 343, 368, 375 (top), 387 (top), 392, 407 (bottom), 427 (top), 468 (bottom), 474, 518, 566 (bottom), 589, 590, 602, 609 and 618 (top) are © Sam Bailey/Hodder Education.

Except where stated above, photographs are by Andrew Callaghan.

Nutritional analysis

New nutritional analysis for this book was carried out by Annemarie Aburrow (Expert Dietitian – Nutrition & Dietetic Consultancy) and Jane Krause (JK Health & Nutrition).

Some of the nutritional analysis was created for earlier editions by Joanne Tucker (University of West London), Jenny Arthur, Dr Jenny Poulter, Jane Cliff and Pat Bacon.

Conversion tables

In this book, metric weights and measures are used. All temperatures are given in degrees Celsius.

Weights and measures

Imperial	Approximate metric equivalent
¼ oz	5 g
½ oz	10 g
1 oz	25 g
2 oz	50 g
3 oz	75 g
4 oz	100 g
5 oz	125 g
6 oz	150 g
7 oz	175 g
8 oz	200 g
9 oz	225 g
10 oz	250 g
11 oz	275 g
12 oz	300 g
13 oz	325 g
14 oz	350 g
15 oz	375 g
16 oz	400 g
2 lb	1 kg
¼ pt	125 ml
½ pt	250 ml
¾ pt	375 ml
1 pt	500 ml
1½ pt	750 ml
2 pt (1 qt)	1 litre
2 qt	2 litres
1 gal	4.5 litres
¼ in	0.5 cm
½ in	1 cm
1 in	2 cm
1½ in	4 cm
2 in	5 cm

Imperial	Approximate metric equivalent
2½ in	6 cm
3 in	8 cm
4 in	10 cm
5 in	12 cm
6 in	15 cm
6½ in	16 cm
7 in	18 cm
12 in	30 cm
18 in	45 cm

Spoons and cups

1 teaspoon (tsp)	5 ml
1 dessertspoon (dsp)	10 ml
1 tablespoon (tbsp)	15 ml
¼ cup	60 ml
⅓ cup	80 ml
½ cup	125 ml
1 cup	250 ml

Oven temperatures

	°C	Gas regulo	°F
slow (cool)	110	¼	225
	130	½	250
	140	1	275
	150	2	300
	160	3	325
moderate	180	4	350
	190	5	375
	200	6	400
hot	220	7	425
	230	8	450
very hot	250	9	475

This chapter is relevant to the following units:
→ Maintain a safe, hygienic and secure working environment.

Every day people are injured at work; some of the injuries may be serious, disabling or even fatal. It is therefore important to always work professionally in a healthy, safe and hygienic way. Safety awareness will help to keep yourself and others that work with you safe. It is also very important to provide a safe environment for customers and visitors.

You must always follow the health and safety procedures that your employer has put in place when you are working; you should not interfere with safety equipment and you must report anything you consider to be a possible hazard.

Personal health and hygiene

All humans are a potential source of food contamination and everyone working with food must be aware of the importance of high standards of appearance and personal hygiene. As well as the important role this plays in avoiding food contamination, it will reflect the professionalism of the individual as well as the establishment they work for, giving a positive impression to customers and guests.

Details on maintaining personal cleanliness, health and hygiene can be found on page 19 in Chapter 3 Maintain food safety. It covers the importance of maintaining good personal hygiene including: wearing smart and appropriate clothing, footwear and head coverings; keeping hair neat and tidy; rules concerning jewellery and cosmetics; and dealing with cuts, grazes, burns and other wounds. Information is also included on the importance of reporting any illness or infections to the appropriate person before you go near any food – this is a legal requirement.

Personal protective equipment (PPE)

Protective clothing is worn to protect food from contamination by food handlers and to protect the wearer from such things as excessive heat, burns and sharp objects.

According to the Personal Protective Equipment (PPE) at Work Regulations, 1992, employees must wear personal protective clothing/equipment suitable for the work they are involved in. For example, chefs wear protective chef's whites, but may add gauntlet gloves and eye goggles if cleaning an oven. See page 19 for more on protective clothing.

A hygienic, safe and secure workplace

Responsibilities under the Health and Safety at Work Act

The **Health and Safety Executive** (HSE) is responsible for enforcing health and safety in the workplace. It has the power to investigate premises; check, dismantle and remove equipment; inspect the records; ask questions; and seize and destroy articles. The HSE can give verbal or written advice, order improvement and issue prohibition notices, and will prosecute, if necessary, which can result in unlimited fines or even imprisonment.

Everyone working in a kitchen needs to know the laws on health and safety, and how they are affected by these laws. The **Health and Safety at Work Act 1974** gives employees and employers certain responsibilities that they must adhere to within their working environment:
- All employees and employers must take reasonable care of their own safety and the safety of others they work with.
- Employees must inform their line manager/supervisor if they see anything they think is unsafe and could cause an accident.
- Any procedure, equipment or protective clothing put in place for safety must be used correctly and never be modified or tampered with.
- Employees must co-operate with their employer on health and safety matters and procedures put in place to keep the working environment safe.

Employers must also ensure that all staff are safe at work and not put staff in dangerous situations where they could injure themselves or others. They must provide safe methods of work for their employees. This includes:

- producing a workplace policy document on health and safety
- completing risk assessments for all equipment and procedures in the workplace
- providing safe equipment and utensils
- training and supervising staff in safe practices
- providing first-aid equipment
- keeping an accurate record of all accidents.

The **Health and Safety Information for Employees Regulations (1989)** also require that employers provide health and safety information for their employees. This could be in the form of leaflets, posters, DVDs and information packs. A selection of these is available from the HSE.

Finding information about health and safety

Information relating to health and safety in your workplace can be obtained in a number of ways. It can be available through:

- induction training, staff training, staff handover and briefing sessions
- posters, booklets, leaflets and signs around the workplace
- line managers, head chefs and supervisors
- health and safety representatives and managers, and human resources departments.

Hazards in the workplace

There can be a number of inherent hazards when working in kitchen areas. For this reason, it is important to work in a safe and systematic way in order to avoid accidents or injury to yourself or anyone else.

The following are some common causes of accidents in the kitchen:

- slipping on a wet or greasy floor
- tripping over objects or walking into objects
- lifting objects wrongly or lifting loads that are too heavy
- being exposed to hazards such as hot or dangerous substances, for example steam or oven-cleaning chemicals
- being hit or hurt by moving objects, such as being cut by a knife when chopping
- injury from machines such as vegetable-cutting machines, liquidisers and mincing machines

- fires and explosions
- electric shocks
- not wearing suitable protective clothing or not wearing it properly
- incidents due to poor lighting
- ignoring or abusing the rules put in place for health and safety.

It is now a legal requirement for all employers to carry out risk assessments for all of the procedures completed in the workplace. The risk assessment must also record the measures in place to keep employees safe and to avoid risk of injury, ill health or harm. Health and safety legislation covers everyone in the premises, including full- and part-time employees, agency staff, contractors, voluntary workers and those on work placement, as well as customers and guests.

Slips, trips and falls

The majority of accidents in kitchens are slips, trips and falls. Therefore, floor surfaces must be of a suitable construction to reduce this risk. A major cause of this kind of accident is spilt water and grease, which can make the floor surface slippery. For this reason any spillage must be cleaned immediately and warning notices put in place, where appropriate, highlighting the danger. Verbal warnings should also be given.

Falls can also be caused when items are left on floors and in passageways or between stoves and tables. People carrying trays and containers may have a restricted view and may not see hazards and so can trip over them. They may fall on to a hot stove, on to a sharp item, or the item they are carrying may be hot. These falls can have severe consequences. Ensure that nothing is left on the floor that may cause an obstruction and be a hazard. If it is necessary to have articles on the floor temporarily, they should be guarded to prevent accidents.

Kitchen personnel should be trained to think and act in a safe manner so as to avoid this kind of accident.

If you become aware of a hazard or potential hazard in your working area, it is important to assess the situation and decide if it is something that you can deal with yourself or if it needs to be reported to someone else, or maybe both (see below). **Do not ignore hazards**: they may have the potential to cause serious injury. It is essential that you do one or more of the following to minimise risk:

- Deal with the hazard yourself where it is safe to do so; an example of this would be dealing with a wet floor and putting up the appropriate signs.

- Warn others of the hazard verbally, for example warning of the wet floor before you have dealt with it. Make sure others working around you are aware of hot surfaces and hot equipment, such as trays you have just taken from the oven.
- Report the problem to another colleague, for example your mentor or someone with responsibility for health and safety.
- Report the problem to a supervisor, head chef or manager.
- Remove dangerous pieces of equipment, for example a hand-held blender with a damaged electrical cord, or place a 'do not use' sign on larger equipment and inform a supervisor, head chef or manager.

Hazard warning signs

Safety signs are used to control a hazard. They should not replace other methods of controlling risks.

Yellow signs – warning signs

These are to warn of various dangers, such as slippery floors, hot oil or hot water. They also warn about hazards such as corrosive material.

Blue signs – mandatory signs

These signs inform about precautions that must be taken, such as how to progress safely through a certain area. They are also used when special precautions need to be taken, such as wearing protective clothing.

Red signs – prohibition or fire-fighting signs

Red signs tell people that they should not enter and are to stop people from doing certain tasks in a hazardous area. Red signs are also used for fire-fighting equipment.

Green signs – safe signs

These are route signs designed to show where fire exits and emergency exits are. Green also tends to be used for first-aid equipment.

Electricity and gas

The majority of kitchens will have a range of electrical equipment and great care must be taken when dealing with electricity. Electrical equipment is covered by **Electricity at Work Regulations (1989)**; under these regulations all electrical equipment must be tested each year by a qualified electrician.

If a person comes into direct contact with electricity an electric shock can occur, which can be very serious and sometimes fatal. If a person has an electric shock, switch off the current. If this is not possible, free the person using something that is dry and that will insulate you from the electricity, such as a thick cloth or something made of wood or rubber. You must take care not to use your bare hands otherwise the electric shock may be transmitted to you.

In the case of electric shock:
- switch off the current
- raise the alarm
- call for medical/first-aid help.

You can give artificial respiration where necessary if you are trained in the procedure.

Gas is often the preferred fuel for industrial stoves and can be potentially hazardous. On leaving the kitchen, make sure that you turn off all gas appliances. It is important to report any gas leaks, faulty equipment or gas smell immediately to a supervisor or line manager.

In some kitchens there are central gas cut-off points where one switch cuts off the gas supply to the whole kitchen. These are used in emergency situations such as a fire.

Hazardous substances

The **Control of Substances Hazardous to Health (COSHH) Regulations (1999)** state that an employer must not carry out work that might expose employees to substances that are hazardous to their health, unless the employer has assessed the risks and put relevant controls in place. These risk assessments must be recorded and available for inspection. All potentially harmful chemicals must be stored, used and then disposed of properly according to COSHH regulations. The hazardous nature of the chemical must be identified on the packaging. Substances that are dangerous to health are labelled as 'very toxic', 'toxic', 'harmful', 'irritant' or 'corrosive'.

This includes the use of recognisable symbols.

Corrosive

Flammable

Harmful

Toxic

Chemicals commonly used in kitchens include: detergents, disinfectants, sanitisers, degreasers, descalers, oven cleaners and pest-control chemicals. These substances could cause injury if not used correctly by getting them on to the skin, in the eyes or mouth, or breathing in through the nose or mouth.

People using chemical substances must be trained to use them properly and safely. This will include:

- wearing the relevant protective clothing, such as aprons, goggles, gloves and facemasks
- following the manufacturer's instructions correctly
- always storing chemicals in their original containers, away from heat and with the lids tightly closed
- not allowing exposure to heat or to naked flames
- never mixing chemicals
- knowing first-aid procedures
- disposing of used chemicals and empty containers correctly.

Incident/accident reporting

If an accident or near-accident occurs in your working area it is important that it is reported to the appropriate person so it can be recorded and measures put in place to prevent it occurring again.

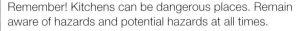

Health and safety

Remember! Kitchens can be dangerous places. Remain aware of hazards and potential hazards at all times.

Health and safety must be monitored regularly in the workplace by the designated health and safety manager/officer. Any accident incidents or near-accidents must be recorded, even if no one was injured.

As an employee all accidents and potential accidents must be reported to your line manager or supervisor. Each accident is recorded in an accident book/file, which must be provided in every business. Below is an example of an incident report form showing all the details required.

RIDDOR (Reporting of Injuries, Diseases and Dangerous Occurrences Regulations) 2013

The law says that all serious work-related accidents, diseases and dangerous occurrences must be recorded and reported to the HSE online (www.hse.gov.uk).

There is also a telephone contact number, but this is only for very serious incidents and fatalities (Incident Contact Centre: 0845 300 9923).

The following injuries must be reported:

- bone fractures (except fingers, thumbs or toes)
- amputation (cutting off) of limbs
- dislocation of a hip, knee or spine
- temporary or permanent loss of sight (blindness)

Full name of injured person:			
Occupation:		Supervisor:	
Time of accident:	Date of accident:	Time of report:	Date of report:
Name of injury or condition:			
Details of hospitalisation:			
Extent of injury (after medical attention):			
Place of accident or dangerous occurrence:			
Injured person's evidence of what happened (include equipment/items and/or other persons):			
Witness evidence (1):		Witness evidence (2):	
Supervisor's recommendations:			
Date:		Supervisor's signature:	

▲ An incident report form

- eye injuries from chemicals getting into the eye, a hot metal burn to the eye or any penetration of the eye
- any injury from electric shock or burning that leads to unconsciousness or the need to resuscitate the person or send them to hospital for more than 24 hours
- any injury resulting in hypothermia (when someone gets too cold), or illness due to heat, that leads to unconsciousness or the need to resuscitate the person or send them to hospital for more than 24 hours (such as an electric shock, or a gas flame blown back and causing burns)
- unconsciousness caused by exposure to a harmful substance or biological agents (such as cleaning products and solvents)

- unconsciousness or illness requiring medical treatment caused by inhaling a harmful substance or absorbing it through the skin (such as breathing in poisonous carbon monoxide leaking from a gas appliance)
- illness requiring medical treatment caused by a biological agent or its toxins or infected material (such as harmful bacteria used in laboratories).

Examples of reportable diseases include:
- dermatitis
- skin cancer
- asthma
- hepatitis
- tuberculosis
- tetanus
- anthrax.

Emergencies in the workplace

Emergencies that might happen in the workplace include:
- serious accidents involving injury
- outbreak of fire or explosion
- threats such as terrorism or riots
- a bomb scare
- failure of a major system, for example water or electricity.

An organisation will have systems in place to deal with emergencies. Key staff are usually trained to lead the procedure in cases of emergency and most organisations will have fire marshals and first-aiders. These people will attend regular update meetings. Evacuation procedures will also be in place, which employees will need to practise (for example, fire drills), and fire alarms will be tested regularly.

First aid

When people are injured or fall ill at work, it is important that immediate help is available and, in serious cases, medical assistance is called.

The arrangements for providing first aid in the workplace are set out in the **Health and Safety (First Aid) Regulations 1981**. Since 1982 it has been a legal requirement that adequate first-aid equipment, facilities and personnel are provided at work.

All kitchen staff need to know who they should call or inform if there is an accident, where the first-aid equipment is located and the procedures they should follow when there is an injury or incident, no matter how small.

First-aid equipment needs to be checked regularly, replenished and maintained; making this procedure part of a job role will ensure that the required items are always available.

All injuries, including minor injuries, must be recorded. This is usually done on individual recording forms that are then kept. Some organisations now record accidents on computer systems – these must also be kept for information and/or inspection.

Dealing with minor cuts and burns

Minor cuts, grazes and burns occur occasionally in kitchens because of the nature of the work. Most minor cuts can usually be treated using the contents of the first-aid box, maybe with the assistance of an appointed first-aider. For more serious cuts and burns it is important to seek advice from the first-aider and get medical help as soon as possible.

Safe lifting and handling

Working in a kitchen often includes the need to move heavy or awkwardly shaped objects. This could include deliveries of food and other items that need to be moved to another area, lifting heavy trays from ovens, manoeuvring large pieces of equipment and using heavy cleaning equipment.

Picking up and carrying heavy or difficult loads can lead to accidents, injury and long-term sickness if it is not done properly. Incorrect lifting or lifting something too heavy is a common cause of back injury. The **Manual Handling Operations Regulations (1992)** cover safe lifting and handling at work. An employer must carry out a risk assessment on all tasks that involve lifting and put procedures in place to make it safe. Staff must then be trained in these procedures.

When lifting, the general rules include:
- assessing the load and not attempting to lift anything that is too heavy
- breaking the load into smaller units if appropriate
- using lifting equipment or moving equipment such as trolleys where available
- requesting help with lifting.

When lifting, it is essential to use a safe lifting technique:
- Assess the load and plan how you are going to lift it.
- Position yourself with your feet apart, back straight and knees bent.
- Grip the item firmly at the base or lifting handles.
- Lift in a smooth movement, keeping the load close to the body.
- Walk carefully, making sure there are no trip hazards.
- Lower or place the load, still keeping the back straight and bending knees if necessary.

> ## Health and safety
>
> Take extra care when **lifting hot items**. This includes large trays from ovens, roasting trays, large pans of liquids, oven or salamander shelves, and a variety of other kitchen items that could be hot and cause burns. When moving a hot item be sure that you can do it safely and that there is a clear space to put it down. Give others working around you verbal warnings. Wrap an oven cloth around hot pan-handles and do not allow hot trays to stick out over the edge of surfaces.

Stage 1 – think before lifting

Stage 2 – adapt a strong, stable position

Stage 3 – place feet slightly apart, straight back, squat over the object with knees slightly bent and feet slightly apart

Stage 4 – keep the load close to the waist

Stage 5 – avoid twisting or leaning sideways

Stage 6 – look ahead

Stage 7 – move object and place down, adjust to the desired position

Fire safety

Everyone working in a kitchen needs to be aware of the potential risk of fire. It is important to work safely to prevent fire, especially around open gas jets and when using fats and oils with cooking appliances. Deep-fat fryers should be thermostatically controlled to prevent overheating and only be used after training has been completed.

All employers have a duty of care for the safety of employees in the event of a fire. The **Regulatory Reform (Fire Safety) Order 2005** emphasises that measures must be taken to prevent fires. All staff must be trained in emergency evacuation with fire action plans clearly displayed to show the correct evacuation routes for staff, customers and visitors. The fire evacuation procedures should be practised at least once a year, the procedure recorded and reviewed regularly to take into account staff changes and any changes to the premises.

Under current health and safety regulations it is a requirement to:

- make sure that the fire precautions, where reasonably practicable, ensure the safety of all employees and others in the building
- complete a fire risk assessment of the premises and specific areas. This must be recorded and be available for inspection. Preventative and protective measures must be reviewed. A fire risk assessment will help to establish the likelihood of a fire occurring and highlight the dangers from fire in the workplace
- make sure that suitable fire detection systems are in place and fire alarms are tested weekly
- clearly sign all escape routes and make sure that they are free from hazards that might slow down or prevent escape.

All fires require heat, fuel and oxygen ('the fire triangle' – see below). Without any one of these elements a fire will not start. Methods of putting fires out concentrate on either cooling it (as in a water extinguisher or fire hose) or depriving it oxygen (as in an extinguisher that uses foam or powder).

Fuel

Flammable gases, liquids or solids

Ignition source

Smoking or naked flames
Hot surfaces
Electrical equipment
Static electricity

Oxygen

Always present in the air
Also comes from oxidising substances

▲ The fire triangle

Fire precautions

Effective measures in the prevention of fire include:

- removing all hazards or reducing them as much as possible
- making sure that measures have been taken to protect from the risk of fire and the likelihood of a fire spreading
- ensuring that all escape routes are safe and used effectively, and that they are well signed and easy to access
- provision of suitable fire-fighting equipment and staff well trained in its use
- providing suitable ways of detecting a fire (for example smoke alarms) and instructions on what to do in case of fire
- arrangements in place for what to do if a fire breaks out – employees must be trained in what to do in the event of a fire
- all precautions provided must be installed and maintained by a competent person.

Fires are classified in accordance with British Standard EN2 as follows:

- **Class A**: fires involving solid materials where burning normally forms glowing embers, for example, wood.
- **Class B**: fires involving liquids, such as methylated spirit or any kind of flammable gel used under a burner.
- **Class C**: fires involving gases.
- **Class D**: fires involving metals.
- **Class F**: fires involving cooking oils or fats.

Different types of fire extinguishers are suitable for different types of fire. Generally, portable fire extinguishers contain one of the following five substances:

- water
- foam
- powder
- carbon dioxide
- vaporising liquids.

The most useful form of general-purpose fire-fighting equipment is the water-type extinguisher or hose reel. Areas of special risk, such as kitchens where oil, fats and electrical equipment are used, may need other types of extinguisher, such as carbon dioxide, wet chemical or dry powder.

Ensure that you know exactly where the fire alarms are in your working area and how they are operated. Also be well aware of the evacuation procedures in your establishment and follow the procedure shown to you. If you need to leave the premises because of fire, the usual steps include:

- Raise the alarm and warn others verbally.
- Turn off gas supplies using a central cut-off point if possible.
- Do not put yourself and others in danger; only tackle the smallest of fires, and only if you know how to do this and you are certain that it is safe to do so.
- Leave by the appointed exits, checking that others are also vacating the building. Guests, visitors and customers may need assisting and directing.
- Go to the appointed assembly point and await further instruction.
- Do not re-enter the building until you are told you can do so.

Security procedures

Security in hospitality premises always remains a high priority. In many hospitality establishments large numbers of people can be present in the building at any one time. These may include: staff, guests, customers, contractors, visitors and others.

As well as providing security and protection for all these people, consideration needs to be given to the buildings and grounds; fixtures, fittings and furniture; decor and decorative items; equipment; clothing and linen; and stock.

The main security concerns include:

- **theft**: where customers' property, employers' property (particularly food, drink and equipment) or employees' property is stolen
- **burglary**: where a burglar comes on to the premises (trespasses) and steals customers', employers' or employees' property
- **robbery**: theft with assault, for example when staff are banking or collecting cash
- **fraud**: false insurance claims; counterfeit money; stolen credit cards
- **assault**: fights between customers; assaults on staff by customers; violence or attacks on staff; verbal abuse
- **vandalism**: damage to property caused by customers, intruders or employees
- **arson**: setting fire to the property
- **undesirable individuals**: having people such as drug dealers on the premises
- **terrorism**: bombs, telephone bomb threats.

The **Management of Health and Safety at Work Regulations 1999** require employers to conduct a risk assessment regarding the safety of staff in the business. Preventing crime is more efficient and less damaging than having to deal with it once it has happened.

Dealing with security

Everyone entering the premises should be monitored. Reception staff should be trained to spot suspicious individuals and those likely to cause problems. Everyone who comes into the building should be asked to sign in at reception and, if they are a legitimate visitor, be given a security badge. It is also essential to make sure that any suspicious person does not re-enter the building.

- All contract workers should be registered and given security badges, and they may be restricted to working in certain areas.
- There should also be good security systems on all doors; those delivering goods need to report to the relevant person.
- All establishments should try to reduce temptation for criminals, for example by reducing the amount of cash that is handled. The use of credit and debit cards is now common and widespread, and reduces the amounts of cash used, so reducing the risk of cash theft. However, credit/debit card fraud and crimes are also a problem.

- Staff who handle money should be trained in simple anti-fraud measures, such as checking bank notes, checking signatures on plastic cards and so on.
- It is impossible to remove all temptation, so equipment (such as computers, fax machines, photocopiers) should be marked with some sort of security tag or identification.
- There are many simple and obvious security measures that can also be taken, such as locking doors and windows.
- Coded key pads on doors are effective in keeping areas safe. Keys should be kept securely and access to them restricted to those who need them.
- Good lighting is also important for security reasons – criminals are less likely to come on to the premises at night if they can be clearly seen. Regular checks should be made of the lighting in all areas. Lighting areas that can be seen by passers-by can also help.
- Closed-circuit television (CCTV) cameras with recordings are also used as a deterrent against crime.
- With regard to staff, a good security measure is checking their references from previous employers.
- Staff are frequently provided with security swipe cards to enter the building; these may also carry a photograph of the staff member.
- Some companies put the 'right to search' into employee contracts – this means that, from time to time, the employer can carry out searches of the employees' lockers, bags and other belongings.

Dealing with customers' property

Customers' property often needs to be looked after, secured or cared for in hospitality establishments. Keeping customers' property safe while on the premises is dealt with by:

- locked rooms
- lockers and locking cupboards
- personal safes in rooms or a central safe that customers can use
- cloakrooms with ticket/token systems
- items left in reception areas or at concierge desks
- items given to staff for safe keeping.

When customers' property has been left behind by mistake the usual procedure is to report it to a supervisor, record the date and a description of the item, and then store it securely. When the identity and whereabouts of the person leaving the item is known they may be contacted to inform them of their lost property.

Most establishments will have set procedures in place with regards to **risks, threats and security**. Make sure that you are aware of these policies and carry them out correctly in line with the establishment's operational procedures. Most employers provide regular training and update sessions for their staff, making sure that everyone is well aware of requirements and that their knowledge is up to date.

Test yourself

1 When you work in a kitchen it is important for you to have an understanding of health and safety issues. Suggest three places that you could find out about health and safety.

2 Suggest three hazards that you may come across in your kitchen that you think may cause an injury or accident. Who would you report these to, and how could you warn others working around you?

3 Describe four signs that you may see around the kitchen to warn or inform you of health and safety issues.

4 Why is it important that everyone in the kitchen knows where to find the first-aid equipment, and why is it important that first-aid supplies are kept topped up?

5 If you were asked to move some large boxes that had been delivered, how could you do this safely?

6 Suggest three possible causes of fire in a kitchen. Which type of fire-fighting equipment could be used on a deep-fat fryer?

7 Suggest three ways that you could reduce the risk of accidental fire when working in the kitchen.

8 If you see an accident or near-accident in your workplace who should you report it to? Why is reporting it important?

9 Describe three of the security procedures you are aware of in your workplace.

10 If a visitor to your kitchen or a customer left some of their property behind, what is the procedure that should be followed?

2 Work effectively as part of a hospitality team

This chapter is relevant to the following units:
→ Work effectively as part of a hospitality team.

When working in a kitchen, or in any hospitality role, you will be working as part of a team. This may include:

- completing tasks on your own but as part of a wider team
- completing tasks with one or two other people as part of a wider team
- working as part of a large team that may be subdivided into sections.

Kitchen teams will include managers, supervisors (head chefs or sous chefs) as well as team members at various levels and those working at the same level as yourself. There will also be people providing support, such as kitchen porters and clerical staff. Kitchen teams vary in size and type depending on the establishment – a large hotel may have an extensive kitchen brigade with a formal structure, but a small restaurant will have a smaller and less formal team.

Planning and organising your work

To be successful as part of a kitchen team you will need to develop the skills to plan and organise your own work. You need to make sure that the instructions and allocated tasks given to you are clearly understood so that mistakes are not made, and time and food are not wasted. If there is something you do not understand, ask for a further explanation or to be shown the procedure again.

The tasks to be completed by each kitchen section and each member of staff needs to be planned and organised so that all work is completed efficiently, to the required standards and on time.

Following instructions

You will be given a number of instructions during your working day and it is important to complete these tasks to the best of your ability and with accuracy. These may be written down as a task list for you to complete or you may receive verbal instruction. Whichever way you are given the instructions, read and/or listen carefully, if possible confirm back what is required of you, and ask for further instruction if you don't understand what you are being asked to do.

With a list of tasks it will be necessary to prioritise which are most important or need to be done first. For example, some vegetables needed for lunch service in an hour's time will need to be dealt with before the preparation of items for dinner or tomorrow's menu.

Also, you need to organise your time efficiently; while something is cooking in the oven you could be working on something else. If you need help or advice on how to prioritise tasks or if you are unsure that you have got it right, ask for guidance. As the day's work progresses it may be necessary to change the order and priority of tasks as some things may become more urgent. Writing down the instructions given to you will help you to work efficiently and professionally.

Types of instructions

- **The recipe**: one of the most important sets of instructions you will use; it is important to follow it accurately. You will frequently need to scale the recipe up or down (multiplying or dividing the amounts) to match the quantities you will need; take care to do this accurately. It is advisable to write down and double check the amended recipe amounts. Read the whole recipe through at least once before starting the task and ask about anything you are unsure of. Assemble the ingredients you will need before starting preparation or cooking, and also assemble all of the tools and equipment you will need.
- **Use of equipment and machinery**: always make sure you have been shown how to prepare and use equipment for specific tasks. For example, does a dessert mould need lining with silicone film? Does a loaf tin need to be greased and floured? Always make sure you have had full instructions and training before using equipment or machinery that you are unsure of.
- **Health and safety/food safety instructions**: follow the guidelines or training given by your employer and any training courses you may have completed. Some of these instructions will be legal requirements and it is your legal responsibility to comply with them. Apart from following the necessary instructions, it is essential that you report anything that may cause problems

in maintaining the required standards of health and safety or food safety. For example, it would be essential to report a refrigerator not maintaining the required temperature (as food at the wrong temperature can cause food poisoning) or an electrical appliance with a damaged flex (which could cause an electric shock or fire).

- **Uniform and personal hygiene**: instructions on the required standards of kitchen uniform and the standards of personal hygiene required must be followed precisely. This will give you pride in your own appearance and professionalism, and will also maintain the standards and reputation of the establishment you work for. You will have been given instructions about reporting any sickness or infection you may have before you start work. It is of the utmost importance, and a legal requirement, that you follow these instructions fully.
- **Emergency procedure instructions**: you will have been told the procedure to follow in an emergency such as a fire. Be aware of the procedures and follow evacuation instruction correctly.
- **Standard operational procedure**: some instructions you are given about the way that you work and complete tasks will be specific to the individual workplace or a group of establishments. It means that all employees will be completing tasks in the same way and will be maintaining the same standards. This is called the 'standard operational procedure' (SOP) and will detail the steps and activities of a process and the required quality and presentation of the finished product. An example would be the way a specific dish was produced, presented, garnished and served at a banqueting event so each plate looks exactly the same.

Efficient use of time

Organising and managing your time well is important because kitchen work is generally more time-specific than many other areas of work. For example, if some office-based data entry was completed an hour later than planned it may not be too much of a problem but, if someone ordered lunch that was an hour late, the customer would rightly have cause for complaint and would probably not come back again. To meet the time constraints of a busy kitchen careful planning and organisation is essential.

Keeping the work area clean, tidy and organised

It is important to keep your own work area clean tidy and well organised as you work. Completing tasks hygienically and protecting food from contamination are legal food

safety requirements, as well as allowing you to work efficiently and professionally. 'Clean as you go' must be standard practice in all food preparation areas.

Do not allow waste to build up in work areas; dispose of waste according to the policies practised by the establishment (for example, some items may be placed in specific containers for recycling). General waste should be placed in a lined waste bin with a foot-operated lid. Make sure this is emptied regularly and not allowed to become overfull.

Ensure that food contact surfaces, such as chopping boards, are clean and sanitised before use. Clean well and sanitise areas between tasks. Organise the equipment you will need for the work you are completing and consider the best way to complete each task with maximum efficiency.

Put equipment and ingredients away in the proper places once you have finished using them. Make sure that food items being put away into fridges, freezers and other storage areas are correctly covered or wrapped and labelled and dated according to the establishment's policy.

Working efficiently means that tasks are completed within the time allowed, in a well-organised, clean and tidy way, without causing undue stress or tiredness. There have been many studies on the way people work best and the provision of working conditions that suit the people working with them – this is often referred to as ergonomics.

Keeping waste to a minimum

Careful preparation, storage and cooking methods, as well as good staff training, will help to avoid unnecessary kitchen waste. Waste needs to be avoided for a number of reasons. Firstly wastage means the calculated yield from ingredients will not be achieved; waste is expensive and will affect the overall cost of what is being produced; also, disposal of excessive waste needs to be paid for. Unnecessary waste is now also considered to be ecologically unacceptable, placing strain on the planet's resources.

We all need to be aware of food sustainability. There are ever-increasing demands on world food stocks and efforts are being made to produce food that does not impose long-term harm on the environment, endanger animal or fish species, and provides fair pay and conditions for agricultural workers. Reducing the amounts of food we waste helps to achieve these aims. We are also encouraged to decrease 'food miles' where possible, which means using local produce rather than similar produce imported from across the world. Doing this reduces waste on fuel and storage, and often excess packaging too. Using more locally sourced food may also result in a high-quality fresher product as well as adding local or regional interest to the menu.

Be aware of quantities required before starting preparation. Take care to avoid unnecessary waste, which can be caused by:

- over production
- wrong information or lack of information
- careless preparation, for example peeling vegetables too thickly
- poor cooking procedures, such as overcooking causing excessive shrinkage or food to be completely spoiled
- poor storage and lack of stock rotation, causing food to deteriorate
- allowing food to become contaminated, so it then must be disposed of
- high-risk food at kitchen temperatures for too long, which must then be thrown away.

Asking for help

Working as part of a team means that you will be working together with others to reach the desired goals within a specific time. Variations of requirements and pressures of work in different areas mean that you may need to ask for help from others to reach your targets on time.

You may also need to ask for help or further instruction if you don't understand what you are being asked to do, if you need advice on how to prioritise tasks, or if you are unsure that you have got a task right. You should speak to your supervisor or line manager.

Working effectively with team members

Good teamwork is essential in all working environments and kitchen teams have traditionally worked closely together

in an organised structure to ensure all work is completed to the required standards, on time with all team members understanding their role and responsibilities. Working as part of a team can allow people to feel valued and learn from each other's skills and expertise. In a good team people feel supported in their role allowing for job satisfaction and team achievement. The work is completed on time to high standards and there is a positive and creative working environment.

Offering help to others

On occasions you may need to offer help and assistance to others to make sure the team reaches their targets on time. However, only do this when you have sufficient time and your own work will not suffer by helping others, if the help you offer is within your capabilities, and it does not contradict what a supervisor or senior chef has asked you to do. If you are not sure about any of this, ask your section chef, head chef or line manager.

Remember that it is the outcome and product of the team that defines a successful business or operation and it is less likely that those working in isolation will achieve the necessary goals.

Passing on information

At some time in the day you may be left a message or given information that needs to be passed on to others in the team. It is essential that such information is passed on quickly and accurately. Make sure that the person you are giving the information to fully hears and understands what you are telling them. If a written note has been left or an email sent, make sure it has been seen and read by the relevant person.

Such information may include:

- a message from a member of staff saying they will not be in work or will be late. Record and pass on details such as the time of the call, how late they will be or the reason for absence, and how long they expect to be away from work (a contact number may also be useful)
- a late delivery from a supplier or items that could not be supplied
- bookings or cancellations
- arrival of visitors such as maintenance contractors, inspectors or company representatives
- faulty equipment or supplies running low
- changes in the menu
- information about special dietary requirements or allergies
- changes in timing, for example a buffet lunch required one hour earlier.

Use the most appropriate way to pass on the information (for example verbally, written message, email – see communication methods below).

Behaviour that helps teams to work effectively

Employers value good team members. They will look for employees with the personal qualities to work as part of a successful and productive team, and who are able to develop good working relationships with others. A good team member is:

- reliable, dependable and always punctual
- someone who takes pride in their personal appearance and is clean, smart, tidy and well groomed
- a good communicator, listening to instructions and passing on relevant information clearly and promptly
- someone who completes work on time, asks for help when needed and offers help to others when appropriate
- well organised with the ability to think ahead and prioritise tasks as appropriate
- open to feedback and always willing to learn new skills and techniques, and learns from experience
- someone who has empathy with others and listens to the points of view of other team members
- confident and assertive within the specific job role.

Negative behaviour

Sometimes however, negative behaviour occurs in a workplace. This must be discouraged and dealt with promptly and effectively by someone managing or supervising the area. Negative behaviour can include:

- poor timekeeping and being unreliable
- poor standards of dress and personal appearance
- being inconsiderate to others and unhelpful
- laziness; not completing tasks properly
- use of inappropriate language or swearing
- producing work that is not of the required standard or not produced on time.

Working relationship problems

Occasionally in busy kitchens pressure, workload and personality differences can have negative effects on good working relationships within a team. It is important that you bring any concerns of such problems to the attention of your line manager or supervisor. You will need to discuss what the problem is and why you are concerned, giving specific examples where possible. You should also say when the problems occur and the frequency. Try to remain constructive in your discussion of relationship problems so that a solution can be planned in the most amicable way.

Signs of damaging behaviour within the workplace must be taken very seriously and reported immediately. Examples of this kind of behaviour may include:

- intimidation – deliberately making someone feel frightened or nervous in certain situations
- harassment – annoying or unpleasant behaviour that takes place regularly, for example threats, offensive remarks or even physical attacks
- victimisation – to single someone out and treat them unfairly
- bullying – hurting, frightening, threatening, persecuting or tormenting others; it could also be forcing someone to do something they do not want to do.

The above may take the form of:

- racist comments or gestures
- remarks about religion, belief, gender or sexuality
- remarks about personal characteristics or disabilities
- physical or sexual abuse
- belittling and undermining an individual's achievements
- ignoring individuals and making them feel isolated
- excluding individuals from information and what is going on
- threatening behaviour
- humiliating individuals in front of others
- setting of unrealistic or unachievable targets.

No employee should suffer any of the above and a solution to the problem must be found as soon as possible. Discuss any concerns that you may have with your line manager, supervisor or head chef.

Communicating clearly and effectively

Good communication is essential to a successful kitchen team. There will be many different communication methods used between:

- individuals working together
- other kitchen sections and service staff
- other departments and management
- suppliers and contractors
- customers/guests.

Speaking and listening is the most widely used form of communication in a kitchen, so it is important that it carried out effectively:

- Speak clearly and listen carefully so the message is understood. This is especially important in a noisy kitchen.
- Non-verbal gestures, such as facial expressions and hand gestures, may help to reinforce the message and will confirm understanding.
- Take time to communicate properly; avoid speaking from a distance or speaking while walking past the other person.
- Avoid interrupting and avoid distractions; listen to what is being said then respond.
- Do not shout, swear or use inappropriate language.
- When receiving verbal instruction, ask questions where necessary and summarise the instruction at the end.

However, there are many other ways that communication takes place in kitchens, including:

- **Non-verbal gestures**: non-verbal gestures – such as a nod, a raised hand or 'thumb up' – can be useful, but make sure they are not misunderstood, especially when communicating between different nationalities and cultures.
- **Written communication**: this is very widely used, from formal letters through task lists and brief notes. Make sure they are clearly written so that the recipient will fully understand the meaning.
- **Pictorial communication**: pictures or diagrams are often used in instructions and signs around the kitchen (especially for health and safety instruction). These are often standardised and are recognised internationally. A picture, diagram or sketch could also be used to convey meaning where there is a language barrier.
- **Telephone**: this remains a very widely used method of communication and there may be specific systems used in an establishment (for example land lines or mobile/smart phones).

- **Fax messaging**: this 'older technology' still has numerous uses, especially when exact copies, signed copies, drawings or diagrams need to be sent elsewhere.
- **Electronic systems**: these have become increasingly sophisticated and are very popular. Frequently used systems include email, text messaging, QR codes, electronic ordering systems, data-logging systems and systems designed for specific company use, such as Vocera, Maytas or Opera.

Many employees are now given access to their own company email or other communication system. Increasingly communication takes place through social media such as Twitter, Facebook, LinkedIn and Rehoba.

Developing your skills

Good employees will be keen to learn as much as they can about the job they are employed to do, as well as improving and refining their own knowledge and skills. Development within the job role will lead to progression and promotion, and will also provide interesting challenges.

Improving your knowledge and skills

Improving your knowledge and skills is not only beneficial for you and your career progression but will help to raise the skills within the team and provide variety and diversity within the workplace. You may also encourage others working with you to develop their skills and knowledge too.

The ways that you can develop and progress within your job role include:

- asking questions of others as well as finding things out for yourself
- working with skilled and experienced colleagues
- attending training provided by your employer or asking about courses that interest you
- attending a full-time or part-time college course
- completing a work-based qualification managed by a training provider or college
- asking for feedback and progression advice
- discussing your progress with your managers, supervisors and mentors
- actively participating in formal appraisals, discussing your performance targets and progression
- producing or working to a learning plan (see below).

Seeking feedback on performance and progression

Asking for feedback on your work and progression from your peers, supervisors or senior chefs is a good way of evaluating your performance. Listen to what is said and maybe take notes. When receiving feedback you may like to ask questions and discuss which parts of your work are up to standard and where improvements could be made. Agreements can be made and targets set for future improvement and progression. Recording your progress and achievements in a learning or progression plan is an excellent way to check your progress and allows you to refer back to your initial targets and work towards the final outcome.

A learning/progression plan

A progression plan allows learning and development to be organised, and your progress and achievement can be monitored. The plan needs to have long-term aims of what you ultimately want to achieve as well as short-term aims that are the steps to get you there. Producing, developing and taking interest in your learning plan will show your employer that you are ambitious, proactive and well organised. Planning future progress is a good skill in itself and will help you to focus on planning your career. Having a personal learning or development plan will help you to identify targets and time scales to improve your skills and advance your career for personal and professional success.

A learning plan could be put in place by:
- your employer, human resources department or training department
- your head chef, supervisor or mentor
- a training provider or college managing your learning
- you – you can produce your own learning plan or simply keep a notebook or chart of your goals and achievements. These can then be discussed at appraisal or progress meetings.

Reviewing and updating plans

The progress you are making may be monitored and updated by:
- keeping your own record with dates in a suitable notebook, file, laptop or tablet.
- regular progress meetings with a tutor, head chef or mentor
- verbal and written feedback
- formal appraisals
- letters or emails
- logbooks, charts and electronic tracking systems.

Performance appraisals

Appraisal is a method by which the job performance of an employee is reviewed and evaluated, usually by a manager, supervisor or head chef. An appraisal is a part of guiding and managing career development and is a good opportunity for uninterrupted discussion between an employee and their line manager. Performance appraisals are a time to discuss your recent successes, achievements, personal strengths and weaknesses, and suitability for promotion or further education/training. It is an excellent opportunity to discuss ways to progress and enhance your career prospects. Your learning plan may be something that is useful in helping you to contribute positively to your appraisal.

Test yourself

1   Give three reasons why good, effective teamwork is essential in a kitchen.

2   Why is it important to fully understand exactly what is required from the work you complete? What could go wrong if you did not understand?

3   Give three reasons why it is important to keep your own working area clean and tidy.

4   What are the main reasons for avoiding waste when you are working?

5   Suggest two occasions when you may offer help to someone else in your team. Also, suggest two occasions when you should **not** give help to someone else.

6   When might you ask for help from someone else?

7   Describe four pieces of information you may need to pass on to someone else. What are the ways you could use to pass on the information clearly?

8   Give three examples of positive behaviour in a team and three examples of negative behaviour.

9   If you were concerned about poor working relationships in your kitchen what could you do about it?

10 What are the benefits to you of continuing to improve your work knowledge and skills?

11 How can you get feedback on how you are progressing with your learning and skills? Suggest a good way to keep a record of your targets and achievements.

3 Maintain food safety

This chapter is relevant to the following units:
→ Maintain food safety when storing, preparing and cooking food.

This chapter provides the necessary information to enable you to prepare and cook food safely. It focuses on the key food safety control areas outlined by the Food Standards Agency: cooking, cleaning, chilling and prevention of cross-contamination. It also discusses food safety hazards and the measures necessary to control them, from delivery of food up until the time it is served to the customer, and how to comply with food safety legislation.

What is food safety and why does it matter?

Everyone eating food prepared and cooked for them should reasonably expect to be served safe food that will not cause them illness or harm them in any way. Food poisoning is still a significant problem and it can be serious; food handlers must take great care to prevent it.

Food safety means putting in place all of the measures needed to make sure that food and drinks are suitable, safe and wholesome through all the processes of food provision, from selecting suppliers and delivery of food right through to serving the food to the customer.

Eating 'contaminated' food can result in food poisoning, causing harm, illness and, in some cases, even death.

The number of reported cases of food poisoning in the UK each year remains unacceptably high: between 70,000 and 94,000 cases reported each year. However, as a large number of food poisoning cases are never reported, no one really knows the actual number.

The term 'food poisoning' covers a range of illnesses of the digestive system and is usually caused by eating food that has become contaminated with bacteria and/or the toxins they may produce. However, there are a number of ways that food can become contaminated and cause harm, and all must be avoided.

This chapter covers the various ways that food businesses and food handlers can keep food safe to eat and avoid causing food poisoning.

Although the main reason for adopting high standards of food safety is to prevent the possibility of food poisoning, there are many more benefits a food business can gain by keeping food safety standards high. These include:
- being compliant with food safety law
- reducing food wastage and improving efficiency
- return business from satisfied customers
- building a good reputation and receiving fewer complaints.

Keeping yourself clean and hygienic

All food handlers are a potential source of contamination from food poisoning bacteria and other hazards, so it is very important that they are aware of the importance of high standards of appearance and personal hygiene. As well as the important part this plays in avoiding food contamination, it will reflect the professionalism of the individual as well as the establishment they work for, giving a positive impression of the food business.

All food handlers need to ensure that they have a daily bath or shower, clean underwear every day and use a suitable underarm deodorant.

Protective clothing

Protective clothing is worn to protect food from contamination by food handlers and to protect the wearer from things such as excessive heat, burns and sharp objects.

It is very important that food handlers wear suitable clothing that protects their body; protective footwear should also be worn.

Clothing worn in the kitchen must be strong to make it 'protective' and withstand the hard wear and frequent washing needed. Clothing will also need to be lightweight, comfortable and absorbent to deal with perspiration caused by a hot kitchen.

Kitchen clothing must be clean and changed at least once a day – more frequently if it becomes soiled – to avoid contamination of food, surfaces and equipment. It should cover any other clothing and only be worn in the kitchen area. Outdoor clothing, and other clothing that has been taken off before wearing whites, should be kept in a suitable locker.

According to the **Personal Protective Equipment (PPE) at Work Regulations 1992**, employees must wear personal protective clothing/equipment suitable for the work they are involved in. For example, chefs need to wear protective chef's whites, but they may also need gauntlet gloves and eye goggles if cleaning an oven.

Jackets and trousers

Chef's jackets are usually made of cotton or a cotton mixture, are double-breasted and ideally have long sleeves; these protect the chest and arms from the heat of the stove and prevent hot foods or liquids burning or scalding the body.

Trousers worn as part of a chef's uniform are usually made from a lightweight cotton or coated cotton. They should be loose fitting for both safety and comfort.

White coats

It is good practice to keep these available in kitchen areas to wear over standard kitchen clothing when completing other tasks such as unloading a delivery or unpacking raw meat. A white coat should be worn over other clothing when leaving the kitchen to complete another job or go for a break. It is also good practice to offer white coats to anyone visiting the kitchen to cover their own clothing, which could cause contamination.

Aprons

Aprons are designed to provide extra protection to the body from being scalded or burned, and particularly to protect the legs from any liquids that may be spilled. For this reason the apron should be of sufficient length with long ties, allowing it to be wrapped around the body and tied at the front, so that it can be removed quickly if a hot spillage occurs.

Hats

The main purpose of a hat is to prevent loose hairs from falling into food and to absorb perspiration on the forehead. As well as the traditional chef's toque (tall white hat) a variety of designs are now available, some with a net incorporated to contain the hair completely. Lightweight disposable hats are now used by many establishments.

Footwear

This should be strong and in good repair so as to protect and support the feet. As kitchen staff are on their feet for many hours at a time, care of the feet is essential. Suitable, clean, comfortable kitchen footwear and socks need to be worn. Open-toed shoes and trainers are unsuitable as they would not offer protection from spillage of hot liquids, falling knives or heavy items.

Disposable gloves

These are now available for use in most kitchens. They provide a barrier between the food handler and the food, helping to prevent cross-contamination, for example when handling raw meat or handling high-risk food. They are also useful for the food handler to wear when they have a cut or a burn on the hand and there is a possibility that their blue plaster could fall off, and when completing first-aid tasks. It is important that they are changed frequently.

Hair

Hair can be a source of food poisoning bacteria and contamination from this source must be avoided. Hair falling into food can also be a physical hazard. Hair must be washed regularly, long hair tied back, and kept covered with a suitable kitchen hat and/or net to prevent loose hair falling into food. The hair/head should never be scratched, combed or touched in the kitchen as bacteria and loose hair could be transferred to the food or food preparation equipment.

Jewellery, rings and watches

The wearing of jewellery is not acceptable when handling food. Jewellery can trap particles of food and provide a warm damp environment for bacteria to grow, which can then be transferred to food being prepared. This is particularly relevant to items worn on the hands such as rings and watches. Jewellery or parts of jewellery can also fall into food, especially as some food preparation involves plunging hands into water. (Body piercing items can also be a breeding ground for bacteria, so remove them or completely cover before handling food.)

Fingernails

These should always be kept clean and short as dirt can easily lodge under the nails and be transferred to food, introducing harmful bacteria. Nails must be kept neatly trimmed and nail varnish must never be worn in food areas.

Hand washing

Hands are frequently in contact with food and numerous other items; if they are not kept clean they can very easily transfer harmful bacteria to food, surfaces and equipment.

To avoid contamination from hands they must be washed thoroughly and frequently, particularly after using the toilet, before commencing work, during the handling of food, and especially between different tasks and after dealing with waste. Hand washing must be completed using a basin just for this purpose. It must have hot and cold running water, suitable soap (preferably in a dispenser) and paper towels for drying hands. Some establishments also provide an anti-bacterial gel to apply after hand washing.

To ensure that hands are washed thoroughly:

1 Use a basin provided just for hand washing with hot and cold running water (preferably with a mixer tap).
2 Wet hands under warm running water.
3 Apply liquid soap.
4 Rub hands together thoroughly, remembering to clean between fingers and thumbs.
5 Remember fingertips, nails and wrists.
6 Rinse off under running water.
7 Dry hands on a paper towel and use the paper towel to turn off the tap before disposing of it.

A nail brush may also be used to aid thorough hand washing but always ensure this is clean and disinfected (for example, keep it in a sanitising solution or consider using disposable brushes).

You must wash your hands:

- when you enter the kitchen, before starting work and handling any food
- after a break (especially after using the toilet)
- between different tasks, but especially after handling raw food and before handling ready-to-eat food
- after touching hair, nose or mouth, or using a tissue for sneezing or coughing
- after you apply or change a dressing on a cut or burn
- after cleaning preparation areas, equipment or contaminated surfaces
- after handling kitchen waste, external food packaging, money or flowers.

This will help to reduce the risk of cross-contamination from contact between food and hands.

You can also avoid excessive hand contact with food by using slices, ladles, tongs and spoons where possible, and by using disposable plastic gloves when appropriate (change these frequently, especially between tasks).

Unsafe behaviour

Touching your face, nose or mouth

When working with food it is of great importance not to touch face, nose or mouth, blow your nose or scratch any skin areas. If you do need to do any of these things, wash your hands very thoroughly afterwards.

The nose should not be touched when food is being handled. If a handkerchief/tissue is used, the hands should be washed thoroughly afterwards. The nose is an area where there can be vast numbers of harmful bacteria; it is therefore very important not to sneeze on food, other people, working surfaces or equipment. If a sneeze or cough is unavoidable, turn away and sneeze into the shoulder area.

The mouth also harbours large numbers of bacteria, therefore the mouth or lips should not be touched when working with food.

Ears too are a source of bacteria and should not be touched when handling food.

Chewing gum

Chewing gum is not acceptable when preparing food. It produces more saliva and may involve touching the lips and mouth, which can transfer bacteria to food. It also looks unprofessional.

Eating in the kitchen

As a chef you will frequently need to **taste** the food you cook to assess the flavour, texture and seasonings. This should be done in a controlled and hygienic way, using a clean teaspoon. Use the spoon only once then clean and disinfect it before using again. Alternatively use a disposable plastic spoon then throw it away. Do not use cooking utensils such as wooden spoons for tasting food, nor should fingers be used for this purpose as bacteria may be transferred to the food.

Eating would refer to consuming a meal or a snack while working or in your working area, or picking at the food being prepared. This is a hazard because you are likely to touch the face or mouth, which can then transfer harmful bacteria to the food.

Smoking

Smoking is now illegal in most buildings and certainly where there is food. If food handlers smoke at break times hands must be washed thoroughly afterwards because, when a cigarette is taken from the mouth, bacteria from the mouth can be transferred via the fingers on to food.

Cuts, burns, infections and grazes

It is particularly important to keep all cuts, burns, boils, scratches, grazes and similar abrasions covered with a waterproof dressing (blue plaster) to avoid contaminating food with bacteria. If these become infected there are large numbers of harmful bacteria that must not be allowed to come into contact food. In most cases people suffering in this way should not handle food. Report any infected skin problems or injuries to your supervisor before starting work.

Minor cuts, grazes and burns do occur occasionally in kitchens because of the nature of the work. Most minor cuts can usually be treated using the contents of the first-aid box, maybe with the assistance of an appointed first-aider. For more serious cuts and burns it is important to seek advice from the first-aider and get medical help as soon as possible. It is important to cover any open cuts or burns immediately to prevent bacteria from the wound getting into food.

- **Minor cuts and grazes**: place the cut/graze under cold running water, dry it thoroughly and apply a blue waterproof dressing of suitable size. If necessary, also wear a disposable glove. If the cut continues to bleed and is not being contained by the dressing, seek further help.
- **Minor burns**: place the injury under cold running water and keep it there for a minimum of ten minutes (an ice pack could also be used). If the burn is more serious and/or the skin is broken, cover lightly with a sterile dressing and seek medical help. Do not let adhesive items, creams, antiseptics or kitchen cloths come into contact with the wound.

Reporting illnesses and infections

Good levels of health and fitness are required to work in a kitchen, so attention must be paid to maintaining your health with a good diet, adequate exercise and enough sleep and rest. Many employers now have an occupational health department to support and advise employees in health matters.

It is now a **legal requirement** for all food handlers to report certain illnesses or infections they may have to their line manager/supervisor before starting work as they may be excluded from handling food. This is because with certain conditions, especially stomach-related illnesses, organisms can easily be transferred from the food handler to the food and this could make the person eating the food unwell. Illnesses that must be reported include:

- diarrhoea, vomiting or other symptoms of a food-borne illness – the food handler must not return to food-handling duties until they have been free from symptoms for 48 hours or more
- any skin infections or infected cuts, boils, grazes or burns
- heavy colds and coughs, eye or ear discharges.

Keeping work areas clean and hygienic

Suitable buildings with well-planned fittings, layout and equipment allow for good food safety practices to take place. All surfaces and equipment must be in good condition and kept clean. Certain basics need to be available if a building is to be used for food production:

- there must be an electricity supply and preferably a gas supply
- drinking water and good drainage
- suitable road access for deliveries and refuse collection
- no risk of contamination from the surrounding area and buildings, such as chemicals, smoke, odours or dust.

Layout

When planning food premises a linear workflow should be in place:

delivery → **storage** → **preparation** → **cooking** → **hot holding** → **serving**

This means there will be no crossover of activities that could result in cross-contamination. Clean and dirty – and raw and cooked – processes should be well segregated.

There must be adequate storage areas; proper refrigerated storage is especially important. Cleaning and disinfection should be planned with separate storage areas for cleaning materials and chemicals.

Sufficient, suitable staff hand washing/drying facilities must be provided, as well as personal hygiene facilities for staff, including changing and storage areas for personal clothing and belongings.

All areas should allow for efficient cleaning, disinfection and pest control.

Staff accommodation and offices ← Entrance and goods in → Kitchen waste Empties store

Cold store   Dry goods store
Vegetable store
Equipment store   Cleaning store

Food preparation

Meat and fish   Vegetables and salad
General   Pastry

Cooking

Roasting
Frying Baking   Steaming Boiling
Grilling

Dishing up

Service

Dining area

Waste food
Pot wash

Wash up

Dirties return

▲ Workflow through the areas of the kitchen

Surfaces and equipment

Lighting and ventilation

Lighting (natural and artificial) must be sufficient for the tasks being completed to allow for safe working and so that cleaning can be carried out efficiently.

Good ventilation is also essential in food premises to prevent excessive heat, condensation, circulation of air-borne contaminants, grease vapours and odours.

Drainage

Drainage must be adequate for the work being completed without causing flooding. If channels, grease traps and gullies are used they should allow for frequent and easy cleaning.

Floors

These need to be durable and in good condition; they must be non-porous, non-slip and easy to clean. Suitable materials are: non-slip quarry tiles, epoxy resins, industrial vinyl sheeting and granolithic flooring. Where the materials allow, edges between floor and walls should be coved (curved) to prevent debris collecting in corners.

Walls

Walls need to be non-porous, smooth, easy to clean and preferably light in colour. Suitable wall coverings are: plastic cladding, stainless steel sheeting, ceramic tiles, epoxy resin or rubberised painted plaster or brickwork. Walls should be coved where they join the floor. Lagging and ducting around pipes should be sealed and gaps sealed where pipes enter the building to stop pests getting in.

Ceilings

Ceiling finishes must resist the build-up of condensation, which could encourage mould. They should be of a non-flaking material and be washable. Non-porous ceiling panels and tiles are frequently used and may incorporate lighting.

Windows and doors

Windows and doors provide possibilities for pests to enter the building, so they should be fitted with suitable screening, strip-curtains, metal kick plates, and so on. Doors and windows should also fit well into their frames to stop pests gaining access.

Damaged surfaces and equipment

Damaged surfaces can contaminate food by allowing waste and bacteria to build up in cracks and crevasses. Loose parts, chipped or broken fittings and pieces of broken equipment can also fall into food causing physical contamination.

If you notice that a piece of equipment is damaged, broken, cracked, has loose parts or is not working properly, either remove it from use or – if it's too large to do that – put up a sign warning others not to use it. Report the problem with the equipment to a supervisor or whoever is in charge of food safety immediately. These measures must be taken to prevent injury to the person using the equipment but also to prevent contamination of food and illness or injury to the consumer.

The same applies to damaged surfaces or fittings such as work surfaces, walls, ceilings, floors and furniture. Attention must also be given to serving and display equipment to ensure it is undamaged and in good working order. Cracks and crevasses can hold food debris and bacteria, which can then be transferred to food. Loose parts from broken equipment, cracked tiles or flaking paint can fall into food as it is being prepared. These could cause illness and injury to the person eating the food, so damaged surfaces and equipment must be reported to the responsible person immediately.

Cleaning

Clean food areas are essential in the production of safe food and it is a requirement to plan, record and check all cleaning as part of a **cleaning schedule**.

Clean premises, work areas and equipment are important to:
- control the bacteria that cause food poisoning
- discourage growth of moulds
- reduce the possibility of physical and chemical contamination
- make accidents less likely, for example slips on a greasy floor
- create a positive image for customers, visitors and employees
- comply with the law
- avoid attracting pests to the kitchen.

The cleaning schedule needs to include the following information:
- **what** is to be cleaned
- **who** should do it (name if possible)
- **how** it is to be done and how long it should take
- **when** it should be done (for example, the time of day)

- **materials** to be used, including chemicals, dilution, cleaning equipment and protective clothing to be worn
- **safety** precautions necessary
- **signatures** of cleaner and supervisor checking the work, as well as the date and time.

As a food handler it is important to **clean as you go** and not allow waste to accumulate in the area where you are working; this is because it is very difficult to keep untidy areas clean.

Cleaning products

Different cleaning products are designed for different tasks.

Detergent is designed to remove grease and dirt and hold them in suspension in water. It may be in the form of liquid, powder, gel or foam, and usually needs to be added to water. Detergent will not kill pathogens (but the hot water it is mixed with may help to do this); however, it will clean and degrease so that disinfectant can work properly. Detergents work best with hot water.

Disinfectant is designed to destroy bacteria when used properly; make sure you only use a disinfectant intended for kitchen use. Disinfectants must be left on a clean, grease-free surface for the required amount of time – **contact time** – to be effective. Heat may also be used to disinfect, for example the use of steam cleaners or the hot rinse cycle of a dishwasher.

Sanitiser both cleans and disinfects, and usually comes in spray form. Sanitiser is very useful for work surfaces and equipment, especially between tasks. It is usual to clean surfaces with hot water and detergent before spraying with sanitiser.

Items that should be both cleaned and disinfected include:
- all items that come into contact with food, such as preparation surfaces, chopping boards, bowls, trays, knives, serving equipment and utensils, and food display items
- all hand-contact surfaces, such as door and refrigerator handles, telephones and switches
- all equipment used for cleaning, such as cloths, mops, buckets, brooms, dustpans and hand-brushes.

Cleaning cloths

Take great care with kitchen cloths – they are a growing area for bacteria. Different cloths for different areas will help to reduce cross-contamination and it is certainly good practice to use different cloths for raw food and high-risk food areas. Use of disposable kitchen towel is the most hygienic way to dry utensils and food preparation areas.

If a tea towel is used, treat it with great care: remember that it can easily spread bacteria so don't use it as an 'all-purpose cloth' and don't keep it on your shoulder (the cloth touches neck and hair, picking up bacteria).

Cleaning procedures

Cleaning kitchen surfaces should be planned and all staff need to be trained in a suitable cleaning method, such as one of the following.

Six-stage process for cleaning a surface

1 Remove debris and loose particles.
2 Main clean to remove residue and grease.
3 Rinse using clean hot water and cloth to remove the detergent.
4 Apply disinfectant and leave for the contact time recommended on the container.
5 Rinse off the disinfectant (if recommended).
6 Allow to air dry or use kitchen paper.

Four-stage process for cleaning a surface

1 Remove debris and loose particles.
2 Main clean using hot water, detergent and sanitiser.
3 Rinse using clean hot water and cloth if recommended on instructions.
4 Allow to air dry or use kitchen paper.

Cleaning is essential to prevent hazards but, if not managed properly, can become a hazard in itself. Do not store cleaning chemicals in food preparation and cooking areas, and take care with their use to avoid chemical contamination. Make sure that items such as cloths, paper towels and fibres from mops do not get into open food (physical contamination). Bacterial contamination could occur by using the same cleaning cloths and equipment in raw food areas then in high-risk food areas, or by using dirty cloths and equipment.

Dishwashing

Automatic dishwashing

The most efficient and hygienic method of cleaning dishes and crockery is the use of a dishwashing machine as this will clean and disinfect items that will then air dry, removing the need for cloths. The dishwasher can also be used to clean/disinfect small equipment such as chopping boards. The stages in machine dishwashing are:

1 Remove waste food.
2 Pre-rinse or spray.
3 Load on to the appropriate racks with a space between each item.
4 The wash cycle runs at 50°C to 60°C using a detergent.
5 The rinse cycle runs at 82°C to 88°C which will disinfect items ready for air drying.

Dishwashing by hand

If items need to be washed by hand the recommended way to do this is:

1 Scrape/rinse off residue food.
2 Wash items in a sink of hot water (the temperature should be 50°C to 60°C, which means that rubber gloves need to be worn). Use a dishwashing brush rather than a cloth.
3 Rinse in very hot water – if rinsing can be done at 82°C for 30 seconds it would disinfect the dishes.
4 Allow to air dry; do not use tea towels.

Waste disposal

It is important to deal with kitchen waste quickly, hygienically and safely. If waste is allowed to build up in kitchen areas it can encourage pests, allow for multiplication of bacteria, produce unpleasant odours, and items such as food trimmings and packaging materials could fall into food that is being prepared.

All food handlers should keep areas clear, clean and waste to a minimum. Kitchen waste should be placed in waste bins with lids. They should preferably be foot-operated to reduce contamination to the hands. Bins should be made of a strong material, usually a thick plastic, with a strong plastic liner bag placed inside, be easy to clean and pest proof. To deal with waste hygienically bins should be emptied very regularly to avoid waste build-up; the task of keeping kitchen waste bins emptied and cleaned/disinfected should be listed on the cleaning schedule with a specific person responsible for doing this. An over-full, heavy bin is much more difficult to handle and empty than a bin that is emptied regularly.

Outside waste should be in strong containers with lids to prevent pests getting in. They should preferably be raised from the floor (usually by wheels) and on a hard surface, such as concrete, that can be hosed down and kept clean. Outside waste bins should be emptied regularly.

Pests

When there are reports of food premises being heavily fined or forcibly closed down, an infestation of pests is often the reason. As pests can be a serious source of contamination and disease, they must be eliminated for food safety reasons and to comply with the law. Pests can carry food-poisoning bacteria into food premises from their fur/feathers, feet/paws, saliva, urine and droppings. Other problems caused by pests include damage to food stock and packaging; damage to buildings, equipment and wiring; and blockages in equipment and piping.

Pests are attracted to food premises because there may be food, warmth, shelter, water and possible nesting materials; all reasonable measures must be put in place to keep them out. Any possible signs that pests may be present must be reported to the supervisor or manager immediately.

Common pests that may cause problems in food areas are: rats, mice, cockroaches, wasps, flies, ants (including pharaoh ants), birds and domestic pets. Pest management needs to be planned as part of the food safety management system. Regular visits from a recognised pest control company are advisable because they will offer advice as well as deal with problems arising. Companies conducting a regular audit will provide a pest audit report, which should be kept and could be used as part of the food safety management system.

Table 3.1 Signs of pest presence

Pest	Signs that they are present
Rats and mice	Sightings of rodents, droppings, unpleasant smell, gnawed wires, etc. Greasy marks on lower walls, damaged food stock, paw prints.
Flies and wasps	Sighting of flies and wasps, hearing them, dead insects, maggots.
Cockroaches	Sightings (dead or alive) usually at night, unpleasant smell.
Ants	Sightings and present in food; the tiny, pale-coloured Pharaoh ants are difficult to spot but can still be the source of a variety of pathogens.
Weevils	Sightings of weevils in stored products, e.g. flour or cornflour; may be difficult to see – tiny black insects moving in flour.
Birds	Sightings, droppings, in outside storage areas and around refuse.
Domestic pets	These must be kept out of food areas as they carry pathogens on fur, whiskers, saliva, urine, etc.

Measures to keep pests out of the building are of great importance and need to be planned. Pest control contractors can offer advice on keeping pests out as well as organise eradication systems for any pests that do get in. Some basic guidelines are:

- block entry – for example no holes around pipe work, avoid all gaps and cavities where they could get in, sealed drain covers
- damage to the building or fixtures and fittings should be repaired quickly
- window/door screening/netting should be in place
- check deliveries/packaging for pests
- baits and traps used as appropriate
- electronic fly killer (EFK) in place to deal with flying insects
- use of sealed containers so no open food left out
- not allowing a build up of waste in the kitchen
- outside waste not kept too close to the kitchen
- planned pest management control, surveys and reports.

Flying insets cause problems as they can find their way in through very small spaces or from other parts of the building. They can then spread bacteria around the kitchen and on to open food. To eliminate insects such as flies, bluebottles and wasps, an EFK is recommended. These use ultraviolet light to attract the insects, which are then electrocuted on charged wires and fall into catch trays. Do not position an EFK directly above food preparation areas and make sure the catch trays are emptied regularly.

Pest control measures can also introduce food safety hazards. Bodies of dead insects or even rodents may remain in the kitchen (physical and bacterial contamination). Pesticides, insecticides and baits could cause chemical contamination if not managed properly. Pest control is best managed by professionals.

Storing food safely

Checking food on delivery

For food to remain in top condition and be safe to eat it is essential that food deliveries are carefully checked, that correct storage is in place and that procedures are fully understood by all kitchen staff. Only approved suppliers should be used who can assure that food is delivered in the best condition in suitable, undamaged packaging, properly date coded and at the correct temperature. Food suppliers need to be able to provide information on the product from source through to the time it is delivered to you (traceability). Packaged or processed food of any kind will have a list of ingredients listed on the pack. If the food is removed from this packaging for storage, retain the ingredient lists because they will give essential allergy advice.

- All deliveries should be checked then moved to the appropriate storage area as soon as possible and chilled/frozen food within 15 minutes of delivery.

- Use a food probe to check the temperature of food deliveries; record these temperatures and keep as part of the food safety management system:
  - chilled food should be below 5 °C (reject it if above 8 °C)
  - frozen food should be at or below −18 °C (reject it if above −15 °C).
- Many suppliers now provide a print out of temperatures at which food was delivered, (save these printouts in kitchen records).
- Dry goods should be in undamaged packaging, well within best-before dates, be completely dry and in perfect condition on delivery.

When receiving a delivery of food check:

- the items are the quantity, size and quality ordered
- packaging and food is undamaged
- food is at the required temperature (see above)
- food is within use-by dates or has a suitable best-before date
- there are no signs of deterioration or spoilage of the food
- there are no signs of pests present in the food or packaging
- no cross-contamination is evident in the delivery, for example raw and cooked food packaged together.

Preparing food for storage

It is important to prepare food for storage to ensure there is no risk of cross-contamination and that food is labelled and maintained at correct temperatures. Remove food items from their outer packaging – being careful to check for any possible pests that may have found their way in – before placing the products in a refrigerator, freezer or dry store.

Fresh food, such as meat or fish on trays, should be covered well with cling film, dated and labelled, and then placed in the appropriate refrigerated area.

Segregate any unfit food from other food until it is thrown away or collected by supplier. This is to avoid any possible contamination to other foods.

The storage area

Once a food delivery has been accepted it must be placed in the correct storage area. This will reduce the possibility of cross-contamination and help to ensure that the food remains fresh and in best condition. All storage areas (refrigerators, freezers, cold rooms, dry store areas) must be

kept clean and tidy, and this needs to be planned as part of the cleaning schedule. If you notice that these areas are not clean and tidy report it to a supervisor who can deal with the matter properly.

The multi-use refrigerator

The following guidelines apply if a refrigerator is used to store various types of food:

- It is best practice to keep the refrigerator running between 1 °C and 4 °C (the legal requirement is 8 °C).
- Food must be covered and labelled with name of item and the date.
- Always store raw food at the bottom of the refrigerator with other items above.
- Keep high-risk foods well away from raw foods.
- Never overload a refrigerator – to operate properly cold air must be allowed to circulate between items.
- Wrap strong-smelling foods very well as their smell (and taste) can transfer to other foods, for example milk.
- Record the temperature at which the refrigerator is operating at least once a day. Keep the fridge temperatures with other kitchen records.

Refrigerators must be cleaned regularly:

- Remove food to another refrigerator.
- Clean according to the cleaning schedule using a recommended sanitiser (a solution of bicarbonate of soda and water is also good for cleaning refrigerators).
- Remember to empty and clean any drip trays, and clean door seals thoroughly.
- Rinse then dry with kitchen paper.
- Make sure the refrigerator front and handle is cleaned and disinfected to avoid cross-contamination.
- Make sure the refrigerator is back down to a temperature between 1 °C and 4 °C before replacing the food in the proper positions. Check the dates and condition of all food before replacing.

Correct food storage
Storing raw meat and poultry

Raw meat and poultry should be stored in a separate refrigerator running at temperatures between 1 °C and 4 °C where possible. If not already packaged place on trays, cover well with cling film and label. If it is necessary to store meat or poultry in a multi-use refrigerator, make sure it is covered, labelled and placed at the bottom of the refrigerator, well away from other items.

Storing fish

A separate fish refrigerator running between 1°C and 4°C is best. Remove fresh fish from ice containers and place on trays, cover well with cling film and label. If it is necessary to store fish in a multi-use refrigerator, make sure it is well covered, labelled and placed at the bottom of the refrigerator, well away from other items. Remember that odours from fish can permeate other items such as milk or eggs.

Storing dairy products and eggs

Pasteurised milk and cream, eggs and cheese should be stored in their original containers between 1°C and 4°C. Sterilised or UHT milk can be kept in the dry store following the storage instructions on the label.

After delivery, eggs should be stored at a constant temperature – a refrigerator is the best place.

Storing and defrosting frozen foods

Store frozen food in a freezer running at –18°C or below. Separate raw foods from ready-to-eat foods, and never allow food to be refrozen once it has thawed. (For information on defrosting see 'Preparing, cooking and holding food safely' below.)

Storing fruit, vegetables and salad items

Storage conditions will vary according to type. For example, sacks of potatoes, root vegetables and some fruit can be stored in a cool, well-ventilated store room, but salad items, green vegetables, soft fruit and tropical fruit would be better in refrigerated storage. If possible, a specific refrigerator running at around 8°C would be ideal to avoid any chill damage.

Storing dry goods

Dry goods, such as rice, dried pasta, sugar, flour and grains, should be stored at ambient temperatures (room temperature). They should be kept in clean, covered containers on wheels or in smaller sealed containers on shelves to stop pests getting into them. Storage should be in a cool, well-ventilated dry store area and well-managed stock rotation is essential. Remember to keep packaging information as this may include essential **allergy advice**.

Storing and handling canned products

Cans are usually stored in the dry store area and, once again, rotation of stock is essential. Canned food will carry best-before dates and it is not advisable to use them after this date. 'Blown' cans must never be used, and do not use badly dented or rusty cans. Once opened transfer any unused canned food to a clean bowl, cover and label it, and store it in the refrigerator for up to two days.

Storing cooked and ready-to-eat foods

Foods that are purchased ready-cooked or cooked and then stored include a wide range of items such as cooked meats and fish, pies and other pastry items, pâté, cream cakes, desserts and savoury flans. They will usually be 'high-risk foods' so correct storage is essential. Check the labelling on individual items for specific storage instructions but, generally, keep them refrigerated between 1°C and 4°C. Store carefully, wrapped and labelled, and well away from and above raw foods to avoid any cross-contamination.

Food being held for service must be kept above **63°C (or below 5°C)**. If food is being cooled to serve cold or for reheating at a later time, it must be protected from contamination and cooled quickly, that is, to **8°C within 90 minutes**. The best way to do this is in a blast chiller.

Any food that is to be chilled or frozen must be well wrapped or placed in a suitable container with a lid, (items may also be vacuum packed). Make sure that all food is labelled and dated before chilling or freezing.

Stock rotation

First in – first out

This term is used to describe stock rotation and is applied to all categories of food. It simply means that foods already in storage must be used before new deliveries (providing stock is still within recommended dates and in sound condition). Food deliveries should be labelled with their delivery date and preferably the date by which they should be used (see food labelling codes below). Written stock records should form a part of a food safety management system.

Food labelling codes

- **Use-by dates** appear on perishable foods with a short life. Legally, the food must be used by this date and should not stored or used after it. Food past its use-by date must be thrown away.
- **Best-before dates** apply to foods that are expected to have a longer life, such as dry products or canned food. A best-before date advises that food is at its best before this date; using it after this date is still legal but not advised.

▲ Examples of food labelling

Preparing, cooking and holding food safely

Food safety hazards

There are a number of ways that food could be exposed to hazards that could result in it becoming contaminated. Contaminated food can cause illness or even be fatal to those eating it. It is important to be aware of this and to check food frequently and follow the required procedures from delivery right through until the time it is served.

Contamination of food from pathogenic bacteria (biological contamination) is considered to be the most dangerous hazard of all because food can be dangerously contaminated with bacteria but still look, smell and taste fine. There is increasing concern about allergenic hazards too, especially as these can be hidden ingredients in food but can still cause dangerous reactions.

Biological contamination

Biological contamination can occur from pathogenic bacteria and the toxins they may produce. Viruses, yeasts, moulds, spoilage bacteria and enzymes are all around us: in the environment, on raw food, on humans, animals, birds and insects. Pathogenic bacteria are of most concern as they can multiply to dangerous levels but still not be visible except with a microscope. When pathogenic bacteria multiply in food or use food to get into the human body, illness can result.

Bacteria and food poisoning

Not all bacteria are harmful: some are very useful and are used to good effect in the manufacture of foods and medicines. Making milk into yoghurt and making cheese may use bacteria in the process.

Bacteria that are harmful are called **pathogenic bacteria** and can cause food poisoning. Bacteria are very small – so small that you would need to use a microscope to see them; you would not be able to taste them or smell them on food. This is why pathogenic bacteria are so dangerous: you can't tell if they are in food or not. When bacteria have the conditions they need – food, warmth, moisture and time – they can multiply approximately every 10 to 20 minutes by dividing in half (this is called binary fission).

Common food-poisoning bacteria include the following:

- **Salmonella** used to be the most common cause of food poisoning in the UK but, since measures were put in place to reduce salmonella in chickens and in eggs, food poisoning from this source has reduced. One of the main sources of salmonella now is the human and animal gut and excreta, but it is also found on pests such as rodents, insects and birds and in raw meat and poultry, eggs and shellfish. Salmonella poisoning can also be passed on through human carriers (someone carrying salmonella but not showing any signs of illness).
- **Staphylococcus aureus** is found mainly on the human body and can be present on the skin, hair and scalp, nose and throat. Cuts, spots, burns and boils will also be a source of this organism. When it multiplies in food, a toxin (poison) is produced that is very difficult to kill, even with boiling temperatures. To avoid food poisoning from this organism, food handlers need to maintain very high standards of personal hygiene and report any illness they may have to their supervisor before handling food.
- **Clostridium perfringens** can be present in human and animal faeces and raw meat, poultry and vegetables (as well as insects, soil, dust and sewage). A number of food-poisoning incidents from this organism have occurred when large amounts of meat are brought up to cooking temperatures slowly and then allowed to cool slowly. *Clostridium perfringens* can produce **spores** during this heating/cooling process. Spores are very resistant to any further cooking and allow bacteria to survive in conditions that would usually kill them.
- **Bacillus cereus** is another organism that can produce spores, and it can also produce two different toxins, so it is a very dangerous pathogen. It is often associated with cooking rice in large quantities, cooling it too slowly and then reheating. The reheating temperatures are not enough to destroy the spores and toxins. It has also been linked with other cereal crops, spices, soil and vegetables.
- **Clostridium botulinum** is fortunately rare; the symptoms can be very serious, even fatal. Sources tend to be intestines of fish, soil and vegetables.

Toxins

Toxins (poisons) can be produced by some bacteria as they multiply in food. They are heat resistant and may not be killed by the normal cooking processes that kill bacteria, so they remain in the food and can cause illness. Other bacteria produce toxins as they die, usually in the intestines of the person who has eaten the food.

Spores

Some bacteria are able to form spores when the conditions surrounding them become hostile, such as when temperatures rise or in the presence of chemicals such as disinfectant. A spore forms a protective 'shell' inside the bacteria, protecting the essential parts from the high temperatures of normal cooking, disinfection and dehydration. Once spores are formed the rest of the cell disperses – it cannot divide and multiply as before but simply survives until conditions improve, for example high temperatures drop to a level where the cell can reform and multiplication can start again. Prolonged cooking times and/or very high temperatures are needed to kill spores. Time is very important in preventing the formation of spores. Large amounts of food, such as meat for stewing, when brought slowly to cooking temperature, allows time for spores to form; these are then very difficult to kill. Bring food up to cooking temperature quickly and cool food quickly.

Food-borne illness

Some different organisms from the ones named above are said to cause food-borne illness. These pathogens do not multiply in food but use food to get into the human gut where they then multiply and cause a range of illnesses (some of them serious), including severe abdominal pain, diarrhoea, vomiting, headaches, blurred vision, flu symptoms, septicaemia and miscarriage. These organisms may be transmitted from person-to-person, in water or be airborne, as well as through food.

Food-borne pathogens include:
- **Campylobacter**: causes more food-related illness than any other organism. It is found in raw poultry and meat, sewage, animals, insects and birds.
- **E. coli 0157**: present in the intestines and excreta of animals and humans, raw meat, and can be present on raw vegetables.
- **Listeria**: of concern because it can multiply (slowly) at fridge temperatures, that is, below 5 °C. It has been linked with chilled products such as unpasteurised cheeses, pâté and prepared salads, as well as cook/chill meals.

- **Norovirus**: like all viruses, norovirus will not multiply on food but it may live for a short time on surfaces, utensils and food, and use these to get into the body. The usual way this is spread is airborne, person-to-person, water or sewage.

Chemical contamination

Chemical contamination can occur when chemical items get into food accidentally; these can then make the consumer suffer discomfort or become ill. The kinds of chemical that can get into food could be cleaning fluids, disinfectants, machine oil, degreasers and pesticides. Problems can also occur when there are chemical reactions between things such as metal containers and acidic foods.

Physical contamination

Physical contamination is caused when something gets into foods that should not be there, such as glass; nuts, bolts and oil from machinery; mercury from thermometers; flaking paint; pen tops; threads and buttons from clothing; blue plasters; hair and insects.

Allergenic contamination

An **allergy** is when the immune system in some people reacts to certain food, causing swelling, itching, rashes, breathlessness and even cause anaphylactic shock, (a severe reaction causing swelling of the throat and mouth, which prevents breathing). **Food intolerance** is different and does not involve the immune system, but there may still be a serious reaction to some foods. Foods usually associated with allergies and intolerances are: nuts, dairy products, wheat-based products and gluten, eggs, fish and shellfish. Some people may also have an allergy to some fruits, vegetables, plants and mushrooms.

It is very important for all food handlers to have some knowledge of allergens and the foods or ingredients that could cause allergic reactions. All food businesses must have information and procedures in place for providing safe food for allergy sufferers. Correct allergen information must be given to the customer about the food being served to them. If in doubt seek advice from someone senior in your team and discuss the customer's requirements with them. It is very important that you follow your workplace procedures for allergies and provide accurate information at all times.

Provision of certain food allergy information became mandatory in December 2014: all businesses offering food to customers must now provide this information. Under EU regulation FIR 1169/2011, specific information on 14 allergens/ingredients must be available, irrespective of whether the food is packaged or chosen from a menu, although allergy information about menu items may be provided verbally as long as it is accurate. Statements such as 'may contain nuts' are no longer adequate. For more information and advice go to the Food Standards Agency's website (www.food.gov.uk).

Poisoning from other items

Some foods can be naturally poisonous, such as some types of mushroom and undercooked red kidney beans. Some oily fish can develop toxins if stored at too high a temperature, and occasionally some shellfish can cause illness when they have fed on poisonous plankton.

Some moulds can produce toxins as they grow; these are called **mycotoxins**. Mycotoxins can cause serious illness and have been linked with cancers. Do not use mouldy food (controlled moulds, such as in blue cheeses, are fine).

Food spoilage and food preservation

Most foods have a limited life and will eventually deteriorate due to moulds, yeasts, enzymes or bacteria. Spoilage of food also occurs due to exposure to oxygen, moisture or chemicals; damage by pests; or by poor handling and bad storage.

Unlike bacterial contamination, which is impossible to detect in a normal kitchen situation, food spoilage can usually be observed by sight, smell, taste and touch. Spoilage could include mouldy, slimy, dried-up or over-wet fresh foods. Blown cans and vac-packs and food with freezer burn are also a sign of food spoilage.

Different methods have been developed to prolong the natural life of various foods and keep them fresh. These include:

- **use of heat** – cooking, canning, sterilisation, UHT, pasteurisation
- **use of heat and sealing** – canning, bottling, cooking then vacuum packaging
- **use of low temperatures** – chilling, freezing
- **exclusion of air** – vacuum packaging
- **changing gases surrounding food** – modified atmosphere packaging
- **removal of moisture** – dehydrated foods
- **use of acids, sugar or salt concentrations**
- **food preservatives** – for example, nitrates and sulphates.

Food preservation will often combine methods to ensure effective preservation, for example vacuum-packed fish will also be refrigerated, as would pasteurised milk.

Controlling hazards

As a food handler it is your responsibility, along with those working with you, to assist in the control of food hazards. There are a number of ways that the range of hazards described above can be controlled. These include:

- strict and careful standards of personal hygiene
- reporting of illness to the appropriate person
- keeping work areas clean and hygienic
- storing food correctly and at the appropriate temperatures
- cooking food to the required temperature
- taking care to avoid cross-contamination.

The food handler is also in a good position to notice any possible hazards that could be a risk to food safety. These should be reported immediately to a supervisor, head chef or senior chef, or anyone else with responsibility for food safety in the area.

Cross-contamination

Cross-contamination occurs when bacteria are transferred from one place to another. This is usually from contaminated food (mostly raw food), equipment or surfaces to ready-to-eat food. It is the cause of significant amounts of food poisoning and care must be taken to avoid it. Cross-contamination could be caused by:

- foods touching, for example raw and cooked meat
- raw meat or poultry dripping on to high-risk foods
- soil from dirty vegetables coming into contact with high-risk foods
- dirty cloths, dirty staff uniforms or dirty equipment
- equipment used for raw then cooked food, for example chopping boards or knives
- hands touching raw then cooked food, not washing hands between tasks, and so on
- hands touching items such as door handles, refrigerator handles or telephones
- pests spreading bacteria around the kitchen.

Controlling cross-contamination

Completely separate working areas and storage areas for raw and high-risk foods are strongly recommended. If this is not possible, keep them well away from each other and make sure that working areas are thoroughly cleaned and disinfected between tasks.

Vegetables should be washed before preparation and again afterwards. Leafy vegetables may need to be washed in several changes of cold water to remove all of the soil present.

Good personal hygiene practices by staff, in particular frequent and effective hand washing, is very important in controlling cross-contamination and will avoid the significant amounts of contamination caused by faecal/oral routes (this is when pathogens normally found in faeces are transferred to ready-to-eat foods resulting in cross-contamination and illness). An obvious way that this may happen is when food handlers visit the toilet, do not wash their hands properly, then handle food.

Colour-coded chopping boards are a good way to keep different types of food separate. Worktops and chopping boards come into contact with the food being prepared so need special attention. Make sure that chopping boards are in good condition: cracks and splits could trap bacteria and this could be transferred to food.

As well as colour-coded chopping boards some kitchens also provide colour-coded knives, cloths, cleaning equipment, storage trays, bowls and even staff uniforms to help prevent cross-contamination.

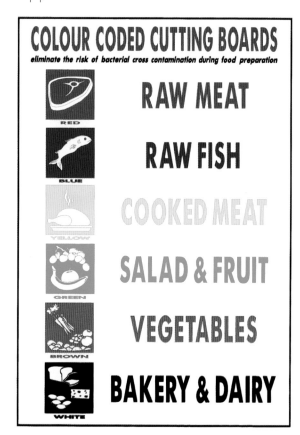

▲ The colour-coding system

Clean and sanitise worktops and chopping boards before working on them and do this again after use, paying particular attention when they have been used for raw foods.

Chopping boards can be disinfected after use by putting them through a dishwasher with a high rinse temperature of 82 °C (high temperatures will kill bacteria).

Small equipment, such as knives, bowls, spoons and tongs, could also be the cause of cross-contamination; it is important to wash them thoroughly (once again a dishwasher does it well). This is especially important when they are used for a variety of cooked and raw food.

Methods, times, temperatures and checks for keeping food safe

Defrosting frozen foods before cooking

Most frozen foods will need to be defrosted before use. This is because, if the food is still frozen or partly frozen, it is unlikely to reach the temperatures required in the centre to kill any bacteria present. The exceptions to this are small or thin foods such as pizza, vegetables, and small items of prepared fish or chicken that would defrost fully in the cooking process.

If you need to defrost frozen food, such as a whole chicken, place it in a deep tray, cover it with film and label, stating what the item is and the date when defrosting was started. Place at the bottom of the refrigerator where thawing liquid can't drip on to anything else. Thaw food completely (no ice crystals on any part), then cook thoroughly within 12 hours. Make sure that you allow enough time for this process – it may take longer than you think! (A 2 kg chicken will take about 24 hours to defrost at 3 °C.)

Cooking and reheating

Thorough cooking is one of the best methods available to control bacteria.

Cooking to **75 °C** and holding that temperature for at least **two minutes** will kill most pathogens (but not spores and toxins). These temperatures are important, especially where large amounts are being cooked or the consumers are in the high-risk categories. However, some popular dishes on hotel and restaurant menus are cooked to a lower temperature than this according to individual dish and customer requirements.

Keep food being held for service **above 63°C**, or cool it rapidly and keep **below 5°C**. Never put hot or warm food into a refrigerator or freezer – this will raise the temperature and put food into the **danger zone**.

Checking food is thoroughly cooked/reheated

Electronic temperature probes are very useful to measure the temperature in the centre of both hot and cold food. They are also very useful for recording the temperature of deliveries and checking food temperatures in refrigerators. Make sure that the probe is clean and disinfected before use (disposable disinfectant wipes are useful for this). Place the probe into the centre of the food, making sure it is not touching bone or the cooking container.

Check regularly that probes are working correctly (calibration). This can be done electronically, but a simple and low-cost check is to place the probe in icy water – the reading should be 0°C. Next, place the probe in boiling water and the temperature reading should be 100°C. In both cases one degree higher or lower is acceptable. If probes read outside of these temperatures they need to be repaired or replaced. When calibration of probes has been completed, record these temperatures and keep as part of the food safety management system.

Cooling/chilling cooked food

If food is being cooled/chilled to serve cold or for reheating at a later time, it must be protected from contamination and cooled quickly to 8°C within 90 minutes. This will help prevent multiplication of any bacteria that may be present and avoids possible problems with spores forming. The best way to cool food is in a blast chiller but, if this is not available, place it in the coolest part of the kitchen, making sure that it is protected from contamination while it is cooling. Any food that has been above 8°C (but below 63°C) for more than two hours must be thrown away.

To freeze cooked food:
- chill it first
- wrap well or place in a suitable covered container
- label and date, then freeze quickly
- defrost before using.

The running temperature of refrigerators, freezers and chill cabinets should be checked and recorded at least once a day. Refrigerators and chill cabinets should be below 5°C and freezers below −18°C.

Systems are now available to automatically log temperatures of all fridges, freezers and display cabinets in a business. Temperatures are recorded and sent to a central computer several times a day. These can then be printed or stored electronically as part of due diligence record keeping. Units not running at correct temperatures will be highlighted by the system.

Holding food for service

Wherever possible food on display should be kept under refrigeration and the temperature should be checked to ensure that it is being maintained at a safe level. Where customers are close to displayed food it should be behind a clear sneeze screen.

Dishes prepared in advance should be covered with cling film and refrigerated at between 1°C and 3°C to keep them safe and stop them drying out.

Table 3.2 Important temperatures when dealing with food

Food	Important temperature
Food stored in a freezer (no bacterial growth but does not kill bacteria, toxins or spores)	Store at –18 °C to –23 °C
Refrigerated food: ● raw meat/poultry ● raw fish and shellfish ● cooked meats/meat products ● cooked fish/fish products ● dairy products/fats ● eggs ● salad items, herbs, leafy vegetables ● cooked foods/high-risk items	Store at 1 °C to 4 °C*
Ambient stored food: ● canned food ● dry goods ● grains ● general grocery items	Store at 10 °C to 15 °C in a cool, well-ventilated place
Cooked hot food (a temperature that will kill bacteria but not spores and probably not toxins)	Core (centre) temperature must reach 75 °C
Cooked fish (Environmental Health Officers may advise a higher temperature)	Core (centre) temperature must reach 63 °C
Reheated food	Core (centre) temperature must reach 75 °C (82 °C in Scotland)
Hot food being held for service	Keep above 63 °C – if below this temperature for more than two hours it must be thrown away

*Although the law says that 'foods which support growth of pathogens or formation of toxins must not be stored above 8 °C' it is recognised best practice to store below 5 °C.

100°C Boiling point of water

75°C Cook most food to this temperature or above for at least 2 minutes to kill most bacteria (spores will not be killed)

63°C Bacteria start to die: hold hot food above this temperature

5–63°C
DANGER ZONE
Bacteria grow particularly quickly between 20 and 50°C

37°C Body temperature: bacteria multiply rapidly

5°C Bacteria could start to multiply slowly

0°C Water freezes

–18°C A freezer should run at this temperature or below. Bacteria will survive but not multiply

Food safety management systems

In line with the Food Standards Agency's commitment to reduce food poisoning, all food businesses are required by law to have a food safety management system and this will be checked by Environmental Health Officers (EHOs) when they inspect premises.

Managing food safety with a good recording system will help to control hazards and keep them at a safe level. If hazards are not controlled, contamination could occur and outbreaks of food poisoning could be the result. All food handlers must be well trained to make them aware of possible hazards and that, in terms of food safety, some hazards are more important than others. They must remain aware of the procedures in their workplace for what to do when things go wrong and how to report potential hazards. As discussed earlier in this chapter, hazards are controlled by: cooking, chilling, cleaning and avoiding cross-contamination.

Hazard Analysis Critical Control Points

All food safety management systems must be based on **Hazard Analysis Critical Control Points (HACCP)**. This is a recognised system that looks at identifying the critical points for stages in any process, the hazards that may occur and how these will be controlled.

All processes in the kitchen must be monitored so it is easier to identify if the procedure is not working properly. Where there are problems, such as food not reaching the required temperature to kill bacteria, systems must be in place for staff to report this so that correct procedures are put in place immediately. The system needs to provide a documented record of the stages **all** food will go through right up to the time it is eaten, and may include:

- purchase and delivery
- receipt of food
- storage
- preparation
- cooking
- cooling
- hot holding
- reheating
- chilled storage
- serving.

Once the hazards have been identified, corrective measures are put in place to control the hazards and keep the food safe.

The system must be updated regularly, especially when new items are introduced to the menu or systems change – specific new controls must be put in place to include them (for example, if a new piece of cooking equipment has been installed).

The HACCP system involves seven stages:

1 Identify hazards – what could go wrong?
2 Identify the CCPs (critical control points) – i.e. the important points where things could go wrong.
3 Set critical limits for each CCP – e.g. temperature requirements on delivery of fresh chicken.
4 Monitor CCPs – put checks in place to stop problems happening.
5 Corrective action – what will be done if something goes wrong?
6 Verification – check that the HACCP plan is working.
7 Documentation – record all of the above.

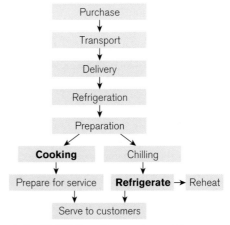

▲ An HACCP flow diagram for cooking a fresh chicken

The example in this diagram relates to the cooking of a chicken. When dealing with a fresh chicken it is necessary to recognise the possible hazards at all of the identified stages:

- **Hazard** – pathogenic bacteria is likely to be present in raw chicken.
- **Control** – the chicken needs to be cooked thoroughly to +75 °C to ensure pathogens are killed.
- **Monitor** – check the temperature where the thigh joins the body with a calibrated temperature probe, make sure no parts of the flesh are pink and juices are running clear, not red or pink.
- **Hot holding** – the chicken must be kept above 63 °C before service; this can be checked with a temperature probe.
- **Or chill and refrigerate** – chill to below 10 °C within 90 minutes. Cover, label and refrigerate below 5 °C.
- **Documentation** – temperatures must be measured and recorded. Hot-holding equipment should be checked and the temperature recorded. Record any corrective measures necessary.

Table 3.3 shows this example in more detail.

Table 3.3 An HACCP control chart for cooking a fresh chicken for later reheating

Process steps	Hazards	Controls	Critical limit	Monitoring	Corrective action
Purchase	Contamination, pathogens, mould or foreign bodies present in food	Approved supplier	Agreed delivery temperatures for chilled/frozen food	All food is to agreed standards	Change supplier
Transport and delivery	Multiplication of harmful bacteria	Refrigerated vehicles	Delivery temperature of chicken below 5°C	Check delivery vehicles, date marks, temperatures	Reject if >8 °C or past 'use by' date
Refrigerate	Bacterial growth Further contamination (bacteria, chemicals, etc.)	Store below 5 °C Separate raw and cooked foods Use within 'use by' date Stock rotation	Store below 5°C	Check and record temperature twice a day Check date marks	Discard if signs of spoilage or past date mark
Prepare	Bacterial growth Further contamination	No more than 30 minutes in 'danger zone' Good personal hygiene Red coded equipment Clean equipment, hygienic premises	Two hours out of refrigeration – discard	Supervisor to audit at regular intervals Visual checks Cleaning schedules	Discard if >8 °C for two hours
Cook	Survival of harmful bacteria	Thorough cooking	75°C on food probe	Check and record temperature/ time	Continue cooking to 75 °C
Prepare for service	Multiplication of bacteria Contamination	No more than 20 minutes in 'danger zone'	Max. two hours	Supervisor to audit at regular intervals	Discard if >8 °C for two hours or more
Chill	Multiplication of bacteria Contamination	Blast chiller	Chill to below 8°C within 90 minutes	Supervisor to audit at regular intervals	Discard if out of refrigeration for two hours or more
Refrigerate	Multiplication of bacteria Contamination	Store below 5 °C Keep away from raw foods	> 8°C within 90 minutes	Check and record temperature twice a day	Discard if >8 °C for two hours or more
Reheat	Survival of bacteria	Reheat to 75 °C in centre	75°C (82°C in Scotland)	Check and record temperature of each batch	Continue reheating to 75 °C

Safer Food Better Business

The HACCP system may seem complicated and difficult to set up for a small or fairly limited business. With this in mind, the Food Standards Agency launched their **Safer Food Better Business** system for England and Wales.

This is based on the principles of HACCP but in an easy-to-understand format with pre-printed pages and charts to enter the relevant information, such as temperatures of individual dishes. It is divided into two parts. The first part is about safe methods, for example avoiding cross-contamination, personal hygiene, cleaning, chilling and cooking. The second part covers opening and closing checks, proving methods are safe, recording safe methods, training records, supervision, stock control and the selection of suppliers and contractors.

Safer Food Better Business is available to download from www.food.gov.uk.

Similar systems have been developed in Scotland (**CookSafe**) and Northern Ireland (**Safe Catering**).

Due diligence

'Due diligence' can be used as defence under food safety legislation when something relating to food safety goes wrong. It involves providing proof that a business took all reasonable care and precaution, and did everything it could to prevent food safety problems: that is, it exercised all due diligence. To prove due diligence accurate and up-to-date written documents are essential. They should include:

- staff training records
- staff sickness records
- temperature records (cooking and cold storage)
- pest control policy and audits
- cleaning schedules and deep-clean reports
- equipment maintenance records
- CCP monitoring activities – changes made, corrective actions and recalls
- modifications to the HACCP system
- customer complaints/investigation results
- calibration of instruments, e.g. temperature probes
- lists of suppliers (traceability of food).

What the law says

The latest laws of importance to food businesses took effect from 1 January 2006. They set out the basic food safety requirements for all aspects of a food business, from premises to personal hygiene of staff, with specific attention to actual temperatures relating to food.

The main difference in the 2006 laws was the requirement to have an approved **food safety management procedure** in place with up-to-date records available.

Legislation concerning food safety covers a wide range of topics including:

- controlling and reducing outbreaks of food poisoning
- registration of premises/vehicles
- content and labelling of food
- preventing manufacture and sale of injurious food
- food imports
- prevention of food contamination and equipment contamination
- training of food handlers
- provision of clean water, sanitary facilities and washing facilities.

For further information on food safety legislation visit: www.food.gov.uk.

Training

Food businesses must ensure that all staff who handle food are supervised and instructed and/or trained in food hygiene appropriate to the work they do. The person responsible for the food safety management of a business must also be responsible for staff training.

Appropriate training can take place in-house or with a training provider. Records of staff training must include the date, level of the training and topics covered. All records of staff training must be kept for possible inspection.

Environmental Health Officers

Food safety standards and legislation is enforced in the UK by Environmental Health Officers (EHOs) and Environmental Health Practitioners (EHPs).

Enforcement officers may visit food premises as a matter of routine, as a follow-up when problems have been identified or after a complaint. The frequency of visits depends on the type of business and food being handled, possible hazards within the business, the risk rating and any previous problems or convictions. Generally, businesses posing a higher risk will be visited more frequently than those considered low risk.

EHO/EHPs can enter a food business at any reasonable time without previous notice or appointment, usually when the business is open. The main purpose of these inspections is to identify any possible risks from the food business and to assess the effectiveness of the business's own food safety management systems, and also to identify any non-compliance of regulations so this can be monitored and corrected.

The role of the EHO/EHP is to:

- offer professional food safety advice to food businesses on routine visits and provide useful information such as leaflets and posters
- advise on new food safety legislation
- investigate complaints about the business
- ensure that food offered for sale is safe and fit for consumption
- monitor food operations within a business and identify possible sources of contamination
- ensure food safety law compliance
- observe the effectiveness of the food safety management system
- deal with food-poisoning outbreaks
- advise on food safety training
- deal with non-compliance by formal action/serving notices. They have the power to:
  - close the business
  - seize/remove food
  - instigate prosecution
  - seize records.

Notices and orders for non-compliance

A **Hygiene Improvement Notice** will be served if the EHO/EHP believes that a food business does not comply with regulations. The notice is served in writing and states the name and address of the business, what is wrong, why it is wrong, what needs to be done to put it right and the time in which this must be completed (usually not less than 14 days).

A **Hygiene Emergency Prohibition Notice** is served if the EHO/EHP believes that there is an imminent risk to health from the business. This would include serious issues such as sewage contamination, lack of water supply, rodent infestation, and so on. Serving this notice means immediate closure of the business for three days, during which time the EHO/EHP must apply to magistrates for a **Hygiene Emergency Prohibition Order** to keep the premises closed. Notices/orders must be displayed in a visible place on the premises. The owner of the business must apply for a **Certificate of Satisfaction** before they can reopen.

A **Hygiene Prohibition Order** prohibits a person (the owner/manager) from working in a food business.

Magistrates' courts can impose fines of up to £5,000, a six-month prison sentence or both. For serious offences, such as knowingly selling food dangerous to health, magistrates could impose fines of up to £20,000. In a crown court unlimited fines and/or two years' imprisonment can be imposed.

The Food Standards Agency

The Food Standards Agency was established in 2000 'to protect public health from risks which may arise in connection with the consumption of food and otherwise to protect the interest of customers in relation to food'. The agency is committed to putting customers first, to being open and accessible, and to being an independent voice on food-related matters.

Scores on the Doors

Scores on the Doors is a strategy introduced by the Food Standards Agency to raise food safety standards and reduce the incidence of food poisoning. When an EHO/EHP inspection has been carried out, a star rating will be awarded ranging from 0 to 5 stars:

Number of stars	Rating
*****	Excellent
****	Very good
***	Good
**	Broadly compliant
*	Poor
none	Very poor

The intention is that the given star rating will be placed in a prominent position on the door or window of premises, but it is not mandatory to do so.

It is hoped that the Scores on Doors scheme will have a lasting, positive impact on food safety standards.

Test yourself

1   Why should long hair be tied back and covered in the kitchen?

2. Describe how to wash your hands safely and give three examples of when your hands must be washed when working with food.

3   There are certain illnesses that a food handler must report to their supervisor before being involved with food. What are they?

4. When cleaning, what do each of the following do:

   a   detergent

   b   sanitiser

   c   disinfectant?

5   Pest control is important.

   a   Why must you keep pests out of food premises?

   b   Suggest three types of pests that could be found in food premises and describe ways that you could keep each of them out.

6   Give four examples of foods that could cause an allergic reaction in some people.

7   Give four examples of how you can avoid cross-contamination in a kitchen.

8   It is essential to keep food above 63 °C or below 5 °C when holding food for service.

   a   Why is this important?

   b   What is the name given to this range of temperatures?

9   What are the temperatures you would recommend storing:

   a   dairy foods

   b   frozen fish

   c   fresh meat

   d   soft fruit

   e   flour?

10 All food businesses are required by law to have a food safety management system.

   a   Why is it important to monitor hazards to food safety in a kitchen?

   b   State the key stages in the monitoring process when cooking a fresh chicken for later reheating.

4 Maintain, handle and clean knives

This chapter is relevant to the following units:
→ Maintain, handle and clean knives.

Knives are essential pieces of equipment in kitchens and have different styles and characteristics to deal with a wide range of culinary tasks. To achieve the best possible results from knives they must be well cared for, cleaned well after use and kept sharp. All chefs need to be trained in the best, safest and most efficient ways to use a range of knives as well as cleavers, scissors and secateurs.

The types, availability and styles of professional knives have developed considerably in recent years. Quality knives are a good investment for a chèf and should be chosen carefully.

You will need to consider:
- the tasks you are completing – for example, if you work in a fish restaurant a good-quality filleting knife would be a good investment
- how the knife feels to hold – they do vary in style, weight and balance
- ease of sharpening
- the cost and what you are prepared to spend
- preferences in style and the materials used to make the knife
- how you are going to clean and store the knife safely.

Knives and related equipment

The professional chef will use a range of knives in the kitchen and a very wide choice is available. The most commonly used knives are straight-bladed and serrated.

Straight-bladed knives

- **Chopping knife (cook's knife or chef's knife):** this will have a broad, rigid blade between 15 and 30 cm long, and a 'heel'. This is probably the chef's most useful knife and is used for a variety of tasks including chopping, cutting, slicing of vegetables, meat, poultry, fish and fruit, as well as tasks such as shredding of salads and vegetables.
- **Paring knife:** a small, multi-purpose knife used mainly for topping, tailing and trimming vegetables, and peeling fruits and vegetables. It may also be used on smaller vegetable cuts and for garnish preparation.
- **Filleting knife:** used for filleting fish. This knife often has a flexible blade, which allows the chef to move the knife easily around the bone structure and between the flesh and bone of the fish.

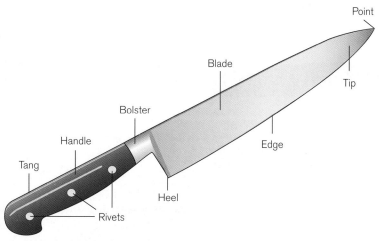

▲ The parts of a knife

- **Boning knife**: a short-bladed knife with a pointed end used for boning meat. The blade is strong and rigid (not flexible) in order to get close to the bones, cut away the meat and manoeuvre between bones safely.
- **Palette knife**: a flat knife with a blunt, rounded end blade. It is used for lifting and turning food, scraping and spreading. It probably has most use in the pastry section but is also used in other kitchen areas.
- **Turning knife**: a small curve-bladed knife used for shaping vegetables in a variety of ways.
- **Carving knife and fork**: a French carving knife has a long, thin blade and is also known as a tranchard. Long strokes with the blade enables neat and efficient carving of meat. A carving fork is two pronged, strong enough to support meats for carving and also for lifting them once carved.

Serrated knives

Serrated knives are used for slicing or for foods that are softer on the inside than the outside, such as crusty bread or tomatoes. A serrated knife allows you to cut neat slices, so is good for slicing bread and pastry items. The serrated blade is used in long strokes with a light sawing action, which does not compress the food. It can also be used to slice foods such as meat or terrines into neat slices. Special palette knives are also available with a serrated edge for slicing cakes, sponges and other pastry goods. Small serrated knives can be used for cutting tomatoes and soft fruits, and a small, pointed serrated knife may also be a cutlery item when serving steaks.

Serrated knifes are not usually sharpened in the kitchen but are sent to a specialist company for sharpening.

▲ A palette knife

▲ A turning knife

▲ A carving fork

Other cutting equipment

Other tools used for cutting in the kitchen include:
- **Butchers' saws**: commonly used in butchery to saw through meat bones; they have serrated blades.

- **Meat cleavers (choppers)**: usually used for heavy chopping tasks, such as bones in meat. The heavy flat blade allows this to be done more easily.
- **Secateurs**: similar to scissors with two long, pointed blades. Some secateurs have the handles set at an angle to the blades to allow for easy and efficient use. Secateurs have a variety of uses including cutting through chicken joints and trimming whole fish.
- **Kitchen scissors**: a wide range of uses including trimming fish, snipping herbs, cutting lengths from filo pastry, cutting paper to line tins and moulds, and opening bags and packets safely.

▲ A butcher's saw

▲ A meat cleaver

Materials used for knives

The materials used for knife blades include:
- **Carbon steel**: easy to sharpen and get a good edge, but can rust and stain easily.
- **Stainless steel**: now very popular for chefs' knives. It is softer than carbon steel so will need sharpening more frequently but is resistant to rust stains.
- **High-carbon stainless steel**: a higher-grade stainless steel with a high carbon content. These knives resist rust and staining, and maintain their sharp edge for longer than standard stainless steel.
- **Laminated** blades are made with a hard steel and a more brittle steel sandwiched together to combine the advantages of a tougher blade that stays sharp for longer.
- **Ceramic** is the hardest material available for knife blades and will hold a sharp edge for the longest time. However, the blade can chip and may break if the knife is dropped. It also needs specialist sharpening. Ceramic knives tend to be lighter than steel and usually have plastic handles.

- **Folded steel** knives are of Japanese origin and have a strong and very sharp blade. The blade is made from numerous layers of soft and hard steel with a central layer of very hard steel forming the cutting edge. The layers are heated, folded and hammered to create soft layers that act as shock absorbers for the hard steel, which tends to be brittle. The techniques used are labour intensive so these knives tend to be relatively expensive.

Knife handles were traditionally made from wood with the blade 'tang' – the metal piece at the end of the blade that goes into the handle – secured by rivets. Although wooden-handled knives are still manufactured, plastics have generally replaced wooden handles.

Knives made in one piece with a stainless steel handle and blade have become increasingly popular. They are forged with hard molybdenum/vanadium stainless steel, which retains a good edge, and are considered to be more hygienic because of the lack of joints. The handles are often of a hollow construction, which may be filled with sand for weight and balance purposes.

Using knives

Knives are essential tools for all chefs but they can cause serious injury to the user or to someone else if they are used wrongly or carelessly. Always use the correct knife for the task you are about to complete. This will make the work easier to complete and you are more likely to achieve a professional finish. Make sure the knife is undamaged, sharpened and that the blade and handle are completely clean and grease free; this will help to avoid accidents. Quality knives that are looked after and treated with care will give good service and will be less likely to cause injury.

Most chefs have their own set of knives that they will clean, sharpen and replace as necessary. However, where knives are provided for you, it is essential to look after them as required by the employer and report any damaged knives to them immediately.

All knives can be potentially dangerous if not used properly. If wrongly used, serious injury can be the result as well as more minor injuries. By following a few simple rules and treating knives with respect, injuries and accidental cuts should be kept to a minimum. Use knives correctly at all times and encourage others around you to do the same.

Any accidents/injuries that do occur when using knives must be reported to supervisor, senior chef or the first-aid person, then properly recorded according to the establishment's operational procedure. This means that there is a record of all accidents and incidents, and when they happened, which is a legal requirement for all workplaces.

Holding a knife

Generally, you should grasp a knife with your fingers around the handle (thumb and index fingers on opposite sides) and well clear of the blade edge. The exact way that you hold the knife will vary depending on the size and design of the knife and the task being carried out. Grasp the knife firmly to give full control. Make sure that the fingers and thumb of the hand not holding the knife are well tucked in, away from the blade edge, to avoid cutting them.

The cutting surface

Most of the cutting and chopping you do will be on a suitable chopping board placed on a working surface. Firstly make sure that the work surface is free from items other than what you actually need for the task, and that it is thoroughly cleaned and sanitised.

Select the correct board for the task you are completing and make sure it is clean and disinfected/sanitised too. This will help to avoid cross-contamination from bacteria, physical items or chemicals and allergens (see the information on colour-coded chopping boards in the Chapter 3 Maintain food safety, page 32). Make sure the board is firmly secured before starting to cut or chop. This is important because, if the board is moves as you use it, you will lose full control of the knife and injury can result. The board can be secured by placing non-slip rubber matting between the board and surface or using damp kitchen paper/damp cloth to do the same thing.

Safety with knives

- When carrying a knife in the kitchen hold it down by the side of your body with the blade pointing down and backwards.
- Never run holding a knife and take care not to trip or slip.
- When handing a knife to someone else, offer them the handle while you hold the top (blunt edge) of the blade.
- Keep the sharp edge of the blade away from you when cleaning or drying knives, and do not run your fingers along the blade edge.
- Do not have more than one knife at a time on the chopping board. When not actually using the knife, place it alongside the board with the blade edge facing inwards.
- Never carry knives around on top of a chopping board; they could slide off and cause injury.
- Do not allow knives to overhang the edge of the work surface; they could be knocked off or fall and cause injury. Never try to catch a falling knife – step back and wait until it reaches the floor.

- Never leave a knife with the blade pointing upwards. You or someone else could put a hand down on the blade. (Many knives are now designed so that it is impossible for them to be placed 'blade upwards'.)
- Keep the knife handle clean, grease free and dry. If the handle is wet or greasy it can slip in use and could cause cuts to the user.
- Keep knives visible – do not leave them under vegetable peelings, packaging or a cloth.
- Store knives carefully, preferably in a box or carrying case with compartments to keep the knives separate and easy to find. Do not place knives loosely into a drawer or locker because you or someone else could grasp the blade by accident.
- Any knives that have become damaged, badly worn or dangerous in any way should be removed from use immediately to avoid injury. Damaged workplace-owned knives must be removed from use and reported to a head chef or supervisor.

Sharpening knives

Sharp knives are safer than blunt knives, provided that they are handled with care. This is because a sharp blade will cut cleanly and efficiently through the food without the need for excessive pressure. A blunt knife is less easy to control. It will need more pressure and force, and is likely to slip sideways, possibly causing injury as well as badly prepared food.

Knives need to be kept sharp by sharpening them frequently with a steel, whetstone or other sharpening tool. Take time to learn how to do this properly and safely.

Steels are used for sharpening knives. The metal shaft may be circular or oval; diamond steels embedded with abrasive diamond particles are considered to be the easiest and best to use. Steels usually have a guard to protect the hands and a handle similar to a knife handle. To sharpen a knife, run the knife at an angle (usually 45 degrees) along the steel edge.

▲ A selection of knives, a steel and an electric sharpener

▲ Sharpening a knife with a steel

Once a blade becomes really blunt it may need to be 'reground' by a specialist. An electric or manually operated grinding wheel is used to replace the lost 'edge' on the knife blade. Arrangements can be made for mobile units to visit your premises to regrind knives or they can be sent away to be reground.

Cleaning knives

Taking care to clean knives well will avoid cross-contamination and make them safer to use (greasy knife handles can cause them to slip and cause injury). Good care and cleaning tends to make knives last for longer.

- Clean knives in hot water with detergent but keep hold of them and take care not to run fingers along the edge of the blade. Remember to clean the handle too.
- Do not leave knives in washing-up water where they are not visible – the blade could be grasped, resulting in cuts to the hand.
- Rinse and dry thoroughly, and store in an appropriate safe place.
- Generally it is not recommended to clean knives in a dishwasher (the blade edge can be damaged).

Food safety and knives

A knife can very easily transfer harmful bacteria from one place to another or from one food to another, making it a vehicle of contamination. It is also very important to remember that an unwashed knife could cause allergen contamination. For example, if a knife is used to chop nuts then – without thorough cleaning – is used to slice cooked chicken, the chicken will have traces of nuts, which could cause a severe allergic reaction in someone with a nut allergy.

- Always make sure that knives and the cutting surface (such as chopping boards) are clean and sanitised before use to avoid possible cross-contamination.
- Wash and dry knives thoroughly between using on different food types to avoid cross-contamination. Some kitchens have knives with colour-coded handles (along with chopping boards and other equipment) to use on foods for allergy sufferers. The equipment intended for use in this way is usually purple. This separate equipment will help to avoid cross-contamination with allergens, which could make an allergy sufferer seriously ill, but also remember that these items need to be cleaned and disinfected.
- Do not use the same cloth to clean knives between tasks when you are preparing raw, high-risk or allergen-related foods.

- When knives have been used on raw meat and poultry, make sure the knife is cleaned and disinfected before using on other tasks. Detergents used in cleaning will remove the grease but disinfectants or very high temperatures are needed to kill bacteria.
- When cleaning knives it is important to clean both the handle and blade well. A dirty handle could contaminate the hands.
- When you have finished working with knives, clean and dry them thoroughly before storing them safely. Bacteria will multiply on wet or dirty knives.

The knife is probably the most important utensil for a chef in the kitchen as it is essential for virtually all food preparation. A good sharp knife will help get the job done more effectively and with greater ease. A good sharp knife is certainly safer and easier to use than a knife with a blunt blade.

Test yourself

1   List a selection of knives that you would need to work in a large kitchen using a range of foods.
2   Describe three straight-bladed knives and say what they are used for.
3   What is the best way to clean a knife after use? Why should knives be clean and grease free?
4   Describe the safest way to carry a knife in the kitchen. How should it be stored after use?
5   Why is it essential to clean a knife thoroughly between use on different foods?
6   Why is a sharp knife safer to use than a blunter knife?
7   What action can be taken with knives and other equipment to prevent allergic reactions in customers?
8   What are the main uses for scissors and secateurs in the kitchen?
9   If you were preparing, cutting and filleting a selection of fish, which knives would you need?
10 Suggest three pieces of equipment you could use to sharpen knives.

5 Stocks, soups and sauces

This chapter is relevant to the following units:
→ Make basic stocks.

→ Prepare, cook and finish basic soups.
→ Prepare, cook and finish basic hot sauces.

Recipes included in this chapter

Stocks

Stock is the basis of all meat sauces, gravies, soups and purées. It is really just the flavour of meat extracted by long and gentle simmering, or the infusion/transfer of flavour from ingredients such as fish, vegetables or shellfish. In making stock, it should be remembered that the object is to draw the goodness out of the materials and into the liquor, imparting the desired level of flavour and other elements that are important to the end product, whether it be a soup, sauce or reduction.

Stocks are the foundation of many important kitchen preparations; for this reason, the greatest possible care should be taken in their production, and stocks, bouillons and nages should only be made with high-quality ingredients. A good, well-flavoured stock cannot be made with inferior ingredients.

- A **bouillon** is another name for meat, fish or vegetable stock. In some cases a bouillon can be distinguished from stock by being meatier and by being seasoned (whereas stock is not seasoned).
- A **nage** is a light but well-flavoured stock, often used for cooking fish and other seafood. The nage will enhance the flavours.

Preparing and cooking stocks

Quality points for ingredients

It is important to choose high-quality ingredients, bones, carcass and vegetables. Do not use ingredients that are past their best as this will affect both the colour and flavour.

- Unsound meat or bones and decaying vegetables will give stock an unpleasant flavour and cause it to deteriorate quickly.
- Scum should be removed, otherwise it will boil into the stock and spoil the colour and flavour.
- Fat should be skimmed off, otherwise the stock will taste greasy.
- Salt should not be added to stock.
- When making chicken stock the bones will need to be soaked first to remove the blood that is in the cavity.

Health and safety

If stocks are not given the correct care and attention, particularly with regard to the soundness of the ingredients used, they can easily become contaminated and a risk to health.

Browning, roasting and boiling

The basic preparation of brown stock involves browning vegetables and bones, usually in the oven. Once browned, they are covered with water, boiled and simmered to give a rich brown colour. White stocks are blanched but not browned, to give a clear white stock.

Simmering

Stock should always simmer gently; if it is allowed to boil quickly, it will evaporate and go cloudy/milky.

Skimming

It is important to skim off the excess fat and impurities with a ladle or perforated spoon to produce a clear and flavoursome stock. If fat is not skimmed off the stock will taste greasy. Stock that is left unattended and not skimmed will become cloudy and may have a bitter taste.

Another way of skimming stock is to use pieces of dish paper dragged across the top of the liquid.

All stock can be chilled down, allowing the fat to settle on the top so that it can be easily removed.

Straining

Stock is poured through a strainer, usually a chinois or muslin, to remove all sediment. This is usually done after the fat has been removed.

Reducing

Stock is placed over a fierce heat and is allowed to evaporate until the volume is reduced to give a more intense flavour.

When cooking predominantly meat stocks, remember that they will contain collagen. This is the main fibrous component of skin, tendons, connective tissue and bones. If you have cooked at a higher heat (e.g. boiling), the collagen content of the sauce will be high, giving you a viscous sauce earlier in the reduction process; due to the thickness of such a sauce, it is impossible to reduce it further without burning.

Glazes

A glaze is a reduced stock that is used to enhance the flavour of soups and sauces. To achieve a glaze, the stock is evaporated on the stove until it is the consistency of treacle or a thick jelly. This thicker consistency is caused by the collagen (which is found in the bones, tendons and connective tissue) breaking down into gelatine as the stock reduces. The result is a more concentrated flavour. Care must be taken not to over reduce the stock otherwise it will become too concentrated and may result in burning. When making a glaze ensure that the base stock used at the start has a medium extraction of collagen. This will give a more flavoursome result and the glaze will be less 'claggy'.

Holding and storing stocks

Once the stock has reached its desired flavour and clarity, strain and chill immediately. Stocks are susceptible to bacterial growth due to their high protein content so special care must be taken in the handling and storage of stocks. Chill the stock rapidly to 5°C in a shallow tray (approximately 3cm to 5cm deep) in a blast chiller before storing in a refrigerator.

If stocks are to be frozen they should be labelled and dated, and stored below −18°C.

When taken from storage, stocks must be boiled for at least two minutes before being used. They must not be reheated more than once.

Ideally, stocks should be made fresh daily and discarded at the end of the day.

Convenience stocks

Today many establishments use prepared stocks to save time and labour, but also to reduce the food safety risks associated with the preparation, production and storage of stocks. These stocks are purchased as a chilled stock, frozen or in a paste or a dry powder. Many of the fresh-chilled products are of a very high quality.

Soups

There are many ways to classify soup – a classic velouté thickened with a liaison, a purée of lentils with ham hock stock, a broth with a clear liquid, or even the crystal clarity of consommé. Up until 15 or 20 years ago, most soups were thickened by either purée or by roux. While hearty soups are still with us today – for example, Scotch broth, minestrone, bouillabaisse, chowder and many more – the foundation of modern dining is a lighter approach, with a reduction in flour and fat, offering a more sophisticated dish.

Types of soup

- **Broth**: a soup in which in which bones, meat, fish, grains or vegetables have been simmered in water or stock. Minestrone, an Italian vegetable-based soup, is an example of a broth.
- **Cream**: a soup finished with cream. These soups can be made from a velouté base, such as cream of chicken and cream of mushroom, but they can also be made from a purée base and finished with cream, for example cream of vegetable soup and cream of green pea soup (*crème St Germain*).
- **Purée**: a soup with a vegetable base that has been puréed in a food mill or blender; it is typically altered after milling with the addition of broth, cream, butter, sour cream or coconut milk.
- **Velouté**: a velvety French sauce made with stock and thickened with a liaison (see thickenings below).
- **Clear (consommé)**: clear, unthickened soups that derive their intense flavour from a stock base. They are clarified by a process of careful straining, resulting in a clear soup. Consommé is a clear soup with an intense flavour derived from meat bones and a good stock.

Dashi is the Japanese equivalent of consommé and is made from giant seaweed (*kombu*), dried bonito and water.

Other types of soup include:

- **Vichyssoise**: a simple, flavourful puréed potato and leek soup, thickened with the potato itself. Traditionally this is called leek and potato soup if served hot, and a little cream or crème fraiche may be added to give it richness; however, when served cold it is classified as vichyssoise – if fat is added to this preparation the dish would leave a fatty residue on the palate and offer a less-than-clear mouth feel.
- **Bisque**: a very rich soup with a creamy consistency, usually made of lobster or shellfish (crab, shrimp, etc.).
- **Bouillabaisse**: a Mediterranean fish soup/stew made of multiple types of seafood, olive oil, water and seasonings such as garlic, onions, tomato and parsley.
- **Chowder**: a hearty North American soup, usually with a seafood base.
- **Gazpacho**: a Spanish tomato and vegetable soup served ice cold.
- **Potage**: a French term referring to a thick soup.

Preparing and cooking soups

Though the perfection of soups can take experience, the basic principles of soup making are quite simple to follow.

Most soup making begins by preparing a stock. The underlying flavours of the foundation ingredients are then enhanced by the herbs and seasonings added. In many cases, this flavour base begins by preparing a mixture of flavouring elements, cooked in a little fat or oil. Because of their aromatic properties and flavours, most soups begin this phase with a combination of onion, garlic, leeks and carrots (this is called a **mirepoix** or **aromats**). The resulting broth is the foundation of all soups.

Quality points for ingredients

When making soups it is important to use fresh, quality ingredients that have been peeled, prepared and weighed as part of the *mise-en-place*.

If you experience any problems with ingredients it is important to inform the supplier. Only use fresh, good-quality ingredients, otherwise the overall flavour of the finished soup will be impaired.

Weighing and measuring

It is important to weigh every ingredient to determine the exact flavour and consistency, but more importantly to determine the exact nutritional content per portion. Measuring the ingredients accurately will also result in the correct yield and less wastage.

Table 5.1 Guide to soups, their preparation and presentation

Soup type	Base	Passed or unpassed	Finish	Example
Broth	Stock Cut vegetables	Unpassed	Chopped herbs	Scotch broth (recipe 11) Minestrone (recipe 10)
Cream	Stock and vegetables Vegetable purée and béchamel velouté	Passed	Cream, milk or yoghurt	Cream of vegetable (recipe 12) Cream of green pea (recipe 13) Cream of tomato (recipe 14)
Purée	Stock Fresh vegetables Pulses	Passed	Croutons	Potato soup (recipe 22) Red lentil soup (recipe 21)
Velouté	Blond roux Vegetables Stock	Passed	Liaison of yolk and cream	Pea velouté (recipe 30)
Clear	Stock	Strained	Usually garnished	Consommé (recipe 32)
Chowder				New England clam chowder (recipe 33)
Bisque	Shellfish Fish stock	Passed	Cream	Prawn bisque (recipe 34)

Blending/liquidising and chopping

Soups can be prepared using stick blenders, liquidisers and food processors. These produce excellent purée soups with a smooth consistency.

For soups that require small cuts of vegetables, such as *paysanne* for minestrone and *gros brunoise* for Scotch broth, the vegetable cutting is usually done by hand, but there are also machines that cut vegetables to the required size available in the market. (For more information on vegetable cuts, see Chapter 12.)

Always use strong, thick-bottomed pans to cook soup to avoid scalding and browning.

Passing and straining

Conical strainers are used to pass soups to obtain a fine consistency. Conical strainers came in a range of sizes, from fine (chinois) to medium. When passing the soup through a chinois, use a ladle to carefully pump the soup through.

Preparing a purée soup

1 Slowly simmer vegetables and seasonings with stock to develop flavours.

2 Purée using a stick blender, liquidiser or food processor.

3 To ensure a smooth consistency, pass the soup through a conical strainer.
4 Use a ladle to carefully pump the soup through.

Finishing soups

Soups may be served for lunch, dinner, supper and snack meals. Depending on their function and purpose, soups are usually served in portions of 250 ml maximum. Sometimes a speciality soup is served as an **amuse-bouche** and the portion size is reduced to approximately 50 ml.

For food safety, serve hot soups at 63 °C or above to control the growth of pathogenic organisms, and discard if not sold after two hours. Cold soups should be served at 5 °C or below. Chill the soups in a blast chiller to below 8 °C within 90 minutes to slow down bacterial growth.

Soups can be served with the following garnishes:
- Croutons: slices of white or brown bread cut into 1 cm dice then carefully shallow fried in vegetable oil or clarified butter.
- Sippets: corners of bread cut from a flat-tin loaf, finely sliced and toasted in the oven. Both croutons and sippets may be flavoured by rubbing chopped garlic on to the bread.
- Toasted flutes (*croûtes de flute*): very small, thin baguette slices, toasted or sprinkled with olive oil or melted butter and baked in the oven until crisp.

Accompaniments that can be served with soup include:
- *brunoise, julienne* or *paysanne* of vegetables
- *concassé*
- fine noodles
- rice
- chopped herbs
- finely diced cooked chicken.

Some soups are finished with cream, crème fraiche, full-cream milk, yoghurt or evaporated milk.

Healthy eating options

With the move towards healthier options, soup offers a very good alternative to other products. Broths and soups containing vegetables, beans and lean protein such as chicken, fish or lean beef, are healthy options that are both light and filling. Minestrone, bouillabaisse and gazpacho are excellent choices. Cream-based soups can often be adapted by using yoghurt or low-fat crème fraiche or fromage frais instead of cream to produce a soup that is lower in fat.

Sauces

A sauce is a liquid that has been thickened by either:

- *beurre manié* (kneaded butter)
- egg yolks
- roux
- cornflour, arrowroot or starch
- cream and/or butter added to reduced stock
- rice (in the case of some shellfish bisques)
- reducing cooking liquor or stock.

Types of sauce

White (béchamel)

Béchamel is a basic white sauce made using butter, flour and milk. Many sauces are derived from a basic béchamel sauce by the addition of appropriate ingredients or garnishes. Parsley, egg, cheese (mornay), soubise, onion, cream, mustard and anchovy are all examples of white sauces.

Velouté

A basic velouté sauce is a blond roux, to which a white stock and chicken, veal, fish, etc. are added. Examples of velouté sauces are caper, suprême, mushroom, ivory and aurora.

Brown (espagnole)

Espagnole is a traditional brown sauce made from brown roux and brown stock, simmered for several hours and skimmed frequently to produce a refined sauce. Because of the lengthy, time-consuming process and a move away from heavy flour-based sauces, in many kitchens a reduced veal stock (see recipe 8) is used as a base for most brown sauces.

Examples of brown sauces include chasseur, devilled, bordelaise, charcutière, Robert, piquant sauce, sherry sauce, Madeira, brown onion, lyonnaise, Italian and pepper sauces.

Demi-glace

Demi-glace is used as the base for a number of derivative sauces. Current practice in most kitchens is to use either stock-reduced sauce, *jus-lié* or a commercially produced powder or granule-based product.

Gravies

Examples of gravies include roast gravy (*jus rôti*) and thickened gravy (*jus-lié*).

A *jus-lié* is a lightly thickened brown stock – traditionally veal – which is flavour-enhanced with tomato and mushroom trimmings and thickened with arrowroot.

Spice-based

Some sauces contain a number of spices used to enhance dishes and to accompany products. Examples include chilli sauce, spicy tomato sauce, curry sauce and Chinese Szechwan sauce.

Purée-based

Purée-based sauces can be fruit based (for example, apple sauce or cranberry sauce), vegetable based (for example, tomato sauce) or herb based (for example, green sauce).

Salsa

Salsa is the Spanish word for a sauce. A wide variety of ingredients can be used and chunky mixtures made to serve with grilled or fried fish, meat and poultry dishes. Recipes 62, 63 and 64 are for salsas.

Butter as a sauce

- **Clarified butter**: clarified butter is butter that has been melted and skimmed. After that, the fat element of the butter is carefully poured off, leaving the milky residue behind. This gives a clear fat that can reach higher temperatures than normal butter without burning, but which can also be used to nap over steamed vegetables or poached or grilled fish.

- ***Beurre noisette***: this basically translates to 'nut butter' and its flavour comes from the caramelisation of the milk element in the butter solids. It is achieved by placing diced hard butter into a moderately hot pan and bringing it to a foam (a good indication that it is ready). Like clarified butter, this can be served with poached or steamed vegetables and fish, but the classic use is with shallow-fried fish. If you take the butter a little further, however, and almost burn the sediment, then add a little vinegar, it is called black butter (*beurre noir*) and is traditionally served with skate.

- ***Beurre fondu***: this is basically an emulsion between fat and liquid – for example, melted butter emulsified with any nage described above will give you a slightly thicker sauce that can be used to coat vegetables or fish. To intensify the flavour, however, if you were to add a *beurre noisette* to the pan, or your cooking medium was clarified butter, you could start cooking the product in the pan with the fat. Once it is half cooked, arrest the cooking by adding a nage and then bring quickly to the boil. Through this boiling process the fat and the stock will become emulsified, which gives an emulsified sauce made in the pan, but with the cooking juices also added.

- **Compound butter sauces**: these are made by mixing the flavouring ingredients (for example, herbs) into softened butter, which can then be shaped into a roll 2 cm in diameter, placed in wet greaseproof paper, foil or cling film, hardened in a refrigerator and cut into 0.5 cm slices when required. Examples include parsley butter (chopped parsley and lemon juice), herb butter (mixed herbs – chives, tarragon, fennel, dill – and lemon juice) and garlic butter (mashed to a paste). Compound butters are served with grilled and some fried fish, and with grilled meats.

Using alcohol in sauces

Take great care when using alcohol in sauces. Alcohol must be used sparingly; it should not dominate the overall flavour, but must blend in with the other ingredients. The alcohol must be cooked out and must not have a raw, harsh taste. Alcohol used correctly will enhance the flavour of the sauce and create pleasant combinations to the dishes.

Quality points for sauces

All sauces should be smooth and glossy in appearance, definite in taste and light in texture; the thickening medium should be used in moderation.

It is important that the ingredients for preparing and cooking sauces are of the best quality, otherwise flavours will be compromised. Wine or alcohol that is used must also be of good quality otherwise the finished products will be impaired.

Thickening sauces

Roux

A roux is a combination of fat and flour that is cooked together. There are three degrees to which a roux may be cooked:

- **White roux**: this is used for white (béchamel) sauce and soups. Equal quantities of butter and flour are cooked together without colouring for a few minutes, to a sandy texture. Alternatively polyunsaturated vegetable margarine or vegetable oil can be used to make a roux, using equal quantities of oil and flour. This does give a slack roux but enables the liquid to be incorporated easily.
- **Blond roux**: this is used for veloutés, tomato sauce and soups. Equal quantities of butter or vegetable oil and flour are cooked for a little longer than a white roux, but without colouring, to a sandy texture.

- **Brown roux**: this is traditionally used for brown (espagnole) sauce and soups, and is slightly browned in the roux-making process.

 Video: making a blond roux and a velouté http://bit.ly/1viPHtG

A boiling liquid should never be added to a hot roux as the result may be lumpy and the person making the sauce may be scalded by the steam produced. If allowed to stand for a time over a moderate heat, a sauce made with a roux may become thin due to a chemical change (dextrinisation) in the flour.

Continental roux is a very easy and straightforward thickening agent that can be frozen and used as a quick thickener during service or à la minute. Mix equal quantities of flour and vegetable oil together to a paste and place in the oven at 140 °C. Cook the mixture, mixing it in on itself continually, until a biscuit texture is achieved. Remove and allow to cool to room temperature. When it is cool enough to handle, form into a sausage shape using a double layer of cling film. Chill, then freeze. To use, remove from the freezer and shave a little off the end of the log. Whisk it into the boiling sauce (it is not necessary to add it slowly to prevent lumping – this will not occur the flour is already cooked). Once the desired thickness has been achieved, pass and serve.

Beurre manié

Beurre manié is a paste made from equal quantities of soft butter and flour, which is then added to a simmering liquid while whisking continuously to prevent lumping.

Egg yolks

This is commonly known as a liaison and is traditionally used to thicken a classic velouté. Both egg yolks and cream are mixed together and added to the sauce/velouté off the boil; this mixture is intended to thicken, however it is essential to keep stirring it, otherwise the eggs will curdle. Once thickening is achieved the sauce/velouté must be served immediately. The liquid must not be allowed to boil or simmer.

Egg yolks are used in mayonnaise (page 577), hollandaise sauce (recipe 60) and custard sauces (page 558). Refer to the appropriate recipe, though, as the yolks are used in a different manner for each sauce. When making mayonnaise (where the yolks are not cooked) or hollandaise (where temperatures remain low), it is advisable to use pasteurised eggs for safety.

Sabayon

A sabayon is a mixture of egg yolks and a little water whisked to the ribbon stage over a gentle heat. The mixture should be the consistency of thick cream. It is added to sauces to assist their glazing.

Cornflour, arrowroot or starch

Cornflour, arrowroot or starch (such as potato starch) is used for thickening gravy and sauces. These are diluted with water, stock or milk, then stirred into the boiling liquid, allowed to reboil for a few minutes and then strained.

Sauce flour

Sauce flour is a specially milled flour that does not require the addition of fat to prevent it from going lumpy. Sauces may be thickened using this flour. It is useful when making sauces for those on a low-fat diet.

Other thickening agents

- Vegetable or fruit purées are known as a coulis. No other thickening agent is used.
- Blood was traditionally used in recipes such as jugged hare, but is used rarely today.
- Cooking liquor from certain dishes and/or stock can be reduced to give a light sauce.

Finishing sauces

When finishing sauces, it is important to check the seasoning and consistency of the finished product. Some hot sauces are finished with cream or crème fraiche. Some are mounted with butter to give them a good shine and smooth consistency: this is known as *monte au beurre*.

Test yourself

1 List the ingredients and describe the cooking methods for brown beef stock.
2 State four quality points you should look for in a white vegetable stock.
3 Give two examples of each of the following soups:
   a purée
   b cream
   c clear
   d broth.
5 Name two alternatives to cream when finishing a soup.
6 At what temperature should hot soup be served?
7 Describe how you would cook lobster bisque.
8 Describe how you would prepare and cook espagnole sauce.
9 Give an example of a dish with which chasseur sauce is traditionally served.
10 Describe how you should store stocks and sauces.

Stock recipes

1 White stock

1 Chop the bones into small pieces, and remove any fat or marrow.
2 Place the bones in a large stock pot, cover with cold water and bring to the boil.
3 Wash off the bones under cold water, then clean the pot.
4 Return the bones to the cleaned pot, add the water and reboil.
5 Skim as and when required, wipe round inside the pot and simmer gently.
6 After 2 hours, add the washed, peeled whole vegetables, bouquet garni and peppercorns.
7 Simmer for 6–8 hours. Skim, strain and, if to be kept, cool quickly and refrigerate.

Ingredient	4.5 litres	10 litres
Raw, meaty bones	1 kg	2.5 kg
Water	5 litres	10.5 litres
Onion, carrot, celery, leek	400 g	1.5 kg
Bouquet garni	½	1½
Peppercorns	8	16

2 White vegetable stock

Ingredient	4 portions	10 portions
Onions	100 g	250 g
Carrots	100 g	250 g
Celery	100 g	250 g
Leeks	100 g	250 g
Water	1.5 litres	3.75 litres

1 Roughly chop all the vegetables.
2 Place all the ingredients into a saucepan, add the water, bring to the boil.
3 Allow to simmer for approximately 1 hour.
4 Skim if necessary. Strain and use.

Energy	Cals	Fat	Sat fat	Carb	Sugar	Protein	Fibre	Sodium
105 kJ	25 kcal	0.3 g	0.1 g	4.9 g	4.0 g	1.0 g	2.4 g	0.0 g

Variation

White fungi stock: add 200–400 g white mushrooms, stalks and trimmings (all well washed) to the recipe.

3 Brown stock

Ingredient	4½ litres	10 litres
Raw, meaty bones	1 kg	2.5 kg
Water	5 litres	10.5 litres
Onion, carrot, celery, leek	400 g	1.5 kg
Bouquet garni	½	1½
Peppercorns	8	16

Energy	Cals	Fat	Sat fat	Carb	Sugar	Protein	Fibre
4 kJ	1 kcal	0.0g	0.0g	0.2g	0.0g	0.0g	0.0g

1 Chop the beef bones and brown well on all sides either by placing in a roasting tin in the oven or carefully browning in a little fat in a frying pan.

2 Drain off any fat and place the bones in a stock pot.

3 Brown any sediment that may be in the bottom of the tray, deglaze (swill out) with half a litre of boiling water, simmer for a few minutes and add to the bones.

4 Add the cold water, bring to the boil and skim. Simmer for 2 hours.

5 Wash, peel and roughly cut the vegetables, fry in a little fat until brown, strain and add to the bones.

6 Add the bouquet garni and peppercorns.

7 Simmer for 6–8 hours. Skim and strain.

Professional tip

A few squashed tomatoes and washed mushroom trimmings can be added to brown stocks to improve flavour, as can a calf's foot and/or a knuckle of bacon. Dishes made with the stock will not be suitable for some religious diets if bacon is used.

Video: making brown stock http://bit.ly/ 1viP8zV

4 White chicken stock

Ingredient	3 litres
Chicken carcass/wings	5 kg
Onions, peeled	1½
Carrots, peeled	2
Cloves of garlic, crushed	2
Leeks, washed and blemishes removed	1
Celery sticks	2
Bay leaf	1
Sprigs of thyme, small	1
Whole white peppercorns	5 g
Water, cold	7 litres

1 Remove any excess fat from the chicken carcasses and wash off under cold water.

2 Place all the bones into a pot that will hold all the ingredients, leaving 5 cm at the top to skim.

3 Add all the other ingredients and cold water, and bring to a simmer; immediately skim all the fat that rises to the surface.

4 Turn the heat off and allow the bones and vegetables to sink. Once this has happened, turn the heat back on, skim and bring to just under a simmer, making as little movement as possible to create more of an infusion than a stock. Skim continuously.

5 Leave to simmer (infuse) for 12 hours then pass through a fine sieve into a clean pan; reduce down rapidly until you have about 3 litres remaining.

5 Fish stock

Ingredient	2 litres
Fish bones, no heads, gills or roe (turbot, sole or brill bones are best)	5 kg
Olive oil	100 ml
Onions, finely chopped	3
Leeks, finely chopped	3
Celery sticks, finely chopped	3
Fennel bulb, finely chopped	1
Dry white wine	350 ml
Parsley stalks	10
Thyme	3 sprigs
White peppercorns	15
Lemons, finely sliced	2

1 Wash off the bones in cold water for 1 hour.

2 Heat the olive oil in a pan that will hold all the ingredients and still have a 1 cm gap at the top for skimming. Add all the vegetables and sweat without colour for 3 minutes.

3 Add the fish bones and sweat for a further 3 minutes.

4 Add the white wine and enough water to cover. Bring to a simmer, skim off the impurities and add the herbs, peppercorns and lemon. Turn off the heat.

5 Infuse for 25 minutes, then pass into another pan and reduce by half. The stock is now ready for use.

6 Brown vegetable stock

Ingredient	4 litres approximately
Onions	300 g
Carrots	300 g
Celery	300 g
Leeks	300 g
Sunflower oil	180 ml
Tomatoes	150 g
Mushroom trimmings	150 g
Peppercorns	18
Water	4 litres
Yeast extract	15 g

1 Cut the vegetables into mirepoix. Fry the mirepoix in the oil until golden brown.
2 Drain and place in a suitable saucepan. Add all the other ingredients except the yeast extract and water.
3 Cover with the water and bring to the boil.
4 Add the yeast extract and simmer gently for approximately 1 hour. Then skim if necessary and use.

Variation

Brown fungi stock: add 200–400 g open or field mushrooms, stalks and trimmings (all well washed) to the recipe.

7 Lamb jus

Ingredient	2 litres
Thyme	bunch
Bay leaves, fresh	4
Garlic	2 bulbs
Red wine	1 litre
Lamb bones	2 kg
Veal bones	1 kg
White onions, peeled	6
Large carrots, peeled	8
Celery sticks	7
Leeks, chopped	4
Tomato purée	6 tbsp

1 Preheat the oven to 175 °C. Place the herbs, garlic and wine in a large, deep container. Place all the bones on to a roasting rack on top of the container of herbs and wine, and roast in the oven for 50–60 minutes. When the bones are completely roasted and have taken on a dark golden-brown appearance, remove from oven.

2 Place all the ingredients in a large pot and cover with cold water. Put the pot on to the heat and bring to the simmer; immediately skim all fat that rises to the surface.

3 Turn the heat off and allow the bones and vegetables to sink. Once this has happened, turn the heat back on and bring to just under a simmer, making as little movement as possible to create more of an infusion than a stock.

4 Skim continuously. Leave to infuse for 12 hours, then pass through a fine sieve, place in the blast chiller until cold and then in the refrigerator overnight. Next day, reduce down rapidly, until you have about 2 litres remaining.

8 Reduced veal stock

1 Brown the bones and calves' feet in a roasting tray in the oven.

2 Place the browned bones in a stock pot, cover with cold water and bring to simmering point.

3 Using the same roasting tray and the fat from the bones, brown off the carrots, onions and celery.

4 Drain off the fat, add the vegetables to the stock and deglaze the tray.

5 Add the remainder of the ingredients; simmer gently for 4–5 hours. Skim frequently.

6 Strain the stock into a clean pan and reduce until a light consistency is achieved.

Ingredient	4 litres
Veal bones, chopped	4 kg
Calves' feet, split lengthways (optional)	2
Water	4 litres
Carrots, roughly chopped	400 g
Onions, roughly chopped	200 g
Celery, roughly chopped	100 g
Tomatoes, blanched, skinned, quartered	1 kg
Mushrooms, chopped	200 g
Large bouquet garni	1
Unpeeled cloves of garlic (optional)	4

Note

No flour is used in the thickening process and consequently a lighter textured sauce is produced. Care needs to be taken when reducing this type of sauce, however, so that the end product is not too strong or bitter.

9 Brown onion soup

Ingredient	4 portions	10 portions
Onions	600 g	1.5 kg
Butter or margarine	25 g	60 g
Clove of garlic, chopped (optional)	1	2–3
Flour, white or wholemeal	10 g	25 g
Brown stock	1 litre	2.5 litres
Salt and pepper		
Flute (thin French stick, 2 cm in diameter)	¼	¾
Grated cheese	50 g	125 g

Energy	Cals	Fat	Sat fat	Carb	Sugar	Protein	Fibre
827 kJ	197 kcal	9.7 g	5.8 g	20.4 g	8.1 g	8.3 g	3.1 g

1 Peel the onions, halve and slice finely.

2 Melt the butter in a thick-bottomed pan, add the onions and garlic, and cook steadily over a good heat until cooked and well browned.

3 Mix in the flour and cook over a gentle heat, browning slightly.

4 Gradually mix in the stock, bring to the boil, skim and season.

5 Simmer for approximately 10 minutes until the onion is soft. Correct the seasoning.

6 Pour into an earthenware tureen or casserole, or individual dishes.

7 Cut the flute (French loaf) into slices and toast on both sides.

8 Sprinkle the toasted slices of bread liberally on the soup.

9 Sprinkle with grated cheese and brown under the salamander.

10 Place on a dish and serve.

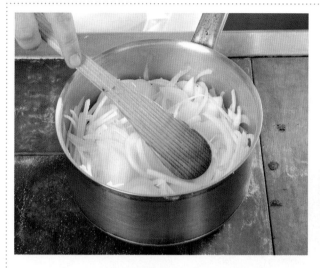

During cooking, the finely sliced onions first become translucent

As the onions continue to cook, they begin to brown without becoming crisp

When the onions are ready, they are well browned

Cook in the flour, and finally the stock

10 Minestrone

Ingredient	4 portions	10 portions
Mixed vegetables (onion, leek, celery, carrot, turnip, cabbage), peeled	300 g	750 g
Butter or oil	50 g	125 g
White stock or water	0.5 litres	1.25 litres
Bouquet garni	1	2
Salt, pepper		
Peas	25 g	60 g
French beans	25 g	60 g
Spaghetti	25 g	60 g
Potatoes, peeled	50 g	125 g
Tomato purée	1 tsp	2½ tsp
Tomatoes, skinned, deseeded, diced	100 g	250 g
Fat bacon (optional)	50 g	125 g
Parsley (optional)	50 g	125 g
Clove of garlic (optional)	1	2½

Energy	Cals	Fat	Sat fat	Carb	Sugar	Protein	Fibre
1,115 kJ	260 kcal	22.9 g	5.8 g	11.9 g	4.2 g	3.8 g	4.1 g

Using sunflower oil.

1 Cut the peeled and washed mixed vegetables into paysanne.

2 Cook slowly without colour in the oil or butter in the pan with a lid on.

3 Add the stock, bouquet garni and seasoning; simmer for approximately 20 minutes.

4 Add the peas and the beans cut into diamonds and simmer for 10 minutes.

5 Add the spaghetti in 2 cm lengths, the potatoes cut into paysanne, the tomato purée and the tomatoes, and simmer gently until all the vegetables are cooked.

6 Meanwhile finely chop the fat bacon, parsley and garlic, if using, and form into a paste.

7 Mould the paste into pellets the size of a pea and drop into the boiling soup.

8 Remove the bouquet garni, correct the seasoning.

9 Serve grated Parmesan cheese and croutons of bread or slices of French bread (flutes) separately.

Healthy eating tips
- Use an unsaturated oil (sunflower or vegetable) to lightly oil the pan. Drain off any excess after the frying is complete and skim the fat from the finished dish.
- Season with the minimum amount of salt as the bacon and cheese are high in salt.

Vegetables chopped into paysanne

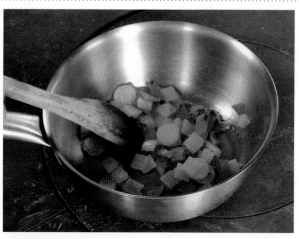

Fry or sweat the vegetables

Simmer the ingredients in the stock

Add the pellets of paste to the soup

11 Scotch broth

Ingredient	4 portions	10 portions
Lean beef (skirt)	200 g	500 g
Beef stock	1 litre	2.5 litres
Barley	25 g	60 g
Vegetables (carrot, turnip, leek, celery, onion), cut into paysanne	200 g	500 g
Bouquet garni	1	2
Salt, pepper		
Chopped parsley		

Energy	Cals	Fat	Sat fat	Carb	Sugar	Protein	Fibre	Sodium
655 kJ	157 kcal	7.8g	3.1g	4.9g	2.7g	16.6g	1.6g	0.2g

1 Place the beef, free from fat, in a saucepan and cover with cold water.

2 Bring to the boil, then immediately wash off under running water.

3 Clean the pan, replace the meat, cover with cold stock, bring to the boil and skim.

4 Add the washed barley, simmer for 1 hour.

5 Add the vegetables, bouquet garni and seasoning.

6 Skim when necessary; simmer for approximately 30 minutes, until tender.

7 Remove the meat, allow to cool and cut from the bone, remove all fat and cut the meat into neat dice the same size as the vegetables; return to the broth.

8 Correct the seasoning, skim off all the fat, add the chopped parsley and serve.

Healthy eating tips
- Remove all fat from the meat.
- Use only a small amount of salt.
- There are lots of healthy vegetables in this dish and the addition of a large bread roll will increase the starchy carbohydrate.

12 Cream of vegetable soup

Ingredient	4 portions	10 portions
Onions, leeks and celery, sliced	100 g	250 g
Other suitable vegetables*, sliced	200 g	500 g
Butter or oil	50 g	125 g
Flour	50 g	125 g
White stock or water	0.5 litres	1.5 litres
Thin béchamel	0.5 litres	1 litre
Bouquet garni	1	2
Salt and pepper		

*Suitable vegetables include Jerusalem artichokes, cauliflower, celery, leeks, onions, parsnips, turnips and fennel.

Analysis based on using butter, cauliflower, turnip and parsnip. 50% stock, 50% semi-skimmed milk used in place of béchamel.

Energy	Cals	Fat	Sat fat	Carb	Sugar	Protein	Fibre	Sodium
862 kJ	206 kcal	12.1g	7.3g	20.0g	8.7g	5.3g	3.4g	0.9g

1 Gently cook all the sliced vegetables in the fat under a lid, without colour.

2 Mix in the flour and cook slowly for a few minutes without colour. Cool slightly.

3 Gradually mix in the hot stock. Stir and bring to the boil.

4 Add the bouquet garni and season.

5 Simmer for approximately 45 minutes; skim when necessary.

6 Remove the bouquet garni; liquidise, blend or pass firmly through a sieve and then through a medium strainer.

7 Return to a clean pan, reheat and correct the seasoning and consistency.

Variation
- Instead of using the béchamel, use an additional 250 ml of stock and then finish the soup with 250 ml milk.
- Alternatively, do this with an additional 375 ml of stock and finish with 125 ml of cream.

---

13 Cream of green pea soup (crème St Germain)

Energy	Cals	Fat	Sat fat	Carb	Sugar	Protein	Fibre
1,356 kJ	323 kcal	23.6g	12.8g	19.6g	8.0g	9.3g	8.3g

Ingredient	4 portions	10 portions
Onion, chopped	25 g	60 g
Leek, chopped	25 g	60 g
Celery, chopped	25 g	60 g
Butter or oil	25 g	60 g
Water or white stock	500 ml	1.25 litres
Peas, fresh (shelled) or frozen	250 ml	625 ml
Sprig of mint		
Bouquet garni	1	2
Thin béchamel	500 ml	1.25 litres
Cream, natural yoghurt or fromage frais	60 ml	150 ml

1 Sweat the onion, leek and celery in the butter or oil.

2 Moisten with water or stock and bring to the boil.

3 Add the peas, mint and bouquet garni, and allow to boil for approximately 5 minutes.

4 Remove the bouquet garni, add the béchamel and bring to the boil.

5 Remove from the heat and liquidise or pass through a sieve. Skim off any fat.

6 Correct the seasoning and pass through medium strainer.

7 Finish with cream, natural yoghurt or fromage frais.

Healthy eating tips
- Use an unsaturated oil (sunflower or vegetable). Lightly oil the pan and drain off any excess after the frying is complete.
- Season with the minimum amount of salt.

Variation

Variations can be made with the addition of:
- a garnish of 25 g cooked and washed tapioca, added at the same time as the cream
- a garnish of 25 g cooked and washed vermicelli and *julienne* of sorrel cooked in butter
- natural yoghurt, skimmed milk or non-dairy cream may be used in place of cream.

See also the variations listed under pulse soup (recipe 16).

14 Cream of tomato soup (crème de tomates fraiche)

Ingredient	4 portions	10 portions
Butter or oil	50 g	125 g
Bacon trimmings, optional	25 g	60 g
Onion, diced	100 g	250 g
Carrot, diced	100 g	250 g
Flour	50 g	125 g
Tomatoes, fresh, fully ripe	1 kg	2.5 kg
Stock	1 litre	2.5 litres
Bouquet garni	1	2
Salt, pepper		
Croutons – sliced stale bread	1	3
Butter	50 g	125 g

Energy	Cals	Fat	Sat fat	Carb	Sugar	Protein	Fibre	Sodium
1159 kJ	277 kcal	16.2g	4.8g	28.5g	13.6g	6.3g	6.6g	0.3g

1 Melt the butter or heat the oil in a thick-bottomed pan.

2 Add the bacon, onion and carrot (mirepoix) and brown lightly.

3 Mix in the flour and cook to a sandy texture.

4 Gradually add the hot stock.

5 Stir to the boil.

6 Remove the eyes from the tomatoes, wash them well, and squeeze them into the soup after it has come to the boil.

7 If colour is lacking, add a little tomato purée soon after the soup comes to the boil.

8 Add the bouquet garni and season lightly.

9 Simmer for approximately 1 hour. Skim when required.

10 Remove the bouquet garni and mirepoix.

11 Liquidise or pass firmly through a sieve, then through a conical strainer.

12 Return to a clean pan, correct the seasoning and consistency. Bring to the boil.

13 Serve fried or toasted croutons separately.

Professional tip

● Flour may be omitted from the recipe if a thinner soup is required.

● A slightly sweet/sharp flavour can be added to the soup by preparing what is known as a gastric (gastrique). In a thick-bottomed pan, reduce 100 ml of malt vinegar and 35 g caster sugar until it is a light caramel colour. Mix this into the completed soup.

● Some tomato purée can be stronger than others, so you may have to add a little more or less when making this soup.

Healthy eating tips

● Use soft margarine or sunflower/vegetable oil in place of the butter.

● Toast the croutons rather than frying them.

● Use the minimum amount of salt – there is plenty in the bacon.

Variation

Without fresh tomatoes: substitute 150 g of tomato purée for the fresh tomatoes (375 g for 10 portions). When reboiling the soup (step 12), add 500 ml of milk or 125 ml of cream, yoghurt or fromage frais.

Try adding the juice and lightly grated peel of 1–2 oranges, cooked rice or a chopped fresh herb, such as chives.

15 Mushroom soup (*crème de champignons*)

Ingredient	4 portions	10 portions
Onion, leek and celery, sliced	100 g	250 g
Butter or oil	50 g	125 g
Flour	50 g	125 g
White stock (preferably chicken)	1 litre	2.5 litres
White mushrooms, washed and chopped	200 g	500 g
Bouquet garni	1	2
Salt, pepper		
Milk (or cream)	125 ml (or 60 ml)	300 ml (or 150 ml)

Energy	Cals	Fat	Sat fat	Carb	Sugar	Protein	Fibre
712 kJ	170 kcal	11.8 g	5.2 g	12.6 g	3.0 g	3.8 g	1.6 g

Using hard margarine.

1 Gently cook the sliced onions, leek and celery in the butter or oil in a thick-bottomed pan, without colouring.

2 Mix in the flour and cook over a gentle heat to a sandy texture without colouring.

3 Remove from the heat and cool slightly.

4 Gradually mix in the hot stock. Stir to the boil.

5 Add the well-washed, chopped mushrooms, the bouquet garni and season.

6 Simmer for 30–45 minutes. Skim when needed.

7 Remove the bouquet garni. Pass through a sieve or liquidise.

8 Pass through a medium strainer. Return to a clean saucepan.

9 Reboil, correct the seasoning and consistency; add the milk or cream.

Variation

Natural yoghurt, skimmed milk or non-dairy cream may be used in place of dairy cream.

A garnish of thinly sliced mushrooms may be added. Wild mushrooms may also be used.

Healthy eating tips

- Use soft margarine or sunflower/vegetable oil in place of the butter.
- Use the minimum amount of salt.
- The least fatty option is to use a combination of semi-skimmed milk and yoghurt or fromage frais – not cream.

16 Pulse soup with croutons

1 Pick and wash the pulses (if pre-soaked, change the water).

2 Place in a thick-bottomed pan; add the stock or water and bring to the boil and skim.

3 Add the remaining ingredients and season lightly.

4 Simmer until tender; skim when necessary.

5 Remove the bouquet garni and ham knuckle (if using).

6 Liquidise and pass through a conical strainer.

7 Return to a clean pan and reboil; correct the seasoning and consistency.

8 Serve accompanied by 0.5 cm-diced bread croutons shallow-fried in butter or olive oil.

Ingredient	4 portions	10 portions
Pulses (soaked overnight if necessary)	200 g	500 g
White stock or water	1.5 litres	3.75 litres
Onions, chopped	50 g	125 g
Carrots, chopped	50 g	125 g
Bouquet garni	1	2
Knuckle of ham or bacon (optional)	50 g	125 g
Salt and pepper		
Croutons		
Stale bread	1 slice	2½ slices
Butter or olive oil	50 g	125 g

Energy	Cals	Fat	Sat fat	Carb	Sugar	Protein	Fibre
728 kJ	177 kcal	1.3 g	0.2 g	32.0 g	3.3 g	11.3 g	3.6 g

One portion (no croutons); one portion (with croutons) provides: 1,223 kJ/291 kcal energy; 111.7 g fat; 6.8 g saturated fat; 36.5 g carbohydrates; 3.6 g sugar; 12.1 g protein; 3.8 g fibre.

Note

Pulses are the dried seeds of plants that form pods. Any type of pulse can be made into soup, for example split green and yellow peas, haricot beans and lentils.

Healthy eating tips

● The fat and salt are reduced if the ham is omitted.
● Try lightly brushing the stale bread with olive oil and oven-baking it with garlic and herbs. Alternatively, serve with sippets.

Variation

Variations can be made with the addition of:
● chopped fresh herbs (parsley, chervil, tarragon, coriander, chives, etc.)
● spices (e.g. garam masala)
● crisp lardons of bacon
● sippets (small, thin pieces of bread, toasted or oven-baked).

17 Chicken soup (*crème de volaille* or *crème reine*)

1 Gently cook the sliced onions, leek and celery in a thick-bottomed pan, in the butter or oil, without colouring.

2 Mix in the flour; cook over a gentle heat to a sandy texture without colouring.

3 Cool slightly; gradually mix in the hot stock. Stir to the boil.

4 Add the bouquet garni and season.

5 Simmer for 30–45 minutes; skim when necessary. Remove the bouquet garni.

6 Liquidise or pass firmly through a fine strainer.

7 Return to a clean pan, reboil and finish with milk or cream; correct the seasoning.

8 Add the chicken garnish and serve.

Ingredient	4 portions	10 portions
Onion, leek and celery, sliced	100 g	250 g
Butter or oil	50 g	125 g
Flour	50 g	125 g
Chicken stock	1 litre	2.5 litres
Bouquet garni	1	2
Salt, pepper		
Milk or cream	250 ml or 125 ml	625 ml or 300 ml
Cooked dice of chicken (garnish)	25 g	60 g

Energy	Cals	Fat	Sat fat	Carb	Sugar	Protein	Fibre	Sodium
900 kJ	217 kcal	16.7 g	10.4 g	12.6 g	2.6 g	4.8 g	1.6 g	0.1 g

Using butter and cream.

Variation

Natural yoghurt, skimmed milk or non-dairy cream may be used in place of dairy cream.

Add cooked small pasta or sliced mushrooms.

Healthy eating tips

● Use soft margarine or sunflower/vegetable oil in place of the butter.
● Use the minimum amount of salt.
● The least fatty option is to use a combination of semi-skimmed milk and yoghurt or fromage frais – not cream.

18 Asparagus soup (*crème d'asperges*)

Ingredient	4 portions	10 portions
Onion, sliced	50 g	125 g
Celery, sliced	50 g	125 g
Butter or oil	50 g	125 g
Flour	50 g	125 g
White stock (preferably chicken)	1 litre	2.5 litres
Asparagus stalk trimmings *or*	200 g	500 g
Tin of asparagus	150 g	325 g
Bouquet garni	1	2
Salt, pepper		
Milk or cream	250 ml or 125 ml	625 ml or 300 ml

Energy	Cals	Fat	Sat fat	Carb	Sugar	Protein	Fibre
919 kJ	223 kcal	13.1 g	8.0 g	18.9 g	8.8 g	8.4 g	2.5 g

Using butter.

1 Gently sweat the onions and celery, without colouring, in the butter or oil.

2 Remove from the heat, mix in the flour, return to a low heat and cook out, without colouring, for a few minutes. Cool.

3 Gradually add the hot stock. Stir to the boil.

4 Add the well-washed asparagus trimmings, or the tin of asparagus, and bouquet garni. Season.

5 Simmer for 30–40 minutes, then remove bouquet garni.

6 Liquidise and pass through a strainer.

7 Return to a clean pan, reboil, correct seasoning and consistency. (Milk with a little cornflour can be added to adjust the consistency.)

8 Add the milk or cream and serve.

Healthy eating tips
- Use an unsaturated oil (sunflower/vegetable) to lightly oil the pan. Drain off any excess after the frying is complete and skim the fat from the finished dish.
- Season with the minimum amount of salt.

19 Cream of spinach and celery soup

Ingredient	4 portions	10 portions
Shallots, peeled and chopped (small mirepoix)	2	5
Leeks, washed and chopped (small mirepoix)	1	2½
Cloves of garlic, peeled and chopped	2	5
Corn oil	2 tbsp	5 tbsp
Celery sticks, washed and chopped (small mirepoix)	4	10
Flour	15 g	35 g
Fresh spinach, well washed	500 g	1.25 kg
Milk	600 ml	1.5 litres
Vegetable stock	600 ml	1.5 litres
Salt, to taste		

Energy	Cals	Fat	Sat fat	Carb	Sugar	Protein	Fibre	Sodium
886 kJ	214 kcal	12.7 g	4.7 g	15.1 g	11.3 g	10.1 g	6.1 g	0.3 g

1 Cook the shallots, leeks and garlic in the oil for a few minutes, without colour.

2 Add the celery and cook for another few minutes until starting to soften.

3 Add the flour and mix well, then throw in the spinach and mix around. Add the milk and vegetable stock slowly, ensuring there are no lumps.

4 Stir continuously, bring to a simmer, then switch off and remove from heat. Cover and leave for a few minutes.

5 Blend until smooth in a food processor. Check seasoning and serve.

20 Vegetable purée soup

1 Gently cook all the sliced vegetables in the fat under a lid, without colour.

2 Mix in the flour and cook slowly for a few minutes without colour. Cool slightly.

3 Gradually mix in the hot stock. Stir to the boil.

4 Add the bouquet garni and season.

5 Simmer for approximately 45 minutes; skim when necessary.

6 Remove the bouquet garni; liquidise or pass firmly through a sieve and then through a medium strainer.

7 Return to a clean pan, reboil, and correct the seasoning and consistency.

Ingredient	4 portions	10 portions
Onions, leek and celery, sliced	100 g	250 g
Other suitable vegetables, sliced	200 g	500 g
Butter or oil	50 g	125 g
Flour	50 g	125 g
White stock or water	1 litre	2.5 litres
Bouquet garni	1	2
Salt, pepper		

Suitable vegetables include Jerusalem artichokes, cauliflower, celery, leeks, onions, parsnips, turnips and fennel.

Energy	Cals	Fat	Sat fat	Carb	Sugar	Protein	Fibre
601 kJ	143 kcal	10.3 g	4.4 g	11.4 g	1.8 g	1.9 g	1.9 g

Using hard margarine.

Variation

Add a little spice, sufficient to give a subtle background flavour, e.g. garam masala with parsnip soup.

Just before serving add a little freshly chopped herb(s), e.g. parsley, chervil, tarragon, coriander.

Healthy eating tips

● Use an unsaturated oil (sunflower or vegetable) to lightly oil the pan. Drain off any excess after the frying is complete and skim the fat from the finished dish.

● Season with the minimum amount of salt.

● Try using more vegetables to thicken the soup in place of the flour.

Video: making a purée soup http://bit.ly/ 17qT0U8

21 Red lentil soup

Ingredient	4 portions	10 portions
Ham hock	320 g	800 g
Onion, peeled	25 g	60 g
Whole carrot, peeled	½	1¼
Baby shallots	1	2½
Leeks	50 g	125 g
Celery	50 g	125 g
Oil	40 ml	100 ml
Red lentils	200 g	500 g
Cooking liquid from the hock	1 litre	2.5 litres
Milk, cream or crème fraiche	120 ml	300 ml

Energy	Cals	Fat	Sat fat	Carb	Sugar	Protein	Fibre
1,807 kJ	432 kcal	71.4 g	43.9 g	6.7 g	1.5 g	5.3 g	1.5 g

1 Place the ham hock, onion and carrot in a pan and cover with about 3 litres of water.

2 Bring to the boil and then turn down to a slow simmer. (When the hock is cooked, the centre bone will slide out in one smooth motion.)

3 Slice the shallots, leek and celery into 1 cm dice.

4 Heat a pan with the oil, add the vegetables and cook until they are slightly coloured; add the lentils and cover them with the ham stock.

5 Bring to the boil, then turn the heat down to a very slow simmer.

6 Cook until all the lentils have broken down.

7 Allow to cool for 10 minutes and then purée until smooth.

8 Correct the consistency as necessary, and finish with boiled milk, cream or crème fraiche.

Variation

Meat-free version: omit the ham hock and use a vegetable stock or water instead of the cooking liquid.

22 Potato soup (*purée parmentier*)

Ingredient	4 portions	10 portions
Butter or oil	25 g	60 g
Onion, peeled and sliced	50 g	125 g
White of leek, washed and sliced	50 g	125 g
White stock or water	1 litre	2.5 litres
Potatoes, peeled and sliced	400 g	1.25 kg
Bouquet garni	1	2
Salt and pepper		
Parsley, chopped		
Croutons		
Stale bread	1 slice	2½ slices
Butter, margarine or oil	50 g	125 g

Energy	Cals	Fat	Sat fat	Carb	Sugar	Protein	Fibre
1,063 kJ	253 kcal	15.7 g	9.8 g	26.1 g	2.1 g	3.6 g	2.9 g

1 Melt the butter or heat the oil in a thick-bottomed pan.

2 Add the onion and leek; cook for a few minutes without colour with the lid on.

3 Add the stock or water, the potatoes and the bouquet garni. Season.

4 Simmer for approximately 30 minutes. Remove the bouquet garni and skim off all fat.

5 Liquidise or pass the soup firmly through a sieve then pass it through a medium conical strainer.

6 Return to a clean pan and reboil. Correct the seasoning and consistency.

7 Serve sprinkled with chopped parsley.

8 Serve fried or toasted croutons separately.

Healthy eating tips
- Use an unsaturated oil (sunflower or vegetable). Lightly oil the pan and drain off any excess after the frying is complete.
- Season with the minimum amount of salt.
- Toast the croutons instead of frying them.

23 Potato and watercress soup

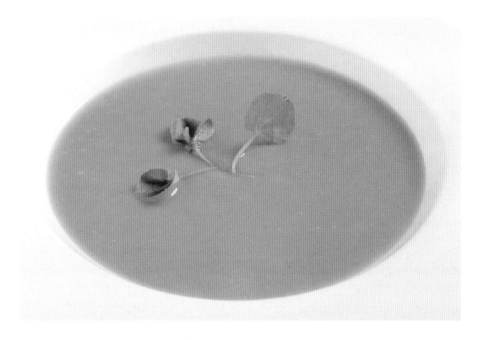

Ingredient	4 portions	10 portions
Butter or oil	25 g	60 g
Onion, peeled and sliced	50 g	125 g
White of leek, sliced	50 g	125 g
White stock or water	1 litre	2.5 litres
Potatoes, peeled and sliced	400 g	1 kg
Watercress	small bunch	small bunch
Bouquet garni		
Salt, pepper		
Parsley, chopped		
Croutons		
Stale bread	1 slice	2½ slices
Butter, margarine or oil	50 g	125 g

Energy	Cals	Fat	Sat fat	Carb	Sugar	Protein	Fibre	Sodium
583 kJ	139 kcal	5.5 g	3.3 g	21.0 g	3.8 g	2.7 g	3.4 g	0.1 g

Using butter.

1 Pick off 12 neat leaves of watercress and plunge into a small pan of boiling water for 1–2 seconds. Refresh under cold water immediately; these leaves are to garnish the finished soup.

2 Melt the butter or heat the oil in a thick-bottomed pan.

3 Add the peeled and washed sliced onion and leek, cook for a few minutes without colour with the lid on.

4 Add the stock, the peeled, washed and sliced potatoes, the rest of the watercress, including the stalks, and the bouquet garni. Season.

5 Simmer for approximately 30 minutes. Remove the bouquet garni, skim off all fat.

6 Liquidise or pass the soup firmly through a sieve then pass through a medium conical strainer.

7 Return to a clean pan, reboil, correct the seasoning and consistency, and serve.

8 Garnish with watercress.

9 Serve fried or toasted croutons separately.

24 Chilled leek and potato soup (vichyssoise)

Ingredient	4 portions	10 portions
Onions, finely sliced	160 g	400 g
Leeks, finely sliced	175 g	430 g
Butter	125 g	300 g
Potatoes, diced small	750 g	1.8 kg
Water/vegetable stock	1.8 litres	4.5 litres
Salt	15 g	30 g
Pepper to taste		
Garnish		
Whipped cream		
Chives, chopped		

Energy	Cals	Fat	Sat fat	Carb	Sugar	Protein	Fibre
1,653 kJ	397 kcal	26.4g	16.3g	36.9g	4.5g	5.3g	4.0g

1 Sweat the sliced onion and leek without colour in the butter. Cook until very tender.

2 Add the potatoes and bring quickly to the boil with the water or vegetable stock.

3 Liquidise in food processor and allow to cool.

4 Check seasoning. Note that seasoning needs to reflect the serving temperature.

5 Serve cold with whipped cream and chopped chives.

25 Gazpacho

Ingredient	4 portions	10 portions
Tomato juice	500 ml	1.25 litres
Tomatoes, skinned, deseeded and diced	100 g	250 g
Cucumber, peeled and diced	100 g	250 g
Green pepper, diced	50 g	125 g
Onion, chopped	50 g	125 g
Mayonnaise	1 tbsp	2–3 tbsp
Vinegar	1 tbsp	2–3 tbsp
Seasoning		
Clove of garlic	1	2–3

Energy	Cals	Fat	Sat fat	Carb	Sugar	Protein	Fibre	Sodium
861 kJ	203 kcal	2.7g	0.8g	40.5g	38.7g	6.7g	12.5g	3.2g

This soup has many regional variations. It is served chilled and has a predominant flavour of cucumber, tomato and garlic.

1 Mix all the ingredients together.
2 Season and add crushed chopped garlic to taste.
3 Stand in a cool place for an hour.
4 Correct the consistency with iced water and serve chilled.

Variation

Instead of serving with all the ingredients finely chopped, the soup can be liquidised and garnished with chopped tomato, cucumber and pepper.

The soup may also be finished with chopped herbs.

A tray of garnishes may accompany the soup, e.g. chopped red and green pepper, chopped onion, tomato, cucumber and croutons.

26 Tomato soup

Energy	Cals	Fat	Sat fat	Carb	Sugar	Protein	Fibre
1,150 kJ	274 kcal	21.3 g	11.2 g	17.1 g	3.7 g	4.6 g	1.0 g

Using hard margarine.

Ingredient	4 portions	10 portions
Butter or oil	50 g	125 g
Bacon trimmings, optional	25 g	60 g
Onion, diced	100 g	250 g
Carrot, diced	100 g	250 g
Flour	50 g	125 g
Tomato purée	150 g	375 g
Stock	1.25 litres	3.5 litres
Bouquet garni	1	2
Salt, pepper		
Croutons		
Slice stale bread	1	3
Butter	50 g	125 g

1 Melt the butter or heat the oil in a thick-bottomed pan.
2 Add the bacon, onion and carrot (mirepoix) and brown lightly.
3 Mix in the flour and cook to a sandy texture.
4 Remove from the heat, mix in the tomato purée.
5 Return to heat and gradually add the hot stock.
6 Stir to the boil. Add the bouquet garni, season lightly.
7 Simmer for approximately 1 hour. Skim when required.
8 Remove the bouquet garni and mirepoix.
9 Liquidise or pass firmly through a sieve, then through a conical strainer.
10 Return to a clean pan, correct the seasoning and consistency. Bring to the boil.
11 Serve fried or toasted croutons separately.

Professional tip

If a slightly sweet/sour flavour is required, reduce 100 ml vinegar and 35 g caster sugar to a light caramel and mix into the completed soup.

Healthy eating tips
● Use soft margarine or sunflower/vegetable oil in place of the butter.
● Toast the croutons rather than frying them.
● Use the minimum amount of salt – there is plenty in the bacon.

Variation

Variations can be made with the addition of:
● juice and lightly grated zest of 1–2 oranges
● tomato concassé
● cooked rice
● chopped fresh coriander, basil or chives
● 200 g peeled, sliced potatoes with the stock.

27 Roasted red pepper and tomato soup

Ingredient	4 portions	10 portions
Red peppers	4	10
Plum tomatoes	400 g	1.25 kg
Butter or oil	50 g	125 g
Onion, chopped	100 g	250 g
Carrot, chopped	100 g	250 g
Stock	500 ml	1.5 litres
Crème fraiche	2 tbsp	5 tbsp
Basil	25 g	75 g
Croutons		
Slice stale bread	1	3
Butter	50 g	125 g

Energy	Cals	Fat	Sat fat	Carb	Sugar	Protein	Fibre
983 kJ	235 kcal	16.8g	7.1g	18.3g	16.4g	3.6g	4.5g

1 Core and deseed the peppers and halve the tomatoes.

2 Lightly sprinkle with oil and place on a tray into a hot oven or under a grill until the pepper skins are blackened.

3 Allow the peppers to cool in a plastic bag.

4 Remove the skins and slice the flesh.

5 Place the butter or oil in a pan, add the onions and carrots and fry gently for 5 minutes.

6 Add the stock, peppers and tomatoes and bring to the boil.

7 Simmer for 30 minutes, correct the seasoning and blend in a food processor until smooth.

8 Add crème fraiche and basil leaves torn into pieces, and serve with croutons.

28 Roasted butternut squash soup

Ingredient	4 portions	10 portions
Butternut squash, peeled and de-seeded	600 g	2 kg
Onion	100 g	250 g
Olive oil	2 tbsp	5 tbsp
Garlic (optional), finely chopped	1 clove	2 cloves
Bacon (back rashers), in small pieces	4	10
Chicken or vegetable stock	625 ml	1.5 litres
Salt and pepper		
Cream or thick natural yoghurt	6 tbsp	15 tbsp

Energy	Cals	Fat	Sat fat	Carb	Sugar	Protein	Fibre
923 kJ	220 kcal	12.0g	3.5g	19.6g	13.1g	9.9g	2.8g

1   Cut the squash into thick pieces, place on a lightly oiled baking sheet and roast for 20–25 minutes in a hot oven until the flesh is soft and golden brown.

2   Sweat the onions and garlic in the olive oil without colouring, for approximately 5 minutes.

3   Add the bacon and lightly brown.

4   Add the roasted squash, pour in the stock, and bring to boil. Simmer for 20 minutes.

5   Allow to cool before liquidising or blending until smooth.

6   Season lightly, add yoghurt or cream, then reheat gently and serve.

Variation

Add three to four saffron strands soaked in one tablespoon hot water at step 4.

Healthy eating tips

● Use unsaturated oil (sunflower or olive); lightly oil the pan to sweat the garlic and onions. Drain off any excess fat after cooking the bacon.

● Use low-fat yoghurt to reduce the fat content. Add a little cornflour to stabilise the yoghurt before adding to the soup.

29 Carrot and butter bean soup

Ingredient	4 portions	10 portions
Onions, peeled and chopped	1	2½
Cloves of garlic, chopped	2	5
Sunflower oil	15 ml	35 ml
Carrots, large to medium, brunoise	250 g	750 g
Vegetable stock	500 ml	1.25 litres
Butter beans, cooked	400 g	1 kg
Seasoning		

Energy	Cals	Fat	Sat fat	Carb	Sugar	Protein	Fibre	Sodium
638 kJ	152 kcal	4.6g	0.6g	21.9g	8.5g	7.0g	9.4g	0.5g

1   Cook the onion and garlic in the oil for a few minutes, without colour, then add the carrots and stir well.

2   Add the vegetable stock. Bring to the boil, turn down to a simmer and cook for about 15 minutes until the carrot is cooked through.

3   Add the beans and cook for a further 5 minutes or so until they are heated through.

4   Liquidise in a food processor until smooth; check seasoning.

Professional tip

With any soup recipe, it is important to simmer the soup gently. Do not let it boil vigorously, because too much water will evaporate. If the soup has boiled, add more stock or water to make up for this.

30 Pea velouté

Ingredient	4 portions	10 portions
Frozen peas	400g	1 kg
Vegetable oil	10 ml	25 ml
Shallots, chopped	1	2
Milk	200 ml	500 ml
Double cream	40 ml	100 ml
Butter or margarine	40g	100g

Energy	Cals	Fat	Sat fat	Carb	Sugar	Protein	Fibre	Sodium
984 kJ	237 kcal	17.8g	9.6g	12.2g	5.5g	7.7g	6.9g	0.1g

1 Blanch the peas in a small pan of boiling water for 3 minutes, then drain.

2 Heat the oil in a large saucepan and cook the shallots without letting them colour.

3 Add the peas to this pan, and cook for a further 2–3 minutes, again without colouring.

4 Add the milk, bring to a simmer and cook until the peas are tender.

5 Cool the mixture slightly, then transfer to a food processor and liquidise until very smooth – this may take a while. At this point, the soup can be cooled completely and stored in an airtight container in the refrigerator until ready to serve.

6 Add the cream and butter just before serving.

31 Pumpkin velouté

Ingredient	4 portions	10 portions
Shallots, sliced	1	2½
Butter	320g	800g
Clove of garlic, sliced (optional)	½	1¼
Large squash or pumpkin (300g), flesh diced	1	2½
Parmesan, grated	30g	75g
Truffle oil	1 tbsp	2½ tbsp
Salt, pepper		
Chicken stock	400–600 ml	1–1.5 litres

Energy	Cals	Fat	Sat fat	Carb	Sugar	Protein	Fibre	Sodium
2,883 kJ	689 kcal	71.4g	43.9g	6.7g	1.5g	5.3g	1.5g	3.0g

Using acorn squash and olive oil.

1 Sweat the shallots in the butter, without colour, until cooked and soft.

2 Add the garlic, pumpkin, Parmesan and truffle oil. Correct the seasoning and cook for 5 minutes.

3 Add the chicken stock, bring to the boil, simmer for 5 minutes.

4 Liquidise, pass, correct the seasoning and serve hot. Blast chill if to be stored.

32 Clear soup (*consommé*)

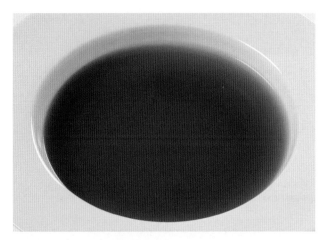

Ingredient	4 portions	10 portions
Chopped or minced beef	200 g	500 g
Salt, to taste		
Egg whites	1–2	3–5
White or brown beef stock, cold	1 litre	2.5 litres
Mixed vegetables (onion, carrot, celery, leek)	100 g	250 g
Bouquet garni	1	2
Peppercorns	3–4	8–10

Energy	Cals	Fat	Sat fat	Carb	Sugar	Protein	Fibre
126 kJ	30 kcal	0.0 g	0.0 g	1.8 g	0.0 g	5.6 g	0.0 g

1 Thoroughly mix the beef, salt, egg white and a quarter of the cold stock in a thick-bottomed pan.
2 Peel, wash and finely chop the vegetables.
3 Add to the beef with the remainder of the stock, the bouquet garni and the peppercorns.

4 Place over a gentle heat and bring slowly to the boil, stirring occasionally.
5 Allow to boil rapidly for 5–10 seconds. Give a final stir.
6 Lower the heat so that the consommé is simmering very gently.
7 Cook for 1½–2 hours without stirring.
8 Strain carefully through a double muslin.

9 Remove all fat, using both sides of 8 cm square pieces of kitchen paper.
10 Correct the seasoning and colour, which should be a delicate amber.
11 Degrease again, if necessary. Bring to the boil and serve.

Healthy eating tips

- This soup is fat free!
- Keep the salt to a minimum and serve as a low-calorie starter for anyone wishing to reduce the fat in their diet.

Variation

Consommés are varied in many ways by altering the flavour of the stock (chicken, chicken and beef, game, etc.), also by the addition of numerous garnishes (julienne or brunoise of vegetables, shredded savoury pancakes or pea-sized profiteroles) added at the last moment before serving, or small pasta.

Cold, lightly jellied consommés, served in cups, with or without garnish (diced tomato), may be served in hot weather.

33 New England clam chowder

Ingredient	4 portions	10 portions
Salt pork or bacon, cut into 0.5 cm dice	50 g	125 g
Onion, finely chopped	50 g	125 g
Cold water	300 ml	750 ml
Potatoes, cut into 0.5 cm dice	500 g	1.25 kg
Fresh trimmed clams, or tinned clams, and their juices	200 g	500 g
Cream	180 ml	450 ml
Thyme, crushed or chopped	1 g	2 g
Salt, white pepper		
Butter, softened	20 g	50 g
Paprika		

Energy	Cals	Fat	Sat fat	Carb	Sugar	Protein	Fibre
1,109 kJ	269 kcal	14.9 g	7.7 g	24.5 g	2.5 g	14.9 g	1.8 g

Using bacon or salt pork.

1 Dry-fry the pork or bacon in a thick-bottomed saucepan for about 3 minutes, stirring constantly until a thin film of fat covers the bottom of the pan.

2 Stir in the chopped onion and cook gently until a light golden brown.

3 Add the water and potatoes, bring to the boil and simmer gently until the potatoes are cooked but not mushy.

4 Add the chopped clams and their juice, the cream and thyme, and heat until almost boiling. Season with salt and pepper.

5 Correct the seasoning, stir in the softened butter and serve, dusting each soup bowl with a little paprika.

The traditional accompaniment is salted cracker biscuits. An obvious variation would be to use scallops in place of clams.

34 Prawn bisque

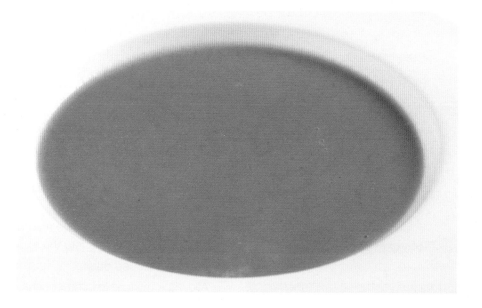

Ingredient	4 portions	10 portions
Oil	50 ml	125 ml
Butter	30 g	75 g
Unshelled prawns	250 g	625 g
Flour	20 g	50 g
Tomato purée	1 tbsp	2 tbsp
Shellfish nage (4 portions)	1 litre	2.5 litres
Fish stock	150 ml	375 ml
Whipping cream	120 ml	300 ml
Dry sherry	75 ml	180 ml
Paprika, pinch		
Seasoning		
Chives, chopped		

Energy	Cals	Fat	Sat fat	Carb	Sugar	Protein	Fibre	Sodium
1,578 kJ	381 kcal	31.2g	13.0g	8.2g	4.0g	12.9g	0.8g	1.0g

1 Heat the oil and the butter. Add the prawns and cook for 3–4 minutes on a moderately high heat.

2 Sprinkle in the flour and cook for a further 2–3 minutes.

3 Add the tomato purée and cook for a further 2 minutes.

4 Meanwhile, bring the nage up to a simmer and, once the tomato purée has been cooked in, slowly add to the prawn mix, being mindful that you have formed a roux; stir in the fish stock to prevent lumping.

5 Once all the stock has been added, bring to the boil and simmer for 3–4 minutes.

6 Pass through a fine sieve, return the shells to the pan and pound to extract more flavour and more colour.

7 Pour over the fish stock, bring to the boil, then pass this back on to the already passed soup.

8 Bring to the boil, add the cream and sherry, correct the seasoning and served with chopped chives.

35 Béchamel sauce (white sauce)

1 Melt the butter or heat the oil in a thick-bottomed pan.
2 Mix in the flour with a heat-proof plastic or wooden spoon.
3 Cook for a few minutes, stirring frequently. As you are making a white roux, do not allow the mixture to colour.
4 Remove the pan from the heat to allow the roux to cool.
5 Return the pan to the stove and, over a low heat, gradually mix the milk into the roux.
6 Add the studded onion.
7 Allow the mixture to simmer gently for 30 minutes, stirring frequently to make sure the sauce does not burn on the bottom.
8 Remove the onion and pass the sauce through a conical strainer.

Ingredient	1 litre	4.5 litres
Butter or oil	100g	400g
Flour	100g	400g
Milk, warmed	1 litre	4.5 litres
Onion, studded with cloves	1	2–3

Variation

For cream sauce, finish with 125ml single cream per litre of béchamel sauce.

Professional tip

To prevent a skin from forming, brush the surface with melted butter. When ready to use, stir this into the sauce. Alternatively, cover the sauce with cling film or greaseproof paper.

36 Reduced-fat béchamel sauce

Ingredient	
Milk	500ml
Sauce flour	40g
Seasoning	

Energy	Cals	Fat	Sat fat	Carb	Sugar	Protein	Fibre
302 kJ	73 kcal	1.8g	1.1g	10.9g	4.8g	4.2g	0.3g

Professional tip

Add a little blended cornflour prior to heating to stabilise the sauce.

1 The milk may be first infused with an onion clouté (an onion studded with cloves and a bay leaf), carrot and a bouquet garni. Allow to cool.
2 Place the milk in a suitable saucepan and gradually whisk in the sauce flour. Bring slowly to the boil until the sauce has thickened.
3 Season and simmer for approximately 5–10 minutes. Use as required.

37 Parsley sauce

Ingredient	Makes 500 ml
Milk	500 ml
Sauce flour	40 g
Parsley, chopped	1 tbsp
Seasoning	

1 The milk may be first infused with a studded onion clouté, carrot and a bouquet garni. Allow to cool.

2 Place the milk in a suitable saucepan, gradually whisk in the sauce flour. Bring slowly to the boil until the sauce has thickened.

3 Season, simmer for approximately 5–10 minutes. Add the parsley. Use as required.

38 Cheese sauce (mornay)

Ingredient	Makes 500 ml
Milk	500 ml
Grated cheese	50 g
Egg yolk	1
Sauce flour	40 g

1 The milk may be first infused with a studded onion clouté, carrot and a bouquet garni. Allow to cool.

2 Place the milk in a suitable saucepan, gradually whisk in the sauce flour. Bring slowly to the boil until the sauce has thickened.

3 Mix in the cheese and egg yolk when the sauce is boiling.

4 Remove from the heat. Strain if necessary.

5 Do not allow the sauce to reboil at any time.

Professional tip

Add a little cornflour prior to heating to stabilise the sauce.

39 Soubise

Ingredient	Makes 500 ml
Onion, chopped or diced	100 g
Milk	500 ml
Sauce flour	40 g
Seasoning	

Note

This recipe, like mornay sauce and parsley sauce (Recipes 37 and 38) uses sauce flour to thicken the sauce, rather than a traditional roux base. This is a simpler method and produces a lower fat content.

1 Cook the onions without colouring them, either by boiling or sweating in butter.

2 The milk may be first infused with a studded onion clouté, carrot and a bouquet garni. Allow to cool.

3 Place the milk in a suitable saucepan, gradually whisk in the sauce flour. Bring slowly to the boil until the sauce has thickened.

4 Add the onions, season, simmer for approximately 5–10 minutes.

5 Blitz well. Pass through a strainer.

40 Suprême sauce

Ingredient	4 portions	10 portions
Margarine, butter or oil	100 g	250 g
Flour	100 g	250 g
Stock (chicken, veal, fish or mutton)	1 litre	2.5 litres
Mushroom trimmings	25 g	60 g
Egg yolk	1	2½
Cream	60 ml	150 ml
Lemon juice	2–3 drops	5–6 drops

Energy	Cals	Fat	Sat fat	Carb	Sugar	Protein	Fibre	Sodium
1339 kJ	322 kcal	25.2 g	15.3 g	21.1 g	1.8 g	4.1 g	1.6 g	0.2 g

Using butter.

1 Melt the fat or oil in a thick-bottomed pan.

2 Add the flour and mix in. Cook to a sandy texture over a gentle heat, without colouring.

3 Allow the roux to cool, then gradually add the boiling stock. Stir until smooth and boiling.

4 Add the mushroom trimmings. Simmer for approximately 1 hour.

5 Pass through a final conical strainer.

6 Finish with a liaison of the egg yolk, cream and lemon juice. Serve immediately.

This sauce can be served hot with boiled chicken, vol-au-vonts, etc., and can also be used for white chaud-froid sauce. The traditional stock base is a good chicken stock.

> **Professional tip**
>
> Once the liaison has been added, do not reboil this sauce.

41 Mushroom sauce

Ingredient	1 litre	4.5 litres
Butter or oil	100 g	400 g
Flour	100 g	400 g
Stock (chicken, veal, fish, mutton) as required	1 litre	4.5 litres
White button mushrooms, well-washed, sliced, sweated	200 g	900 g
Mushroom trimmings	50 g	225 g
Egg yolk	2	9
Cream	120 ml	540 ml
Lemon, juice of	½	1

1 Melt the butter or heat the oil in a thick-bottomed pan.

2 Add the flour and mix in.

3 Cook out to a sandy texture over gentle heat without colouring.

4 Allow the roux to cool.

5 Gradually add the boiling stock.

6 Stir until smooth and boiling.

7 Add the mushrooms and trimmings. Allow to simmer for approximately 1 hour.

8 Pass it through a fine conical strainer.

9 Simmer for 10 minutes, then add the egg yolk, cream and lemon juice.

42 Ivory sauce

Ingredient	4 portions	10 portions
Chicken or veal velouté	250 ml	625 ml
Mushroom trimmings, washed and dried	50 g	125 g
Cream, single or double	50 ml	125 ml
Lemon, juice of	½	1½
Chicken or beef meat glaze	1 tbsp	2½ tbsp
Seasoning		

1 Place the velouté into a suitable saucepan and bring to the boil.
2 Add the mushroom trimmings; simmer for 10 minutes.
3 Pass the sauce through a fine chinois.
4 Add the meat glaze; stir well to achieve an ivory colour.
5 Add the lemon juice and finish with cream. Correct the seasoning.

Serve with grilled veal or pork chops, grilled or poached chicken.

Energy	Cals	Fat	Sat fat	Carb	Sugar	Protein	Fibre	Sodium
351 kJ	85 kcal	6.8g	4.3g	4.9g	0.8g	1.3g	0.6g	0.0g

Using butter and single cream.

43 Aurora sauce

Ingredient	4 portions	10 portions
Chicken or veal velouté	250 ml	625 ml
Mushroom trimmings, washed and dried	50 g	125 g
Fresh cream, double or single	50 ml	125 mls
Egg yolks	1	3
Lemon, juice of	½	1½
Tomato purée	1 tbsp	1½ tbsp
Seasoning		

Energy	Cals	Fat	Sat fat	Carb	Sugar	Protein	Fibre	Sodium
247 kJ	59 kcal	4.0g	1.9g	3.0g	2.7g	3.1g	0.4g	0.0g

Using single cream, and chicken soup in place of velouté.

1. Place the velouté in a suitable saucepan and bring to the boil.
2. Add the mushroom trimmings. Allow to simmer for 10 minutes.
3. Add the tomato purée; mix well.
4. Strain through a fine chinois.
5. In a basin mix the egg yolks and cream.
6. Add a little of the hot sauce to this mix; whisk well.
7. Return to the main sauce and stir. Do NOT allow to re-boil.
8. Finish with lemon juice.

Serve with poached chicken or poached eggs. If serving with poached or steamed fish use fish velouté.

44 Chasseur sauce

Ingredient	4 portions	10 portions
Butter or oil	25 g	60 g
Shallots, chopped	10 g	25 g
Clove of garlic, chopped (optional)	1	1
Button mushrooms, sliced	50 g	125 g
White wine, dry	60 ml	150 ml
Tomatoes, skinned, deseeded, diced	100 g	250 g
Demi-glace, *jus-lié* or reduced stock	250 ml	625 ml
Parsley and tarragon, chopped		

Energy	Cals	Fat	Sat fat	Carb	Sugar	Protein	Fibre
227 kJ	55 kcal	5.3 g	2.5 g	1.4 g	1.2 g	0.5 g	0.5 g

1. Melt the butter or heat the oil in a small sauteuse.
2. Add the shallots and cook gently for 2–3 minutes without colour.
3. Add the garlic and the mushrooms, cover and cook gently for 2–3 minutes.
4. Strain off the fat.
5. Add the wine and reduce by half. Add the tomatoes.
6. Add the demi-glace; simmer for 5–10 minutes.
7. Correct the seasoning. Add the tarragon and parsley.

May be served with fried steaks, chops, chicken, etc.

Healthy eating tips
- Use an unsaturated oil (sunflower or vegetable). Lightly oil the pan.
- Skim the fat from the finished dish.
- Season with the minimum amount of salt.

45 Devilled sauce (*sauce diable*)

Ingredient	Makes 250 g
Butter	25 g
Shallots, finely chopped	25 g
Dry white wine	150 ml
Reduced brown stock or *jus-lié*	250 ml
Cayenne pepper	2 grams

1 In a suitable pan, add the butter and gently sweat the shallots without colour.

2 Add the white wine; reduce by half.

3 Add the brown stock or *jus-lié*; bring to the boil and simmer for 2 minutes.

4 Season with cayenne pepper. Correct the seasoning and consistency.

Serve with grilled chicken and steaks.

> **Professional tip**
>
> The sauce should have a background flavour of white wine, with a sharp after taste from the cayenne pepper. The sauce may also be improved with the addition of 15 g of soft butter before serving.

46 Robert sauce

Ingredient	4 portions	10 portions
Oil or butter	20 g	50 g
Onions, finely chipped	10 g	25 g
Vinegar	60 ml	150 g
Demi-glace, *jus-lié* or reduced stock	250 ml	625 ml
English or continental mustard	1 level tbsp	2½ level tbsp
Caster sugar	1 level tbsp	2½ level tbsp

Energy	Cals	Fat	Sat fat	Carb	Sugar	Protein	Fibre	Sodium
401 kJ	96 kcal	5.7 g	3.1 g	8.3 g	6.5 g	2.5 g	0.4 g	0.2 g

Using butter.

1 Melt the fat or oil in a small sauteuse.

2 Add the onions. Cook gently without colour.

3 Add the vinegar and reduce completely.

4 Add the demi-glace; simmer for 5–10 minutes.

5 Remove from the heat and add the mustard, diluted with a little water and the sugar; do not boil.

6 Skim and correct the seasoning.

May be served with fried sausages and burgers or grilled pork chops.

Healthy eating tips

- Use unsaturated oil (sunflower or olive). Lightly oil the pan and drain off any excess after the frying is complete. Skim the fat from the finished dish.
- Season with the minimum amount of salt.

47 Piquant sauce

Ingredient	4 portions	10 portions
Vinegar	60 ml	150 ml
Shallots, chopped	50 g	125 g
Demi-glace, *jus-lié* or reduced stock	250 ml	625 ml
Gherkins, chopped	25 g	60 g
Capers, chopped	10 g	25 g
Chervil, tarragon and parsley, chopped	½ tbsp	1½ tbsp

Energy	Cals	Fat	Sat fat	Carb	Sugar	Protein	Fibre	Sodium
151 kJ	36 kcal	1.3 g	0.5 g	3.0 g	1.3 g	2.4 g	0.7 g	0.0 g

1 Place the vinegar and shallots in a small sauteuse and reduce by half.

2 Add the demi-glace; simmer for 15–20 minutes.

3 Add the rest of the ingredients.

4 Skim and correct the seasoning.

May be served with made-up dishes, sausages and grilled meats.

48 Madeira sauce

Ingredient	4 portions	10 portions
Demi-glace, *jus-lié* or reduced stock	250 ml	625 ml
Madeira wine	2 tbsp	5 tbsp
Butter	25 g	60 g

Energy	Cals	Fat	Sat fat	Carb	Sugar	Protein	Fibre	Sodium
365 kJ	88 kcal	6.4 g	3.7 g	3.5 g	1.4 g	2.1 g	0.3 g	0.1 g

1 Boil the demi-glace in a small sauteuse.
2 Add the Madeira and reboil.
3 Correct the seasoning.
4 Pass through a fine conical strainer.
5 Gradually mix in the butter.

May be served with braised ox tongue or ham.

Variation

Dry sherry or port wine may be substituted for Madeira (and the sauce renamed accordingly).

49 Brown onion sauce (*sauce lyonnaise*)

Ingredient	4 portions	10 portions
Margarine, oil or butter	25 g	60 g
Onions, sliced	100 g	250 g
Vinegar	2 tbsp	5 tbsp
Demi-glace, *jus-lié* or reduced stock	250 ml	625 ml

1 Melt the fat or oil in a sauteuse.
2 Add the onions; cover with a lid and cook gently until tender and golden in colour.
3 Remove the lid and colour lightly.
4 Add the vinegar and completely reduce.
5 Add the demi-glace; simmer for 5–10 minutes.
6 Skim and correct the seasoning.

May be served with burgers, fried liver or sausages.

Energy	Cals	Fat	Sat fat	Carb	Sugar	Protein	Fibre	Sodium
374 kJ	90 kcal	6.8 g	3.9 g	3.5 g	1.8 g	3.7 g	1.0 g	0.1 g

Using butter.

Healthy eating tips
- Use unsaturated oil (sunflower or olive). Lightly oil the pan and drain off any excess after the frying is complete. Skim the fat from the finished dish.
- Season with the minimum amount of salt.

50 Italian sauce

Ingredient	4 portions	10 portions
Margarine, oil or butter	25 g	60 g
Shallots, chopped	10 g	25 g
Mushrooms, chopped	50 g	125 g
Demi-glace, *jus-lié* or reduced stock	250 ml	625 ml
Lean ham, chopped	25 g	60 g
Tomatoes, skinned, deseeded	100 g	250 g
Diced parsley, chervil and tarragon, chopped		

Healthy eating tips
- Use unsaturated oil (sunflower or olive). Lightly oil the pan and drain off any excess after the frying is complete.
- Trim as much fat as possible from the ham.
- The ham is salty, so do not add more salt; flavour will come from the herbs.
- Skim all fat from the finished sauce.

Energy	Cals	Fat	Sat fat	Carb	Sugar	Protein	Fibre	Sodium
359 kJ	86 kcal	6.5 g	3.7 g	4.4 g	2.2 g	2.4 g	0.8 g	0.1 g

Using butter.

1 Melt the fat or oil in a small sauteuse.

2 To make a duxelle, add the shallots and cook gently for 2–3 minutes.

3 Add the mushrooms and cook gently for a further 2–3 minutes.

4 Add the demi-glace, ham and tomatoes. Simmer for 5–10 minutes.

5 Correct the seasoning; add the chopped herbs.

51 Pepper sauce (*sauce poivrade*)

Ingredient	4 portions	10 portions
Butter, margarine or oil	25 g	60 g
Onions, chopped into mirepoix	50 g	125 g
Carrots, chopped into mirepoix	50 g	125 g
Celery, chopped into mirepoix	50 g	125 g
Bay leaf	1	1
Sprig of thyme		
White wine	2 tbsp	5 tbsp
Vinegar	2 tbsp	5 tbsp
Mignonette pepper	5 g	12 g
Demi-glace, *jus-lié* or reduced stock	250 ml	625 ml
Cream (optional, to finish)	25 ml	65 ml

Energy	Cals	Fat	Sat fat	Carb	Sugar	Protein	Fibre
247 kJ	60 kcal	5.3 g	2.5 g	2.6 g	2.0 g	0.5 g	0.6 g

1 Melt the fat or heat the oil in a small sauteuse.

2 Add the vegetables (mirepoix) and herbs, and allow to brown.

3 Add the wine, vinegar and pepper. Reduce by half.

4 Add the demi-glace and simmer for 20–30 minutes.

5 Pass through a fine conical strainer.

6 Correct the seasoning.

7 Finish with cream if desired.

Note

Mignonette pepper is coarsely ground black pepper. Softer green or pink peppercorns may be used instead. This sauce is usually served with joints or cuts of venison.

Healthy eating tips

● Use an unsaturated oil (sunflower or vegetable). Lightly oil the pan.
● Skim the fat from the finished dish.
● Season with the minimum amount of salt.

52 Beef jus

Ingredient	1 litre
Mushrooms, finely sliced	750 g
Butter	100 g
Shallots, finely sliced	350 g
Beef trim, diced	350 g
Sherry vinegar	100 ml
Red wine	700 ml
Chicken stock	500 ml
Beef stock	1 litre

1 Caramelise the mushrooms in foaming butter, strain, then put aside in pan.

2 Caramelise the shallots in foaming butter, strain, then put aside in pan.

3 In another pan, caramelise the beef trim until golden brown.

4 Place the mushrooms, shallots and beef trim in one of the pans. Deglaze the other two pans with the vinegar, then add to the pan with the beef, shallots and mushrooms in it.

5 In a separate pan, reduce the wine by half and add to the main pan.

6 Add the stock, then reduce to sauce consistency.

7 Pass through a sieve, then chill and store until needed.

53 Roast chicken jus

Ingredient	1 litre
Chicken stock	600 ml
Lamb jus	600 ml
Chicken wings, chopped small	300 g
Vegetable oil	60 ml
Shallots, sliced	100 g
Butter	50 g
Tomatoes, chopped	200 g
White wine vinegar	40 ml
Red wine vinegar	75 ml
Tarragon	1 tsp
Chervil	1 tsp

1 Put the jus and stock in a pan and reduce to 1 litre.

2 Roast the chicken wings in oil until slightly golden.

3 Add the shallots and butter, and cook until lightly browned (do not allow the butter to burn).

4 Strain off the butter and return the bones to the pan; deglaze with the vinegar and add tomatoes.

5 Ensure the bottom of the pan is clean. Add the reduced stock/jus and simmer for 15 minutes.

6 Pass through a sieve, then reduce to sauce consistency.

7 Remove from the heat and infuse with the aromats for 5 minutes.

8 Pass through a chinois and then muslin cloth.

54 Red wine jus

Ingredient	1 litre
Shallots, sliced	150 g
Butter	50 g
Garlic, halved	10 g
Red wine vinegar	100 ml
Red wine	250 ml
Chicken stock	350 ml
Lamb or beef jus	250 ml
Bay leaves	2
Sprig of thyme	1

1 Caramelise the shallots in foaming butter until golden, adding the garlic at the end.
2 Strain through a colander and then put back into the pan and deglaze with the vinegar.
3 Reduce the red wine by half along with the stock and jus, at the same time as colouring the shallots.
4 When everything is done, combine and simmer for 20 minutes.
5 Pass through a sieve and reduce to sauce consistency.
6 Infuse the aromats for 5 minutes.
7 Pass through muslin cloth and store until needed.

55 Roast gravy (*jus rôti*)

Ingredient	4 portions	10 portions
Raw veal bones or beef and veal trimmings	200 g	500 g
Stock or water	500 ml	1.25 litres
Onions, chopped	50 g	125 g
Celery, chopped	25 g	60 g
Carrots, chopped	50 g	125 g

Energy	Cals	Fat	Sat fat	Carb	Sugar	Protein	Fibre	Sodium
309 kJ	74 kcal	3.9 g	1.5 g	3.3 g	2.7 g	6.2 g	1.3 g	0.1 g

1 Chop the bones and brown in the oven, or brown in a little oil on top of the stove in a frying pan. Drain off all the fat.

2 Place the bones in a saucepan with the stock or water.

3 Bring to the boil, skim and allow to simmer.

4 Add the lightly browned vegetables, which may be fried in a little fat in a frying pan or added to the bones when partly browned.

5 Simmer for 1½–2 hours.

6 Remove the joint from the roasting tin when cooked.

7 Return the tray to a low heat to allow the sediment to settle.

8 Carefully strain off the fat, leaving the sediment in the tin.

9 Return the joint to the stove and brown carefully; deglaze with the brown stock.

10 Allow to simmer for a few minutes.

11 Correct the colour and seasoning. Strain and skim off all fat.

Professional tip

For preference, use beef bones for roast beef gravy and the appropriate bones for lamb, veal, mutton and pork.

Healthy eating tips
- Use an unsaturated oil (sunflower or vegetable). Lightly oil the pan.
- Season with the minimum amount of salt.

56 Thickened gravy (*jus-lié*)

1 Start with roast gravy (recipe 55) or reduced veal stock (recipe 8). Add a little tomato purée, a few mushroom trimmings and a pinch of thyme and simmer for 10–15 minutes.

2 Stir some arrowroot diluted in cold water into the simmering gravy.

3 Reboil, simmer for 5–10 minutes and pass through a strainer.

Energy	Cals	Fat	Sat fat	Carb	Sugar	Protein	Fibre	Sodium
247 kJ	59 kcal	2.6g	1.0g	4.7g	1.4g	4.1g	0.7g	0.1g

Variation

Add a little rosemary, thyme or lavender.

57 Apple sauce

Ingredient	8 portions
Cooking apples	400 g
Sugar	50 g
Butter or margarine	25 g

Energy	Cals	Fat	Sat fat	Carb	Sugar	Protein	Fibre	Sodium
276 kJ	65 kcal	2.6g	1.6g	11.0g	11.0g	0.2g	1.1g	0.0g

Using butter.

1 Peel, core and wash the apples.
2 Place with other ingredients in a covered pan and cook to a purée.
3 Pass through a sieve or liquidise.

58 Tomato sauce (*sauce tomate*)

Ingredient	Makes 500 ml
Carrots, chopped into mirepoix	90 g
Celery, chopped into mirepoix	30 g
Clove of garlic, chopped	½
Vegetable oil	25 g
Butter	25 g
Thyme	1 g
Bay leaf	½
Tomato purée	12 g
Plum tomatoes	200 g
Chicken stock	750 g
Juniper berries	2
Cream	75 g
Gastric (50/50 sherry vinegar and sugar, heated to dissolve the sugar)	5 g

1 Sweat the carrots, celery and garlic in the oil and butter.
2 Add the thyme, bay leaf and tomato purée, and cook for 5 minutes.
3 Add the plum tomatoes and cook for 5 minutes.
4 Add the chicken stock and juniper berries, reduce by a third.
5 Remove the mirepoix. Strain through a chinois.
6 Finish with the cream, bring to the boil and blitz.
7 Season with salt and gastric.

59 Cranberry sauce

Ingredient	8 portions
Cranberries	400g
Water	100ml
Sugar	50g

1 Simmer all ingredients together in a covered pan (not iron or aluminium) until soft.

2 The sauce may be sieved or liquidised if required.

Variation

Half orange juice and half water, plus some grated orange zest, may be used. Alternatively, use half orange juice and half port wine.

Energy	Cals	Fat	Sat fat	Carb	Sugar	Protein	Fibre	Sodium
138 kJ	32 kcal	0.1g	0.0g	8.3g	8.3g	0.2g	1.9g	0.0g

60 Hollandaise sauce

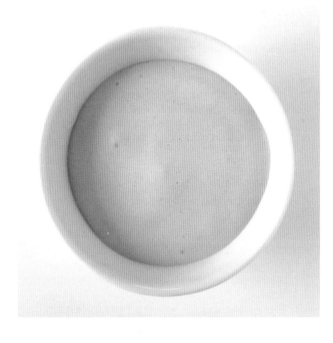

Ingredient	Makes 500g
Peppercorns, crushed	12
White wine vinegar	3 tbsp
Egg yolks	6
Melted butter	325g
Salt and cayenne pepper	

1 Place the peppercorns and vinegar in a small pan and reduce to one-third.

2 Add 1 tablespoon of cold water and allow to cool. Add the egg yolks.

3 Put on a bain-marie and whisk continuously to a sabayon consistency.

4 Remove from the heat and gradually whisk in the melted butter.

5 Add seasoning and pass through muslin or a fine chinois.

6 Store in an appropriate container at room temperature.

Note

Egg-based sauces should not be kept warm for more than two hours. After this time, they should be thrown away. They are best made fresh to order.

Variation

- Mousseline sauce – a hollandaise base with lightly whipped cream.
- Maltaise sauce – a hollandaise base with lightly grated zest and juice of one blood orange.

Faults

If you add oil or butter too fast when making hollandaise or mayonnaise, the sauce may curdle because the lecithin has had insufficient time to coat the droplets. This can be rectified by adding the broken sauce to more egg yolks.

61 Béarnaise sauce

1 Place the shallots, tarragon, peppercorns and vinegar in a small pan and reduce to one-third.
2 Add 1 tablespoon of cold water and allow to cool. Add the egg yolks.
3 Put on a bain-marie and whisk continuously to a sabayon consistency.
4 Remove from the heat and gradually whisk in the melted butter.
5 Add seasoning. Pass through muslin or a fine chinois.
6 To finish, add the chopped chervil and tarragon.
7 Store in an appropriate container.

Note

Egg-based sauces should not be kept warm for more than two hours. After this time, they should be thrown away. They are best made fresh to order.

Professional tip

This sauce should be twice as thick as hollandaise.

Variation

- Choron sauce – add 200 g tomato concassé, well dried. Do not add the chopped tarragon and chervil to finish.
- Foyot or valois sauce – add 25 g warm meat glaze.
- Paloise sauce – use chopped mint stalks in place or the tarragon in the reduction. To finish, add chopped mint instead of the chervil and tarragon.

Ingredient	Makes 500 ml
Shallots, chopped	50 g
Tarragon	10 g
Peppercorns, crushed	12
White wine vinegar	3 tbsp
Egg yolks	6
Melted butter	325 g
Salt and cayenne pepper	
Chervil and tarragon to finish, chopped	

62 Salsa verde

Ingredient	8 portions
Mint, coarsely chopped	1 tbsp
Parsley, coarsely chopped	3 tbsp
Capers, coarsely chopped	3
Clove of garlic (optional)	1
Dijon mustard	1 tsp
Lemon, juice of	½
Extra virgin olive oil	120 ml
Salt	

Energy	Cals	Fat	Sat fat	Carb	Sugar	Protein	Fibre
281 kJ	69 kcal	7.5g	1.1g	0.2g	0.1g	0.1g	0.0g

Per tablespoon.

1 In a large bowl, mix all the ingredients together and check the seasoning.

Serve with grilled fish.

63 Tomato and cucumber salsa

Ingredient	8 portions
Ripe tomatoes, skinned, deseeded, chopped	400g
Cucumber, peeled, chopped	½
Spring onions, chopped	6
Fresh basil, chopped	1 tbsp
Fresh parsley, chopped	1 tbsp
Olive oil	3 tbsp
Lemon or lime, juice of	1
Salt and pepper	

1 Mix all the ingredients together in a large bowl.

2 Correct seasoning and serve.

Energy	Cals	Fat	Sat fat	Carb	Sugar	Protein	Fibre
202 kJ	49 kcal	4.3g	0.7g	2.0g	2.0g	0.6g	0.7g

Healthy eating tips

Rely on the herbs for flavour, with the minimum amount of salt.

Variation

This recipe may be varied by using any chopped salad ingredients and fresh herbs (e.g. tarragon, chervil). Do not be afraid to experiment.

Extra vegetables can be added and the salsa used liberally with grilled fish or chicken. Rice could be served with this, or the salsa used to fill a tortilla.

64 Avocado and coriander salsa

Ingredient	8 portions
Ripe avocado, peeled and diced	1
Ripe tomatoes, peeled, deseeded and diced	3
Shallot, peeled and cut into rings	1
Fresh coriander, chopped	1 tsp
Pine kernels, toasted	10 g
Cucumber, diced	25 g
Lemon or lime, juice of	1
Virgin olive oil	3 tbsp
Salt and pepper to taste	

Energy	Cals	Fat	Sat fat	Carb	Sugar	Protein	Fibre
361 kJ	87 kcal	8.6g	1.4g	1.8g	1.4g	0.8g	1.0g

1 Mix all the ingredients together in a large bowl.

2 Check the seasoning and serve.

Use with cold dishes such as salads or terrines.

Healthy eating tips
- Although avocado is rich in fat, it is unsaturated fat and therefore healthier.
- Try using the salsa to fill a tortilla, and add grilled fish or chicken to make a healthy meal.

65 Melted butter sauce (*beurre fondu*)

Ingredient	4 portions	10 portions
Butter	200 g	500 g
Water or white wine	2 tbsp	5 tbsp

- **Method 1**: boil the butter and water together gently until combined, then pass through a fine strainer.
- **Method 2**: melt the butter in the water and carefully strain off the fat, leaving the water and sediment in the pan.

Note

Usually served with poached fish and certain vegetables (e.g. blue trout, salmon, asparagus, sea kale).

Energy	Cals	Fat	Sat fat	Carb	Sugar	Protein	Fibre
388 kJ	94 kcal	10.3g	6.5g	0.1g	0.1g	0.1g	0.0g

66 Horseradish sauce (*sauce raifort*)

Ingredient	8 portions
Horseradish	25 g
Vinegar or lemon juice	1 tbsp
Salt, pepper	
Cream or crème fraiche, lightly whipped	125 ml

1 Wash, peel and rewash the horseradish. Grate finely.

2 Mix all the ingredients together.

Serve with roast beef, smoked trout, eel or halibut.

Professional tip

It is essential to blend the ingredients without over-mixing them, in order to get a good flavour.

Energy	Cals	Fat	Sat fat	Carb	Sugar	Protein	Fibre	Sodium
135 kJ	33 kcal	3.0g	1.9g	0.7g	0.6g	0.7g	0.3g	0.0g

Using cream.

67 Sweet and sour sauce

Ingredient	4 portions	10 portions
White vinegar	375 ml	1 litre
Brown sugar	150 g	375 g
Tomato ketchup	125 ml	300 ml
Light soy sauce	1 tbsp	2½ tbsp
Seasoning		

1 Boil the vinegar and sugar in a suitable pan.

2 Add the tomato ketchup, soy sauce and seasoning.

3 Simmer for a few minutes then use as required. This sauce may also be lightly thickened with cornflour or another thickening agent.

Energy	Cals	Fat	Sat fat	Carb	Sugar	Protein	Fibre	Sodium
823 kJ	194 kcal	0.0g	0.0g	47.8g	47.4g	1.0g	0.4g	0.8g

68 Gribiche sauce

Ingredient	500 g
Hard-boiled eggs, sieved	2
Vegetable oil	325 ml
French mustard	1 tsp
White wine vinegar	100 ml
Capers, chopped	30 g
Gherkins, chopped	30 g
Parsley, chopped	½ tsp
Chives, chopped	½ tsp
Basil, chopped	½ tsp
Seasoning	

This is an emulsified sauce. The mustard is a natural emulsifying agent.

1 Place the sieved egg yolks in a basin and add the mustard and vinegar.
2 Whisk together with a balloon whisk.
3 Slowly add the oil, whisking continuously.
4 When the emulsion is formed, add the remainder of the ingredients and season.

Serve with steamed fish, fried fish, cold meats, chicken and gammon.

6 Eggs

This chapter is relevant to the following units:
→ Prepare, cook and finish basic egg dishes.

Recipes included in this chapter

Eggs are a very versatile ingredient and are used extensively in hors d'oeuvres, meat and poultry dishes, soups, pasta, egg dishes, salads, fish dishes, sweets and pastries, sauces and savouries. They are useful as a main dish as they provide the energy, fat, minerals and vitamins needed for growth and repair of the body.

Fried, scrambled, poached and boiled eggs, and omelettes, are mainly served at breakfast, but a variety of egg dishes may also be served for lunch, high tea, supper and snacks.

Most egg products are available in liquid, frozen or spray-dried form. Whole eggs are used primarily for cake production, where their foaming and coagulation properties are required. Egg whites are used for meringues and light sponges, where their foaming property is crucial.

The structure of eggs

The outer shell of an egg is composed mainly of calcium carbonate; they are lined with membranes and have a number of pores for gas exchange. These pores are covered by a wax-like layer known as the cuticle. This cuticle protects against microbial invasion and controls water loss.

The egg white is divided into a thick layer around the yolk and a thinner layer next to the shell. The thick layer anchors the yolk, together with the chalaza, in the middle of the egg, where it is less vulnerable to microbial attack. The egg white has an important function as it possesses special antibacterial properties, which, under normal circumstances, prevent the growth and multiplication of micro-organisms that have entered the shell. The yolk is rich in nutrients and is the part of the egg that is most vulnerable to micro-organisms.

Egg yolks are high in saturated fat, while egg whites are made up of protein and water.

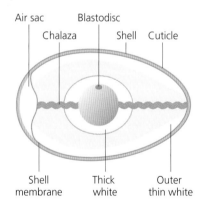

Table 6.1 The composition of eggs (approximate percentages)

	Whole egg	White	Yolk
Water	73	87	47
Protein	12	10	15
Fat	11	0	33
Minerals	1	0.5	2
Vitamins	3	2.5	3

Types of eggs

Almost all of the eggs used for culinary purposes come from hens, but eggs from turkeys, geese, ducks, guinea fowl, quail and gulls are also edible.

Quails' eggs are used in a variety of ways, for example: as a garnish on many hot and cold dishes; and as a starter or main course, such as a salad of assorted leaves with hot wild mushrooms and poached quail eggs, or tartlet of quail eggs on chopped mushrooms coated with hollandaise sauce.

Purchasing and quality points

When buying eggs the following points should be noted:
- The eggshell should be clean, well shaped, strong and slightly rough.
- When eggs are broken there should be a high proportion of thick white to thin white. If an egg is kept, the thick white gradually changes into thin white, and water passes from the white into the yolk.
- The yolk should be firm, round (not flattened) and of a good, even colour. As eggs are kept the yolk loses strength and begins to flatten, water evaporates from the egg and is replaced by air.
- Hens can pass salmonella bacteria into their eggs and therefore cause food poisoning. To reduce this risk, pasteurised eggs may be used where appropriate (pasteurised eggs are washed, sanitised and then broken into sterilised containers; with the yolks and whites either separated or together they are strained and pasteurised – that is, heated to 63 °C for one minute – then rapidly cooled).
- Always purchase fresh eggs from sources where there is no salmonella contamination or from a low-risk supplier. Look for the 'Lion' quality mark on the egg shell and egg box – it shows that the eggs have been produced to the highest standards of food safety, including a programme of vaccination against *Salmonella enteritidis*. Always buy eggs from a reputable retailer where they will have been transported and stored at the correct temperature (below 20 °C).
- Cracked eggs should not be used.

Candling of eggs is a method that is used for checking the quality of eggs. The egg is illuminated with a light so the flaws can be seen, including the yolk position and size, the size of the air sac and the presence of blood or meat spots.

The Code of Practice for Lion Quality eggs covers breeding flocks and hatcheries, pullet rearing and laying birds, including both hygiene and animal welfare requirements, farm handling of eggs, distribution of eggs from farms, feeding, hen disposal, packing centres, procedures, advice to retailers, consumers and caterers, and environmental policy and enforcement. For more information on the British Lion Quality mark see www.lioneggfarms.co.uk.

Quality grading

Under European law eggs are graded for quality using the following system:
- Grade A – naturally clean, fresh eggs, internally perfect with intact shells and an air sac not exceeding 6 mm in depth.
- Grade B – eggs that have been downgraded because they have been cleaned or preserved, or because they are internally imperfect, cracked or have an air sac exceeding 6 mm but not more than 9 mm in depth. Grade B eggs are broken out and pasteurised.
- Grade C – eggs that are fit for breaking for manufacturing purposes but cannot be sold in their shells to the public.

Sizes

Hens' eggs are now graded in four sizes in the UK – small, medium, large and very large – as shown in Table 6.2 below.

Table 6.2 Hens' egg sizes

Egg size	Weight	Old size
Very large	73 g	Size 0 to size 1
Large	63–73 g	Size 1 to size 3
Medium	53–63 g	Size 3 to size 5
Small	53 g and under	Size 5 to size 7

The size of the eggs does not affect their quality, but it does affect their price. Once eggs have been tested for quality, then weighed and graded (see Purchasing and quality points below) they are packed into boxes. The wholesale price of eggs is quoted per 'long hundred' (120). All egg boxes leaving the packing station are dated.

Preparing and cooking eggs

Make sure the eggs are fresh and always cook them according to the recipe. Take special care when undercooking eggs so that the yolks are soft.

Cooking eggs using different methods will affect the taste and texture. Egg dishes can be very flavoursome and use a range of herbs and spices, especially when preparing scrambled eggs and omelettes.

Environmental officers advise that eggs should be cooked well done and should reach an internal temperature of 72 °C. However, eggs cooked to this temperature are overcooked and often have a rubbery texture. Most people expect eggs to be served at a lower temperature, but they should be cooked thoroughly to reduce the risk of food poisoning from salmonella.

Always choose the correct tools and equipment when cooking egg dishes, especially when scrambling, poaching, frying, boiling and baking. Always have the correct equipment to hand.

Health and safety

- Hands should be washed before and after handling eggs.
- Preparation surfaces, utensils and containers should be cleaned regularly and always cleaned between preparation of different dishes.

Healthy options when making egg dishes

When preparing egg dishes such as omelettes, scrambled eggs or eggs sur le plat, use olive oil instead of butter. When finishing egg dishes, fromage frais or natural yoghurt can be used instead of cream in some recipes.

Holding and serving temperatures

When possible, always serve eggs to order. Do not have egg dishes such as fried eggs and scrambled eggs on a buffet for long periods as they will tend to loose moisture and dry out, changing their texture and flavour and therefore becoming inedible.

As explained above, it is best that eggs are cooked to order and are cooked through. Do not leave eggs cooked and on a hot buffet for long periods – leave for no more than 20 minutes.

Egg dishes should be consumed as soon as possible after preparation or, if not for immediate use, refrigerated at 5 °C or below.

Storing eggs

Eggs should be stored in a cool but not too dry place (0–5 °C is ideal) where the humidity of the air and the amount of carbon dioxide present are controlled. Eggs will keep for up to nine months under these conditions.

Most eggs have date stamps and must not be used after that date. Stocks should be rotated: first in, first out.

Because eggshells are porous, eggs will absorb any strong odours; therefore, they should not be stored near strong-smelling foods such as onions, fish and cheese.

Test yourself

1 State four quality points to look for when buying fresh eggs.
2 Describe the process for cooking a poached egg.
3 State what you could do when preparing and cooking scrambled eggs to make the dish healthier.
4 At what temperature should egg dishes be held for service?
5 How should an egg dish not for immediate use be stored?

Egg recipes

1 Soft-boiled eggs in the shell (*oeufs à la coque*)

Allow 1 or 2 eggs per portion.

Method 1 (soft)

1 Place the eggs in cold water and bring to the boil.
2 Simmer for 2–2½ minutes, then remove from the water.
3 Serve at once in an egg cup.

Method 2 (medium soft)

1 Plunge the eggs in boiling water, then reboil.
2 Simmer for 4–5 minutes.
3 Serve at once in an egg cup.

Energy	Cals	Fat	Sat fat	Carb	Sugar	Protein	Fibre
340 kJ	81 kcal	6.0g	1.9g	0.0g	0.0g	6.8g	0.0g

Using 1 egg per portion.

2 Soft-boiled eggs out of the shell (*oeufs mollets*)

Hard-boiled eggs (left) and soft-boiled eggs (right) – recipes 2 and 3

Energy	Cals	Fat	Sat fat	Carb	Sugar	Protein	Fibre
1,052 kJ	251 kcal	18.9g	8.7g	8.0g	3.3g	12.5g	1.2g

Using 1 egg per portion.

Allow 1 or 2 eggs per portion.

1 Plunge the eggs into boiling water, then bring back to the boil.
2 Simmer for 4½–5 minutes. Refresh immediately.
3 Remove the shells carefully.
4 Reheat when required for 30 seconds in hot salted water.

3 Hard-boiled eggs (*oeufs durs*)

Energy	Cals	Fat	Sat fat	Carb	Sugar	Protein	Fibre
753 kJ	181 kcal	13.5g	3.8g	0.0g	0.0g	15.0g	0.0g

Allow 1 or 2 eggs per portion.

1 Plunge the eggs into a pan of boiling water.

2 Reboil and simmer for 8–10 minutes.

3 Refresh until cold under running water.

4 Remove the shell carefully if required.

Note

If high temperatures or a long cooking time are used to cook eggs, iron in the yolk and sulphur compounds in the white are released to form an unsightly blackish ring around the yolk. Stale eggs will also show a black ring round the yolk.

4 Fried eggs (*oeufs frits*)

Allow 1 or 2 eggs per portion.

1 Melt a little fat in a frying pan. Add the eggs.

2 Cook gently until lightly set. Serve on a plate or flat dish.

Professional tip

To prepare an excellent fried egg, it is essential to use a fresh high-quality egg, to maintain a controlled low heat and to use a high-quality fat (butter or oil, such as sunflower oil).

Health and safety

Lightly cooked eggs do not reach high enough temperatures to kill all bacteria that may be present. Do not serve lightly cooked eggs to people in high-risk groups: very young children, elderly people, pregnant women or people who are ill.

Energy	Cals	Fat	Sat fat	Carb	Sugar	Protein	Fibre
536 kJ	128 kcal	31.0g	9.8g	0.0g	0.0g	7.6g	0.0g

Fried in sunflower oil.

5 Scrambled eggs (*oeufs brouillés*)

1 Break the eggs in a basin, add milk (if using), lightly season with salt and pepper and thoroughly mix with a whisk.
2 Melt half the butter in a thick-bottomed pan, add the eggs and cook over a gentle heat, stirring continuously until the eggs are lightly cooked.
3 Remove from the heat, correct the seasoning and mix in the remaining butter. (A tablespoon of cream may also be added at this point.)

Serve in individual egg dishes or on a slice of freshly butter toast with the crust removed.

Ingredient	4 portions	10 portions
Eggs	6–8	15–20
Milk (optional)	2 tbsp	5 tbsp
Salt, pepper		
Butter or oil	50g	125g

Energy	Cals	Fat	Sat fat	Carb	Sugar	Protein	Fibre
1,105 kJ	263 kcal	22.9g	8.7g	0.5g	0.5g	13.9g	0.0g

Using hard margarine instead of butter.

Variation

Scrambled eggs may be served with smoked salmon (as shown).

Note

If scrambled eggs are cooked too quickly or for too long the protein will toughen, the eggs will discolour because of the iron and sulphur compounds being released, and syneresis (separation of water from the eggs) will occur. This means that they will be unpleasant to eat. The heat from the pan will continue to cook the eggs after it has been removed from the stove; therefore, the pan should be removed from the heat just before the eggs are cooked.

Healthy eating tips

● Try to keep the butter used in cooking to a minimum and serve with unbuttered toast.
● Garnish with a grilled tomato.

6 Eggs Benedict

Ingredient	4 portions	10 portions
Cooking medium (see note)		
Large eggs	8	20
Butter, unsalted	2 tbsp	5 tbsp
Plain English muffins, split and toasted	4	10
Smoked bacon or sweet cure bacon, cooked	12 slices	30 slices
Hollandaise sauce	200g	500g

Energy	Cals	Fat	Sat fat	Carb	Sugar	Protein	Fibre	Sodium
3910 kJ	943 kcal	77.0g	37.8g	24.8g	2.2g	39.2g	1.4g	2.1g

1 Bring the cooking medium to a slight simmer.

2 Crack an egg into a cup and carefully slide it into the hot poaching liquid. Quickly repeat with all the eggs.

3 Poach the eggs for 3 minutes, turning them occasionally with a spoon, until the whites are firm.

4 Using a slotted spoon, remove the eggs and transfer to a kitchen towel. Lightly dab the eggs with the towel to remove any excess water.

5 While the eggs are poaching, butter the muffins and place two halves on each plate.

6 Reheat the bacon and place on top of the muffins, then top with the drained eggs.

7 To finish, lightly spoon over a generous helping of warm hollandaise sauce and serve immediately, or serve the hollandaise separately.

Note

The cooking bath must be deep and must have a minimum of 15 per cent distilled or white wine vinegar added.

7 Eggs en cocotte

1 Butter the appropriate number of egg cocottes.

2 Break an egg carefully into each and season.

3 Place the cocottes in a sauté pan containing 1 cm water.

4 Cover with a tight-fitting lid, place on a fierce heat so that the water boils rapidly.

5 Cook for 2–3 minutes until the eggs are lightly set, then serve.

Variation

● Half a minute before the cooking is completed, add 1 tsp of cream to each egg and complete the cooking.
● When cooked, add 1 tsp of *jus-lié* to each egg.
● Place diced cooked chicken, mixed with cream, in the bottom of the cocottes; break the eggs on top of the chicken and cook.
● As above, using tomato concassé in place of chicken.

Ingredient	4 portions	10 portions
Butter	25 g	60 g
Eggs	4	10
Salt, pepper		

Energy	Cals	Fat	Sat fat	Carb	Sugar	Protein	Fibre
534 kJ	127 kcal	11.2 g	5.2 g	0.0 g	0.0 g	6.8 g	0.0 g

8 Eggs sur le plat

Allow 1 or 2 eggs per portion.

1 Take a china *sur le plat* dish. Add a teaspoon of olive oil or butter. Heat it on the side of the stove, until it is moderately hot.

2 Break in 1 or 2 eggs. Allow them to set on the stove.

3 Transfer to the oven for 2–4 minutes to finish cooking.

Note

A *sur le plat* dish is a shallow porcelain dish used for cooking and serving eggs.

Energy	Cals	Fat	Sat fat	Carb	Sugar	Protein	Fibre	Sodium
875 kJ	211 kcal	16.9g	6.3g	0.0g	0.0g	14.8g	0.0g	0.2g

Using butter and two eggs.

9 Scotch eggs

1 Place the eggs, still in their shells, in a pan of water.

2 Place over a high heat and bring to the boil, then reduce the heat to simmer for approximately 9 minutes.

3 Drain and refresh the eggs under cold running water, then peel.

4 Mix the sausage meat with the thyme, parsley and spring onion in a bowl, season well with salt and freshly ground black pepper.

5 Divide the sausage meat mixture into four and flatten each out on a clean surface into ovals about 12 cm long and 8 cm at the widest point.

6 Roll the boiled egg in the seasoned flour.

7 Place each egg on to a sausage meat oval, then wrap the sausage meat around the egg, making sure the coating is smooth and completely covers the egg.

8 Dip each meat-coated egg in the beaten egg, covering the entire surface area.

9 Roll in the breadcrumbs to coat completely.

10 Heat the oil in a deep heavy-bottomed pan, to 180 °C.

Ingredient	4 portions	10 portions
Eggs	4	10
Pork sausage meat	275 g	700 g
Fresh thyme leaves	1 tsp	2½ tsp
Fresh parsley, chopped	1 tsp	2½ tsp
Spring onion, very finely chopped	1	2½
Plain flour, seasoned	125 g	300 g
Egg, beaten	1	2½
Breadcrumbs	250 g	625 g
Salt and freshly ground black pepper		
Vegetable oil for deep-frying		

11 Carefully place each Scotch egg into the hot oil and deep fry for 6–8 minutes, until golden and crisp and the sausage meat is completely cooked.

12 Carefully remove from the oil with a slotted spoon and drain on kitchen paper.

To serve, cut the egg in half and season slightly with rock salt. Scotch eggs can be served hot, warm or cold.

Variation

For a **vegetarian** version of the traditional pork Scotch egg, follow the same method as above, replacing the sausage meat with 350 g of dry mashed potato.

A **fish** version can be made. Follow the same method as above, using 300 g fish mousse (this works best using salmon) instead of sausage meat.

Energy	Cals	Fat	Sat fat	Carb	Sugar	Protein	Fibre	Sodium
2906 kJ	692 kcal	30.9g	8.5g	80.2g	4.7g	28.2g	2.0g	1.2g

1 Flatten out an oval of the sausage meat mixture.

2 Flour the egg and wrap the meat around it until it is completely covered.

3 Dip in flour, then beaten egg.

4 Roll the egg in the breadcrumbs.

5 The egg should be completely coated in breadcrumbs, ready for frying.

10 Omelette (*omelette nature*)

Ingredient	1 portion
Eggs	2–3
Salt, pepper	
Butter or oil	10 g

Energy	Cals	Fat	Sat fat	Carb	Sugar	Protein	Fibre
990 kJ	236 kcal	20.2 g	9.1 g	0.0 g	0.0 g	13.6 g	0.0 g

1 Break the eggs into a basin, season lightly with salt and pepper.

2 Beat well with a fork, or whisk until the yolks and whites are thoroughly combined and no streaks of white can be seen.

3 Heat the omelette pan; wipe thoroughly clean with a dry cloth.

4 Add the butter; heat until foaming but not brown.

5 Add the eggs and cook quickly, moving the mixture continuously with a fork until lightly set; remove from the heat.

6 Half fold the mixture over at right angles to the handle.

7 Tap the bottom of the pan to bring up the edge of the omelette.

8 With care, tilt the pan completely over so as to allow the omelette to fall into the centre of the dish or plate.

9 Neaten the shape if necessary and serve immediately.

1 Whisk the eggs until the yolks and whites are combined.

2 Move the mixture continuously while it cooks.

3 Carefully tip the omelette out of the pan.

Variation

Variations to omelettes can easily be made by adding the ingredient that the guest or dish may require. For example:
- fine herbs (chopped parsley, chervil and chives)
- mushroom (cooked, sliced, wild or cultivated)
- cheese (25 g grated cheese added before folding)
- tomato (incision made down centre of cooked omelette, filled with hot tomato concassé; served with tomato sauce)
- bacon (grill and then julienne into small strips and fold in at the end).

Healthy eating tips
- Use salt sparingly and serve with plenty of starchy carbohydrate and vegetables or salad.

Video: making an omelette http://bit.ly/ 1MxDy9I

11 Spanish omelette

Ingredient	1 portion
Eggs	2–3
Salt, pepper	
Butter, or oil	10 g
Tomato concassé	50 g
Onions, cooked	100 g
Red pepper, diced	100 g
Parsley, chopped	

Energy	Cals	Fat	Sat fat	Carb	Sugar	Protein	Fibre	Sodium
1,726 kJ	416 kcal	30.9g	11.2g	10.9g	8.2g	24.6g	2.5g	0.8g

1 Make up an omelette following recipe 10, steps 1 to 5, but including the tomato, onion, red pepper and parsley with the eggs.

2 Sharply tap the pan on the stove to loosen the omelette and toss it over as for a pancake.

This omelette is cooked and served flat. Many other flat omelettes can be served with a variety of ingredients.

When the butter is foaming, add the egg mixture

The omelette is tipped out flat

12 Feta, mint, lentil and pistachio omelette

Ingredient	4 portions	10 portions
Vegetable oil	4 tbsp	10 tbsp
Brown lentils, cooked	400 g	1 kg
Sorrel	20 leaves approximately	50 leaves
Seasoning		
Feta cheese, crumbled	50 g	125 g
Fresh mint, chopped	2 tbsp	5 tbsp
Pistachio nuts, toasted	2 tbsp	5 tbsp
Eggs	12	30

Energy	Cals	Fat	Sat fat	Carb	Sugar	Protein	Fibre	Sodium
2007 kJ	481 kcal	32.8g	8.1g	17.5g	0.8g	30.3g	5.4g	0.4g

For the filling:

1 Heat the oil in a pan. Add the lentils and the sorrel, season with salt and pepper. Stir until the sorrel is wilted.

2 Remove from the heat; add the feta cheese, mint and pistachio nuts.

For the omelette:

1 Beat the eggs well, add a teaspoon of water or cream to every three eggs.

2 Heat sufficient oil or butter in an omelette pan and proceed to make the omelettes.

3 When nearly cooked through, tilt the omelette pan and start to fold the omelette.

4 Add the filling and continue to finish folding the omelette.

Serve on plates garnished with mint leaves and wedges of lemon or lime.

Rice, pulses and grains

This chapter is relevant to the following units:
→ Prepare, cook and finish basic rice dishes.

→ Prepare, cook and finish basic pulse dishes.
→ Prepare, cook and finish basic grain dishes.

Recipes included in this chapter

Rice

Rice is one of the world's most important crops: it is the main food crop for about half the world's population. A hot, wet atmosphere is required for the cultivation of rice, and it is grown chiefly in India, Southeast Asia, South America, Italy and the southern states of the USA. In order to grow, it needs more water than any other cereal crop.

Rice is used in a variety of dishes, both starters and main courses.

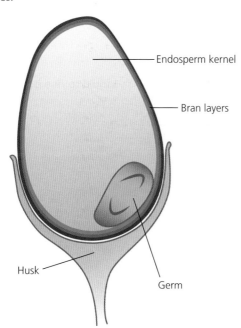

Endosperm kernel

Bran layers

Husk

Germ

▲ The structure of a grain of rice

Rice varieties

There are around 250 different varieties of rice. The main ones are described below.

- **Long-grain**: a narrow, pointed grain that has had the full bran and most of the germ removed so that it is less fibrous than brown rice. Because of its firm structure, which helps to keep the grains separate when cooked, it is suitable for plain boiling and savoury dishes such as kedgeree and curry.
- **Short-grain**: a short, rounded grain with a soft texture, suitable for sweet dishes and risotto.
- **Round**: rice which has an even, round grain.
- **Brown grain**: any rice that has had the outer covering removed, but retains its bran and, as a result, is more nutritious and contains more fibre. It takes longer to cook than long-grain rice. The nutty flavour of brown rice lends itself to some recipes but does not substitute well in traditional dishes such as paella, risotto or puddings.

Many other types of rice are now widely available, which can add different colours and textures to dishes. Some of these are described below.

- **Arborio**: an Italian short-grain rice. It is used in risottos because it can absorb a good deal of cooking liquid without becoming too soft.
- **Basmati**: a narrow long-grain rice with a distinctive flavour, suitable for serving with Indian dishes. Basmati rice should be soaked before being cooked to remove excess starch.

- **Wholegrain rice**: the whole unprocessed grain of the rice.
- **Wild rice**: this is actually an aquatic grass, not a rice.
- **Easy-cook rice**: traditional rice is milled direct from the field; this rice is steamed under pressure before it is milled, which hardens the grain and reduces the possibility of overcooking. The raw rice is golden in colour and turns white during cooking.
- **Aromatic rice**: special rice with a distinct flavour and aroma. Its quality and flavour can differ from one year to the next based on the harvest and climate change.
- **Jasmine rice**: this aromatic rice originates from Thailand; it is soft and sticky when cooked and is sometimes known as sticky rice.

> **Professional tip**
>
> Many chefs prefer to use jasmine rice when making sushi as it sticks together and therefore is easier to shape.

- **American aromatic rice**: this type of aromatic rice is now becoming available in several varieties.
- **Japonica rice**: this rice is grown in California and available as red, brown and black rice. It is commonly used in Japanese culinary work and Caribbean cuisine. When cooked it is moist, sticky and firm.

Other rice products include:

- **Rice paper**: edible paper made from milled rice, used in pastry work for nougat and macaroons, etc.
- **Rice wine**: made from fermented wine; sake is the most famous rice wine and is drunk extensively in Japan. Mirin is a sweet rice wine used in rice dishes and culinary work. Shaoxing is a Chinese rice wine.
- **Rice cakes**: rice cakes are best known in Japan and the countries of the Pacific Rim, where rice production is the economic staple and the grain forms the basis for many meals and foods.
- **Rice noodles**: these are made from rice flour. They come in a range of shapes and sizes and styles similar to pasta shapes. They are made by blending rice flour and water, rolling out the mixture, cutting or extruding it. The noodles are then usually dried. Fresh noodles are often cut into wide ribbons that are used in soups and stir fries. Sometimes ingredients such as mung bean flour may be added to rice noodles to change their consistency and appearance. The noodles cook up slightly transparent, and tend to be chewy and slightly resilient. Examples include laksa noodles, rice fluke noodles, rice sticks, rice vermicelli and rice river noodles.

Quality points to look for in rice

- No split grains.
- Good colour.
- Free from infestation, moisture and foreign bodies.

Preparing and cooking rice

Most rice purchased today does not require washing. However, the washing and soaking of rice removes any excess starch, which tends to cloud the cooking medium. Washing impure rice removes debris, dirt and impurities.

Rice grains are porous and absorb water easily. Rice should be slightly undercooked (to the bite), known professionally as al denté, unless if the rice is being moulded.

When boiling rice, cook in a large quantity of water and drain well. Often the rice is refreshed in cold running water or ice water then drained and stored in the refrigerator. However, it is not advisable to reheat rice due to the risk of food poisoning with *Bacillus cereus*.

Rice introduces texture, flavour and carbohydrate content to dishes. The resulting texture and flavour depends on the cooking method and temperature used. The following cooking methods can be used when cooking rice dishes:

- boiling
- steaming
- frying
- stewing
- braising
- microwaving
- baking.

Rice absorbs liquid easily. Use the information in Table 7.1 as a guide to liquid absorption to achieve the exact texture and overall result required.

Table 7.1 Liquid to rice proportions

Cooking method	Liquid to rice proportion
Boiling	3:1 or 4:1
Pilaff (braised)	2:1
Risotto	3:1
Paella	4:1
Sushi	1:5
Wild rice	4:1

As the grains cook, starch is released and naturally thickens the liquid. This is particularly important when making risotto and sushi.

Cooking risotto

When cooking risotto (for example, see recipe 5), arborio is the easiest rice to find, but vialone and carnaroli are other Italian types that can be used. Do not attempt to use pudding, patna or Japanese rice, despite their similar appearance to Italian rice.

A perfect risotto is not a pile of stodgy rice on a plate, sitting like a glutinous mound, nor is it a soupy liquid mess lying flat on the plate. It should be just about moundable, fighting to hold its little peaks from collapsing back into the rest. All the liquid should be combined with the rice to give a creamy-type consistency. Finish with butter and cream.

Storage

Uncooked rice can be stored on the shelf in a tightly sealed container. The shelf life of brown rice is shorter than that of white rice (the bran layers contain oil that can become rancid). Refrigerator storage is recommended for longer shelf life. Cooked rice can be refrigerated for up to seven days or stored in the freezer for six months.

Once cooked, keep rice hot (above 65 °C for no longer than two hours) or cool it quickly (within 90 minutes) and keep it cool, below 5 °C. If this is not done, the spores of *Bacillus cereus* (a bacterium found in the soil) may revert to bacteria and multiply in the cooked rice.

Pulses

Pulses are one of the most versatile commodities. They can be used extensively in a wide range of dishes. Imaginative and experimental use of different herbs, spices, flavourings and vegetables can give individual variation to pulse recipes.

Pulses are defined as annual leguminous crops, which yield from 1 to 12 grains or seeds of variable size, shape and colour within a pod. The term 'pulse' is reserved for crops harvested solely for the dry grain. This therefore excludes green beans and green peas, which are considered vegetable crops. Also excluded are crops that are grown mainly for oil extraction (oil seeds such as soybeans and peanuts), and crops that are used exclusively for sowing (for example clovers and alfalfa).

All pulses, except for soybeans, are very similar in nutritional content. They are rich in protein, carbohydrate and fibre, and low in fat, which is mostly of the unsaturated kind. They are also an important source of some B vitamins and contain iron. Fresh pulses contain vitamin C, but this declines after harvesting and virtually all is lost from dried pulses. They are 20 to 25 per cent protein, which is double that found in wheat and three times that found in rice.

Types of pulses

Beans

- **Aduki**: small, round, deep red, shiny, nutty and sweet (they are used in Japanese confectionery).
- **Black**: glistening black skins, creamy flesh.
- **Black-eyed**: small white beans with a savoury, creamy flavour, and with a black 'scar' where they were joined to the pod. Used a lot in American and African cooking, they are the essential ingredient in the traditional southern-style dish 'Hoppin John' – a mixture of black-eyed beans, bacon and white rice traditionally eaten on New Year's Day.
- **Broad**: also known as fava beans; strongly flavoured.
- **Borlotti**: Italian beans with a mild, bittersweet flavour; they're used in regional stews and often mixed with rice, and are particularly good in soups such as minestrone and *pasta e fagioli*.
- **Butter**: also known as lima beans, available large or small.
- **Cannellini**: Italian haricot, slightly larger than the English.
- **Dutch brown**: light brown in colour.
- **Flageolet**: pale green, kidney-shaped with a delicate flavour.
- **Ful mesdames**: also known as Egyptian brown beans; small, brown and knobbly, known as the field bean in the UK.
- **Haricot**: white, smooth and oval; used for baked beans.
- **Mung**: small and olive green in colour; good flavour; available split, whole and skinless. Widely used sprouted for their shoots.
- **Pinto**: the original ingredient of Mexican refried beans; an orange-pink bean with rust-coloured specks that grows freely across South America and throughout the American southwest; the bean is creamy-white in colour with a fluffy texture when cooked, and is good in soups, salads and rich stews.
- **Red kidney**: normally dark red-brown, this kidney-shaped bean holds its shape and colour and is therefore great in mixed bean salads and stews, including the traditional chilli con carne.
- **Soissons**: finest haricot beans.
- **Soy**: soybeans are very high in nutrients, especially protein, and they contain all the essential amino acids. They are processed into many forms: soy flour, TVP (meat substitute), tofu (curd), oils, margarine, soy milk and soy sauce.

Peas

- **Blue**: also known as marrowfat peas; pleasant flavour, floury texture, retain shape when cooked.
- **Chickpeas**: shaped like hazelnuts, they have a tasty nutty flavour when cooked. Chickpeas are used all over the world in dishes such as the Indian *kabli chana* or Spanish *caldo gallego*. Chickpeas are a key ingredient of hummus – a traditional Greek dip of cooked chickpeas, tahini (sesame seed paste), oil and garlic. They can be bought and soaked from dried, but canned chickpeas do just as well for most recipes.
- **Split green**: a sweeter variety than the blue pea; cook to a purée easily.
- **Split yellow**: cook to a purée easily.

Both yellow and green split peas are used for vegetable purées and soups.

Lentils

Lentils, varying in size and colour, can form a nutritious basis for a meal. Larger brown or green lentils retain their shape during cooking and are particularly good in soups. Red and yellow lentils cook down well, can be puréed, and are used a great deal in Indian cooking (such as in a spicy dhal). Tiny green puy lentils have a distinctive flavour and also keep their shape and colour when cooked.

- **Orange**: several types, which vary in size and shade, and may be sold whole or split.
- **Green or continental**: retain shape after cooking, available in small or large varieties.
- **Yellow**: of Asian origin, often used as a dhal accompaniment to curry dishes.
- **Red**: purée easily, used for soups and stews, etc.
- **Indian brown**: red lentils from which the seed coat has not been removed; they purée easily.
- **Puy**: dark French lentils, which vary in size; they retain their shape when cooked and are considered the best of their type.
- **Dhal**: the Hindi word for dried peas and beans; also the name of a spicy lentil dish.

Preparing and cooking pulses

Allow about 55 g dry weight per person – once soaked and cooked they will at least double in weight.

Most dried pulses need soaking for several hours before they can be cooked; exceptions are all lentils, green and yellow split peas, black-eyed beans and mung beans. Soaking times vary from 4 to 12 hours. It is usually most convenient to soak pulses overnight.

Always discard the soaking water, rinse the pulses and cook them in fresh water without any salt (salt toughens the skins and makes for longer cooking). Changing the water will also help to reduce the flatulence some people suffer after eating pulses. Adding a pinch of aniseed, caraway, dill or fennel seeds is also supposed to help with this.

Dried kidney beans need to be cooked carefully – soak them for at least eight hours. After soaking, drain and rinse them, discarding the soaking water. Put them into a pan with cold water to cover and bring to the boil – the beans must be boiled for 10 minutes to destroy toxins; after this, simmer until cooked (approximately 45–60 minutes). The beans should have an even, creamy texture throughout – if the centre is still hard and white, they require longer cooking.

Soybeans should be soaked for at least 12 hours, drained and rinsed then covered with fresh water and brought to the boil. Soybeans should be boiled for the first hour of cooking; they can then be simmered for the remaining two to three hours that it takes to cook them.

Health and safety ⚠

It is not safe to eat raw or undercooked kidney beans or soybeans.

When preparing pulses and lentils, cook them in sparkling bottled water. The sparkling motion helps ensure even cooking through momentum; the reason for using bottled water over tap water is the reduced calcium. In hard-water areas there is a lot of calcium, which blocks the pores of pulses, causing beans to 'boil in their jackets' and burst, making the pulses undesirable. Bottled water allows the fluid to pass through the tiny pores and cook evenly.

Storage

One advantage of dried pulses is that they store very well for long periods if kept in a dry, airtight container away from light. However, it is best to eat them as fresh as possible. Pulses toughen on storage and older ones will take longer to cook.

- Store fresh pulses in a refrigerator at a temperature below 5 °C.
- Store frozen pulses in a freezer at a temperature below −18 °C.
- Store dried pulses in clean airtight containers off the floor in the dry store.
- Unpack tinned pulses and check that the tins are sound and undamaged.
- When storing cooked pulses, keep them covered and in a refrigerator at a temperature below 5 °C.
- To prevent the risk of cross-contamination, store cooked pulses away from any raw foods.

Grains

Cereals are important crops and are the oldest farmed agricultural products. Grain is the name given to the edible fruit of cereals. In many countries grains are the main staple food, as they are inexpensive and readily available. Cereals are used in a range of dishes and food products, including breads, soups and stews.

Grains are a rich source of carbohydrate and supply most of their food energy as starch. They are also a significant source of protein. Wholegrain cereals are good sources of dietary fibre, essential fatty acids and other important nutrients.

The whole grain is made up of three parts: the bran, the endosperm and the germ:

- The bran is the outer layers of the cereal. Bran contains a high amount of dietary fibre and some B vitamins (B_1, thiamine, and B_3, niacin). It also contains the minerals zinc, copper and iron, as well as protein and other chemicals.
- The endosperm is the middle layer and is the largest section of the grain. It is the main energy supply and is rich in carbohydrates, protein and B vitamins.
- The germ is the smallest part of the grain. As the name suggests, it develops into the new plant. It is rich in B vitamins, minerals, vitamin E and other chemicals.

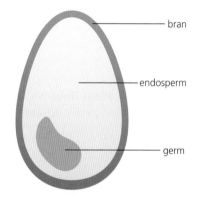

Types of grain

Barley

Barley grows in a wider variety of climatic conditions than any other cereal. Usually found in the shops as **whole** or **pot barley** (or **polished pearl barley**) you can also buy **barley flakes** or **kernels**. It can be cooked on its own (one part grain to three parts water for 45–60 minutes) as an alternative to rice, pasta or potatoes, or added to stews. Malt extract is made from sprouted barley grains.

Barley must have its fibrous hull removed before it is eaten (hulled barley). Hulled barley still has its bran and germ and is considered to be a whole grain, making it a popular health food. Pearl barley is hulled barley that has been processed further to remove the bran.

Buckwheat

When roasted, the seeds of buckwheat are dark reddish-brown. It can be cooked (one part grain to two parts water for 6 minutes, leave to stand for 6 minutes) and served like rice, or it can be added to stews and casseroles. **Buckwheat flour** can be added to cakes, muffins and pancakes, where it imparts a distinctive flavour. Soba noodles, made from buckwheat, are an essential ingredient in Japanese cooking. Buckwheat is gluten free.

Corn/maize

Fresh corn – available in the form of sweetcorn and corn on the cob – is eaten as a vegetable. The dried grain is most often eaten as cornflakes or popcorn. The flour made from corn (**cornmeal**) is used to make Italian polenta, and can be added to soups, pancakes and muffins. Cook polenta (one part grain to three parts water, for 15–20 minutes), stirring carefully to avoid lumps. Use it like mashed potato: it is quite bland, so try stirring in tasty ingredients such as Gorgonzola

▲ From left to right: barley, millet and buckwheat

or Parmesan and fresh herbs, or press it when cold, cut into slices, brush with garlicky olive oil and grill. You can also get ready-made polenta. Tortillas are made from maize meal, as are quite a lot of snack foods. Don't confuse cornmeal with **refined corn starch/flour**, used for thickening. Corn is gluten free.

Oats

There are various grades of **oatmeal**, including **rolled oats** and **jumbo oat flakes**. All forms can be used to make porridge, combined with nuts to make a nut roast, or added to stews. Oatmeal is low in gluten so can't be used to make bread, but can be mixed with wheat flour to add flavour and texture to bread, muffins and pancakes. Oatmeal contains some oils and can become rancid, so watch the best-before date.

Oatmeal is created by grinding oats into a coarse powder; various grades are available depending on the thoroughness of the grinding (including coarse, pinhead and fine). The main uses of oats are:

- as an ingredient in baking
- in the manufacture of bannocks or oatcakes
- as a stuffing for poultry
- as a coating for some cheeses
- as an ingredient of black pudding
- for making traditional porridge.

Millet

Millet is a group of small-seeded cereal crops or grains widely grown around the world for food and fodder. The main millet varieties are:

- pearl millet
- foxtail millet
- proso millet (also known as common millet, broom corn millet, hog millet or white millet)
- finger millet.

Coeliac patients can replace certain cereal grains (such as wheat) in their diets by consuming millets in various forms, including breakfast cereals.

In western India, millet flour (called 'bajari' in Marathi) has been commonly used with 'jowar' (sorghum) flour for hundreds of years to make the local staple flatbread, 'bhakri'.

Millet can often be used in place of buckwheat, rice or quinoa.

The protein content in millet is very close to that of wheat; both provide about 11 per cent protein by weight. Millets are rich in B vitamins – especially B_3 (niacin), B_6 and B_9 (folic acid) – calcium, iron, potassium, magnesium and zinc. Millets contain no gluten, so they cannot rise to make bread. When combined with wheat or xanthan gum (for those who have coeliac disease), though, they can be used to make raised bread. Alone, they are suited to flatbread.

Millet is an alternative to rice but the tiny grains need to be cracked before they will absorb water easily. Before boiling, sauté them with a little vegetable oil for 2–3 minutes until some are seen to crack, then add water carefully (one part grain to three parts water). Bring to the boil and simmer for 15–20 minutes until fluffy. **Millet flakes** can be made into porridge or added to muesli. **Millet flour** is available, and it is sometimes also made into pasta.

Wheat

This is the most familiar cereal in the UK today, used for bread, cakes, biscuits, pastry, breakfast cereals and pasta. **Wheat grains** can be eaten whole (cook one part grain to three parts water for 40–60 minutes) and have a satisfying, chewy texture. **Cracked** or **kibbled wheat** is the dried whole grains cut by steel blades. **Bulgar wheat** is parboiled before cracking, has a light texture and only needs rehydrating by soaking in boiling water or stock. **Semolina** is a grainy yellow flour ground from durum or hard wheat, and is the main ingredient of dried Italian pasta. **Couscous** is made from semolina grains that have been rolled, dampened and coated with finer wheat flour. Soak in two parts of water/stock to rehydrate; traditionally, it is steamed after soaking. **Strong wheat flour** (with a high gluten content) is required for yeasted breadmaking. **Plain flour** is used for general cooking including cakes and pastry. **Wheat flakes** can be used for porridge, muesli and flapjacks.

Quinoa

Quinoa is an ancient crop that fed the South American Aztecs for thousands of years, and has recently been cultivated in the UK. It's a seed that is high in protein, making it useful for vegetarians.

The small, round grains look similar to millet but are pale brown in colour. The taste is mild and the texture firm and slightly chewy. It can be cooked like millet and absorbs twice its volume in liquid. Cook for 15 minutes (one part grain to three parts water); it's ready when all the grains have turned from white to transparent, and the spiral-like germ has separated. Use in place of more common cereals or pasta, or in risottos, pilaff and vegetable stuffings. It may be used in place of rice and is served in salads and some stuffings.

Rye

Rye is the only cereal (apart from wheat and barley) that has enough gluten to make a yeasted loaf. However, with less gluten than wheat, **rye flour** makes a denser, richer-flavoured bread. It's more usual to mix rye flour with wheat flour. **Rye grains** should be cooked using one part grain to three parts water for 45–60 minutes. **Kibbled rye** is often added to granary-type loaves. Rye grains can be added to stews, and **rye flakes** are good in muesli.

Spelt

Originating in the Middle East, Spelt is closely related to common wheat and has been popular for decades in eastern Europe. It has an intense nutty, wheaty flavour. The flour is excellent for breadmaking and spelt pasta is becoming more widely available.

Quality points to look for in grains

Grains should always look and smell faintly sweet or have no aroma at all. If you detect a musty or oily scent, the grains have passed their peak and should not be purchased.

Buy grains that are well packaged and sealed tightly. Check the use-by date.

Preparing and cooking grains

Grains should first be washed under cold water in a colander to remove any dust or foreign bodies. Look for any unusual infestation such as insects. The dry grain does not need to be soaked.

Grains can vary in cooking time depending on the age of the grain. Grains are usually boiled, or steamed, but may be braised or stewed. As the grain is heated, it absorbs the water, swells and bursts, cooking at between 60°C and 70°C. Grains such as couscous, bulgar wheat and millet only usually require boiling water to be poured on to them, stirred and cooled. Cooking softens the grains. Whole grains take longer to cook than grains that have been processed.

Grains may be cooked in water or soaked in wine or fruit juice; they may also be steamed. Consider too the trend of baking porridge oats and oat flakes, polenta and cornmeal, soaked or parboiled, poured into a lined baking sheet, usually on a silicone mat, and baked in the oven. As the grains are baked the water will cook the product, evaporate and the result is a dry baked grain.

Storage

Cereals are best stored in airtight containers in a cool, dark, dry place. Whole grains can be stored for up to two years; flaked or cracked grains and flours should be used within two to three months of purchase.

Whole grains must be stored more carefully than refined grains, since the healthy oils found largely in the germ of the whole grain can be negatively affected by heat, light and moisture. Because each grain has a different fat content, their shelf life varies.

Intact grains will keep for up to six months in a cool dry store, or up to one year in a freezer.

Wholegrain flours and meals spoil more quickly than intact grains because their protective bran layer has been broken up and air can reach all parts of the grain, causing oxidation. If stored properly they will keep for one to three months in a cool, dry store, or up to two to six months in a freezer.

Test yourself

1. State three quality points to look for when buying rice.
2. How much liquid to rice would you use when cooking risotto?
3. Describe how to store uncooked rice.
4. Describe how you would prepare dried chickpeas before cooking.
5. Describe how to store dried pulses.
6. Describe the preparation and cooking process for red kidney beans.
7. List three quality points to look for when buying grains.
8. State two foods for which barley can be used as an alternative.
9. Describe how to cook polenta by boiling.
10. What is an appropriate cooking method for rye?

Rice recipes

1 Plain boiled rice

Allow 100g of rice (dry weight) for 4 portions.

1 Pick and wash the long-grain rice. Add to plenty of boiling salted water.

2 Stir to the boil and simmer gently until tender (approximately 12–15 minutes).

3 Pour into a sieve and rinse well under cold running water, then boiling water. Drain and leave in the sieve, placed over a bowl and covered with a cloth.

4 Place on a tray in the hotplate and keep hot.

5 Serve separately in a vegetable dish.

Energy	Cals	Fat	Sat fat	Carb	Sugar	Protein	Fibre
37 kJ	90 kcal	0.1 g	0.0 g	20.0 g	0.0 g	1.9 g	0.0 g

2 Steamed rice

Allow 100g of rice (dry weight) for 4 portions.

1 Place the washed rice into a saucepan and add water until the water level is 2.5cm above the rice.

2 Bring to the boil over a fierce heat until most of the water has evaporated.

3 Turn the heat down as low as possible, cover the pan with a lid and allow the rice to complete cooking in the steam.

4 Once cooked, the rice should be allowed to stand in the covered steamer for 10 minutes.

Energy	Cals	Fat	Sat fat	Carb	Sugar	Protein	Fibre
1277 kJ	305 kcal	1.4 g	0.0 g	63.7 g	0.0 g	7.1 g	0.0 g

3 Braised or pilaff rice

Ingredient	4 portions	10 portions
Butter or oil	50 g	125 g
Onion, chopped	25 g	60 g
Rice, long grain, white or brown	100 g	250 g
White stock (preferably chicken)	200 ml	500 ml
Salt, mill pepper		

Energy	Cals	Fat	Sat fat	Carb	Sugar	Protein	Fibre
774 kJ	184 kcal	10.4 g	4.5 g	22.1 g	0.3 g	1.9 g	0.6 g

Using white rice and hard margarine. Using brown rice and hard margarine, 1 portion provides: 769 kJ/183 kcal energy, 10.9 g fat, 4.6 g saturated fat, 20.7 g carbohydrates, 0.7 g sugar, 1.9 g protein and 1.0 g fibre.

1 Place half the butter or oil into a small sauteuse. Add the onion.

2 Cook gently without colouring for 2–3 minutes. Add the rice.

3 Cook gently without colouring for 2–3 minutes.

4 Add twice the amount of stock to rice.

5 Season, cover with buttered paper, bring to the boil.

6 Place in a hot oven (230–250 °C) for approximately 15 minutes, until cooked.

7 Remove immediately into a cool sauteuse.

8 Carefully mix in the remaining butter or oil with a two-pronged fork.

9 Correct the seasoning and serve.

Cook the rice gently without colouring

Add the stock

Cover with buttered paper, with a small hole at the centre

Note

It is usual to use long-grain rice for pilaff because the grains are firm and there is less likelihood of them breaking up and becoming mushy. During cooking, the long-grain rice absorbs more liquid, loses less starch and retains its shape as it swells; short or medium grains may split at the ends and become less distinct in outline.

Variation

Pilaff may also be infused with herbs and spices such as cardamom.

Professional tip

Cook the rice for the exact time specified in the recipe. If it cooks for longer, it will be overcooked and the grains will not separate.

Healthy eating tips

● Use an unsaturated oil (sunflower or olive). Lightly oil the pan and drain off any excess after the frying is complete.
● Keep the added salt to a minimum.

4 Braised rice with mushrooms (*riz pilaff aux champignons*)

Ingredients are as for braised or pilaff rice (recipe 3) with the addition of 50–100g well-washed, sliced button mushrooms (or wild mushrooms).

1 Place 25g butter in a small sauteuse. Add the onion.

2 Cook gently without colour for 2–3 minutes.

3 Add the rice and button mushrooms.

4 Complete as for braised or pilaff rice (recipe 3) from step 4.

Energy	Cals	Fat	Sat fat	Carb	Sugar	Protein	Fibre	Sodium
849 kJ	203 kcal	11.7g	6.9g	22.0g	0.5g	3.5g	0.9g	0.2g

Using 75g of button mushrooms.

5 Risotto with Parmesan (*risotto con Parmigiano*)

1 Bring the stock to a simmer, next to where you will cook the risotto. Take a wide, heavy-bottomed pan or casserole, put half the butter in over a medium heat and melt.

2 Add the onion and sweat until it softens and becomes slightly translucent.

3 Add the rice and stir with a heat-resistant spatula until it is thoroughly coated in butter (about 2 minutes). Then take a soup ladle of hot stock and pour it into the rice.

4 Continue to cook and stir until this liquid addition is completely absorbed (about 3 minutes).

5 Repeat this procedure several times until the rice has swollen and is nearly tender. The rice should not be soft but neither should it be chalky. Taste and wait: if it is undercooked, it will leave a gritty, chalky residue in your mouth.

6 Normally the rice is ready about 20 minutes after the first addition of stock.

7 Add the other half of the butter and half the Parmesan off the heat. Stir these in, season and cover. Leave to rest and swell a little more for 3 minutes. Serve immediately after this in soup plates, with more Parmesan offered separately.

This is the classic risotto.

Ingredient	4 portions	10 portions
Chicken stock	1.2 litres	3 litres
Butter	80g	200g
Onion, peeled and finely chopped	½	1¼
Arborio rice	240g	600g
Parmesan, freshly grated	75g	180g
Salt, pepper		

Energy	Cals	Fat	Sat fat	Carb	Sugar	Protein	Fibre
2,598 kJ	621 kcal	36.2g	14.1g	49.9g	4.2g	23.0g	0.3g

Healthy eating tips

- Use an unsaturated oil (sunflower or olive), instead of butter, to sweat the onion. Lightly oil the pan and drain off any excess after the frying is complete.
- Additional salt is not necessary.
- Serve with a large salad and tomato bread.

Professional tip

Add the stock slowly, to give the rice time to absorb the liquid.

Stir regularly during cooking.

Variation

Risotto variations include:

- **saffron or Milanese-style**: soak ¼ teaspoon saffron in a little hot stock and mix into the risotto near the end of the cooking time; bone marrow is also sometimes added.
- **seafood**: add any one or a mixture of cooked mussels, shrimp, prawns, etc., just before the rice is cooked; also use half fish stock, half chicken stock.
- **mushroom**: garnish with cooked mushrooms
- **asparagus**: garnish with freshly cooked asparagus heads.

Risotto may be served as an *amuse-bouche* (bite-sized appetiser).

Video: making risotto
http://bit.ly/
1vGih2Q

6 Indian-style rice (pilau)

Energy	Cals	Fat	Sat fat	Carb	Sugar	Protein	Fibre
1,315 kJ	315 kcal	5.8g	3.3g	60.0g	0.0g	.59g	0.0g

Ingredient	4 portions	10 portions
Basmati rice	300 g	750 g
Ghee	1 tbsp	2½ tbsp
Bay leaves	2	5
Cloves	5	12
Green cardamom pods	5	12
Cassia bark (5 cm piece)	1	2
Fennel seeds	1 tsp	2½ tsp
Cumin seeds	½ tsp	1 tsp
Brown cardamom pods	1	2
Star anise	1	2
Water, boiling	570 ml	1,425 ml

1. Wash and drain the rice.
2. Heat the ghee in a large thick-based saucepan and stir fry the spices for 30 seconds.
3. Add the rice and very gently stir fry, being careful not to breaking the grains of rice.
4. Add to the boiling water and stir around.
5. Place a lid on top and turn down to the lowest heat.
6. Leave for 8 minutes – the water should have been completely absorbed.
7. Check the rice. If it is done, remove from the heat and gently fluff up with a fork.
8. If the rice is still brittle in the middle, replace the lid and leave for a further 2 minutes, adding a little more water if necessary.

Pulse recipes

7 Bean goulash

Ingredient	4 portions	10 portions
Red kidney or haricot beans, dried	200 g	500 g
Sunflower oil	60 ml	150 ml
Onion, finely chopped	50 g	125 g
Clove of garlic, crushed	1	2–3
Paprika	25 g	60 g
Red peppers	2	5
Green pepper	1	2–3
Yellow pepper	1	2–3
Button mushrooms, sliced	200 g	500 g
Tomato purée	50 g	125 g
Vegetable stock	750 ml	2 litre
Bouquet garni	1	2
Seasoning		
Small turned potatoes, cooked	8	20
Parsley, chopped, to serve		

Energy	Cals	Fat	Sat fat	Carb	Sugar	Protein	Fibre
1,728 kJ	411 kcal	17.9 g	2.7 g	50.0 g	7.3 g	17.3 g	18.5 g

1 Soak the beans for 24 hours in cold water. Drain, place into a saucepan. Cover with cold water, boil for at least 10 minutes and then simmer until tender.

2 Heat the oil in a sauté pan, sweat the onion and garlic without colour for 2–3 minutes; add the paprika and sweat for a further 2–3 minutes.

3 Add the peppers (cut in halves, with seeds removed and cut into 1 cm dice). Add the button mushrooms; sweat for a further 2 minutes.

4 Add the tomato purée, vegetable stock and bouquet garni. Bring to the boil and simmer until the pepper and mushrooms are cooked.

5 Remove the bouquet garni. Add the drained cooked beans, correct the seasoning and stir.

6 Garnish with potatoes (or gnocchi) and chopped parsley.

7 Serve wholegrain pilaff or wholemeal noodles separately.

Healthy eating tips
- Use less sunflower oil to sweat the onions.
- Add only a pinch of salt.
- Serve with rice or noodles and a green salad or mixed vegetables.

8 Mexican bean pot

Ingredient	4 portions	10 portions
Red kidney or haricot beans, dried	300 g	750 g
Onions, finely chopped	100 g	250 g
Carrots, sliced	100 g	250 g
Tomato, skinned, deseeded and diced	200 g	500 g
Cloves of garlic, crushed and chopped	2	5
Paprika	10 g	25 g
Dried marjoram	3 g	9 g
Small fresh chilli, finely chopped	1	2–3
Small red pepper, finely diced	1	2–3
Yeast extract	5 g	12 g
Chives, chopped		
Seasoning		

1 Soak the beans in cold water for 24 hours. Drain. Place into a saucepan, cover with cold water, bring to the boil and simmer gently.

2 When three-quarters cooked, add all the other ingredients except the chopped chives.

3 Continue to simmer until all is completely cooked.

4 Serve sprinkled with chopped chives.

Healthy eating tips
- No added salt is needed; there is plenty in the yeast extract.
- Serve with a selection of colourful vegetables.

Energy	Cals	Fat	Sat fat	Carb	Sugar	Protein	Fibre
672 kJ	161 kcal	1.2 g	0.2 g	27.0 g	4.6 g	12.3 g	14.0 g

9 Crisp polenta and roasted Mediterranean vegetables

Ingredient	4 portions	10 portions
Polenta		
Water	200 ml	500 ml
Butter	30 g	75 g
Polenta flour	65 g	160 g
Parmesan, grated	25 g	60 g
Egg yolks	1	2
Crème fraiche	110 g	275 g
Seasoning		
Roasted vegetables		
Red peppers	2	5
Yellow peppers	2	5
Courgettes	2	5
Red onions	2	5
Vegetable oil	200 ml	500 ml
Seasoning		
Clove of garlic	1	3
Thyme, sprigs	2	5

To make the polenta:

1 Bring the water and the butter to the boil.

2 Season the water well and whisk in the polenta flour.

3 Continue to whisk until very thick.

4 Remove from the heat and add the Parmesan, egg yolk and crème fraiche.

5 Whisk until all incorporated; check the seasoning.

6 Set in a lined tray.

7 Once set, cut using a round cutter or cut into squares.

8 Reserve until required.

To make the roasted vegetables:

1 Roughly chop the vegetables into large chunks. Ensure the seeds are removed from the peppers.

2 Toss the cut vegetables in the oil and season well.

3 Place the vegetables in an oven with the aromats for 30 minutes at 180 °C.

4 Remove from the oven and drain. Reserve until required.

To serve:

1 To serve the dish, shallow-fry the polenta in a non-stick pan until golden on both sides.

2 Warm the roasted vegetables and place them in the middle of the plate. Place the polenta on top.

3 Finish with rocket salad and balsamic dressing.

Professional tip

Line the tray with cling film and silicone paper before pouring in the polenta – this will stop it from sticking to the tray when it sets.

Energy	Cals	Fat	Sat fat	Carb	Sugar	Protein	Fibre	Sodium
3,267 kJ	790 kcal	71.4 g	18.9 g	28.6 g	14.0 g	10.1 g	6.6 g	0.1 g

10 Polenta and lentil cakes with roasted vegetables and cucumber and yoghurt sauce

Ingredient	4 portions	10 portions
Puy lentils	250 g	625 g
Vegetable stock	250 ml	625 ml
Fine polenta	75 g	187 g
Parmesan cheese, grated	25 g	62 g
Egg, beaten	1	3
Salt and pepper		
Leeks, finely chopped and blanched	75 g	187 g
Clove of garlic, crushed and finely chopped	1	3
Olive oil	3 tbsp	8 tbsp
Sauce		
Cucumber, peeled	250 g	625 g
Natural yoghurt	250 ml	625 ml
Mint, chopped	¼ tsp	1¼ tsp
Chives, chopped	1 tsp	2½ tsp

Energy	Cals	Fat	Sat fat	Carb	Sugar	Protein	Fibre
1,898 kJ	452 kcal	15.2 g	4.1 g	55.6 g	7.9 g	25.2 g	4.3 g

1 Wash the lentils and cook in salted water for about 25 minutes until tender but still firm. Drain well, refresh and drain again. Dry on a suitable cloth.

2 Bring the vegetable stock to the boil, add the polenta and cook gently, stirring until thickened.

3 Add the Parmesan and beaten egg; season.

4 Mix the lentils, polenta, leeks and garlic together.

5 Correct the seasoning, cool and shape into four (or ten) round cakes.

6 Place in the fridge and chill well for at least 1 hour.

7 Heat the olive oil in a suitable pan; gently fry the cakes for about 3–4 minutes on each side until heated through and well browned.

8 To make the sauce, liquidise the peeled cucumber with the yoghurt, and finish with chopped mint and chives.

9 To serve, place a small amount of the sauce on to a plate and place the cakes on top. Garnish the plate with freshly roasted vegetables.

Healthy eating tips
- No additional salt is needed.
- Use less olive oil to fry the cakes, and drain on kitchen paper.

11 Couscous with meat and vegetables

Ingredient	4 portions	10 portions
Couscous	200 g	500 g
Lean stewing lamb	400 g	1 kg
Stewing beef *or* chicken, cut for sauté	200 g	500 g
Olive oil	2 tbsp	5 tbsp
Onion, finely chopped	50 g	125 g
Clove of garlic, crushed and chopped	1	2–3
Celery, sliced	100 g	250 g
Leek, sliced	100 g	250 g
Carrot, diced (1 cm)	100 g	250 g
Chickpeas	25 g	60 g
Ground ginger (optional)	¼ tsp	½ tsp
Saffron (optional)	¼ tsp	½ tsp
Raisins	50 g	125 g
Courgettes, diced	100 g	250 g
Tomatoes, skinned, deseeded and diced	50 g	125 g
Parsley, chopped		
Tomato purée	50 g	125 g
Cayenne pepper		
Paprika	½ tsp	1 tsp
Butter	50 g	125 g

Energy	Cals	Fat	Sat fat	Carb	Sugar	Protein	Fibre
2,146 kJ	515 kcal	28.5 g	12.6 g	42.2 g	14.7 g	25.3 g	2.8 g

Using lamb and butter.

1 Soak the couscous in warm water for 10 minutes.

2 Fry the meat in the oil until browned and sealed. Remove quickly.

3 Fry the onions and garlic, then remove and drain.

4 Place the meat, onions and garlic into a saucepan, and add the celery, leeks, carrots and chickpeas. Cover with water and season.

5 Add the ginger and saffron, if using; bring to the boil and simmer for about 1 hour.

6 Drain the couscous, place in the top part of the couscousier and steam for 30 minutes. Alternatively, place the couscous in a metal colander lined with muslin. Fit into the top of the saucepan, making sure that the liquid from the stew does not touch the steamer as the couscous will become lumpy. Stir occasionally.

7 Add the raisins and courgettes to the stew, followed by the tomatoes, chopped parsley and tomato purée. Cook for a further 30 minutes.

8 Remove approx. 250 ml (625 ml) sauce from the stew and stir enough cayenne pepper in to it to make it strong and fiery. Finish with paprika.

9 To serve, pile the couscous into a suitable serving dish, preferably earthenware, add knobs of butter and work into the grains with a fork.

10 Carefully arrange the meat and vegetables over the couscous and pour the broth over. Serve the hot peppery sauce separately.

11 Alternatively, the couscous, meat and vegetables, broth and peppery sauce can be served in separate bowls.

Note

Pre-cooked couscous is also available.

Healthy eating tips
● No additional salt is needed.
● Add only a small amount of fat to the couscous before adding the meat and vegetables.
● The fat content will be reduced if skinned chicken is used or less lamb/beef and more vegetables.

12 Couscous fritters with feta (*amuse bouche*)

Ingredient	4 portions	10 portions
Couscous	80 g	200 g
Vegetable stock	100 ml	250 ml
Beaten egg	½	1¼
Natural yoghurt	1 tbsp	2½ tbsp
Feta cheese, cut into 1 cm dice	40 g	100 g
Tomatoes, skinned, deseeded and cut into small dice	25 g	60 g
Spring onions, finely chopped	2	5
Vegetable oil	1 tbsp	2½ tbsp

Energy	Cals	Fat	Sat fat	Carb	Sugar	Protein	Fibre	Sodium
533 kJ	128 kcal	6.9g	2.3g	11.8g	1.5g	5.2g	0.3g	0.2g

1 Place the couscous in a suitable bowl; pour in the boiling stock and stir. Allow to stand until the couscous absorbs the stock.

2 Add the egg and yoghurt, mix well and season. Fold in the feta cheese, tomatoes and spring onions.

3 Divide the mixture into the number of portions and shape into small cakes.

4 Shallow fry the fritters in vegetable oil on both sides until golden brown.

5 Serve as an *amuse bouche* on a fresh tomato sauce seasoned with chilli. Garnish each fritter with a suitable chutney, red onion, beetroot or fig.

This chapter is relevant to the following units:
→ Prepare, cook and finish basic pasta dishes.
→ Prepare, cook and finish noodle dishes.

Recipes included in this chapter

Pasta

Pasta is made from durum wheat, which has a 15 per cent protein content. This makes it a good alternative to rice and potatoes for vegetarians. Pasta also contains carbohydrates in the form of starch, which gives the body energy. Eating more pasta is in line with the recommendation to 'eat more starchy carbohydrates'.

Traditionally, pasta was eaten as a starter, but it is now used much more as a main course or stand-alone dish.

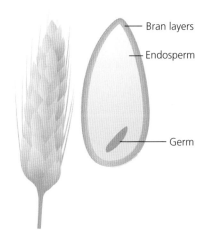

▲ The structure of a grain of wheat

Types of pasta

There are basically four types of pasta, each of which may be plain or flavoured with spinach or tomato:

1 dried durum wheat pasta
2 fresh egg pasta
3 semolina pasta
4 wholewheat pasta.

Dried pasta

There are an almost infinite number of types of dried pasta, especially if you include all the regional variations. Almost 90 per cent of the pasta eaten in Italy is dried.

Fresh pasta

Fresh pasta has a short shelf life as it contains eggs.

Stuffed pasta

Pasta that is to be stuffed must be rolled as thinly as possible. The stuffing should be pleasant in taste and plentiful in quantity. The edges of the pasta must be thoroughly sealed otherwise the stuffing will seep out during poaching.

The list of possible stuffings is almost endless as every district in Italy has its own variations and, with thought and experimentation, many more can be produced.

Examples of stuffed pasta include the following:

- **Agnolini**: small half-moon shapes, usually filled with ham and cheese or minced meat.
- **Cannelloni**: large tubes of pasta, poached that may be stuffed with a variety of fillings (e.g. ricotta cheese and spinach) and finished with an appropriate sauce.
- **Cappelletti**: shaped like little hats and usually filled as agnolini; they are available dried.
- **Ravioli**: usually square with serrated edges. A wide variety of fillings can be used (fish, meat, vegetarian, cheese, etc.).
- **Ravolini**: 'little ravioli', half the size of ravioli.
- **Tortellini**: a slightly larger version of cappelletti; also available in dried form.
- **Tortelloni**: a double-sized version of tortellini.

Quality points

When purchasing dried pasta the box or container should be sealed and the pasta unbroken. Check the 'best before' date. Dried pasta must be dry and not damp, have a good even colour with no signs of infestation. If you experience problems with the ingredients inform the supplier or your manger immediately. If in doubt, do not use them.

When purchasing fresh pasta it must be at or below 5 °C, evenly coloured, intact and not torn or damaged. The pasta must separate easily.

Ingredients for pasta dishes

A huge variety of ingredients may be used in pasta dishes. The list is almost endless, but may include:

- fish, e.g. smoked salmon, anchovies, tuna
- shellfish, e.g. shrimps, prawns, scallops, lobster, crab, cockles
- meat, e.g. smoked ham, sausage, salami, bacon, beef, chicken, duck
- offal, e.g. tongue, chicken livers
- herbs, e.g. parsley, rosemary, basil, tarragon, chives, marjoram
- spices, e.g. chillies, saffron, grated nutmeg
- vegetables, e.g. mushrooms, tomatoes, onions, fennel, courgettes, spring onions, peas, spinach, peppers, broad beans, broccoli
- nuts, e.g. pine nuts, walnuts, hazelnuts
- fruit, e.g. stoned olives, avocado, sultanas, lemon zest
- eggs
- capers
- cooked, dried beans
- Balsamic vinegar.

It is important to know what ingredients blend well together and complement the pasta without overpowering the main ingredient. Customers must also know what ingredients are in the dish in case they suffer from an allergy (see Chapter 17).

Preparing and cooking pasta dishes

Dried pasta

A rule of thumb for cooking dried pasta is to allow 80–100 g per portion as a starter course; increase accordingly if larger portions are required.

Bring plenty of water (at least 4 litres for every 600 g of dry pasta) to a rolling boil. Add about 1 tbsp of salt per 4 litres of water, if desired. Add the pasta in small quantities to maintain the rolling boil. Stir frequently to prevent sticking. Do not cover the pan. Follow package directions for cooking time. Do not overcook. Pasta should be *al dente* (meaning literally 'to the tooth' – tender, yet firm). It should be slightly resistant to the bite, but cooked through. Drain pasta to stop the cooking action but do not rinse it unless the recipe specifically says to do so. For salads, drain and rinse pasta with cold water.

Fresh egg pasta

This requires less cooking time than dried pasta. When cooking fresh pasta, the addition of a few drops of olive oil in the water will help prevent the pasta pieces from sticking together.

Straining

Always strain pasta carefully as it is a delicate product. Use a colander or a spider.

▲ Pasta-making equipment, left to right: pasta machine, ravioli cutter, ravioli tray and rolling pin

Making fresh pasta

1 Sift 400g strong flour together with a pinch of salt.

2 Make a well in the flour; pour 4 beaten eggs into the well.

3 Gradually incorporate the flour.

4 Mix until a dough is formed. Add olive oil to adjust to the required consistency. The amount of oil will vary according to the type of flour and the size of the eggs.

5 Pull and knead the dough until it is of a smooth elastic consistency.
6 Cover the dough and allow to rest in a cool place for 30 minutes.

7 After resting, knead the dough again.
8 Roll the dough out on a well-floured surface to a thickness of 0.5mm.
9 Trim the sides and cut as required using a large knife.

Other cooking methods for pasta dishes

- **Baking**: this technique is used for dishes such as cannelloni and pasta bakes. These dishes have usually been cooked previously and require baking to finish the product. This technique requires the dish to cook evenly to give a well-distributed colour. After cooking, clean the dish before presenting it to the customer. Always check the internal temperature using a probe to ensure that it reaches a safe 72 °C.
- **Grilling**: this method is used to finish cooked pasta dishes that include a sauce topped with grated cheese.
- **Deep frying**: some pasta dishes may be deep fried; the pasta is first boiled and then coated before deep frying. An example is stuffed ravioli dipped in egg wash or butter milk, coated in breadcrumbs and then deep fried.

Sauces and accompaniments

Always mix sauces into pasta in a large bowl or saucepan to enable the ingredients to be well distributed throughout it. This is best done with a large spoon or, if cold, the pasta can be mixed by hand (make sure hands have been thoroughly washed; alternatively use food gloves).

Examples of sauces to go with pasta include:
- tomato sauce
- cream, butter or béchamel-based sauces
- rich meat sauce, e.g. bolognaise
- olive oil and garlic
- soft white or blue cheese
- pesto.

Cheeses used when pasta cooking include the following:
- **Parmesan**: the most popular hard cheese for use with pasta, ideal for grating. The flavour is best when it is freshly grated. If bought ready grated, or if it is grated and stored, the flavour deteriorates.
- **Pecorino**: a strong ewes' milk cheese, sometimes studded with peppercorns. Used for strongly flavoured dishes, it can be grated or thinly sliced.
- **Ricotta**: a creamy-white cheese made from the discarded whey of other cheeses. It is widely used in fillings for pasta such as cannelloni and ravioli, and for sauces.
- **Mozzarella**: traditionally made from the milk of the water buffalo. Mozzarella is pure white and creamy, with a mild but distinctive flavour, and usually round or pear-shaped. It will keep for only a few days in a container half-filled with milk and water.
- **Gorgonzola and dolcelatte**: distinctive blue cheeses that can be used in sauces.

All stuffed pasta should be served in or coated with a suitable sauce and, depending on the type of recipe, may be finished 'au gratin' by sprinkling with freshly grated Parmesan and browning lightly under the salamander.

Storing pasta

Dry pasta can be stored almost indefinitely, if kept in a tightly sealed package or a covered container in a cool, dry place, but you must observe the best-before date on the packaging.

Fresh egg pasta should be stored in the refrigerator at or below 5 °C; if it is not for immediate use it must be stored in a cool, dry place. Allow it to dry then keep it in a clean, dry container or bowl in a cool, dry store.

If cooked pasta is not to be used immediately, drain and rinse thoroughly with cold water. If the pasta is left to sit in water, it will continue to absorb water and become mushy. When the pasta is cool, drain and toss lightly with salad oil to prevent it from sticking and drying out. Cover tightly and refrigerate or freeze. Refrigerate the pasta and sauce separately or the pasta will become soggy. To reheat, put pasta in a colander and immerse in rapidly boiling water just long enough to heat through. Do not allow the pasta to continue to cook. Pasta may also be reheated in a microwave.

Always make sure you refresh the pasta in plenty of water so that the pasta is free flowing and does not stick together.

Shaped raw pasta is best stored in large containers sprinkled with semolina, layered with sheets of greaseproof or silicone paper or sheets of plastic in an airtight container.

Stuffed fresh pasta should be blanched, drained, frozen or chilled in small amounts which allows for easy separation. Frozen pasta will keep for up to three months but it is recommended that it is used within one month.

Health and safety !

Remember to store fresh pasta in the refrigerator at 5 °C. When cooked the core temperature must be 72 °C.

Noodles

Noodles are probably the world's oldest fast food; they are versatile and quick to cook. They may be steamed, boiled, pan-fried, stir fried or deep fried. Noodles are a staple food in southeast Asia but they are also very popular in the West.

Noodles are high in starch (carbohydrate). They provide some protein, especially those made from hard wheat and beans. The addition of egg also increases noodles' protein content.

Examples of the nutritional content of some noodles are given in Table 8.1.

Noodles can be made fresh or purchased dried.

Quality points

The basic quality points for dried noodles are:

- even and of a good colour
- no sign of moisture or discolouration.

Fresh noodles must:

- have a good colour
- be evenly cut and of the right thickness throughout.

Cooking noodles

As noodles take very little time to cook it is best to cook them to order.

Storing noodles

Store fresh noodles in a vacuum pouch or in a plastic sealed bag in the refrigerator. Dried noodles should be kept in a tightly sealed package or a covered container in a cool, dry place, but you must observe the best-before date on the packaging.

Table 8.1 Nutritional content of noodles

100 g dry weight	Calories	Carbohydrates	Protein	Fat	Sodium
Rice sticks	380	88%	6%	0	
Rice vermicelli	363	85.5%	7.3%	0	
Egg noodles	341	70%	11%	1.9%	0.8%
Wheat noodles	308	60% (plus fibre 10%)	12.5%	2%	0.8%
Bean thread	320	65%	20%	0	
Pasta	350	75%	11.5%	0.3%	

Source: Pat Chapman (1998) *Pat Chapman's Noodle Book*, Hodder & Stoughton Ltd.

Test yourself

1. State three quality points to look for when buying dried pasta.
2. State three pieces of equipment you would use when preparing fresh pasta.
3. Describe how to prepare fresh egg pasta dough.
4. What is the minimum legal temperature for holding cooked lasagne hot for service?
5. Describe how to store cooked pasta which is not for immediate use.
6. State two quality points to look for when buying fresh noodles.
7. Describe how to store uncooked fresh noodles.
8. Name three types of noodle.

Pasta recipes

1 Fresh egg pasta dough

Ingredient	4 portions	10 portions
Pasta flour	175 g	350 g
Whole eggs	1	2
Egg yolks	3	6

Energy	Cals	Fat	Sat fat	Carb	Sugar	Protein	Fibre
1,672 kJ	400 kcal	17.2 g	9.4 g	50.0 g	10.2 g	11.8 g	4.0 g

This is an alternative method to the one given earlier in the chapter.

1 Place all the ingredients into a food processor and mix quickly until a wet crumb mix appears; this should take no more than 30–45 seconds.

2 Tip the mix out on to a clean surface; this is where the working of the pasta begins. Knead it lightly.

3 The pasta dough may feel wet at this stage, however the working of the gluten will take the moisture back into the dry mass, leaving a velvety-smooth finish that is malleable and easy to work; most of this process should be carried out using a pasta machine.

4 Rest the dough for 30 minutes and then it is ready to use.

5 For a classic noodle shape, roll out to a thin rectangle 45 × 15 cm. Cut into 0.5 cm strips. Leave to dry.

Professional tip

- Do not knead the dough too much or it will become tough.
- Let it rest before rolling it out.
- The best way to roll out pasta dough to the correct thickness is to use a pasta machine.

Combine the ingredients into a wet crumb mix

Work and roll out the pasta using a pasta machine

A pasta machine with an attachment can be used to cut noodles

Video: making fresh pasta http://bit.ly/ 1MxDxCK

2 Spaghetti with tomato sauce (*spaghetti alla pomodoro*)

1 Plunge the spaghetti into a saucepan containing boiling salted water. Allow to boil gently.
2 Stir occasionally with a wooden spoon. Cook for approximately 12–15 minutes, until *al dente*.
3 Drain well in a colander. Return to a clean, dry pan.
4 Mix in the butter and add the tomato sauce. Correct the seasoning.
5 Add the tomato concassé and 4–5 leaves of flat parsley or fresh basil torn into pieces with your fingers, and serve with grated cheese.

Professional tip

Cook pasta to an *al dente* texture.

Ingredient	4 portions	10 portions
Spaghetti	100 g	250 g
Butter (optional) or olive oil	25 g	60 g
Tomato sauce (page 98)	250 ml	625 ml
Salt, mill pepper		
Tomato concassée, to serve		
Fresh basil or flat parsley, to serve		
Grated cheese, to serve		

Healthy eating tips
- Use very little or no salt as there is already plenty from the cheese.
- Reduce or omit the butter and serve with a large green salad.

Energy	Cals	Fat	Sat fat	Carb	Sugar	Protein	Fibre
1,672 kJ	400 kcal	17.2 g	9.4 g	50.0 g	10.2 g	11.8 g	4.0 g

Using hard margarine instead of butter.

Place the spaghetti into boiling water

Drain the cooked pasta

Add the sauce to the pasta

3 Spaghetti bolognaise (*spaghetti alla bolognese*)

1 Place half the butter or oil in a sauteuse.
2 Add the chopped onion and garlic, and cook for 4–5 minutes without colour.
3 Add the beef and cook, colouring lightly.
4 Add the *jus-lié*, the tomato purée and the herbs.
5 Simmer until tender.
6 Add the mushrooms and simmer for 5 minutes. Correct the seasoning.
7 Meanwhile, cook the spaghetti in plenty of boiling salted water.
8 Allow to boil gently, stirring occasionally with a wooden spoon.
9 Cook for approximately 12–15 minutes. Drain well in a colander.
10 Return to a clean pan containing the rest of the butter or oil (optional).
11 Correct the seasoning.
12 Serve with the sauce in centre of the spaghetti.
13 Serve grated cheese separately.

Ingredient	4 portions	10 portions
Butter or oil	20 g	50 g
Onion, chopped	50 g	125 g
Clove of garlic, chopped	1	2
Lean minced beef or tail end fillet, cut into 3 mm dice	400 g	1 kg
Jus-lié	125 ml	300 ml
Tomato purée	1 tbsp	2½ tbsp
Marjoram or oregano	Pinch	½ tsp
Mushrooms, diced	100 g	250 g
Salt, mill pepper		
Spaghetti	100 g	250 g
Grated cheese, to serve		

Energy	Cals	Fat	Sat fat	Carb	Sugar	Protein	Fibre	Sodium
1741 kJ	416 kcal	22.7 g	12.0 g	21.7 g	2.7 g	32.5 g	2.0 g	0.4 g

Using butter.

Variation

There are many variations on bolognaise sauce, e.g. substitute lean beef with pork mince or use a combination of both; add 50 g each of chopped carrot and celery; add 100 g chopped pancetta or bacon.

Healthy eating tips

- Use an unsaturated oil (sunflower or olive). Lightly oil the pan and drain off any excess after the frying is complete. Skim the fat from the finished dish.
- Season with the minimum amount of salt.
- Try using more pasta and extending the sauce with tomatoes.
- Serve with a large green salad.

Alternative recipe for bolognaise sauce

Ingredient	4 portions	10 portions
Olive oil	1 tbsp	2½ tbsp
Beef mince and pork mince	270 g	700 g
Onion, chopped	½	1
Mushrooms, sliced	100 g	250 g
Carrots, peeled and cut as for paysanne	1	2
Red wine	75 ml	180 ml
Beef stock or meat stock, reduced	100 ml	250 ml
Tomato purée	1 tbsp	2 tbsp
Tabasco sauce (optional)	½ tsp	1 tsp
Salt and freshly ground black pepper, to taste		
Fresh parsley, chopped	2 tbsp	5 tbsp
Fresh chives, chopped, to garnish		

1 Heat the olive oil in a frying pan, over a medium heat.

2 Add the beef and pork mince and the chopped onion and pan-fry for 4–6 minutes, stirring well, until the mince has browned and the onion has softened.

3 Add the mushrooms and carrots and cook for a further minute before adding the red wine, beef stock and tomato purée.

4 Add the Tabasco sauce and season to taste (optional).

5 Add the chopped parsley and cook for 2–4 minutes more to allow the wine and stock to reduce a little.

6 When mixing the pasta into the sauce, first drain the water thoroughly from the pasta then place into the bolognaise sauce.

7 Toss well, to evenly coat, then spoon into a serving bowl.

8 Garnish with the chopped chives, to serve (optional).

4 Penne arrabiata

Energy	Cals	Fat	Sat fat	Carb	Sugar	Protein	Fibre
2,263 kJ	539 kcal	24.1 g	4.4 g	65.7 g	10.2 g	19.3 g	2.8 g

Ingredient	4 portions	10 portions
Extra virgin olive oil	90 ml	225 ml
Onion, chopped	1	2½
Medium hot chillies, finely chopped	2	5
Cloves of garlic, chopped	1	2
Bacon lardons	100 g	250 g
Canned chopped plum tomatoes	600 g	1.5 kg
Tomato purée	1 tbsp	2½ tbsp
Salt, to taste		
Fresh/dried penne rigate pasta	400 g	1 kg
Basil leaves, shredded	5	12
Parmesan shavings, to serve		

1 Gently heat the olive oil in a frying pan. Add the onion, chilli and garlic and fry while stirring for one minute. Add the lardons and cook until golden.

2 Add the chopped tomatoes and tomato purée to the frying pan and simmer for 10–15 minutes, until the sauce has thickened a little. Season with salt to taste.

3 While the sauce is cooking, cook the pasta in large saucepan of boiling, salted water until *al dente* (fresh pasta will cook much more quickly than dried pasta). Drain the pasta and drizzle it with oil.

4 Add the basil to the sauce. Mix in the drained pasta.

5 Serve with shavings of Parmesan.

5 Macaroni cheese

Ingredient	4 portions	10 portions
Macaroni	100 g	250 g
Butter or oil, optional	25 g	60 g
Grated cheese	100 g	250 g
Thin béchamel sauce	500 ml	1.25 litres
Diluted English or continental mustard	¼ tsp	1 tsp
Salt, mill pepper		

Energy	Cals	Fat	Sat fat	Carb	Sugar	Protein	Fibre
1,899 kJ	452 kcal	29.2 g	16.1 g	34.2 g	6.7 g	15.0 g	1.7 g

1 Plunge the macaroni into a saucepan containing plenty of boiling salted water.

2 Allow to boil gently and stir occasionally with a wooden spoon.

3 Cook for approximately 15 minutes and drain well in a colander.

4 Return to a clean pan containing the butter.

5 Mix with half the cheese and add the béchamel and mustard. Season.

6 Place in an earthenware dish and sprinkle with the remainder of the cheese.

7 Brown lightly under the salamander and serve.

Browning the macaroni well gives it a good flavour, texture and presentation.

Healthy eating tips
- Half the grated cheese could be replaced with a small amount of Parmesan (more flavour and less fat).
- Use semi-skimmed milk for the béchamel. No added salt is necessary.

Variation

Variations include the addition of cooked, sliced mushrooms, diced ham, sweetcorn, tomato, and so on. Macaroni may also be prepared and served as for any of the spaghetti dishes.

6 Spinach fettuccine with ham and cream cheese (*fettuccine verdi con salsa cremona*)

Ingredient	4 portions	10 portions
Spinach fettuccine or other pasta	400 g	1 kg
Cream cheese, mashed	200 g	500 g
Single cream	2 tbsp	5 tbsp
Parmesan cheese, grated	50 g	125 g
Salt and pepper		
Butter, melted	50 g	125 g
Lean cooked ham, cut into thick julienne	100 g	250 g

Energy	Cals	Fat	Sat fat	Carb	Sugar	Protein	Fibre
3,183 kJ	760 kcal	42.2 g	25.4 g	76.3 g	2.7 g	23.7 g	3.1 g

1 Cook the fettuccine in plenty of boiling salted water.

2 Mix the cream cheese, cream and Parmesan, and season with salt and pepper.

3 Drain the fettuccine and return it to the pan.

4 Mix in the butter and cream cheese mixture. Add the ham. Toss and serve.

> **Healthy eating tips**
> ● This sauce is high in fat and salt, so additional butter and salt is not necessary.
> ● For a lower-fat version, use a 'light' cream cheese.
> ● Serve with a large green salad.

7 Tagliatelle carbonara

Ingredient	4 portions	10 portions
Tagliatelle	300 g	750 g
Olive oil	1 tbsp	2½ tbsp
Cloves of garlic, peeled and crushed	2	5
Smoked bacon, diced	200 g	500 g
Eggs	4	10
Double or single cream	4 tbsp	150 ml
Parmesan cheese	4 tbsp	150 ml

Energy	Cals	Fat	Sat fat	Carb	Sugar	Protein	Fibre	Sodium
2,911 kJ	698 kcal	44.8 g	20.8 g	43.0 g	1.9 g	33.4 g	0.2 g	1.0 g

1 Cook the tagliatelle in boiling salted water until *al dente*. Refresh and drain.

2 Heat the oil in a suitable pan. Fry the crushed and chopped garlic. Add the diced, smoked bacon.

3 Mix together the beaten eggs, cream and Parmesan. Season with black pepper.

4 Add the tagliatelle to the garlic and bacon. Add the eggs and cream, stirring until the eggs cook in the heat. Serve immediately.

8 Ravioli

Ingredient	4 portions	10 portions
Flour	200 g	500 g
Salt		
Olive oil	35 ml	150 ml
Water	100 ml	250 ml

Energy	Cals	Fat	Sat fat	Carb	Sugar	Protein	Fibre
1,027 kJ	249 kcal	9.4 g	1.4 g	38.9 g	0.8 g	4.8 g	1.6 g

1 Sieve the flour and salt. Make a well. Add the liquid.

2 Knead to a smooth dough. Rest for at least 30 minutes in a cool place.

3 Roll out to a very thin oblong: 30 cm × 45 cm.

4 Cut in half and egg wash.

5 Place the stuffing in a piping bag with a large plain tube.

6 Pipe out the filling in small pieces, each about the size of a cherry, approximately 4 cm apart, on to one half of the paste.

7 Carefully cover with the other half of the paste and seal, taking care to avoid air pockets.

8 Mark each with the back of a plain cutter.

9 Cut in between each line of filling, down and across with a serrated pastry wheel.

10 Separate on a well-floured tray.

11 Poach in gently boiling salted water for approximately 10 minutes. Drain well.

12 Place in an earthenware serving dish.

13 Cover with 250 ml *jus-lié*, demi-glace or tomato sauce.

14 Sprinkle with 50 g grated cheese.

15 Brown under the salamander and serve.

Fresh egg pasta dough can also be used. If you have prepared the dough, start this recipe at step 3.

The photo shows ravioli stuffed with spinach and ricotta cheese, then poached. The ravioli has been drizzled with olive oil and garnished with micro herbs and slices of Parmesan.

Possible fillings

Here are some examples of stuffing for ravioli, tortellini and other pastas. Each recipe provides enough stuffing to use with 400 g of pasta.

Fish	
Fish, chopped, cooked	200 g
Mushrooms, chopped, cooked	100 g
Parsley, chopped	
Anchovy paste	

Spinach and ricotta	
Dry spinach, cooked, puréed	200 g
Ricotta cheese	200 g
Butter	25 g
Nutmeg	
Salt and pepper	

Pork and veal	
Lean pork mince, cooked	200 g
Lean veal mince, cooked	200 g
Butter	25 g
Cheese, grated	25 g
2 yolks or 1 egg	
Fresh white breadcrumbs	25 g
Salt and pepper	

Ricotta and Parmesan	
Marjoram, chopped	Pinch
Ricotta cheese	150 g
Parmesan, grated	75 g
Egg	1
Nutmeg	
Salt and pepper	

Beef	
Beef or pork mince, cooked	200 g
Spinach, cooked	100 g
Onion, chopped, cooked	50 g
Oregano	
Salt and pepper	

Chicken	
Chicken, cooked, minced	200 g
Ham, minced	100 g
Butter	25 g
2 yolks or 1 egg	
Cheese, grated	25 g
Nutmeg, grated	pinch
Salt and pepper	
Fresh white breadcrumbs	25 g

9 Ravioli of squash and spinach with wild mushroom sauce

For the ravioli

1 Peel the butternut squash, remove the seeds and chop the flesh roughly.
2 Cook the squash in the butter with the salt over a medium heat until soft.
3 Add the spinach and cook for a further minute.
4 Drain off the butter and chill the mixture until firm.
5 Once the mixture is firm, roll out and cut into 1 cm pieces.
6 Roll the pasta dough and make the ravioli to the required shape.
7 Place on a floured tray and reserve until required.

For the sauce

1 Sweat down the onions, fresh mushrooms, garlic and herbs in the butter for 10 minutes.
2 Add the dried cep and sweat for a further 5 minutes.
3 Add the Noilly Prat and reduce completely.
4 Add the vegetable stock and reduce by three-quarters.
5 Add the cream and bring to the boil. Remove the thyme and bay leaf.
6 Blitz the sauce until smooth, season and reserve until required.

To serve

1 Blanch the ravioli in simmering, salted water for 3 minutes.
2 Heat the sauce gently in a pan. Drain the ravioli and add to the sauce.
3 Garnish with the squash (reheated in the oven).
4 Finish with chopped chives and serve as required.

Ingredient	4 portions	10 portions
Squash and spinach ravioli		
Butternut squash	500 g	1.25 kg
Butter	100 g	250 g
Salt	10 g	25 g
Spinach	250 g	625 g
Pasta dough	400 g	1 kg
Wild mushroom sauce		
Onions, finely sliced	50 g	125 g
Button mushrooms, finely sliced	75 g	185 g
Wild mushrooms, sliced	60 g	150 g
Clove of garlic	½	1
Bay leaf	1	2
Sprig of thyme	1	2
Butter	10 g	25 g
Dried cep	5 g	12 g
Noilly Prat (dry vermouth)	75 g	185 g
Vegetable stock	200 ml	500 ml
Single cream	100 g	250 g
Salt and pepper		
Chives, chopped		

Energy	Cals	Fat	Sat fat	Carb	Sugar	Protein	Fibre	Sodium
2,469 kJ	590 kcal	30.8 g	17.6 g	62.0 g	6.6 g	15.8 g	4.2 g	1.3 g

10 Ricotta and spinach cannelloni with tomato and basil sauce

Ingredient	4 portions	10 portions
Dried plain or spinach lasagne sheets	12	30
Fresh spinach	350 g	850 g
Ricotta cheese	200 g	500 g
Salt and pepper		
Tomato sauce (page 98)	200 ml	500 ml
Basil, shredded	1 tbsp	2 tbsp
Parmesan cheese, grated	50 g	125 g

Energy	Cals	Fat	Sat fat	Carb	Sugar	Protein	Fibre	Sodium
1,913 kJ	454 kcal	14.6 g	6.3 g	61.0 g	6.5 g	23.8 g	3.1 g	0.3 g

1 Preheat the oven to 190 °C.

2 Cook the lasagne sheets in a large pan of boiling, salted water for the time stated on the packaging. Refresh immediately in ice-cold water.

3 Pick the spinach to de-branch it. Blanch by plunging it into rapidly boiling water for 20 seconds before refreshing it in ice-cold water.

4 Drain the spinach and squeeze out the excess water, then chop roughly.

5 Beat the ricotta with a spoon until soft, stir in the spinach and season well with salt and pepper.

6 Using a piping bag, pipe the ricotta mixture down one side of each lasagne sheet and roll it up to form a filled tube. Cover and chill in a refrigerator.

7 Place the cannelloni into a lightly oiled baking dish.

8 Pour the tomato sauce over the prepared cannelloni, and sprinkle with freshly shredded basil and the grated Parmesan.

9 Bake at 190 °C for 20 minutes and serve.

De-branch the spinach

Stir the chopped spinach into the beaten ricotta

Pipe the ricotta mixture down one side of the lasagne sheet

Carefully lift the edge of the sheet with a knife, then roll the cannelloni by hand

11 Lasagne

Ingredient	4 portions	10 portions
Lasagne sheets	200 g	500 g
Oil	1 tbsp	2½ tbsp
Streaky bacon, thin strips of	50 g	125 g
Onion, chopped	100 g	250 g
Carrot, chopped	50 g	125 g
Celery, chopped	50 g	125 g
Minced beef	200 g	500 g
Tomato purée	1 tbsp	2½ tbsp
Jus-lié or demi-glace	375 ml	1 litre
Clove of garlic	1	2½
Salt, pepper		
Marjoram	½ tsp	1½ tsp
Mushrooms, sliced	100 g	250 g
Béchamel sauce	250 ml	600 ml
Parmesan or Cheddar cheese, grated	25 g	125 g

Energy	Cals	Fat	Sat fat	Carb	Sugar	Protein	Fibre
2,416 kJ	575 kcal	28.7 g	11.4 g	56.1 g	10.0 g	26.7 g	5.8 g

1 Prepare the fresh egg pasta dough and roll out to 1 mm thick.

2 Cut into 6 cm squares.

3 Allow to rest in a cool place and dry slightly on a cloth dusted with flour.

4 Whether using fresh or ready-bought lasagne, cook in gently simmering salted water for approximately 3 minutes (fresh pasta) or 10 minutes (dried).

5 Refresh in cold water, then drain on a cloth.

6 Gently heat the oil in a thick-bottomed pan, add the bacon and cook for 2–3 minutes.

7 Add the onion, carrot and celery, cover the pan with a lid and cook for 5 minutes.

8 Add the minced beef, increase the heat and stir until lightly brown.

9 Remove from the heat and mix in the tomato purée.

10 Return to the heat, mix in the *jus-lié* or demi-glace, stir to boil.

11 Add the garlic, salt, pepper and marjoram, and simmer for 15 minutes. Remove the garlic.

12 Mix in the mushrooms, reboil for 2 minutes, then remove from the heat.

13 Butter an ovenproof dish and cover the bottom with a layer of the meat sauce.

14 Add a layer of lasagne and cover with meat sauce.

15 Add another layer of lasagne and cover with the remainder of the meat sauce.

16 Cover with the béchamel.

17 Sprinkle with cheese, cover with a lid and place in a moderately hot oven at 190 °C for approximately 20 minutes.

18 Remove the lid, cook for a further 15 minutes and serve in the cleaned ovenproof dish.

Note

This recipe can be made using 200 g of ready-bought lasagne or it can be prepared fresh using 200 g flour noodle paste. Wholemeal lasagne can be made using noodle paste made with 100 g wholemeal flour and 100 g strong flour.

Brown the minced beef in a thick-bottomed pan

Place a layer of lasagne over a layer of meat sauce

Cover the final layer with béchamel

Variation

Traditionally, pasta dishes are substantial in quantity but because they are so popular they are also sometimes requested as lighter dishes. Obviously the portion size can be reduced but other variations can also be considered.

For example, freshly made pasta cut into 8–10 cm rounds or squares, rectangles or diamonds, lightly poached or steamed, well drained and placed on a light tasty mixture (e.g. a tablespoon of mousse of chicken or fish or shellfish, well-cooked dried spinach flavoured with toasted pine nuts and grated nutmeg or a duxelle mixture) using just the one piece of pasta on top or a piece top and bottom. A light sauce should be used (e.g. a measure of well-reduced chicken stock with a little skimmed milk, blitzed to a froth just before serving, pesto sauce, a drizzle of good-quality olive oil, or a light tomato sauce). The dish can be finished with a suitable garnish (e.g. lightly fried wild or cultivated sliced mushrooms).

Fillings for lasagne can be varied in many ways. Tomato sauce may be used instead of *jus-lié*.

Healthy eating tips

- Use an unsaturated oil (sunflower or olive). Lightly oil the pan and drain off any excess after the frying is complete. Skim the fat from the finished meat sauce.
- Season with the minimum amount of salt.
- The fat content can be proportionally reduced by increasing the ratio of pasta to sauce and thinning the béchamel.

12 Vegetarian lasagne

1 Cook the lasagne sheets in boiling, salted water until *al dente*; refresh and drain.

2 Heat half the oil and sweat the onion and garlic.

3 Add the mushrooms and continue to cook without colour. Season.

4 Heat the remaining oil in a sauteuse, add the courgettes and lightly fry; sprinkle with the oregano. Cook until crisp, then add the tomatoes and tomato purée.

5 Add the broccoli and carrots, then mix in the pine kernels.

6 Make a cheese sauce using the béchamel and half the grated cheese; finish with the natural yoghurt.

7 Grease a suitable ovenproof dish well with the sunflower oil and place a layer of lasagne in the bottom.

8 Cover with a layer of mushrooms, then a layer of lasagne, then the broccoli and tomato mixture, then lasagne, then cheese sauce. Continue to do this, finishing with a layer of cheese sauce on the top.

9 Sprinkle with the remaining grated Parmesan.

10 Bake in a preheated oven at 180 °C for 20–25 minutes.

Ingredient	4 portions	10 portions
Sheets of lasagne	10	30
Sunflower oil	125 ml	300 ml
Onions, finely chopped	100 g	250 g
Cloves of garlic, chopped	2	5
Mushrooms, sliced	200 g	500 g
Salt and pepper		
Medium-sized courgettes, cut into 1 cm dice	2	5
Oregano	3 g	9 g
Tomatoes, skinned, deseeded and diced	200 g	500 g
Tomato purée	2 tbsp	5 tbsp
Broccoli, cut into small florets, blanched and refreshed	300 g	750 g
Carrots, cut into 0.5 cm dice, blanched and refreshed	100 g	250 g
Pine nuts	25 g	60 g
Béchamel sauce	250 ml	625 ml
Parmesan cheese, grated	50 g	125 g
Natural yoghurt	250 ml	625 ml

Healthy eating tips
- Try using a mixture of white and green lasagne.
- Use as little oil as possible to sweat the onion.
- Make the béchamel with semi-skimmed milk.
- No added salt is needed.

Energy	Cals	Fat	Sat fat	Carb	Sugar	Protein	Fibre
2,993 kJ	713 kcal	46.2 g	8.5 g	54.6 g	16.5 g	22.9 g	11.8 g

Gnocchi recipes

13 Potato gnocchi (*gnocchi piemontese*)

Ingredient	4 portions	10 portions
Potatoes	300 g	1 kg
Flour, white or wholemeal	100 g	250 g
Egg and egg yolk, beaten	1	2
Butter	25 g	60 g
Salt and pepper		
Nutmeg, grated		
Tomato sauce (page 98)	250 ml	625 ml
Grated cheese, to serve		

Energy	Cals	Fat	Sat fat	Carb	Sugar	Protein	Fibre
1,045 kJ	248 kcal	9.7 g	4.7 g	35.2 g	2.1 g	7.2 g	2.1 g

Using white flour.

1 Bake or boil the potatoes in their jackets.
2 Remove the skins and mash with a fork or pass through a sieve.
3 Mix with the flour, egg, butter and seasoning while hot.
4 Mould into balls the size of walnuts.
5 Dust well with flour and flatten slightly with a fork.
6 Poach in gently boiling water until they rise to the surface. Drain carefully.
7 Dress in a buttered earthenware dish, cover with tomato or any other pasta sauce.
8 Sprinkle with grated cheese, brown lightly under the salamander and serve.

Healthy eating tips

No added salt is necessary.

Ingredients for gnocchi

Combine the mashed potato with the other ingredients while hot

Mould the mixture into balls, then flatten with a fork

Drop the gnocchi into gently boiling water and poach them

14 Parmesan gnocchi and tomato sauce

Ingredient	4 portions	10 portions
Parmesan gnocchi		
Desiree potatoes, cooked	350 g	875 g
Parmesan cheese	75 g	185 g
Egg yolks	2	5
Butter	10 g	25 g
Salt and pepper		
Pasta flour	125 g	300 g
Tomato sauce		
Carrot	75 g	185 g
Celery	20 g	50 g
Butter	25 g	60 g
Vegetable oil	25 g	60 g
Clove of garlic	½	1
Sprig of thyme	1	2
Juniper berries	1	2
Bay leaf	1	2
Plum tomatoes	200 g	500 g
Tomato purée	10 g	25 g
Vegetable stock	500 ml	1.25 litres
Cream	25 g	60 g
Sherry vinegar, to taste		
Fresh herbs, e.g. basil, and Parmesan to finish		

For the Parmesan gnocchi:

1 Place the potatoes in an oven at 180 °C for 1 hour.
2 Grate the Parmesan using a fine grater.
3 Discard the potato skins and pass the cooked potato through a drum sieve.
4 Add the Parmesan, egg yolks, butter and seasoning.
5 Mix until smooth but do not overwork.
6 Incorporate the flour until it is all absorbed.
7 Wrap the dough in cling film and allow to rest for 30 minutes.
8 Roll and shape into 1 cm pieces.
9 Blanch the gnocchi in simmering water until they float.
10 Refresh the gnocchi and reserve until required.

For the tomato sauce:

1 Cut the carrot and celery into small pieces.
2 Heat the butter and oil in a pan, sweat down the carrot and celery with the garlic, thyme, juniper berries and bay leaf for 10 minutes.
3 Roughly chop the tomatoes and add to the pan with the tomato purée. Cook for 15 minutes.
4 Add the vegetable stock and reduce by half.
5 Add the cream and reduce by half.
6 Remove the bay leaf and thyme, add the sherry vinegar, then blitz until smooth.
7 Reserve until required.

To finish:

1 Gently sauté the gnocchi in a little oil, and warm the sauce gently.
2 Combine the two together and finish with fresh herbs and shaved Parmesan.

Energy	Cals	Fat	Sat fat	Carb	Sugar	Protein	Fibre	Sodium
1814 kJ	433 kcal	25.0 g	11.1 g	41.0 g	6.4 g	14.7 g	4.0 g	0.7 g

Excluding juniper berries; using ¼ tsp sherry vinegar and 10 g shaved Parmesan to garnish per 4 portions.

This chapter is relevant to the following units:
→ Prepare fish for basic dishes.
→ Prepare shellfish for basic dishes.

→ Cook and finish basic fish dishes.
→ Cook and finish basic shellfish dishes.

Recipes included in this chapter

Fish

Types and varieties

Fish are vertebrates (animals with a backbone) and are split into two primary groups: **flat** and **round** fish. From this they can be split again into subgroups or secondary groups:

- **Oily fish** have bodies that are round in shape and include herring, mackerel, salmon, tuna and sardines. They are **pelagic** fish, which means that they are found midwater.
- **White fish** can be round, such as cod, whiting, hake, pollock and sea bass, or flat, such as plaice, sole and turbot. They are **demersal** fish, which means that they are found at or near the bottom of the sea.
- **Shellfish** (see page 169).

Many people choose to eat fish in preference to meat because of health considerations and, consequently, consumption of fish has been steadily increasing. This popularity has resulted in a far greater selection becoming available and, due to swift and efficient transport, well over 200 types of fish are on sale throughout the year.

Fish is plentiful in the UK because it is surrounded by water, although overfishing and pollution are having a detrimental effect on supplies of certain fish. Most catches are made off Iceland or Scotland, in the North Sea, Irish Sea and the English Channel. Salmon are caught in certain English and Scottish rivers, and are also extensively farmed. Frozen fish is imported from Scandinavia, Canada and Japan, and other countries worldwide; Canada and Japan both export frozen salmon to Britain.

Unfortunately, due to overfishing, the supply of fish is not unlimited and it is now necessary to have fish farms (such as those for trout and salmon, turbot, bass and cod) to supplement natural sources. This is not the only problem: due to contamination by humans and industry, seas and rivers are becoming increasingly polluted, affecting both the supply and the suitability of fish – particularly shellfish – for human consumption.

Quality points when choosing and buying fish

Fresh fish can be bought by the kilogram, number of fillets or number of whole fish of the weight that is required. For example, 30 kg of salmon could be ordered as 2 × 15 kg, 3 × 10 kg or 6 × 5 kg, the number of whole fish, or portions such as fillets, suprêmes or darnes. Frozen fish can be purchased whole (gutted), filleted, cut or prepared in a wide variety of different ways. The checklists below summarise the main points to look for when choosing and buying fish.

Whole fish

These should have:

- clear, bright eyes, not sunken
- bright red gills
- no missing scales; scales should be firmly attached to the skin
- moist skin (fresh fish feels slightly slippery)
- shiny skin with bright natural colouring
- a stiff tail
- firm flesh
- a fresh sea smell and no trace of ammonia smell.

Fish fillets

These should be:

- neatly trimmed with firm flesh
- firm and closely packed together, not ragged or gaping
- a translucent white colour if they are from a white fish, with no discoloration.

Smoked fish

These should have:

- a glossy appearance
- firm flesh and not sticky
- a pleasant, smoky smell.

Frozen fish

This should:

- be frozen hard with no signs of thawing
- be in packaging that is not damaged
- show no evidence of freezer burn (this shows as dull, white, dry patches).

Seasonality

The quality of fish can vary due to local climatic and environmental conditions. Generally, all fish spawn over a period of four to six weeks. During spawning, they use up a lot of their reserves of fat and protein in the production of eggs. This has the effect of making their flesh watery and soft. Fish in this condition are termed 'spent fish'. This takes anything between one and two months, depending on local environmental conditions.

Availability

Naturally, prevailing weather conditions have an enormous bearing on fishing activities. The full range of species may not always be available during stormy weather, for instance.

Dealing with problems with fish

If you find there are problems with fish or shellfish and they are not of the quality, quantity, cut or type required, inform a supervisor or head chef immediately. This applies when checking deliveries or when you are about to use fish already in storage.

Table 9.1 Seasonality of fish

Legend: ● = Available (dark fish) · ◎ = At best (white fish on dark) · ○ = Spawning and roeing (outline fish)

	JAN	FEB	MAR	APR	MAY	JUN	JUL	AUG	SEP	OCT	NOV	DEC
Bream	●	●	●	●	○	○	○	●	●	●	●	●
Brill	◎	◎	●	●	○	◎	◎	◎	◎	◎	◎	◎
Cod	◎	◎	○	○	●	●	●	●	●	◎	◎	◎
Eel						●	◎	◎	◎	◎	●	
Grey mullet	●	●	○	○	●	●	●	●	●	●	●	●
Gurnard	●	●	●	●	●	●	●	●	●	●	●	●
Haddock	◎	◎	◎	◎	●	●	●	●	◎	◎	◎	◎
Hake	●	●	○	○	○	●	●	◎	◎	◎	◎	◎
Halibut	◎	◎	◎	○	○	●	●	◎	◎	◎	◎	◎
Herring	●	●	●	●	●	●	●	◎	◎	◎	◎	◎
John Dory	●	●	●	○	○	○	○	●	●	●	●	●
Mackerel	●	●	●	○	●	●	●	●	●	●	●	●
Monkfish	●	●	●	●	●	●	●	●	●	●	●	●
Plaice	●	●	○	○	●	●	●	●	●	●	●	●
Red mullet			●	●	◎	◎	◎	◎	◎	●	●	
Salmon (farmed)	●	●	●	●	●	●	●	●	●	●	●	●
Salmon (wild)				◎	◎	◎	◎	◎				
Sardines	◎	◎	◎	●					◎	◎	◎	◎
Sea bass	●	●	●	○	○	●	●	●	●	●	●	●
Sea trout					●	◎	◎	◎	○	○	○	○
Skate	●	●			●	●	●	●		●	●	●
Squid	●								●	●	●	●
Sole (Dover)	◎	●	●						◎	●	●	●
Sole (lemon)	◎	◎	◎	◎	◎	◎	◎	◎	◎	◎	◎	◎
Trout					●	●	●	●	●	●	●	
Tuna	●	●	●	●	●	●	●	●	●	●	●	●
Turbot	◎	◎	●	○	○	○	●	●	●	●	●	●
Whiting	◎	◎								●	●	●

Key:

Available

At best

Spawning and roeing – this can deprive the flesh of nutrients and will decrease the yield.

Storing fish

Once caught, fish has a shelf life of 10 to 12 days if properly refrigerated at a temperature between 0 °C and 4 °C. If the fish is delivered whole with the innards still in the fish, it should be gutted and the cavity washed well before it is stored.

Use the fish as soon as possible after delivery, but it can be stored overnight. Rinse, pat dry, cover with cling film and store in a refrigerator just for fish or at the bottom of a multi-use refrigerator. Make sure the fish is covered or wrapped, labelled and dated. Fish may also be vacuum packed before chilling. For fish products that do not need to be used immediately, use in rotation: this means using older items before the newly delivered items.

Ready-to-eat cooked fish, such as hot-smoked mackerel, cooked prawns and crab, should be stored on shelves above other raw foodstuffs to avoid cross-contamination.

Preservation of fish

Fish deteriorates quickly after it has been caught and over many years ways have been sought to preserve fish for longer. The following are some of the ways that fish (and shellfish) can be preserved.

Freezing

Fish is either frozen at sea or as soon as possible after reaching port. The freezing process should be fast because the longer it takes to freeze, the larger and more angular the ice crystals become, which breaks the protein strands. This results in liquid leaking out when the fish is defrosted, leaving an inferior product. When fish is frozen quickly, the ice crystals are small, and there is less leakage and less damage. Most fish should be defrosted before being cooked but some prepared fish products, such as frozen, breadcrumbed scampi or plaice, can be cooked from frozen. Plaice, halibut, turbot, haddock, pollack, sole, cod, trout, salmon, herring, whiting, scampi, smoked haddock and kippers, as well as a wide range of prepared products, are available frozen.

Frozen fish should be checked for:
- no evidence of freezer burn
- undamaged packaging
- minimum fluid loss during defrosting
- flesh still firm after defrosting.

Frozen fish should be stored at −18 °C to −20 °C and defrosted overnight in a refrigerator. It should *not* be defrosted in water as this spoils the taste and texture of the fish, and valuable water-soluble nutrients are lost. Fish should not be refrozen as this will impair its taste and texture, as well as being a food safety risk.

Canning

It is usually the oily fish that are canned. Sardines, salmon, anchovies, pilchards, tuna, herring and herring roe (eggs) are canned in either their own juice (e.g. salmon), in oil, a sauce, brine or spring water. In some countries bottling is popular for fish such as herrings; this is a similar process to canning.

Salting

In the UK, the salting of fish is usually accompanied by a smoking process.
- Cured herrings are packed in salt.
- Caviar – the slightly salted roe of the sturgeon – is sieved, canned and refrigerated.

In some Caribbean countries salted dried fish, especially cod, has been popular for many years and this is now available in numerous other countries. It needs to be soaked in plenty of cold water for several hours before use.

Pickling

Herrings pickled in vinegar are filleted, rolled and skewered, and known as rollmops.

Smoking

Fish that is to be smoked may be gutted or left whole. It is then soaked in a strong salt solution (brine) and, in some cases, a dye is added to improve colour. After this, it is drained, hung on racks in a kiln and exposed to smoke for five or six hours.

Smoked fish should be wrapped well and kept separate from other fish to prevent the smell and dye penetrating other foods.

Cold smoking takes place at a temperature of no more than 33 °C (this is to avoid cooking the flesh). Therefore, all cold-smoked fish is raw and is usually cooked before being eaten, the exceptions being smoked salmon and cold-smoked trout.

Hot-smoked fish is cured at a temperature between 70 °C and 80 °C in order to cook the flesh, so does not require further cooking.

Choose fish with a pleasant smoky smell and a bright glossy surface. The flesh should be firm; sticky or soggy flesh means that the fish may have been of low quality or under smoked. Smoked fish still needs refrigeration or freezing.

Healthy eating tips
Salted, pickled and smoked fish has a high salt content so there is no need to add additional salt when cooking.

Preparation

When preparing fish and shellfish it is important to always select the correct tools and equipment to enable you to work professionally and achieve a good finish. Fish is a delicate product and some, such as fillets of flat white fish, can be very delicate. Choosing your equipment well and handling the fish carefully will help to prevent damage and wastage. Do not over handle the fish and, when prepared, place neatly on a tray, cover and refrigerate until needed. Correct equipment will also allow for safe working practices and reduce the risks of cross-contamination.

Preparation equipment may include: chef's knife, filleting knife, oyster knife, scissors/secateurs, fish tweezers, chopping boards, bowls, trays, spoons and other items as required. Assemble all of your equipment before you start the task.

Unless otherwise stated, as a guide allow 100 g fish off the bone and approximately 200 to 300 g on the bone for a portion (check the recipe).

All fish should be washed under running cold water before and after preparation.

> ## Health and safety
>
> - Use the correct colour-coded boards; blue for preparing raw fish and yellow for cooked fish. Keep the boards clean and disinfect by putting through a dishwasher or spray with sanitiser.
> - If possible keep other equipment used just for raw fish use. If this is not possible, wash and sanitise equipment before and immediately after each use.
> - Unhygienic equipment, utensils and preparation areas increase the risk of cross-contamination.
> - Use a dishwasher to clean and disinfect equipment after use and wash hands thoroughly.
> - For cleaning, use disposable single-use cloths where possible along with sanitiser.

There are various methods of preparing, cutting and filleting fish and these are described below.

Trimming and scaling

Whole fish are trimmed to remove the scales, fins and head using fish scissors and a knife. If the head is to be left on (as in the case of a salmon for a cold buffet), the gills and the eyes are removed.

Gutting

If the fish needs to be gutted, the following procedure should be used.

1 Cut from the vent to two-thirds along the fish.
2 Draw out the intestines with the fingers or, in the case of a large fish, use the hook handle of a utensil such as a ladle.
3 Ensure that the blood lying along the main bone is removed, then wash and drain thoroughly.
4 If the fish is to be stuffed then it may be gutted by removing the innards through the gill slits, so leaving the stomach skin intact, forming a pouch in which to put the stuffing. When this method is used, care must be taken to ensure that the inside of the fish is clear of all traces of blood.

Skinning and filleting

The following sequences demonstrate how to prepare and fillet a round or flat fish, and how to skin and prepare a whole Dover sole. These fish have already been gutted and cleaned.

When you fillet a fish, remove the first fillet by cutting along the backbone from head to tail. Then reverse the fish and remove the second fillet by cutting from tail to head.

Coating and marinating

Fish and shellfish can be coated with items such as flour, egg and breadcrumbs (*pane*), milk and flour or batter before cooking. They may also be marinated – placed in a prepared mixture which may include herbs, spices, seasonings, fruit juice or zest, oil, wine and other ingredients – to achieve the required flavour.

Filleting a round fish (salmon)

1 Remove the head and clean thoroughly.

2 Remove the first fillet by cutting along the backbone from head to tail. Keeping the knife close to the bone, remove the fillet.

3 After both fillets have been removed, remove the rib cavity bones and trim the fish neatly.

Boning a round fish (trout)

Remove the pin bones from the fillet

Video: filleting a round fish http://bit.ly/ 1aikddT

Filleting a flat fish (turbot)

1 Using a filleting knife, make an incision from the head to tail. Cut around the gill and backbone.

2 Remove the first fillet, holding the knife almost parallel to the work surface and keeping the knife close to the bone.

3 Repeat for the second fillet.

4 Turn the fish over and repeat, removing the last two fillets.

5 Hold the fillet firmly at the tail end. Cut the flesh as close to the tail as possible, as far as the skin. Keep the knife parallel to the work surface, grip the skin firmly and move the knife from side to side to remove the skin.

6 Trim the fillets neatly.

Video: filleting a flat fish
http://bit.ly/17grHfz

Preparing a whole Dover sole

1 Score the skin just above the tail.

2 Hold the tail firmly, then cut and scrape the skin until sufficient is lifted to be gripped.

3 Pull the skin away from the tail to the head. Both the black and white skins may be removed in this way.

4 Trim the tail and side fins with fish scissors.
5 Remove the eyes. Clean and wash the fish thoroughly. The fish is shown here with all the parts that were removed.

Cuts of fish

Fish may be cut and portioned depending on their size, shape and the menu requirements. The usual fish cuts are:

- **Fillets**: cuts of fish free from bone. There will be two fillets from a round fish (one from each side of the spine) and four from a flat fish (two from each side).
- **Steaks**: thick slices of fish on or off the bone.
- **Darnes**: steaks of round fish (salmon, cod) cut through the bone.
- **Tronçons**: steaks of flat fish (turbot, halibut) cut through the bone. If cut from a large fish, these may then be cut into halves or quarters..
- **Suprêmes**: prime cuts of fish without bone and skin, for example cut from skinless fillets of salmon, turbot or brill.

- **Goujons**: filleted fish cut into strips approximately 8 × 0.5 cm.
- **Délice**: fillets of fish neatly folded with the skinned side facing inwards.
- **Paupiette**: fillets of fish, such as sole, plaice or whiting, spread with a stuffing and rolled.
- **Plaited** (*en tresse*): for example, sole fillets cut into three even pieces lengthwise to within 1 cm of the top, and neatly plaited.

 Video: cutting fish into darnes http://bit.ly/1zOtrmN

▲ Cuts of fish: (clockwise from top left) darne, tronçon, fillet, paupiettes, suprême, goujons

Portion control

There are a number of ways that can be used to achieve good portion control with fish, for example:

- specified size and weight of a whole fish, such as trout, sea bass or dover sole per portion
- specified cut sizes of darnes, tronçons and suprêmes used as a portion
- number of fillets from small fish, for example two fillets from a plaice as a portion
- number of shellfish items, for example six king prawns, four scallops or half a lobster making a portion
- number and size of paupiettes or délice offered as a portion
- dividing a fish pie into equal-sized portions
- filling an individual pie dish or serving dish or pastry case
- using a ladle to measure the portion size of a fish stew or soup.

Professional tip

The fish or shellfish dish you cook needs to meet the dish requirements as required by your supervisor or head chef. It must also meet the requirements and descriptions on the menu (this is a legal requirement). So if the menu says Dover sole you cannot use lemon sole instead unless you change the menu. You must also meet cooking method requirements, when a menu states grilled fish it must be grilled not oven baked. The customer too will have expectations of the dish you are preparing and cooking, and it is important to achieve the required quality to meet those expectations.

Cooking methods

The texture of various fish and shellfish varies greatly: some are very fragile and can break easily when cooking, so handle carefully and choose a suitable cooking method. For example, plaice fillets are very soft and delicate so are not suitable for stewing or roasting. Your recipes will provide good guidelines to suitable cooking methods.

Fish is very economical on fuel because it cooks quickly. When cooked, fish loses its translucent look and takes on an opaque appearance. It will also flake easily, so should be handled with care to stop it breaking up.

Fish can easily become dry and lose its flavour if overcooked, so it is important to consider methods of cookery carefully. Overcooked, dry fish will be far less enjoyable to eat and is less attractive than fish that is cooked properly. The correct cooking method must also be selected to ensure the fish meets dish requirements and menu descriptions.

To maintain the quality and food safety of fish dishes it is advisable to check the internal temperature using a temperature probe. It is recommended that all fish should be cooked to a minimum internal temperature of 63 °C. This is for whole fish and cuts of fish. Prepared fish dishes such as fish pie or fishcakes should be cooked to a minimum of 75 °C.

Because fish cooks so quickly, an experienced chef will be able to tell when certain types of fish are cooked by touch (touch temperature).

The following are the main cooking methods used for fish.

Frying

Frying is probably the most popular method of cooking fish. Described below are the three main types of frying.

Shallow frying

The fish should be seasoned and lightly coated with flour before frying, in order to protect it and seal in the flavour. Use a mixture of oil and butter when frying, and turn the fish only once during cooking, to avoid it breaking up.

This method is suitable for small whole fish, cuts or fillets cooked in oil or fat in a frying pan. The fish can also be lightly coated with semolina, matzo meal, oatmeal or breadcrumbs before frying. If the frying medium is to be butter, it must be clarified otherwise there is a risk that the fish may burn. Oil is the best medium, to which a little butter may be added for flavour.

Deep frying

This method is suitable for small whole white fish, cuts and fillets, as well as made-up items such as fishcakes. All white fish are suitable for deep frying in batter, including cod, pollack, haddock and skate. Depending on size, the fish may be left whole or may be portioned or filleted.

The fish should be seasoned and coated before frying, usually with a batter or an egg and breadcrumb mixture to form a surface that prevents penetration of the cooking fat or oil into the fish. It also adds a crisp texture to the fish. Use a thermostatically controlled deep fryer no more than half-filled with oil; heat the oil to 175 °C. Test the temperature before serving the fish. Drain the fish on absorbent paper after cooking.

Coatings can be either:
- flour, egg and breadcrumbs (*pane*)
- milk and flour
- batter.

Stir-frying

This is a very fast and popular method of cooking where the fish is cooked along with suitable vegetables and perhaps noodles, bean shoots or rice. Spices, flavourings

and suitable sauces may also be added. Use a wok or deep frying pan and a high cooking temperature. Food should be cut into thin strips and all prepared before cooking begins. This method is well suited to firm-fleshed fish cut into strips or shellfish.

Grilling

Grilling, or griddling, is cooking under radiant heat, and is a fast and convenient method suitable for fillets or small whole fish. When grilling whole fish, trim and prepare neatly and descale. Cut through the flesh at the thickest part of the fish to allow even cooking. Lightly oil and season fish or fillets and, to avoid breaking, do not turn more than once.

Poaching

Poaching is suitable for:
- whole fish such as salmon, trout or bass
- certain cuts on the bone such as salmon, turbot, brill, halibut, cod and skate
- fillets, suprêmes or fish prepared into délice or paupiette.

In each case, the prepared fish should be completely immersed in the cooking liquid, which can be either water, water and milk, or fish stock (for white fish), or a court bouillon (water, vinegar, onion, carrot, thyme, bay leaf, parsley stalks and peppercorns) for oily fish. Most kinds of fish can be cooked in this way and should be poached gently for 5–8 minutes, depending on the thickness of the fish.

Whole fish are covered with a cold liquid and brought to the boil, then cooked just below simmering point. Cut fish are usually placed in the liquid when it is at simmering point then cooked just below simmering point. The resulting liquid is ideal for use in sauces and soups.

When poaching smoked fish, place in cold, unsalted water and bring to simmering point, then lower the temperature slightly. This liquid will be salty and may not be suitable for use in stocks and sauces.

Sous-vide

This method, where the fish is sealed in a vacuum pack and cooked in a water bath, has become a popular way to cook fish. It helps to reduce moisture loss and also allows the fish to cook with a marinade or sauce if required.

Boiling

Boiling is used mainly for shellfish and, as many shellfish are sold already cooked, this is often done at sea or soon after landing because shellfish can deteriorate quickly.

Shellfish are often boiled from live and include: lobsters, crabs, oysters, langoustines, crayfish, clams, cockles, mussels, prawns and shrimps.

Roasting

Roast fish frequently appears on restaurant menus but, because fish is much more delicate than meat, only whole fish or larger, firmer cuts are suitable for roasting and care must be taken not to overcook. The fish may be brushed with oil or clarified butter before cooking and may be raised a little from the base of the pan using vegetables. More usually the fish is placed skin down in the hot cooking pan to add colour and texture, or the skin is seared in hot oil first then cooked skin side up. The fish is usually basted with the pan juices as it cooks.

When the fish is cooked and removed, the tray can be deglazed with a suitable wine (usually a dry white) and fish stock to form the base of an accompanying sauce.

Fish can also be coated in a light crust of breadcrumbs mixed with a good oil, butter, lemon juice, freshly chopped herbs (such as parsley, tarragon, chervil or rosemary), a duxelle-based mixture or a light coating of creamed horseradish.

The cooked fish may be served with a sauce or salsa, or placed on a bed of creamed or flavoured mashed potato with a compound butter sauce and quarters of lemon.

Baking

Many fish (whole, portioned or filleted) may be oven-baked. To retain their natural moisture it is necessary to protect the fish from direct heat and this may be done by coating. Prepared fish dishes, such as fish pies and en croute items, are also finished by baking.

There are various ways of preparing fish for baking:
- whole fish need to be scaled, gutted and washed, then may be stuffed with items such as a duxelle-based mixture, flavoured breadcrumbs, fish mousses, herbs or vegetables, such as onion or fennel
- wrapped in pastry (puff or filo)
- coated with a crumb mixture
- completely covered with a thick coating of dampened sea salt, which is removed before serving
- topping or finishing a prepared dish such as a fish pie or seafood with puff pastry, mashed potato or a sauce.

For a whole fish or cuts of fish proceed as follows:
1 Depending on the size and shape of the fish, 100 to 150g thick portions can be cut, leaving the skin on (this helps to retain the natural moisture of the fish).
2 Place the prepared portions in a greased ovenproof dish, brush with oil and bake slowly, skin side up (this may be seared in hot oil first); alternatively, place skin side down in a hot pan to sear it.
3 Add herbs such as parsley, rosemary or thyme, and finely sliced vegetables such as mushrooms, onions, shallots.
4 The fish can then be served, for example on a bed of creamy or flavoured mashed potato with a suitable sauce, a compound butter or a salsa.

Steaming

Small whole fish, fish cuts or fillets are good cooked in this way. Preparation is usually simple, with the fish just being seasoned then placed in a steamer tray lined with greaseproof paper or in a small steamer over simmering water covered with a lid. Cook for 10 to 15 minutes, depending on the thickness of the fish or the fillets.

Steaming can also be done by putting the food between two plates and placing the plates over a pan of simmering water.

Fish is prepared as for poaching. Any fish that can be poached or boiled may also be cooked by steaming. This method has a number of advantages:
- it is an easy method of cooking
- because it is quick, it conserves flavour, colour and nutrients
- it is suitable for large-scale cookery.

Any cooking liquor from the steamed fish may be strained off, reduced and incorporated into a sauce. Preparation can also include adding finely cut ingredients (such as ginger, spring onions, garlic, mushrooms and soft herbs), lemon juice and dry white wine, either to the fish on the steamer dish before cooking or when the fish is served.

Braising and stewing

These tend to be less popular methods for cooking fish but generally whole fish or larger cuts of fish can be braised in a closed container covering or half covering the fish with a suitable liquid (such as those used for poaching). Vegetables such as onion, shallot and fennel may be added along with herbs, spices, lemon or lime.

Stewing of fish may be similar to braising but in many countries there are traditional fish stews using a variety of fish and shellfish along with onions, shallots, tomatoes, garlic and a variety of other ingredients. Examples of these would be bouillabaisse from France, cataplana from Portugal, the Italian-American dish cioppino, and moqueca from Brazil.

Table 9.2 gives examples of some of the 200-plus fish types that are available, divided into oily and white varieties. It also shows which methods of cookery are suitable for each fish.

Table 9.2 Examples of fish types available and suitable cooking methods

	Baking	Boiling	Deep frying	Grilling	Poaching	Roasting	Shallow (pan) frying	Steaming	Stir-frying
Oily fish									
Barracuda				✔			✔		
Dorade (red sea bream)	✔			✔			✔		✔
Emperor bream	✔			✔			✔		
Herring				✔			✔		
Mackerel	✔			✔	✔				
Marlin	✔			✔	✔		✔		
Monkfish	✔					✔	✔		✔
Red mullet	✔			✔		✔	✔		
Red snapper	✔			✔			✔		
Salmon	✔	✔		✔	✔	✔	✔	✔	✔
Sardines				✔			✔		
Trout	✔			✔			✔		
Tuna				✔	✔		✔		✔
Whitebait			✔						
White fish									
Cod	✔	✔	✔	✔	✔	✔	✔	✔	
Coley		✔	✔	✔			✔		
Dover sole			✔	✔	✔		✔		
Grouper				✔		✔	✔		
Haddock	✔		✔	✔	✔		✔		
Hake	✔			✔	✔		✔		
Halibut	✔			✔	✔	✔	✔	✔	✔
Huss			✔	✔	✔		✔		
John Dory	✔				✔		✔		
Lemon sole	✔		✔	✔	✔		✔		
Plaice	✔		✔	✔			✔		
Pollock	✔	✔		✔	✔		✔	✔	
Sea bass	✔			✔	✔		✔	✔	
Shark	✔			✔	✔		✔		✔
Skate		✔	✔		✔		✔		
Swordfish	✔			✔			✔		
Turbot	✔	✔	✔	✔	✔	✔	✔		✔

Healthy eating options when preparing and cooking fish (and shellfish)

Fish is a naturally healthy food because it is a high protein food that is low in fat; in fact it is as good a source of protein as meat. Oily fish (sardines, mackerel, herring, salmon, sardines) contain the fat-soluble vitamins A and D in their flesh as well as omega-3 fatty acids (the unsaturated fatty acids that are essential for good health). It is recommended that we eat more oily fish. Owing to its fat content, oily fish is not as easily digestible as white fish, however.

The flesh of white fish does not contain any fat (and vitamins A and D are only present in the liver, which is why it is used in cod liver or halibut liver oil).

If the small bones in sardines, whitebait and canned salmon are eaten they provide calcium and phosphorus.

The preparation and cooking methods selected can change the nutritional content of a fish dish however. For example, by taking white fish and seasoning it, coating it in batter and deep frying it, you have increased the salt, carbohydrate and fat content significantly.

Healthy options when preparing and cooking fish include:
- Do not add salt in preparation, cooking and finishing.
- Use low-fat cooking options such as steaming, poaching and grilling.
- Reduce fat and salt content in coatings and marinades.
- Use oils and butter sparingly when grilling or baking fish.
- Avoid high-fat, salty sauces and adding extra butter before serving.

Shellfish

Shellfish, such as lobsters and crabs, are all invertebrates, which means that they do not have an internal skeleton. They are split into two main groups:
- **Molluscs** have either an external hinged double shell (for example, scallops and mussels) or a single spiral shell (for example, winkles and whelks), or have soft bodies with an internal shell, such as squid and octopus (these are called cephalopods).
- **Crustaceans** have tough outer shells that act like armour, and also have flexible joints to allow quick movement (for example, crab and lobster).

Choosing and buying shellfish

Shellfish are prized for their tender, fine-textured flesh, which can be prepared in a variety of ways. They are prone to rapid spoilage however, because they contain quantities of certain proteins (amino acids) that encourage bacterial growth.

To ensure freshness and best flavour it may be preferable to choose live shellfish and cook them yourself. This is increasingly possible with modern transportation, especially air freight, which allows shellfish to be transported around the world quickly.

Consider the following points when choosing shellfish:
- The shells should not be cracked or broken.
- The shells of mussels and oysters should be tightly shut; open shells that do not close when tapped sharply should be discarded.
- Lobsters, crabs and prawns should have a good colour and be heavy for their size.
- Lobsters and crabs should have all their limbs in place.

Storing shellfish

All shellfish start to spoil as soon as they have been removed from their natural environment, therefore the longer shellfish are stored the more they will deteriorate due to the bacteria present (see the guidelines on choosing and buying, above). Best practice would be to cook immediately and store as for cooked fish. Shellfish can be blanched quickly to remove the shell and membrane (especially in lobsters), but they will still need to be stored as a raw product as they will require further cooking.

Bear in mind the following quality, purchasing and storage points:
- Where possible, shellfish should be purchased live to ensure freshness.
- Shellfish should be kept in suitable containers, covered with cling film or damp cloths, and stored in a refrigerator.
- Shellfish should be cooked as soon as possible after purchasing.

Cooking shellfish

The flesh of fish and shellfish is different to meat and, as a consequence, their muscle make-up is very different too, making the connective tissue very fragile, the muscle

Table 9.3 Seasonality of shellfish

Key: ● = Available, ○ = At best

	JAN	FEB	MAR	APR	MAY	JUN	JUL	AUG	SEP	OCT	NOV	DEC
Crab (brown cock)	○	○	○	○	●	●	●	●	●	●		
Crab (spider)	●	●	●	●	○	○	○	○	○	○	●	●
Crab (brown hen)	○	○	●	●	●	●	○	○	○	●	●	●
Clams	●	●	●	●	●	●	●	●	●	●	●	
Cockles	●	●	●	●	●	●	●	●	●	●	●	
Crayfish (signal)				●	●	●	●	●	●	●		
Lobster	○	○	●	●	●	●	●	●	●	●	●	
Langoustines			●	●	●	●	●	●	●	●		
Mussels	●	●	●	●	●	●	●	●	○	○	○	○
Oysters (rock)	○	○	○	○	●	●	●	●	○	○	○	○
Oysters (native)	○	○	○	○					●	●	●	●
Prawns							●	●	●	●	●	○
Scallops	○	○	○	○	○	●	●	●	○	○	○	●

Key:

Available	●
At best	○

fibres shorter and the fat content relatively low. Generally, care should be taken when cooking and shellfish should be cooked as little as possible, to the point that the protein in the muscle groups just coagulates. Beyond this point the flesh tends to dry out, leading to toughening and a dry texture. Shellfish are known for their dramatic colour change when being cooked, from blue/grey to a vibrant orange colour. This is because they contain red and yellow pigments called carotenoids, bound to molecules of protein. Once heat is applied, the bonds are broken and the bright colour appears.

Shrimps and prawns

These are often bought cooked, either in the shells or peeled. Smell is a good guide to freshness. Shrimps and prawns can be used for garnishes, decorating fish dishes, cocktails, sauces, salads, hors d'oeuvres, omelettes, and snack and savoury dishes. They can also be used for a variety of hot dishes, including stir-fries, risotto and curries. Potted shrimps are also a popular dish. Freshly cooked prawns in their shells may also be served cold accompanied by a mayonnaise-based sauce, such as garlic mayonnaise. **King prawns** are a larger variety that can also be used in any of the above ways.

Raw and cooked shrimps and prawns are prepared by having the head, carapace (upper shell), legs, tail section and the dark intestinal vein running down the back removed.

Scampi, crayfish and Dublin Bay prawns

Scampi, crayfish and Dublin Bay prawns are also known as Norway lobster or langoustine, and are sold fresh, frozen, raw or cooked. Their tails are prepared like shrimps and they are used in a variety of ways: salads, rice dishes, stir-fries, deep-fried, poached and served with a number of different sauces. They are also used as garnishes for hot and cold fish dishes.

Freshwater crayfish are also known as *écrevisse*. These are small freshwater crustaceans with claws, found in lakes and lowland streams. They are prepared and cooked like shrimps and prawns, and used in many dishes, including soup. They are often used whole to garnish hot and cold fish dishes.

▲ Remove the cord from each langoustine before cooking

Lobster

Although there many different lobster varieties around the world, the two main ones are the American lobster, which tends to be the largest, and the European lobster, which is usually smaller. Their preferred habitat is hard surfaces or crevices on the sea bed at depths of around 20 to 60 metres. Lobsters grow very slowly and can live up to 100 years. As they grow they shed their hard shell and form another one. Maturity is reached at about five years old and at a length of 18 to 20 cm. They can weigh up to 9 kg but are usually around 2 to 3 kg. They have ten limbs (decapods), two of which are the two large front claws (one is used for cutting and one for crushing).

Purchasing points

Purchase alive, with both claws attached, to ensure freshness.
- Lobsters should be heavy in proportion to their size.
- The coral of the hen lobster is necessary to give the required colour for certain soups, sauces and lobster dishes.

- Hen lobsters are distinguished from cock lobsters by their broader tails.

Cooking lobsters

1 Wash then plunge the lobsters into a pan of boiling salted water containing 60 ml vinegar to 1 litre of water.
2 Cover with a lid, reboil, then allow to simmer for 15 to 20 minutes according to size.
3 Overcooking can cause the tail flesh to toughen and the claw meat to become hard and fibrous.
4 Allow to cool in the cooking liquid when possible.

Some advice for the humane killing of lobsters is to place them in the freezer for one hour before cooking to numb them. Some chefs prefer to kill the lobster instantly by plunging the tip of a sharp knife straight down and through the lobster, right behind the eyes. There is also a device called the Crustastun, which uses an electric current to stun and painlessly kill shellfish such as lobsters, crabs and langoustines before cooking. The machine can make a large crustacean unconscious in less than 0.3 seconds and kill it in five to ten.

Cleaning a cooked lobster

1 Remove the claws and the pincers from the claws.
2 Crack the claws and joints, and remove the meat.
3 Cut the lobster in half by inserting the point of a large knife 2 cm above the tail on the natural central line.
4 Cut through the tail firmly.
5 Turn the lobster around and cut through the upper shell (carapace).
6 Remove the halves of the sac (which contains grit) from each half. This is situated at the top, near the head.
7 Using a small knife, remove the intestinal trace from the tail and wash if necessary.

Preparing a cooked lobster

Remove the claws and legs

Cut the lobster in half

Remove the meat from the cleaned lobster

Uses

Lobsters are served cold in cocktails, lobster mayonnaise, hors d'oeuvres, salads, sandwiches and in halves on cold buffets. They are used hot in soups, sauces, rice dishes, stir-fry dishes and in numerous ways served in the half-shell with various sauces. They are also used to garnish fish dishes.

Crawfish

These are sometimes referred to as 'spiny lobsters' but, unlike lobsters, they have no claws and their meat is solely in the tail. Crawfish vary considerably in size from 1 to 3 kg; they are cooked as for lobsters and the tail meat can be used in any of the lobster recipes. Because of their impressive appearance whole dressed crawfish are sometimes used on special cold buffets. They are very expensive and are also available frozen.

Squid

Squid is a cephalopod; they are traditionally popular in Mediterranean cuisine but have increased in popularity through the rest of Europe. It is available all year round fresh or frozen. Squid vary in size, from 5 to 7 cm in length, to up to 25 cm. The ink sac and transparent cartilage need to be removed and the main body is often cut into rings for cooking. Squid needs to be cooked very quickly or by a slow moist method otherwise it can be tough.

1 Pull the head away from the body, together with the innards.

2 Taking care not to break the ink bag, remove the long transparent blade of cartilage (the backbone or quill).

3 Cut the tentacles just below the eye and remove the small round cartilage at the base of the tentacles.

4 Scrape or peel off the reddish membrane that covers the pouch, rub with salt and wash under cold water.

5 Discard the head, innards and pieces of cartilage. Cut up the squid as required.

Crab

There are an estimated 4,000 species of edible of crab. The meat from crab is very different in the claws and the main body. Crab claws have a sweet, dense white meat similar to lobster while the flesh from under the main body shell is soft, rich and brown. Male crabs tend to have larger claws and more white meat.

European brown crabs, the most widely available across Europe and available year-round, reach 20 to 25 cm across and have large front claws with dark pincers, a red or brown shell and red legs.

Atlantic blue crabs have a blue/brown shell and tend to be smaller than European brown crabs at 10 to 15 cm.

Dungeness crabs can reach up to 20 cm and have plenty of good white, dense meat in the claws. The meat in the shell tends to be different from other crabs and is pale grey/green in colour. It is popular in the west of the United States.

Spider crabs are popular in France and Spain, and do look like a big spider. The meat has a good flavour but it has no large claws (so no white claw meat).

Purchasing points
- Buy alive where possible to ensure freshness.
- Ensure that both claws are attached.
- Crabs should be heavy in relation to size.

Cooking
Cook as for lobsters (see above).

Uses
Crab meat can be served simply with bread and salad, used cold for hors d'oeuvres, cocktails, salads, sandwiches and dressed crab. Used hot, it can be covered with a suitable sauce and served with rice, in *bouchées* or pancakes, or made into crab fishcakes.

Cockles

Cockles are enclosed in small, attractive, cream-coloured shells. As they live in sand it is essential to purge them by washing well under cold running water and leaving them in cold salted water (changed frequently) until no traces of sand remain.

Cockles can be cooked either by steaming, boiling in unsalted water, on a preheated griddle, or as for any mussel recipe. They should be cooked only until the shells open.

They can be used in soups, sauces, salads, stir-fries and rice dishes, and as garnish for fish dishes.

Mussels

Mussels are bivalves, which means they have a double outer shell hinged at the top. Mussels can be from either sea or freshwater (rivers and lakes) but the sea varieties are by far the most widely used. Mussels are now extensively farmed, cultivated on wooden frames in the sea, producing tender, delicately flavoured plump flesh. They are produced off British coasts and also imported from France, Holland and Belgium. French mussels are small; Dutch and Belgian mussels are plumper. The production of mussels is considered to be ecologically sound, which means that the species is not threatened or damaging to the environment.

Purchasing points
- The shells must be tightly closed, indicating the mussels are alive.
- They should be of a good size.
- There should not be an excessive number of barnacles attached.
- They should smell fresh.

Storage
Mussels should be kept in containers, covered with damp cloths or cling film, and stored in a refrigerator. Do not store mussels in water.

Cooking
1. Scrape the shells to remove any barnacles, etc. Remove the byssus threads ('beards').
2. Wash well in several changes of water and drain in a colander.
3. Prepare a cooking liquid of shallots, butter, garlic and herbs along with fish stock.
4. Cook the mussels in the liquid in a large pan with a tightly fitting lid until they open, which usually takes 4 to 5 minutes. Remove the mussels and check they have all opened; throw away any that are still closed.
5. Strain the liquid, whisk in some cream and serve with the mussels still in their shells.

Alternatively, place 25 g chopped shallot or onion for each litre of mussels into a thick-bottomed pan with a tight-fitting lid. Add the mussels, cover with the lid and cook on a fierce heat for 4 to 5 minutes until the shells open completely. Remove the mussels from their shells. Retain the carefully strained liquid to make a sauce to serve with the mussels.

Uses
Mussels can be used for soups, sauces and salads, and cooked in a wide variety of hot dishes.

Scallops

Scallops are bivalves with a fan-shaped shell. They vary in size from 15 cm for great scallops, around 8 cm for bay scallops, and to queen scallops that are the size of cockles. Inside is the round white flesh and the orange coral (the roe), which is often discarded. Scallops are popular and the prices tend to remain high, especially for hand-dived scallops rather than those caught by a dredging trawler. They are prepared by prising the two halves of the shell apart and removing the white flesh and the orange roe if required.

Scallops in their shells should be covered with damp cloths and kept in a refrigerated cold room or fish refrigerator.

Cooking

Scallops should only be cooked lightly, otherwise they shrink and toughen.

- Poach gently for two to three minutes in fish stock or dry white wine with a little onion, carrot, thyme, bay leaf and parsley. Serve with a suitable sauce (for example white wine or mornay).
- Lightly fry on both sides for a few seconds in butter or oil in a very hot pan (if the scallops are very thick they can be cut in half sideways) and serve with a suitable garnish (sliced wild or cultivated mushrooms, or a fine brunoise of vegetables and tomato) and a liquid that need not be thickened (white wine and fish stock, or a cream- or butter-mounted sauce). Fried scallops can also be served hot on a plate of salad leaves.
- Deep-fry, either egg and crumbed or passed through a light batter and served with segments of lemon and a suitable sauce.
- Wrap in thin streaky bacon and place on skewers for grilling or barbecuing.

Whelks

The common whelk is familiar around the coast of Britain. It is actually a gastropod, which means it has a large, strong flat foot to move around on. Whelks are also equipped with a siphon, which is used for breathing and feeling around for food.

British winkles

The main types of British winkle, which can be readily identified on rocky shores, are:

- small periwinkle: approximately 4 mm
- rough periwinkle: at least four different subspecies, with the largest reaching 30 mm
- flat periwinkle.

Video: buying shellfish http:// bit.ly/1DCYHek

Oysters

Oysters are highly regarded saltwater bivalves found near the bottom of the sea; the upper shell (valve) is flattish and attached by a ligament hinge to the lower, bowl-shaped shell. A number of different species available, including native, flat or rock oysters, with Colchester and Whitstable being significant oyster areas in the UK. Traditionally oysters are eaten raw so it is essential that they are very fresh and cleaned/purged well. Preparation usually involves prising the two halves of the shell apart with a small, pointed oyster knife. The oysters may then be served with lemon and other condiments.

Oysters are high in protein and low in fat; they are rich in zinc and contain many other nutrients such as calcium, iron, copper, iodine, magnesium and selenium.

Purchasing points

They should smell fresh and the shells should be clean, bright and unbroken. The shells should be tightly closed or should close when tapped.

Storage

Oysters should be stored at a low temperature (1 °C to 2 °C). Unopened live oysters can be kept in the fish refrigerator covered with wet cloths or cling film for two to three days; discard any that open. Do not store in an airtight container or under fresh water as this will cause them to die. Shucked oysters (ones that have been removed from their shells) can be kept refrigerated in a sealed container for four to five days.

Ready prepared shellfish

Shellfish are increasingly available ready prepared in a number of ways, such as breadcrumbed and frozen prawns and scampi, or shellfish wrapped in puff or filo pastry, mussels, cooked and vacuum packed in a sauce, crab cakes, sushi and many more. Shellfish are great favourite for canapés and many of these are now available ready prepared.

Test yourself

1 What are the differences between oily and white fish? Give three examples of each.
2 At what temperatures should a) fresh fish and b) frozen fish be stored?
3 How would you defrost fish that has been frozen?
4 Describe how you would skin a Dover sole.
5 What are the quality points you would look for in a delivery of fresh fish? If you thought there were problems with the quality, what would you do?
6 If you had been asked to fillet and skin five whole plaice, what equipment would you get ready?
7 List four cooking methods that could be used for white fish and four for oily fish.
8 List five types of fish suitable for deep frying.
9 Describe the following cuts of fish and suggest a method for cooking each of them:
   a délice
   b tronçon
   c darne
   d goujon.
10 Describe how you would prepare mussels for cooking.
11 How would you prepare and cook scallops?
12 What are the quality points you would look for with lobsters? How would you prepare them?

Grilled fish recipes

1 Grilled fillets of sole, plaice or haddock

1 Remove the black skin from sole and plaice. Wash the fillets and dry them well.

2 Pass through flour, shake off surplus and brush with oil.

3 Place on hot grill bars, a griddle or a greased baking sheet if grilling under a salamander. Brush occasionally with oil. Turn the fish carefully and grill on both sides. Do not overcook.

Serve with lemon slices with the rind removed.

Professional tip

Oil the grill bars well, so that the fish does not stick.

Energy	Cals	Fat	Sat fat	Carb	Sugar	Protein	Fibre	Sodium
802 kJ	191 kcal	7.8g	1.0g	3.9g	0.1g	26.6g	0.2g	0.1g

2 Grilled tuna, rocket and fennel salad

Energy	Cals	Fat	Sat fat	Carb	Sugar	Protein	Fibre	Sodium
1,619 kJ	388 kcal	24.3g	4.3g	4.2g	3.7g	38.4g	4.5g	0.6g

Ingredient	4 portions	10 portions
For the salad		
Rocket salad, washed and picked	400 g	1 kg
Fennel bulb	1	2
Green beans, cooked and refreshed	200 g	500 g
Baby spinach	100 g	250 g
Coriander, picked	50 g	125 g
For the dressing		
Dijon mustard	1 tsp	3 tsp
Cider vinegar	1 tsp	3 tsp
Olive oil	3 tbsp	7 tbsp
Sunflower oil	3 tbsp	7 tbsp
Lemon juice	1 tsp	2 tsp
Lime juice	1 tsp	2 tsp
Seasoning		
For the fish		
Tuna steaks (150 g, no skin or blood line)	4	10
Olive oil	50 ml	125 ml
Sea salt, fresh milled black pepper		
Lemon	1	2

For the salad:

1 Ensure all the leaves are well washed and picked.

2 Cut the root and top off the fennel, leaving the main bulb.

3 Thinly slice the fennel on a mandolin. Place in cold water with plenty of ice (this will make the fennel very crisp and curly, giving the salad some height).

4 Place all the salad ingredients into a large bowl ready to dress with the dressing.

For the dressing:

1 Place the mustard and vinegar in a bowl then slowly whisk in the oil.

2 To finish, adjust the taste with the lemon juice, lime juice and seasoning.

3 To dress, mix the salad and dressing well, check the seasoning and divide the salad equally between four/ten plates.

For the tuna:

1 Before you start to cook the tuna, ensure that the salad is dressed and on the serving plate.

2 Lightly brush the tuna steaks with the oil and season.

3 Ensure the grill is hot. Place two steaks on at a time (this is manageable as the tuna cooks very quickly).

4 Turn after 30 seconds and cook until the centre half of the tuna is still pink.

5 Remove and place on the salad. Repeat for the other steaks. Serve with a wedge of lemon.

Note

This recipe lends itself well to other fish such as salmon, sea bass, turbot, trout, hake and monkfish.

3 Whole grilled mackerel with tomatoes, basil and shaved fennel

Energy	Cals	Fat	Sat fat	Carb	Sugar	Protein	Fibre	Sodium
2,067 kJ	497 kcal	39.4g	7.8g	3.9g	3.8g	32.4g	2.2g	0.2g

Based on sardines rather than mackerel.

Ingredient	4 portions	10 portions
For the mackerel		
Medium mackerel, head and guts removed	4	10
Olive oil	50 ml	125 ml
Freshly milled pepper		
For the salad		
Olive oil	50 ml	125 ml
Baby plum tomatoes, cut in half	400 g	1 kg
Fennel bulb, shaved on a mandolin	1	2
Baby spinach	100 g	250 g
Lemon, juice of	1	2
Basil leaves, torn	6	15

For the mackerel:

1 Ensure that the fish is clean. Score the flesh of each fish in the deepest part (near the head), about 3 mm into the fish but not through to the bone. (This scoring is called *ciseler* – it helps the fish to cook more evenly and can be used with most methods of cooking whole fish.)

2 Brush with the oil and place on a moderate grill. (Wrap the tail in foil to ensure that it doesn't burn.)

3 Turn the fish over to cook the other side, removing the foil. At this point, start making the salad.

4 Once the fish is cooked, dress the plates with the salad and lay the fish on top. Drizzle the pan juices over and around the fish and serve.

For the salad:

1 Heat the oil in a pan and add the tomatoes and fennel. Cook on a hot heat.

2 Remove from the heat, stir in the spinach and allow it to wilt.

3 Season with salt, pepper and a dash of lemon juice. Finish with basil leaves.

4 Whole sole grilled with traditional accompaniments

1 Ensure the fish is clean of roe, scales and skin.

2 Place on a buttered grilling tray and rub soft butter into the flesh.

3 Season and place under the grill.

4 When the butter starts to brown slightly, remove from the grill and turn the fish over carefully, using a roasting fork or a long pallet knife.

5 With a spoon, baste the flesh of the uncooked side and continue cooking. The tail end will cook faster than the head end – the tail should therefore be cooked in the less-hot area towards the front of the grill.

6 To check whether the fish is done, place your thumb just behind the gill area and you should feel the flesh ease away from the bone.

7 Finish with parsley butter and a wedge of lemon.

Ingredient	4 portions	10 portions
Whole sole, skin removed	4	10
Butter for grilling	200 g	500 g
Seasoning		
Parsley butter	100 g	250 g
Lemons, peeled and cut into wedges	1	3

Energy	Cals	Fat	Sat fat	Carb	Sugar	Protein	Fibre	Sodium
3,058 kJ	740 kcal	65.4 g	39.1 g	1.0 g	0.9 g	36.9 g	0.3 g	0.7 g

Professional tip

Remember that sole is a delicate fish, so be careful not to overcook it. This is a classic recipe for slip, Dover and lemon sole – there is no need to modernise it.

5 Sardines with tapenade

Ingredient	4 portions	10 portions
Sardines	8–12	20–30
For the tapenade		
Kalamata olives	20	50
Capers	1 tbsp	2½ tbsp
Lemon juice	1 tsp	2½ tsp
Olive oil	2 tsp	5 tsp
Anchovy paste (optional)	½ tsp	1¼ tsp
Freshly ground black pepper		

Energy	Cals	Fat	Sat fat	Carb	Sugar	Protein	Fibre	Sodium
3,167 kJ	757 kcal	44.0g	12.4g	0.0g	0.0g	90.5g	0.8g	1.0g

Using additional olives in place of capers.

1 Finely chop the olives and capers. Add the lemon juice, olive oil, anchovy paste and black pepper. Mix well.

2 Allow 2–3 sardines per portion. Clean the sardines and grill them on both sides, either on an open flame grill or under the salamander.

3 When cooked, smear the tapenade on top. The tapenade can be heated slightly before spreading.

Variation

A little chopped basil and a crushed chopped clove of garlic may also be added to the tapenade.

Cleaned sardines

Grilled sardines, before the tapenade is added

6 Poached salmon

Depending on the size of the salmon, either a whole or half a darne would be served as a portion.

See page 606 for a court bouillon recipe.

1 Place the prepared and washed darnes of salmon in a court bouillon, just below simmering, for approximately 5 minutes.

2 Drain well and carefully remove the centre bone and outer skin. Ensure that the fish is cleaned of any cooked blood.

Serve with a suitable sauce (e.g. hollandaise or pesto) or melted herb butter, and thinly sliced cucumber.

Energy	Cals	Fat	Sat fat	Carb	Sugar	Protein	Fibre	Sodium
1,284 kJ	309 kcal	20.6 g	5.5 g	0.3 g	0.3 g	30.4 g	0.1 g	0.1 g

7 Poached smoked haddock

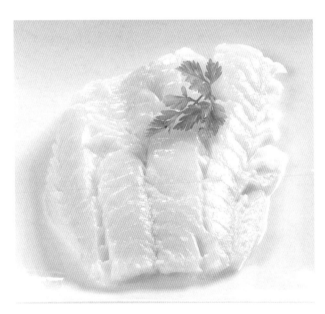

Ingredient	4 portions	10 portions
Smoked haddock fillets	400–600 g	1–1.5 kg
Milk and water, mixed		

This is a popular breakfast dish and is also served as a lunch and a snack dish.

1 Cut fillets into even portions, place into a shallow pan and just cover with half milk and water.

2 Poach gently for a few minutes until cooked.

3 Drain well and serve.

Variation
● When cooked, garnish with slices of peeled tomato or tomato concassé, lightly coat with cream, flash under the salamander and serve.
● Top with a poached egg.
● When cooked, lightly coat with Welsh rarebit mixture, brown under the salamander and garnish with peeled slices of tomato or tomato concassé.

Energy	Cals	Fat	Sat fat	Carb	Sugar	Protein	Fibre	Sodium
702 kJ	168 kcal	7.6 g	4.6 g	1.4 g	1.4 g	23.4 g	0.0 g	1.0 g

For a 125 g portion.

8 Poached turbot, brill, halibut or cod (on the bone)

1 Place the prepared fish into a shallow pan of simmering, lightly salted water containing lemon juice (the citric acid helps to make the flesh firm and white and gives a gentle flavour).

2 Allow to poach gently. The cooking time depends on the thickness of the fish. Do not overcook.

3 Remove with a fish slice, remove the skin, drain and serve.

4 Garnish with picked parsley and plain boiled potatoes, and serve with a suitable sauce (e.g. hollandaise, herb butter, shrimp or mushroom).

Energy	Cals	Fat	Sat fat	Carb	Sugar	Protein	Fibre	Sodium
1,412 kJ	353 kcal	9.5g	2.5g	0.3g	0.3g	62.0g	0.0g	0.2g

Place the fish into the gently simmering liquid

Allow the fish to poach

Lift out the fish and remove any black skin

9 Délice of flat white fish Dugléré

Ingredient	4 portions	10 portions
Fillets of flat white fish (e.g. sole, plaice)	400–600 g	1–1.5 kg
Fish stock for poaching	approx. 200 ml	approx. 500 ml
For the sauce		
Butter	25 g	60 g
Shallots, finely chopped	20 g	50 g
Fish stock	60 ml	150 ml
Dry white wine	60 ml	150 ml
Whipping cream	200 ml	500 ml
Butter, sliced and kept cold on ice	50 g	125 g
Tomatoes, skinned and neatly diced (concassé)	2	5
Parsley, chopped finely	10 g	20 g

Energy	Cals	Fat	Sat fat	Carb	Sugar	Protein	Fibre	Sodium
1974 kJ	475 kcal	38.0g	23.0g	3.5g	3.2g	28.0g	0.7g	0.6g

Using 150 g plaice.

1 Skin the fish, trim and wash.

2 Fold the fillets neatly, ensuring the skinned side is facing inwards (délice).

3 Using a wide, shallow pan, poach the délice gently in fish stock for 4–6 minutes (depending on the thickness of the fillet).

4 To make the sauce, sweat the finely chopped shallots with the butter in a saucepan, until translucent.

5 Add the fish stock and reduce by one-third.

6 Add the dry white wine and reduce again by half.

7 Add the whipping cream and reduce by one-third, until the cream starts to thicken the sauce to a coating consistency.

8 Add the cold, sliced butter and ripple the sauce over the butter until the butter has emulsified into the sauce (monté). Check the seasoning and adjust accordingly. Do not allow the sauce to reboil as the butter will split and the sauce will become greasy.

9 Add the neatly cut tomato concassé and finely chopped parsley to the sauce.

10 To serve, drain the fish well and place neatly on a plate; carefully coat each délice with the sauce and serve.

Fold each fillet into a délice

Sweat the finely chopped shallots

Coat each délice with sauce

10 Fillets of fish in white wine sauce (*filets de poisson vin blanc*)

Ingredient	4 portions	10 portions
Fillets of white fish (100–150 g)	4	10
Butter, for dish and greaseproof paper		
Shallots, finely chopped and sweated	10 g	25 g
Fish stock	60 ml	150 ml
Dry white wine	60 ml	150 ml
Lemon, juice of	¼	½
Fish velouté	250 ml	625 ml
Butter	50 g	125 g
Cream, lightly whipped	2 tbsp	5 tbsp

Energy	Cals	Fat	Sat fat	Carb	Sugar	Protein	Fibre
1,421 kJ	342 kcal	24.0 g	12.8 g	5.8 g	0.9 g	25.9 g	0.2 g

1 Skin and fillet the fish, trim and wash.
2 Butter and season an earthenware dish.
3 Sprinkle with the sweated chopped shallots and add the fillets of fish.
4 Season, add the fish stock, wine and lemon juice.
5 Cover with buttered greaseproof paper.
6 Poach in a moderate oven at 150–200 °C for 7–10 minutes.
7 Drain the fish well; dress neatly on a flat dish or clean earthenware dish.
8 Bring the cooking liquor to the boil with the velouté.
9 Correct the seasoning and consistency and pass through double muslin or a fine strainer.
10 Mix in the butter then, finally, add the cream.
11 Coat the fillets with the sauce. Garnish with flat parsley or *fleurons* (puff paste crescents).

Professional tip

In this recipe, the shallots should be sweated before use; however, if they are very finely chopped, they could be added raw.

Healthy eating tips
● Keep the added salt to a minimum.
● Reduce the amount of butter and cream added to finish the sauce.
● Less sauce could be added, plus a large portion of potatoes and vegetables.

Variation

Add to the fish before cooking:
● fish *bonne-femme:* 100 g thinly sliced white button mushrooms and chopped parsley
● fish *bréval:* as for *bonne-femme* plus 100 g diced, peeled and deseeded tomatoes.

11 Fillets of fish mornay (*filets de poisson mornay*)

1 Prepare the fillets; place in a buttered, seasoned earthenware dish or shallow pan, such as a sauté pan.

2 Add the fish stock, cover with buttered paper.

3 Cook in a moderate oven at 150–200 °C for approximately 5–10 minutes.

4 Drain the fish well, place in a clean earthenware or flat dish.

5 Bring the béchamel to the boil, add the reduced cooking liquor, whisk in the egg yolk and remove from the heat. Add half of the cheese and correct the consistency. Do not reboil, otherwise the egg will curdle.

6 Correct the seasoning and pass through a fine strainer.

7 Mix in the butter and cream; check the consistency.

8 Mask the fish with the sauce, sprinkle with the remaining grated cheese and gratinate under the salamander.

Ingredient	4 portions	10 portions
White fish fillets	500–600 g	1.5 kg
Butter, for dish and greaseproof paper		
Fish stock	125 ml	300 ml
Béchamel sauce	250 ml	625 ml
Egg yolk or sabayon	1	3
Grated cheese, preferably Gruyère or Parmesan	50 g	125 g
Salt and cayenne pepper		
Butter	25 g	60 g
Cream, lightly whipped	2 tbsp	5 tbsp

Energy	Cals	Fat	Sat fat	Carb	Sugar	Protein	Fibre
1,309 kJ	315 kcal	19.3 g	9.3 g	5.5 g	0.7 g	29.9 g	0.2 g

Healthy eating tips

- Reduce the amount of butter and cream added to finish the sauce.
- Less sauce could be served, plus a large portion of potatoes and vegetables.

Variation

Classical variations include:
- Fillets of fish Walewska – place a slice of cooked lobster on each fish fillet before coating with the sauce; after the dish is browned decorate each fillet with a slice of truffle.
- Fillets of fish Florentine – proceed as for fillets mornay, placing the cooked fish on a bed of well-drained and heated dry leaf spinach.

12 Fillets of fish Véronique

1 Skin and fillet the fish, trim and wash.

2 Butter and season an earthenware dish.

3 Sprinkle with the sweated chopped shallots and add the fillets of fish.

4 Season, add the fish stock, wine and lemon juice.

5 Cover with buttered greaseproof paper.

6 Poach in a moderate oven at 150–200 °C for 7–10 minutes.

7 Drain the fish well and retain the cooking liquor. Dress the fish neatly on a flat dish or clean earthenware dish.

8 Bring the cooking liquor to the boil with the velouté and egg yolk or sabayon.

9 Correct the seasoning and consistency, and pass through double muslin or a fine strainer.

10 Mix in the butter then, finally, add the cream.

11 Coat the fillets with the sauce. Glaze under the salamander.

12 Arrange the grapes neatly on the dish.

Ingredient	4 portions	10 portions
Fillets of white fish (100–150 g)	4	10
Butter, for dish and greaseproof paper		
Shallots, finely chopped, sweated in a little butter/oil	10 g	25 g
Fish stock	60 ml	150 ml
Dry white wine	60 ml	150 ml
Lemon, juice of	½	1
Fish velouté	250 ml	625 ml
Egg yolk or spoonful of sabayon	1	2½
Butter	50 g	125 g
Cream, lightly whipped	2 tbsp	5 tbsp
White grapes, blanched, skinned and pipped	50 g	125 g

Professional tip

Plaice and sole are very good in this dish.

Chill the grapes well before use, so that they provide a real contrast of flavour.

Healthy eating tips
● Keep the added salt to a minimum.
● Reduce the amount of butter and cream added to finish the sauce.
● Less sauce could be added plus a large portion of potatoes and vegetables.

Energy	Cals	Fat	Sat fat	Carb	Sugar	Protein	Fibre
1,077 kJ	256 kcal	19.3 g	10.7 g	6.9 g	2.1 g	11.8 g	0.4 g

13 Fish kedgeree

Ingredient	4 portions	10 portions
Fish (usually smoked haddock or fresh salmon)	400 g	1 kg
Milk for poaching		
Rice pilaff (see page 125)	200 g	500 g
Eggs, hard-boiled	2	5
Butter	50 g	125 g
Salt, pepper		
Chives, chopped	1 tsp	2 tsp
Curry sauce, to serve	250 ml	625 ml

Energy	Cals	Fat	Sat fat	Carb	Sugar	Protein	Fibre
1,974 kJ	472 kcal	28.2 g	15.3 g	29.3 g	4.7 g	25.7 g	1.2 g

Using smoked haddock.

This dish is traditionally served for breakfast, lunch or supper. The fish used should be named on the menu (e.g. salmon kedgeree).

1 Poach the fish in milk. Remove all skin and bone. Flake the fish.

2 Cook the rice pilaff. Cut the eggs into dice.

3 Combine the eggs, fish and rice and heat in the butter. Correct the seasoning and add the chives.

Serve hot with a sauceboat of curry sauce.

Healthy eating tips
- Reduce the amount of butter used to heat the rice, fish and eggs.
- Garnish with grilled tomatoes and serve with bread or toast.

Remove the skin from the poached fish

Flake the fish

Dice the hard-boiled eggs

Baked fish dishes

14 Baked cod with a herb crust

1 Place the prepared, washed and dried fish on a greased baking tray or ovenproof dish.

2 Combine the ingredients for the herb crust (the mustard, breadcrumbs, butter, margarine or oil, cheese, parsley and seasoning) and press evenly over the fish.

3 Bake in the oven at 180 °C for approximately 15–20 minutes until cooked and the crust is a light golden-brown.

Serve either with lemon quarters or a suitable salsa (see page 101) or sauce, e.g. tomato or egg.

Ingredient	4 portions	10 portions
Cod fillets, 100–150 g each	4	10
Herb mustard	1 tsp	2½ tsp
Fresh breadcrumbs	100 g	250 g
Butter, margarine or oil	100 g	250 g
Cheddar cheese, grated	100 g	250 g
Parsley, chopped	1 tsp	1 tbsp
Salt, pepper		

Professional tip

Add a little bit of beaten egg to the breadcrumb mixture; this will help bind the mixture together.

Healthy eating tips
- Use a little sunflower oil when making the herb crust.
- Cheese is salty – no added salt is needed.
- Serve with a large portion of tomato or cucumber salsa and new potatoes.

Energy	Cals	Fat	Sat fat	Carb	Sugar	Protein	Fibre
1,882 kJ	452 kcal	30.8 g	18.7 g	12.7 g	0.8 g	31.7 g	0.4 g

Using mustard powder (1 tsp) for herb mustard.

15 Baked hake with tomatoes and olives

Ingredient	4 portions	10 portions
Baby plum vine tomatoes	300 g	750 g
Olive oil	100 ml	250 ml
Cloves of garlic, unpeeled	6	15
Black olives, stoned	16	40
Hake fillets (200 g, skin on, bones removed)	4	10

Energy	Cals	Fat	Sat fat	Carb	Sugar	Protein	Fibre	Sodium
1,659 kJ	400 kcal	29.9 g	4.3 g	4.3 g	2.5 g	28.6 g	2.1 g	0.4 g

1 Preheat the oven to 175 °C.

2 Put the tomatoes in a small roasting pan, drizzle with the olive oil and add the garlic.

3 Roast for 15 minutes, then add the olives.

4 Move the mixture aside and add the hake fillets to the pan, skin side down.

5 Baste them with a little of the olive oil in the pan and bake for 8–10 minutes, depending on the thickness of the fillets, until just firm and flaking easily.

6 Remove the pan from the oven and squeeze the roasted garlic cloves out of their skins.

7 Gently mix them with the tomatoes and olives, trying not to break up the tomatoes too much.

8 Season the tomato mixture and spoon on to four plates. Place a piece of baked hake on top of each.

9 Serve with braised cabbage and mashed potato.

Note

Kalamata olives are best – they have a subtle flavour.

Cod, pollock or haddock may be used instead of hake.

16 Cod boulangère

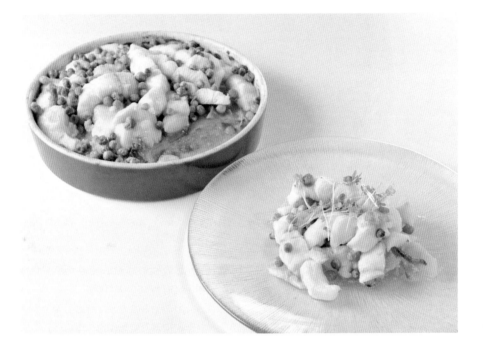

Ingredient	4 portions	10 portions
Onion	1	2
Oil	50 ml	125 ml
Sea salt, freshly milled black pepper		
Potatoes	750 g	2 kg
Thyme		
Lemon, zest and juice of	1	2
Fish stock, hot	400 ml	1 litre
Butter	100 g	250 g
Cod fillets (100 g, skinless, boneless)	4	10
Fresh peas	300 g	750 g
Chives, chopped		

Energy	Cals	Fat	Sat fat	Carb	Sugar	Protein	Fibre	Sodium
2,650 kJ	636 kcal	35.7 g	15.1 g	44.1 g	5.4 g	37.3 g	8.7 g	0.6 g

1 Peel the onions and slice them approximately 3 mm thick.

2 Heat the oil in a thick-bottomed pan, place in the onions and cook slowly until a light golden-brown. (Do not fast-fry the onions – this is a caramelisation process to reveal their natural sugars.)

3 Meanwhile, preheat the oven to 190 °C.

4 Grease a shallow baking tin with a little butter and season well with freshly milled black pepper and sea salt.

5 Peel the potatoes and slice them finely (3 mm thick).

6 Once the onions are softened, arrange the potato and onion in alternate layers on the bottom of the baking dish, also adding the thyme throughout.

7 Mix the lemon juice and zest with the hot fish stock and pour over the potatoes and onion.

8 Randomly place knobs of butter over the top of the potatoes.

9 Cover the baking dish with foil and bake in the oven for 55 minutes.

10 While the potatoes are cooking, prepare the cod by cutting it into large, bite-sized chunks and place in the fridge.

11 When the potatoes are cooked (check with the point of a knife), arrange the fish over the top of the potatoes, recover with the foil and cook for another 10 minutes.

12 Remove the foil and sprinkle over the peas, recover and place back in the oven for a further 3 minutes.

13 Remove from the oven, take off the foil, clean the outer rim of the dish if required, sprinkle with the chopped chives and serve.

17 Fish pie

Ingredient	4 portions	10 portions
Béchamel (thin) (see page 84)	250 ml	625 ml
Cooked fish (free from skin and bone)	200 g	500 g
Mushrooms, cooked and diced	50 g	125 g
Egg, hard-boiled and chopped	1	2½
Parsley, chopped		
Salt, pepper		
Potatoes, mashed or duchess	200 g	500 g
Egg wash or milk, to finish		

Energy	Cals	Fat	Sat fat	Carb	Sugar	Protein	Fibre
879 kJ	209 kcal	12.0 g	5.3 g	11.9 g	3.2 g	14.1 g	0.9 g

1 Bring the béchamel to the boil.

2 Add the fish, mushrooms, egg and parsley. Correct the seasoning.

3 Place in a buttered pie dish.

4 Carefully spread or pipe the potato on top. Brush with egg wash or milk.

5 Brown in a hot oven and use a food probe to check that the temperature is 75 °C.

Cook the fish, mushrooms and egg in the béchamel

Pipe mashed potato over the top before baking

Healthy eating tips
- Keep the added salt to a minimum.
- This is a healthy main course dish, particularly when served with plenty of vegetables.

Variations

Suitable fish include cod, haddock, pollock, plaice, sole, gurnard and monkfish.

Many variations can be made to this recipe with the addition of:
- prawns or shrimps
- herbs such as dill, tarragon or fennel
- raw fish poached in white wine, the cooking liquor strained off, double cream added in place of béchamel and reduced to a light consistency.

Steamed fish dishes

18 Salmon en papillote with crushed new potatoes

Ingredient	4 portions	10 portions
For the potatoes		
New potatoes	20	50
Olive oil	50 ml	125 ml
Dill, finely chopped	1 tsp	2 tsp
Sea salt, freshly milled black pepper		
For the salmon		
Olive oil	2 tbsp	5 tbsp
Cloves of garlic, thinly sliced	2	5
Red chilli, deseeded, finely chopped	1	2
Large shallots, thinly sliced	1	2
Carrot, peeled and cut into thin matchsticks	1	2
Sugarsnap peas, halved lengthways	16	40
Purple sprouting broccoli stems	8	20
Flat-leaf parsley stems	2	5
Suprêmes of salmon (200 g, skin on, pin boned)	4	10
Rock salt		
White wine	200 ml	500 ml

Energy	Cals	Fat	Sat fat	Carb	Sugar	Protein	Fibre
3,032 kJ	727 kcal	41.4 g	6.7 g	36.1 g	7.2 g	46.8 g	6.9 g

1 Preheat one oven to 190 °C and another to 220 °C.

2 For timing purposes, start with the potatoes. Boil them until they are just cooked but not soft.

3 Crush roughly with the back of a fork and place on a lightly oiled baking tray. Sprinkle with the olive oil and black pepper. Put aside until the salmon is in the oven.

4 Cut two pieces of tin foil per portion, each measuring about 23 cm².

5 Place half of the foil squares on a work surface and drizzle with the olive oil.

6 Sprinkle over the garlic, chilli and shallots and arrange the vegetables and salmon suprêmes on top.

7 Season with the rock salt.

8 Place the remaining foil squares on top of the fish, lining up with the base foil.

9 Bring together the edges of the bottom foil with the top and fold together, then repeat to form a watertight seal (this is the essence of the cooking method). Before making the last fold to seal each parcel, pour in 50 ml of white wine.

10 Place on a baking sheet and bake at 190 °C for 10–12 minutes. Meanwhile, in the hotter oven, further cook the potatoes for 12 minutes until crisp and golden.

11 To serve, sprinkle the potatoes with the chopped dill and serve with the parcels of salmon.

Note

The term 'en papillotte' means 'butterfly' and traditionally this method of cookery was all about the theatre at the restaurant table.

The ingredients were placed on a piece of parchment paper (today's greaseproof paper, or aluminium foil), shaped like a heart or a butterfly (both sides symmetrical). The edges of the paper were brushed with oil and crimped together, forming a waterproof seal. Once placed in the oven, the moisture from the ingredients inflates the parchment pouch like a pillow and cooks the dish in its own juices. This is then taken straight to the table and opened in front of the diner, allowing the aromas to escape, creating great theatre and sensory stimulation.

This method of cookery still has its place in the modern world of gastronomy, however there is less theatre in the room. The parcel is likely to be opened in the kitchen and served on the plate, thus harnessing the natural cooking juices from the ingredients to create a naturally light and clean-tasting dish.

19 Steamed fish with garlic, spring onions and ginger

1 Wash and dry the fish well; rub *lightly* with salt on both sides.
2 Put the fish on to plates, scatter the ginger evenly on top.
3 Cover the plates tightly, place into the steamer and steam gently until just cooked (5–15 minutes, according to the thickness of the fish).
4 Remove the plates, sprinkle on the spring onions and soy sauce.
5 Brown the garlic slices in the hot oil and pour over the dish.

Garlic and ginger have intense flavours, so they must be chopped very finely.

Ingredient	4 portions	10 portions
White fish fillets, e.g. cod, sole	400 g	1 kg
Salt		
Fresh ginger, freshly chopped	1 tbsp	2½ tbsp
Spring onions, finely chopped	2 tbsp	5 tbsp
Light soy sauce	1 tbsp	2½ tbsp
Cloves of garlic, peeled and thinly sliced	4	10
Oil	1 tbsp	2½ tbsp

Energy	Cals	Fat	Sat fat	Carb	Sugar	Protein	Fibre
468 kJ	112 kcal	3.5g	0.7g	1.2g	0.4g	18.7g	0.1g

Using two cloves of garlic.

Healthy eating tips
- Steaming is a healthy way of cooking.
- Serve with a large portion of rice or noodles and stir-fried vegetables.

Variation

This is a Chinese recipe that can be adapted in many ways – for example, replace the spring onions and garlic and use thinly sliced mushrooms, diced tomato (skinned and deseeded), finely chopped shallots, lemon juice, white wine, chopped parsley, dill or chervil.

20 Steamed halibut with lime and fennel

Ingredient	4 portions	10 portions
Halibut fillet, skinned (or use any other white fish such as pollack, cod, haddock)	4 × 100 g	10 × 100 g
Spring onions, thinly sliced	4	10
Salt and black pepper		
Red chilli, deseeded and cut into very thin slices	½	1½
Lime juice	3 tbsp	8 tbsp
Olive oil or sunflower oil	3 tbsp	8 tbsp
Limes cut into rounds	1	3
Bay leaves	2	6
Cloves of garlic, finely chopped	1	2½
Coriander, chopped	1 tbsp	2½ tbsp
Fennel bulb, very thinly sliced	1	2½
Thai fish sauce (Nam Pla)	1 tbsp	2½ tbsp

1 Mix together the lime juice, oil, garlic and fish sauce and marinate the fish in this for 30 minutes, spooning the mixture over the fish frequently.

2 Remove the fish from the marinade and scatter each piece with spring onion, coriander, chilli and a slice of lime.

3 Season the fennel and place in a steamer tray, small steamer or between two plates over simmering water.

4 Top with the fish, make sure it is well covered and steam gently for 5–10 minutes until the fish is cooked and the fennel tender.

5 Remove the fish and continue to cook the fennel if necessary.

6 Divide the fennel between the plates and top each with fish.

Energy	Cals	Fat	Sat fat	Carb	Sugar	Protein	Fibre	Sodium
914 kJ	219 kcal	13.3g	1.9g	2.2g	1.6g	22.8g	2.1g	0.1g

21 Frying batters (*pâtes à frire*) for fish

Recipe A

Ingredient	4 portions	10 portions
Flour	200 g	500 g
Salt		
Yeast	10 g	25 g
Water or milk	250 ml	625 ml

1 Sift the flour and salt into a basin.
2 Dissolve the yeast in a little of the water.
3 Make a well in the flour. Add the yeast and the liquid.
4 Gradually incorporate the flour and beat to a smooth mixture.
5 Allow to rest for at least 1 hour before using.

Batter mixed to the right consistency

Recipe B

Ingredient	4 portions	10 portions
Flour	200 g	500 g
Salt		
Egg	1	2–3
Water or milk	250 ml	625 ml
Oil	2 tbsp	5 tbsp

1 Sift the flour and salt into a basin. Make a well. Add the egg and the liquid.
2 Gradually incorporate the flour and beat to a smooth mixture.
3 Mix in the oil. Allow to rest before using.

Recipe C

Ingredient	4 portions	10 portions
Flour	200 g	500 g
Salt		
Water or milk	250 ml	625 ml
Oil	2 tbsp	5 tbsp
Egg whites, stiffly beaten	2	5 tbsp

1 As for Recipe B, but fold in the egg whites just before using.

Note

Other ingredients can be added to batter, for example chopped fresh herbs, grated ginger, garam masala or beer.

22 Fried fish in batter

1 Pass the prepared, washed and well-dried fish through flour, shake off the surplus and pass through the batter (see Recipe 21).

2 Place carefully away from you into the hot deep-fryer at 175 °C until the fish turns a golden-brown. Remove and drain well.

Serve with lemon quarters and tartare sauce.

> **Professional tip**
>
> Remove any excess batter before frying; too much batter will make the dish too heavy.

Energy	Cals	Fat	Sat fat	Carb	Sugar	Protein	Fibre
1,736 kJ	415 kcal	14.0g	1.8g	41.6g	3.5g	33.2g	2.1g

Pass the prepared fish through the batter

Shake off any excess and then lower carefully into the fryer

23 Deep-fried fish coated with breadcrumbs

1 Pass the fillets through flour, beaten egg and fresh white breadcrumbs. (Pat the surfaces well to avoid loose crumbs falling into the oil, burning and spoiling both the oil and the fish.)

2 Deep-fry at 175 °C, until the fish turns a golden-brown. Remove and drain well.

3 Serve with lemon wedges and tartare sauce.

Energy	Cals	Fat	Sat fat	Carb	Sugar	Protein	Fibre	Sodium
1,356 kJ	324 kcal	19.5g	2.0g	14.0g	0.5g	24.2g	0.8g	0.2g

24 Goujons of plaice

1 Cut fillets of plaice into strips approximately 8 × 0.5 cm. Wash and dry well.

2 Pass through flour, beaten egg and fresh white breadcrumbs. Pat the surfaces well so that there are no loose crumbs which could fall into the oil and burn.

3 Deep-fry at 175–180 °C, then drain well.

Serve with lemon quarters and a suitable sauce (e.g. tartare).

Professional tip

Keep the coating ingredients (flour, egg and breadcrumbs) separate. Shake off any excess flour and egg before dipping the fish into the breadcrumbs.

Other fish, e.g. sole or salmon, may be used instead of plaice.

Energy	Cals	Fat	Sat fat	Carb	Sugar	Protein	Fibre	Sodium
1,094 kJ	261 kcal	13.8g	0.0g	13.8g	0.0g	21.3g	0.6g	0.3g

25 Salmon fishcakes

Ingredient	4 portions	10 portions
Salmon fillet, skinned and boneless	400 g	1 kg
Butter	50 g	125 g
Lemon, juice of	1	2
Spring onions	3	8
Flat leaf parsley	10 g	25 g
Dill	sprig	sprig
Cooked mashed potato (make sure this is fairly dry)	225 g	560 g
Eggs, beaten	1	2
Crème fraiche	1 tbsp	2½ tbsp
Thai fish sauce (*nam pla*) – optional	Few drops	1 tsp
Plain flour, seasoned		
Eggs, beaten		
Breadcrumbs		

Energy	Cals	Fat	Sat fat	Carb	Sugar	Protein	Fibre
1,821 kJ	438 kcal	30.2g	13.6g	18.0g	1.5g	24.5g	1.6g

1 Place the salmon in an oiled roasting tin, season with salt and pepper, dot with butter and squeeze the lemon juice over.

2 Bake at 200 °C for approximately 7 minutes.

3 Allow the salmon to cool a little, then flake into bite-sized pieces.

4 Chop the spring onions and herbs.

5 Add the salmon to the mashed potato, and mix in the herbs, spring onion, beaten egg and crème fraiche. Add a little *nam pla* if using and season.

6 Form into neat, even-sized cake shapes (a ring mould could be used), place on a tray lined with cling film and chill thoroughly for several hours.

7 Coat with seasoned flour, egg and breadcrumbs (*pané*), chill well again or the formed cakes can be frozen.

8 Cook in a deep fryer as required and drain on kitchen paper.

9 Serve with a suitable sauce or salsa and/or mixed salad leaves.

One way to divide the mixture is to form it into a long roll

Divide the roll into even pieces

Mould each piece into a ball

Pass the balls through seasoned flour, beaten egg and breadcrumbs

Flatten each cake firmly and shake off surplus crumbs

Deep fry until golden brown

Shallow-fried fish dishes

26 Shallow-fried fish

1 Prepare, clean, wash and dry the fish well.

2 Pass through flour and shake off all surplus. (If using non-stick pans it is not necessary to flour the fish.)

3 Heat the frying medium, such as oil, in a frying pan.

4 Shallow-fry on both sides (presentation side first), then serve.

Professional tip

Do not overcrowd the pan because this may cause the temperature of the oil to fall, which will affect the efficient cooking of the fish.

Energy	Cals	Fat	Sat fat	Carb	Sugar	Protein	Fibre	Sodium
1,056 kJ	251 kcal	13.2g	1.7g	7.8g	0.2g	26.0g	0.4g	0.2g

Pass the fish through seasoned flour

Place carefully into the pan, presentation side first

Turn the fish gently, once, during cooking

Variation

When cooked, sprinkle with a mixture of grated lemon zest, finely chopped garlic and chopped parsley (known as gremolata).

27 Shallow-fried sole with shrimp and caper dressing

Ingredient	4 portions	10 portions
Lemon sole (350 g)	4	10
Ground cumin, toasted	5 g	12 g
Sea salt, freshly milled black pepper		
Plain flour	200 g	500 g
Sunflower oil	100 ml	250 ml
For the dressing		
Shrimps, cooked and peeled	100 g	250 g
Small capers	75 g	200 g
Butter, cut into small cubes	150 g	375 g
Olive oil	50 ml	125 ml
Parsley, chopped	2 tbsp	5 tbsp
Lemon, juice of	1	2

Energy	Cals	Fat	Sat fat	Carb	Sugar	Protein	Fibre	Sodium
4,655 kJ	1117 kcal	74.9 g	25.2 g	39.7 g	1.6 g	74.5 g	2.3 g	1.0 g

1 Fillet the fish and trim the fillets to neaten them.

2 Mix the cumin, salt, pepper and flour together.

3 Before you start cooking the fish, make sure the other components of the dish are ready, as the sole will cook quickly.

4 Heat the oil in a non-stick pan large enough to cook one portion (four fillets). Pass the fillets through the flour, ensuring that the whole fillet is coated.

5 Place the fillets into the hot oil, presentation side first, and cook until golden. Turn and cook for a further 10 seconds, remove and place on an oven tray (they will be flashed in the oven just before serving).

6 Repeat the process for the other portions.

7 Add the dressing ingredients, except the parsley and lemon juice, to the pan, and heat until the butter foams and brings out the flavour of the capers.

8 Squeeze in the lemon juice and add the parsley.

9 Flash the sole in a moderate oven. Spoon the dressing over the sole to serve. Accompany with purple sprouting broccoli or green salad.

28 Fish meunière

Healthy eating tips
- Use a small amount of unsaturated oil to fry the fish.
- Use less *beurre noisette* per portion. Some customers will prefer the finished dish without the additional fat.

Variation

Variations include the following:
- **Fish meunière with almonds**: as for fish meunière, adding 10g of almonds cut in short julienne or coarsely chopped into the meunière butter just before it begins to turn brown. This method is usually applied to trout.
- **Fish belle meunière**: as for fish meunière, with the addition of a grilled mushroom, a slice of peeled tomato and a soft herring roe (passed through flour and shallow-fried), all neatly dressed on each portion of fish.
- **Fish Doria**: as for fish meunière, with a sprinkling of small turned pieces of cucumber carefully cooked in 25g of butter in a small covered pan, or blanched in boiling salted water.
- **Fish Grenobloise**: as for fish meunière, the peeled lemon being cut into segments, neatly dressed on the fish, with a few capers sprinkled over.
- **Fish Bretonne**: as for fish meunière, with a few picked shrimps and cooked sliced mushrooms sprinkled over the fish.

For each of these classical dishes, chefs may wish to add some chopped herbs for flavour; for example, add chopped dill to fish Doria.

	4 portions	10 portions
White fish fillets, skinned	400–600g	1–1.5kg
Large lemons	2	5
Clarified butter	100g	250g
Parsley, chopped	1 tsp	2 tsp

Energy	Cals	Fat	Sat fat	Carb	Sugar	Protein	Fibre
1,314 kJ	313 kcal	24.1g	10.3g	3.1g	0.0g	21.2g	0.1g

Many fish, whole or filleted, may be cooked by this method: for example, sole, sea bass, bream, fillets of plaice, trout, brill, cod, turbot, herring and scampi.

1 Prepare and clean the fish, wash and drain.
2 Pass through seasoned flour, shaking off all surplus.
3 Shallow-fry on both sides, presentation side first, in hot clarified butter or oil.
4 Dress neatly on an oval flat dish or plate/plates.
5 Peel a lemon, removing the peel, white pith and pips.
6 Cut the lemon into slices and place one on each portion.
7 Squeeze some lemon juice on the fish.
8 Allow 10–25g butter per portion and colour in a clean frying pan to the nut-brown stage (*beurre noisette*).
9 Pour over the fish.
10 Sprinkle with chopped parsley and serve.

29 Pan-fried fillets of sole with rocket and broad beans

Ingredient	4 portions	10 portions
Oil for frying		
Sole fillets, trimmed	16	40
Seasoning		
Butter	200 g	500 g
Broad beans, cooked and shelled	250 g	625 g
Rocket, picked and washed	300 g	750 g
Vinaigrette	50 ml	125 ml

Energy	Cals	Fat	Sat fat	Carb	Sugar	Protein	Fibre	Sodium
2,710 kJ	654 kcal	54.2 g	28.0 g	5.1 g	1.4 g	36.6 g	6.6 g	0.6 g

Note

This is a very simple and quick dish. Any salad or greens, if they are quickly cooked or lightly dressed, can go with this dish.

1 Heat a little oil in a non-stick pan.

2 Place the fillets of sole on a tray and season on both sides.

3 Place the fish in the pan carefully (presentation side down).

4 Cook for 1 minute on a medium/high heat, and then carefully turn the fish, remove the pan from the heat and allow the residual heat to finish the cooking.

5 Place the sole fillets (four per portion) on serving plates and keep warm.

6 Place the butter in the cooking pan, heat to the *noisette* stage, add the broad beans and cook for 30 seconds to 1 minute just to reheat them.

7 Mask the fish with the *noisette* butter and the beans. Finish with a dressed rocket salad.

30 Pan-fried skate with capers and *beurre noir*

1 Place a skillet on the hottest part of the stove and an empty sauté pan to the side of the stove, achieving a moderate heat (this is for the *beurre noir*).

2 Ensure the skate wings are fresh, and free from ammonia aromas and skin. Season them with salt and pepper.

3 Add the vegetable oil to the skillet and place in the skate wings; cook with colour for 1–2 minutes and then carefully turn. At this point, ease the skillet to a cooler point of the stove while the *beurre noir* cooks.

4 Place the butter in the sauté pan and allow to foam (at this point remove the skate and place on the serving dish).

5 Add the lemon, parsley and capers to the *beurre noir* and stir well.

6 To finish, nap over the skate wing and serve.

Note

Because skate pass urine through their wings, if they are not extremely fresh they will start to smell of ammonia after three to four days. This is a key indicator of their freshness.

Ingredient	4 portions	10 portions
Skate, skinless fillets (approx. 160 g each)	4	10
Seasoning		
Vegetable oil	50 ml	125 ml
Butter	175 g	450 g
Lemons, juice of	2	5
Flat leaf parsley, chopped	2 tbsp	5 tbsp
Small capers	100 g	250 g

Energy	Cals	Fat	Sat fat	Carb	Sugar	Protein	Fibre	Sodium
2,395 kJ	579 kcal	51.9 g	24.7 g	0.8 g	0.8 g	27.1 g	1.2 g	1.0 g

Based on olives in place of capers.

31 Nage of red mullet with baby leeks

Ingredient	4 portions	10 portions
Mussels, cooked and removed from shell	16	40
Lemons, juice of	2	5
Baby spinach	200 g	500 g
Baby leeks	12	30
Baby asparagus, spears of	12	30
Green beans, pieces of	2 tbsp	5 tbsp
Red mullet fillets (approximately 120 g each), pin bones and scales removed	4	10
Nage		
Large onion	1	3
Carrots, peeled	2	5
Celery sticks	2	5
Leeks	2	5
Cloves of garlic	1	3
Half white and half pink peppercorns	12	30
Star anise	1	3
White wine	375 ml	950 ml
Noilly Prat	375 ml	950 ml
Chervil	10 g	25 g
Parsley	10 g	25 g
Tarragon	10 g	25 g
Chives, chopped	1 tbsp	3 tbsp

Energy	Cals	Fat	Sat fat	Carb	Sugar	Protein	Fibre	Sodium
2,172 kJ	519 kcal	9.2 g	0.9 g	26.8 g	19.7 g	46.2 g	13.1 g	0.6 g

1 In a large pan place the onions, carrots, celery and leeks, which have been cut into 2 cm pieces.

2 Just cover the vegetables with water. Bring to the boil. Simmer for 4–5 minutes. Remove from the heat and add the rest of the ingredients.

3 Cover with cling film and allow to cool to room temperature. Place into a plastic container and store in the fridge overnight to develop flavour.

4 Pass through a fine sieve. Any surplus nage can be frozen for later use.

5 To finish, place 500 ml of the vegetable nage in a pan, add the mussels, a squeeze of lemon, spinach, baby leeks, asparagus and green beans.

6 Bring to the boil, check the seasoning and retain.

7 Heat a non-stick pan with a little vegetable oil. Season the mullet fillets and cook for 1 minute on each side (thickness dependent), starting with the skin side down.

8 Divide the vegetable garnish between the bowls. Place the red mullet on top of the vegetable garnish and, returning the pan the mullet was cooked in to the stove, pour in the nage.

9 When the nage has returned to the boil, spoon over the fish and garnish. Serve immediately.

Professional tip

This dish is open to many substitutions of fish and shellfish but one key point to remember is that the nage should not be allowed to overpower the main ingredients.

32 Barramundi with garlic, ginger and lemon butter and pak choi

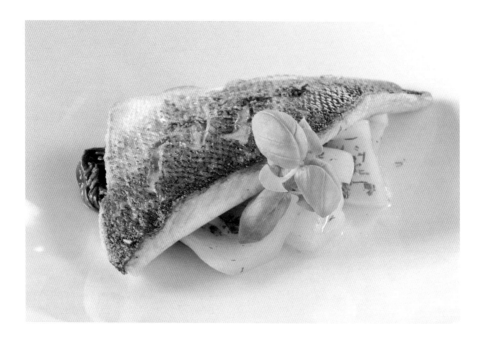

Ingredient	4 portions	10 portions
Olive oil	75 ml	200 ml
Barramundi fillets (200 g, skin off)	4	10
Seasoning		
Small heads of pak choi	8	20
Salted butter	100 g	250 g
Garlic, small cloves, chopped	1	2
Root ginger, cut into 2–3/6–8 pieces	50 g	125 g
Fresh lemon juice	3 tbsp	7 tbsp
Fresh basil leaves, chopped	5	12

Energy	Cals	Fat	Sat fat	Carb	Sugar	Protein	Fibre	Sodium
3,174 kJ	766 kcal	62.2g	19.7g	7.9g	6.9g	44.3g	6.8g	0.3g

Using spring greens instead of pak choi.

Note

Barramundi can be used in any recipe calling for a white fish such as cod, bass or haddock, or red snapper.

1 Bring a pan of salted water to the boil.

2 Heat the oil in a non-stick frying pan.

3 Season the fish fillets and place in the hot oil. Cook for 2 minutes and then turn, removing the pan from the heat. Allow the residual heat to finish the cooking process.

4 Meanwhile, blanch the pak choi for 2 minutes in the boiling water, until vibrant green. Drain.

5 Remove the fish from the pan and keep it warm. Return the pan to the heat and add the butter, garlic and ginger. Cook for 2 minutes until the garlic is soft and the ginger has imparted its flavour. Remove the ginger and add the lemon juice and basil.

6 Mix well and add the pak choi. Ensure that all the flavours are incorporated well.

7 Serve the fish and pak choi with the dressing from the pan over the top.

33 Thai fishcakes

Ingredient	4 portions	10 portions
Salmon, filleted and skinned	100 g	250 g
Cod, filleted and skinned	100 g	250 g
Sesame oil	½ tsp	1¼ tsp
Cloves of garlic	2	5
Root ginger, grated	1 tbsp	2¼ tbsp
Red chillies (small)	½	1
Soy sauce	1 tsp	1½ tsp
Lemon grass	12 g	30 g
Salt	2 g	5 g
Pepper	2 g	5 g
Lime juice	2 tsp	5 tsp
Sunflower oil for cooking	2 tsp	5 tsp

Energy	Cals	Fat	Sat fat	Carb	Sugar	Protein	Fibre
395 kJ	95 kcal	5.8 g	0.9 g	0.7 g	0.2 g	10.0 g	0.1 g

1 Place all ingredients, except the oil for cooking, in a food processor, blend until bound together and smooth.

2 Turn out and divide into 12 small cakes for four portions (30 for ten portions). The cakes should be at least 2 cm thick.

3 Heat the oil in a suitable pan. Place the fish cakes in, allowing approximately 3 minutes each side. Drain on kitchen paper after frying.

4 Serve immediately garnished with flat leaf parsley and Thai cucumber salad.

Healthy eating tips
● No added salt is needed.
● Serve with plenty of fragrant Thai rice and extra vegetables.

Boiled shellfish dishes

34 Mussels in white wine sauce (*moules marinière*)

Ingredient	4 portions	10 portions
Shallots, chopped	50 g	125 g
Parsley, chopped	1 tbsp	2 tbsp
White wine	60 ml	150 ml
Strong fish stock	200 ml	500 ml
Mussels	2 kg	5 kg
Butter	25 g	60 g
Flour	25 g	60 g
Seasoning		

Energy	Cals	Fat	Sat fat	Carb	Sugar	Protein	Fibre	Sodium
1,900 kJ	452 kcal	14.3g	5.3g	18.1g	0.9g	61.4g	0.6g	1.5g

1 Take a thick-bottomed pan and add the shallots, parsley, wine, fish stock and the cleaned mussels.

2 Cover with a tight-fitting lid and cook over a high heat until the shells open.

3 Drain off all the cooking liquor in a colander set over a clean bowl to retain the cooking juices.

4 Carefully check the mussels and discard any that have not opened.

5 Place in a dish and cover to keep warm.

6 Make a roux from the flour and butter; pour over the cooking liquor, ensuring it is free from sand and stirring continuously to avoid lumps.

7 Correct the seasoning and garnish with more chopped parsley.

8 Pour over the mussels and serve.

Variation

For an eastern influence add a little red chilli and replace the parsley with coriander.

35 Crab cakes with chilli lime dipping sauce

Ingredient	30–40 cakes
Crab cakes	
Crab meat	350g
Uncooked prawns, shelled and deveined	650g
Red curry paste	1 tbsp
Egg	1
Spring onions	2
Fresh coriander, finely chopped	2 tbsp
Lemon grass, finely chopped	2 tsp
Red Thai chilli, deseeded and chopped	1
Vegetable oil	2 tbsp
Dipping sauce	
Lime juice	2 tbsp
Water	2 tbsp
Fish sauce (*nam pla*)	2 tsp
Kaffir lime leaf, chopped	1
Red Thai chilli, deseeded and finely chopped	1

Energy	Cals	Fat	Sat fat	Carb	Sugar	Protein	Fibre
557 kJ	133 kcal	5.6g	0.7g	1.2g	0.4g	19.6g	0.1g

For the crab cakes:

1 In a food processor, place the crab, prawns, curry paste, egg, spring onion, coriander, lemon grass and chilli. Combine all ingredients until mixed together.

2 Shape into small cakes.

3 Heat the oil in a shallow pan and fry the crab cakes on both sides until golden brown. Drain, then place on a suitable dish with the dipping sauce (see below).

For the dipping sauce:

1 Combine all ingredients in a suitable bowl.

2 Stir well.

36 Crab cakes with rocket salad and lemon dressing

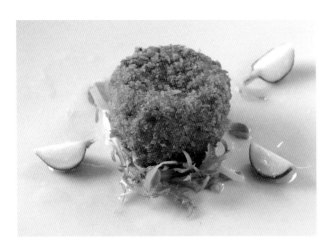

For the crab cakes:

1 Mix the shallots, spring onions and the fish glaze with the hand-picked crab meat.

2 Add the mayonnaise, lemon juice, tomato concassé and mustard, check and adjust the seasoning.

3 Allow to rest for 30 minutes in the refrigerator.

4 Scale into 80–90 g balls and shape into discs 1.5 cm high, place in the freezer for 30 minutes to harden.

5 When firm to the touch, coat in breadcrumbs using the flour, egg and breadcrumbs.

6 Allow to rest for a further 30 minutes.

7 Heat a little oil in a non-stick pan, carefully place the cakes in and cook on each side until golden brown.

For the salad and dressing:

1 Combine the oil, vinegar and lemon juice together, check the seasoning.

2 Place the rocket and Parmesan in a large bowl and add a little dressing, just to coat.

3 Place this in the centre of each plate, top with the crab cakes and serve. Alternatively, present the salad on top of the crab cakes.

Ingredient	4 portions	10 portions
Crab cakes		
Shallots, finely chopped	25 g	60 g
Spring onions, finely chopped	4	10
Fish/shellfish glaze	75 ml	185 ml
Crab meat	400 g	1 kg
Mayonnaise	75 g	185 g
Lemons, juice of	1	3
Plum tomatoes skinned, cut into concassé	2	5
Wholegrain mustard	1 tsp	3 tsp
Seasoning		
Fresh white breadcrumbs	200 g	500 g
Eggs, beaten with 100 ml of milk	2	5
Salad and lemon dressing		
Vegetable oil	170 ml	425 ml
White wine vinegar	25 ml	60 ml
Lemons, juice of	1	2½
Seasoning		
Rocket, washed and picked	100 g	250 g
Parmesan, shaved	100 g	250 g

> **Professional tip**
>
> Any excess crab meat can be used up in this recipe – a quick, classic dish. The crab can be exchanged for salmon or most fresh fish trimmings.

Energy	Cals	Fat	Sat fat	Carb	Sugar	Protein	Fibre
3,002 kJ	719 kcal	43.9 g	10.5 g	41.9 g	4.4 g	41.4 g	4.1 g

37 Lobster beignets with tomato chutney

Energy	Cals	Fat	Sat fat	Carb	Sugar	Protein	Fibre	Sodium
1,914 kJ	451 kcal	3.3 g	0.6 g	77.4 g	26.1 g	28.1 g	7.8 g	0.3 g

Note

This can be served as a quick, hot and spicy bar dish.

Ingredient	4 portions	10 portions
For the chutney		
Oil	1 tbsp	2½ tbsp
Onion, peeled and chopped	1	2
Tomatoes, peeled, seeded and diced (concassé)	1 kg	2.5 kg
Red wine vinegar	70 ml	175 ml
Cup sugar	50 g	125 g
Coriander powder	1 tbsp	2 tbsp
Paprika	1 tbsp	2 tbsp
For the lobster beignets		
Cooked lobster tails	4	10
Plain flour (plus a little extra for coating)	145 g	360 g
Fecule (potato starch)	120 g	300 g
Active dry yeast	1 tbsp	2½ tbsp
Salt	½ tsp	1¼ tsp
Real ale or beer	300 ml	750 ml

For the chutney:

1 Warm the oil in a large pot over a medium-low heat.

2 Add onion and cook, stirring occasionally, until tender (5–10 minutes).

3 Add tomatoes, vinegar, sugar, coriander and paprika; bring to a simmer, stirring occasionally, until thickened (45–55 minutes).

4 Remove from the heat and allow to cool.

For the lobster beignets:

1 Slice lobster meat crosswise into 0.5 cm-thick medallions; keep chilled.

2 Heat the oil in a deep fryer to 180 °C.

3 In a bowl, combine the flour, starch, yeast and salt; stir to mix. Stir in the beer to make the batter.

4 Coat a lobster medallion in a little flour and then in the batter. Deep-fry until crispy and golden, 2–3 minutes.

5 Fry three or four at a time (do not crowd the fryer). Drain well. Sprinkle beignets lightly with salt and serve hot with chutney.

38 Prawns with chilli and garlic

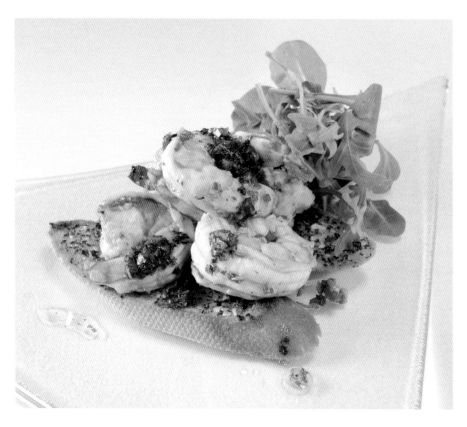

Ingredient	4 portions	10 portions
Clove of garlic, crushed	1	3
Lime, juice of	1	2½
Lemon, juice of	½	1¼
Mild red chillies, deseeded and finely chopped	2	5
Olive oil	1 tbsp	3 tbsp
Honey	1 tbsp	3 tbsp
Extra large prawns, raw, shells on, heads removed	32	80
Black pepper		
To serve		
Salsa verde (see page 101)	100 ml	250 ml
Garlic bread	4 slices	10 slices
Green salad		

Energy	Cals	Fat	Sat fat	Carb	Sugar	Protein	Fibre	Sodium
728 kJ	173 kcal	3.8g	0.6g	6.6g	6.3g	28.6g	0.1g	0.3g

1 In a shallow dish, mix together the garlic, lime juice, lemon juice, chillies, olive oil and honey.

2 Make an incision (don't cut all the way through – leave the prawn intact) in the back of each prawn and remove the entrails. Wash and dry well.

3 Add the prawns to the oil/chilli mix, season with black pepper and marinate in the fridge for 30 minutes.

4 Meanwhile, prepare the green salad, salsa verde and garlic bread.

5 Remove the prawns from the marinade and heat a small amount of oil in a non-stick frying pan.

6 Place the prawns in the pan and cook until pink and cooked through, basting with any leftover marinade while cooking.

7 To serve, place warm garlic bread on plates and pile the prawns up on top, allowing the cooking juices to run into the bread. Drizzle with salsa verde and serve with the salad.

Grilled shellfish dishes

39 Scallops and bacon

Ingredient	4 portions	10 portions
Large scallops, shelled, roe and skirt removed, washed	12	30
Pancetta bacon rashers (rind off)	12	30
Olive oil	50 ml	125 ml
Lemon	1	2½
Asparagus sticks, peeled, blanched for 1 minute and refreshed	16	40
Seasoning		

Energy	Cals	Fat	Sat fat	Carb	Sugar	Protein	Fibre	Sodium
1,705 kJ	410 kcal	26.8g	6.9g	5.9g	2.8g	36.4g	2.3g	1.3g

1 Wrap the scallops in the pancetta, pin with a cocktail stick and season (be mindful that the pancetta is salty).

2 Heat the oil in a non-stick pan, place the scallops in and cook until golden-brown. Squeeze the lemon over the scallops and allow the juice to evaporate slightly.

3 Remove from the pan and retain with all the pan juices.

4 Return the pan to the heat and add the asparagus, cooking for a further 2 minutes.

5 To serve, divide the asparagus on to plates. Top with the scallops, pour over the pan juices and serve.

10 Meat and offal

This chapter is relevant to the following units:
→ Prepare meat for basic dishes.
→ Prepare offal for basic dishes.

→ Cook and finish basic meat dishes.
→ Cook and finish basic offal dishes.

Recipes included in this chapter

Meat

Butcher's meat used today is largely a product of selective breeding and feeding techniques – animals are reared carefully to reach high standards and meet specific needs. Present-day demand is for lean and tender meat – modern cattle, sheep and pigs are well-fleshed yet compact creatures, and there is an increase in use of specific-named breeds on restaurant tables.

Full information on meat, including cattle, sheep and pigs, can be found at:

- www.qmscotland.co.uk
- www.eblex.org.uk
- www.bpex.org.uk.

The structure of meat

Meat and its fat content varies considerably. The fat is found round the outside of meat, in **marbling** (the white flecks of fat throughout the lean muscle) and inside the meat fibres. The visible fat (saturated) should be trimmed off as much as possible before cooking.

To cook meat properly it is important to understand its structure:

- Meat comprises fibres bound by connective tissue.
- Connective tissue (elastin) is yellow and collagen white.
- Yellow tissue needs to be removed.
- Small fibres are present in tender cuts and younger animals.
- Coarser fibres are present in tougher cuts and older animals.
- Fat assists in providing flavour and moistens meat during roasting and grilling.
- Tenderness, flavour and moistness are increased if meat is hung after slaughter and before being used.

Quality points when choosing and buying meat

Meat is a natural product and therefore not uniform, varying in quality from carcass to carcass. Flavour, texture and appearance are determined by the type of animal and the way it has been fed.

There is no reason to think that flavour is obtained only in meat that possesses a higher proportion of fat, although fat does give a characteristic flavour to meat and helps to keep it moist during roasting. Neither is the colour of meat any guide to quality. Consumers are inclined to choose light-coloured meat – bright-red beef, for example – because they think that it will be fresher than an alternative dark-red piece. Freshly butchered beef is bright red because the pigment in the tissues, myoglobin, has been chemically affected by the oxygen in the air. After several hours the colour changes to dark red or brown as the pigment is further oxidised to become metamyoglobin. The colour of fat can vary from almost pure white in lamb to bright yellow in beef. Colour depends on the feed, on the breed and, to a certain extent, on the time of year.

The most useful guide to tenderness and quality is knowledge of the cuts of meat and their location on the carcass. The various cuts are described below, but in principle the leanest and most tender cuts – the **prime cuts** – come from the hindquarters. The **coarse cuts** – meat from the neck, legs and forequarters; those parts of the animal that have had plenty of muscular exercise and where fibres have become hardened – provide meat for braising and stewing. Many consider these cuts to have more flavour, although they require slow cooking to make them tender. The meat from young animals is generally more tender.

Animals may be injected before slaughter with an enzyme, such as papin, which softens the fibres and muscles. This speeds up a natural process: meat contains its own enzymes that gradually break down the protein cell walls as the carcass ages; that is why meat is hung for 10 to 20 days in controlled conditions of temperature and humidity before being offered for sale. Meat that has been aged longer is more expensive as the cost of refrigeration is high and the meat itself shrinks because of evaporation and the trimming of the outside hardened edges.

Kosher and halal meat

Meat that is sold as kosher or halal must have been slaughtered according to the food laws of Judaism (kosher) or Islam (halal).

Kosher slaughter is done by a quick, deep stroke across the throat with a sharp blade. This is considered painless, causes unconsciousness within two seconds and is widely recognised as the most humane method of slaughter possible. The animal is bled completely, and the meat soaked in suet and water to remove any residual blood, because blood must not be consumed in a kosher diet.

Halal slaughter is done by cutting the throat or piercing the hollow of the throat, causing a quick death with the least pain possible. The blood is completely drained from the carcass. Halal slaughter is preceded by a prayer.

Storing meat

Meat that is chilled is kept at a temperature just above freezing point in a controlled atmosphere. Meat should be hung and stored between 0 °C and 1 °C.

Chilled meat cannot be kept in the usual type of cold room for more than a few days, although sufficient time must be allowed for the meat to hang, enabling it to become tender. Beef can be stored for up to three weeks, veal for one to three weeks, lamb for 10 to 15 days, and pork 7 to 14 days.

> ### Health and safety ⚠️
> Store uncooked meat, offal and poultry on trays to prevent dripping, ideally in separate refrigerators, at a temperature of 1 °C to 4 °C. If separate refrigerators are not available, then store in separate areas of the refrigerator, with uncooked meat at the bottom and cooked meat above it.

Other preservation methods

Freezing

Small carcasses, such as lamb and mutton, can be frozen without affecting their quality. They can be kept frozen until required and then thawed out before being used. Some beef is frozen, but it is inferior in quality to chilled beef.

Canning

Large quantities of meat are canned; corned beef is an example with a very high protein content. Pork is used for tinned luncheon meat. Ham cuts are also available in cans.

Salting

The salt draws out moisture and creates an environment in which bacteria find it difficult to multiply. If salted in cold weather (so that the meat does not spoil while the salt has time to take effect), salted meat can last for years. Salting is still used with bacon, before the meat is smoked, and hams. It is also used for some beef products, for example dried beef, corned beef and pastrami, which are made by soaking beef in a 10 per cent salt water brine for several weeks. Meat can be pickled in brine; this method of preservation may be applied to silverside, brisket and ox tongues.

Preparing meat

Refer to the sections on different types of meat below for further detail on preparation methods. The following food safety points should be taken into account to reduce the risk of cross-contamination when preparing meat:

- When preparing uncooked meat, offal or poultry, and then cooked food, or changing from one type of meat, offal or poultry to another, equipment, working areas and utensils must be thoroughly cleaned or changed.
- Where colour-coded boards are used, it is essential to always use the correct colour-coded boards for the preparation of foods, and different ones for cooked foods.
- Clean all work surfaces with detergent and sanitiser to kill bacteria. This is particularly important when handling poultry and pork.

For information on maintaining a safe and secure working environment; a professional and hygienic appearance; and clean food production areas, equipment and utensils, as well as food hygiene, please refer to Chapters 1 and 3.

Cooking meat

Meat is an extremely versatile product that can be cooked in a multitude of ways and matched with practically any vegetable, fruit and herb. The cut (shin, steak, brisket and so on), the method of cooking (roasting, braising, grilling) and the time and temperature all affect the way the meat will taste.

Raw meat is difficult to chew because the muscle fibre contains an elastic protein (collagen), which is softened only by mincing – as in steak tartare – or by cooking. When you cook meat, the protein gradually **coagulates** as the internal temperature increases. At 77 °C coagulation is complete, the protein begins to harden and further cooking makes the meat tougher.

> ### Professional tip
>
> Meat bones are useful for giving flavour to soups and stocks, especially beef ones with plenty of marrow. Veal bones are gelatinous and help to enrich and thicken soups and sauces. Fat can be rendered down for frying or used as an ingredient, such as suet or lard used in pastry.

Time and temperature in meat cookery

Since tenderness combined with flavour is the aim in meat cookery, much depends on the ratio of time and temperature. In principle, slow cooking retains the juices and produces a more tender result than fast cooking at high temperatures. There are, of course, occasions when high temperatures are essential: for instance, you need to grill a steak under a hot flame for a very limited time to obtain a crisp, brown surface and a pink, juicy interior – using a low temperature would not give you the desired result. But, in potentially tough cuts, such as breast, or where there is a quantity of connective tissue (e.g. neck of lamb), a slow rate of cooking converts the tissues to gelatine and helps to make the meat more tender. Meat containing bone will take longer to cook because bone is a poor conductor of heat.

Tough or coarse cuts of meat should be cooked by braising, pot roasting or stewing. Marinating in a suitable marinade, such as wine and wine vinegar, helps to tenderise the meat and imparts an additional flavour. Searing meat in hot fat or in a hot oven before roasting or stewing helps to produce a crisp exterior by coagulating the protein but does not, as is widely supposed, seal in the juices. However, if the external temperature is too high and cooking prolonged, rapid evaporation and contraction of the meat will cause considerable loss of juices and fat. Salt sprinkled on meat before cooking will also hasten loss of moisture since salt absorbs water.

When fibrous proteins are heated they contract and squeeze out the associated water. For example, when a steak is cooked the proteins contract, therefore squeezing out all the water/juices. If the heat is increased or continues, the steak will become dry and the eating quality will be impaired. Cuts of meat also contain elastin and collagen: elastin (the muscle group associated with tendons and arteries) is extremely stretchy and further cooking adds to its strength; collagen (the main muscle proteins, which amount to the highest proportion of mass in the muscle) is tough and chewy. Meat that has a higher proportion of both, usually from the major and highly worked muscle groups, would not be suitable for prime cooking (e.g. grilling or frying). However, these cuts of meat may be cooked for longer at the correct temperature (braising), dissolving the collagen as it is water soluble, forming gelatine and offering a tasty joint of meat.

Prime cuts, such as beef fillets, have little collagen in their make-up (approximately 3 per cent) and do not require long cooking to tenderise them. Although most chefs would adopt a high temperature for a short period on the prime cuts, this does not always lead to a perfect result. Due to the lack of fat and collagen in such cuts of meat, high heat will dry out the muscle fibres and, consequently, the eating quality is impaired. A lower temperature and longer in the oven will produce a gradual heat, therefore there is less extreme coagulation in the tissues and less fluid will be squeezed out in the process.

Sirloin of beef has more collagen than fillet (it is essentially a worked muscle group) and is generally cooked on a high heat, either roasted or pan-fried. Using a slow cooking method, however, you can prepare sirloin that is extremely tender, full of moisture, with a roasted outer and a flavoursome roasted meat taste. An average sirloin joint for roasting can weigh from 2 kg to 5 kg whole off the bone. The method is to seal the meat on the outside, as you would normally, place into a preheated oven at 180 °C, cook for 10 minutes, then reduce the temperature to 64 °C (the oven door will need to be open at this stage). Once the oven has come down to 64 °C, close the door and cook for a further 1 hour and 50 minutes. This will give you an extremely tender piece of sirloin.

To maintain the quality and safety of meat and poultry dishes, it is advisable to check internal temperatures using a probe. The recommended temperatures are shown in Table 10.1.

Table 10.1 Recommended internal temperatures

Meat	Recommended internal temperature
Beef	rare 52 °C, medium 57 °C, well done 62 °C
Duck	pink 57 °C; well done 62 °C
Lamb	pink 57 °C, well done 62 °C
Pork	73 °C
Turkey/chicken	77 °C
Veal	62 °C

Environmental health officers may require higher temperatures.

The Maillard reaction

A series of chemical reactions, known as the Maillard reaction, happen when proteins are heated with sugars to temperatures above 140 °C. This is why a good flavour develops when meat cooks.

Always ensure that the outside of the meat is cooked at a high temperature (until it is a dark brown colour), in order to develop the flavour. Cook meats with little connective tissue for only a short time. Seal the outside so that it is browned and so that the inside does not become tough (e.g. by grilling, frying or roasting).

Meats with lots of connective tissue should be cooked for longer so that all the connective tissue breaks down and the bundles of coagulated muscle proteins fall apart, tenderising the meat (e.g. by stewing or braising).

Lamb and mutton

Lamb is the meat from a sheep under a year old; above that age the animal is called a 'hogget' and its meat becomes mutton. The lamb carcass provides smaller cuts of more tender meat than mutton. Mutton needs to be well ripened by long hanging before cooking and, as it is usually fatty, needs a good deal of trimming as well.

Lamb has a very thin, parchment-like covering on the carcass, known as the 'fell', which is usually left on roasts to help them maintain their shape during cooking. It should, however, be removed from chops. The flesh of a younger lamb is usually more tender. A good way to judge age is through weight – especially with legs of lamb: the highest quality weighs about 2.3 kg and never more than 4 kg. Smaller chops are also more tender and, therefore, more expensive.

> **Professional tip**
>
> Mutton fell out of favour in the UK for some years but has recently become more popular, backed by the Mutton Renaissance campaign, which was supported by several well-known chefs and the Prince of Wales. Using mutton is good for food sustainability – because the animals are not killed young they are larger than lambs and have a higher yield.

Quality points

- Good-quality lamb should have fine, white fat, with pink flesh where freshly cut; in mutton the flesh is a deeper colour.
- A good-quality animal should be compact and evenly fleshed.
- The lean flesh should be firm, of a pleasing dull-red colour and of a fine texture or grain.
- There should be an even distribution of surface fat, which should be hard, brittle and flaky in structure and a clear white colour.
- In a young animal the bones should be pink and porous, so that when cut a degree of blood is shown in their structure. As the sheep grows older, the bones become hard, dense and white, and inclined to splinter when chopped.

Portions and cuts

As a guide, when ordering allow approximately 100 g meat off the bone per portion, and 150 g on the bone per portion. It must be clearly understood, however, that the weights given can only be approximate. They must vary according to the quality of the meat and also according to the purpose for which the meat is being butchered. For example, a chef will often cut differently from a shop butcher (a chef frequently needs to consider the presentation of the particular joint, while the butcher is more often concerned with economical cutting). In the text that follows, simple orders of dissection are given for each carcass. In general, bones need to be removed only when preparing joints, so as to facilitate carving. The bones are used for stock and the excess fat can be rendered down for second-class dripping.

▲ Joints of lamb, viewed from different angles – see Table 10.2 for an explanation of the numbers

Table 10.2 Lamb and mutton joints, their uses and weights

Joint	Uses	Approx. weight (kg)	
		Lamb	Mutton
Whole carcass		16	25
Shoulder (1)	Roasting, stewing	3	4.5
Leg (2)	Roasting (mutton boiled)	3.5	5.5
Breast (3)	Roasting, stewing	1.5	2.5
Middle neck (4)	Stewing	2	3
Scrag-end (5)	Stewing, broth	0.5	1
Best end/ rack (6)	Roasting, grilling, frying	2	3
Saddle (7)	Roasting, grilling, frying	3.5	5.5

The order of dissection of a lamb carcass:
1 Remove the shoulders.
2 Remove the breasts.
3 Remove the middle neck and scrag.
4 Remove the legs.
5 Divide the saddle from the best end.

Table 10.3 Common cooking methods for lamb

Joint	Methods of cookery
Saddle	Roast, pot roast
Loin	Roast
Fillet	Grill, fry
Loin chop	Grill, fry, stew, braise
Chump chop	Grill, fry, stew, braise
Kidney	Grill, sauté

Preparing a shoulder of lamb

- **Boning**: remove the blade bone and upper arm bone (see diagram) and tie with string; the shoulder may be stuffed before tying.
- **Cutting for stews**: bone out, cut into even 25–50 g pieces.
- **For roasting**: remove the pelvic or aitchbone; clean and trim the knucklebone so as to leave approximately 3 cm of clean bone; trim off excess fat and tie with string if necessary.

Video: making brown lamb stew http://bit.ly/ 1CIMkfD

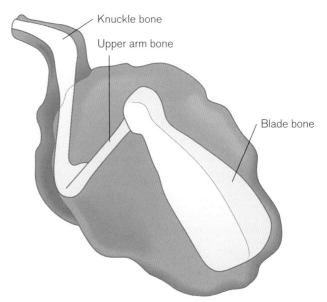

▲ Shoulder of lamb, showing three bones

Preparing breasts of lamb

- Remove excess fat and skin.
- **For roasting**: bone, stuff and roll; tie with string.
- **For stewing**: cut into even 25–50 g pieces.

Preparing middle neck

- **For stewing**: remove excess fat, excess bone and gristle; cut into even 50 g pieces; this joint, when correctly butchered, can give good uncovered second-class cutlets.

Preparing scrag-end

- **For stewing**: this can be chopped down the centre, the excess bone, fat and gristle removed, and cut into even 50 g pieces, or boned out and cut into pieces.

Preparing a saddle of lamb

The saddle may be divided as follows:

- remove the skin, starting from head to tail and from breast to back
- split down the centre of the backbone to produce two loins
- each loin can be roasted whole, boned and stuffed, or cut into loin and chump chops.

A full saddle is illustrated below. For large banquets it is sometimes better to remove the chumps and use short saddles. Saddles may also be boned and stuffed.

▲ Saddle of lamb

If the saddle is to be roasted:

- skin and remove the kidney
- trim the excess fat and sinew
- cut off the flaps, leaving about 15 cm each side so as to meet in the middle under the saddle
- remove the aitch, or pelvic, bone
- score neatly and tie with string.

For presentation the tail may be left on, protected with foil and tied back. The saddle can also be completely boned, stuffed and tied.

Preparing a loin of lamb

If the loin is to be roasted:

- skin and remove excess fat and sinew
- remove the pelvic bone and tie with string.

If the loin is to be boned and stuffed:

- remove the skin, excess fat and sinew
- bone out
- replace the fillet, season and stuff if required, and tie with string.

Preparing lamb chops

- **Loin chops**: skin the loin, remove the excess fat and sinew, then cut into chops approximately 100–150 g in weight. A first-class loin chop should have a piece of kidney skewered in the centre.
- **Double loin chop (Barnsley chop)**: these are cut approximately 2 cm across a saddle on the bone. When trimmed they are secured with a skewer and may include a piece of kidney in the centre of each chop.
- **Chump chops**: these are cut from the chump end of the loin. Cut into approximately 150 g chops and trim where necessary.
- **Noisettes**: this is a cut from a boned-out loin. Cut slantwise into approximately 2 cm thick slices, bat out slightly, and trim into a cutlet shape.
- **Rosettes**: this is a cut from a boned-out loin approximately 2 cm thick. It is shaped round and tied with string.
- **Valentine**: this is a cut from a boned-out loin. Cut slantwise into approximately 4 cm thick slices, then cut in half through top, about two-thirds through but keeping the meat connected at bottom, and fold out into heart shape (often called a butterfly cut).

▲ Lamb loin chops

▲ Left to right: rosette, valentine, noisette, Barnsley (double loin) chop

Preparing a best end (rack) of lamb

1 Remove the bark/skin, working from head to tail and from breast to back. Leave as much fat as possible on the joint.

2 Mark or score the fat, 2 cm from the end of the bones.

3 Score down the middle of the back of each bone, scoring the cartilage.

4 Pull the skin fat and meat from the bone (to bring out the bone ends – this is an alternative to scraping them).

5 Remove the elastin as shown, then clean the sinew from between the rib bones.

6 Trim the overall length of the bones to two and a half times the length of the nut of meat. Score the fat neatly to approximately 2 mm deep and tie the joint.

To make the best end into cutlets, prepare as for roasting, excluding the scoring, and divide evenly between the bones. Alternatively, the cutlets can be cut from the best end and prepared separately.

A single cutlet consists of one bone, and a double cutlet two bones, so a six-bone best end yields six single or three double cutlets.

▲ Lamb cutlets

220

Carving and serving roast lamb

Roast leg

Holding the bone, carve with a sharp knife at an angle of 45 degrees and take off each slice as it is cut. Continue in this manner along the joint, turning it from side to side as the slices get wider.

Shoulder

To obtain reasonable-sized slices of meat, carve the flesh side, not the skin side, of the joint. Having obtained the slices, carve round the bones. Due to the awkward shape of the bone structure, the shoulder is normally boned out, rolled and tied before cooking to facilitate carving.

Roast saddle

- **Carving on the bone**: there are two usual ways of carving the saddle, one is by carving lengthways either side of the backbone, the other by making a deep cut lengthwise either side of the backbone and then slicing across each loin. It is usual to carve the saddle in thick slices.
- **Carving off the bone**: for economical kitchen carving it is often best to bone the loins out whole, carve into slices, then reform on the saddle bone.
- The fillets may be left on the saddle or removed; in either case they are carved and served with the rest of the meat.

Roast loin

- **On the bone**: proceed as for the saddle.
- **Boned-out**: cut in slices across the joint; the slices are cut slightly thicker when stuffed.

Roast best end (rack)

Divide into cutlets by cutting between bones.

Service

All roast joints are served garnished with watercress and a sauceboat of roast gravy separately. When carved, serve a little gravy over the slices as well as offering a sauceboat of gravy. Mint sauce should be served with roast lamb and redcurrant jelly should be available. For roast mutton, redcurrant jelly and/or onion sauce should be served, with mint sauce available.

Beef

Quality points

- The lean meat should be bright red with small flecks of white fat (marbled).
- The fat should be firm, brittle in texture, creamy-white in colour and odourless. Older animals and dairy breeds have fat that is usually a deeper-yellow colour.

Butchery

A side of beef weighs approximately 180 kg. A whole side is divided between the wing ribs and the fore ribs.

Video: beef hindquarter joints
http://bit.ly/1G36Ecv

▲ A side of beef

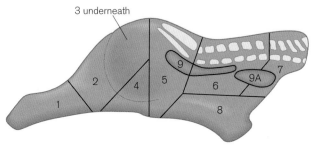

▲ A hindquarter of beef in more detail

1	Shin	9A	Fat and kidney
2	Topside	10	Fore rib
3	Silverside	11	Middle rib
4	Thick flank	12	Chuck rib
5	Rump	13	Sticking piece
6	Sirloin	14	Plate
7	Wing ribs	15	Brisket
8	Thin flank	16	Leg of mutton cut
9	Fillet	17	Shank

Dissection of a hindquarter of beef

1 Remove the rump suet and kidney.
2 Remove the thin flank.
3 Divide the loin and rump from the leg (topside, silverside, thick flank and shin).
4 Remove the fillet.
5 Divide the rump from the sirloin.
6 Remove the wing ribs.
7 Remove the shin.
8 Bone out the aitchbone.
9 Divide the leg into the three remaining joints (silverside, topside and thick flank).

Table 10.4 Joints, uses and weights of a hindquarter of beef

Joint	Uses	Approx. weight (kg)
Shin	Consommé, beef tea, stewing	7
Topside	Braising, stewing, second-class roasting	10
Silverside	Pickled in brine then boiled	14
Thick flank	Braising and stewing	12
Rump	Grilling and frying as steaks, braised in the piece	10
Sirloin	Roasting, grilling and frying in steaks	9
Wing ribs	Roasting, grilling and frying in steaks	5
Thin flank	Stewing, boiling, sausages	10
Fillet	Roasting, grilling and frying in steaks	3
Fat and kidney	Fat: rendered for frying and basting, using in pastry	10
	Kidney: pies, puddings, braising	

Preparing joints from a hindquarter of beef

- **Shin**: bone out, remove excess sinew; cut or chop as required.
- **Topside**: for roasting and braising remove excess fat, cut into joints and tie with string; for stewing cut into dice or steaks as required.
- **Silverside**: remove the thigh bone; this joint is usually kept whole and pickled in brine prior to boning.
- **Thick flank**: as for topside.
- **Rump**: bone out; cut off the first outside slice for pies and puddings. Cut into approximately 1.5 cm slices for steaks. The point steak – considered the most tender – is cut from the pointed end of the slice.

Dissection of a forequarter of beef

1 Remove the shank.
2 Divide in half down the centre.
3 Take off the fore ribs.
4 Divide into joints.

Table 10.5 Joints, uses and weights of a forequarter of beef

Joint	Uses	Approx. weight (kg)
Fore rib	Roasting and braising	8
Middle rib	Roasting and braising	10
Chuck rib	Stewing and braising	15
Sticking piece	Stewing and sausages	9
Plate	Stewing and sausages	10
Brisket	Pickled in brine and boiled, pressed beef	19
Leg of mutton cut	Braising and stewing	11
Shank	Consommé, beef tea	6

Preparing cuts of beef

The cuts of beef vary considerably, from very tender fillet steak through to tough brisket or shin, and there is a greater variety of cuts in beef than for any other type of meat. While their names may vary, there are 14 primary cuts from a side of beef, each one composed of muscle, fat, bone and connective tissue. The least developed muscles, usually from the inner areas, can be roasted or grilled, while leaner and more sinewy meat is cut from the more highly developed external muscles. Exceptions are rib and loin cuts, which come from external but basically immobile muscles.

Knowing where the cuts come from helps to designate the cooking method.

- **Fillet** is taken from the back of the animal; this is the most tender part, cut from the centre of the sirloin. It is usually cut into steaks and can be fried or grilled.
- **Sirloin** is either roasted as a joint or cut into boneless steaks; it is more tender than rump but not as tender as fillet. Sirloin steaks are suitable for grilling or frying.
- **Rump** is a good-quality cut though it is less tender than fillet or sirloin. It is suitable for roasting, grilling or frying.
- **Rib** is sold on the bone or unboned and rolled. It is suitable for roasting.
- **Topside** is a lean, tender cut from the hindquarters. It is suitable for braising or pot roasting.

- **Silverside** is taken from the hindquarters; this is a cut from the round. It can be pot roasted or used for traditional boiled beef.
- **Flank** is a boneless cut from the mid-to-hindquarters; it is suitable for braising or stewing.
- **Skirt** is a boneless, rather gristly cut. It is usually stewed or made into mince.
- **Brisket** is a cut from the fore end of the animal, below the shoulder. Quite a fatty joint, it is sold on or off the bone or salted. It is suitable for slow roasting.

▲ Fillet and loin of beef

Sirloin

If the sirloin is to be roasted whole on the bone (*l'aloyau de boeuf*):

- Saw through the chine bone.
- Lift back the covering fat in one piece for approximately 10 cm.
- Trim off the sinew and replace the covering fat.
- Tie with string if necessary.
- Ensure that the fillet has been removed.

To roast the whole sirloin boned out:

- Remove the fillet and bone out the sirloin. Remove the sinew.
- Remove the excess fat and sinew from the boned side.
- This joint may be roasted open or rolled and tied with string.

Sirloin may be cut into various steaks for grilling or frying:

- **Minute steaks**: cut into 1 cm slices, flatten with a cutlet bat dipped in water, making as thin as possible, then trim.
- **Sirloin steaks (entrecôte)**: cut into 1 cm-thick slices and trim (approximate weight 150 g).
- **Double sirloin steaks**: cut into 2 cm-thick slices and trim (approximate weight 250–300 g).

- **Porterhouse steaks**: cut including the bone from the rib end of the sirloin.
- **T-bone steaks**: cut from the rump end of the sirloin, including the bone and fillet.

▲ T-bone steaks

Fillet

As a fillet of beef can vary from 2.5–4.5 kg it follows that there must be considerable variation in the number of steaks obtained from it. In this list of the different fillet steaks, it is assumed that a 3 kg fillet is used.

- **Chateaubriand**: double fillet steak 3 to 10 cm thick, two to four portions (average weight 300 g to 1 kg). Cut from the head of the fillet, trim off all the nerves and leave a little fat on the steak.
- **Fillet steaks**: approximately four steaks of 100 to 150 g each, 1.5 to 2 cm thick. These are trimmed as for chateaubriand.
- **Tournedos**: approximately six to eight at 100 g each, 2 to 4 cm thick. Continue cutting down the fillet. Remove all the nerve and fat tissue, and tie each tournedos with string.
- **Tail of fillet** is another possible cut. The tail of a 3 kg fillet will weigh approximately 0.5 kg. Remove all fat and sinew, and slice or mince as required. This cut is useful for dishes that need small pieces of tender beef, such as stir-fries.

▲ Cuts of fillet of beef

The whole fillet may be roasted or pot roasted (*poêlé*). Remove the head and tail of the fillet, leaving an even centre piece from which all the nerve and fat is removed. This may be larded by inserting pieces of fat bacon, cut into long strips, with a larding needle.

Wing rib (*côte de boeuf*)

This joint usually consists of the last three rib bones, which, because of their curved shape, act as a natural trivet. Because of its prime quality it is a first-class roasting joint, hot or cold, particularly when it is to be carved in front of the customer.

To prepare, the chine needs to be removed from the joint

Cut seven-eighths of the way through the spine or chine bone and remove the nerve

Saw through the rib bones on the underside, 5–10 cm from the end, to finish removing the chine

Trim and clean the top bone

Remove the elastin

Tie the bone firmly back with string; it will act as a trivet

Fore ribs and middle ribs from the forequarter are prepared in the same way as wing rib.

Other cuts

- **Thin flank** from the hindquarter: trim off excessive fat and cut or roll as required.
- **Chuck ribs, sticking piece, brisket, plate, leg of mutton cut** and **shank** are all cuts from the forequarter. Bone out, remove excess fat and sinew, and use as required.

Barbecue cooking

1 **Choice of meat**: some fat is required for flavour, but not too much. Ensure size and thickness are uniform to allow even cooking. Suitable cuts include: T-bone steaks, rib steaks, double lamb chops and noisettes, well-trimmed pork cutlets and steaks.

2 **Seasoning**: add salt and pepper, and brush lightly with oil before placing on the barbecue. Take care when using marinades as some may contain glucose, which burns easily. Try marinating with wine and herbs; avoid marinating oils, which may ignite and spoil the barbecue.

3 **Choice and preparation of barbecue**: gas is the preferred choice for temperature control. Allow time to preheat the barbecue (30 minutes for gas, 1½ hours for charcoal). If cooking on charcoal, always wait for the flames to go out and the embers to start glowing before starting to cook.
   - Secure a layer of tinfoil over the barbecue.
   - Wait until the grill bars are hot or the charcoal embers glow.
   - Remove tin foil and brush the grill bars with a firm, long-handled wire brush to remove any unwanted debris.

4 **Cooking**: place the seasoned and lightly oiled meat at a 45° angle on the barbecue and seal one side. Rotate through another 45°, allow to cook, then turn the meat and repeat the process: this creates attractive markings on the meat. Control the temperature and do not let the meat burn or blacken unnecessarily. Only cook as much meat as required at one time; if left for too long it will dry out and become tough. Use a meat probe to ensure the desired internal temperature is reached. 'Made-up' items such as burgers and sausages must be cooked thoroughly to the centre.

5 Serve with fresh, crisp vegetables or salads and traditional barbecue dips and sauces.

> ### Health and safety ⚠
> Burgers and sausages should be cut open, checked and cooked for longer if necessary. Barbecued food may look well cooked when it isn't.

Testing whether beef is cooked

Roast joints

When using a temperature probe, insert it into the part of the joint that was thickest before the food was placed in the oven. The internal temperature reached should be as follows:

- rare meat: 55–60 °C
- medium done: 66–71 °C
- well done: 78–80 °C.

To test without a temperature probe:

- remove the joint from the oven and place on a plate or dish
- firmly press the surface of the meat so that some juice issues
- check the colour of the juice: *red* indicates the meat is underdone; *pink* indicates the meat is medium done; *clear* indicates that the meat is cooked through.

Grilled beef

The degrees of cooking for grilled meat are:

- very rare (or blue): cooked over a fierce heat for a few seconds on each side
- rare: the cooked meat has a reddish tinge
- medium: the cooked meat is slightly pinkish
- well done: thoroughly cooked with no sign of pinkness.

When using a temperature probe, insert it into the part of the meat that was thickest before the food was placed under the grill. The internal temperature reached should be as follows:

- rare: 45–50 °C
- medium: 55–60 °C
- well done: 75–77 °C.

You can also check how well done grilled meat is by using finger pressure. The springiness, or resilience, of the meat and the amount of blood issuing from it indicates the degree to which it is cooked. This calls for experience, but if the meat is placed on a plate and tested, then the more underdone the steak, the greater the springiness and the more blood will be shown on the plate.

Veal

Veal is obtained from good-quality carcasses weighing around 100 kg. This quality of veal is required for first-class cookery and is produced from calves slaughtered at between 12 and 24 weeks.

Veal is available all year round.

Quality points

- The flesh should be pale pink in colour and firm in structure – not soft or flabby.
- Cut surfaces should be slightly moist, not dry.
- Bones, in young animals, should be pinkish white, porous and with a degree of blood in their structure.
- The fat should be firm and pinkish white.
- The kidney should be firm and well covered with fat.

Where applicable, when offering veal on a menu, give the origin and breed of the veal.

The veal carcass

The average weight of English or Dutch milk-fed veal calves is 18 kg. The joints of veal are shown in the diagram and Table 10.6.

The order of dissection for a veal carcass is as follows:

1 Remove the shoulders.
2 Remove the breast.
3 Take off the leg.
4 Divide the loin and best end from the scrag and neck end.
5 Divide the loin from the best end.

▲ A side of veal – see Table 10.6 for an explanation of the numbers

Table 10.6 Uses and weights of veal joints and offal

Joint	Uses	Approx. weight (kg)
Knuckle (1)	Osso buco, sauté, stock	2
Leg (2)	Roasting, braising, escalopes, sauté	5
Loin (3)	Roasting, frying, grilling	3.5
Best end (4)	Roasting, frying, grilling	3
Shoulder (5)	Braising, stewing	5
Neck end (6)	Stewing, sauté	2.5
Scrag (7)	Stewing, stock	1.5
Breast (8)	Stewing, roasting	2.5
Kidneys	Stewing (pies and puddings), sauté	–
Liver	Frying	–
Sweetbreads	Braising, frying	–
Head	Boiling, soup	4
Brains	Boiling, frying	–
Bones	Stock	–

Dissecting a leg of veal

1 Remove the knuckle by dividing the knee joint (at A on the diagram) and cut through the meat away from the cushion line (from A to B).
2 Remove the aitchbone at thick end of the leg, separating it at the ball and socket joint.
3 Remove all the outside skin and fat, thus exposing the natural seams. It will now be seen that the thigh bone divides the meat into two-thirds and one-third (thick flank).
4 Stand the leg on the thick flank with point D (on the diagram) uppermost. Divide the cushion from the under cushion, following the natural seam, using the hand and the point of a knife. Having reached the thigh bone, remove it completely.

5 When the boned leg falls open, the three joints can easily be seen joined only by membrane. Separate and trim the cushion, removing the loose flap of meat.
6 Trim the under cushion, removing the layer of thick gristle. Separate into three small joints through the natural seams. It will be seen that one of these will correspond with the round in silverside of beef.
7 Trim the thick flank by laying it on its round side and making a cut along the length about 2.5 cm deep. A seam is reached and the two trimmings can be removed.

The anticipated yield of escalopes from this size of leg would be 6.25 kg, that is, 55 × 100 g or 75 × 80 g, serving 1 or 2 escalopes per portion.

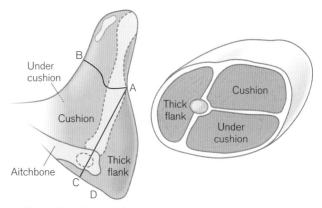

▲ Dissection of a leg of veal

Preparing joints and cuts of veal

Shin
● For stewing (on the bone; *osso buco*): cut and saw into 2–4 cm thick slices through the knuckle.
● For sauté: bone out and trim, then cut into even 25 g pieces.

Leg
● For braising or roasting whole: remove the aitch bone, clean and trim 4 cm off the knuckle bone. Trim off the excess sinew.

Table 10.7 Joints of a leg of veal

Cuts	Weight	Proportion	Uses	Corresponding joint in beef
Cushion or nut	2.75 kg	15%	Escalopes, roasting, braising, sauté	Topside
Under cushion or under nut	3 kg	17%	Escalopes, roasting, braising, sauté	Silverside
Thick flank	2.5 kg	14%	Escalopes, roasting, braising, sauté	Thick flank
Knuckle (whole)	2.5 kg	14%	Osso buco, sauté	
Bones (thigh and aitch)	2.5 kg	14%	Stock, *jus-lié*, sauces	
Usable trimmings	2 kg	11%	Pies, stewing	

- To braise or roast the nut: remove all the sinew; if there is insufficient fat on the joint then bard (tie fat around it, for example, bacon) thinly and secure with string.
- Escalopes: remove all the sinew, cut into large 50–75 g slices against the grain and bat out thinly.
- For sauté: remove all the sinew and cut into 25 g pieces.

Loin and best end

- For roasting: bone out and trim the flap, roll out and secure with string. This joint may be stuffed before rolling.
- For frying: trim and cut into cutlets.

▲ Veal escalopes

Boning a loin of veal

The loin

Using a boning knife, carefully remove the fillet

The joint and the fillet

Bring the loin down from the rib to the backbone, and trim the rib bones

Trim the excess fat and sinew from the meat

The fillet, boned loin and bones (which can be used for stock)

Shoulder

- For braising: bone out as for lamb; usually stuffed.
- For stewing: bone out, remove all the sinew and cut into 25 g pieces.

Neck end and scrag

For stewing or sauté: bone out and remove all the sinew; cut into approximately 25 g pieces.

Breast

- For stewing: as for neck end.
- For roasting: bone out, season, stuff and roll up, then tie with string.

Pork

The keeping quality of pork is less than that of other meat; therefore it must be handled, prepared and cooked with great care. Pork should always be well cooked, reaching at least 75 °C in the centre.

Where applicable, name the origin and breed of the pork (e.g. Gloucester Old Spot, Tamworth) on the menu.

Quality points

- Lean flesh should be pale pink, firm and of a fine texture.
- The fat should be white, firm, smooth and not excessive.
- Bones should be small, fine and pinkish.
- The skin or rind should be smooth.

The pork carcass

The cuts of pork are shown in the diagram below and their uses in Table 10.8.

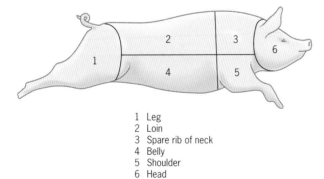

1 Leg
2 Loin
3 Spare rib of neck
4 Belly
5 Shoulder
6 Head

▲ Pig carcass dissection

Table 10.8 Joints, uses and weights of pork

Joint	Uses	Approx. weight (kg)
Leg	Roasting, boiling	5
Loin	Roasting, frying, grilling	6
Spare rib	Roasting, pies	1.5
Belly	Pickling, boiling, stuffed, rolled and roasted	2
Shoulder	Roasting, sausages, pies	3
Head	Brawn	4
Trotters	Grilling, boiling	
Kidneys	Sauté, grilling	
Liver	Frying, pâté	

At five to six weeks old a piglet is known as a sucking or suckling pig. Its weight is then between 5 and 10 kg.

The order of dissection for a pig carcass is:

1 Remove the head.
2 Remove the trotters.
3 Remove the leg.
4 Remove the shoulder.
5 Remove the spare ribs.
6 Divide the loin from the belly.

Preparing joints and cuts of pork

Leg

- **For roasting**: remove the pelvic or aitch bone, trim and score the rind neatly – that is, with a sharp-pointed knife make a series of 3 mm-deep incisions approximately 2 cm apart all over the skin of the joint; trim and clean the knuckle bone.
- **For boiling**: it is usual to pickle the joint either by rubbing dry salt and saltpetre (potassium nitrate) into the meat or by soaking it in a brine solution (see recipe 21); then remove the pelvic bone, trim and secure with string if necessary.

Loin

- **For roasting (on the bone)**: saw down the chine bone in order to facilitate carving; trim the excess fat and sinew and score the rind in the direction that the joint will be carved; season and secure with string.
- **For roasting (boned out)**: remove the fillets and bone out carefully; trim off the excess fat and sinew, score the rind and neaten the flap. Season, replace the filet mignon, roll up and secure the string. This joint is sometimes stuffed.

- **Chops for grilling or frying**: remove the skin, excess fat and sinew, then cut and saw or chop through the loin in approximately 1 cm-thick slices; remove the excess bone and trim neatly.

▲ Boned leg of pork

▲ Loin of pork

▲ Pork chops

Spare rib

- **For roasting**: remove the excess fat, bone and sinew, and trim neatly.
- **For grilling**: remove the excess fat, bone and sinew, cut into individual ribs or leave as a rack, and marinade for at least 2 hours.
- **For pies**: remove the excess fat and sinew, bone out and cut as required.

Shoulder

- **For roasting**: the shoulder is usually boned out, the excess fat and sinew removed, seasoned, scored and rolled with string; it may be stuffed and can also be divided into two smaller joints.
- **For sausages or pies**: skin, bone out and remove the excess fat and sinew; cut into even pieces or mince.

Belly

Boning a pork belly

Pork belly before it is prepared for roasting

Remove all the small rib bones

Cut the fat

Score the fat

Season with salt, pepper and chopped sage

Roll and secure with string; this joint may be stuffed

Bacon

Bacon is the cured flesh of a bacon-weight pig that is specifically reared for bacon (because its shape and size yield economic bacon joints). Bacon is cured either by dry salting and then smoking or by soaking in brine followed by smoking. Green bacon is brine-cured but not smoked; it has a milder flavour but does not keep for as long as smoked bacon.

Depending on the degree of salting during the curing process, bacon joints may or may not require soaking in cold water before being cooked.

Do not confuse ham with gammon. Ham is meat taken from the carcass *before* salting or smoking and cooking, where gammon is taken from the carcass *after* brining and smoking.

Quality

- There should be no sign of stickiness.
- There should be a pleasant smell.
- The rind should be thin, smooth and free from wrinkles.
- The fat should be white, smooth and not excessive in proportion to the lean meat.
- The lean meat should be a deep-pink colour and firm.

Preparing bacon joints and cuts

1 Collar
2 Hock
3 Back
4 Streaky
5 Gammon

Grilling cuts

Gammon

▲ A side of bacon

Table 10.9 Cuts, uses and weights of bacon

Joint	Uses	Approx. weight (kg)
Collar	Boiling, grilling	4.5
Hock	Boiling, grilling	4.5
Back	Grilling, frying	9
Streaky	Grilling, frying	4.5
Gammon	Boiling, grilling, frying	7.5

Collar

- **For boiling**: remove bone (if any) and tie with string.
- **Rashers for grilling**: remove the rind, trim off the outside surface and cut into thin slices (rashers) across the joint.

Hock

Leave whole or bone out and secure with string. The hock is usually boiled.

Back and streaky bacon

- **Rashers for grilling**: remove all bones and rind, and cut into thin rashers.
- **Rashers or chops for frying**: remove the rind, trim off the outside surface and cut into rashers or chops of the required thickness.

Gammon

Cut fairly thick slices from the middle of the gammon. Trim them and remove the rind. Slices of gammon are usually grilled or fried.

▲ Gammon

▲ Gammon steaks

Offal and other edible parts of the carcass

Offal is the name given to the edible parts taken from the inside of a carcass of meat, including the liver, kidneys, heart and sweetbreads. Tripe, brains, tongue, head and oxtail are also sometimes included under this term.

Fresh offal (unfrozen) should be purchased as required and can be refrigerated under hygienic conditions at a temperature of 1–4 °C. Frozen offal must be kept in a deep freeze at −18 °C or below, and defrosted in a refrigerator as required.

Preparing kidneys for grilling

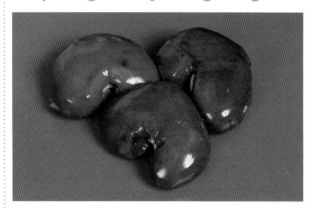

Skin the kidneys, and remove any fat and gristle

Split the kidney three-quarters of the way through, and open it up

Lift up and cut out the white sinew in the centre

Kidneys before, during and after preparation

Liver

Liver is low in fat, a good source of protein and iron, and also contains vitamins A and D.

- **Calf's liver** is considered the best in terms of tenderness and flavour. It is also the most expensive.
- **Lamb's liver** is mild in flavour, light in colour and tender. Sheep's liver, being from an older animal, is firmer in substance, deeper in colour and has a stronger flavour.
- **Ox** or **beef liver** is the cheapest and, if taken from an older animal, can be coarse in texture and strong in flavour. It is usually braised.
- **Pig's liver** has a strong, full flavour and is used mainly for pâté recipes.

Quality points

- Liver should look fresh, moist and smooth, with a pleasant colour and no unpleasant smell.
- Liver should not be dry or contain an excessive number of tubes.

Preparing liver

- Remove the skin if possible.
- Remove the gristle and tubes.
- Cut into thin slices on the slant.

Kidneys

The nutritional value of kidney is similar to that of liver.

- **Lamb's kidneys** are light in colour, delicate in flavour and ideal for grilling and frying.
- **Sheep's kidneys** are darker in colour and stronger in flavour.
- **Calf's kidneys** are light in colour, delicate in flavour and used in a variety of dishes.
- **Ox kidney** is dark in colour, strong in flavour, and is either braised or used in pies and puddings (mixed with beef).
- **Pig's kidneys** are smooth, long and flat, and have a strong flavour.

Quality points

- Suet – the saturated fat in which kidneys are encased – should be left on, otherwise the kidneys will dry out. The suet should be removed when kidneys are being prepared for cooking.
- Both suet and kidneys should be moist and have no unpleasant smell.

Preparing kidneys

Skin them and remove the fat and gristle, then cut as required:

- **For grilling**: split the kidney three-quarters of the way through lengthwise. Cut out and discard the gristle. Skewer.
- **For sauté**: cut slantways.
- **For calves' or pigs' kidneys**: cut down the middle lengthwise. Remove the sinew. Cut into thin slices or neat dice.

▲ Veal kidneys

Hearts

Hearts are a good source of protein, which is needed for growth and repair of the body.

- **Lamb's hearts** are small and light; they are normally served whole.
- **Sheep's hearts** are dark and solid; they can be dry and tough unless cooked carefully.
- **Ox** or **beef hearts** are dark coloured and solid, and tend to be dry and tough.
- **Calf's hearts**, coming from a younger animal, are lighter in colour and more tender.

Before cooking, remove the arterial tubes and excess fat. Most hearts need slow braising to tenderise them.

Quality points

- Hearts should not be too fatty and should not contain too many tubes.
- When cut they should be moist, not sticky, and with no unpleasant smell.

Sweetbreads

Sweetbreads are the pancreas gland (heart bread) and thymus gland (neck bread). The heart bread is round, plump and of better quality than the neck bread, which is long and uneven in shape. Calf's heart bread, considered the best, weighs up to 600 g, while lamb's heart bread weighs up to 100 g.

Sweetbreads are an easily digested source of protein, which makes them valuable for use in invalid diets.

Quality points

- Heart and neck breads should be fleshy and of a good size.
- They should be creamy-white in colour and have no unpleasant smell.

Preparing sweetbreads

- Soak in cold salted water for two to three hours to remove blood, which would darken the sweetbreads during cooking. Use several changes of water for calves' sweetbreads.
- Wash well, blanch, trim and refresh.
- For calves' sweetbreads, peel off the membrane and connective tissue.
- The sweetbreads can then be pressed between two trays with a weight on top, and refrigerated.

▲ Veal sweetbreads

Tripe

Tripe is the stomach lining or white muscle of the ox, consisting of the rumen or paunch and the honeycomb tripe (considered the best). Sheep tripe, which is darker in colour, is obtainable in some areas. Tripe contains protein, is low in fat and high in calcium.

Tripe should be fresh, with no signs of stickiness or unpleasant smell. To prepare it, wash it well and soak in cold water, then cut into even pieces. Boil or simmer until tender.

Tongues

Ox, lamb and sheep tongues are those most used in cooking. Ox tongues are usually salted then soaked before being cooked. Lamb tongues are cooked fresh.

Tongues must be fresh and have no unpleasant smell and there should not be an excess of waste at the root end. To prepare them for cooking remove the bone and gristle from the throat end and soak in cold water for two to four hours. If salted, soak for three to four hours.

Oxtail

Oxtails usually weigh 1.5–2 kg and should be lean with not too much fat. There should be no sign of stickiness and no unpleasant smell. To prepare the tail, cut between the natural joints then trim off excess fat. The large pieces may be split in two.

Suet

Suet is the fat that surrounds the kidneys. Beef suet should be creamy-white, brittle and dry. Other meat fat should be fresh, not sticky, and with no unpleasant smell.

Bone marrow

Marrow is obtained from the bones of the leg of beef. It should be of good size, firm, creamy-white and odourless. Sliced, poached marrow may be used as a garnish for some meat dishes and savouries.

Bones

Bones must be fresh, not sticky, with no unpleasant smell, and preferably meaty (as they are used for stock, the foundation for so many preparations).

Pigs' trotters

To prepare trotters, boil in water for a few minutes then scrape with the back of a knife to remove the hairs. Wash off in cold water and split in half.

Table 10.10 Uses of beef offal

Offal	Uses
Bones	Beef stocks
Heart	Braising
Kidney	Stewing, soup
Liver	Braising, frying
Suet	Suet paste and stuffing, or rendered down for first-class dripping
Sweetbread	Braising, frying
Tail	Braising, soup
Tongue	Pickled in brine, boiling, braising
Tripe	Boiling, braising

Other meat preparations

Forcemeat

This is a term given to numerous mixtures of meats (usually veal and pork) and poultry, game, fish, vegetables and bread. Forcemeats range from a simple sausagemeat to the finer mixtures used in the making of hot mousses (ham, chicken, fish) and soufflés. Also included are mixtures of bread, vegetables and herbs, which are alternatively referred to as stuffings.

Forcemeats are used for galantines, raised pies, terrines, meatballs and a wide variety of other dishes.

Crépinettes

These are small sausages, usually made from a forcemeat of veal, lamb, pork or chicken, encased either in caul (a thin membrane of fat from the intestines) or paper-thin slices of salt pork. Other ingredients are sometimes added (e.g. chopped mushrooms or truffles). Crépinettes are usually covered with melted butter or good quality oil, coated with fresh white breadcrumbs and grilled, sautéed or cooked in the oven. Traditionally they are served with potato purée and a well-flavoured demi-glace sauce.

Test yourself

1   List two quality points to look for when buying beef.

2   Describe how to store uncooked meat in a refrigerator.

3   Describe the stages in the preparation of a best end of lamb.

4   What are the benefits of sealing meat before cooking?

5   Give two reasons why braising is a suitable cooking method for neck of veal.

6   Describe the stages in the preparation and cooking of a leg of pork.

7   List four quality points to look for when buying pork.

8   List two quality points to look for when buying calves' liver.

9   Why is braising the most appropriate cooking method for hearts?

10 Describe how to prepare sweetbreads for cooking.

Lamb dishes

1 Grilled lamb cutlets (*côtelettes d'agneau grillées*)

1 Season the cutlets lightly with salt and mill pepper.
2 Brush with oil or fat.
3 If the grill is heated from below, place the prepared cutlet on the greased, preheated bars. Cook for approximately 5 minutes, turn and complete the cooking.
4 If using a salamander, place the cutlets on a greased tray, cook for approximately 5 minutes, turn and complete the cooking.
5 Serve dressed, garnished with a deep-fried potato and watercress. A compound butter (e.g. parsley, herb or garlic) may also be served.
6 Each cutlet bone may be capped with a cutlet frill.

Healthy eating tips

When served with boiled new potatoes and boiled or steamed vegetables, the dish becomes more 'balanced'.

Energy	Cals	Fat	Sat fat	Carb	Sugar	Protein	Fibre	Sodium
1,493 kJ	357 kcal	20.7 g	9.8 g	0.0 g	0.0 g	42.8 g	0.0 g	0.1 g

2 Mixed grill

Ingredient	4 portions	10 portions
Sausages	4	10
Cutlets	4	10
Kidneys	4	10
Tomatoes	4	10
Mushrooms	4	10
Streaky bacon, rashers	4	10
Deep-fried potato, to serve		
Watercress, to serve		
Parsley butter, to serve		

Energy	Cals	Fat	Sat fat	Carb	Sugar	Protein	Fibre
2,050 kJ	488 kcal	40.8 g	19.3 g	0.0 g	0.0 g	30.4 g	0.0 g

1 portion (2 cutlets). With deep-fried potatoes, parsley and watercress, 1 portion provides: 3,050 kJ/726 kcal energy, 59.2 g fat, 26.6 g saturated fat, 20.2 g carbohydrates, 2.5 g sugar, 29.5 g protein and 4.9 g fibre.

These are the usually accepted items for a mixed grill, but it will be found that there are many variations to this list (e.g. steaks, liver, a Welsh rarebit and fried egg).

1 Grill in the order listed above.

2 Dress neatly on an oval flat dish or plates.

Garnish with deep-fried potato, watercress and a slice of compound butter on each kidney or offered separately.

> **Professional tip**
>
> The items must be cooked in the order listed above, so that they are all fully and evenly cooked at the end.

Healthy eating tips
Add only a small amount of compound butter and serve with plenty of potatoes and vegetables.

3 Lamb kebabs (*shish kebab*)

Energy	Cals	Fat	Sat fat	Carb	Sugar	Protein	Fibre	Sodium
1,544 kJ	372 kcal	25.1 g	9.9 g	7.2 g	5.9 g	29.6 g	2.0 g	0.1 g

1 Cut the meat into cubes and place on skewers with squares of green pepper, tomato, onion and bay leaves in between. The pieces of lamb and vegetables must be cut evenly so that they will cook evenly

2 Sprinkle with chopped thyme and cook over a hot grill.

Serve with pilaff rice, or with chickpeas and finely sliced raw onion.

Note

Kebabs, a dish of Turkish origin, are pieces of food impaled and cooked on skewers over a grill or barbecue. There are many variations and different flavours can be added by marinating the kebabs in oil, wine, vinegar or lemon juice with spices and herbs for 1–2 hours before cooking.

Kebabs can be made using tender cuts, or mince of lamb and beef, pork, liver, kidney, bacon, ham, sausage and chicken, using either the meats individually or combining two or three. Vegetables and fruit can also be added (e.g. onion, apple, pineapple, peppers, tomatoes, aubergine). Kebabs can be made using vegetables exclusively (e.g. peppers, onion, aubergine, tomatoes). Kebabs are usually served with a pilaff rice (see page 125).

The ideal cuts of lamb are the nut of the lean meat of the loin, best end or boned-out meat from a young shoulder of lamb.

Variation

Miniature kebabs (one mouthful) can be made, impaled on cocktail sticks, grilled and served as an amuse-bouche, or as a hot snack at receptions.

Fish kebabs can be made using a firm fish, such as monkfish or tuna, and marinating in olive oil, lemon or lime juice, chopped fennel or dill, garlic and a dash of Tabasco or Worcester sauce.

4 Lamb satay

Ingredient	To make 10	To make 20
Lamb fillets or loin of lamb	250 g	500 g
Clove of garlic, crushed and chopped	1	2
Thai fish sauce	1 tsp	2 tsp
Sweet chilli sauce	1 tbsp	2 tbsp
Fresh ginger, grated	1 tsp	2 tsp
Lime juice	30 ml	60 ml
Peanut butter (coarse)	1 tbsp	2 tbsp
Ground cumin	½ tsp	1 tsp
Ground turmeric	½ tsp	1 tsp
Sauce		
White vinegar	30 ml	60 ml
Caster sugar	1 tbsp	2 tbsp
Sweet chilli sauce	3 tsp	1 tbsp
Unsalted, roasted peanuts	3 tsp	1 tbsp
Fresh coriander leaves, finely chopped	3 tsp	1 tbsp

Energy	Cals	Fat	Sat fat	Carb	Sugar	Protein	Fibre	Sodium
1,624 kJ	391 kcal	29.3 g	10.2 g	13.3 g	11.7 g	19.6 g	2.4 g	0.7 g

1 Prepare the lamb, cutting it into thin strips.

2 In a bowl place the garlic, sauces, ginger, lime juice, peanut butter and spices. Mix well.

3 Put the lamb into the marinade, stir and put in refrigerator for 3 hours or overnight.

4 Meanwhile, soak some bamboo skewers in water for about an hour to prevent scorching.

5 Thread the lamb on to the skewers. Grill the lamb skewers, turning once until cooked and nicely coloured.

6 Prepare the sauce by placing the vinegar and sugar in a small pan, stirring until the sugar has dissolved. Bring to the boil and simmer for 2 minutes. Stir in the remaining ingredients.

7 Serve the lamb on a suitable platter on banana leaves (optional) with the dipping sauce in a bowl in the centre.

5 Grilled loin or chump chops, or noisettes of lamb

1 Season the chops or noisettes lightly with salt and mill pepper.

2 Brush with oil and place on hot greased grill bars or place on a greased baking tray.

3 Cook quickly for the first 2–3 minutes on each side, in order to seal the pores of the meat.

4 Continue cooking steadily, allowing approximately 12–15 minutes in all.

A compound butter may also be served, together with deep-fried potatoes.

Variation

Sprigs of rosemary or other herbs may be laid on the chops during the last few minutes of grilling to impart flavour.

Energy	Cals	Fat	Sat fat	Carb	Sugar	Protein	Fibre	Sodium
1,338 kJ	320 kcal	16.1 g	7.4 g	0.0 g	0.0 g	43.8 g	0.0 g	0.1 g

6 Lamb rosettes with thyme and blueberries

Ingredient	4 portions	10 portions
Lamb rosettes	8	20
Olive oil	2 tbsp	5 tbsp
Red wine	250 ml	625 ml
Fresh thyme	4 sprigs	10 sprigs
Lamb stock	250 ml	625 ml
Blueberries	200 g	500 g
Salt and pepper		

Energy	Cals	Fat	Sat fat	Carb	Sugar	Protein	Fibre	Sodium
3197 kJ	771 kcal	63.0 g	28.0 g	6.1 g	4.6 g	35.0 g	1.3 g	0.4 g

Using lamb cutlets and beef stock.

1 Shallow-fry the rosettes in the olive oil.

2 Deglaze the pan with the wine, then add the thyme.

3 Add the lamb stock and reduce to a sauce consistency.

4 Add the blueberries, then season.

5 Serve the lamb with the blueberries and the sauce.

Note

Risotto makes a suitable accompaniment.

7 Noisettes of lamb with baby ratatouille

Ingredient	4 portions	10 portions
Noisettes of lamb	8	20
Vegetable oil for frying		
Baby ratatouille (see recipe on page 406, but cut the vegetables into 0.75 cm dice)	400 g	1 kg

Energy	Cals	Fat	Sat fat	Carb	Sugar	Protein	Fibre
1,666 kJ	400 kcal	29.3 g	9.3 g	3.8 g	3.2 g	30.7 g	2.4 g

1 Prepare the noisettes of lamb.

2 Shallow-fry the seasoned noisettes in vegetable oil on both sides until just pink.

3 Drain on kitchen paper. Serve on a bed of baby ratatouille.

4 Garnish with fresh basil or some fresh chopped mixed herbs (parsley, chervil, tarragon, etc).

8 Lamb valentine steaks with fresh pea hummus

Ingredient	4 portions	10 portions
Lamb steaks	8	20
Olive oil	2 tbsp	5 tbsp
For the hummus		
Peas	600 g	1.5 kg
Cloves of garlic, crushed and chopped	4	10
Ground cumin	1 tsp	2½ tsp
Lemon juice	½ tsp	1¼ tsp
Mint leaves, chopped	1 tsp	2½ tsp
Extra virgin olive oil	10 tbsp	25 tbsp
Tahini paste	2 tbsp	5 tbsp

Energy	Cals	Fat	Sat fat	Carb	Sugar	Protein	Fibre	Sodium
4152 kJ	1002 kcal	86.0 g	26.0 g	15.4 g	4.2 g	43.0 g	1.0 g	0.3 g

Using 90 g lamb loin chops.

1 Prepare the valentine steaks.

2 To make the hummus, cook the peas in boiling salted water and drain well. Purée in a food processor with the garlic, cumin, lemon juice, mint, olive oil and tahini paste.

3 Lightly season the valentines. Shallow-fry in olive oil until golden brown and slightly pink.

4 Serve on individual plates on a bed of pea hummus, garnished with fresh mint. Alternatively, serve the steaks on plates with the pea hummus piped as a rosette, and a circle of lamb jus around.

9 Samosas

Energy	Cals	Fat	Sat fat	Carb	Sugar	Protein	Fibre	Sodium
2,740 kJ	682 kcal	43.9g	15.2g	49.5g	2.0g	25.5g	3.0g	0.5g

Using short paste and lamb filling.

Filling 1: potato

Ingredient	4 portions	10 portions
Potatoes, peeled	200g	500g
Vegetable oil	1½ tsp	3¾ tsp
Black mustard seeds	½ tsp	1¼ tsp
Onions, finely chopped	50g	125g
Fresh ginger, finely chopped	12g	30g
Fennel seeds	1 tsp	2½ tsp
Cumin seeds	¼ tsp	1 tsp
Turmeric	¼ tsp	1 tsp
Frozen peas	75g	187g
Salt, to taste		
Water	1 tbsp	2½ tbsp
Fresh coriander, finely chopped	1 tsp	2½ tsp
Garam masala	½ tsp	2½ tsp
Pinch of cayenne pepper		

1 Cut the potatoes into 0.5 cm dice; cook in water until only just cooked.

2 Heat the oil in a suitable pan, add the mustard seeds and cook until they pop.

3 Add the onions and ginger. Fry for 7–8 minutes, stirring continuously until golden brown.

4 Stir in the fennel, cumin and turmeric; add the potatoes, peas, salt and water.

5 Reduce to a low heat, cover the pan and cook for 5 minutes.

6 Stir in the coriander; cook for a further 5 minutes.

7 Remove from the heat, stir in the garam masala and the cayenne seasoning.

8 Remove from the pan, place into a suitable bowl to cool before using.

Filling 2: lamb

Ingredient	4 portions	10 portions
Saffron	½ tsp	1¼ tsp
Boiling water	2½ tsp	6¼ tsp
Vegetable oil	3 tsp	7½ tsp
Fresh ginger, finely chopped	12g	30g
Cloves of garlic, crushed and chopped	2	5
Onions, finely chopped	50g	125g
Salt, to taste		
Lean lamb, minced	400g	1 kg
Pinch of cayenne pepper		
Garam masala	1 tsp	2½ tsp

1 Infuse the saffron in the boiling water; allow to stand for 10 minutes.

2 Heat the vegetable oil in a suitable pan. Add the ginger, garlic, onions and salt, stirring continuously. Fry for 7–8 minutes, until the onions are soft and golden brown.

3 Stir in the lamb, add the saffron with the water. Cook, stirring the lamb until it is cooked.

4 Add the cayenne and garam masala, reduce the heat and allow to cook gently for a further 10 minutes.

5 The mixture should be fairly tight with very little moisture.

6 Transfer to a bowl and allow to cool before using.

To make the samosas

Ingredient	16–20 pasties	40–50 pasties
Short pastry made from ghee fat and fairly strong flour (the dough must be fairly elastic)	400 g	1 kg
Or filo or spring roll pastry		

Healthy eating tips
- Use the minimum of salt in the potato filling. No added salt is necessary with the lamb.
- Use a small amount of unsaturated oil to fry the mustard seeds, onions and lamb.
- Drain off the excess fat before adding the water.

Note

Allow 4 or 5 samosas for a portion. They can also be served individually as finger food.

The samosas may be made in advance, covered with cling film or plastic, and refrigerated before being deep-fried.

Samosas can be garnished with coriander leaves and served with chutney.

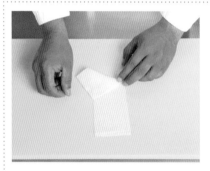

1 Cut the paste into strips approx. 18 × 7 cm. Fold over the end of the pastry.

2 Eggwash the upper side of the pastry, then fold over the top part to form a pocket.

3 Flip over the pocket, ease it open and fill it.

4 Once completely full, eggwash the top edge and the flap of pastry.

5 Fold over the pastry and wrap it round the seal the samosa.

6 Deep-fry until golden brown and crisp.

10 Braised lamb chump chops (*chop d'agneau braisées*)

1 Fry the seasoned chops in a sauté pan quickly on both sides in hot fat.

2 When turning the chops, add the mirepoix (onion and carrot).

3 Draw aside and drain off the surplus fat.

4 Add the flour and mix in, singe in the oven or on top of the stove. (Alternatively, use flour that has been browned in the oven.)

5 Add the tomato purée and the hot stock, and stir with a kitchen spoon until thoroughly mixed.

6 Add the bouquet garni and garlic, if using. Season, skim and allow to simmer; cover with a lid.

7 Cook (preferably in the oven), skimming off all oil and scum.

8 When cooked, transfer the chops to a clean pan.

9 Correct the seasoning and consistency of the sauce.

10 Skim off any oil and pass the sauce through a fine strainer over the chops.

11 Serve sprinkled with chopped parsley.

Ingredient	4 portions	10 portions
Lamb chops	4	10
Salt and pepper		
Sunflower or olive oil		
Onion, diced	100 g	250 g
Carrot, diced	100 g	250 g
Flour (white or wholemeal)	25 g	60 g
Tomato purée	1 level tsp	2½ level tsp
Brown stock	500 ml	1.25 litre
Bouquet garni	1	2
Clove of garlic, optional	1	2½
Parsley, chopped		

Energy	Cals	Fat	Sat fat	Carb	Sugar	Protein	Fibre
1,452 kJ	349 kcal	23.4 g	10.8 g	9.4 g	3.8 g	25.8 g	1.2 g

Healthy eating tips
- Trim fat from the chops before frying.
- Use the minimum amount of salt.
- Lightly oil the pan with an unsaturated oil to fry the chops. Drain off any excess fat after the frying is complete.
- Serve with a large portion of vegetables.

Variation

Lamb steaks cut from the chump end of the leg can also be cooked in this way. Variations include the following additions after the sauce has been strained:
- cooked pulses (e.g. haricot, butter or flageolet beans)
- neatly cut cooked vegetables (e.g. carrots, turnips, swede, green beans or peas).

11 Braised lamb shanks

Ingredient	4 portions	10 portions
Lamb shanks	4	10
Olive oil for braising (to fill casserole about 1 cm deep)		
Leeks, roughly chopped	1	2½
Celery sticks, roughly chopped	2	5
Carrots, roughly chopped	2	5
Onions, roughly chopped	2	5
Garlic head, broken into cloves (unpeeled)	1	2½
Bay leaf	1	2½
Thyme sprig	1	2½
Rosemary sprig	1	2½
Red wine	375 ml	1 litre
Chicken stock	600 ml	1.5 litres

Energy	Cals	Fat	Sat fat	Carb	Sugar	Protein	Fibre	Sodium
3098 kJ	742 kcal	24.2g	7.4g	10.5g	8.1g	98.3g	4.0g	0.3g

1 Take a casserole (or oven-proof dish) and place on the hob over a high heat. Pour in the olive oil and, when hot, add the lamb shanks, turning occasionally until brown.

2 Once browned, remove the lamb from the pot and tip in the leek, celery, carrot, onion and garlic cloves. Stir them all together and add the bay leaf, thyme and rosemary. These ingredients will all add flavour to the dish but won't be served at the end.

3 Once the vegetables are lightly browned, place the lamb back into the pot, allowing it to rest on top of the vegetables.

4 Pour in the red wine and chicken stock and bring to the boil.

5 Cover the pot with a lid or kitchen foil and place in the oven at 150 °C to braise for 2 hours 30 minutes, or up to 5 hours depending on the amount of lamb being used. When the meat is cooked, the bone can easily be turned out of the meat (if you would like to present the bone, only give it a small turn to check if the lamb is ready, as it will be difficult to re-insert the bone once removed).

6 Pass the cooking stock through a fine sieve and reduce to the correct consistency (coats the back of a spoon).

7 Serve the lamb shanks with the cooking juices poured over the top.

The lamb can be served with mashed potato and roast vegetables.

12 Hot pot of lamb or mutton

Ingredient	4 portions	10 portions
Stewing lamb	500 g	1.25 kg
Salt, pepper		
Onions, thinly sliced	100 g	250 g
Potatoes, thinly sliced	400 g	1 kg
Brown stock	1 litre	2.5 litres
Oil (optional)	25 g	60 g
Parsley, chopped		

Energy	Cals	Fat	Sat fat	Carb	Sugar	Protein	Fibre
1,505 kJ	360 kcal	17.0 g	6.4 g	22.0 g	1.8 g	29.0 g	2.5 g

Using sunflower oil.

1 Trim the meat and cut into even pieces.

2 Place in a deep earthenware dish. Season with salt and pepper.

3 Lightly sauté the onions in the oil, if desired. Mix the onion and approximately three-quarters of the potatoes together.

4 Season and place on top of the meat; cover three parts with stock.

5 Neatly arrange an overlapping layer of the remaining potatoes on top, sliced about 2 mm thick.

6 Thoroughly clean the edges of the dish and place to cook in a hot oven at 230–250 °C until lightly coloured.

7 Reduce the heat and continue cooking for approximately 1½–2 hours.

8 Press the potatoes down occasionally during cooking.

9 Serve with the potatoes brushed with butter or margarine and sprinkle with the chopped parsley.

Note

Neck chops or neck fillet make a succulent dish.

When the dish is ready, the top layer of potatoes should be golden brown.

Variation

Try:
- using leek in place of onion
- adding 200 g lambs' kidneys
- quickly frying off the meat and sweating the onions before putting in the pot
- adding 100–200 g sliced mushrooms
- adding a small tin of baked beans or a layer of thickly sliced tomatoes before adding the potatoes
- using sausages in place of lamb.

Chop the lamb into even-sized pieces

Layer the potatoes over the lamb

Pour over the stock

13 Brown lamb or mutton stew

Ingredient	4 portions	10 portions
Stewing lamb or mutton	500 g	1.25 kg
Oil	2 tbsp	5 tbsp
Salt, pepper		
Carrot, chopped	100 g	250 g
Onion, chopped	100 g	250 g
Clove of garlic (if desired)	1	2½
Flour (white or wholemeal)	25 g	60 g
Tomato purée	1 level tbsp	2½ level tbsp
Brown stock (mutton stock or water)	500 g	1.25 litre
Bouquet garni		
Parsley, chopped, to serve		

Energy	Cals	Fat	Sat fat	Carb	Sugar	Protein	Fibre
1,320 kJ	314 kcal	18.7 g	6.2 g	9.4 g	3.2 g	27.9 g	1.3 g

Using sunflower oil.

1 Trim the meat and cut into even pieces.

2 Partly fry off the seasoned meat in the oil, then add the carrot, onion and garlic, and continue frying.

3 Drain off the surplus fat, add the flour and mix.

4 Singe in the oven or brown on top of the stove for a few minutes, or add previously browned flour.

5 Add the tomato purée and stir with a wooden spoon.

6 Add the stock and season.

7 Add the bouquet garni, bring to the boil, skim and cover with a lid.

8 Simmer gently until cooked (preferably in the oven) for approximately 1–2 hours, until the lamb is tender.

9 When cooked, place the meat in a clean pan.

10 Correct the sauce and pass it on to the meat.

11 Serve sprinkled with chopped parsley.

Fry the lamb, onions and carrots

Mix in the flour

Add the stock and bring to the boil

Healthy eating tips
- Trim off as much fat as possible before frying.
- Use the minimum amount of salt to season the meat.
- Serve with plenty of potatoes and vegetables.

Professional tip
- Make sure the oil is hot before placing the meat in the pan to brown quickly all over.
- Do not allow the meat to boil in the oil, because this will spoil the flavour and texture.

14 Irish stew

Ingredient	4 portions	10 portions
Stewing lamb (scrag, middle neck or shoulder)	500 g	1.25 kg
Salt, pepper		
Bouquet garni		
Potatoes	400 g	1 kg
Onions	100 g	250 g
Celery	100 g	250 g
Savoy cabbage	100 g	250 g
Leeks	100 g	250 g
Button onions	100 g	250 g
Parsley, chopped		

Energy	Cals	Fat	Sat fat	Carb	Sugar	Protein	Fibre
1,339 kJ	319 kcal	11.2 g	5.2 g	26.1 g	5.7 g	30.2 g	5.0 g

1 Trim the meat and cut into even pieces. Blanch and refresh.

2 Place in a shallow saucepan, cover with water, bring to the boil, season with salt and skim. If tough meat is being used, allow ½–1 hour stewing time before adding any vegetables.

3 Add the bouquet garni. Turn the potatoes into barrel shapes.

4 Cut the potato trimmings, onions, celery, cabbage and leeks into small neat pieces and add to the meat; simmer for 30 minutes.

5 Add the button onions and simmer for a further 30 minutes.

6 Add the potatoes and simmer gently with a lid on the pan until cooked.

7 Correct the seasoning and skim off all fat.

8 Serve sprinkled with chopped parsley.

Professional tip

Keep the meat and vegetables covered with liquid during cooking, to keep the dish consistent and tasty.

Variation

Alternatively, a more modern approach is to cook the meat for 1½–2 hours until almost tender, then add the vegetables and cook until all are tender. Optional accompaniments include Worcester sauce and/or pickled red cabbage (see page 587).

Healthy eating tips
- Trim as much fat as possible from the stewing lamb.
- Use the minimum amount of salt.
- Serve with colourful seasonal vegetables to create a 'healthy' dish.

Ingredients for Irish stew

Boil the meat

Add the vegetables

15 Roast leg of lamb with mint, lemon and cumin

Ingredient	4 portions	10 portions
Mint	25 g	62.5 g
Lemons, juice of	2	5
Cumin	2 tsp	5 tsp
Olive oil	4 tbsp	10 tbsp
Leg of lamb	3.5 kg	2 × 3.5 kg

Energy	Cals	Fat	Sat fat	Carb	Sugar	Protein	Fibre
2,192 kJ	524 kcal	39.1 g	13.7 g	0.3 g	0.3 g	29.7 g	0.0 g

Using a 225 g portion of lamb.

1 Place the mint, lemon juice, cumin and olive oil in a food processor. Carefully blend the mint, lemon juice, cumin and olive oil to give maximum flavour.

2 Rub the mixture into the lamb and place in a suitable roasting tray.

3 Roast the lamb in the normal way at 200 °C.
Serve on a bed of boulangère potatoes or dauphinoise potatoes and a suitable green vegetable, e.g. leaf spinach with toasted pine nuts, or with a couscous salad.

Ingredients for roast leg of lamb with mint, lemon and cumin

Place the leg of lamb in a roasting tray and rub with the mint and lemon mixture

Carving a leg of lamb

16 Roast saddle of lamb with rosemary mash

Ingredient	4 portions	10 portions
Saddle of lamb, boned		
Milk	250 ml	625 ml
Rosemary	2 sprigs	5 sprigs
Potatoes, mashed	1.3 kg	3.25 kg

Energy	Cals	Fat	Sat fat	Carb	Sugar	Protein	Fibre	Sodium
3,215 kJ	770 kcal	45.7 g	22.1 g	58.9 g	4.7 g	34.4 g	5.6 g	0.2 g

1 Bone the saddle of lamb and roast in the normal way.

2 Bring the milk to the boil with the rosemary. Remove from the heat, cover and leave to infuse for 10–15 minutes.

3 To make the rosemary mash, prepare a potato purée using the milk infused with rosemary.

17 Best end of lamb with breadcrumbs and parsley

	6 portions
Best end of lamb, French trimmed	2
Oil	
Seasoning	
Fresh white breadcrumbs	50 g
Parsley, chopped	2 tbsp
Egg	1
Butter or margarine, melted	50 g

Energy	Cals	Fat	Sat fat	Carb	Sugar	Protein	Fibre	Sodium
2530 kJ	612 kcal	51.3g	24.2g	6.6g	0.5g	31.2g	0.2g	0.2g

Using butter.

1 Lightly brush the joint with oil and season it.

2 Roast the best end at 220 °C for 15–20 minutes.

3 Cover the fat surface of the meat with a mixture of the fresh white breadcrumbs mixed with plenty of chopped parsley, an egg and the melted butter or margarine.

4 Return to the oven for approximately 10 minutes to complete the cooking, browning carefully.

Professional tip

Cook the lamb until it is pink. Carefully bind the breadcrumbs with herbs and beaten egg, so that they will hold together during cooking.

Variation

Try:
- mixed fresh herbs used in addition to parsley
- adding finely chopped garlic
- chopped fresh herbs, shallots and mustard.

18 Slow-cooked shoulder of lamb with potatoes boulangère

Ingredient	4 portions	10 portions
Boned shoulder of lamb, rolled and tied	1	3
Olive oil	1 tbsp	3 tbsp
Salt, pepper		
Rosemary, sprigs	6	18
Thyme, sprigs	6	18
Cloves of garlic	4	10
Mirepoix	400 g	1 kg
Bay leaves	1	3
Red wine or dry cider	250 ml	625 ml
Brown stock	300 ml	750 ml
Redcurrant jelly	1 tbsp	2 tbsp

Energy	Cals	Fat	Sat fat	Carb	Sugar	Protein	Fibre	Sodium
1,815 kJ	437 kcal	30.8 g	14.5 g	2.2 g	0.3 g	27.6 g	0.4 g	0.6 g

1 For instructions on how to prepare potatoes boulangère for baking, see page 379.

2 Rub the lamb with oil, and season with salt and pepper. Place in a suitable roasting tray and cook in an oven at 200 °C for 15 minutes.

3 Remove from the oven and reduce the temperature to 140 °C.

4 Add the remaining ingredients to the roasting tray.

5 Cook for 2 hours, basting every 20 minutes.

6 Remove the lamb from the roasting tray and return it to the oven on a rack. Place the potatoes boulangère directly below the lamb. Cook for ½–1 hour, until the lamb is tender and sticky.

7 To finish the sauce, once the lamb is removed from the roasting tray, reduce the cooking liquor to the required consistency. Add the strained redcurrant jelly, mix well, correct seasoning, then strain.

19 Pot-roast shoulder of lamb with gratin forcemeat

Energy	Cals	Fat	Sat fat	Carb	Sugar	Protein	Fibre	Sodium
3537 kJ	850 kcal	54.0g	24.0g	42.0g	12.5g	51.0g	6.2g	0.6g

Using beef stock and chicken liver.

Ingredient	10 portions
Lamb shoulder, boned	3 kg
Gratin forcemeat (see below)	300 g
Salt	1 tsp
Pepper	½ tsp
Wholewheat flour	3 tbsp
Oil	3 tbsp
Brown stock	500 mls
Potatoes, turned	10
Carrots, turned	10
Button onions	10
Worcestershire sauce	1 tsp

1 Preheat the oven to 160 °C.

2 Stuff shoulder with forcemeat and tie.

3 Dredge the lamb with seasoned flour.

4 Heat oil in a large roast pot over medium high heat.

5 Add the floured lamb to hot pan and brown evenly on all sides.

6 Pour stock to cover lamb.

7 Cover the pot and place in the preheated oven. Slow cook the lamb for 2½ to 3 hours.

8 During the last 45 minutes, add the vegetables to the pot. Cover and continue to cook until meat and vegetables are tender.

9 Remove the cooked lamb and vegetables from the pot to a serving platter.

10 Strain the cooking liquor and adjust the consistency; this can be thickened if desired.

11 Finish with Worcestershire sauce and season to taste.

Sautéed forcemeat (gratin forcemeat)

Ingredient	Makes 300 g
Chicken liver or calves' liver (free from skin and sinews)	150 g
Pork fat, diced	5 g
Mushroom trimmings	50 g
Sautéed shallots	25 g
Butter	50 g
Spice salt	5 g
Pinch thyme and marjoram	
Brandy	10 mls

1 Brown the pork fat in the butter, to set firm. Remove from pan and set to one side.

2 Sauté the liver in the same pan to set.

3 Return pork back to the pan.

4 Add mushrooms, sautéed shallots and seasonings.

5 Sauté all together, then flame with brandy.

6 Remove from heat and allow to cool.

7 Place all ingredients in food processor and blend. The forcemeat is then ready to use.

Professional tip

This forcemeat could also be used to stuff a loin of lamb or skirt of beef rolled and then pot roasted, or served on croutons to accompany poultry or game dishes.

20   Shepherd's pie

Ingredient	4 portions	10 portions
Onions, chopped	100 g	250 g
Oil	35 ml	100 ml
Lamb or mutton (minced), cooked	400 g	1 kg
Salt, pepper		
Worcester sauce	2–3 drops	5 drops
Potatoes, cooked	400 g	1 kg
Butter or margarine	25 g	60 g
Milk or egg wash		
Jus-lié or demi-glace	125–250 ml	300–600 ml

Energy	Cals	Fat	Sat fat	Carb	Sugar	Protein	Fibre
1,744 kJ	415 kcal	25.3 g	9.1 g	22.1 g	2.5 g	26.3 g	1.6 g

Using sunflower oil, with hard margarine in topping.

1 Cook the onion in the oil without colouring.
2 Add the cooked meat from which all fat and gristle has been removed.
3 Season and add Worcester sauce (sufficient to bind).
4 Bring to the boil; simmer for 10–15 minutes.
5 Place in an earthenware or pie dish.
6 Prepare the potatoes – mix with the butter or margarine, then mash and pipe, or arrange neatly on top.
7 Brush with the milk or egg wash.
8 Colour lightly under a salamander or in a hot oven.
9 Serve accompanied with a sauceboat of *jus-lié*.

Note

This dish prepared with cooked beef is known as **cottage pie**.

Pipe the potato carefully so that the meat is completely covered.

When using reheated meats, care must be taken to heat thoroughly and quickly.

Healthy eating tips
● Use an oil rich in unsaturates (olive or sunflower) to lightly oil the pan.
● Drain off any excess fat after the lamb has been fried.
● Try replacing some of the meat with baked beans or lentils, and add tomatoes and/or mushrooms to the dish.
● When served with a large portion of green vegetables, a healthy balance is created.

Variation
Try:
● adding 100–200 g sliced mushrooms
● adding a layer of thickly sliced tomatoes, then sprinkling with rosemary
● mixing a tin of baked beans in with the meat
● sprinkling with grated cheese and browning under a salamander
● varying the flavour of the mince by adding herbs or spices
● varying the potato topping by mixing in grated cheese, chopped spring onions or herbs, or by using duchess potato mixture
● serving lightly sprinkled with garam masala and with grilled pitta bread.

Beef dishes

21 Grilled beef

The following cuts may be cooked in this way:
- rump steak
- point steak
- double fillet steak (chateaubriand)
- fillet steak
- tournedos
- porterhouse or T-bone steak
- sirloin steak (entrecôte)
- double sirloin steak
- minute steak
- rib eye steak.

Allow approximately 100–150 g per portion, although in many establishments these weights will be exceeded.

Energy	Cals	Fat	Sat fat	Carb	Sugar	Protein	Fibre
706 kJ	168 kcal	6.0g	2.7g	0.0g	0.0g	28.6g	0.0g

1 Lightly season the steaks with salt and pepper, and brush on both sides with oil.

2 Place on hot, preheated and greased grill bars.

3 Turn halfway through the cooking and brush occasionally with oil. Cook to the degree ordered by the customer (see page 225).

4 Serve garnished with watercress and deep-fried potatoes, and offer a suitable sauce such as compound butter or sauce béarnaise.

22 Hamburger, American style

Energy	Cals	Fat	Sat fat	Carb	Sugar	Protein	Fibre	Sodium
1,868 kJ	450 kcal	32.4g	13.9g	0.0g	0.0g	39.4g	0.0g	0.2g

Hamburgers – now more commonly known as burgers – were originally made using 200 g of minced beef per portion.

The meat used should be pure beef with 20–25 per cent beef fat by weight. Less fat than this will result in a tough, dry hamburger. If more fat is used the hamburgers will be unpalatable, nutritionally undesirable and will shrink considerably during cooking.

1 Pass the meat through a mincer twice. This makes a more tender product.

2 Lightly mix the mince with any desired seasoning or ingredients (over-mixing will make the hamburger tough).

3 Mould the mixture into patties. Mark the top with crossed lines using a knife.

4 Grill until cooked thoroughly to the centre, reaching 75 °C. Do not prick the hamburgers while cooking, as the juices will seep out leaving a dry product.

Note

Mini burgers (one mouthful) can be served as hot canapés at receptions.

Variation

Variations in seasonings and ingredients can be added to the minced beef, but traditionally the sauces and garnishes offered are sufficient. These can include: ketchup, mustard, mayonnaise, chilli sauce, horseradish, cheese, raw onion rings, lettuce, avocado slices, bacon, and various pickles and relishes. Freshly fried chips and/or cut pieces of raw vegetables (e.g. carrot, celery, spring onions) can be added.

The bun may be plain or seeded (sesame seeds).

Alternative fillings can include:
- cheese – either on its own or added to the beef
- egg – a freshly fried egg, or added to the beef
- chicken – a freshly grilled portion of chicken, either minced or in the piece
- fish – a freshly grilled portion of a whole fish (cod or haddock)
- vegetables – a selection of freshly grilled or fried vegetables (e.g. onions, peppers, aubergines, mushrooms).

Mould the mixture into shape

Mark the top of each burger before grilling it

23 Tournedos

Energy	Cals	Fat	Sat fat	Carb	Sugar	Protein	Fibre	Sodium
1,540 kJ	366 kcal	13.2g	4.8g	0.0g	0.0g	61.8g	0.0g	0.2g

Tournedos are cut from the middle of a fillet of beef and are usually 100–150g in weight.

1 Lightly season and shallow-fry on both sides in a sauté pan.

2 Serve with an appropriate garnish or sauce (see Variation).

Note

Traditionally, tournedos are cooked underdone and served on a round croûte of bread fried in butter.

Healthy eating tips
- Use little or no salt to season the steaks.
- Fry in a small amount of an unsaturated oil and drain off all excess fat after frying.
- Serve with plenty of boiled new potatoes or a jacket potato and a selection of vegetables.

Variation

Tournedos can be served with a variety of sauces, such as chasseur, red wine or mushroom, and numerous garnishes (e.g. diced cubed potatoes, wild or cultivated mushrooms). The photo shows **tournedos Rossini** – the tournedos are served with foie gras, Parma ham, girolles, truffle and a Madeira jelly.

24 Sirloin steak with red wine (*entrecôte bordelaise*)

Ingredient	4 portions	10 portions
Butter or oil	50g	125g
Sirloin steaks (approximately 150–200g each)	4	10
Red wine	60ml	150ml
Red wine sauce (see page 96)	250ml	625ml
Parsley, chopped		

Energy	Cals	Fat	Sat fat	Carb	Sugar	Protein	Fibre
3,013 kJ	717 kcal	62.2g	21.6g	6.0g	3.0g	26.1g	1.4g

Using sunflower oil and 150g raw steak per portion. Using sunflower oil and 200g raw steak per portion provides: 3584 kJ/853 kcal energy, 73.6g fat, 26.2g saturated fat, 6.0g carbohydrates, 3.0g sugar, 34.4g protein and 1.4g fibre.

1 Heat the butter or oil in a sauté pan.

2 Lightly season the steaks on both sides with salt and pepper.

3 Fry the steaks quickly on both sides, keeping them underdone.

4 Dress the steaks on a serving dish.

5 Pour off the fat from the pan.

6 Deglaze with the red wine. Reduce by half and strain.

7 Add the red wine sauce, reboil and correct the seasoning.

8 Coat the steaks with the sauce.

9 Sprinkle with chopped parsley and serve.

Traditionally, two slices of beef bone marrow, poached in stock for 2–3 minutes, would be placed on each steak.

Professional tip

Cook the steaks to order (and make the sauce by deglazing the pan and reducing), not in advance.

Healthy eating tips
- Use little or no salt to season the steaks.
- Fry in a small amount of an unsaturated oil and drain off all excess fat after frying.
- Serve with plenty of boiled new potatoes or a jacket potato and a selection of vegetables.

25 Beef stroganoff

1 Cut the meat into strips approximately 1 × 5 cm.

2 Place the butter or oil in a sauteuse over a fierce heat.

3 Add the beef strips, lightly season with salt and pepper, and allow to cook rapidly for a few seconds. The beef should be brown but underdone.

4 Drain the beef into a colander. Pour the butter back into the pan.

5 Add the shallots, cover with a lid and allow to cook gently until tender.

6 Drain off the fat, add the wine and reduce to one-third.

7 Add the cream and reduce by a quarter.

8 Add the lemon juice and the beef strips; do not reboil. Correct the seasoning.

9 Serve lightly sprinkled with chopped parsley. Accompany with rice pilaff (see page 125).

Ingredient	4 portions	10 portions
Fillet of beef (tail end)	400 g	1 kg
Butter or oil	50 g	125 g
Salt, pepper		
Shallots, finely chopped	25 g	60 g
Dry white wine	125 ml	300 ml
Cream	125 ml	300 ml
Lemon, juice of	¼	½
Parsley, chopped		

Healthy eating tips
- Use little or no salt to season the meat.
- Fry in a small amount of an unsaturated oil.
- Serve with a large portion of rice and a salad.

Energy	Cals	Fat	Sat fat	Carb	Sugar	Protein	Fibre
1,364 kJ	325 kcal	23.7 g	7.9 g	1.7 g	1.7 g	21.2 g	0.3 g

Using sunflower oil.

26 Hamburg or Vienna steak

Ingredient	4 portions	10 portions
Onion, finely chopped	25 g	60 g
Butter or oil	10 g	25 g
Lean minced beef	200 g	500 g
Small egg	1	2–3
Breadcrumbs	100 g	250 g
Cold water or milk	2 tbsp (approximately)	60 ml (approximately)

Energy	Cals	Fat	Sat fat	Carb	Sugar	Protein	Fibre
681 kJ	162 kcal	6.7 g	1.9 g	12.7 g	1.0 g	13.8 g	1.0 g

1 Cook the onion in the fat without colour, then allow to cool.

2 Add to the rest of the ingredients and mix in well.

3 Divide into even pieces and, using a little flour, make into balls, flatten and shape round.

4 Shallow-fry in hot fat on both sides, reducing the heat after the first few minutes, making certain they are cooked right through.

5 Serve with a light sauce, such as piquant sauce (see page 91).

The 'steaks' may be garnished with French-fried onions and sometimes with a fried egg.

Healthy eating tips
● Use a small amount of an unsaturated oil to cook the onion and to shallow-fry the meat.
● The minced beef will produce more fat, which should be drained off.
● Serve with plenty of starchy carbohydrate and vegetables.

27 Carbonnade of beef

Ingredient	4 portions	10 portions
Lean beef (topside)	400 g	1 kg
Salt, pepper		
Flour (white or wholemeal)	25 g	60 g
Dripping or oil	25 g	60 g
Onions, sliced	200 g	500 g
Beer	250 ml	625 ml
Caster sugar	10 g	25 g
Tomato purée	25 g	60 g
Brown stock		

Energy	Cals	Fat	Sat fat	Carb	Sugar	Protein	Fibre
1,037 kJ	247 kcal	9.1 g	1.8 g	14.0 g	8.1 g	24.7 g	1.1 g

1 Cut the meat into thin slices.

2 Season with salt and pepper and pass through the flour.

3 Quickly colour on both sides in hot fat and place in a casserole.

4 Fry the onions to a light brown colour. Add to the meat.

5 Add the beer, sugar and tomato purée and sufficient brown stock to cover the meat.

6 Cover with a tight-fitting lid and simmer gently in a moderate oven at 150–200 °C until the meat is tender (approximately 2 hours).

7 Skim, correct the seasoning and serve.

Slice the meat thinly

Pass each slice through the flour

Pour the liquid over the browned meat and onions

Healthy eating tips

- Trim off as much fat as possible before frying and drain off all surplus fat after frying.
- Use the minimum amount of salt to season the meat.
- Skim all fat from the finished sauce.
- Serve with plenty of potatoes and vegetables.

Note

Carbonnade of beef is usually served with braised red cabbage. Serve separately.

28 Beef bourguignon

Ingredient	4 portions	10 portions
Beef		
Beef shin pre-soaked in red wine (see below) for 12 hours	600 g	1.5 kg
Inexpensive red Bordeaux wine	1 bottle	2 bottles
Olive oil	50 ml	125 ml
Onion	100 g	250 g
Carrot	100 g	250 g
Celery sticks	75 g	180 g
Leek	100 g	250 g
Cloves of garlic	2	5
Sprig fresh thyme	1	2
Bay leaf	1	2
Seasoning		
Veal/brown stock to cover		
Garnish		
Button onions, cooked	150 g	300 g
Cooked bacon lardons	150 g	300 g
Button mushrooms, cooked	150 g	300 g
Parsley, chopped	2 tsp	5 tsp
To finish		
Mashed potato	300 g	750 g
Washed, picked spinach	300 g	750 g
Cooked green beans	250 g	625 g

Energy	Cals	Fat	Sat fat	Carb	Sugar	Protein	Fibre	Sodium
2,838 kJ	681 kcal	33.3 g	9.1 g	20.1 g	7.2 g	44.9 g	8.0 g	0.9 g

1 Preheat the oven to 180 °C.

2 Remove the meat from the wine. Trim the beef shin of all fat and sinew, and cut into 2.5 cm-thick rondelles.

3 Heat a little oil in a thick-bottomed pan and seal/brown the skin. Place in a large ovenproof dish.

4 Meanwhile, reduce the red wine by half.

5 Peel and trim the vegetables as appropriate, then add them to the pan that the beef has just come out of and gently brown the edges. Then place this, along with the garlic and herbs, in the ovenproof dish with the meat.

6 Add the reduced red wine to the casserole, then pour in enough stock to cover the meat and vegetables. Bring to the boil, then cook in the oven preheated to 180 °C for 40 minutes; after that, turn the oven down to 90–95 °C and cook for a further 4 hours until tender.

7 Remove from the oven and allow the meat to cool in the liquor. When cold, remove any fat. Reheat gently at the same temperature to serve.

8 Heat the garnish elements separately and sprinkle over each portion. Serve with a mound of mashed potato, wilted spinach and buttered green beans. Finish the whole dish with chopped parsley.

Variation

Other joints of beef can be used here; beef or veal cheek can be used, reducing the time for the veal, or modernise the dish by using the slow-cooked fillet preparation and serving the same garnish.

Professional tip

Shallow fry the beef in hot oil to brown it all over, but do not let it boil in the oil. Then allow it to stew gently in the red wine.

Marinate the beef

Gently brown the vegetables

Brown the meat

Pour in stock to cover the meat and vegetables

29 Braised beef (*boeuf braisé*)

Energy	Cals	Fat	Sat fat	Carb	Sugar	Protein	Fibre
1,380 kJ	329 kcal	14.3 g	3.3 g	26.8 g	4.7 g	24.7 g	2.4 g

Using sunflower oil.

Ingredient	4 portions	10 portions
Lean beef (topside or thick flank)	400 g	1 kg
Dripping or oil	25 g	60 g
Onions, sliced and lightly fried	100 g	250 g
Carrots, sliced and lightly fried	100 g	250 g
Brown stock	500 ml	1.25 litres
Salt and pepper		
Bouquet garni	1	2
Tomato purée	25 g	60 g
Demi-glace or *jus-lié*	250 ml	625 ml

Method 1

1 Trim and tie the joint securely.

2 Season and colour quickly on all sides in hot fat to seal the joint.

3 Place the lightly fried, sliced vegetables into a small braising pan (any pan with a tight-fitting lid that may be placed in the oven) or in a casserole.

4 Place the joint on to the vegetables.

5 Add the stock, which should come two-thirds of the way up the meat, and season lightly.

6 Add the bouquet garni and tomato purée and, if available, add a few mushroom trimmings.

7 Bring to the boil, skim and cover with a lid. Cook in a moderate oven at 150–200 °C.

8 After approximately 1½ hours' cooking, remove the meat.

9 Add the demi-glace or *jus-lié*, reboil, skim and strain.

10 Replace the meat; do not cover, but baste frequently and continue cooking for approximately 2–2½ hours in all. Braised beef should be well cooked (allow 35 minutes per 0.5 kg plus 35 minutes). To test if cooked, pierce with a trussing needle – it should penetrate the meat easily and there should be no sign of blood.

11 Remove the joint and correct the colour, seasoning and consistency of the sauce.

12 To serve: remove the string and carve slices across the grain. Pour some of the sauce over the slices and serve the remainder of the sauce in a sauceboat.

Method 2

As for Method 1, but when the joint and vegetables are browned, sprinkle with 25 g (60 g for 10 portions) flour and singe in the oven; add the tomato purée, stock and bouquet garni; season and complete the recipe.

Trim the joint neatly

Tie the joint securely before braising it

Place the joint in the pan on a layer of vegetables

Note

Suitable garnishes include spring vegetables or pasta. Red wine may be used in place of stock.

Healthy eating tips

- Trim off as much fat as possible before frying and drain off all surplus fat after frying.
- Use the minimum amount of salt.
- Skim all fat from the finished sauce.
- Serve with plenty of potatoes and vegetables.

30 Boiled silverside, carrots and dumplings

Ingredient	4 portions	10 portions
Silverside, pre-soaked in brine	400 g	1 kg
Onions	200 g	500 g
Carrots	200 g	500 g
Suet paste	100 g	250 g

Energy	Cals	Fat	Sat fat	Carb	Sugar	Protein	Fibre
1,068 kJ	254 kcal	10.17 g	4.6 g	15.5 g	5.5 g	26.3 g	2.6 g

1 Soak the meat in cold water for 1–2 hours to remove excess brine.

2 Place in a saucepan and cover with cold water, bring to the boil, skim and simmer for 45 minutes.

3 Add the whole prepared onions and carrots and simmer until cooked.

4 Divide the suet paste into even pieces and lightly mould into balls (dumplings).

5 Add the dumplings and simmer for a further 15–20 minutes.

6 Serve by carving the meat across the grain, garnish with carrots, onions and dumplings, and moisten with a little of the cooking liquor.

Note

A large joint of silverside is approximately 6 kg; for this size of joint, soak it overnight and allow 25 minutes cooking time per 0.5 kg plus 25 minutes.

The beef is salted because this gives the desired flavour. The meat is usually salted before it is delivered to the kitchen.

Healthy eating tips

Adding carrots, onions, boiled potatoes and a green vegetable will give a healthy balance.

Variation

Herbs can be added to the dumplings.

Boiled brisket and tongue can be served with the silverside.

French-style boiled beef is prepared using unsalted thin flank or brisket with onions, carrots, leeks, celery, cabbage and a bouquet garni, all cooked and served together, accompanied with pickled gherkins and coarse salt.

31 Steak pudding

Ingredient	4 portions	10 portions
Suet paste (see page 464)	200 g	500 g
Prepared stewing beef (chuck steak)	400 g	1 kg
Worcester sauce	1 tsp	2½ tsp
Parsley, chopped	1 tsp	2½ tsp
Salt, pepper		
Onion, chopped (optional)	50–100 g	125–250 g
Water	125 ml approximately	300 ml approximately.

Energy	Cals	Fat	Sat fat	Carb	Sugar	Protein	Fibre
1,369 kJ	326 kcal	17.3g	7.8g	20.6g	1.0g	23.0g	1.1g

1 Line a greased ½ litre basin with three-quarters of the suet paste and retain one-quarter for the top.

2 Mix all the other ingredients, except the water, together.

3 Place in the basin with the water to within 1 cm of the top.

4 Moisten the edge of the suet paste, cover with the top and seal firmly.

5 Cover with greased greaseproof paper and also, if possible, foil or a pudding cloth tied securely with string.

6 Cook in a steamer for at least 3½ hours for a four-portion pudding, or approximately 1½ hours for individual puddings.

7 Serve with the paper and cloth removed, clean the basin, place on a round flat dish and fasten a napkin round the basin.

Extra gravy should be served separately. If the gravy in the pudding is to be thickened, the meat can be lightly floured.

Healthy eating tips
- Use little or no salt as the Worcester sauce contains salt.
- Trim off as much fat as possible from the raw stewing beef.
- Serve with plenty of potatoes and vegetables.

Variation

Try:
- adding 50–100 g ox or sheep's kidneys cut in pieces with skin and gristle removed
- adding 50–100 g sliced or quartered mushrooms
- making the steak pudding with a cooked filling; in which case, simmer the meat until cooked in brown stock with onions, parsley, Worcester sauce and seasoning; cool quickly and proceed as above, steaming for 1–1½ hours.

Line the basin with suet paste

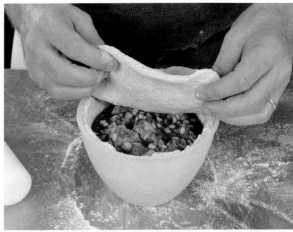

Fill the basin, then cover the top with paste

Make a foil cover for the basin, with a fold to allow it to expand

Tie the cover over the basin securely

32 Goulash

1 Remove excess fat from the beef. Cut into 2 cm square pieces.

2 Season and fry in the hot fat until slightly coloured. Add the chopped onion.

3 Cover with a lid and sweat gently for 3–4 minutes.

4 Add the flour and paprika and mix in with a wooden spoon.

5 Cook out in the oven or on top of the stove. Add the tomato purée, mix in.

6 Gradually add the stock, stir to the boil, skim, season and cover.

7 Allow to simmer, preferably in the oven, for approximately 1½–2 hours until the meat is tender.

8 Add the potatoes and check that they are covered with the sauce. (Add more stock if required.)

9 Re-cover with the lid and cook gently until the potatoes are cooked.

10 Skim and correct the seasoning and consistency. A little cream or yoghurt may be added at the last moment.

11 Serve sprinkled with a few gnocchis made from choux paste (see page 459), reheated in hot salted water or lightly tossed in butter or margarine. Alternatively, garnish with turned potatoes.

Ingredient	4 portions	10 portions
Prepared stewing beef	400 g	1 kg
Lard or oil	35 g	100 g
Onions, chopped	100 g	250 g
Flour	25 g	60 g
Paprika	10–25 g	25–60 g
Tomato purée	25 g	60 g
Stock or water	750 ml (approximately)	2 litres (approximately)
Turned potatoes or small new potatoes	8	20
Choux paste (see page 459)	125 ml	300 ml

Healthy eating tips
- Trim off as much fat as possible before frying and drain all surplus fat after frying.
- Use the minimum amount of salt to season the meat.
- Serve with a large side salad.

Energy	Cals	Fat	Sat fat	Carb	Sugar	Protein	Fibre
1,625 kJ	389 kcal	20.4 g	6.0 g	26.1 g	3.9 g	26.9 g	1.7 g

33 Cornish pasties

Ingredient	4 portions	10 portions
Short paste (see page 446)	200 g	500 g
Potato (raw), finely diced	100 g	250 g
Raw beef, chuck or skirt, cut into thin pieces	100 g	250 g
Onion or leeks, chopped	50 g	125 g
Swede (raw), finely diced (optional)	50 g	125 g
Egg wash		

Energy	Cals	Fat	Sat fat	Carb	Sugar	Protein	Fibre
1,217 kJ	290 kcal	16.2 g	6.0 g	29.3 g	1.2 g	8.7 g	1.8 g

1 Roll out the short paste to 3 mm thick and cut into rounds 12 cm in diameter.
2 Mix the remaining ingredients together, moisten with a little water and place in the rounds in piles. Brush the edges with egg wash.
3 Fold in half and seal; flute the edge and brush evenly with egg wash.
4 Cook in a moderate oven at 150–200 °C for ½–1 hour.
5 Serve with a suitable sauce/gravy, or hot or cold as a snack.

Note

The filling can be made from cooked meat that has been quickly chilled and held at 3 °C.

Healthy eating tips
● Adding baked beans, tomatoes and/or mushrooms will 'dilute' the fat from the meat.
● Serve with a large portion of vegetables.

Variation

Variations include:
● potato, onion or leek, and turnip or swede, with fresh herbs
● bacon, hard-boiled eggs and leeks
● lamb, carrot and potato
● apples, cinnamon, cloves, brown sugar, cider
● puff pastry.

Ingredients for Cornish pasties

Place the filling on to the pastry

Fold the pastry over and seal the edge

34 Steak pie

Ingredient	4 portions	10 portions
Prepared stewing beef (chuck steak)	400 g	1 kg
Oil or dripping	50 ml	125 ml
Onion, chopped (optional)	100 g	250 g
Worcester sauce, few drops		
Parsley, chopped	1 tsp	2½ tsp
Water, stock, red wine or dark beer	125 ml	300 ml
Salt, pepper		
Cornflour	10 g	25 g
Short, puff or rough puff paste (see pages 446, 465 and 467)	100 g	250 g

Energy	Cals	Fat	Sat fat	Carb	Sugar	Protein	Fibre
1,442 kJ	346 kcal	22.2 g	2.9 g	13.6 g	1.8 g	24.3 g	0.4 g

Using puff pastry (McCance data).

1 Cut the meat into 2 cm strips then cut into squares.
2 Heat the oil in a frying pan until smoking, add the meat and quickly brown on all sides.
3 Drain the meat off in a colander.
4 Lightly fry the onion.
5 Place the meat, onion, Worcester sauce, parsley and the liquid in a pan, season lightly with salt and pepper.
6 Bring to the boil, skim, then allow to simmer gently until the meat is tender.
7 Dilute the cornflour with a little water, stir into the simmering mixture, reboil and correct seasoning.
8 Place the mixture into a pie dish and allow to cool.
9 Cover with the paste, egg wash and bake at 200 °C for approximately 30–45 minutes.

Dice the steak evenly

Coat the meat in cornflour before frying it

Cover the top with paste and trim off the excess

Press gently to ensure a seal between the paste and the dish

Healthy eating tips

- Use little or no salt as the Worcester sauce contains salt.
- Fry in a small amount of an unsaturated oil and drain off all excess fat after frying.
- There will be less fat in the dish if short paste is used.
- Serve with boiled potatoes and plenty of vegetables.

Variation

Try:

- adding 50–100 g ox or sheep's kidneys with skin and gristle removed and cut into neat pieces
- adding 50–100 g sliced or quartered mushrooms
- adding 1 heaped teaspoon of tomato purée and some mixed herbs
- in place of cornflour, the meat can be tossed in flour before frying off
- in place of plain flour, 25–50 per cent wholemeal flour may be used in the pastry.

35 Roast wing of beef

Ingredient	10 portions
Wing rib of beef	1 × 2 kg
Beef dripping	25 g
Yorkshire puddings (see recipe 36), prepared English mustard or horseradish sauce, to serve	
Gravy	
Carrots (for the mirepoix)	50 g
Onion (for the mirepoix)	50 g
Red wine	200 ml
Plain flour	30 g
Beef stock	300 ml

Energy	Cals	Fat	Sat fat	Carb	Sugar	Protein	Fibre
3,185 kJ	758 kcal	31.0 g	13.0 g	31.6 g	4.5 g	90.0 g	1.6 g

1 Preheat the oven to 195 °C.

2 Place the dripping in a heavy roasting tray and heat on the stove top.

3 Place the beef in the tray and brown well on all sides.

4 Place in the oven on 195 °C for 15 minutes then turn down to 75 °C for 2 hours.

5 Remove and allow to rest before carving.

For the gravy

1 Remove the beef. Place the tray with the fat, sediment and the juice back on the stove.

2 Add the mirepoix and brown well.

3 Add the red wine and reduce by two-thirds.

4 Mix the flour and a little stock together to form a viscous batter-like mix.

5 Add the stock to the roasting tray and bring to the boil.

6 Pour in the flour mix and whisk into the liquid in the tray.

7 Bring to the boil, simmer and correct the seasoning.

8 Pass through a sieve and retain for service.

To complete

Slice the beef and warm the Yorkshire puddings (see recipe 37), serve with the gravy, horseradish and mustard.

> **Professional tip**
>
> This dish would work well with most vegetables or potatoes. As an alternative, why not add slightly blanched root vegetables to the roasting tray at the start of the beef cooking, remove and reheat for service? They will obtain maximum flavour from the beef and juices.

36 Yorkshire pudding

Ingredient	4 portions	10 portions
Flour	85 g	215 g
Eggs	2	5
Milk	85 ml	215 ml
Water	40 ml	100 ml
Dripping or oil	20 g	50 g

Energy	Cals	Fat	Sat fat	Carb	Sugar	Protein	Fibre	Sodium
730 kJ	174 kcal	9.3 g	2.1 g	17.5 g	1.3 g	6.3 g	0.9 g	0.1 g

1 Place the flour and eggs into a mixing bowl and mix to a smooth paste.

2 Gradually whisk in the milk and water and place in the refrigerator for 1 hour. Preheat the oven to 190 °C.

3 Heat the pudding trays in the oven with a little dripping or oil in each well.

4 Carefully ladle the mixture in, up to about two-thirds full.

5 Place in the oven and slowly close the door (if you have a glass-fronted door it will be easy to monitor progress; if not, after about 30 minutes check the puddings). The myth about opening the door during cooking has an element of truth in it – however, it is slamming and the speed at which the door is opened that have most effect, so have just a small, careful peek to check and see if they are ready.

6 For the last 10 minutes of cooking, invert the puddings (take out and turn upside down in the tray) to dry out the base.

7 Serve immediately.

Professional tip

The oven, and the oil, must be very hot before the mixture is placed into the pudding tray; if they are not hot enough, the puddings will not rise.

37 Slow-cooked sirloin with lyonnaise onions and carrot purée

Ingredient	4 portions	10 portions
Beef		
Sirloin, outer skin removed, with fat tied back on	1 kg	3 kg
Oil	50 ml	125 ml
Clove of garlic, sliced	1	2
Sprigs of thyme	1	2
Bay leaves	1	2
Lyonnaise onions		
Onions	200 g	500 g
Seasoning		
Carrot purée		
Medium-sized carrots	600 g	1.5 kg
Star anise	1	2
To serve		
Jus de viande (meat juice)	150 ml	375 ml
Sprigs of chervil		

Energy	Cals	Fat	Sat fat	Carb	Sugar	Protein	Fibre	Sodium
2,436 kJ	584 kcal	26.9 g	7.4 g	13.5 g	11.2 g	72.5 g	5.9 g	0.8 g

For the beef:

1 Preheat the oven to 180 °C. Season the beef and heat the oil in the pan. Add the garlic, thyme, bay leaves and the beef.

2 Place the beef in the oven for 15 minutes. Remove and turn the oven down to 70 °C. When the oven has reached this new temperature, return the beef to it for a further 1 hour 10 minutes.

3 While the beef is cooking, make the lyonnaise onions and carrot purée (see below) and keep warm.

For the onions:

1 Finely slice the onions and put them into a large induction pan while cold.

2 Put on medium heat and season.

3 When the onions are starting to colour, turn down and cook slowly for approximately 2 hours.

4 Cool and refrigerate.

For the carrot purée:

1 Peel the carrots. Liquidise half of them into carrot juice and place the juice into a small pan.

2 Cut the remaining carrots into equal slices of about 1 cm and place into the carrot juice.

3 Boil the carrots, ensuring that you scrape down the sides of the pan.

4 For the last 8 minutes of cooking, before all the liquid has completely evaporated, drop in the star anise. Pass, retaining the juice.

5 Remove the star anise and blitz the purée for 7 minutes, adding the retained juice.

To finish:

1 When the beef is cooked, remove from the oven and carve evenly. Place a portion of carrot purée and lyonnaise onions on each plate. Top with the beef and pour over the jus de viande (meat juice), garnish with sprigs of chervil and serve.

Veal dishes

38 Escalope of veal

Veal escalope Holstein

Ingredient	4 portions	10 portions
Nut or cushion of veal	400 g	1 kg
Seasoned flour	25 g	60 g
Egg	1	2½
Breadcrumbs	50 g	125 g
Oil, for frying	50 g	125 g
Butter, for frying	50 g	125 g
Beurre noisette (optional)	50 g	125 g
Jus-lié (page 97)	60 ml	150 ml

Energy	Cals	Fat	Sat fat	Carb	Sugar	Protein	Fibre
2,079 kJ	495 kcal	39.8 g	11.4 g	10.3 g	0.5 g	24.7 g	1.0 g

Fried in sunflower oil, using butter to finish.

1 Trim and remove all sinew from the veal.

2 Cut into four even slices and bat out thinly using a little water.

3 Flour, egg and crumb. Shake off surplus crumbs. Mark with a palette knife.

4 Place the escalopes into shallow hot fat and cook quickly for a few minutes on each side.

5 Dress on a serving dish or plate.

6 An optional finish is to pour over 50 g *beurre noisette* (nut-brown butter) and finish with a cordon of *jus-lié*.

The escalopes need to be batted out thinly. Excess breadcrumbs must be shaken off before the escalopes are placed into the hot fat.

Healthy eating tips

● Use an unsaturated oil to fry the veal.
● Make sure the fat is hot so that less will be absorbed into the crumb.
● Drain the cooked escalope on kitchen paper.
● Use the minimum amount of salt.
● Serve with plenty of starchy carbohydrate and vegetables.

Variation

Escalope of veal Viennoise: as for this recipe, but garnish the dish with chopped yolk and white of egg and chopped parsley; on top of each escalope place a slice of peeled lemon decorated with chopped egg yolk, egg white and parsley, an anchovy fillet and a stoned olive; finish with a little lemon juice and nut-brown butter.

Veal escalope Holstein: prepare and cook the escalopes as for this recipe; add an egg fried in butter or oil, and place two neat fillets of anchovy criss-crossed on each egg; serve.

Escalope of veal with spaghetti and tomato sauce: prepare escalopes as for this recipe, then garnish with spaghetti with tomato sauce (page 141), allowing 10 g spaghetti per portion.

39 Breadcrumbed veal escalope with ham and cheese (*escalope de veau cordon bleu*)

1 Trim and remove all sinew from the veal.

2 Cut into eight even slices (20 slices for ten portions) and bat out thinly using a little water.

3 Place a slice of ham and a slice of cheese on to four of the veal slices (ten slices for ten portions), cover with the remaining veal slices and press together firmly.

4 Flour, egg and crumb. Shake off all surplus crumbs and shape like a diamond. Mark on one side with crossed lines using a palette knife.

5 Place the escalopes marked side down into the hot oil (with butter if desired) and cook quickly for a few minutes on each side, until golden brown.

6 An optional finish is to serve coated with *beurre noisette* (nut-brown butter) and a cordon of *jus-lié*.

Note

Veal escalopes may be cooked plain (not crumbed), in which case they are only slightly batted out.

Healthy eating tips

● No added salt is needed as there is plenty in the ham and cheese.
● This is a high-fat dish so serve with plenty of starchy carbohydrates and vegetables to 'dilute' the fat.

Ingredient	4 portions	10 portions
Nut or cushion of veal	400 g	1 kg
Cooked ham, sliced	4	10
Gruyère cheese, sliced	4	10
Seasoned flour	25 g	60 g
Egg, beaten	1	2½
Breadcrumbs	50 g	125 g
Oil	50 g	125 g
Butter (optional)	100 g	250 g
Beurre noisette (optional)	50 g	125 g
Jus-lié	60 ml	150 ml

Energy	Cals	Fat	Sat fat	Carb	Sugar	Protein	Fibre
2,632 kJ	627 kcal	48.1 g	16.3 g	12.0 g	1.3 g	37.1 g	0.7 g

Fried in sunflower oil, using butter to finish.

Bat out the escalopes

Layer the veal, ham and cheese

Coat the escalope with breadcrumbs and mark on one side

40 Veal escalope with Parma ham and mozzarella cheese (*involtini di vitello*)

1 Sprinkle each slice of veal lightly with flour and flatten.

2 Place a slice of Parma ham on each escalope.

3 Add several slices of mozzarella cheese to each.

4 Add a sage leaf or a light sprinkling of dried sage.

5 Season, roll up each escalope and secure with a toothpick or cocktail stick. Make sure the ham and cheese are well sealed within the escalope before cooking.

6 Melt the butter in a sauté pan, add the escalopes and brown on all sides.

7 Transfer the escalopes and butter to a suitably sized ovenproof dish.

8 Sprinkle generously with grated Parmesan cheese and bake in a moderately hot oven at 190 °C for 10 minutes.

9 Clean the edges of the dish and serve.

Ingredient	4 portions	10 portions
Small, thin veal escalopes	400 g (8 in total)	1 kg (20 in total)
Flour (for dusting)		
Parma ham, thinly sliced	100 g	250 g
Mozzarella cheese, thinly sliced	200 g	500 g
Fresh sage leaves	8	20
or		
dried sage	1 tsp	2½ tsp
Salt, pepper		
Butter or oil	50 g	125 g
Parmesan cheese, grated		

Healthy eating tips
● Use a small amount of oil to fry the escalopes and drain the cooked escalopes on kitchen paper.
● No added salt is necessary as there is plenty of salt in the cheese.
● Serve with plenty of vegetables.

Energy	Cals	Fat	Sat fat	Carb	Sugar	Protein	Fibre
1,642 kJ	394 kcal	26.1 g	15.5 g	0.1 g	0.1 g	39.8 g	0.0 g

Layer the veal, ham and cheese, then roll them up

Transfer the fried escalopes to an ovenproof dish and sprinkle with cheese

41 Fricassée of veal

Ingredient	4 portions	10 portions
Boned stewing veal (shoulder or breast)	400 g	1 kg
Butter or oil	35 g	90 g
Flour	25 g	60 g
White veal stock	500 ml	1.25 litres
Salt, pepper		
Egg yolk	1	2–3
Cream (dairy or vegetable)	2–3 tbsp	5–7 tbsp
Squeeze of lemon juice		
Parsley, chopped, to finish		

Energy	Cals	Fat	Sat fat	Carb	Sugar	Protein	Fibre
992 kJ	236 kcal	13.6 g	7.5 g	5.3 g	0.4 g	23.3 g	0.2 g

Using butter.

1 Trim the meat. Cut into even 25 g pieces.

2 Sweat the meat gently in the butter without colour in a sauté pan.

3 Mix in the flour and cook out without colour.

4 Allow to cool.

5 Gradually add boiling stock just to cover the meat, stir until smooth.

6 Season, bring to the boil, skim.

7 Cover and simmer gently on the stove until tender (approximately 1½–2 hours).

8 Pick out the meat into a clean pan. Correct the sauce.

9 Pass on to the meat and reboil. Mix the yolk and cream in a basin.

10 Add a little of the boiling sauce, mix in and pour back on to the meat, shaking the pan until thoroughly mixed; do not reboil. Add the lemon juice.

11 Serve, finished with chopped parsley and heart-shaped croutons fried in butter or oil.

> **Professional tip**
>
> After adding the flour, cook carefully so that it does not colour.
>
> Add the liaison of yolks and cream carefully. Do not allow the sauce to boil after this, because it will curdle.

Ingredients for fricassée of veal

Cook the meat and flour

Add the stock and continue to cook

Add the liaison of egg yolk and cream

Healthy eating tips

● Add the minimum amount of salt.
● Brush the croutons with olive oil and bake them, or serve with sippets (small, thin pieces of toasted bread).
● A large serving of starchy carbohydrates and vegetables will help to proportionally reduce the fat content.

Variation

Add mushrooms and button onions. Proceed as for this recipe but, after 1 hour's cooking, pick out the meat, strain the sauce back on to the meat and add 2 small button onions per portion. Simmer for 15 minutes, add 2 small white button mushrooms per portion, washed and peeled if necessary, then complete the cooking. Finish and serve as in this recipe. This is known as *fricassée de veau à l'ancienne*.

42 Braised shin of veal (*osso buco*)

Ingredient	4 portions	10 portions
Salt and ground pepper		
Plain flour	45 g	112 g
Thick slices of veal shin on the bone	4 × 200 g	10 × 200 g
Butter	50 g	125 g
Oil	2 tbsp	5 tbsp
White wine	150 ml	375 ml
Plum tomatoes	450 g	1.1 kg
Light veal or chicken stock	300 ml	750 ml
Sprigs of parsley and thyme		
Bay leaf	1	1

Energy	Cals	Fat	Sat fat	Carb	Sugar	Protein	Fibre
1,732 kJ	413 kcal	19.7 g	8.5 g	12.5 g	3.9 g	47.3 g	1.5 g

1 Preheat the oven to 180 °C.

2 Season the flour and use to coat the meat well on both sides.

3 Heat the butter and oil in a casserole, add the veal and fry, turning once, until browned on both sides. Add the wine and cook, uncovered, for 10 minutes. Blanch, peel and chop the tomatoes, and add along with the stock and herbs.

4 Cover and cook in the centre of the oven until the meat is very tender and falls away from the marrow bone in the middle.

Delicious served with sauté potatoes or with a *risotto alla Milanese*.

Note

Part of the attraction of this dish is the marrow found in the bones. Although very rich, it is a special treat. Traditionally, *osso buco* is served with a gremolata, which is a combination of chopped parsley, garlic and lemon zest that is added to the dish at the very end. It has been omitted from this recipe, offering you a simple base.

Pork dishes

43 Pork escalope with calvados sauce

Ingredient	4 portions	10 portions
Crisp eating apples (e.g. russet)	2	5
Cinnamon	¼ tsp	¾ tsp
Lemon juice	1 tbsp	2½ tbsp
Brown sugar	2 tsp	5 tsp
Butter, melted	25 g	60 g
Pork escalopes	4 × 100 g	10 × 100 g
Butter or oil	50 g	125 g
Shallots or onions, finely chopped	50 g	125 g
Calvados	30 ml	75 ml
Double cream or natural yoghurt	125 ml	300 ml
Salt, cayenne pepper		
Basil, sage or rosemary, chopped		

Energy	Cals	Fat	Sat fat	Carb	Sugar	Protein	Fibre
1,856 kJ	447 kcal	34.2 g	20.3 g	12.7 g	12.5 g	22.8 g	1.1 g

Using lean meat only, and double cream.

Variation

Calvados can be replaced with twice the amount of cider and reduced by three-quarters as an alternative.

Add a crushed clove of garlic and 1 tablespoon of continental mustard (2–3 cloves and 2½ tablespoons for 10 portions).

1 Core and peel the apples.

2 Cut into 0.5 cm-thick rings and sprinkle with a little cinnamon and a few drops of lemon juice.

3 Place on a baking sheet, sprinkle with brown sugar and a little melted butter, and caramelise under the salamander or in the top of a hot oven.

4 Lightly sauté the escalopes on both sides in the butter.

5 Remove from the pan and keep warm.

6 Add the chopped shallots to the same pan, cover with a lid and cook gently without colouring (use a little more butter if necessary).

7 Strain off the fat, leaving the shallots in the pan, and deglaze with the calvados.

8 Reduce by a half and then add the cream or yoghurt, seasoning and herbs.

9 Reboil, correct the seasoning and consistency, and pass through a fine strainer on to the meat.

10 Garnish with slices of caramelised apple.

Special care must be taken not to overheat if using yoghurt, otherwise the sauce will curdle.

Healthy eating tips
- Use a little unsaturated oil to sauté the escalopes.
- Add the minimum amount of salt.
- Try using yoghurt stabilised with a little cornflour, or half cream and half yoghurt.

44 Sweet and sour pork

Ingredient	4 portions	10 portions
Loin of pork, boned	250 g	600 g
Sugar	12 g	30 g
Dry sherry	70 ml	180 ml
Soy sauce	70 ml	180 ml
Cornflour	50 g	125 g
Vegetable oil, for frying	70 ml	180 ml
Oil	2 tbsp	5 tbsp
Clove of garlic	1	2½
Fresh root ginger	50 g	125 g
Onion, chopped	75 g	180 g
Green pepper, in 1 cm dice	1	2½
Chillies, chopped	2	5
Sweet and sour sauce (see page 103)	210 ml	500 ml
Pineapple rings (fresh or canned)	1	3
Spring onions	2	5

Energy	Cals	Fat	Sat fat	Carb	Sugar	Protein	Fibre
3,067 kJ	730 kcal	43.9 g	9.2 g	69.7 g	54.7 g	13.4 g	1.6 g

1 Cut the boned loin of pork into 2 cm pieces.

2 Marinate the pork for 30 minutes in the sugar, sherry and soy sauce.

3 Pass the pork through cornflour, pressing the cornflour in well.

4 Deep-fry the pork pieces in oil at 190 °C until golden brown, then drain. Add the tablespoons of oil to a sauté pan.

5 Add the garlic and ginger, and fry until fragrant.

6 Add the onion, pepper and chillies, sauté for a few minutes.

7 Stir in the sweet and sour sauce, bring to the boil.

8 Add the pineapple cut into small chunks, thicken slightly with diluted cornflour. Simmer for 2 minutes.

9 Deep-fry the pork again until crisp. Drain, mix into the vegetables and sauce or serve separately.

10 Serve garnished with rings of spring onions or button onions.

> **Professional tip**
>
> It is important to allow the pork enough time to marinate.

45 Stir-fried pork fillet

Ingredient	4 portions	10 portions
Shallots, finely chopped	2	5
Clove of garlic (optional), chopped	1	2½
Button mushrooms, sliced	200 g	500 g
Olive oil		
Pork fillet	400 g	1 kg
Chinese five-spice powder	1 pinch	2½ pinches
Soy sauce	1 tbsp	2½ tbsp
Clear honey	2 tsp	5 tsp
Dry white wine	2 tbsp	5 tbsp
Salt, pepper		

Energy	Cals	Fat	Sat fat	Carb	Sugar	Protein	Fibre
831 kJ	199 kcal	9.8 g	2.2 g	5.1 g	4.2 g	22.9 g	0.8 g

1 Gently fry the shallots, garlic and sliced mushrooms in a little oil in a frying pan or wok.

2 Add the pork cut into strips, stir well, increase the heat, season and add the Chinese five-spice powder; cook for 3–4 minutes then reduce the heat.

3 Add the soy sauce, honey and wine, and reduce for 2–3 minutes.

4 Correct the seasoning and serve.

Healthy eating tips
- No extra salt is needed, as soy sauce is added.
- Adding more vegetables and a large portion of rice or noodles can reduce the overall fat content.

46 Sauerkraut, ham hocks and lentils

Sauerkraut is made by a process of pickling called lacto-fermentation. The bacteria and yeasts needed for the fermentation process are found on the cabbage leaves. No additional bacteria are added for this reaction to take place.

The process of making sauerkraut begins by washing and finely slicing white cabbage. It is put into a large pot, a specific amount of salt is mixed in and it is mashed with a cabbage masher. This allows the cabbage juices to be extracted: it produces enough to cover the cabbage in liquid. It is important for the cabbage to be completely covered in liquid to keep air out – any cabbage exposed to air would spoil during the fermentation process.

Using salt in this way is a process that can extract the natural juices of many ingredients by breaking down the cell structure. In meat, this 'tightening action' affects the myosin protein, while in vegetables it breaks down the cell wall structure – commonly done when preparing cauliflower for piccalilli or aubergine for ratatouille.

The cabbage, covered with its juices, is put into a large, covered, airtight container and allowed to ferment for four to six weeks. The bacteria and yeast begin the fermentation process. Over time, the lactic acid bacteria become active, converting the sugars in the cabbage into lactic acid. The sauerkraut is ready when the desired 'sourness' is obtained.

Sauerkraut can keep for several months if it is stored in an airtight container and stored at or below 13°C. Refrigeration is not essential, but it greatly increases the shelf life of the sauerkraut. Many commercial producers also use pasteurisation to further increase its shelf life.

If you can plan ahead, then this is a worthwhile recipe to make. It highlights some of the near-forgotten culinary techniques that are making a comeback at every level of gastronomy.

Below there are two methods for making sauerkraut: traditional and modern. Alternatively, use 600g of ready-made sauerkraut for this ham hock recipe.

Sauerkraut – traditional method

Ingredient	8–10 portions
Head of white cabbage	1
Salt	40g

1 Finely slice the cabbage. Mix with the salt and mash down, encouraging the cell structure to break down and extracting the natural liquid from the cabbage.

2 Ensure that the cabbage is completely covered with the liquid.

3 Place the cabbage in a covered container (not air sealed as the bacteria need air movement) for four to six weeks, until the cabbage takes on the natural sourness.

4 Store in an airtight jar for up to six months at 13°C, or place in the fridge if a longer shelf life is required.

Sauerkraut – modern interpretation

Ingredient	8–10 portions
Head of white cabbage	1
Salt	10g
Oil	50ml
Butter	50g
Streaky bacon, cut into lardons	300g
Shallots, sliced	2
Juniper berries	5
Alsace-style wine	250ml
Chicken stock	1 litre

1 Shred the cabbage and place in a colander over a dish. Sprinkle with the salt and leave to extract the liquid for an hour.

2 Squeeze out the remaining liquid by hand, wash the cabbage and pat dry with kitchen towel.

3 Heat the oil and butter in a pan and add the bacon. Cook until the bacon is crisp and has released its fat into the pan.

4 Add the cabbage and cook until soft, without colour.

5 Add the juniper, and then deglaze with the wine and reduce until half the liquid has evaporated.

6 Add the chicken stock and reduce the heat until the cabbage mix is soft and has absorbed the liquid (you may have to regularly top up with a little water to aid the cooking).

For the ham hocks

Ingredient	8–10 portions
Ham hocks, about 1.3 kg	2
Onion, quartered	1
Carrots, quartered lengthways	2
Celery sticks, cut into thirds crossways	2
Fresh thyme, few sprigs	
Bay leaf	

1 Before starting the cooking process, blanch the hocks to rinse away any impurities and excess salt.

2 Put the joints in a large saucepan, cover with cold water and bring to the boil.

3 Reduce the heat and simmer for 1 minute, then carefully move the pan to the sink and drain off the hot water.

4 Refresh the hams under cold running water for a minute or so, then tip out the water.

5 Put the blanched hams in the pan, and add the onion, carrots, celery sticks, thyme and bay leaf.

6 Pour in enough fresh cold water to cover and bring to a simmer.

7 The pan can now be covered with its lid and the hams cooked, keeping the liquor at a gentle simmer for 3 hours.

8 To check if the hams are cooked, pull out the small bone close to the large one – it should be loose and come out easily.

9 Rest the hams in the stock for 15–20 minutes.

10 Lift out the hams and set aside until cool enough to handle. Wrap in cling film to retain the moisture.

11 Retain 900 ml of the stock to cook the lentils.

12 About 10 minutes before the lentils are ready, strip off the skin and fat from the hams with a knife, then remove the meat from the bones and cut it into rough pieces or shred it with your fingers.

For the lentils

Ingredient	8–10 portions
Puy lentils	250 g
Butter	75 g
Large onion, peeled and finely diced	1
Large carrot, peeled and finely diced	1
Celery stick, finely diced	1
Fresh parsley, coarsely chopped	1 heaped tbsp
Stock from cooking the hams, strained	900 ml

1 First blanch the lentils by plunging them into a pan of boiling water, then drain into a sieve and refresh under the cold tap. (This process not only rinses the lentils well, it also speeds up the entire braising process and stops the lentils breaking before the cooking process has finished.)

2 Melt the butter in a medium saucepan. Add the diced onion, carrot and celery, cover the pan and cook without colouring for 5–6 minutes.

3 Tip in the blanched lentils, then pour in the reserved stock from the hams.

4 Bring the lentils to a simmer and cook for about 30 minutes, until tender. Check occasionally and top up with more stock if needed.

To finish

Warm the sauerkraut gently in a pan and place on a large serving plate. Scatter the shredded ham over the top of the cabbage. Add the coarsely chopped parsley to the lentils, and season with a twist of pepper, then scatter the lentils over the dish and serve with crusty sourdough bread.

Energy	Cals	Fat	Sat fat	Carb	Sugar	Protein	Fibre	Sodium
2295 kJ	550 kcal	31.0 g	12.4 g	29.0 g	12.4 g	40.0 g	10.7 g	2.4 g

Using the traditional method and a pork leg joint.

47 Boiled bacon

1 Soak the bacon in cold water for 24 hours before cooking. Change the water.

2 Bring to the boil, skim and simmer gently (approximately 25 minutes per 0.5 kg, plus another 25 minutes). Allow to cool in the liquid.

3 Remove the rind and brown skin; carve.

4 Serve with a little of the cooking liquor.

Boiled bacon may be served with pease pudding (a purée of yellow split peas) and a suitable sauce such as parsley (see page 85). It may also be served cold, or used as an ingredient in other dishes.

Energy	Cals	Fat	Sat fat	Carb	Sugar	Protein	Fibre
1,543 kJ	367 kcal	30.5 g	12.2 g	0.0 g	0.0 g	23.1 g	0.0 g

Using 113 g per portion.

48 Roast leg of pork

Energy	Cals	Fat	Sat fat	Carb	Sugar	Protein	Fibre
1,357 kJ	323 kcal	22.4 g	8.9 g	0.0 g	0.0 g	30.4 g	0.0 g

113 g portion.

1 Prepare leg for roasting (see page 228).

2 Moisten with water, oil, cider, wine or butter and lard, then sprinkle with salt, rubbing it well into the cracks of the skin. This will make the crackling crisp.

3 Place on a trivet in a roasting tin with a little oil or dripping on top.

4 Start to cook in a hot oven at 230–250 °C, basting frequently.

5 Gradually reduce the heat to 180–185 °C, allowing approximately 25 minutes per 0.5 kg plus another 25 minutes. Pork must always be well cooked. If using a probe, the minimum temperature should be 75 °C for 2 minutes.

6 When cooked, remove from the pan and prepare a roast gravy from the sediment (see page 96).

7 Remove the crackling and cut into even pieces for serving.

Serve the joint garnished with picked watercress and accompanied by roast gravy, sage and onion dressing and apple sauce. If to be carved, proceed as for roast lamb (see page 221).

Variation

Other joints can also be used for roasting (e.g. loin, shoulder and spare rib).

49 Roast pork belly with shallots and champ potatoes

Ingredient	4 portions	10 portions
Pork belly	1.2 kg	3 kg
Salt, pepper		
Olive oil	1 tbsp	2½ tbsp
Shallots	20	50
Butter	70 g	175 g
Potatoes, peeled and chopped	1 kg	2.5 kg
Spring onions, chopped	8	20
Double cream	4 tbsp	10 tbsp

Energy	Cals	Fat	Sat fat	Carb	Sugar	Protein	Fibre	Sodium
2,680 kJ	645 kcal	50.5 g	18.3 g	0.0 g	0.0 g	47.8 g	0.0 g	0.2 g

1 Place the pork on a rack in a roasting tray; season and oil. Roast in the oven for 10 minutes at 200 °C and then for 3–3½ hours at 140 °C.

2 Peel the shallots, fry gently in half the butter until caramelised. Keep warm.

3 Purée the potatoes.

4 Melt the remaining butter in a pan and sauté the spring onions until soft. Add the spring onion and the butter to the potato purée.

5 Add the cream and mix well.

6 Serve the pork with the caramelised shallots and potato.

7 Serve with a reduced brown stock flavoured with cider; alternatively, a red wine sauce may be served.

50 Slow-roast belly of pork

Ingredient	4 portions	10 portions
Pork belly	1.2 kg	3 kg
Salt and pepper		

1 Preheat the oven to 145 °C.
2 Season the pork with salt and pepper.
3 Place on a rack in a large roasting tray, skin-side up.
4 Roast for 4½–5 hours, then remove from the tray.
5 Pour off excess fat and make a gravy.
6 Carve into thick slices and serve with apple sauce, sage and onion dressing and a suitable potato and vegetable.

Energy	Cals	Fat	Sat fat	Carb	Sugar	Protein	Fibre
3,216 kJ	774 kcal	60.6g	21.9g	0.0g	0.0g	57.3g	0.0g

51 Sage and onion dressing for pork

	4 portions	10 portions
Onion, chopped	50 g	125 g
Pork dripping	50 g	125 g
White breadcrumbs	100 g	250 g
Chopped parsley, pinch		
Powdered sage, good pinch		
Salt, pepper		

Healthy eating tips
- Use a small amount of unsaturated oil instead of dripping.
- Add the minimum amount of salt.

Energy	Cals	Fat	Sat fat	Carb	Sugar	Protein	Fibre	Sodium
865 kJ	204 kcal	12.9g	6.3g	20.6g	1.9g	2.7g	0.2g	0.2g

1 Cook the onion in the dripping without colour.
2 Combine all the ingredients. Dressing is usually served separately.

Professional tip
Modern practice is to refer to this as a dressing if served separately to the meat, but as stuffing if used to stuff the meat.

52 Spare ribs in barbecue sauce

Ingredient	4 portions	10 portions
Onion, finely chopped	100 g	250 g
Clove of garlic, chopped	1	2
Oil	60 ml	150 ml
Vinegar	60 ml	150 ml
Tomato purée	150 g	375 g
Honey	60 ml	150 ml
Brown stock	250 ml	625 ml
Worcester sauce	4 tbsp	10 tbsp
Dry mustard	1 tsp	2½ tsp
Pinch thyme		
Salt		
Spare ribs of pork	2 kg	5 kg

Energy	Cals	Fat	Sat fat	Carb	Sugar	Protein	Fibre
6,151 kJ	1,465 kcal	12.6 g	37.3 g	20.3 g	17.1 g	63.5 g	0.3 g

Using sunflower oil.

1 Sweat the onion and garlic in the oil without colour.

2 Mix in the vinegar, tomato purée, honey, stock, Worcester sauce, mustard and thyme, and season with salt.

3 Allow the barbecue sauce to simmer for 10–15 minutes.

4 Place the prepared spare ribs fat side up on a trivet in a roasting tin.

5 Brush the spare ribs liberally with the barbecue sauce.

6 Place in a moderately hot oven: 180–200 °C.

7 Cook for ¾–1 hour.

8 Baste generously with the barbecue sauce every 10–15 minutes.

9 The cooked spare ribs should be brown and crisp.

10 Cut the spare ribs into individual portions and serve.

Professional tip

Apply plenty of barbecue sauce before and during cooking, to give the ribs a good flavour.

Healthy eating tips
- Sweat the onion and garlic in a little unsaturated oil.
- No added salt is necessary as the Worcester sauce is salty.

53 Roasted joint of bacon

Energy	Cals	Fat	Sat fat	Carb	Sugar	Protein	Fibre
1,021 kJ	245 kcal	14.8g	4.9g	0.0g	0.0g	28.0g	0.0g

1 Soak the joint in cold water for 24 hours.
2 Remove from the water. Dry well.
3 Place on a roasting tray and roast for approximately 25 minutes per 0.5 kg, plus another 25 minutes.
4 Remove from the oven and allow to stand for 5 minutes before carving.
5 Use the sediment to make roast gravy (see page 96), having checked for saltiness.
6 The joint may be cooked in foil and, for the last 25–30 minutes, cooked out of the foil.

54 Meat cured in brine (*saumure*)

Ingredient	To make 2.5 litres of brine
Cold water	2.5 litres
Saltpetre	15g
Salt	850g
Bay leaf	1
Juniper berries	6
Brown sugar	50g
Peppercorns	6

1 Boil all the ingredients together for 10 minutes, skimming frequently.
2 Strain into a china, wooden or earthenware container.
3 When the brine is cold, add the meat.
4 Immerse the meat for up to 10 days under refrigeration.

Ingredients for brine

Strain the liquid

Immerse the meat in the brine

Offal dishes

55 Calf's liver and bacon (*foie de veau au lard*)

Ingredient	4 portions	10 portions
Calf's liver	300 g	750 g
Flour		
Oil, for frying	50 g	125 g
Streaky bacon	50 g	125 g
Jus-lié	125 ml	300 ml

Energy	Cals	Fat	Sat fat	Carb	Sugar	Protein	Fibre
998 kJ	238 kcal	13.4 g	5.0 g	2.8 g	2.7 g	26.9 g	1.1 g

1 Skin the liver and remove the gristle.
2 Cut in slices on the slant.
3 Pass the slices of liver through flour and shake off the excess.
4 Quickly fry on both sides in hot oil.
5 Remove the rind and bone from the bacon and grill on both sides.
6 Serve the liver and bacon with a cordon of *jus-lié* and a separate sauceboat of *jus-lié*.

Note

Liver dishes are often cooked so that the liver is still pink in the centre. It is safer to cook to a higher core temperature, especially if the dish is for anyone in a high-risk group (see Chapter 3).

Variation

Lamb's liver may be cooked in the same way. Variations include the following:
● Fry in butter and sprinkle with powdered sage or chopped fresh sage.
● Fry in butter, remove the liver then deglaze the pan with raspberry vinegar and powdered thyme.
● When cooked, sprinkle with chopped parsley and a few drops of lemon juice.
● Flour, egg and breadcrumb the liver before cooking.
● The liver may be lightly brushed with oil and grilled.

Healthy eating tips
● Bacon is salty, so no added salt is needed.
● Use a little unsaturated oil to fry the liver, and drain off any excess fat.
● Serve with boiled new potatoes and a variety of vegetables.

56 Grilled lambs' kidneys (*rognons grillés*)

1 Season the prepared skewered kidneys (as for lamb kebabs, see recipe 3).

2 Brush with melted butter or oil.

3 Place on preheated, greased grill bars or on a greased baking tray.

4 Grill fairly quickly on both sides (approximately 5–10 minutes depending on size).

5 Serve with parsley butter, picked watercress and straw potatoes.

Energy	Cals	Fat	Sat fat	Carb	Sugar	Protein	Fibre
614 kJ	147 kcal	10.3 g	5.9 g	0.1 g	0.1 g	13.7 g	0.0 g

Healthy eating tips
- Use the minimum amount of salt.
- Serve with plenty of starchy carbohydrates and vegetables.

57 Devilled lambs' kidneys

Energy	Cals	Fat	Sat fat	Carb	Sugar	Protein	Fibre	Sodium
692 kJ	165 kcal	8.1 g	2.7 g	2.5 g	2.4 g	17.3 g	0.0 g	0.4 g

Ingredient	4 portions	10 portions
Lambs' kidneys	8	20
Olive oil	1 tbsp	2½ tbsp
Salt, pepper		
Amontillado sherry	60 ml	150 ml
White wine vinegar	1 tbsp	2½ tbsp
Redcurrant jelly	1 tsp	2½ tsp
Worcester sauce	3 drops	7 drops
Double cream	1 tbsp	2½ tbsp
English mustard	1 tsp	2½ tsp
Mixed herbs, chopped		

1 Prepare the kidneys: cut in half, remove the white ducts then cut into quarters.

2 Heat the oil in the pan. Season the kidneys and place in the pan. When cooked, remove.

3 Add the sherry to the pan and bring to the boil, then add the vinegar and redcurrant jelly.

4 Add the Worcester sauce and season.

5 Add the cream and mustard. Simmer and reduce to a sauce consistency.

6 Add the kidneys and warm through.

7 Serve on a bed of pilaff rice (see page 125), garnished with chopped herbs.

58 Braised calf's cheeks with vegetables

Ingredient	4 portions	10 portions
Calf's cheeks	800 g	2 kg
Salt, pepper		
Olive oil or vegetable oil	2 tbsp	5 tbsp
Ground cumin	½ tsp	1¼ tsp
White peppercorns	½ tsp	1¼ tsp
Cloves	4	10
Celery, 5 mm dice	1 stick	2½ sticks
Bay leaves	2	5
Cloves of garlic	8	20
Leeks, finely shredded	1	2½
Onions, chopped	1	2½
Shallots, quartered	2	5
Savoy cabbage	400 g	1 kg
Dry white wine	500 ml	1.25 litres
Cider	350 ml	875 ml
Chopped chives	½ tsp	1¼ tsp

Energy	Cals	Fat	Sat fat	Carb	Sugar	Protein	Fibre	Sodium
2208 kJ	527 kcal	20.0g	6.3g	13.5g	10.8g	49.0g	6.0g	0.4g

Using stewing steak in place of cheeks.

1 Season the cheeks.

2 Heat the oil in a suitable pan. Sear the cheeks on all sides. Remove and keep warm. Add to the pan the cumin, peppercorns, cloves, celery, bay leaves, garlic, leeks, onions and shallots. Cook until the vegetables start to brown.

3 Add the cabbage and cook until wilted and slightly brown.

4 Add half the white wine and three-quarters of the cider.

5 Return the cheeks to the pan. Cover and braise in the oven for about 2½ hours, until the meat is tender.

6 Remove the cheeks and vegetables from the juices. Set aside and keep warm.

7 Strain the juices and return to the pan. Then add the remaining wine and cider. Bring to the boil and reduce to a sauce consistency.

8 Return the cheeks to the pan and simmer, basting with the sauce until it is syrupy and the meat is glazed.

9 To serve, place the vegetables on plates with the cheeks on top. Mask with the sauce and sprinkle with chopped chives.

10 Serve with polenta or couscous.

59 Braised oxtail (*ragoût de queue de boeuf*)

Ingredient	4 portions	10 portions
Oxtail	1 kg	2.5 kg
Dripping or oil	50 g	125 g
Onion	100 g	250 g
Carrot	100 g	250 g
Flour, browned in the oven	35 g	100 g
Tomato purée	25 g	60 g
Brown stock	1 litre	2.5 litres
Bouquet garni		
Clove of garlic	1	2½
Salt, pepper		
Parsley, chopped		

Energy	Cals	Fat	Sat fat	Carb	Sugar	Protein	Fibre
2,481 kJ	595 kcal	38.0 g	12.0 g	12.3 g	4.7 g	51.6 g	1.4 g

1 Cut the oxtail into sections. Remove the excess fat.

2 Fry on all sides in hot fat.

3 Place in a braising pan or casserole.

4 Roughly cut the onion and carrot. Fry them, then add them to the braising pan.

5 Mix in the flour.

6 Add tomato purée, brown stock, bouquet garni and garlic, and season lightly.

7 Bring to the boil, then skim.

8 Cover with a lid and simmer in the oven until tender (approximately 3 hours).

9 Remove the meat from the sauce, place in a clean pan.

10 Correct the sauce, pass on to the meat and reboil.

11 Serve sprinkled with chopped parsley.

Brown the pieces of oxtail

Mix in the flour

Note

This is usually garnished with glazed turned or neatly cut carrots and turnips, button onions, peas and diamonds of beans. Oxtail must be very well cooked so that the meat comes away from the bone easily.

Variation

Haricot oxtail can be made using the same recipe with the addition of 100 g (250 g for 10 portions) cooked haricot beans, added approximately ½ hour before the oxtail has completed cooking.

Healthy eating tips
● Keep added salt to a minimum.
● Fry in a small amount of an unsaturated oil and drain off all excess fat after frying.
● Serve with mashed potato and additional green vegetables.

60 Shallow-fried lambs' sweetbreads

Ingredient	4 portions	10 portions
Sweetbreads	8	20
Seasoned flour		
Oil	50 ml	125 ml
Butter	50 g	125 g
Lemon, juice of	1	2½
Parsley, chopped	½ tsp	1¼ tsp

1 Trim the sweetbreads, then blanch them for 30 seconds. Pass through seasoned flour.

2 Shallow-fry in oil for 2 minutes, turning.

3 Add butter to pan (*beurre noisette*), then add the lemon juice and chopped parsley.

4 Drain and serve.

Energy	Cals	Fat	Sat fat	Carb	Sugar	Protein	Fibre	Sodium
1,635 kJ	396 kcal	36.0 g	11.0 g	0.4 g	0.4 g	17.6 g	0.1 g	0.4 g

11 Poultry and game

This chapter is relevant to the following units:
→ Prepare poultry for basic dishes.
→ Prepare game for basic dishes.
→ Cook and finish basic poultry dishes.
→ Cook and finish basic game dishes.

Recipes included in this chapter

Poultry

The term 'poultry' is applied to all domestic fowl bred for food, and includes turkeys, geese, ducks, fowls and pigeons.

The flesh of poultry is more easily digested than that of butchers' meat. It contains protein and is therefore useful for building and repairing body tissues and providing heat and energy. The fat content is low and it contains a high percentage of unsaturated fatty acids.

Originally, fowl were classified according to size and feeding by specific names as shown in Table 11.1.

Table 11.1 Traditional classification of fowl

Fowl	Weight (kg)	Number of portions
Single baby chicken (poussin)	0.3–0.5	1
Double baby chicken (poussin)	0.5–0.75	2
Small roasting chicken	0.75–1	3–4
Medium roasting chicken	1–2	4–6
Large roasting or boiling chicken	2–3	6–8
Capon	3–4.5	8–12
Old boiling fowl	2.5–4	

There is approximately 15 to 20 per cent bone in poultry.

Storing poultry

Chilled birds should be stored between 1 °C and 4 °C. Oven-ready birds are eviscerated (gutted and cleaned) and should be stored in a refrigerator. Frozen birds must be kept in a deep freeze until required, but must be completely thawed, preferably in a refrigerator, before being cooked. This procedure is essential to reduce the risk of food poisoning: chickens are potential carriers of salmonella and campylobacter, and if birds are cooked from the frozen state there is a risk that the centre of the bird will not reach the required degree of heat to kill off these pathogens.

When using frozen poultry, check that:
- the packaging is undamaged
- there are no signs of freezer burn, which is indicated by white patches on the skin
- frozen birds are defrosted by moving them from the freezer to a refrigerator.

Preparing poultry

Refer to the sections below for different types of poultry for specific preparation methods. For information on maintaining a safe and secure working environment; a professional and hygienic appearance; clean food production areas, equipment and utensils; and food hygiene when preparing and cooking poultry, please refer to Chapters 1 and 3.

Additional health and safety points to reduce the risk of cross-contamination when preparing poultry are as follows:
- When preparing uncooked poultry or game and then cooked food – or changing from one type of meat, poultry or game to another – equipment, working areas and utensils must be thoroughly cleaned or changed.
- If colour-coded boards are used, it is essential that you always use the correct colour-coded boards for the preparation of raw or cooked poultry.

- Unhygienic equipment, utensils and preparation areas increase the risk of cross-contamination and danger to health.
- Store uncooked poultry and game on trays to prevent dripping, in a separate refrigerator, at a temperature of 1–4 °C, preferably at the lower temperature. When separate refrigerators are not available then store in the bottom of the refrigerator.
- Wash all work surfaces with a bactericidal detergent to kill bacteria. This is particularly important when handling poultry and game.

Cooking, holding and serving poultry

Refer to Chapter 10 for the principles related to cooking meat. All poultry must be cooked until it reaches a core temperature of 75 °C, even if this is not stated in the recipe. When holding cooked poultry and game dishes this should be above 65 °C.

Chicken

The different types of chicken are:
- **Spring chickens**: poussin 4–6 weeks old, used for roasting and grilling.
- **Broiler chickens**: 3–4 months old, used for roasting, grilling and casseroles.
- **Medium roasting chickens**: fully grown, tender, prime birds, used for roasting, grilling, sauté, casseroles, suprêmes and pies.
- **Large roasting or boiling chickens**: used for roasting, boiling, casseroles and galantine.
- **Capons**: specially bred, fattened cock birds used for roasting.
- **Old hens**: used for stocks and soups.

Quality points

- Plump breast, pliable breast bone and firm flesh.
- Skin white and unbroken. Broiler chickens have a faint bluish tint.
- Corn-fed are yellow. Free-range have more colour, a firmer texture and more flavour.
- Bresse chickens are specially bred in France and are highly regarded for their quality and flavour.
- Old birds have coarse scales, large spurs on the legs and long hairs on the skin.

Trussing

To truss a bird for roasting:

Video: buying poultry http://bit.ly/1ClMF1V

1 Place the bird on its back.

2 To facilitate carving, remove the wishbone.

3 Insert a trussing needle through the bird, midway between the leg joints.

4 Thread the needle through the tendon and breast.

5 The needle comes out by the wing.

6 Turn over the chicken.
7 Run the needle under the skin through the wing, crown and other wing.

8 The string ends at the same place it started. Tie the ends of the string securely.

9 The trussed bird will hold its shape during roasting.

To truss for boiling or pot roasting:

● Proceed as for roasting.
● Cut the leg sinew just below the joint.
● Bend back the legs so that they lie parallel to the breast and secure when trussing, *or* insert the legs through incisions made in the skin at the rear end of the bird, and secure when trussing.

Cutting chicken

Chicken is cut into pieces as shown in the diagram. The leg is cut into two parts: drumstick and thigh.

1 Wing   2 Breast   3 Thigh
4 Drumstick   5 Winglet   6 Carcass

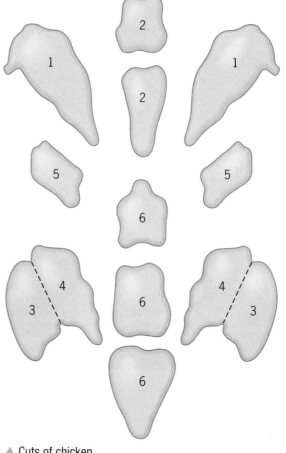

▲ Cuts of chicken

Cutting chicken for sauté, fricassée, pies, etc.

1 Remove the winglets.

2 Remove the legs from the carcass, cutting around the oyster.

3 Cut off the feet.

4 Separate the thigh from the drumstick.

5 Trim the drumstick neatly.

6 Remove each breast from the carcass.

7 Separate the wing from the breast and trim it.

8 Cut into the cavity, splitting the carcass (this may be used for stock).

9 Cut each breast in half.

10 Chicken cut for sauté, on the bone: thighs, drumsticks, breasts, winglets and wings.

Video: cutting chicken for sauté http://bit.ly/ 1Fy3JaY

Preparing a spatchcock chicken

To prepare chicken for grilling:
- Remove the wishbone.
- Cut off the claws at the first joint.
- Place the bird on its back.
- Insert a large knife through the neck end and out of the vent.
- Cut through the backbone and open out.
- Remove back and rib bones.

The chicken may then be grilled whole (spatchcock, see recipe 2) or cut into pieces.

Insert the knife through the neck end

Remove the backbone

Spatchcock chicken ready for cooking

Preparing chicken suprêmes

A suprême is the wing and half the breast of a chicken with the trimmed wing bone attached to the white meat. One chicken yields two suprêmes. To cut suprêmes, use a chicken weighing 1.25 to 1.5 kg. Removing the skin is optional.

1 Cut off both the legs.

2 Scrape the wing bone bare, adjoining the breasts. Cut off the winglets near the joints, leaving 1.5 to 2 cm of bare bone attached. Then remove the wishbone.

3 Cut the breasts close to the breastbone and follow the bone down to the wing joint.

4 Cut through the joint. Pull the suprêmes off, using the knife to assist.

5 To finish, lift the fillets from the suprêmes and remove the sinew from each. Make an incision lengthways, along the thick side of the suprêmes; open and place the fillets inside. Close, lightly flatten with a bat moistened with water, and trim if necessary.

Stuffing and tying a ballotine

A ballotine is a boned, stuffed leg of bird.

Cut the leg open around the bone.

Start to separate the knuckle from the meat. (Scrape the bone.)

Lift the knuckle away (tunnel boning).

Cut the bone below the knuckle.

Fill the cavity of the thigh and drumstick with stuffing.

Close up in a neat shape and secure with string.

Ballotines of chicken may be cooked and served using any of the recipes for chicken sauté presented in this chapter.

Cutting cooked chicken

To cut up a cooked chicken (roasted or boiled):
- Remove the legs and cut in two (drumstick and thigh).
- Remove the wings.
- Separate the breast from the carcass and divide in two.
- Serve a drumstick with a wing and the thigh with the breast.

Turkey

Turkeys can vary in weight from 3.5 to 20 kg. They are trussed in the same way as chicken for roasting. The wishbone should always be removed before trussing in order to facilitate carving. The sinews should be drawn out of the legs. Allow 200 g per portion raw weight.

When cooking a large turkey, the legs are often removed, boned, rolled and tied before roasting. The whole breast still on the bone is known as a crown. Suprêmes can be removed as for other poultry and then used in similar ways, slicing across the breast to form an escalope which would normally be batted out with a cutlet bat to gain an even slice that can then be filled, coated and cooked.

Stuffings may be rolled in foil, steamed or baked and thickly sliced. If a firmer stuffing is required, mix in one or two raw eggs before cooking.

Quality points

- Large full breast with undamaged skin and no signs of stickiness.
- Legs smooth with supple feet and a short spur.
- As birds age the legs turn scaly and the feet harden.

Preparing a large turkey for roasting

1 Remove the legs; cooking them separately will reduce the cooking time and enable the legs and breast to cook more evenly.

2 Remove the leg bones.

3 Stuff and roll each leg if required.

4 Tie the stuffed legs securely.

5 Cut the remainder of the bird in half, again to reduce the cooking time.

6 The two halves, ready for roasting, with one leg left whole and the other boned, stuffed and rolled.

Preparing a chicken or turkey crown

1 Cut off the legs.

2 Sever the leg at the joint with a sharp tap of the knife.

3 Cut off the front of the bird, leaving the crown.

4 A prepared crown: this is useful for roasting when only a few portions are required or the legs are not wanted.

Tunnel boning a turkey or chicken

1 Cut around the exposed end of the bone.

2 Scrape and cut, gently parting the flesh from the bone.

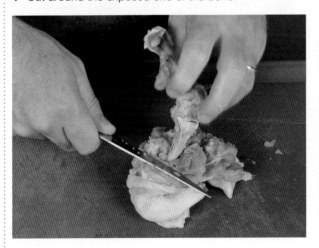

3 Push the meat down as it is freed, and lift the bone out.

4 The de-boned leg.

Ducks and geese

Approximate sizes are as follows:

- **duckling**: 1.5–2 kg
- **duck**: 3–4 kg
- **gosling**: 3 kg
- **goose**: 6 kg.

Quality points

- Plump breasts.
- Webbed feet tear easily.
- Lower back bends easily.
- Feet and bill should be yellow.

Ducks and geese are prepared for roasting in the same way as chickens. The gizzard is not split but trimmed off with a knife.

Video: preparing a duck http://bit.ly/ 1EoOFMD

Game

The word game is used, for culinary purposes, to describe animals or birds that are hunted for food, although many birds and animals categorised as game are now being bred domestically, such as squab (pigeon), duck and venison. There are two types of game:

1. **Feathered**: often purchased plucked and dressed ready for cooking.
2. **Furred**: purchased skinned and pre-jointed in most kitchens.

Wild animals, because of their diet and general lifestyle, have more of certain enzymes in their tissues than poultry, which break down or metabolise meat proteins; they become active about 24 hours after the animal has been killed, softening the meat and making it gelatinous and more palatable (as well as giving the characteristic 'gamey' flavour). They also contain micro-organisms (anaerobes), which also help to break down the proteins.

Choosing and buying

The most important factor when buying game is to know its 'life age' and its 'hanging age', since this will determine the method of cookery to be used. Indications of age are by no means infallible, but there are some general guidelines when buying young birds – soft-textured feet, pliable breastbones – and young partridges have pointed flight feathers (the first large feather of the wing), while in older birds these feathers are more rounded. There are many other distinctive guidelines you can use when selecting game, however the grading of game is a specialised subject and best left to the experts.

The seasons for game are shown in Table 11.2.

Table 11.2 Seasonality of game

	JAN	FEB	MAR	APR	MAY	JUN	JUL	AUG	SEP	OCT	NOV	DEC
Furred												
Hare	At best	At best	Available	Available	Available	Available	At best	At best	At best	At best	At best	At best
Rabbit	Available	Available	Available	Available	Available	Available	Available	Available	Available	Available	Available	Available
Venison	Available	Available	Available	Available	Available	Available	Available	Available	Available	Available	Available	Available
Feathered												
Goose (wild)	Available									At best	At best	At best
Goose (farmed)	Available								Available	At best	At best	At best
Grouse								At best (12th)	At best	At best	At best	
Mallard	Available								At best	At best	At best	At best
Moorhen	Available								At best	At best	At best	At best
Partridge (English grey leg)	At best								At best	At best	At best	At best
Partridge (French red leg)	Available								At best	At best	At best	At best
Pheasant	At best									At best	At best	At best
Pigeon (farmed)	Available	Available	Available	Available	Available	Available	Available	Available	Available	Available	Available	Available
Pigeon (English wood)	Available	Available	Available	At best	At best	At best	At best	At best	Available	Available	Available	Available
Quail	Available	Available	Available	Available	At best	At best	At best	At best	Available	Available	Available	Available
Snipe	At best							At best (12th)	At best	At best	At best	At best
Teal	Available											
Woodcock	At best									At best	At best	At best

Key:

Available	
At best	

Storing and hanging game

Game bought from a game dealer will probably have been hung correctly. If, however, you require your game (or any other meat that benefits from hanging) to be hung specifically for you, speak to your butcher or game dealer. The general rules are to hang in a cool, dry, airy place, protected from flies to prevent maggot infestation. You should hang the carcass until you detect the first whiff of tainting. In Britain, birds are usually hung from their heads, feet down, and rabbits and other game are hung with their heads down.

However, there is no real need to hang game, due to the metabolic enzymes present so, if you object to the strong flavour that hanging promotes, a short hanging period (or no hanging at all) may be preferable.

Current legislation does not allow the hanging or plucking of game in a normal kitchen environment.

Game should be well wrapped and careful consideration given to its age; strict labelling is essential because, when in prime condition, the meat may have a slightly tainted smell, which may be difficult to discern from the smell that denotes the meat is past its best.

Drawing and washing

This is the process that is carried out when the bird is sold with all its entrails still inside. To remove, make a small lateral incision into the backside of the bird, then insert your forefinger and index finger, and roll them around the inner cavity of the bird. This loosens the membrane that holds in the innards. When loose, remove from the wider backside and discard. Ensure that all the innards are removed, that the cavity is empty, then wash and dry well.

Check for any shot that could be present and remove before completing preparations ready for cooking.

Cooking game

Game meat responds best to roasting. Young game birds in particular should be trussed and roasted; it is traditional to leave them unstuffed. Due to the low fat content of game, especially wild non-domestic varieties, added fat in the form of sliced streaky bacon, lardons and the like can be wrapped around the bird to help baste it while cooking and therefore retain moisture. Older, tougher game or high-worked muscle groups, such as a haunch of venison, should be casseroled/stewed or made into pies or terrines. Marinating in oil, vinegar or wine with herbs and spices helps to make tough meat more tender; it may also enhance the taste and it speeds up the action of the metabolic enzyme that breaks game down.

As game birds are deficient in fat, a thin slice of fat bacon (bard) should be tied over the breast during cooking to prevent it from drying out; this is also placed on the breast when serving.

The preparation techniques for poultry, such as stuffing ballotines, also apply to game birds.

Roast game birds are served with gravy; bread sauce and browned breadcrumbs (toasted or fried) are served separately.

Roast pheasant, partridge or grouse may also be served in the traditional manner: on a croûte of fried bread, garnished with thick round pieces of toasted French bread spread with game farce, game chips and picked watercress.

Game birds

Pheasant

One of the most common game birds, pheasants are found in the hedgerows and open farmland across the country. Young birds are reared and then released. An average weight of 1.5 to 2 kg will serve two; they are often served roasted although chefs sometimes remove the legs and cook separately.

Partridge

Two varieties are used in the UK, with the red-legged being slightly larger than the grey-legged. They have an average weight of around 500 g per bird and are cooked as for pheasant.

Grouse

Red grouse are found in the hills and mountains feeding on heather. The grouse season starts on the 12th of August each year, which is considered to be the start of the hunting season for game. With an average weight of around 750 g per bird, they are served roasted or pot roasted with appropriate garnishes and sauce.

Pigeon

As pigeons do not have gall bladders it is not necessary to remove their livers when they are drawn and cleaned. Tender young pigeons (less than 12 months old) can be roasted, pot roasted or split open and grilled and served (for example, with a Robert, charcutière or devilled sauce).

Young pigeons can be cut in half, flattened slightly, seasoned, shallow-fried in butter, and cooked and finished as for sautés of chicken (for example, chasseur, bordelaise).

Quail

Only plump birds with firm white fat should be selected. When prepared the entrails are drawn, but the heart and liver are retained inside the birds. They may be roasted, spit roasted, cooked 'en casserole' or poached in a rich, well-flavoured chicken or veal stock (or a combination of both). Quails may also be boned out from the back and stuffed with a forcemeat.

Hare and rabbits

The rabbit is distinguished from the hare by its shorter ears, feet and body. The ears of good-quality hare and rabbits should tear easily. With old hare, the lip is more pronounced than in young animals.

Preparation of wild rabbit

1 Carefully remove the fur.
2 Cut an incision along the belly.
3 Remove the intestines.
4 Clean out the forequarter, removing all traces of blood.

Venison

Venison is the name given to the meat of deer, with the main types available being red deer, fallow deer and roe deer. Of these three, the meat of the roebuck is considered to have the best and most delicate eating quality. The prime cuts are the legs, loins and best ends. The shoulder of young animals can be boned, rolled and roasted but, if in any doubt as to its tenderness, it should be cut up and used for stewed or braised dishes.

Venison is available from most catering butchers. The cuts and joints of venison are shown in the diagram and Table 11.3.

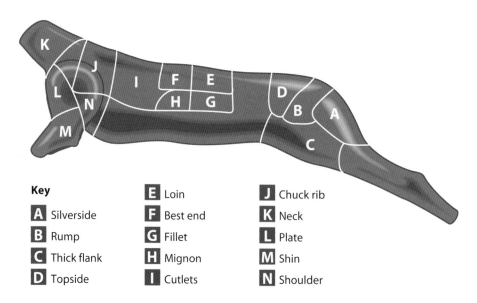

Key

A Silverside	**E** Loin	**J** Chuck rib
B Rump	**F** Best end	**K** Neck
C Thick flank	**G** Fillet	**L** Plate
D Topside	**H** Mignon	**M** Shin
	I Cutlets	**N** Shoulder

▲ Cuts and joints of venison

Table 11.3 Cuts and joints of venison

Cut	Joints	Approx. weight	Uses
Haunch	Silverside	2 kg	Stewing, braising
	Topside	2 kg	Roasting, braising
	Thick flank	1.5 kg	Stewing
	Rump dice, escalopes	1.5 kg	Roasting, braising, frying
Saddle	Saddle	8 kg	Roasting, braising, frying
	Loin	1.4 kg	
	Noisettes	1 kg	
	Chops	1 kg	
	Filet mignon	0.5 kg	
Best end	Best end cutlets	1.5 kg	Frying, roasting, braising
Fillet	Fillet	1 kg	Escalopes, medallions, steaks
Shin	Shin	0.5 kg	Dice, mince, stewing
Neck	Neck	2 kg	Grilling, dice, mince, stewing
Shoulder	Shoulder	4 kg	Roasting/stewing, braising, dice, mince, burgers, sausages
	Chuck rib	2 kg	

The nutritional value of venison is compared with other meats in Table 11.4. It is a good meat to use when planning healthier menus as it contains very little fat. The fat in venison is mainly polyunsaturated and therefore lower in cholesterol.

Venison is also a good source of protein, as 100 g of venison supplies 68.5 per cent of the daily value for protein for only 179 calories and 1.4 g of saturated fat. It is also a source of iron, vitamin B_{12} and other B vitamins.

Quality points

- The flesh should be dark red in colour.
- The flesh should be dry and firm.
- The carcass should have a good amount of flesh and a close grain texture.
- The flesh should be lean, with little fat.
- There should be no unpleasant smell.

After slaughter, carcasses should be hung well in a cool place for several days and, when cut into joints, are usually marinated before being cooked. Joints of venison should be well fleshed and a dark brownish-red colour.

Cooking and serving cutlets

Venison cutlets (cut from the best end) and chops (cut from the loin) are usually well trimmed and cooked by shallow-frying, provided that the meat is tender. If in doubt, they should be braised.

After they are cooked they should be removed from the pan, the fat poured off and the pan deglazed with stock, red wine, brandy, Madeira or sherry, which is then added to the accompanying sauce.

A spicy, peppery sauce is usually offered, which can be varied by the addition of extra ingredients (for example, cream,

Table 11.4 Nutritional information: venison and other meats

Meat	Fat g/100 g	Protein g/100 g	Iron mg/100 g	Cholesterol mg/100 g
Venison	1.6	22.2	3.3	29
Chicken	2.1	22.3	0.7	90
Pork	2.2	21.7	0.8	64
Lamb	12.3	19.0	0.25	78
Beef	12.9	20.4	1.3	48

yoghurt, redcurrant jelly, cooked beetroot, sliced button or wild mushrooms, cooked pieces of chestnut, and so on).

Accompaniments can include, for example, a purée of a root vegetable (e.g. celeriac, turnip, swede, carrot, parsnip, or any combination of these).

Cooking and serving steaks

Venison steaks, or escalopes, are cut from the boned-out nuts of meat from the loins, trimmed well and thinned slightly with a meat bat.

The escalopes can be quickly shallow-fried and finished as for cutlets and chops, and served with a variety of accompanying sauces and garnishes.

Cooking and serving haunch of venison

The haunch may be roasted or braised. It is popular served hot or cold.

Wild boar

For good quality, buy animals obtained from suppliers using as near as possible 100 per cent pure breeding stock wild boars that are free to roam and forage for food, rather than those that have been penned and fed.

Animals aged between 12 and 18 months old, weighing 60 to 75 kg on the hoof, are best slaughtered in the late summer when their fat content is lower. The meat should be hung for seven to ten days before being used.

Young boar up to the age of six months are sufficiently tender for cooking in noisettes and cutlets, and joints for roasting. The prime cuts of older animals (e.g. leg, loin, best end) can be marinated and braised.

Boar's head is prepared by boning the head and stuffing it with a forcemeat to which strips of ox tongue, foie gras, truffles and pistachio nuts can be added. The head is tied securely in a cloth and simmered gently. When cooled it is completely coated and the tusks are re-inserted. Boar's head is a traditional Christmas cold buffet dish served with a spicy sauce (e.g. Cumberland).

Test yourself

1. List five quality points for a good quality chicken.
2. At what temperature should prepared poultry be chilled for storage?
3. State three considerations when roasting a chicken.
4. What is the safe internal temperature required for cooked poultry?
5. Explain why shallow frying is an appropriate cooking method for turkey escalopes.
6. Briefly describe how to truss a turkey.
7. State why you would baste a whole duck when roasting.
8. Describe how to store game birds.
9. List three quality points you should look for when buying venison.
10. Describe how you can keep game birds moist during cooking.

Chicken dishes

1 Grilled chicken (*poulet grillé*)

Energy	Cals	Fat	Sat fat	Carb	Sugar	Protein	Fibre
975 kJ	234 kcal	15.7g	4.3g	0.0g	0.0g	23.3g	0.0g

Based on chicken with bone, wing and leg quarters.

1 Season the chicken with salt and mill pepper, and prepare for grilling (see page 299).

2 Brush with oil or melted butter or margarine, and place on preheated greased grill bars or on a barbecue or a flat baking tray under a salamander.

3 Brush frequently with melted fat during cooking; allow approximately 15–20 minutes each side.

4 Test if cooked by piercing the drumstick with a skewer or trussing needle; there should be no sign of blood issuing from the leg.

5 Serve garnished with picked watercress and offer a suitable sauce separately.

Healthy eating tips
- Use a minimum of salt and an unsaturated oil.
- Garnish with grilled tomatoes and mushrooms.
- Serve with Delmonico potatoes and green vegetables.

Variation

Grilled chicken is frequently garnished with streaky bacon, tomatoes and mushrooms.

The chicken may be marinated for 2–3 hours before grilling, in a mixture of oil, lemon juice, spices, herbs, freshly grated ginger, finely chopped garlic, salt and pepper. Chicken or turkey portions can also be grilled and marinated beforehand if wished (breasts or boned-out lightly battened thighs of chicken).

2 Chicken spatchcock (*poulet grillé à la crapaudine*)

Ingredient	4 portions	10 portions
Chicken, 1.25–1.5 kg	1	2½

Energy	Cals	Fat	Sat fat	Carb	Sugar	Protein	Fibre
1,560 kJ	372 kcal	24.1 g	8.0 g	0.0 g	0.0 g	38.9 g	0.0 g

Healthy eating tips
- Use a minimum amount of salt to season the chicken.
- The fat content can be reduced if the skin is removed from the chicken.
- Use a small amount of an unsaturated oil to brush the chicken.
- Serve with a large portion of potatoes and vegetables.

1 Cut horizontally from below the point of the breast over the top of the legs down to the wing joints, without removing the breasts. Fold back the breasts.

2 Snap and reverse the backbone into the opposite direction so that the point of the breast now extends forward.

3 Flatten slightly. Remove any small bones.

4 Skewer the wings and legs in position.

5 Season with salt and mill pepper.

6 Brush with oil or melted butter.

7 Place on preheated grill bars or on a flat tray under a salamander.

8 Brush frequently with melted fat or oil during cooking and allow approximately 15–20 minutes on each side.

9 Test if cooked by piercing the drumstick with a needle or skewer – there should be no sign of blood.

Serve garnished with picked watercress and offer a suitable sauce separately (e.g. devilled sauce or a compound butter).

3 Chicken sauté chasseur

Ingredient	4 portions	10 portions
Butter or oil	50 g	125 g
Salt, pepper		
Chicken, 1.25–1.5 kg, cut for sauté	1	2½
Shallots, chopped	10 g	25 g
Button mushrooms, washed and sliced	100 g	250 g
Dry white wine	3 tbsp	8 tbsp
Jus-lié, demi-glace or reduced brown stock	250 ml	625 ml
Tomato concassé	200 g	500 g
Parsley and tarragon, chopped		

Energy	Cals	Fat	Sat fat	Carb	Sugar	Protein	Fibre
2,430 kJ	579 kcal	45.8 g	20.7 g	2.1 g	1.6 g	37.6 g	1.5 g

Using butter.

1. Place the butter or oil in a sauté pan on a fairly hot stove.

2. Season the pieces of chicken and place in the pan in the following order: drumsticks, thighs, wings and breast.

3. Cook to a golden brown on both sides.

4. Cover with a lid and cook on the stove or in the oven until tender. Dress neatly in a suitable dish.

5. Add the shallots to the sauté pan, rubbing them into the pan sediment to extract the flavour. Cover with a lid and cook on a gentle heat for 1–2 minutes.

6. Add the washed, sliced mushrooms and cover with a lid. Cook gently for 3–4 minutes, without colour. Drain off the fat.

7. Add the white wine and reduce by half. Add the *jus-lié*, demi-glace or reduced stock.

8. Add the tomatoes. Simmer for 5 minutes.

9. Correct the seasoning and pour over the chicken.

10. Sprinkle with chopped parsley and tarragon and serve.

Ballotines of chicken chasseur can be prepared as above or lightly braised (as shown).

Place the chicken into the hot pan

Cook the shallots in the pan that was used for the chicken – they will pick up the sediment and flavour

Professional tip

The leg meat takes longer to cook than the breast meat, which is why the drumsticks and thighs should be added first.

Add the soft herbs and tomatoes just before serving.

Healthy eating tips
- Use a minimum amount of salt to season the chicken.
- The fat content can be reduced if the skin is removed from the chicken.
- Use a little unsaturated oil to cook the chicken, and drain off all excess fat from the cooked chicken.
- Serve with a large portion of new potatoes and seasonal vegetables.

4 Crumbed breast of chicken with asparagus (*suprême de volaille aux pointes d'asperges*)

Ingredient	4 portions	10 portions
Suprêmes of chicken	4 × 125 g	10 × 125 g
Egg	1	2
Breadcrumbs (white or wholemeal)	50 g	125 g
Oil	50 g	125 g
Butter or margarine	100 g	250 g
Jus-lié	60 ml	150 ml
Asparagus	200 g	500 g

Energy	Cals	Fat	Sat fat	Carb	Sugar	Protein	Fibre
1,831 kJ	439 kcal	26.4 g	8.9 g	15.7 g	1.5 g	35.5 g	1.3 g

1 Pané the chicken suprêmes. Shake off all surplus crumbs.

2 Neaten and mark on one side with a palette knife.

3 Heat the oil and 50 g (125 g for 10 portions) of the butter or margarine in a sauté pan.

4 Gently fry the suprêmes to a golden brown on both sides (6–8 minutes). Use a probe to check that the centre has reached 75 °C.

5 Dress the suprêmes on a flat dish and keep warm.

6 Mask the suprêmes with the remaining butter cooked to the nut-brown stage.

7 Surround the suprêmes with a cordon of *jus-lié*.

8 Garnish each suprême with a neat bundle of asparagus points (previously cooked, refreshed and reheated with a little butter).

Healthy eating tips
- Use a minimum amount of salt.
- Remove the skin from the suprêmes and fry in a little unsaturated vegetable oil. Drain on kitchen paper.
- Try omitting the additional cooked butter.
- Serve with plenty of boiled new potatoes and vegetables.

5 Paella

Ingredient	4 portions	10 portions
Lobster, cooked	400 g	1 kg
Squid	200 g	500 g
Gambas (Mediterranean prawns), cooked	400 g	1 kg
Mussels	400 g	1 kg
White stock	1 litre	2.5 litres
Pinch of saffron		
Onion, finely chopped	50 g	125 g
Clove of garlic, finely chopped	1	2–3
Red pepper, diced	50 g	125 g
Green pepper, diced	50 g	125 g
Roasting chicken, cut for sauté	1.5 kg	3.75 kg
Olive oil	60 ml	150 ml
Short-grain rice	200 g	500 g
Thyme		
Bay leaf		
Seasoning		
Tomatoes, skinned, deseeded and diced	200 g	500 g
Lemon wedges, to finish		

Energy	Cals	Fat	Sat fat	Carb	Sugar	Protein	Fibre
3,383 kJ	804 kcal	31.0g	6.2g	48.8g	3.8g	85.7g	1.3g

Using chicken.

1 Prepare the lobster: cut it in half, remove the claws and legs, discard the sac and trail. Remove the meat from the claws and cut the tail into 3–4 pieces, leaving the meat in the shell.

2 Clean the squid: pull the body and head apart, and extract the transparent 'pen' from the body. Rinse well, pulling off the thin purple membrane on the outside. Remove the ink sac. Cut the body into rings and the tentacles into 1 cm lengths.

3 Prepare the gambas by shelling the body.

4 Boil the mussels in water or white stock until the shells open. Shell the mussels and retain the cooking liquid.

5 Boil the white stock and mussel liquor together, infused with saffron. Simmer for 5–10 minutes.

6 Sweat the finely chopped onion in a little oil in a suitable pan, without colour. Add the garlic and the peppers.

7 Sauté the chicken in olive oil until cooked and golden brown, then drain.

8 Add the rice to the onions and garlic and sweat for 2 minutes.

9 Add about 200 ml white stock and mussel liquor.

10 Add the thyme, bay leaf and seasoning. Bring to the boil then cover with lightly oiled greaseproof paper and a lid. Cook for 5–8 minutes in a moderate oven (180 °C).

11 Add the squid and cook for another 5 minutes.

12 Add the tomatoes, chicken and lobster pieces, mussels and gambas. Stir gently, cover with a lid and reheat the rice in the oven.

11 Correct the consistency of the rice if necessary by adding more stock, so that it looks sufficiently moist without being too wet. Correct the seasoning.

12 When all is reheated and cooked, place in a suitable serving dish, decorate with four (ten) gambas and four (ten) mussels halved and shelled. Finish with wedges of lemon.

Healthy eating tips
- To reduce the fat, skin the chicken and use a little unsaturated oil to sweat the onions and fry the chicken.
- No added salt is necessary.
- Serve with a large green salad.

6 Chicken palak (chicken fried with spinach and spices)

Ingredient	4 portions	10 portions
Chicken, 1.5 kg, cut for sauté	1	2
Ghee, butter or oil	50 g	125 g
Onion, finely chopped	50 g	125 g
Clove of garlic, crushed and chopped	1	2–3
Fresh ginger	25 g	60 g
Green chilli	1	2½
Ground cumin	1 tsp	2½ tsp
Ground coriander	1 tsp	2½ tsp
Spinach, washed and finely chopped	250 g	625 g
Tomatoes, skinned, deseeded and diced	200 g	500 g
Chicken stock	250 ml	625 ml

Energy	Cals	Fat	Sat fat	Carb	Sugar	Protein	Fibre
1,575 kJ	378 kcal	21.9 g	9.5 g	4.4 g	3.5 g	41.3 g	1.9 g

Estimated edible meat used; butter used.

Healthy eating tips
- Skin the chicken and fry in a small amount of unsaturated oil.
- Skim excess fat from the finished dish.
- Serve with plenty of rice, dhal, chapatis and a vegetable dish.

1 Gently fry the chicken in the fat until golden brown.

2 Remove the chicken; fry the onion and garlic until lightly browned. Add the ginger, chilli and spices, and sweat for 3 minutes.

3 Stir in the spinach, add the tomatoes and season. Add the chicken pieces.

4 Add the chicken stock and bring to the boil.

5 Cover with a lid and cook in a moderate oven (180 °C) for 30 minutes or until the chicken is tender. Stir occasionally, adding more stock if necessary.

6 Serve in a suitable dish with rice, chapatis and dhal.

7 Deep-fried chicken

1 Cut the chicken as for sauté. Alternatively, the chicken may be boned.

2 Coat with flour, egg and crumbs (pané), or pass them through a light batter (see page 408) to which herbs can be added.

3 Deep-fry in hot oil (approx. 170–180 °C) until golden brown and cooked through – about 5 minutes. When the chicken is cooked, a probe in the thickest part will read 75 °C+, and the juices will run clear when the chicken is pierced.

For suprêmes, make an incision, stuff with a compound butter, flour, egg and crumb, and deep-fry as in chicken Kiev (recipe 8).

Healthy eating tips
The fat content can be reduced if the skin is removed from the chicken.

Energy	Cals	Fat	Sat fat	Carb	Sugar	Protein	Fibre
1,754 kJ	421 kcal	28.6g	6.1g	14.5g	0.4g	27.2g	0.5g

8 Chicken Kiev

Ingredient	4 portions	10 portions
Suprêmes of chicken	4 × 150 g	10 × 150 g
Butter	100 g	250 g
Seasoned flour	25 g	65 g
Eggs	2	5
Breadcrumbs	100 g	250 g

1 Make an incision along the thick sides of the suprêmes. Insert 25 g cold butter into each. Season.

2 Pass through seasoned flour, egg wash and crumbs, ensuring complete coverage. Egg wash and crumb twice if necessary.

3 Deep-fry until completely cooked. When the chicken is cooked, a probe in the thickest part will read 75 °C+, and the juices will run clear when the chicken is pierced. Drain and serve.

Energy	Cals	Fat	Sat fat	Carb	Sugar	Protein	Fibre	Sodium
2,094 kJ	500 kcal	26.1g	14.4g	24.4g	0.9g	43.4g	1.0g	0.5g

Carefully make an incision in the top of the suprême	Stuff with softened butter	Dip the chicken in egg and flour and then coat with breadcrumbs

Variation

Additional ingredients may be added to the butter before insertion:

- chopped garlic and parsley
- fine herbs such as tarragon or chives
- liver paté.

Professional tip

The butter must be pushed well into the suprême, and the incision must be sealed, or the butter will leak out during cooking.

9 Braised chicken leg forestière

Energy	Cals	Fat	Sat fat	Carb	Sugar	Protein	Fibre	Sodium
1,878 kJ	448 kcal	15.9g	3.9g	16.9g	8.7g	49.9g	3.6g	1.0g

Note

These quantities will produce a moderate portion to be served as part of a three-course meal. Allow two chicken legs per person for a hearty portion.

Ingredient	4 portions	10 portions
Chicken legs	4	10
Salt and pepper		
Olive oil	2 tbsp	5 tbsp
Onions, sliced fairly thickly	2	5
Smoked bacon, thickly sliced rashers cut into lardons	3	8
Clove of garlic, crushed	1	2
Whole button or small chestnut mushrooms (if larger, cut in half)	100 g	250 g
Oyster mushrooms, sliced in half	100 g	250 g
Plain flour	1½ tbsp	4 tbsp
Tomato purée	1 tbsp	2½ tbsp
Red wine	250 ml	625 ml
Brown chicken stock	400 ml	1 litre
Tomatoes, blanched, peeled, concassé	3	7½
Fresh tarragon and parsley, chopped	15 g	35 g

1 Season the chicken with salt and pepper. Heat the olive oil in a lidded sauté pan or shallow casserole and pan-fry the chicken over a medium-high heat, turning, until golden on both sides.

2 Remove from the pan and keep to one side. You will need about 2 tablespoons of fat left in the pan to cook the onions so, if the legs have released a lot of fat, drain off the excess.

3 Add the onions and fry for 2–3 minutes before adding the bacon, garlic and mushrooms to the pan. Continue to stir until they have a little colour and the mushrooms are beginning to soften.

4 Sprinkle over the flour and stir until the flour has lightly browned.

5 Stir in the tomato purée and then gradually add the red wine and chicken stock, stirring until the liquid has fully mixed into the flour and purée paste.

6 Return the chicken to the pan and bring to a simmer. Place a lid on the pan and continue to cook, allowing the sauce to just simmer for about 1 hour, or until the meat is completely tender.

7 To finish, remove the chicken legs, place on to a plate or tray and keep in a warm place, e.g. the side of the stove. Skim the sauce of any further excess fat and adjust the consistency as necessary.

8 Adjust the seasoning before adding the tomatoes.

9 Place the chicken legs back into the sauce and scatter over the chopped herbs before serving.

10 Steamed ballotine of chicken with herb stuffing and red wine jus

Ingredient	4 portions	10 portions
Chicken legs	4	10
Forcemeat		
Minced chicken	120 g	300 g
Parsley	1 tsp	2½ tsp
Tarragon	1 tsp	2½ tsp
Chives	1 tsp	2½ tsp
Chervil	1 tsp	2½ tsp
Salt and pepper		
Red wine jus		
Shallots, sliced	75 g	190 g
Butter	25 g	60 g
Garlic, finely chopped	5 g	10 g
Red wine	175 ml	440 ml
Chicken stock	175 ml	440 ml
Veal or beef jus	125 ml	310 ml
Bay leaves	1	2½
Thyme, sprigs	½	1

Variation

Instead of the traditional chicken legs, ballotines can be made using:
- chicken suprêmes, batted out, stuffed and rolled
- chicken breasts: make an incision in the thicker part and fill this with forcemeat.

These ballotines are cooked in the same way.

Energy	Cals	Fat	Sat fat	Carb	Sugar	Protein	Fibre	Sodium
1,626 kJ	390 kcal	24.9 g	8.5 g	1.8 g	0.9 g	33.4 g	0.5 g	1.1 g

1 Remove the thighbone and the knuckle joint from the chicken legs.

2 Prepare the forcemeat by mixing all of the herbs with the minced chicken. Season the mix and divide it evenly between the chicken legs.

3 Season the legs then stuff them with the forcemeat. Roll the leg into a neat cylinder and either tie the leg in place or roll tightly in cling film and tie off the ends.

4 Steam the legs for 30–45 minutes or until the core temperature reaches 84 °C.

5 Allow the chicken legs to rest so they will stay in shape.

6 When the chicken legs have rested and cooled slightly, remove the string or cling film and dry them.

7 Heat a sauté pan with oil and butter, add the chicken legs and brown the skin. Slice and serve with the sauce.

For the red wine jus:

1 Caramelise the shallots in the butter until golden, adding the garlic at the end.

2 Strain off any excess butter, deglaze the pan with the red wine and reduce by half.

3 Add the chicken stock and veal jus and reduce to a sauce consistency, adding the aromats for the last 5 minutes.

4 Pass through a muslin cloth and serve over the sliced ballotines.

11 Fricassée of chicken

1 Cut the chicken as for sauté (page 298); season with salt and pepper.

2 Place the butter in a sauté pan. Heat gently.

3 Add the pieces of chicken. Cover with a lid.

4 Cook gently on both sides without colouring. Mix in the flour.

5 Cook out carefully without colouring. Gradually mix in the stock.

6 Bring to the boil and skim. Allow to simmer gently until cooked.

7 Mix the yolks and cream in a basin (liaison).

8 Pick out the chicken into a clean pan.

9 Pour a little boiling sauce on to the yolks and cream and mix well.

10 Pour all back into the sauce, combine thoroughly but do not reboil.

11 Correct the seasoning and pass through a fine strainer.

12 Pour over the chicken, reheat without boiling.

13 Serve sprinkled with chopped parsley and garnish with heart-shaped croutons, fried in butter, if desired.

Ingredient	4 portions	10 portions
Chicken, 1.25–1.5 kg	1	2–3
Salt, pepper		
Butter, margarine or oil	50 g	125 g
Flour	35 g	90 g
Chicken stock	0.5 litre	1.25 litres
Egg yolks	2	5
Cream or non-dairy cream	4 tbsp	10 tbsp
Parsley, chopped		

Energy	Cals	Fat	Sat fat	Carb	Sugar	Protein	Fibre
2,699 kJ	643 kcal	51.3g	23.3g	7.4g	0.6g	38.2g	0.4g

Using butter.

> **Professional tip**
>
> Sauté the chicken lightly. Add the liaison of yolks and cream carefully. Do not allow the sauce to come back to the boil once the liaison has been added, or it will curdle.

Variation

Fricassée de volaille à l'ancienne: a fricassée of chicken with button onions and mushrooms can be made in a similar way, with the addition of 50–100g button onions and 50–100g button mushrooms. They are peeled and the mushrooms left whole, turned or quartered depending on size and quality. The onions are added to the chicken as soon as it comes to the boil and the mushrooms 15 minutes later. Heart-shaped croutons may be used to garnish. This is a classic dish.

Healthy eating tips

- Keep added salt to a minimum throughout the cooking.
- Use a little unsaturated oil to cook the chicken, and drain off all excess fat after cooking.
- Try oven-baking the croutons brushed with olive oil.
- The sauce is high in fat, so serve with plenty of starchy carbohydrate and vegetables.

12 Chicken à la king

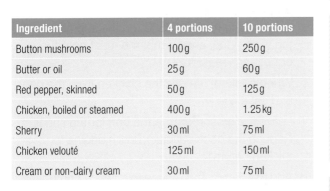

1 Wash, peel and slice the mushrooms.
2 Cook them without colour in the butter or oil.
3 If using raw pepper, discard the seeds, cut the pepper into dice and cook with the mushrooms.
4 Cut the chicken into small, neat slices.
5 Add the chicken to the mushrooms and pepper.
6 Drain off the fat. Add the sherry.
7 Add the velouté and bring to the boil.
8 Finish with the cream and correct the seasoning.
9 Place in a serving dish and decorate with small strips of cooked pepper.

Use a velouté with a good chicken flavour, to create the best sauce.

Variation

Try adding 1 or 2 egg yolks to form a liaison with the cream, mixed into the boiling mixture at the last possible moment and immediately removed from the heat.

Chicken à la king may be served in a border of golden-brown duchess potato, or a pilaff of rice (see page 125) may be offered as an accompaniment. It is suitable for a hot buffet dish.

Ingredient	4 portions	10 portions
Button mushrooms	100 g	250 g
Butter or oil	25 g	60 g
Red pepper, skinned	50 g	125 g
Chicken, boiled or steamed	400 g	1.25 kg
Sherry	30 ml	75 ml
Chicken velouté	125 ml	150 ml
Cream or non-dairy cream	30 ml	75 ml

Energy	Cals	Fat	Sat fat	Carb	Sugar	Protein	Fibre
1,226 kJ	292 kcal	16.7 g	7.8 g	3.2 g	0.8 g	30.4 g	0.9 g

Using butter or hard margarine.

Healthy eating tips

- Use the minimum amount of salt.
- Remove the skin from the cooked chicken.
- Try reducing or omitting the cream used to finish the sauce.
- Serve with plenty of rice and vegetables or salad.

Slice the mushrooms and dice the red pepper Neatly slice the cooked chicken Add the velouté during cooking

13 Poached suprême of chicken with Madeira and mushroom café cream sauce

1 Sauté the shallots and mushrooms in butter until golden brown.

2 Divide the mushroom and shallots into equal piles in a shallow pan – place each of the trimmed chicken suprêmes on to one pile.

3 Add the Madeira and bring to the boil.

4 Add the reduced chicken stock, bring back to the boil and cover with buttered greaseproof paper.

5 Place the chicken in a preheated oven at 170 °C and cook for 12 minutes, or until the core temperature reaches 75 °C. (In the suprême with the wing bone, ensure that the meat near the bone reaches 82 °C.)

6 When cooked, remove the chicken from the pan and set aside.

7 Leave the mushrooms in the pan for the sauce. Reduce the cooking liquor until it begins to thicken naturally.

8 Add the cream and reduce to a sauce consistency.

9 Season and serve with the chicken suprêmes.

Note

The café cream sauce of Madeira wine, chicken stock and double cream is also known as café au lait.

Ingredient	4 portions	10 portions
Shallots, finely chopped	40 g	100 g
Button mushrooms, sliced	160 g	400 g
Butter	40 g	100 g
Chicken suprêmes	4	10
Madeira wine	2 tbsp	5 tbsp
Brown chicken stock	250 ml	625 ml
Double cream	200 ml	500 ml

Energy	Cals	Fat	Sat fat	Carb	Sugar	Protein	Fibre
2,126 kJ	512 kcal	37.3g	22.4g	2.5g	2.2g	38.2g	0.8g

14 Confit chicken leg with leeks and artichokes

1 Gently heat the confit oil, add the garlic, bay and thyme.

2 Put the chicken legs in the oil and place on a medium to low heat, ensuring the legs are covered.

3 Cook gently for 3–3½ hours.

4 To test if the legs are cooked, squeeze the flesh on the thigh bone and it should just fall away.

5 When cooked, remove the legs carefully and place on a draining tray.

6 Heat the vegetable oil in a medium sauté pan, add the artichokes and leeks, colour slightly and then add the brown chicken stock.

7 Reduce the heat to a simmer and cook for 4–5 minutes; meanwhile place the confit leg on a baking tray and place in a preheated oven at 210 °C; remove when the skin is golden brown (approximately 5 minutes), taking care as the meat is delicate.

8 Place the chicken in a serving dish or on a plate, check the leeks and artichokes are cooked through, and bring the stock to a rapid boil, working in the butter to form an emulsion.

9 Add the chopped chives to the sauce and nap over the chicken legs.

Ingredient	4 portions	10 portions
Confit oil	1 litre	2.5 litres
Cloves of garlic	4	10
Bay leaf	1	3
Sprig of thyme		
Chicken legs, 200 g	4	10
Vegetable oil	50 ml	125 ml
Globe artichokes, prepared, cooked and cut into quarters	4	10
Whole leeks, blanched	2	5
Brown chicken stock	250 ml	625 ml
Butter	50 g	125 g
Chives, chopped	1 tbsp	2½ tbsp
Seasoning		

Note

Confit oil is half olive oil and half vegetable oil, infused with herbs, garlic, whole spices or any specific flavour you wish to impart into the oil. The foodstuff picks up the flavour through slow cooking in the oil.

Energy	Cals	Fat	Sat fat	Carb	Sugar	Protein	Fibre	Sodium
3,622 kJ	875 kcal	75.9g	3.6g	43.3g	3.6g	43.3g	2.6g	0.8g

Professional tip

This dish utilises the less popular chicken legs; it is not only very cost-effective but has great depth of flavour due to the work the muscle group has done.

After cooking in oil, squeeze the thigh to determine whether it is done

Remove from the oven when the chicken is golden brown

Add butter to the stock to form an emulsion

15 Chicken in red wine (*coq au vin*)

Ingredient	4 portions	10 portions
Roasting chicken, 1.5 kg	1	2–3
Lardons	50 g	125 g
Small chipolatas	4	10
Button mushrooms	50 g	125 g
Butter	50 g	125 g
Sunflower oil	3 tbsp	7 tbsp
Small button onions	12	30
Red wine	500 ml	900 ml
Beurre manié		
Butter	25 g	60 g
Flour	10 g	25 g

Energy	Cals	Fat	Sat fat	Carb	Sugar	Protein	Fibre
4,794 kJ	1,141 kcal	95.7 g	32.9 g	16.6 g	2.3 g	49.0 g	1.7 g

Using sunflower oil and hard margarine.

1 Cut the chicken as for sauté (see page 298). Blanch the lardons.

2 If the chipolatas are large, divide into two.

3 Wash and cut the mushrooms into quarters.

4 Sauté the lardons, mushrooms and chipolatas in a mixture of butter and oil. Remove when cooked.

5 Lightly season the pieces of chicken and place in the pan in the correct order (see recipe 1) with button onions. Sauté until almost cooked.

6 Place in a casserole with the mushrooms and lardons.

7 Drain off the fat from the sauté pan. Deglaze with the red wine and stock; bring to the boil.

8 Transfer the liquid to the casserole (just covering the chicken); cover with a lid and finish cooking.

9 Remove the chicken and onions, place into a clean pan.

10 Lightly thicken the liquor with a *beurre manié* of butter and flour by whisking small pieces of it into the simmering liquid.

11 Pass the sauce over the chicken and onions, add the mushrooms, chipolatas and lardons. Correct the seasoning and reheat.

12 Add the *beurre manié* slowly, mixing well, to create a thick, smooth sauce.

Healthy eating tips

● Use a well-seasoned pan to dry-fry the lardons and chipolatas, then add the mushrooms.
● Use the minimum amount of added salt.
● Drain all the fat from the cooked chicken.
● Garnish with oven-baked croutons and serve with plenty of starchy carbohydrate and vegetables.

Sauté the other ingredients before the chicken

Sauté the chicken pieces and onion in the same pan

Add a *beurre manié*

16 Chicken pie

Ingredient	4 portions	10 portions
Chicken, 1.25–1.5 kg	1	2–3
Salt, pepper		
Streaky bacon	100 g	250 g
Button mushrooms, washed and sliced	100 g	250 g
Onion, chopped	1	2½
Chicken stock	250 ml	625 ml
Chopped parsley, pinch		
Hard-boiled egg, chopped	1	2½
Cold chicken stock		
Puff pastry (page 465)	200 g	500 g

1 Cut the chicken as for sauté (see page 298) or bone out completely and cut into 4 × 1 cm pieces.

2 Season lightly with salt and pepper.

3 Wrap each piece in very thin streaky bacon. Place in a pie dish.

4 Add the mushrooms and remainder of the ingredients, except the pastry.

5 Add sufficient cold stock to barely cover the chicken.

6 Cover with puff pastry and allow to rest in a refrigerator.

7 Egg wash and bake at 200 °C for approximately 30 minutes, until the pastry has set and the juice is simmering.

8 Reduce the heat to 160–180 °C and continue cooking for 1 hour.

Note

If the pie is to be served cold, a soaked leaf of gelatine can be laid on the chicken before covering with pastry.

Healthy eating tips
- Add little or no salt – the bacon is salty.
- Remove the skin from the chicken.
- Serve with plenty of starchy carbohydrates and a large mixed salad.

Energy	Cals	Fat	Sat fat	Carb	Sugar	Protein	Fibre
3,357 kJ	799 kcal	62.6 g	25.1 g	16.4 g	1.9 g	43.3 g	1.8 g

Using hard margarine in the pastry.

Wrap the chicken pieces in bacon

Pour stock over the pie filling

Egg wash the edge of the pie dish and lay the pastry over

Press down gently at the edges to form a seal

Trim off the excess and then crimp the edges with your fingers

17 Tandoori chicken

Energy	Cals	Fat	Sat fat	Carb	Sugar	Protein	Fibre
1,436 kJ	342 kcal	14.1 g	4.6 g	10.1 g	8.6 g	44.6 g	0.3 g

Estimated edible meat used; vegetable oil used.

Ingredient	4 portions	10 portions
Chicken, cut as for sauté (page 298)	1.25–1.5 kg	3–4 kg
Salt	1 tsp	2½ tsp
Lemon, juice of	1	2½
Natural yoghurt	300 ml	850 ml
Small onion, chopped	1	2½
Clove of garlic, peeled	1	2½
Ginger, piece of, peeled and quartered	5 cm	12 cm
Fresh hot green chilli, sliced	½	1
Garam masala	2 tsp	5 tsp
Ground cumin	1 tsp	2½ tsp
Red and yellow colouring, few drops each		

Professional tip

If cooking in a tandoor oven, make sure the chicken is secure on the skewer, so that it cannot slip off during cooking.

Healthy eating tips
- Skin the chicken and reduce the salt by half.
- Serve with rice and vegetables.

1 Cut slits bone-deep in the chicken pieces.

2 Sprinkle the salt and lemon juice on both sides of the pieces, lightly rubbing into the slits; leave for 20 minutes.

3 Combine the remaining ingredients in a blender or food processor.

4 Brush the chicken pieces on both sides, ensuring the marinade goes into the slits. Cover and refrigerate for 6–24 hours.

5 Preheat the oven to the maximum temperature.

6 Shake off as much of the marinade as possible from the chicken pieces; place on skewers and bake for 15–20 minutes or until cooked.

Serve with red onion rings and lime or lemon wedges.

18 Roast chicken with dressing (*poulet rôti à l'anglaise*)

1 Lightly season the chicken inside and out with salt.

2 Place on its side in a roasting tin.

3 Cover with 50 g of the oil or butter.

4 Place in a hot oven for approximately 20–25 minutes, then turn on to the other side.

5 Cook for a further 20–25 minutes. Baste frequently.

6 To test whether the chicken is fully cooked, pierce it with a fork between the drumstick and thigh, and hold it over a plate. The juice issuing from the chicken should not show any sign of blood. If using a temperature probe, insert in the thickest part of the leg; it should read 75 °C. Place the cooked chicken breast-side down to retain all the cooking juices.

7 To make the dressing, gently cook the onion in the remaining oil or butter without colour.

8 Season and add the herbs and breadcrumbs.

9 Mix in the liver if using.

10 Correct the seasoning and bake or steam the dressing separately, for approximately 20 minutes, until thoroughly cooked and reaching 75 °C.

Ingredient	4 portions (per chicken)
Chicken, 1.25–1.5 kg	1
Salt and pepper	
Oil or butter	100 g
Onion, chopped	25 g
Chopped parsley, pinch	
Powdered thyme, pinch	
Breadcrumbs (white or wholemeal)	50 g
Liver from the chicken, raw, chopped (optional)	

Energy	Cals	Fat	Sat fat	Carb	Sugar	Protein	Fibre
1,363 kJ	327 kcal	20.4 g	3.7 g	6.7 g	0.7 g	29.5 g	0.3 g

Based on average edible portion of roasted meat (100 g).

Professional tip

Arranging the chicken so that it cooks sitting on one leg, then the other, and then the breast, ensures that the whole bird cooks evenly.

Healthy eating tips
● Use unsaturated oil to cook the onion.
● Keep the added salt to a minimum.
● Serve with plenty of potatoes and vegetables.

19 Turkey escalopes

1 Cut 100g slices from boned-out turkey breast and lightly flour. Gently cook on both sides in butter or oil with a minimum of colour; alternatively flour, egg and crumb the slices and shallow fry.

2 Serve with a suitable sauce and/or garnish (e.g. pan-fried turkey escalope cooked with oyster mushrooms and finished with white wine and cream).

Professional tip

The oil or fat must be hot enough before the escalopes are placed in the pan. If it is too cool, the breadcrumbs will absorb the fat and the dish will be greasy.

Energy	Cals	Fat	Sat fat	Carb	Sugar	Protein	Fibre	Sodium
1,712 kJ	414 kcal	37.0g	14.0g	5.9g	0.2g	14.8g	0.3g	0.1g

20 Roast turkey

Ingredient	4 portions	10 portions
Turkey, with legs on	1 small bird	4–5 kg
Sea salt and freshly ground black pepper		
Unsalted butter, melted	250 g	625 g

Energy	Cals	Fat	Sat fat	Carb	Sugar	Protein	Fibre
1,076 kJ	257 kcal	9.6g	3.2g	0.0g	0.0g	42.0g	0.0g

Professional tip

The secret to keeping turkey moist is to baste as much as you can and, when the turkey is cooked, place it on its breast, breast-side down, allowing all the cavity juices to penetrate the meat.

1   Adjust an oven rack to its lowest position and remove the other racks in the oven. Preheat to 165 °C.

2   Remove turkey parts from neck and breast cavities and reserve for other uses, if desired. Dry bird well with paper towels, inside and out. Salt and pepper inside the breast cavity.

3   Set the bird on a roasting rack in a roasting pan, breast-side up, brush generously with half the butter and season with salt and pepper. Tent the bird with foil.

4   Roast the turkey for 2 hours. Remove the foil and baste with the remaining butter. Increase the oven temperature to 220 °C and continue to roast until an instant-read thermometer registers 74 °C in the thigh of the bird, about 45 minutes more.

5   Remove turkey from the oven and set aside to rest for 15 minutes before carving. Carve and serve with roast gravy, cranberry sauce, bread sauce, and either or both sausage meat and chestnut dressing and parsley and thyme dressing. Chipolata sausages and rolled rashers of grilled bacon may also be served.

Duck dishes

21 Duck breast steaks with cherries

Ingredient	4 portions	10 portions
Duck breasts, skinned and scored	4	10
Olive oil for frying		
Cherries	300 g	750 g
Raspberry vinegar	4 tbsp	10 tbsp
Bramble jelly or redcurrant jelly	4 tbsp	10 tbsp
Extra virgin olive oil	2 tbsp	5 tbsp

Energy	Cals	Fat	Sat fat	Carb	Sugar	Protein	Fibre	Sodium
1,432 kJ	341 kcal	15.3g	3.8g	21.5g	21.5g	30.3g	0.9g	0.2g

1   Season and shallow-fry the duck breasts in olive oil, skin side down, and finish in the oven at 200 °C if required.

2   Meanwhile, place the cherries, vinegar and jelly in a pan and heat gently until the jelly has melted. Simmer and remove from the heat.

3   Stir in the extra virgin olive oil.

4   Carve the breasts into slices and serve on top of the sauce with the cherries and an accompaniment of vegetables.

22 Confit duck leg with red cabbage and green beans

1 Gently heat the confit oil, add the garlic, bay leaf and thyme.

2 Put the duck legs in the oil and place on a medium to low heat, ensuring the legs are covered.

3 Cook gently for 4–4½ hours (if using goose, 5–6½ hours may be needed).

4 To test if the legs are cooked, squeeze the flesh on the thigh bone and it should just fall away.

5 When cooked, remove the legs carefully and place on a draining tray.

6 When drained, put the confit leg on a baking tray and place in a preheated oven at 210 °C; remove when the skin is golden brown (approximately 9–10 minutes), taking care as the meat is delicate.

7 Heat the butter in a medium sauté pan and reheat the green beans.

8 Place the braised cabbage in a small pan and reheat slowly.

9 Place the duck leg in a serving dish or plate along with the red cabbage and green beans.

Ingredient	4 portions	10 portions
Confit oil	1 litre	2.5 litres
Cloves of garlic	4	10
Bay leaf	1	3
Sprig of thyme	1	2
Duck legs	4 × 200 g	10 × 200 g
Butter	50 g	125 g
Green beans, cooked and trimmed	300 g	750 g
Braised red cabbage	250 g	625 g
Seasoning		

Energy	Cals	Fat	Sat fat	Carb	Sugar	Protein	Fibre	Sodium
3859 kJ	932 kcal	83.0g	28.0g	7.7g	6.4g	39.2g	4.2g	0.3g

Professional tip

Confit oil is 50/50 olive oil and vegetable oil infused with herbs, garlic, whole spice or any specific flavour you wish to impart into the oil; then, through slow cooking in the oil, the foodstuff picks up the flavour.

Confit duck legs can be prepared up to three or four days in advance. Remove them carefully from the fat they are stored in, clean off any excess fat and place directly into the oven. This is a great timesaver in a busy service.

23 Roast duck or duckling (*canard ou caneton rôti*)

1 Lightly season the duck inside and out with salt.

2 Truss and brush lightly with oil.

3 Place on its side in a roasting tin, with a few drops of water.

4 Place in a hot oven for 20–25 minutes.

5 Turn on to the other side.

6 Cook for a further 20–25 minutes. Baste frequently.

7 To test if cooked, pierce with a fork between the drumstick and thigh and hold over a plate. The juice issuing from the duck should not show any signs of blood. If using a probe, the temperature should be 62 °C. If the duck is required pink, the temperature should be 57 °C.

8 Prepare the roast gravy with the stock and the sediment in the roasting tray. Correct the seasoning, remove the surface fat.

9 Serve garnished with picked watercress. Accompany with a sauceboat of hot apple sauce, a sauceboat of gravy, and game chips. Also serve a sauceboat of sage and onion dressing (recipe 24).

Ingredient	4 portions	10 portions
Duck	1	2–3
Salt		
Oil		
Brown stock	0.25 litres	600 ml
Salt, pepper		
Watercress, bunch	1	2
Apple sauce (page 98)	125 ml	300 ml

Energy	Cals	Fat	Sat fat	Carb	Sugar	Protein	Fibre
3,083 kJ	734 kcal	60.5g	16.9g	8.2g	7.8g	40.0g	1.4g

With apple sauce and watercress.

Note

Arrange the duck to cook sitting on one leg, then the other leg and then the breast, so the whole bird cooks evenly.

The temperatures in this recipe reflect industry standards for cooking duck. For food safety reasons, it is advisable to cook duck to higher temperatures.

Healthy eating tips

● Use the minimum amount of salt to season the duck and the roast gravy.
● Take care to remove all the fat from the roasting tray before making the gravy.
● This dish is high in fat and should be served with plenty of boiled new potatoes and a variety of vegetables.

24 Sage and onion dressing for duck

Ingredient	4 portions	10 portions
Onion, chopped	100 g	250 g
Duck fat or butter	100 g	250 g
Powdered sage	¼ tsp	½ tsp
Parsley, chopped	¼ tsp	½ tsp
Salt, pepper		
White or wholemeal breadcrumbs	100 g	250 g
Duck liver (optional), chopped	50 g	125 g

Energy	Cals	Fat	Sat fat	Carb	Sugar	Protein	Fibre	Sodium
1346 kJ	320 kcal	26.0 g	8.4 g	22.0 g	2.7 g	2.9 g	1.0 g	0.2 g

Using duck fat and omitting liver.

1 Gently cook the onion in the fat without colour. Add the chopped liver (if required) and fry until cooked.

2 Add the herbs and seasoning. Mix in the crumbs. Form into thick sausage shapes, in foil.

3 Place in a tray and finish in a hot oven at 180 °C for approximately 5–10 minutes. Check with a probe that the centre has reached 75 °C.

Serve separately with roast duck.

25 Cranberry and orange dressing for duck

Ingredient	4 portions	10 portions
Cranberries	400 g	1 kg
Granulated sugar	50 g	125 g
Red wine	125 ml	310 ml
Red wine vinegar	2 tbsp	5 tbsp
Orange zest and juice	2	5

Energy	Cals	Fat	Sat fat	Carb	Sugar	Protein	Fibre
398 kJ	93 kcal	0.2 g	0.0 g	22.7 g	22.7 g	1.3 g	4.2 g

1 Place the cranberries in a suitable saucepan with the rest of the ingredients.

2 Bring to the boil and simmer gently for approximately 1 hour, stirring from time to time.

3 Remove from the heat and leave to cool. Use as required.

Note

The dressing may be liquidised if a smooth texture is required.

Goose dish

26 Roast goose

The average weight of a goose is 5–6 kg.

1 Clean and truss the goose as for a chicken (see page 297).

2 Roast the goose using the same procedure for roasting a duck (recipe 23), with the oven at 200–230 °C. Turn it down to 180 °C after 20 minutes. Allow 15–20 minutes per 0.5 kg.

Energy	Cals	Fat	Sat fat	Carb	Sugar	Protein	Fibre
9,541 kJ	2,305 kcal	210.5 g	60.0 g	0.0 g	0.0 g	103.1 g	0.0 g

Guinea fowl dish

27 Suprêmes of guinea fowl with a pepper and basil coulis

Ingredient	4 portions	10 portions
Red peppers	3	7½
Olive oil	150 ml	375 ml
Fresh basil, chopped	2 tbsp	5 tbsp
Salt, pepper		
Guinea fowl suprêmes (approximately 150 g each)	4	10

Energy	Cals	Fat	Sat fat	Carb	Sugar	Protein	Fibre
904 kJ	216 kcal	4.7 g	1.3 g	7.8 g	7.3 g	35.8 g	0.5 g

Using chicken instead of guinea fowl.

1 Skin the peppers by brushing with oil and gently scorching in the oven or under the grill. Alternatively, use a blowtorch with great care. Once scorched, peel the skin from the peppers, cut in half and deseed.

2 Place the skinned and deseeded peppers in a food processor, blend with the olive oil and pass through a strainer.

3 Add the chopped basil and season.

4 Season the guinea fowl and either shallow-fry or grill.

5 Pour the coulis on to individual plates. Place the guinea fowl on top and serve immediately.

Cold dish

28 Terrine of chicken with vegetables

Ingredient	8–10 portions
Carrots, turnips and swedes, peeled and cut into 7 mm dice	50 g of each
Broccoli, small florets	50 g
Baby corn, cut into 7 mm rounds	50 g
French beans, cut into 7 mm lengths	50 g
Chicken (white meat only), minced	400 g
Egg whites	2
Double cream	200 ml
Salt, mill pepper	

Energy	Cals	Fat	Sat fat	Carb	Sugar	Protein	Fibre
930 kJ	226 kcal	17.3 g	9.4 g	2.0 g	1.8 g	15.5 g	0.9 g

1 Blanch all the vegetables individually in boiling salted water, ensuring that they remain firm. Refresh in cold water, and drain well.

2 Blend the chicken and egg whites in a food processor until smooth. Turn out into a large mixing bowl and gradually beat in the double cream.

3 Season with salt and mill pepper, and fold in the vegetables.

4 Line a lightly greased 1-litre terrine with cling film.

5 Spoon the farce into the mould and overlap the cling film.

6 Cover with foil, put the lid on and cook in a bain-marie in a moderate oven for about 45 minutes. Use a temperature probe to check that the centre has reached 70 °C.

7 When cooked, remove the lid and leave to cool overnight.

Healthy eating tips
● Keep the added salt to a minimum.
● Serve with plenty of salad vegetables and bread or toast (optional butter or spread).

Cut the vegetables into neat dice, rounds and florets

Line the terrine with cling film and spoon in the mixture

Cover the mixture with cling film and press down gently

Game dishes

29 Pot au feu of pigeon

Ingredient	4 portions	10 portions
Squabs, legs removed	6 (approx. 2 kg)	10 (approx. 3.5 kg)
Carrot, peeled and cut into 4 laterally	1	3
Celery stick, cut into 4	1	3
Baby turnips	8	20
Medium turnips, peeled and blanched	2	4
Leek, washed, cut in rounds	1	3
Small shallots, peeled and left whole	8	20
Smoked streaky bacon, rind removed	100g	250g
Chicken/game stock	400 ml	1 litre
Bouquet garni with 4 black peppercorns and 1 clove of garlic	1	3
Salt		

Energy	Cals	Fat	Sat fat	Carb	Sugar	Protein	Fibre
1,545 kJ	367 kcal	11.2g	3.4g	11.1g	10.0g	56.2g	4.8g

1 Place the squab legs in a large casserole and arrange the vegetables tightly in one layer with the legs, add the bacon then cover with the stock to about 4 cm above the ingredients (you may need to top this up with water).

2 Add the muslin-wrapped bouquet garni. Season with salt and bring to a gentle boil.

3 Skim off any impurities, cover with a lid (leaving a small gap) and simmer gently for 50 minutes.

4 Skim off any fat or impurities, then add the squab breasts and cook for a further 12 minutes.

Note

This is a social dish, designed to be placed in the middle of the table and served with warm, crusty bread, mashed potato or buttered new potatoes.

333

Arrange the squab legs and vegetables in the pan

Cover with stock

Add the breasts later, as they need less time to cook

30 Roast partridge

Ingredient	4 portions	10 portions
Grey-legged partridges (approx. 400g each), oven-ready, with livers	4	10
Unsalted butter	20g	50g
Groundnut oil or vegetable oil	20g	50g
Salt and freshly ground pepper		
Roasting juices from veal, pork or beef	70ml	175ml
Water	50ml	125ml

Energy	Cals	Fat	Sat fat	Carb	Sugar	Protein	Fibre
2,495 kJ	596 kcal	26.7g	7.6g	0.3g	0.1g	88.5g	0.0g

Note

Simply roasted partridge is a great autumnal or winter base for most accompaniments: braised cabbage, roast carrots, parsnips and so on.

1 Shorten the wings and sear the partridges under a flame to remove the feather stubs. Remove any trace of gall from the liver. Wash briefly, pat dry and reserve.

2 In a roasting tray sear the wing bones and the partridges in the butter and oil for 2 minutes on each side and 2 minutes on the breast (6 minutes in total) until they are brown.

3 Season with salt and pepper, and roast in the preheated oven for 5–10 minutes, according to the size of the partridges.

4 Remove from the oven and place the partridges on a cooling wire, breast-side down. Cover loosely with aluminium foil and allow to rest.

5 In the same roasting tray, fry the livers in the remaining butter and oil until well done, and reserve. Spoon out the excess fat and add the roasting juices and water to the winglets, bring to the boil then simmer for 5 minutes.

6 Taste and season with salt and pepper, then strain through a fine sieve.

7 Serve with roasted seasonal vegetables (e.g. roast parsnips, carrots and braised cabbage). Suggested accompaniments include bread sauce, roast gravy, watercress and game chips. The fried livers may be puréed and served on croûtes of toasted bread as an accompaniment.

31 Traditional-contemporary roast grouse

Ingredient	4 portions	10 portions
Grouse		
Young grouse (approx. 750 g each)	4	10
Sage leaves	4	10
Butter	20 g	50 g
Salt and pepper		
Stock		
Oil	30 ml	75 ml
Reserved grouse wings and giblets		
Large onion, diced	1	2½
Celery stick, diced	1	2½
Carrot, diced	1	2½
Red wine	250 ml	625 ml
Water		
Thyme, sprig of		
Bay leaf	1	2½
Brandy		
Toast		
Small slices of bread	16	40
Duck fat		
To serve		
Bread sauce		
Watercress, bunches	1	2
Game chips		

Energy	Cals	Fat	Sat fat	Carb	Sugar	Protein	Fibre
3,932 kJ	943 kcal	24.7 g	7.1 g	63.8 g	9.5 g	107.4 g	5.6 g

Nutritional analysis includes accompaniments.

Note

Good-quality grouse that has not been over-hung is essential. The meat will already have a strong, pungent flavour from the birds' diet of heather.

1 Trim the wings from the young grouse, draw and reserve the livers, hearts and giblets. Season birds liberally inside and out, and put the livers and hearts back in with a sage leaf and a knob of butter. Preheat the oven to 210 °C.

2 Brown the wings and the remaining giblets in the oil with the onion, celery and carrot. Deglaze pan with red wine, cover with water and simmer for 30 minutes with the thyme and bay leaf. Strain and reserve.

3 Meanwhile, fry the bread in duck fat. Make the bread sauce and pick through the watercress.

4 Seal the birds in a little hot oil until golden, then place them at the top of the oven and roast. Cook until a probe inserted between the leg and the cavity reads 75 °C, or until the juices run clear.

5 Remove from the pan and leave the birds to rest for 10 minutes.

6 Put the roasting tray over a flame, add a splash of brandy and the stock, and allow to bubble down to a thin gravy.

7 A traditional way to serve grouse is to scoop out the livers and hearts, mash these up and serve on the toast. Place a bunch of the watercress into the grouse's cavity and put the bird and toast on to a plate with some bread sauce and game chips. Pour a little of the gravy over each bird and serve the remaining gravy separately. Alternatively, serve with apple sauce.

Bread sauce

Milk	600 ml
Onion, studded with cloves and bay leaf	1
Peppercorns	6
Fresh white breadcrumbs	100 g
Butter	50 g

1 Heat the milk to boiling point. Infuse the onion and peppercorns in the milk for 30 minutes, then remove.

2 Strain the milk and stir in the breadcrumbs.

3 Heat gently for 10 minutes until thick.

4 Stir in the butter and season.

32 Pot-roasted quail with roast carrots and mashed potato

Ingredient	4 portions	10 portions
Quails (approx. 75 g each)	8	20
Pancetta, thinly sliced	8 slices (approx. 160 g)	20 slices (approx. 420 g)
Fresh sage leaves	8	20
Vegetable oil	15 ml	40 ml
Butter	20 g	50 g
Salt and freshly ground pepper		
Carrots, peeled and cut into quarters	100 g	250 g
Oil	30 ml	75 ml
Dry white wine	125 ml	310 ml
Red wine	125 ml	310 ml
Brown stock	250 ml	625 ml
Unsalted butter	50 g	125 g
Portions of mashed potato	4 (200 g)	10 (500 g)
Chives, chopped	1 tsp	2 ½tsp

Energy	Cals	Fat	Sat fat	Carb	Sugar	Protein	Fibre	Sodium
3076 kJ	742 kcal	56.0g	19.7g	11.5g	3.9g	38.0g	1.2g	1.2g

Chicken was used in place of quail.

1 Wash the quails thoroughly inside and out, then place them in a large colander to drain for at least 20 minutes; pat the quail dry.

2 Stuff the cavity of each bird with 1 slice of pancetta and 1 sage leaf.

3 Put the oil in a large, thick-bottomed roasting pan on a high heat. When the fat is hot, add all of the quails in a single layer and cook until browned on one side, gradually turning them, and continue cooking until they are evenly browned all over.

4 Lightly sprinkle the quails with salt and pepper, then add the carrots and cook for a couple of minutes until a slight colour appears.

5 Add the wine and brown stock then turn the birds once; let the wine bubble for about 1 minute then lower the heat to moderate and partially cover the pan. Cook the quail until the meat feels very tender when poked with a fork and comes away from the bone (approximately 35 minutes).

6 Check from time to time that there are sufficient juices in the pan to keep the birds from sticking; if this does occur, add 1 to 2 tablespoons of water at a time. When the quails are done, transfer them to a warmed tray and reserve.

7 Turn up the heat and reduce the cooking juices to a glaze – enough to coat all the birds, scraping the bottom of the pan with a spoon to loosen any cooking residues.

8 Add the unsalted butter and whisk in to form an emulsion; at this point, if the sauce splits or is too thick, add a little water and reboil.

9 Remove the carrots from the pan and place neatly on the plate with the mashed potato.

10 Pass the juices then pour them over the quail, sprinkle with chopped chives and serve immediately.

Stuff the cavity of the quail

33 Braised baron of rabbit with olives and tomatoes

Ingredient	4 portions	10 portions
Farm-raised rabbit barons (approx. 750–800 g each), including bones and trim for gravy	2	5
Carrot	1	2½
Onion	1	2½
Celery stick	1	2½
Olive oil	90 ml	225 ml
Balsamic vinegar	15 ml	40 ml
Caster sugar	10 g	25 g
Dry white wine	750 ml	1.9 litres
Butter, to brown the meat	125 ml	310 ml
Basil leaves	12	30
Black olives	32	80
Sun-dried tomato pieces	8	20
Salt and pepper		

Energy	Cals	Fat	Sat fat	Carb	Sugar	Protein	Fibre
2,365 kJ	568 kcal	41.0 g	8.4 g	5.5 g	4.8 g	44.6 g	0.9 g

Variation

The ingredients that give this recipe a Mediterranean influence (basil, olives and sun-dried tomatoes) can be omitted or substituted with a British theme – for example woodland mushrooms and parsnips – and served with braised cabbage.

1 Prepare the rabbits well ahead of time: cut the rabbits across at the point where the ribs end and chop the forequarters into small pieces.

2 Cut the vegetables into a mirepoix.

3 In a large saucepan, brown the bones and mirepoix in 2 tablespoons (or 5 tablespoons) of the olive oil.

4 Add the vinegar and sugar, and toss to coat. Cook until light brown.

5 Pour over almost all the white wine, reserving about 150 ml (or 375 ml) for deglazing the roasting pan later. Boil hard to reduce until the liquid has a syrupy consistency.

6 Just cover with cold water, return to the boil and skim.

7 Simmer for 1½ hours.

8 Pass the resulting stock into a bowl, wash out the saucepan and return the stock to it.

9 Bring back to the boil, skim again and, once more, return to a slow simmer until reduced by half. Reserve.

10 Cut the rabbit legs into two (thigh and drumstick), and the rack into two.

11 In a large saucepan, brown the meat cuts in foaming butter; when golden brown, add the finished stock and cook for a further 1½ hours (approximately).

12 When cooked, pass the sauce through a fine strainer, bring to the boil and reduce by half.

13 While reducing, put the rabbit into a casserole/serving dish, julienne the basil and remove the stones from the olives.

14 When the sauce is reduced by half, add the tomatoes, olives and basil. Correct the seasoning, pour over the rabbit and serve.

Note

A baron is the rear end of the rabbit – the rack and the two hind legs.

34 German-style saddle of hare

Ingredient	4 portions	10 portions
For the marinade		
Carrot, finely sliced	200 g	400 g
Onion, finely sliced	200 g	400 g
Celery, finely sliced	100 g	200 g
Cloves of garlic	2	5
Parsley stalks	25 g	60 g
Sprig of thyme		
Bay leaf	½	1
Cloves	2	5
Peppercorns	12	30
Red wine	500 ml	1.25 litres
Wine vinegar	125 ml	310 ml
Oil	125 ml	310 ml
For the hare		
Saddles of hare	2–4	5–10
Salt, pepper		
Cream	125 ml	310 ml
Lemon juice		

Energy	Cals	Fat	Sat fat	Carb	Sugar	Protein	Fibre
3,561 kJ	859 kcal	60.6 g	14.3 g	9.4 g	7.1 g	47.3 g	3.6 g

Variation
- After the saddle is removed, the roasting tray can be deglazed with brandy, whisky or gin.
- Sliced mushrooms (cultivated or wild) can be added to the sauce.

1 Season the hare with salt and pepper, and place into a suitable container (e.g. stainless steel or china).

2 Cover with the marinade ingredients.

3 Refrigerate, turning the joints over frequently, for approximately 24 hours.

4 Remove the saddles from the marinade and dry thoroughly.

5 Remove the vegetables from the marinade and place into a roasting tray. Place the saddles on top of the vegetables and roast in the oven at 180 °C.

6 When the saddle is three-quarters cooked, remove the vegetables.

7 Add the cream to the roasting tray and continue cooking. Baste the meat frequently with the cream. Keep the meat pink.

8 Remove the saddles from the tray. Separate the meat from the bone and slice each side into four pieces.

9 Add a few drops of lemon juice to the cooking liquor, correct the seasoning and consistency, and pass through a fine strainer. Serve the sauce with the saddles.

Suitable accompaniments include: cabbage; braised chestnuts or chestnut purée; Brussels sprouts with chestnuts; purée of celeriac, celeriac and parsnips or celeriac and onion; buttered noodles.

Note

The saddle is a joint cut from the back of the hare, usually in a similar way to a short saddle of lamb – that is, a pair of uncut loins. All skin and sinew must be removed and the joint trimmed before use. If desired, the joint may be larded with pork fat.

A saddle of hare yields one or two portions, depending on its size.

It is not essential to marinade the saddle if obtained from a young hare but, if there is any doubt as to its tenderness, or if it is to be kept for a few days, then the joint should be marinated, as in this recipe.

12 Vegetables and vegetable protein

This chapter is relevant to the following units:
→ Prepare vegetables for basic dishes.
→ Cook and finish basic vegetable dishes.
→ Prepare, cook and finish vegetable protein dishes.

Recipes included in this chapter

Vegetables

Vegetable is a culinary term that generally refers to the edible part of a plant. All parts of herbaceous plants eaten as food by humans, in whole or in part, are normally considered to be vegetables. Mushrooms, though categorised as fungi, are also commonly considered vegetables. In general, vegetables are thought of as being savoury, not sweet, although there are many exceptions. In most countries they are associated with poultry, meat or fish as part of a meal or as an ingredient. Nuts, grains, herbs, spices and culinary fruits (see below) are not normally considered to be vegetables. Some vegetables are botanically classed as fruits – tomatoes are berries and avocados are drupes – but both are commonly used as vegetables because they are not sweet.

Vegetables can include leaves (lettuce), stems (asparagus), roots (carrots), flowers (broccoli), bulbs (garlic), seeds (peas and beans) and vegetable fruits (such as cucumbers, squash, pumpkins and capsicums).

- A **root** is the part of the plant growing down into the soil to support the plant and take up water and nutrients.
- A **stem** is the part of the plant usually above the ground that bears the buds, leaves, flowers and fruit (although it can be underground). A young stem is called a shoot.
- A **bulb** is an organ in some plants which consist of an underground axis with many thick overlapping leaves.
- A **flower** is the reproductive part of the plant, often brightly coloured to attract insects.
- A **tuber** is an underground stem used for storing food; it is also able to produce new plants.
- A **leaf** is the part of the plant that makes food by photosynthesis.
- A **pod** is the part in some plants where the seeds are developed, for example pea pods.
- A **seed** is the reproductive mechanism of the plant.
- **Fruits** are the part of the flowering plant that contains the seeds.

Vegetables are an important part of our diet, so it is essential to pay attention to quality, purchasing, storage and efficient preparation and cooking if the nutritional content of vegetables is to be conserved.

The nutrient content of different types of vegetables varies considerably. With the exception of pulses, vegetables provide little protein or fat, but they do contain water-soluble vitamins such as vitamin B and vitamin C, fat-soluble vitamins including vitamin A and vitamin D, as well as carbohydrates and minerals. Root vegetables contain starch or sugar for energy, a small but valuable amount of protein, some mineral salts and vitamins. They are also useful sources of cellulose and water. Green vegetables are rich in mineral salts and vitamins, particularly vitamin C and carotene. The greener the leaf, the larger the quantity of vitamins present. The chief mineral salts are calcium and iron.

Vegetables are also an excellent source of antioxidants, which can lower the risk of heart disease, cancer and diabetes-related damage, and even slow down the body's natural ageing process.

Purchasing and selection

The purchasing of vegetables is affected by:
- the perishable nature of the products
- varying availability owing to seasonal fluctuations, and supply and demand
- the effects of preservation (for example, freezing, drying and canning).

Fresh vegetables are living organisms and will lose quality quickly if not stored and handled properly. Automation in harvesting and packaging speeds the handling process and helps retain quality.

Quality points

Root vegetables must be:
- clean, free from soil
- firm, not soft or spongy
- sound
- free from blemishes
- of an even size
- of an even shape.

Green vegetables must be absolutely fresh and have leaves that are bright in colour, crisp and not wilted. In addition:
- cabbages and Brussels sprouts should be compact and firm
- cauliflowers should have closely grown flowers, a firm white head and not too much stalk or too many outer leaves
- peas and beans should be crisp and of medium size; pea pods should be full and beans not stringy
- blanched stems must be firm, white, crisp and free from soil.

Potatoes must be inspected and selected before buying or on delivery.
- Choose firm, smooth ones.
- Avoid excessively wrinkled, withered, cracked potatoes.
- Do not buy those that have a lot of sprouts or green areas.

Table 12.1 UK vegetable availability according to season

Spring (March, April, May)	Summer (June, July, August)	Autumn (September, October, November)	Winter (December, January, February)
Asparagus	Aubergine	Beetroot	Beetroot
Cauliflower	Beetroot	Carrots	Brussels sprouts
Cucumber	Broad beans	Celeriac	Cabbage
Jersey royal new potatoes	Broccoli	Fennel	Cauliflower
Purple sprouting broccoli	Carrots	Field mushrooms	Celeriac
Radishes	Courgettes	Kale	Chicory
Savoy cabbage	Cucumber	Leeks	Fennel
Sorrel	Fennel	Lettuce	Jerusalem artichokes
Spinach	Fresh peas	Marrows	Kale
Spring greens	Garlic	Potatoes	Leeks
Spring onions	Green beans	Pumpkins	Parsnips
Watercress	Lettuce and salad leaves	Rocket	Potatoes
	New potatoes	Sorrel	Red cabbage
	Radishes	Squashes	Swede
	Rocket	Sweet corn	Turnips
	Runner beans	Tomatoes	
	Salad onions	Watercress	
	Sorrel		
	Tomatoes		
	Watercress		

Source: www.lovebritishfood.co.uk

Grading

The EU vegetable quality grading system is as follows:

● **Extra class**: produce of the highest quality
● **Class 1**: produce of good quality
● **Class 2**: produce of reasonably good quality
● **Class 3**: produce of low market quality.

Video: vegetable quality points http://bit.ly/17qTnOH

Seasonal availability

With the advances and development of transportation and refrigeration, fruit and vegetables can be purchased from all over the world and therefore, in many cases, seasons do not exist: for example, we can enjoy strawberries all year round. However, the UK strawberry season starts in late May/early June – local strawberries are full of flavour, while often imported strawberries lack flavour. For this reason, purchasing locally from local farms and specialist growers is popular, so knowing when vegetables are in season is important.

Provenance (knowing where our food comes from) has also become increasingly important as the consumer is now more concerned about the environment and carbon omissions; restricting the amount of food travelling around the world as aircraft cargo has become an important issue. Consumers are also interested in the traceability of food – where it comes from, how it is grown and the welfare of farm workers. EU regulations require the food industry to trace the food, how food is farmed and how the animals are looked after and fed.

Storing vegetables

The fresher the vegetables, the better the flavour, so ideally they should not be stored at all. However, as storage is necessary in many cases, it should be for the shortest time possible.

Many root and non-root vegetables that grow underground can be stored over winter in a root cellar or other similarly cool, dark and dry place, to prevent the growth of mould, greening and sprouting. Care should be taken to understand the properties and vulnerabilities of the particular roots to be stored. These vegetables can last through to early spring and be almost as nutritious as when fresh.

Leafy vegetables lose moisture, and vitamin C degrades rapidly, during storage. They should be stored for as short a time as possible in a cool place in either a plastic bag or sealed plastic container. Green vegetables lose vitamin C quickly if they are bruised, damaged, stored for too long, prepared too early or overcooked.

● Store all vegetables in a cool, dry, well-ventilated room at an even temperature of 4–8 °C, which will help to minimise spoilage. Check vegetables daily and discard any that are unsound.
● Remove root vegetables from their sacks and store in bins or racks.
● Store green vegetables on well-ventilated racks.
● Store salad vegetables in a cool place and leave in their containers.
● Store frozen vegetables between −18 °C and −20 °C. Keep a check on use-by dates, damaged packages and any signs of freezer burn.
● You can store potatoes for several months without affecting their quality; they should be stored at a constant temperature (3 °C). If it is not possible to store them in this way, buying fresh potatoes regularly is best practice. There are three essential rules to bear in mind when storing potatoes: dry, dark and cool. You should avoid light as this will cause sprouting and, eventually, the greening effect, which contains mild toxins; if you have inadvertently purchased potatoes with this green tinge, remove the green bits and the rest of the potato is then fine to use. The storage of a potato is perhaps the most important aspect of its life – the closer the temperature is to freezing point, the quicker the potato starch coverts to sugar, producing a sweet flesh, but a loss of structure and, often, discoloration.

Health and safety !

● If vegetables are stored at the incorrect temperature micro-organisms may develop.
● If vegetables are stored in damp conditions moulds may develop.
● To prevent bacteria from raw vegetables passing on to cooked vegetables, store them in separate areas.
● Thaw out frozen vegetables correctly and *never* refreeze them once they have thawed out.

Preparing vegetables

Vegetables should be washed to remove any residue, chemicals and impurities before peeling. Peeling removes the outer skin of the vegetable or fruit; not all vegetables and fruit require peeling – this will depend on the type of fruit and vegetables and the recipe.

Cuts of vegetables

The size and shape to which the vegetables are cut may vary according to their type and use.

1 Large mirepoix
2 Small mirepoix
3 Paysanne
4 Sliced courgette
5 Turned vegetables
6 Finely diced onion
7 Tomato petals
8 Tomato concassé (gros brunoise)

9 Carrot block
10 Carrot strips
11 Julienne
12 Brunoise
13 Large block of mooli
14 Flat block
15 Jardinière
16 Macédoine

▲ Cuts of vegetables

Cutting vegetables into julienne (strips)

1 Cut the vegetables into 2 cm lengths (short julienne).

2 Cut the lengths into thin slices.

3 Cut the slices into thin strips.

4 Double the length gives a long julienne, used for garnishing (e.g. salads, meats, fish and poultry dishes).

Cutting vegetables into brunoise (small dice)

1 Cut the vegetables into convenient-sized lengths.

2 Cut the lengths into 2 mm slices.

3 Cut the slices into 2 mm strips.

4 Cut the strips into 2 mm squares.

Cutting vegetables into macédoine (0.5 cm dice)

1 Cut the vegetables into convenient lengths.

2 Cut the lengths into 0.5 cm slices.

3 Cut the slices into 0.5 cm strips.

4 Cut the strips into 0.5 cm squares.

Video: cutting vegetables into macédoine http://bit.ly/ 1znW8rU

Cutting vegetables into jardinière (batons)

1 Cut the vegetables into 1.5 cm lengths.

2 Cut the lengths into 3 mm slices.

3 Cut the slices into batons (3 × 3 × 18 mm).

There are at least four accepted methods of cutting **paysanne**. In order to cut economically, the shape of the vegetables should dictate which method to choose. All are cut thinly.

- 1 cm sided triangles.
- 1 cm sided squares.
- 1 cm diameter rounds.
- 1 cm diameter rough-sided rounds.

Concassé means roughly chopped. Skinned and deseeded tomatoes are roughly chopped for many food preparations (see recipe 66). The term is also used to refer to skinned and deseeded tomatoes that are cut into neat strips or cubes and used as a garnish.

Ready-prepared potatoes

Potatoes are obtainable in many convenience forms: peeled, turned, cut into various shapes for frying, or scooped into balls (*Parisienne*) or olive shaped.

- Chips are available fresh, frozen, chilled or vacuum packed.
- Frozen potatoes are available as croquettes, hash browns, sauté and roast.
- Mashed potato powder and flakes are also available.

Cooking vegetables

Approximate times only are given in the recipes in this chapter for the cooking of vegetables, as quality, age, freshness and size all affect the length of cooking time required. Young, freshly picked vegetables will need to be cooked for a shorter time than vegetables that have been allowed to grow older and that may have been stored after picking.

As a general rule, all root vegetables (with the exception of new potatoes) are started off by cooking in cold salted water. Vegetables that grow above the ground are started in boiling salted water; this is so that they may be cooked as quickly as possible for the minimum period of time, so that maximum flavour, food value and colour are retained.

Blanching

Delicate vegetables – particularly green vegetables – can be blanched in salted boiling water and then refreshed in ice-cold water to arrest the cooking process. The main reason for this is because, between the temperatures of 66 °C and 77 °C, chlorophyll is unstable. Chlorophyll is the green pigment in any plant that photosynthesises. For this reason it is important to get through this temperature zone as quickly as possible.

Steaming

All vegetables cooked by boiling may also be cooked by steaming. The vegetables are prepared in exactly the same way as for boiling, placed into steamer trays, lightly seasoned with salt and steamed under pressure for the minimum period of time in order to conserve maximum food value and retain colour. High-speed steam cookers are ideal for this purpose and, because of the speed of cooking they offer, batch cooking (cooking in small quantities throughout the service) can be practised instead of cooking large quantities prior to service, refreshing and reheating.

Frying

Many vegetables are cooked from raw by the stir-fry method, a quick and nutritious method of cooking. Vegetables may also be deep fried with a protective coating, such as tempura vegetables in a tempura batter. Vegetables may also be shallow fried in butter or vegetable oil, for example shallow-fried courgettes.

Health and safety !

Make sure that vegetables are dry before being placed into hot oil. Make sure that every chef knows the fire drill and that they are confident in the procedures and systems for frying. Always have a spider and basket at hand when you are deep frying in order to remove the food quickly and safely if there is a problem. Always wear protective clothing when frying: it is safer to wear a chefs' jacket with long sleeves rather than short sleeves.

Stewing

Stewing is an old, traditional method of cooking vegetables. The vegetables are cut into even pieces, gently sweated on the stove in a little oil, then a stock or tomato juice is added and allowed to simmer on the stove or in an oven.

The stewed vegetables may be flavoured with chopped herbs and/or spices. A classical stewed vegetable dish is ratatouille, which consists of aubergines, peppers, courgettes, onions and tomatoes in their juices.

Braising

Vegetables that are most suitable for braising include potatoes, onions, cabbage, fennel, and celery. In most cases vegetables are blanched (potatoes are the exception) and placed in a shallow pan with stock to come two-thirds of the way up, so not covering the vegetable.

Healthy eating tips

- Cook vegetables *al dente*.
- Cook, reheat and serve immediately.
- Use olive oil in place of butter.
- Avoid the use of cream – use fromage frais or yoghurt instead.
- Do not over-season – reduce the amount of salt used in cooking vegetables.

Cooking potatoes

Potatoes are tubers. They can have white, brown, purple or red skin, and white or golden flesh. Several named varieties of potato are grown in the UK and these will be available according to the season. The different varieties have differing characteristics and some are more suitable for certain methods of cooking than others (see chart and Table 12.2). The careful selection of potatoes to suit the job in hand is essential.

Cooked potatoes may have different textures, depending on whether they are 'waxy' or 'floury' varieties. This is due to changes that happen to the potato cells during cooking. These differences influence the performance of the potato when cooked in different ways (for example, boiling versus roasting).

Source: Potato Council

- 'Waxy' potatoes are more solid than floury potatoes and hold their shape when boiled, but do not mash well. They are particularly suitable for baked and layered potato dishes such as boulangère potatoes. Popular varieties include Cara and Charlotte. Waxy potatoes are translucent and may have a moist and pasty feel.
- 'Floury' potatoes are especially popular in the UK. They are brighter and granular in appearance, leaving a drier feel. They are suitable for baking, mashing and chipping as they have a soft, dry texture when cooked. They are not suitable for boiling, however, because they tend to disintegrate. Popular varieties of floury potato include King Edward and Maris Piper.

During cooking, the starch in the potato starts to absorb water and swell in size. Potatoes need to be cooked for sufficient time to gelatinise the starch or they will look and taste undercooked.

Table 12.2 Potato varieties and recommended cooking methods

Variety	Methods of cookery
Cara	Boil, bake, chip, wedge
Charlotte	Boil, salad use
Desiree	Boil, roast, bake, chip, mash, wedge
Golden Wonder	Boil, roast, crisps
King Edward	Boil, bake, roast, mash, chip
Maris Piper	Boil, roast, bake, chip
Pink Fir Apple	Boil, salad use
Premiere	Boil
Record	Crisps
Romano	Boil, bake, roast, mash
Saxon	Boil, bake, chip
Wilja	Boil, bake, chip, mash

- **Baking**: long slow cooking is best for baked potatoes. The skin becomes very crisp and turns darker because the starch just below the skin converts to sugar, which browns in heat. Make sure you cut a slit in the potato as soon as it comes out of the oven so the interior doesn't steam, which makes for a heavier consistency.
- **Mashing**: mashed potatoes can be made from many varieties of potato. The starch in the potatoes, once again, absorbs water and swells during the cooking process. Then, when the potato is mashed or riced, the cells break open, releasing more starch, which makes the potatoes creamy and smooth. If you boil potatoes for mashing, return them to the hot pan after draining and shake over a medium heat for 2–3 minutes to dry the potatoes. Whatever the cooking method, add butter when you begin mashing. The butter coats the

cells and the starch so they absorb less liquid, making the potatoes less gluey and fluffier. The slower the mash is cooked the better for the starch as it has more structure in the final mixing process, allowing the potato to hold in more fat/liquid than if cooked by the more traditional quicker method. Bring the potatoes up to the boil from cold as normal and boil for 2–3 minutes, remove and rinse in cold water, then repeat the process of boiling from cold and turn the heat down, not even to a simmer. This will obviously take longer but will reduce the water absorption rate dramatically due to the starch wall created by the first process.

- **Roasting**: roast potatoes are simply cut into chunks and parboiled slowly until just cooked on the inside. Drain and toss in a liberal amount of olive oil and seasoning, then roast at a high temperature (220°C) for 15 minutes. Remove, turn the temperature down to 180°C and baste every 5 minutes to ensure a crisp coat all over. Once cooked serve immediately, as prolonged holding will inevitably cause the inside to steam, making the outside soft and leathery.

Yield

- 0.5 kg of old potatoes will yield approximately three portions.
- 0.5 kg of new potatoes will yield approximately four portions.
- 1.5 kg of old potatoes will yield approximately ten portions.
- 1.25 kg of new potatoes will yield approximately ten portions.

Finishing vegetable dishes

It is important to finish vegetable dishes at the point of service to retain their temperature and, for green vegetables, so that they retain their colour. There are a variety of finishes for vegetable dishes based on the individual recipes. Some vegetables are simply brushed with butter or olive oil, while some are finished with pine nuts, chopped mixed herbs, cream, cheese sauce, toasted almonds or toasted breadcrumbs with mixed herbs.

Holding and serving

As soon as vegetables have been cooked or reheated for service, serve immediately at the correct temperature (at least 65°C). Vegetables such as French beans, broccoli and carrots loose heat very quickly. Vegetables on a buffet service must be served in batches and replenished regularly. Do not leave vegetables out on a hotplate for long periods as green vegetables will lose their colour as well as their vitamin C content.

Vegetable protein

According to the Vegetarian Society, vegetarian diets are consistent with dietary guidelines and can meet recommended dietary allowances for nutrients. You can get enough protein from a vegetarian diet as long as the variety of foods and the amounts consumed are adequate. Alternative sources of essential nutrients when following a vegetarian diet include fruits and vegetables; cereals, grains and pulses; nuts and seeds; dairy products such as milk, cheese and eggs; and vegetable protein. (For more information on vegetarian diets see Chapter 17.)

Soya products

The soybean is an important global food source from which many products are made. Its leguminous seeds are high in protein and contain important amino acids, which are essential and cannot be made in the body. Soya flour is used to boost the protein content of a variety of dishes.

Tofu

Tofu (also known as bean curd) is a product of the soybean and is generally available in two forms: silken tofu (soft or Japanese-style tofu), made from lightly pressed soybean curd; and firm tofu (or Chinese-style tofu), which is more heavily pressed. Silken tofu, with its softer consistency is used in soups, sauces and desserts, and is seen as a healthier option to cream. Regular tofu is more common than silken tofu.

To produce tofu, soybeans are boiled, puréed and pressed through a sieve to produce soya milk. The milk is then processed in a similar way to soft cheese.

Always keep tofu in a refrigerator and follow the instructions on the packet from the supplier.

Tempeh

Tempeh is a fermented soybean product that is cooked and pressed. It is similar to tofu but has a firmer texture and is purchased chilled.

Textured vegetable protein (TVP)

This meat substitute is manufactured from protein derived from wheat, oats, cottonseed, soybean and other sources. The main source of TVP is the soybean, due to its high protein content.

TVP is used mainly as a meat extender, replacing from 10 to 60 per cent of fresh meat. Some caterers on very tight budgets make use of it, but its main use is in food manufacturing.

By partially replacing the meat in certain dishes – such as casseroles, stews, pies, pasties, sausage rolls, hamburgers, meat loaf and pâté – it is possible to reduce costs, meet nutritional targets and serve food that is acceptable in appearance.

Soya protein can also be useful when making vegetarian dishes.

Mycoprotein

This meat substitute is produced from a plant that is a distant relative of the mushroom. Mycoprotein contains protein and fibre, and is the result of a fermentation process similar to the way yoghurt is made. It may be used as an alternative to chicken or beef or in vegetarian dishes. The most common brand is Quorn.

It is a low-fat, high-protein food that can be used in a variety of dishes (for example, oriental stir-fries) and does not shrink during preparation and cooking. Quorn mince or pieces can be substituted for chicken or minced meats. Its mild savoury flavour means that it complements the herbs and spices in a recipe and it is able to absorb flavour. Frozen Quorn may be cooked straight from the freezer or may be defrosted overnight in the refrigerator. Once thawed, it must be stored in the refrigerator and used within 24 hours.

Seitan

Seitan (also called wheat meat or wheat gluten) is produced from wheat and has a high gluten content. It can be used as a vegetarian alternative and as a meat substitute, and is high in protein. Asian restaurants use seitan as 'mock meat'.

Seitan can be prepared by hand using either wholewheat flour or vital wheat gluten; it is made by rinsing away the starch in the wheat, leaving high-protein gluten.

Quality points for vegetable protein

- Check the expiry date.
- There should be no unpleasant smell.
- There should be no discoloration (good colour).
- Tofu should be kept in the refrigerator.
- Soya must be free from foreign bodies.
- Packaging should be undamaged.

Test yourself

1　State two quality points to look for when buying leeks.

2　List five vegetables that are in season in autumn.

3　Describe the following cuts of vegetables:

   a　macédoine

   b　jardinière

   c　julienne

   d　paysanne.

4　Describe the preparation and cooking of braised red cabbage.

5　How should fresh green vegetables be stored?

6　What is meant by 'blanching' of vegetables and why is it done?

7　Describe two ways to make vegetable dishes healthier.

8　What is the difference between the method of boiling for green vegetables, such as broccoli, and root vegetables, such as potatoes?

9　Describe how tofu should be stored.

10　List three quality points you should look for when buying soya.

Root vegetables

1 Buttered carrots (*carottes au beurre*)

Ingredient	4 portions	10 portions
Carrots	400 g	1 kg
Salt		
Sugar		
Butter	25 g	60 g
Parsley, chopped		

Energy	Cals	Fat	Sat fat	Carb	Sugar	Protein	Fibre
297 kJ	71 kcal	5.1 g	3.3 g	5.8 g	5.8 g	0.7 g	2.8 g

Healthy eating tips
Use the minimum amount of salt.

1 Peel and wash the carrots.

2 Cut into neat, even pieces, turned barrel shapes or batons.

3 Place in a pan with a little salt, a pinch of sugar and the butter. Barely cover with water.

4 Cover with buttered paper and allow to boil steadily in order to evaporate all the water.

5 When the water has completely evaporated check that the carrots are cooked; if not, add a little more water and continue cooking. Do not overcook.

6 Toss the carrots over a fierce heat for 1–2 minutes in order to give them a glaze.

7 Serve sprinkled with chopped parsley.

2 Carrots in cream sauce (*carottes à la crème*)

Ingredient	4 portions	10 portions
Carrots	400 g	1 kg
Salt		
Butter	25 g	60 g
Parsley, chopped		
Cream sauce (page 84)	100 ml	250 ml

1 Prepare and cook carrots as for buttered carrots (see recipe 1).

2 Mix with the cream sauce, correct the seasoning and serve.

Energy	Cals	Fat	Sat fat	Carb	Sugar	Protein	Fibre
511 kJ	123 kcal	8.2 g	4.6 g	11.5 g	7.8 g	1.4 g	2.5 g

Using a cream sauce based on béchamel with single cream added 40:10.

Note

The cream sauce can be based on a béchamel sauce with single cream added in a ratio of 40:10. It could be made with wholemeal flour, skimmed milk and natural yoghurt.

Healthy eating tips
- Use the minimum amount of salt.
- Try replacing half the cream sauce with natural yoghurt.

3 Purée of carrots (*purée de carottes*)

Ingredient	4 portions	10 portions
Carrots	600 g	1.5 kg
Salt, pepper		
Butter	25 g	60 g

1 Wash, peel and rewash the carrots. Cut into pieces.
2 Barely cover with water, add a little salt. Simmer gently or steam until tender.
3 Drain well. Pass through a sieve or mouli.
4 Return to the pan, reheat and mix in the butter, correct the seasoning and serve.

Healthy eating tips
Use the minimum amount of salt.

Energy	Cals	Fat	Sat fat	Carb	Sugar	Protein	Fibre
410 kJ	99 kcal	5.6 g	3.4 g	11.9 g	11.1 g	0.9 g	3.6 g

4 Beetroot (*betterave*)

1 Select medium-sized or small beetroots; carefully twist off the green leaves (do not cut).
2 Wash well in cold water, cover with water and simmer gently until the skin is easily removed by rubbing between the fingers.

Note

Do not cut or prick with a knife as the beetroots will 'bleed' and turn pale.

Variation

Beetroot may also be cooked in a steamer, or baked.

It may be served hot:
- in cream sauce
- coated in herb-flavoured oil
- coated in butter and marmalade.

Energy	Cals	Fat	Sat fat	Carb	Sugar	Protein	Fibre
92 kJ	22 kcal	0.0 g	0.0 g	5.0 g	5.0 g	0.9 g	1.3 g

Peel the cooked beetroot, wearing gloves to avoid staining your skin

Cut into neat dice

5 Goats' cheese and beetroot tarts with salad of watercress

Ingredient	4 portions	10 portions
Puff pastry	400 g	1 kg
Shallots	150 g	375 g
Beetroot, cooked	200 g	500 g
Goats' cheese	200 g	500 g
Watercress, bunch	1	2

Energy	Cals	Fat	Sat fat	Carb	Sugar	Protein	Fibre
2,377 kJ	568 kcal	37.7 g	9.0 g	43.6 g	7.5 g	18.6 g	1.8 g

1 Roll the puff pastry to a thickness of 3 mm.

2 Chill the rolled puff pastry for 10 minutes.

3 Finely slice the shallots and sweat down without colour.

4 Cut the puff pastry into 4 discs approximately 150 mm in diameter.

5 Chill the pastry discs for 10 minutes.

6 Dice the cooked beetroot into pieces 10 × 10 mm.

7 To make the tarts, place the shallots on the pastry discs.

8 Cook at 180 °C for 12 minutes.

9 Once cooked, remove from the oven and top with the diced beetroot and crumbled goats' cheese.

10 To finish the dish, place the tarts on plates and finish with picked watercress and vinaigrette.

6 Parsnips (*panais*)

1 Wash well. Peel the parsnips and rewash well.

2 Cut into quarters lengthwise, remove the centre root if tough.

3 Cut into neat pieces and cook in lightly salted water until tender, or steam.

4 Drain and serve with melted butter or in a cream sauce.

Variation

Parsnips may be roasted in the oven in a little fat (as shown here) or in with a joint, and can be cooked and prepared as a purée.

Professional tip

For great roast parsnips, blanch them for 2 minutes, drain, then roast in hot olive oil.

Energy	Cals	Fat	Sat fat	Carb	Sugar	Protein	Fibre
235 kJ	56 kcal	0.0g	0.0g	13.5g	2.7g	1.3g	2.5g

7 Buttered celeriac, turnip or swede

1 Peel and wash the vegetables.

2 Cut into neat pieces or turn barrel shaped.

3 Place in a pan with a little salt, a pinch of sugar and the butter. Barely cover with water.

4 Cover with a buttered paper and allow to boil steadily in order to evaporate all the water.

5 When the water has completely evaporated, check that the vegetables are cooked; if not, add a little more water and continue cooking. Do not overcook.

6 Toss the vegetables over a fierce heat for 1–2 minutes to glaze.

7 Drain well, and serve sprinkled with chopped parsley.

Ingredient	4 portions	10 portions
Celeriac, turnips or swedes	400g	1kg
Salt, sugar		
Butter	25g	60g
Parsley, chopped		

Energy	Cals	Fat	Sat fat	Carb	Sugar	Protein	Fibre
253 kJ	60 kcal	5.4g	3.3g	2.5g	2.5g	0.7g	1.9g

8 Purée of celeriac, turnips, swede or parsnips

Ingredient	4 portions	10 portions
Celeriac, turnips, swede or parsnips	600 g	1.5 kg
Salt, pepper		
Butter	25 g	60 g

1 Wash, peel and rewash the vegetables. Cut into pieces if necessary.
2 Barely cover with water; add a little salt.
3 Simmer gently until tender, or steam. Drain well.
4 Pass through a sieve or mouli, or use a food processor.
5 Return to the pan, reheat and mix in the butter; correct the seasoning and serve.

Energy	Cals	Fat	Sat fat	Carb	Sugar	Protein	Fibre
395 kJ	95 kcal	5.9 g	3.3 g	9.2 g	6.4 g	1.8 g	4.7 g

Using mixed vegetables and 25 g butter.

Variation

Combination vegetable purées can include, for example, swede and carrot, and parsnip and potato.

9 Salsify

Ingredient	4 portions	10 portions
Flour	10 g	20 g
Cold water	0.5 litres	1 litre
Salt, to taste		
Lemon, juice of	½	1

Energy	Cals	Fat	Sat fat	Carb	Sugar	Protein	Fibre
76 kJ	18 kcal	0.0 g	0.0 g	2.8 g	2.8 g	1.9 g	0.0 g

0.5 kg will yield 2–3 portions.
1 Wash, peel and rewash the salsify.
2 Cut into 5 cm lengths.
3 Cook in a blanc (see below). Do not overcook. Salsify may then be served brushed with melted butter, or coated in mornay sauce (see page 85), sprinkled with grated cheese and browned under a salamander. It may also be passed through batter and deep fried.

To make the blanc:
1 Mix the flour and water together.
2 Add the salt and lemon juice. Pass through a strainer.
3 Place in a pan, bring to the boil, stirring continuously.

10 Fried onions (*oignons sautées ou oignons lyonnaise*)

Ingredient	2 portions	4 portions
Onions	500 g	1 kg
Oil	25–50 g	50–100 g
Salt		

1 Peel and wash the onions; cut into halves and slice finely.

2 Cook slowly in the oil in a frying pan, turning frequently until tender and browned; season lightly with salt.

Healthy eating tips
- Use a little unsaturated oil to cook the onion.
- Use the minimum amount of salt.

Energy	Cals	Fat	Sat fat	Carb	Sugar	Protein	Fibre
681 kJ	162 kcal	12.9 g	2.4 g	10.4 g	10.4 g	1.8 g	2.6 g

Using peanut oil.

11 French-fried onions (*oignons frites à la française*)

1 Peel and wash the onions.

2 Cut into 2 mm slices, against the grain. Separate into rings.

3 Pass through milk and seasoned flour.

4 Shake off the surplus. Deep-fry in hot fat at 185 °C.

5 Drain well on kitchen paper, season lightly with salt and serve.

Healthy eating tips
- Make sure the oil is hot so that less is absorbed into the onions.
- Drain on kitchen paper.
- Use the minimum amount of salt.

Energy	Cals	Fat	Sat fat	Carb	Sugar	Protein	Fibre
661 kJ	159 kcal	11.7 g	1.6 g	12.3 g	3.5 g	2.0 g	1.0 g

Using 50 g onions, to give 83.5 g finished weight.

Slice the onions thinly

Pass each piece through milk and then seasoned flour

12 Caramelised button onions

Ingredient	4 portions	10 portions
Butter or vegetable oil	50 g	125 g
Button onions	250 g	700 g
Water or brown stock	100 ml	250 ml
Sugar	50 g	125 g

Energy	Cals	Fat	Sat fat	Carb	Sugar	Protein	Fibre	Sodium
713 kJ	171 kcal	10.8g	6.5g	18.4g	16.7g	1.2g	1.2g	0.5g

1 Place the butter or oil in a shallow pan.

2 Fry the button onions quickly to a light golden brown colour.

3 Barely cover with water or brown stock. Add the sugar. Cook the button onions until they are tender and the liquid has reduced with the sugar to a light caramel glaze. Carefully coat the onions with the glaze.

Professional tip

The important thing is to reduce the stock and sugar until they form a light caramel syrup.

13 Braised fennel with black olives and cardamom

Ingredient	4 portions	10 portions
Fennel bulbs, medium	2	5
Olive or vegetable oil	2 tbsp	5 tbsp
Cloves of garlic, crushed or chopped	1	2½
Black olives, stoned and halved	8	20
Cardamom pods	2	5
Thyme, sprigs	1	2½
Chicken stock	300 ml	750 ml
White wine	300 ml	750 ml
Seasoning		

Energy	Cals	Fat	Sat fat	Carb	Sugar	Protein	Fibre	Sodium
531 kJ	128 kcal	6.9g	0.9g	3.3g	2.6g	1.7g	4.2g	0.6g

1 Prepare the fennel: remove any tough outer leaves and cut into quarters vertically.

2 Heat the oil in a suitable pan, add the fennel, and sweat without colour for 5–10 minutes.

3 Add the garlic, olives, cardamom and thyme. Add the stock and white wine, and season. Bring to the boil.

4 Cover with a lid and braise in an oven at 180–200 °C for approximately 1 hour, until tender.

5 When cooked, remove.

Note

Braised fennel may be served with a variety of meat and fish dishes. It may be coated with a cream, cheese, red wine or Madeira sauce.

Variation
- The fennel can be blanched for 2 minutes in boiling water and refreshed before sweating.
- Cinnamon or mixed spice may be used in place of cardamom.

14 Braised leeks with garlic and olives

Ingredient	4 portions	10 portions
Leeks, large	4	10
Butter	50 g	125 g
Cloves of garlic, crushed or chopped	4	10
Chicken stock	250 ml	625 ml
Thyme, sprigs	1	2½
Bay leaves	1	2½
White wine	125 ml	310 ml
Salt and pepper		
Green olives, quartered	50 g	125 g

Energy	Cals	Fat	Sat fat	Carb	Sugar	Protein	Fibre	Sodium
778 kJ	188 kcal	13.2g	7.1g	7.5g	5.5g	5.1g	5.0g	0.7g

1 Trim the leeks and discard any withered leaves.

2 Cut the leeks in half lengthways, but keeping them attached at the root. Wash well.

3 Blanch the leeks in boiling water for 2 minutes, then refresh.

4 Melt the butter in a suitable pan. Sweat the garlic.

5 Place the leeks in the pan; add all other ingredients except the olives. The chicken stock should almost cover the leeks. Season.

6 Bring to the boil and cover.

7 Place in a moderate oven at 180 °C for approximately 20 minutes.

8 When cooked, remove the thyme and bay leaf, and add the olives.

9 Serve as a vegetable or as a garnish to accompany roast meats, fish or pasta.

Note

After blanching the leeks it may be necessary to fold them in half before braising.

Variation

- Leeks may also be boiled in salted water for approximately 10–15 minutes.
- Leeks may be served with a cream sauce, parsley sauce or a cheese sauce.
- Coat the leeks with a red wine sauce, sometimes garnished with mushrooms.

Flower heads

15 Broccoli

1 Cook in lightly salted water, or steam.

1 kg of raw broccoli yields approximately 8 portions.

Because of their size, green and purple broccoli need less cooking time than cauliflower. Broccoli is usually broken down into florets and, as such, requires very little cooking: once brought to the boil, 1–2 minutes should be sufficient. This leaves the broccoli slightly crisp. Tenderstem broccoli is increasingly popular. It has long, slim, evenly sized stems and small flower heads, so it cooks quickly. The distinctive flavour is similar to asparagus. Green and purple varieties are available, and, because of the uniform shape, they can be presented very attractively.

Energy	Cals	Fat	Sat fat	Carb	Sugar	Protein	Fibre	Sodium
125 kJ	30 kcal	1.0g	0.3g	1.4g	1.1g	3.9g	4.6g	0.2g

16 Cauliflower (*chou-fleur nature*)

Variation
- **Boiled or steamed cauliflower** may be served with 250 ml of cream sauce, 100 g of melted butter or 125 ml of hollandaise sauce. Serve the sauce in a sauceboat.
- **Buttered cauliflower** is brushed with 25–50 g melted butter before serving and can be sprinkled with chopped parsley.
- **Fried cauliflower**: cut the cooked cauliflower into four portions then lightly colour on all sides in 25–50 g butter.

Video: boiling vegetables http://bit.ly/ 1E6f57O

Energy	Cals	Fat	Sat fat	Carb	Sugar	Protein	Fibre
142 kJ	34 kcal	0.9g	0.2g	3.0g	2.5g	3.6g	1.8g

Using no additions.

Allow one medium-sized cauliflower for four portions.

1 Trim the stem and remove the outer leaves.

2 Hollow out the stem with a peeler or cut into florets. Wash.

3 Cook in lightly salted boiling water, or steam, for approximately 10–15 minutes. Do not overcook (if cut into florets, cook for only 3–5 minutes).

4 Drain well and serve cut into four even portions.

17 Cauliflower au gratin

1 Cut the cooked cauliflower into four.

2 Reheat in a pan of hot salted water (*chauffant*), or reheat in butter in a suitable pan.

3 Place in vegetable dish or on a greased tray.

4 Coat with 250 ml of mornay sauce (see page 85).

5 Sprinkle with grated cheese.

6 Brown under the salamander and serve.

Healthy eating tips
No additional salt is needed as cheese is added.

Energy	Cals	Fat	Sat fat	Carb	Sugar	Protein	Fibre
632 kJ	150 kcal	10.4g	3.9g	8.6g	3.8g	6.3g	2.0g

Fungi

18 Grilled mushrooms (*champignons grillés*)

Ingredient	4 portions	10 portions
Grilling mushrooms (flat mushrooms)	200 g	500 g
Salt, pepper		
Butter, margarine or oil	50 g	125 g

1 Peel the mushrooms, remove the stalks; wash and drain well.

2 Place on a tray and season lightly with salt and pepper.

3 Brush with melted fat or oil and grill on both sides for 3–4 minutes. Serve with picked parsley.

Energy	Cals	Fat	Sat fat	Carb	Sugar	Protein	Fibre
499 kJ	119 kcal	12.8 g	1.7 g	0.0 g	0.0 g	0.9 g	1.3 g

Using sunflower oil.

Healthy eating tips
Use the minimum amount of salt.

19 Stuffed mushrooms (*champignons farcis*)

1 Peel the mushrooms, remove stalks and wash well.

2 Retain 8 or 12 of the best mushrooms (20 to 30 for ten portions). Finely chop the remainder with the well-washed peelings and stalks.

3 Cook the shallots, without colour, in a little fat.

4 Add the chopped mushrooms and cook for 3–4 minutes (duxelle).

5 Grill the mushrooms as in recipe 18.

6 Place the duxelle in the centre of each mushroom.

7 Sprinkle with a few breadcrumbs and some melted butter.

8 Reheat in the oven or under the salamander and serve.

Ingredient	4 portions	10 portions
Grilling mushrooms	300 g	750 g
Shallots, chopped	10 g	25 g
Butter, margarine or oil	50 g	125 g
Breadcrumbs	25 g	60 g

Energy	Cals	Fat	Sat fat	Carb	Sugar	Protein	Fibre
577 kJ	137 kcal	13.1 g	1.8 g	3.2 g	0.3 g	1.9 g	2.1 g

Using sunflower oil.

Healthy eating tips
Use a little unsaturated oil to cook the shallots.

Variation

Mushrooms may be stuffed with ratatouille or a forcemeat.

Seeds and pods

20 Broad beans

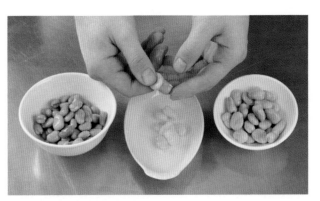

Remove the inner shells of broad beans

Energy	Cals	Fat	Sat fat	Carb	Sugar	Protein	Fibre
344 kJ	81 kcal	0.6g	0.1g	5.0g	0.4g	7.9g	6.5g

100g portion.

0.5kg will yield about 2 portions.

1 Shell the beans and cook in boiling salted water for 10–15 minutes until tender. Do not overcook.

2 If the inner shells are tough, remove before serving.

Professional tip

The modern technique is to take the beans out of their pod and outer skin before serving – this reveals the bright green, tender beans.

Variation

Try:
- brushing with butter
- brushing with butter then sprinkling with chopped parsley
- binding with 500ml cream sauce or fresh cream.

21 Mangetout

0.5kg of mangetout will yield 4–6 portions.

1 Top and tail, wash and drain.

2 Cook in boiling salted water for 2–3 minutes, until slightly crisp.

3 Serve whole, brushed with butter.

Video: boiling vegetables http://bit.ly/ 1E6f57O

Energy	Cals	Fat	Sat fat	Carb	Sugar	Protein	Fibre	Sodium
94 kJ	22 kcal	0.1g	0.0g	2.8g	2.4g	3.1g	0.0g	0.0g

22 French beans (*haricots verts*)

0.5 kg will yield 3–4 portions.

1 Top and tail the beans, carefully and economically.
2 Using a large sharp knife cut the beans into strips 5 cm × 3 mm.
3 Wash.
4 Cook in lightly salted boiling water, or steam, for 5–10 minutes, until tender.
5 Do not overcook. Drain well and serve.

Energy	Cals	Fat	Sat fat	Carb	Sugar	Protein	Fibre
646 kJ	154 kcal	2.9g	0.5g	28.5g	2.1g	5.1g	5.9g

Variation

Variations include:
- brushing the beans with butter
- gently tossing the cooked beans in butter over heat without colour
- combining 400 g cooked French beans with 50 g shallow-fried onions
- combining 400 g cooked French beans with 100 g cooked flageolet beans.

23 French-style peas (*petit pois à la française*)

Ingredient	4 portions	10 portions
Peas (in the pod)	1 kg	2.5 kg
Spring or button onions	12	40
Lettuce, small	1	2–3
Butter	25g	60g
Salt		
Caster sugar	½ tsp	1 tsp
Flour	5g	12g

Energy	Cals	Fat	Sat fat	Carb	Sugar	Protein	Fibre
515 kJ	123 kcal	5.6g	3.4g	12.9g	5.8g	5.9g	5.7g

1 Shell and wash the peas and place in a sauteuse.
2 Peel and wash the onions, shred the lettuce and add to the peas with half the butter, a little salt and the sugar.
3 Barely cover with water. Cover with a lid and cook steadily, preferably in the oven, until tender.
4 Correct the seasoning.
5 Mix the remaining butter with the flour, making a *beurre manié*, and place it into the boiling peas in small pieces until thoroughly mixed; serve.

When using frozen peas, allow the onions to almost cook before adding the peas.

Shell the peas and discard the pods

Place the prepared ingredients into the sauteuse

Add a *beurre manié* at the end of the cooking time

24 Corn on the cob

Allow 1 cob per portion.

1 Trim the stem.

2 Cook in lightly salted boiling water for 10–20 minutes or until the corn is tender. Do not overcook.

3 Remove the outer leaves and fibres.

4 Serve with a sauceboat of melted butter.

Creamed sweetcorn can be made by removing the corn from the cooked cobs, draining well and binding lightly with cream (fresh or non-dairy), béchamel sauce or yoghurt.

Energy	Cals	Fat	Sat fat	Carb	Sugar	Protein	Fibre
646 kJ	154 kcal	2.9g	0.5g	28.5g	2.1g	5.1g	5.9g

25 Okra in cream sauce

1 Top and tail the okra.

2 Blanch in lightly salted boiling water, or steam; drain.

3 Sweat in the margarine or butter for 5–10 minutes, or until tender.

4 Carefully add the cream sauce.

5 Bring to the boil, correct the seasoning and serve in a suitable dish.

Okra may also be served brushed with butter or sprinkled with chopped parsley.

Professional tip

Okra can become glutinous (slimy) when it is cooked in a sauce. To avoid this, wash the okra and let them dry before cooking.

Ingredient	4 portions	10 portions
Okra ('ladies' fingers')	400g	1.25kg
Butter or margarine	50g	125g
Cream sauce	250ml	625ml

Energy	Cals	Fat	Sat fat	Carb	Sugar	Protein	Fibre
928kJ	221kcal	20.2g	9.8g	5.7g	5.7g	4.4g	3.2g

Using hard margarine.

Healthy eating tips
- Use a little unsaturated oil to sweat the okra.
- Try using half cream sauce and half yoghurt, adding very little salt.

26 Okra curry

Ingredient	4 portions	10 portions
Okra, small	450g	1.15kg
Vegetable oil	2 tbsp	5 tbsp
Cumin seeds	2 tsp	5 tsp
Onions, finely chopped	110g	275g
Mild curry paste	1 tbsp	2½ tbsp
Tomatoes, medium, skinned, deseeded, finely chopped	3	8
Fresh coriander, chopped	1 tbsp	2½ tbsp
Red pepper, diced	½	1¼
Green pepper, diced	½	1¼
Fresh red chillies, finely sliced	2	5
Brown sugar	1 tbsp	2½ tbsp
Salt, to taste		

Energy	Cals	Fat	Sat fat	Carb	Sugar	Protein	Fibre	Sodium
722kJ	173kcal	10.4g	1.1g	16.3g	14.3g	5.3g	8.2g	0.3g

1 Very carefully and lightly wash the okra. Pat dry and leave intact.

2 Heat the oil in a wok or frying pan to a medium heat, add the cumin seeds and fry for 30 seconds.

3 Add the onion and curry paste and stir-fry for 5 minutes.

4 Add the tomato, coriander, peppers, chillies and sugar, and continue to stir-fry for 5 minutes.

5 While stir-frying, trim the okra to remove the tops and tails.

6 Add the trimmed okra to the other ingredients and gently stir-fry until cooked through (approximately 3–4 minutes).

7 Season and serve.

Tubers

27 Plain boiled potatoes (*pommes nature*)

1 Wash, peel and rewash the potatoes.

2 Cut or turn into even-sized pieces, allowing 2–3 pieces per portion.

3 Cook carefully in lightly salted water for approximately 20 minutes.

4 Drain well and serve.

Energy	Cals	Fat	Sat fat	Carb	Sugar	Protein	Fibre
487 kJ	116 kcal	0.1 g	0.0 g	28.6 g	0.6 g	2.0 g	1.5 g

Using old potatoes.

28 Parsley potatoes (*pommes persillées*)

1 Wash, peel and rewash the potatoes.

2 Cut or turn into even-sized pieces, allowing 2–3 pieces per portion.

3 Cook carefully in lightly salted water for approximately 20 minutes.

4 Drain well. Brush with melted butter and sprinkle with chopped parsley.

Energy	Cals	Fat	Sat fat	Carb	Sugar	Protein	Fibre
798 kJ	190 kcal	8.3 g	5.2 g	28.6 g	0.6 g	2.1 g	1.5 g

Using old potatoes and 10 g butter per portion.

29 New potatoes (*pommes nouvelles*)

Method 1

1 Wash the potatoes, and boil or steam in their jackets until cooked.

2 Cool slightly, peel while warm and place in a pan of cold water.

3 When required for service add a little salt and a bunch of mint to the potatoes; heat through slowly.

4 Drain well; serve brushed with melted butter and sprinkled with chopped mint, or decorate with blanched, refreshed mint leaves.

Method 2

1 Scrape the potatoes and wash well.

2 Place in a pan of lightly salted boiling water with a bunch of mint and boil gently until cooked (about 20 minutes). Serve as above.

Energy	Cals	Fat	Sat fat	Carb	Sugar	Protein	Fibre
383 kJ	91 kcal	0.1g	0.0g	22.0g	0.8g	1.9g	2.4g

Note

The starch cells of new potatoes are immature; to help break down these cells new potatoes are cooked in water that is already boiling. This also helps to preserve vitamin C (ascorbic acid) in the potatoes.

30 Mashed potatoes (*pommes purées*)

Ingredient	4 portions	10 portions
Floury potatoes	0.5 kg	1.25 kg
Butter	25 g	60 g
Milk, warm	30 ml	85 ml

Energy	Cals	Fat	Sat fat	Carb	Sugar	Protein	Fibre
763 kJ	182 kcal	7.1 g	4.4 g	29.0 g	1.1 g	2.4 g	1.5 g

Using old potatoes, butter and whole milk.

1 Wash, peel and rewash the potatoes. Cut to an even size.

2 Cook in lightly salted water, or steam.

3 Drain off the water, cover and return to a low heat to dry out the potatoes.

4 Pass through a medium sieve or a ricer.

5 Return the potatoes to a clean pan.

6 Add the butter and mix in with a wooden spoon.

7 Gradually add warm milk, stirring continuously until a smooth creamy consistency is reached.

8 Correct the seasoning and serve.

Professional tip

Drain the potatoes as soon as they are cooked. If they are left standing in water, they will become too wet and spoil the texture of the dish.

Healthy eating tips
- Add a minimum amount of salt.
- Add a little olive oil in place of the butter, and use semi-skimmed milk.

Variation

Try:
- dressing in a serving dish and surrounding with a cordon of fresh cream
- placing in a serving dish, sprinkling with grated cheese and melted butter, and browning under a salamander
- adding 50 g diced cooked lean ham, 25 g diced red pepper and chopped parsley
- adding lightly sweated chopped spring onions
- using a good-quality olive oil in place of butter
- adding a little garlic juice (use a garlic press)
- adding a little fresh chopped rosemary or chives
- mixing with equal quantities of parsnip
- adding a little freshly grated horseradish or horseradish cream.

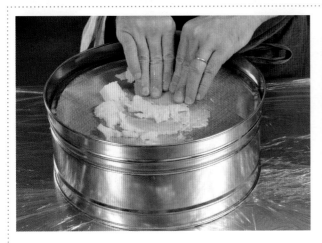

Pass the cooked potato through a sieve

Add milk to the potatoes and combine

31 Duchess potatoes

Ingredient	4 portions	10 portions
Floury potatoes	600 g	1.5 kg
Egg yolks	1	3
Butter	25 g	60 g
Salt, pepper		

Energy	Cals	Fat	Sat fat	Carb	Sugar	Protein	Fibre
819 kJ	195 kcal	8.2 g	3.3 g	28.6 g	0.6 g	3.5 g	1.5 g

Using old potatoes, whole milk, hard margarine.

1 Wash, peel and rewash the potatoes. Cut to an even size.

2 Cook in lightly salted water.

3 Drain off the water, cover and return to a low heat to dry out the potatoes.

4 Pass through a medium sieve or a special potato ricer or mouli.

5 Place the potatoes in a clean pan.

6 Add the egg yolks and stir in vigorously with a kitchen spoon.

7 Mix in the butter. Correct the seasoning.

8 Place in a piping bag with a large star tube and pipe out into neat spirals, about 2 cm in diameter and 5 cm tall, on to a lightly greased baking sheet.

9 Place in a hot oven at 230 °C for 2–3 minutes in order to firm the edges slightly.

10 Remove from the oven and brush with egg wash.

11 Brown lightly in a hot oven or under the salamander.

Note

At step 3, it is important to return the drained potatoes to the heat, so that they are as dry as possible.

Add egg yolks to the mashed potato

Pipe the potato into neat spirals, ready for baking

32 Steamed potatoes in their jackets (*pommes vapeur*)

Energy	Cals	Fat	Sat fat	Carb	Sugar	Protein	Fibre	Sodium
424 kJ	150 kcal	0.3g	0.0g	23.1g	0.8g	2.7g	2.3g	0.1g

1 Wash the potatoes well.

2 Place the potatoes into a steamer tray, sprinkle with salt and steam until tender.

3 When steaming new potatoes, add some sprigs of mint.

4 Drain before serving or peeling for sauté.

Professional tip

- Choose the most suitable varieties for steaming: Saxon, Nadine, Estima, Maris Piper or Desiree. Steaming retains more flavour than boiling.
- Always choose evenly sized potatoes so that they will cook in the same amount of time.
- If the potato is going to be cooked further, e.g. sauté, it is best to leave the skin on during steaming. The skin will protect the flesh of the potato from the steam.

33 Baked jacket potatoes (*pommes au four*)

Energy	Cals	Fat	Sat fat	Carb	Sugar	Protein	Fibre
401 kJ	94 kcal	0.2g	0.0g	21.8g	0.9g	2.7g	1.6g

Using medium potato, 180g analysis given per potato.

1 Select good-sized potatoes; allow 1 potato per portion.

2 Scrub well and make a 2 mm-deep incision round the potato.

3 Place the potato, on a small mound of ground (sea) salt to help keep the base dry, on a tray in a hot oven at 230–250 °C for about 1 hour. Turn the potatoes over after 30 minutes.

4 Test by holding the potato in a cloth and squeezing gently; if cooked it should feel soft.

Healthy eating tips

- Potatoes can be baked without sea salt.
- Fillings based on vegetables with little or no cheese or meat make a healthy snack meal.

Professional tip

Lightly scoring the potatoes will help to make sure that they cook evenly.

The potatoes can also be microwaved. Prick the skins first. Cook on full power for 5 minutes per potato. Wrap in foil and leave to rest for 3 minutes.

Variation

Split and filled with any of the following: grated cheese, minced beef or chicken, baked beans, chilli con carne, cream cheese and chives, mushrooms, bacon, ratatouille, prawns in mayonnaise, coleslaw, and so on.

The cooked potatoes can also be cut in halves lengthwise, the potato spooned out from the skins, seasoned, mashed with butter, returned to the skins, sprinkled with grated cheese and reheated in an oven or under the grill.

34 Roast potatoes (*pommes rôties*)

1 Wash, peel and rewash the potatoes.
2 Cut into even-sized pieces (allow 3–4 pieces per portion).
3 Heat a good measure of oil or dripping in a roasting tray.
4 Add the well-dried potatoes and lightly brown on all sides.
5 Season lightly with salt and cook for about 1 hour in a hot oven at 230–250 °C.
6 Turn the potatoes over after 30 minutes.
7 Cook to a golden brown. Drain and serve.

Professional tip

Roast potatoes can be parboiled for 10 minutes, refreshed and well dried before roasting. This will cut down on the cooking time and can also give a crisper potato.

Energy	Cals	Fat	Sat fat	Carb	Sugar	Protein	Fibre
956 kJ	228 kcal	7.0g	1.1g	39.6g	0.9g	4.1g	1.5g

Using old potatoes and peanut oil for 1 portion (125 g raw potato).

Healthy eating tips
- Brush the potatoes with peanut or sunflower oil, with only a little in the roasting tray.
- Drain off all the fat when cooked.

35 Chateau potatoes

1 Select small, even-sized potatoes and wash them.
2 Turn the potatoes into barrel-shaped pieces about the same size as fondant potatoes (recipe 43).
3 Place in a saucepan of boiling water for 2–3 minutes, then refresh immediately. Drain in a colander.
4 Finish as for roast potatoes. Use a non-stick tray, lightly oiled greaseproof paper or non-stick mat for the roasting.

Energy	Cals	Fat	Sat fat	Carb	Sugar	Protein	Fibre	Sodium
839 kJ	200 kcal	5.9g	0.7g	34.4g	1.2g	4.2g	3.5g	0.0g

36 Fried or chipped potatoes

Energy	Cals	Fat	Sat fat	Carb	Sugar	Protein	Fibre
1,541 kJ	367 kcal	15.8 g	2.8 g	54.1 g	0.0 g	5.5 g	1.5 g

Using old potatoes and peanut oil.

1 Prepare and wash the potatoes.

2 Cut into slices 1 cm thick and 5 cm long.

3 Cut the slices into strips 5 × 1 × 1 cm.

4 Wash well and dry in a cloth.

5 Cook in a frying basket without colour in moderately hot oil (165 °C).

6 Drain and place on kitchen paper on trays until required.

7 When required, place in a frying basket and cook in hot oil (185 °C) until crisp and golden.

8 Drain well, season lightly with salt and serve.

Note

Because chips are so popular, the following advice from the Potato Marketing Board is useful.

● Cook chips in small quantities; this will allow the oil to regain its temperature more quickly; chips will then cook faster and absorb less fat.

● Do not let the temperature of the oil exceed 199 °C as this will accelerate the fat breakdown.

● Use oils high in polyunsaturates for a healthier chip.

● Ideally use a separate fryer for chips and ensure that it has the capacity to raise the fat temperature rapidly to the correct degree when frying chilled or frozen chips.

● Although the majority of chipped potatoes are purchased frozen, the Potato Marketing Board recommends the following potatoes for those who prefer to make their own chips: Maris Piper, Cara and Desiree. King Edward and Santé are also good choices.

Healthy eating tips

● Chipped potatoes may be blanched twice, first at 140 °C, followed by a re-blanch at 160 °C until lightly coloured.

● Blanch in a steamer until just cooked, drain and dry well – final temperature 165 °C.

37 Sauté potatoes

1 Select medium even-sized potatoes. Scrub well.

2 Plain boil or cook in the steamer. Cool slightly and peel.

3 Cut into 3 mm slices.

4 Toss in hot shallow oil in a frying pan until lightly coloured; season lightly with salt.

5 Serve sprinkled with chopped parsley.

Maris piper or Cara potatoes are good varieties for this dish.

Energy	Cals	Fat	Sat fat	Carb	Sugar	Protein	Fibre
1,249 kJ	297 kcal	11.4g	1.3g	46.8g	0.4g	4.9g	1.7g

Using old potatoes and sunflower oil.

Healthy eating tips
- Use a little hot sunflower oil to fry the potatoes.
- Add little or no salt; the customer can add more if required.

Cut the potatoes into 3 mm slices

Toss the slices in hot oil to cook (sauté)

38 Sauté potatoes with onions (*pommes lyonnaise*)

Allow 0.25 kg onion to 0.5 kg potatoes.

1 Shallow-fry the onions slowly in 25–50 g oil, turning frequently, until tender and nicely browned; season lightly with salt.

2 Prepare sauté potatoes as for recipe 37.

3 Combine the two and toss together.

4 Serve as for sauté potatoes.

Energy	Cals	Fat	Sat fat	Carb	Sugar	Protein	Fibre	Sodium
1,098 kJ	261 kcal	9.4g	1.1g	41.5g	6.4g	5.4g	5.3g	0.3g

Finely slice the onions

Sauté the potatoes and onions together

39 New potato rissoles (*pommes nouvelles rissolées*)

1 Boil or steam new potatoes, then drain them.
2 Fry to a golden brown in oil or butter, or a combination of both.

Energy	Cals	Fat	Sat fat	Carb	Sugar	Protein	Fibre
610 kJ	145 kcal	6.1 g	1.1 g	22.0 g	0.8 g	1.9 g	2.4 g

40 Parmentier potatoes

0.5 kg will yield 2–3 portions.

1 Select medium to large potatoes.
2 Wash, peel and rewash.
3 Trim on three sides and cut into 1 cm slices.
4 Cut the slices into 1 cm strips.
5 Cut the strips into 1 cm dice.
6 Wash well and dry in a cloth.
7 Cook in hot shallow oil in a frying pan until golden brown.
8 Drain, season lightly and serve sprinkled with chopped parsley (optional).

Energy	Cals	Fat	Sat fat	Carb	Sugar	Protein	Fibre
1,819 kJ	433 kcal	33.5 g	6.3 g	32.8 g	0.7 g	2.3 g	1.7 g

Using peanut oil.

41 Noisette potatoes (*pommes noisettes*)

0.5 kg will yield two portions.

1 Wash, peel and rewash the potatoes.

2 Scoop out balls with a noisette spoon. Blanch the balls in boiling water.

3 Cook in a little oil in a sauté pan or frying pan. Colour on top of the stove and finish cooking in the oven at 230–250 °C.

Energy	Cals	Fat	Sat fat	Carb	Sugar	Protein	Fibre	Sodium
993 kJ	236 kcal	6.3g	0.7g	42.0g	1.5g	5.1g	3.4g	0.0g

Using 1 tbsp of vegetable oil.

42 Cocotte potatoes (*pommes cocotte*)

1 Proceed as for chateau potatoes (recipe 35), but with the potatoes a quarter the size.

2 Cook in a sauté pan or frying pan.

Energy	Cals	Fat	Sat fat	Carb	Sugar	Protein	Fibre	Sodium
839 kJ	200 kcal	5.9g	0.7g	34.4g	1.2g	4.2g	3.5g	0.0g

43 Fondant potatoes

Energy	Cals	Fat	Sat fat	Carb	Sugar	Protein	Fibre
956 kJ	228 kcal	7.0g	2.1g	39.6g	0.9g	4.1g	1.5g

Using old potatoes and hard margarine for 1 portion (125g raw potato).

Professional tip

To give the potatoes a good glaze, use a high-quality stock and baste during cooking.

Video: making fondant potatoes http://bit.ly/1ASKJEX

1 Select small or even-sized medium potatoes.

2 Wash, peel and rewash.

3 Turn into 8-sided barrel shapes, allowing 2–3 per portion, about 5cm long, end diameter 1.5cm, centre diameter 2.5cm.

4 Brush with melted butter or oil.

5 Place in a pan suitable for the oven.

6 Half cover with white stock, season lightly with salt and pepper.

7 Cook in a hot oven at 230–250°C, brushing the potatoes frequently with melted butter or oil.

8 When cooked, the stock should be completely absorbed by the potatoes.

9 Brush with melted butter or oil and serve.

Variation

Fondant potatoes can be lightly sprinkled with:
- thyme, rosemary or oregano (or this can be added to the stock)
- grated cheese (Gruyère and Parmesan or Cheddar)
- chicken stock in place of white stock.

Healthy eating tips
- Use a little unsaturated oil to brush over the potatoes before and after cooking.
- No added salt is needed; rely on the stock for flavour.

Turn the potatoes into barrel shapes

Place in a pan, half covered with stock, to cook

44 Savoury potatoes (*pommes boulangères*)

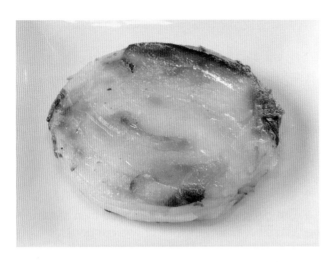

Energy	Cals	Fat	Sat fat	Carb	Sugar	Protein	Fibre
595 kJ	142 kcal	5.3 g	2.2 g	22.3 g	1.8 g	2.8 g	2.4 g

Using 25 g hard margarine (using 50 g hard margarine: 787 kJ/187 kcal energy, 10.3 g fat, 4.4 g saturated fat, 22.3 g carbohydrates, 1.8 g sugar, 2.8 g protein and 2.4 g fibre).

Ingredient	4 portions	10 portions
Potatoes	400 g	1 kg
Onions	100 g	250 g
Salt, pepper		
White stock	125 ml	310 ml
Butter or oil	25–50 g	60–125 g
Parsley, chopped		

Healthy eating tips

- Use an unsaturated oil.
- Add the minimum amount of salt; the stock provides flavour.
- This dish can be used to accompany fattier meat dishes and will help to dilute the fat.

1 Cut the potatoes into 2 mm slices on a mandolin. Set aside the best slices to use for the top.
2 Peel, halve and finely slice the onions.
3 Mix the onions and potatoes together and season lightly with salt and pepper.
4 Place in a well-buttered shallow earthenware dish or roasting tin.
5 Barely cover with stock.
6 Neatly arrange overlapping slices of potato on top.
7 Brush lightly with oil.
8 Place in a hot oven at 230–250 °C for 20 minutes until lightly coloured.
9 Reduce the heat and allow to cook steadily, pressing down firmly from time to time with a flat-bottomed pan.
10 All of the stock should be cooked into the potato when it is ready. Allow approximately 1½ hours cooking time in all.
11 Serve sprinkled with chopped parsley. If cooked in an earthenware dish, clean the edges of the dish with a cloth dipped in salt, and serve in the dish.

Variation

This potato dish can be cooked under a joint of lamb (shoulder or leg). Place an oven rack with the meat on above the potatoes for the final 1½ hours of cooking. The juices from the meat will baste the potatoes as it cooks, then serve the lamb on top of the potato if the style of the restaurant dictates.

Leeks can be used in place of onions for variety.

45 Macaire potatoes (potato cakes, *pommes Macaire*)

Energy	Cals	Fat	Sat fat	Carb	Sugar	Protein	Fibre
4,392 kJ	1,047 kcal	65.7 g	14.7 g	109.8 g	2.7 g	11.4 g	10.8 g

Using hard margarine and sunflower oil.

0.5 kg will yield 2–3 portions.

1 Prepare and cook as for baked jacket potatoes (recipe 33).

2 Cut in halves, remove the centre with a spoon, and place in a basin.

3 Add 25 g butter per 0.5 kg, a little salt and milled pepper.

4 Mash and mix as lightly as possible with a fork.

5 Using a little flour, mould into a roll, then divide into pieces, allowing one or two per portion.

6 Mould into 2 cm round cakes. Quadrille with the back of a palette knife. Flour lightly.

7 Shallow-fry on both sides in very hot oil and serve.

Professional tip

Make sure the potato mixture is firm enough to be shaped, and fry the cakes in very hot oil, or they will lose their shape.

Variation

Additions to potato cakes can include:
- chopped parsley, fresh herbs or chives, or duxelle
- cooked chopped onion
- grated cheese.

Place the potatoes on a baking tray with salt

Once baked, cut in half and scoop out the centre

Mould the potato into cakes

46 Byron potatoes (*pommes Byron*)

1 Prepare and cook as for Macaire potatoes (recipe 45).

2 Using the back of a dessertspoon make a shallow impression on each potato.

3 Carefully sprinkle the centres with grated cheese. Make sure no cheese is on the edge of the potato.

4 Cover the cheese with cream.

5 Brown lightly under the salamander and serve.

Note

This is a classical variation on Macaire potatoes.

Energy	Cals	Fat	Sat fat	Carb	Sugar	Protein	Fibre
2,099 kJ	505 kcal	39.0g	18.7g	33.4g	1.8g	7.1g	2.4g

Analysis given per potato, using 1 tbsp each of cheese and double cream per person.

47 Swiss potato cakes (*rösti*)

1 Parboil in salted water (or steam) for approximately 5 minutes.

2 Cool, then shred into large flakes on a grater.

3 Heat the oil or butter in a frying pan.

4 Add the potatoes, and season lightly with salt and pepper.

5 Press the potato together and cook on both sides until brown and crisp.

Note

The potato can be made in a 4-portion cake or into individual rounds.

Ingredient	4 portions	10 portions
Potatoes, unpeeled	400g	1 kg
Oil or butter	50g	125g
Salt, pepper		

Energy	Cals	Fat	Sat fat	Carb	Sugar	Protein	Fibre
700 kJ	168 kcal	10.5g	6.5g	17.3g	0.7g	2.2g	1.3g

Using butter.

Healthy eating tips
- Lightly oil a well-seasoned pan with sunflower oil to fry the rösti.
- Use the minimum amount of salt.

Variation
- The potato cakes may also be made from raw potatoes.
- Add sweated chopped onion.
- Add sweated lardons of bacon.
- Use two parts of grated potato to one part grated apple.

Shred the parboiled potatoes on a grater

Press into shape in the frying pan

Turn out carefully after cooking

48 Croquette potatoes

1 Use a duchess mixture (see recipe 31) moulded into cylinder shapes 5 × 2 cm.

2 Pass through flour, egg wash and breadcrumbs. Chill.

3 Reshape with a palette knife and chill. Deep fry in hot deep oil (185 °C) in a frying basket.

4 When the potatoes are a golden colour, drain well and serve.

Energy	Cals	Fat	Sat fat	Carb	Sugar	Protein	Fibre
1,699 kJ	405 kcal	25.4g	6.6g	40.8g	1.1g	6.0g	2.2g

Healthy eating tips
- Add the minimum amount of salt.
- Use peanut or sunflower oil to fry the croquettes, and drain on kitchen paper.

49 Potatoes cooked in milk with cheese

Ingredient	4 portions	10 portions
Potatoes	500 g	1.25 kg
Milk	250 ml	625 ml
Salt and pepper		
Grated cheese	50 g	125 g

1 Slice the peeled potatoes to 0.5 cm thick.

2 Place in an ovenproof dish and just cover with milk.

3 Season, sprinkle with grated cheese and cook in a moderate oven (190 °C) until the potatoes are cooked and golden brown.

Energy	Cals	Fat	Sat fat	Carb	Sugar	Protein	Fibre	Sodium
734 kJ	174 kcal	5.6g	3.4g	24.0g	3.7g	8.0g	1.8g	0.4g

50 Potatoes with bacon and onions

Ingredient	4 portions	10 portions
Potatoes, peeled	400 g	1.25 kg
Streaky bacon (lardons)	100 g	250 g
Button onions	100 g	250 g
White stock	250 ml	625 ml
Salt, pepper		
Parsley, chopped		

Energy	Cals	Fat	Sat fat	Carb	Sugar	Protein	Fibre
836 kJ	199 kcal	10.1 g	3.8 g	22.2 g	1.8 g	6.4 g	2.5 g

Using old potatoes.

1 Cut the potatoes into 1 cm dice.

2 Cut the bacon into 0.5 cm lardons; lightly fry in a little fat together with the onions and brown lightly.

3 Add the potatoes, half cover with stock, season lightly with salt and pepper. Cover with a lid and cook steadily in the oven at 230–250 °C for approximately 30 minutes.

4 Correct the seasoning, serve in a vegetable dish, sprinkled with chopped parsley.

Healthy eating tips
● Dry-fry the bacon in a well-seasoned pan and drain off any excess fat.
● Add little or no salt.

51 Delmonico potatoes

1 Wash, peel and rewash the potatoes.

2 Cut into 6 mm dice.

3 Barely cover with milk, season lightly with salt and pepper and allow to cook for 30–40 minutes.

4 Place in an earthenware dish, sprinkle with breadcrumbs and melted butter, brown in the oven or under the salamander and serve.

Energy	Cals	Fat	Sat fat	Carb	Sugar	Protein	Fibre
900 kJ	214 kcal	6.3 g	3.7 g	37.5 g	2.7 g	4.4 g	2.0 g

Using old potatoes and whole milk.

Dice the potatoes

Place in a dish, barely covered with milk, to cook

After baking, sprinkle with breadcrumbs and gratinate

52 Jerusalem artichokes in cream sauce (*topinambours à la crème*)

1 Wash and peel the artichokes, then rewash. Cut to an even size.

2 Barely cover with water, add a little salt and simmer until tender; do not overcook.

3 Drain well and add 250 ml (600 ml for 10 portions) cream sauce (see page 84).

Note

Cream sauce may be made using skimmed milk and natural yoghurt.

Energy	Cals	Fat	Sat fat	Carb	Sugar	Protein	Fibre	Sodium
641 kJ	141 kcal	5.6g	2.1g	21.4g	5.1g	4.9g	7.1g	0.5g

Healthy eating tips

● Use the minimum amount of salt.
● Try replacing half the cream sauce with natural yoghurt.

Leafy vegetables

53 Spring greens (*choux de printemps*)

0.5 kg will serve 3–4 portions; 1.25 kg will serve 8–10 portions.

Prepare and cook as for cabbage (recipe 56), for 10–15 minutes according to age and type. Do not overcook.

Energy	Cals	Fat	Sat fat	Carb	Sugar	Protein	Fibre	Sodium
103 kJ	25 kcal	0.9 g	0.1 g	2.0 g	1.8 g	2.4 g	4.3 g	0.1 g

54 Leaf spinach (*épinards en branches*)

0.5 kg will yield two portions.

1 Remove the stems and discard them.

2 Wash the leaves carefully in plenty of water, several times if necessary.

3 Cook in lightly salted boiling water for 3–5 minutes; do not overcook.

4 Refresh under cold water, squeeze dry into a ball.

5 When required for service, either reheat and serve plain or place into a pan containing 25–50 g butter, loosen with a fork and reheat quickly without colouring.

Energy	Cals	Fat	Sat fat	Carb	Sugar	Protein	Fibre
512 kJ	123 kcal	10.8 g	6.6 g	1.4 g	1.2 g	5.2 g	6.3 g

Using 25 g butter per 0.5 kg.

55 Spinach purée

Variation

Creamed spinach purée can be made by mixing in 30 ml cream and 60 ml béchamel or natural yoghurt before serving. Serve with a border of cream.

An addition would be 1 cm triangle-shaped croutons fried in butter.

Spinach may also be served with toasted pine kernels or finely chopped garlic.

Energy	Cals	Fat	Sat fat	Carb	Sugar	Protein	Fibre
588 kJ	143 kcal	11.9g	6.7g	3.3g	3.1g	5.7g	4.2g

Using 25 g butter per 0.5 kg.

0.5 kg will yield 2 portions.

1 Remove the stems and discard them.
2 Wash the leaves very carefully in plenty of water, several times if necessary.
3 Wilt for 2–3 minutes, taking care not to overcook.
4 Place on a tray and allow to cool.
5 Pass through a sieve or mouli, or use a food processor.
6 Reheat in 25–50 g butter, mix with a kitchen spoon, correct the seasoning and serve.

56 Cabbage (*chou vert*)

0.5 kg will serve 3–4 portions; 1.25 kg will serve 8–10 portions.

1 Cut the cabbage in quarters.
2 Remove the centre stalk and outside leaves.
3 Shred and wash well.
4 Place into lightly salted boiling water.
5 Boil steadily or steam until cooked (approximately 5–10 minutes, according to age and type). Do not overcook.
6 Drain immediately in a colander and serve.

Energy	Cals	Fat	Sat fat	Carb	Sugar	Protein	Fibre
38 kJ	9 kcal	0.0g	0.0g	1.1g	1.1g	1.3g	2.5g

Note

Overcooking will lessen the vitamin content and also spoil the colour. This applies to cooking any green vegetable.

57 Braised red cabbage (*choux à la flamande*)

1 Quarter, trim and shred the cabbage. Wash well and drain.

2 Season lightly with salt and pepper.

3 Place in a well-buttered casserole or pan suitable for placing in the oven (not aluminium or iron, because these metals will cause a chemical reaction that will discolour the cabbage).

4 Add the peeled and cored apples. Cut into 1 cm dice and sugar.

5 Add the vinegar and bacon (if using), cover with a buttered paper and lid.

6 Cook in a moderate oven at 150–200 °C for 1½ hours.

7 Remove the bacon (if used) and serve.

Energy	Cals	Fat	Sat fat	Carb	Sugar	Protein	Fibre
754 kJ	180 kcal	15.2 g	8.4 g	7.8 g	7.7 g	3.4 g	3.2 g

Ingredient	4 portions	10 portions
Red cabbage	300 g	750 g
Salt, pepper		
Butter	50 g	125 g
Cooking apples, peeled and cored	100 g	250 g
Caster sugar	10 g	25 g
Vinegar or red wine	125 ml	310 ml
Bacon trimmings (optional)	50 g	125 g

Strain off most of the liquid after braising

Variation

Other flavourings include 50 g sultanas, grated zest of one orange, pinch of ground cinnamon.

Healthy eating tips

The fat and salt content will be reduced by omitting the bacon.

58 Brussels sprouts (*choux de bruxelles*)

0.5 kg will serve 3–4 portions; 1.25 kg will serve 8–10 portions.

1 Using a small knife, trim the stems; remove any discoloured outer leaves. Wash well.

2 Cook in lightly salted boiling water, or steam, for 5–10 minutes according to size. Do not overcook.

3 Drain well in a colander and serve.

Note

Brussels sprouts with butter are cooked and served as outlined here, but brushed with 25–50 g melted butter (60–125 g for 10 portions). For Brussels sprouts with chestnuts, to every 400 g of sprouts add 100 g cooked peeled chestnuts.

Energy	Cals	Fat	Sat fat	Carb	Sugar	Protein	Fibre
82 kJ	20 kcal	0.0 g	0.0 g	1.9 g	1.8 g	3.1 g	3.2 g

Stems

59 Artichoke bottoms

1 Cut off the stalk and pull out all the underneath leaves.

2 With a large knife, cut through the artichoke leaving only 1.5 cm at the bottom of the vegetable.

3 With a small, sharp knife, while holding the artichoke upside down, peel carefully, removing all the leaf and any green part, keeping the bottom as smooth as possible. If necessary, smooth with a peeler.

4 Rub immediately with lemon and keep in lemon water or ascorbic acid solution.

5 Using a spoon or the thumb, remove the centre furry part, which is called the choke. The choke is sometimes removed after cooking.

6 Artichoke bottoms should always be cooked in a blanc (see below).

Energy	Cals	Fat	Sat fat	Carb	Sugar	Protein	Fibre	Sodium
100 kJ	23 kcal	0.2 g	0.1 g	4.2 g	1.2 g	2.5 g	0.9 g	0.1 g

Using blanc version 1.

Pull out the stalk of the artichoke

Alternatively, cut the stalk off

Pull off the leaves at the bottom

Peel the artichoke

Remove the choke

Note

Artichoke bases may be served as a vegetable; they are sometimes filled with another vegetable (e.g. peas, spinach). When they are served ungarnished they are usually cut into quarters.

Blanc (version 1)

Ingredient	4 portions	10 portions
Flour	10 g	25 g
Cold water	0.5 litres	1.25 litre
Salt, to taste		
Lemon, juice of	½	1¼

1 Mix the flour and water together.
2 Add the salt and lemon juice. Pass through a strainer.
3 Place in a pan, bring to the boil, stirring continuously.

Blanc (version 2)

Ingredient	4 portions	10 portions
Water	0.5 litres	1.25 litres
Vitamin C (ascorbic acid) tablets	2	5
Oil	30 ml	75 ml
Salt		

1 Combine the ingredients.

Healthy eating tips
● Use the minimum amount of salt.

389

60 Globe artichokes

Energy	Cals	Fat	Sat fat	Carb	Sugar	Protein	Fibre
32 kJ	8 kcal	0.0g	0.0g	1.4g	1.4g	0.6g	0.0g

Not including sauce.

Allow 1 artichoke per portion.

1 Cut off the stems close to the leaves.

2 Cut off about 2 cm across the tops of the leaves.

3 Trim the remainder of the leaves with scissors or a small knife.

4 Place a slice of lemon at the bottom of each artichoke.

5 Secure with string.

6 Simmer in gently boiling, lightly salted water (to which a little ascorbic acid – one vitamin C tablet – may be added) until the bottom is tender (20–30 minutes).

7 Refresh under running water until cold.

8 Remove the centre of the artichoke carefully.

9 Scrape away all the furry inside (the choke) and leave clean.

10 Replace the centre, upside down.

11 Reheat by placing in a pan of boiling salted water for 3–4 minutes.

12 Drain and serve accompanied by a suitable sauce.

Artichokes may also be served cold with vinaigrette sauce.

> **Professional tip**
>
> Do not cook artichokes in an iron or aluminium pan because these metals cause a chemical reaction that will discolour them.

61 Asparagus points or tips

Energy	Cals	Fat	Sat fat	Carb	Sugar	Protein	Fibre	Sodium
124 kJ	29 kcal	0.9g	0.1g	1.6g	1.6g	3.5g	1.6g	0.1g

1 kg of asparagus will yield approximately 8 portions.

1 Using the back of a small knife, carefully remove the tips of the leaves.

2 Scrape the stem, either with the blade of a small knife or a peeler.

3 Wash well. Tie into bundles of about 12 heads.

4 Cut off the excess stem.

5 Cook in lightly salted boiling water for approximately 5–8 minutes.

6 Test if cooked by gently pressing the green part of the stem, which should be tender; do not overcook.

7 Lift carefully out of the water. Remove the string, drain well and serve.

Note

Young thin asparagus, 50 pieces to the bundle, is known as sprew or sprue. It is prepared in the same way as asparagus except that, when it is very thin, the removal of the leaf tips is dispensed with. It may be served as a vegetable, perhaps brushed with butter.

Asparagus tips are also used in numerous garnishes for soups, egg dishes, fish, meat and poultry dishes, cold dishes, salad, and so on.

Professional tip

As the flavour of asparagus is mild and can be leached out very easily through the cooking medium, a method of cookery that ensures that no flavour is lost in the cooking process is microwaving.

1 To microwave, place a piece of cling film over a plate that will fit in the microwave and, more importantly, is microwave safe.

2 Spread the cling film with a little oil and salt, evenly place the asparagus on the plate in a single layer.

3 Cover the plate and asparagus with another piece of cling film, and microwave for 30-second stints until the asparagus is tender; serve immediately.

The benefit of this method is that it retains flavour and colour, and it can be cooked in minutes, as opposed to batch cooking, which will, invariably, cause the asparagus to lose flavour and colour the longer it is stored.

If larger-scale cooking is required, the more traditional method, boiling in lightly salted water, should be used: cooking, say, 100 portions of asparagus in the microwave should be avoided for obvious reasons!

62 Asparagus wrapped in puff pastry with Gruyère

Ingredient	4 portions	10 portions
Gruyère cheese	175 g	440 g
Parmesan, freshly grated	3 tbsp	7½ tbsp
Crème fraiche	250 ml	625 ml
Puff pastry (page 465)	350 g	875 g
Egg wash or milk, for brushing		
Asparagus, freshly cooked	350 g	875 g
Salt, pepper		
Watercress, to garnish		

Energy	Cals	Fat	Sat fat	Carb	Sugar	Protein	Fibre
2,017 kJ	485 kcal	37.7 g	15.0 g	23.4 g	2.5 g	15.9 g	0.8 g

1 Cut the Gruyère cheese into 1 cm dice. In a suitable bowl, mix the Parmesan cheese and crème fraiche; season.

2 Roll out the puff pastry to approximately 0.25 cm thick and cut into squares approximately 18 × 18 cm.

3 Brush the edges with egg wash or milk.

4 Divide the crème fraiche, putting equal amounts on to the centre of each square. Lay the asparagus on top. Place the diced Gruyère cheese firmly between the asparagus.

5 Fold the opposite corners of each square to meet in the centre, like an envelope. Firmly pinch the seams together to seal them. Make a small hole in the centre of each one to allow the steam to escape. Place on a lightly greased baking sheet.

6 Allow to relax for 20 minutes in the refrigerator. Brush with egg wash or milk, sprinkle with Parmesan.

7 Bake in a hot oven at 200 °C for approximately 20–25 minutes until golden brown.

8 Serve garnished with watercress.

Professional tip

Make sure the pastry parcels are well sealed so that the mixture does not escape during cooking.

Healthy eating tips

The puff pastry and cheese make this dish high in fat. Serve with plenty of starchy carbohydrate to dilute it.

63 Braised chicory

Ingredient	4 portions	10 portions
Fish or chicken stock	200 ml	500 ml
Chicory, medium heads	8	20
Fresh lemon juice	3 tbsp	7½ tbsp
Caster sugar	3 tbsp	7½ tbsp
Sea salt and freshly ground black pepper		
Butter	25 g	60 g

Energy	Cals	Fat	Sat fat	Carb	Sugar	Protein	Fibre
476 kJ	114 kcal	6.3 g	3.7 g	17.8 g	13.5 g	1.1 g	1.8 g

1 Have the stock ready and set aside.

2 Trim the chicory of any bruised outside leaves, then trim the ends and use a small, sharp knife to remove the bitter core at the base of each head.

3 Bring a pan of water to the boil and add the lemon juice, 1 tablespoon of the sugar and salt to taste. Blanch the chicory for 8–10 minutes and drain well.

4 Drain all the liquid from the chicory and, in a large frying pan, heat the butter and brown the chicory on all sides; deglaze with a little stock and simmer for a few minutes, basting the chicory at all times.

5 Arrange the heads in a single layer on a platter, sprinkle with the remaining sugar, and season with salt and pepper. Leave to cool for about 10 minutes.

64 Shallow-fried chicory

Ingredient	
Lemon juice	
Sugar	1 tbsp
Salt	
Chicory	
Butter	
Stock	
Nut-brown butter, lemon juice and chopped parsley, to serve	

Energy	Cals	Fat	Sat fat	Carb	Sugar	Protein	Fibre
484 kJ	118 kcal	12.0 g	7.3 g	4.8 g	1.3 g	0.9 g	1.5 g

Using 37.5 g butter.

1 Trim the stem, remove any discoloured leaves, wash.

2 Bring a pan of water to the boil and add the lemon juice, sugar, and salt to taste. Blanch the chicory in this for 8–10 minutes and drain well.

3 Drain all the liquid from the chicory. In a large frying pan, heat the butter and brown the chicory on all sides. Deglaze with a little stock and simmer for a few minutes, basting the chicory at all times.

4 Serve with 10 g per portion nut-brown butter, lemon juice and chopped parsley.

65 Kohlrabi

1 Trim off the stems and leaves – these may be used for soups.
2 Peel thickly at the root end and thinly at the top end. Wash.
3 Cut into even-sized pieces. Young kohlrabi can be cooked whole.
4 Simmer in well-flavoured stock until tender.

Variations
● Serve kohlrabi with cream sauce.
● Kohlrabi may be baked and stuffed.

Note

Kohlrabi is a stem that swells to a turnip shape above the ground. When grown under glass it is pale green in colour; when grown outdoors it is purplish.

Select kohlrabi with tops that are green, young and fresh. If the globes are too large they may be woody and tough.

It can be added to casseroles and stews.

Energy	Cals	Fat	Sat fat	Carb	Sugar	Protein	Fibre
77 kJ	18 kcal	0.2g	0.0g	3.1g	3.0g	1.2g	1.9g

Vegetable fruits

66 Tomato concassé

Ingredient	4 portions	10 portions
Tomatoes	400g	1.25kg
Shallots or onions, chopped	25g	60g
Butter or oil	25g	60g
Salt, pepper		

Energy	Cals	Fat	Sat fat	Carb	Sugar	Protein	Fibre	Sodium
237 kJ	57 kcal	5.3g	3.3g	2.1g	1.9g	0.5g	0.7g	0.3g

Using butter and onions.

1 Plunge the tomatoes into boiling water for 5–10 seconds – the riper the tomatoes, the less time is required. Refresh immediately.

2 Remove the skins, cut in quarters and remove all the seeds.

3 Roughly chop the flesh of the tomatoes.

4 Meanwhile, cook the chopped onion or shallots without colour in the butter or oil.

5 Add the tomatoes and season lightly.

6 Simmer gently on the side of the stove until the moisture is evaporated.

Note

This is a cooked preparation that is usually included in the normal *mise-en-place* of a kitchen as it is used in a great number of dishes.

Uncooked tomato concassée is often used for *mise-en-place*.

Blanch the tomatoes and then peel them

Cut each tomato into quarters

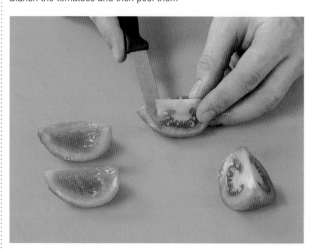
Remove the seeds from each petal

Roughly chop the tomatoes

67 Stuffed tomatoes

1 Wash the tomatoes, remove the eyes.

2 Remove the top quarter of each tomato with a sharp knife.

3 Carefully empty out the seeds without damaging the flesh.

4 Place on a greased baking tray.

5 Cook the shallots in a little butter or oil without colour.

6 Add the washed chopped mushrooms; season with salt and pepper; add the garlic if using. Cook for 2–3 minutes.

7 Add a little of the strained tomato juice, the breadcrumbs and the parsley; mix to a piping consistency. Correct the seasoning. At this stage, several additions may be made (e.g. chopped ham, cooked rice).

8 Place the mixture in a piping bag with a large plain tube and pipe into the tomato shells. Replace the tops.

9 Brush with oil, season lightly with salt and pepper.

10 Cook in a moderate oven at 180–200 °C for 4–5 minutes.

11 Serve garnished with picked parsley or fresh basil or rosemary.

Ingredient	4 portions	10 portions
Tomatoes, medium-sized	8	20
Duxelle		
Shallots, chopped	10 g	25 g
Butter or oil	25 g	60 g
Mushrooms	150 g	375 g
Salt, pepper		
Clove of garlic, crushed (optional)	1	2–3
Breadcrumbs (white or wholemeal)	25 g	60 g
Parsley, chopped		

Energy	Cals	Fat	Sat fat	Carb	Sugar	Protein	Fibre
430 kJ	102 kcal	5.9 g	3.5 g	10.6 g	5.7 g	2.5 g	2.2 g

Healthy eating tips
- Use a small amount of an unsaturated oil to cook the shallots and brush over the stuffed tomatoes.
- Add the minimum amount of salt.
- Adding cooked rice to the stuffing will increase the amount of starchy carbohydrate.

Cut out the eye of the tomato

Slice off the top and remove the seeds from inside

Pipe in the filling and then replace the top

68 Fried aubergine (*aubergine frite*)

Allow half an aubergine per portion.

1 Remove alternate strips with a peeler.
2 Cut into 0.5 cm slices on the slant.
3 Pass through seasoned flour or milk and flour.
4 Shake off all surplus flour.
5 Deep-fry in hot fat at 185 °C. Drain well and serve.

Energy	Cals	Fat	Sat fat	Carb	Sugar	Protein	Fibre
994 kJ	225 kcal	20.0g	3.8g	10.1g	5.9g	1.9g	5.2g

Note

Aubergines may also be shallow-fried, grilled or griddled.

69 Stuffed aubergine

Ingredient	4 portions	10 portions
Aubergines	2	5
Shallots, chopped	10g	25g
Oil or fat, to fry		
Mushrooms	100g	250g
Parsley, chopped		
Tomato concassé	100g	250g
Salt, pepper		
Demi-glace or *jus-lié*	125ml	300ml

Energy	Cals	Fat	Sat fat	Carb	Sugar	Protein	Fibre	Sodium
557 kJ	134 kcal	12.2g	1.5g	4.3g	3.8g	2.4g	4.5g	0.7g

1 Cut the aubergines in two lengthwise.
2 With the point of a small knife, make a cut round the halves approximately 0.5 cm from the edge, then make several cuts 0.5 cm deep in the centre.
3 Deep fry in hot fat at 185 °C for 2–3 minutes; drain well.
4 Scoop out the centre pulp and chop it finely.
5 Cook the shallots in a little oil or fat without colouring.

6 Add the well-washed mushrooms. Cook gently for a few minutes.
7 Mix in the pulp, parsley and tomato; season. Replace in the aubergine skins.
8 Sprinkle with breadcrumbs and melted butter. Brown under the salamander.
9 Serve with a cordon of demi-glace or *jus-lié*.

70 Marrow

1 Peel the marrow with a peeler or small knife.
2 Cut in half lengthwise.
3 Remove the seeds with a spoon.
4 Cut into even pieces, approximately 5 cm square.
5 Cook in lightly salted boiling water, or steam, for 10–15 minutes. Do not overcook.
6 Drain well and serve.

Variation

All the variations for cauliflower (recipes 16 and 17) may be used with marrow.

Energy	Cals	Fat	Sat fat	Carb	Sugar	Protein	Fibre
44 kJ	11 kcal	0.0g	0.0g	2.1g	2.0g	0.6g	0.9g

71 Marrow provençale

Ingredient	4 portions	10 portions
Marrow	400g	1 kg
Onion, chopped	50g	125g
Clove of garlic, chopped	1	2–3
Oil or butter	50g	125g
Salt, pepper		
Tomato concassé	400g	1 kg
Parsley, chopped		

Energy	Cals	Fat	Sat fat	Carb	Sugar	Protein	Fibre
524 kJ	126 kcal	10.6g	6.5g	6.4g	5.7g	1.8g	1.4g

1 Lightly peel the marrow, remove the seeds and cut into 2 cm dice.
2 Cook the onion and garlic in the oil in a pan for 2–3 minutes without colour.
3 Add the marrow and season lightly with salt and pepper.
4 Add the tomato concassé.
5 Cover with a lid and cook gently in the oven or on the side of the stove for 1 hour or until tender.
6 Sprinkle with chopped parsley and serve.

Note

Baby marrows may be served similarly, but reduce the cooking time to 5–10 minutes.

Healthy eating tips
● Use a little unsaturated oil to cook the onion.
● Use the minimum amount of salt.

72 Shallow-fried courgettes

1 Wash. Top and tail, and cut into round slices 3–6 cm thick.

2 Gently fry in hot oil or butter for 2 or 3 minutes, drain and serve.

Energy	Cals	Fat	Sat fat	Carb	Sugar	Protein	Fibre
456 kJ	111 kcal	10.7 g	6.6 g	1.9 g	1.8 g	1.9 g	0.9 g

Using butter.

73 Deep-fried courgettes

1 Wash. Top and tail, and cut into round slices 3–6 cm thick.

2 Pass through flour, or milk and flour, or batter, and deep-fry in hot oil at 185 °C. Drain well and serve.

Energy	Cals	Fat	Sat fat	Carb	Sugar	Protein	Fibre
481 kJ	111 kcal	11.4 g	1.4 g	1.8 g	1.7 g	1.8 g	0.9 g

Using vegetable oil.

Professional tip

Make sure the oil is very hot before adding the courgette. Fry it quickly and drain it before serving.

74 Fettuccine of courgette with chopped basil and balsamic vinegar

Ingredient	4 portions	10 portions
Courgettes, large	2	5
Olive oil	50 ml	125 ml
Olive oil, to finish	20 ml	50 ml
Balsamic vinegar, to finish	20 ml	50 ml
Basil leaves, shredded	2	5

1 Slice the courgettes finely lengthwise, using a mandolin (Japanese slicer).

2 Heat the olive oil in a suitable pan. Sauté the courgette slices quickly without colour for 35 seconds.

3 Place on suitable plates. Drizzle with olive oil and balsamic vinegar, and top with shredded basil leaves.

This may be served as a vegetarian starter or as a garnish for fish and meat dishes.

Energy	Cals	Fat	Sat fat	Carb	Sugar	Protein	Fibre	Sodium
745 kJ	181 kcal	17.9g	2.6g	1.9g	1.8g	1.8g	1.2g	0.0g

75 Courgette flowers

Ingredient	4 portions	10 portions
Flowering courgettes	4	10
Fish mousse (or other mousse, e.g. chicken, veal)	100 g	250 g
Corn oil		
Plain flour for dusting		
Batter		

Energy	Cals	Fat	Sat fat	Carb	Sugar	Protein	Fibre	Sodium
810 kJ	193 kcal	6.6g	1.2g	27.4g	2.2g	7.5g	1.5g	0.0g

1 Gently break off the flowers from the courgettes, ensuring they stay intact.

2 Carefully snap out and discard the stigma from the flowers.

3 Place the fish mousse in a bowl, season lightly and mix.

4 Once the mousse is ready, place into a disposable piping bag.

5 Gently open the courgette flowers a little and pipe in the mousse until the flower is half full.

6 Twist the ends of the petals to seal in the mousse.

7 Place the filled flowers into a steamer or steaming basket over a pan of boiling water.

8 Steam for 2–3 minutes, then carefully immerse into a bowl of iced water to stop the cooking process.

9 Remove from the water, pat dry and store in an airtight container in the fridge for up to 2 hours.

10 Heat the oil for deep-frying to 180°C.

11 Roll the filled courgette flowers in plain flour; shake off the excess.

12 Dip them into batter then place them into the fryer for 1 minute until golden brown.

13 Drain briefly on some kitchen paper and serve.

Courgettes with flowers

76 Roast butternut squash

1 Peel the squash and cut it into thick, even pieces.

2 Place on a lightly oiled roasting tray and roast for approximately 20–25 minutes in a hot oven, until the flesh is soft and golden brown.

Energy	Cals	Fat	Sat fat	Carb	Sugar	Protein	Fibre	Sodium
342 kJ	81 kcal	4.1 g	0.5 g	10.4 g	5.6 g	1.4 g	2.5 g	0.0 g

Using 125 g of squash and 1 tsp vegetable oil per portion.

77 Roast squash or pumpkin with cinnamon and ginger

Ingredient	4 portions	10 portions
Butternut squash or pumpkin	500 g	1.25 kg
Butter or margarine	25 g	60 g
Olive oil	2 tbsp	5 tbsp
Ginger, peeled and freshly chopped	½ tsp	1¼ tsp
Ground cinnamon	½ tsp	1¼ tsp
Salt		
Caster sugar	10 g	25 g
Lemon, juice of	½	1¼

Energy	Cals	Fat	Sat fat	Carb	Sugar	Protein	Fibre	Sodium
519 kJ	125 kcal	11.0g	4.2g	6.0g	5.3g	1.1g	1.7g	0.0g

1 Peel the squash, cut it in half and remove the seeds.

2 Cut the squash into 1.5 cm dice or into small wedges.

3 Place the butter into a suitable roasting pan and heat gently. Add the olive oil, ginger and cinnamon.

4 Add the squash gently and stir until the squash is coated in the spice mixture. Season and add the sugar.

5 Place in an oven at 200 °C until tender and golden brown.

6 When cooked, sprinkle with lemon juice.

Note

Garlic may be added to the spice mixture, and mixed spice may be used in place of cinnamon.

Peel and halve the squash, then remove the seeds

Cut the squash into even pieces

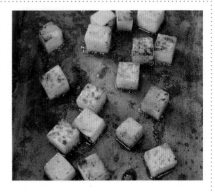

Stir the squash pieces into the warm butter and spices before roasting

78 Stuffed peppers (*piment farci*)

Ingredient	4 portions	10 portions
Red peppers, medium-sized	4	10
Carrots, sliced	50 g	125 g
Onions, sliced	50 g	125 g
Bouquet garni		
White stock	0.5 litres	1.25 litres
Salt, pepper		
Pilaff		
Rice (long grain)	200 g	500 g
Salt, pepper		
Onion, chopped	50 g	125 g
Butter	50 g	125 g

Energy	Cals	Fat	Sat fat	Carb	Sugar	Protein	Fibre
1,291 kJ	308 kcal	11.4 g	6.7 g	48.8 g	5.3 g	5.4 g	3.1 g

1 Place the peppers on a tray in the oven or under the salamander for a few minutes, or deep-fry in hot oil at 180 °C, until the skin blisters.

2 Remove the skin; carefully cut off the top and empty out all the seeds.

3 Stuff with a well-seasoned pilaff of rice (ingredients as listed above), which may be varied by the addition of mushrooms, tomatoes, ham, and so on.

4 Replace the top of the peppers.

5 Place the peppers on the sliced carrot and onion in a pan suitable for the oven; add the bouquet garni, stock and seasoning. Cover with a buttered paper and a lid.

6 Cook in a moderate oven at 180–200 °C for 1 hour or until tender.

7 Serve garnished with picked parsley.

Healthy eating tips
- This dish is low in fat if the peppers are placed in the oven or under the salamander, not deep-fried, and the butter/oil is kept to a minimum.
- Add little or no salt.
- If extra vegetables are added to the rice, and a vegetable stock used, this dish can be a useful vegetarian starter.

Briefly heat the peppers and then peel them

Cut off the top and empty out the seeds

Fill the pepper and then replace the stem

Seaweed and sea vegetables

79 Baked salmon salad with sea vegetables

Ingredient	4 portions	10 portions
Salmon fillets	4 × 150g	10 × 150g
Salt and pepper		
Olive oil, for sprinkling		
Lime	2	5
Stale bread, diced	100g	250g
Olive oil	2 tbsp	5 tbsp
Basil leaves, chopped	1 tbsp	2½ tbsp
Mayonnaise	4 tbsp	10 tbsp
Broad beans	200g	500g
Sea kale	100g	250g
Samphire	100g	250g
Salad leaves, rocket		
Lime wedges	4	10

Energy	Cals	Fat	Sat fat	Carb	Sugar	Protein	Fibre	Sodium
2548 kJ	613 kcal	45.0g	6.9g	18.3g	1.8g	37.5g	2.8g	0.8g

Variation

Use roasted flaked almonds as an alternative to breadcrumbs.

1 Place the salmon on a suitable tray (on parchment paper or a non-stick tray) season with salt and pepper, sprinkle with olive oil and squeeze the juice of a lime on top. Cover with foil and gently bake in a preheated oven at 200 °C for approximately 15 minutes.

2 Place the diced bread in a food processor with the olive oil. Blitz until the bread becomes breadcrumbs, place on a tray and bake the crumbs until golden brown.

3 Add the basil leaves to the mayonnaise; add a squeeze of lime juice.

4 The broad beans and sea kale should be blanched in boiling water for 3-4 minutes. Refresh in cold water and drain. Place in a bowl, sprinkle with olive oil and lime juice, and season.

5 Dress the cooked salmon on a suitable plate, mask with the basil mayonnaise and sprinkle with breadcrumbs.

6 Garnish with the broad beans, sea kale and samphire, finish with the salad leaves and lime wedges.

80 Japanese sea vegetable and noodle salad

Ingredient	4 portions	10 portions
Arame, dried	125 g	320 g
Green cabbage, shredded	500 g	1.25 kg
Parsley, coarsely chopped	2 tbsp	5 tbsp
Carrots, cut into julienne	125 g	320 g
Celery, finely chopped	50 g	125 g
Chives, chopped	50 g	125 g
Udon noodles, cooked	400 g	1 kg
Sesame oil	2 tbsp	5 tbsp
Rice vinegar	3 tbsp	7 tbsp
Smoked tofu, 1 cm dice	75 g	180 g

Energy	Cals	Fat	Sat fat	Carb	Sugar	Protein	Fibre	Sodium
1138 kJ	271 kcal	9.4 g	1.3 g	39.0 g	8.3 g	10.2 g	7.5 g	0.4 g

1 In a large bowl, cover the arame with water and soak for 10 minutes. Drain well.

2 Place the arame back in the bowl, add the cabbage, parsley, carrots, celery, chives and mix well.

3 Add the cooked noodles, oil and vinegar; season and mix well.

4 Serve garnished with diced tofu.

Mixed vegetable dishes

81 Mixed vegetables (*macédoine* or *jardinière de légumes*)

Ingredient	4 portions	10 portions
Carrots	100 g	250 g
Turnips	50 g	125 g
Salt		
French beans	50 g	125 g
Peas	50 g	125 g

Energy	Cals	Fat	Sat fat	Carb	Sugar	Protein	Fibre
58 kJ	14 kcal	0.1 g	0.0 g	2.5 g	1.7 g	1.0 g	2.1 g

1 Peel and wash the carrots and turnips; cut into 0.5 cm dice (macédoine) or batons (jardinière); cook separately in lightly salted water, do not overcook. Refresh.

2 Top and tail the beans; cut into 0.5 cm dice, cook and refresh, do not overcook.

3 Cook the peas and refresh.

4 Mix the vegetables and, when required, reheat in hot salted water.

5 Drain well, serve brushed with melted butter.

12

Ratatouille

Ingredient	4 portions	10 portions
Baby marrow (courgette)	200 g	500 g
Aubergines	200 g	500 g
Tomatoes	200 g	500 g
Oil	50 ml	125 ml
Onions, finely sliced	50 g	125 g
Clove of garlic, peeled and chopped	1	2
Red peppers, diced	50 g	125 g
Green peppers, diced	50 g	125 g
Salt, pepper		
Parsley, chopped	1 tsp	2–3 tsp

Energy	Cals	Fat	Sat fat	Carb	Sugar	Protein	Fibre
579 kJ	138 kcal	12.6 g	1.7 g	5.2 g	4.6 g	1.3 g	2.4 g

1 Trim off both ends of the marrow and aubergines.

2 Remove the skin using a peeler.

3 Cut into 3 mm slices.

4 Concassé the tomatoes (peel, remove seeds, roughly chop).

5 Place the oil in a thick-bottomed pan and add the onions.

6 Cover with a lid and allow to cook gently for 5–7 minutes without colour.

7 Add the garlic, marrow and aubergine slices, and the peppers.

8 Season lightly with salt and mill pepper.

9 Allow to cook gently for 4–5 minutes, toss occasionally and keep covered.

10 Add the tomato and continue cooking for 20–30 minutes or until tender.

11 Mix in the parsley, correct the seasoning and serve.

The vegetables need to be cut evenly so that they will cook evenly; it also improves the texture of the dish.

Healthy eating tips
- Use a little unsaturated oil to cook the onions.
- Use the minimum amount of salt.

Ingredients for ratatouille

Add the tomato to the vegetables during cooking (step 10)

83 Ratatouille pancakes with a cheese sauce

1 Prepare and make the pancakes (one per portion).

2 Prepare the ratatouille (see recipe 82) and cheese sauce (see page 85).

3 Season with salt and cayenne pepper.

4 Fill the pancakes with the ratatouille, roll up and place on individual plates or on a service dish.

5 Coat with the cheese sauce and sprinkle with grated Parmesan. Finish by gratinating under the salamander.

Ingredient	4 portions	10 portions
Ratatouille (recipe 82)		
Pancake batter		
Flour	100 g	250 g
Skimmed milk	250 ml	625 ml
Egg	1	2–3
Pinch of salt		
Sunflower margarine or butter, melted	10 g	25 g
Cheese sauce		
Skimmed milk	500 ml	1.25 litres
Sunflower oil	50 g	125 g
Flour	50 g	125 g
Onion, studded with cloves	1	2–3
Parmesan, grated	25 g	60 g
Egg yolk	1	2–3
Seasoning, cayenne		

Energy	Cals	Fat	Sat fat	Carb	Sugar	Protein	Fibre
2,398 kJ	571 kcal	35.8g	6.5g	46.1g	19.0g	19.6g	6.5g

Using margarine.

84 Roasted vegetables

Ingredient	4 portions	10 portions
Red onions, small	1	3
Red peppers	1	3
Yellow peppers	1	3
Courgettes	2	5
Aubergines	1	3
Cloves of garlic, coarsely chopped	1–2	2–4
Olive oil	1 tbsp	2½ tbsp
Balsamic vinegar	1 tbsp	2½ tbsp
Sea salt and freshly milled black pepper		
Fresh rosemary, roughly chopped		
Fresh basil, roughly chopped		

Energy	Cals	Fat	Sat fat	Carb	Sugar	Protein	Fibre
343 kJ	82 kcal	3.6g	0.6g	10.0g	8.6g	3.0g	3.8g

1 Peel the onions and cut into eight pieces. Cut the peppers into halves, deseed and cut each into approximately 4–6 even pieces. Cut the courgettes into 2 × 1 cm batons. Cut the aubergine into 2 × 1 cm batons.

2 Place all the vegetables (and the garlic) into a suitable roasting dish, sprinkle with the olive oil and balsamic vinegar.

3 Season lightly with sea salt and pepper.

4 Sprinkle with rosemary and basil.

5 Place in a preheated oven at 180 °C for approximately 15 minutes.

6 Serve immediately.

Note

These vegetables may also be chilled and served with a salad as a starter.

Healthy eating tips
Lightly brush the vegetables with the olive oil and add the minimum amount of salt.

85 Tempura

Energy	Cals	Fat	Sat fat	Carb	Sugar	Protein	Fibre
3,397 kJ	815 kcal	55.9g	7.4g	67.4g	5.3g	14.8g	5.0g

Ingredient	4 portions
Vegetable oil	500 ml
Courgettes, sliced	2
Sweet potato, scrubbed and sliced	1
Green pepper, seeds removed and cut into strips	1
Shiitake mushroom, stalks removed and halved if large	4
Onion, sliced as half moons	1
Parsley sprigs, to garnish	4
Batter **(all ingredients must be stored in the fridge until just before mixing)**	
Egg yolk	1
Ice-cold sparkling water	200 ml
Plain flour, sifted	100 g
Tentsuyu dipping sauce (optional)	
Dashi stock	200 ml
Mirin	3 tbsp
Soy sauce	3 tbsp
Ginger, grated	½ tsp

1 To prevent splattering during the frying, make sure to dry all deep-fry ingredients thoroughly first with a kitchen towel.

2 For the batter, beat the egg yolk lightly and mix with the ice-cold water.

3 Add half the flour to the egg and water mixture. Give the mixture a few strokes. Add the rest of the flour all at once. Stroke the mixture a few times with chopsticks or a fork until the ingredients are loosely combined. The batter should be very lumpy. If over-mixed, tempura will be oily and heavy.

4 Heat the oil to 160 °C.

5 Dip the vegetables into plain flour and then into the batter, a few pieces at a time. Fry until just crisp and golden (about 1½ minutes).

6 Drain the cooked vegetables on a kitchen towel.

7 Serve immediately with a pinch of salt, garnished with parsley sprigs and lemon wedges, dry-roasted salt or with Tentsuyu dipping sauce in a small bowl with grated ginger. This dish can also be served with an accompaniment of grated white radish.

8 To make the Tentsuyu sauce (if required), combine the ingredients in a small saucepan; heat it through and leave to one side.

Any vegetables with a firm texture may be used for tempura.

> **Professional tip**
>
> The water and other batter ingredients must be ice cold.
>
> The batter should be lumpy to give it texture. Do not over-mix it; this will make it oily and heavy.
>
> Only fry a few pieces at once.

Healthy eating tips
Use sunflower or groundnut oil for frying.

Use sparkling water to make tempura batter

Cut a variety of vegetables into even pieces

Dip each piece into the batter and then deep-fry it

86 Vegetable biryani

Ingredient	4 portions	10 portions
Basmati rice	400 g	1.25 kg
Oil	2 tbsp	5 tbsp
Cinnamon stick	½	1¼
Cardamom pods	4	10
Cloves	4	10
Onions, sliced	100 g	250 g
Cloves of garlic, crushed	1	2–3
Green chilli, finely chopped	1	2–3
Root ginger, grated	1 tbsp	2–3 tbsp
Mixed vegetables (e.g. carrots, celery, cauliflower, broccoli, French beans)	600 g	1.5 kg
Tomatoes, blanched, deseeded and chopped, or canned plum tomatoes	400 g	1.25 kg
Tomato purée	25 g	60 g
Salt, pepper		
Coriander leaves, chopped		

Energy	Cals	Fat	Sat fat	Carb	Sugar	Protein	Fibre
2,014 kJ	482 kcal	7.3 g	0.9 g	91.3 g	9.9 g	12.2 g	4.6 g

1 Wash, soak and drain the rice.

2 Partly cook the rice in boiling salted water for 3 minutes. Refresh and drain well.

3 Heat the oil in a suitably sized pan. Add the crushed cinnamon, cardamom and cloves, and sweat for 2 minutes.

4 Add the sliced onions, garlic, chilli and ginger. Continue to sweat until soft.

5 Prepare the vegetables: cut the carrots and celery into batons, the cauliflower and broccoli into florets and the French beans into 2.5 cm lengths.

6 Add the vegetables to the pan and fry for 2–3 minutes.

7 Add the tomatoes and tomato purée. Season.

8 Make sure there is sufficient moisture in the pan to cook the vegetables; usually a little water needs to be added. Ideally, though, the vegetables should cook in their own juices, combined with the tomatoes.

9 When the vegetables are partly cooked, layer them in a casserole or suitable pan with the rice. (Make sure that there is sufficient liquid to cook the rice.)

10 Cover the casserole and finish cooking in a moderate oven at 180 °C for about 20 minutes, or until the rice is tender.

11 Sprinkle with chopped coriander leaves and serve.

Note

A biryani is usually served with a side dish of vegetable curry.

Healthy eating tips
● Keep added salt to a minimum.
● Use a little unsaturated oil to sweat the spices, onions and vegetables.

87 Vegetable curry with rice pilaff

5 Add the curry sauce, bring to the boil and simmer gently until all the vegetables are cooked but still crunchy in texture.

6 Make the rice pilaff according to the recipe on page 125. Add the roasted flaked almonds after cooking.

7 Serve the curry in a suitable dish with the rice pilaff, poppadoms and a curry tray with mango chutney.

Curry sauce

Ingredient	4 portions	10 portions
Onion, chopped	50 g	125 g
Clove of garlic, crushed	¼	½
Butter or oil	10 g	25 g
Flour	10 g	25 g
Curry powder	5 g	12 g
Tomato purée	5 g	12 g
Stock	375 ml	1 litre
Apple, chopped	25 g	60 g
Chutney, chopped	1 tbsp	2 tbsp
Desiccated coconut	5 g	12 g
Sultanas	10 g	25 g
Ginger root, grated or	10 g	25 g
Ground ginger	5 g	12 g
Salt		

Ingredient	4 portions	10 portions
Mixed vegetables (e.g. cauliflower, broccoli, peppers, carrots, courgettes, mushrooms, aubergines)	600 g	1.5 kg
Butter or oil	100 g	250 g
Onions, chopped finely	150 g	375 g
Garam masala	25 g	60 g
Creamed coconut (or 50 g/125 g desiccated coconut)	25 g	60 g
Curry sauce made using vegetable stock	500 ml	1.5 litre
Rice pilaff (page 125)	100 g	250 g
Flaked almonds, roasted	50 g	125 g

Energy	Cals	Fat	Sat fat	Carb	Sugar	Protein	Fibre
1,814 kJ	432 kcal	35.5 g	7.4 g	23.5 g	16.3 g	6.4 g	6.7 g

1 Prepare the vegetables: cut the cauliflower and broccoli into small florets, blanch and refresh; cut the peppers in half, remove the seeds, cut into 1 cm dice; cut the carrots into large dice, blanch and refresh; and cut the courgettes into 1 cm dice. Leave the mushrooms whole; cut the aubergines into 1 cm dice.

2 Heat the butter or oil and sweat the onion.

3 Add the garam masala; sweat for approximately 2 minutes and add the coconut.

4 Add all the vegetables; sweat together for approximately 5 minutes.

1 Gently cook the onion and garlic in the fat in a small sauteuse without colouring.

2 Mix in the flour and curry powder. Cook gently to a sandy mixture.

3 Mix in the tomato purée, cool.

4 Gradually add the boiling stock and mix to a smooth sauce.

5 Add the remainder of the ingredients, season with salt, and simmer for 30 minutes. Skim and correct the seasoning.

Healthy eating tips
- Use a small amount of an unsaturated oil to sweat the onions.
- No added salt is necessary if the stock used contains yeast extract.

Vegetable protein

88 Crispy deep-fried tofu

Allow 50 g of firm tofu per portion.

1 Cut the firm tofu into cubes.

2 Coat the tofu cubes with any of the following: flour, egg and breadcrumbs; milk and flour; cornstarch; arrowroot.

3 Deep-fry the tofu at 180 °C until golden brown. Drain.

4 Serve garnished with freshly grated ginger and julienne of herbs.

Serve with a tomato sauce flavoured with coriander.

Healthy eating tips
● Use an unsaturated oil to fry the tofu.
● Make sure the oil is hot so that less is absorbed.
● Alternatively, try dry-frying the tofu.

Energy	Cals	Fat	Sat fat	Carb	Sugar	Protein	Fibre
543 kJ	131 kcal	8.9g	0.0g	1.0g	0.5g	11.8g	0.0g

For a 50 g portion.

89 Chinese vegetable and seitan stir-fry

Ingredient	4 portions	10 portions
Hoisin sauce	70 ml	175 ml
Vegetable oil	30 ml	75 ml
Soy sauce	60 ml	150 ml
Rice vinegar	30 ml	75 ml
Sugar	30 g	75 g
Vegetable stock	400 ml	1 litre
Cornflour	30 g	75 g
Garlic cloves, chopped	3	7½
Fresh ginger, chopped	2 tsp	5 tsp
Seitan (see page 350), cut into 2 cm pieces	500 g	1.25 kg
Spring onions, chopped	8	20
Red pepper, shredded	2	5
Yellow pepper, shredded	2	5
Broccoli, cut into small florets	250 g	625 g
French beans	250 g	625 g

1 In a suitable saucepan whisk together the hoisin sauce, half the vegetable oil, half the soy sauce, the rice vinegar, sugar and vegetable stock. Bring to boil and add the cornflour (diluted in a little water to make a slurry). Add the garlic and ginger. Stir.

2 In a suitable wok, stir fry the seitan in the remaining vegetable oil, then add the remaining soy sauce. Stir fry for approximately 3 minutes. Add the spring onions, peppers, broccoli and French beans. Stir fry for a further 3 minutes.

3 Add the sauce mixture to the stir-fry; cooking until the vegetables are *al dente*.

4 Serve with freshly cooked noodles or pilaff rice.

Other vegetarian dishes

90 Cheese fritters (*beignets au fromage*)

1 Bring the water and butter to the boil in a thick-based pan. Remove from the heat.

2 Add the flour; mix with a kitchen spoon.

3 Return to a gentle heat and mix well until the mixture leaves the sides of the pan. Remove from the heat. Allow to cool slightly.

4 Gradually add the eggs, beating well. Add the cheese and season.

5 Using a spoon, scoop the mixture in pieces the size of a walnut and place into deep hot fat at 185°C.

6 Allow to cook, with the minimum of handling, for about 10 minutes.

7 Drain and serve sprinkled with grated Parmesan.

Ingredient	4 portions	10 portions
Water	125 ml	310 ml
Butter	50 g	125 g
Flour, white or wholemeal	60 g	200 g
Eggs, medium	2	5
Parmesan cheese, grated	50 g	125 g
Salt, cayenne		

Healthy eating tips
- Use sunflower margarine for the fritters.
- No extra salt is needed as the cheese has salt in it.
- Fry in hot sunflower oil and drain on kitchen paper.

Energy	Cals	Fat	Sat fat	Carb	Sugar	Protein	Fibre
1,409 kJ	340 kcal	28.4 g	11.2 g	11.8 g	0.4 g	9.9 g	0.5 g

91 Cheese soufflé (*soufflé au fromage*)

Ingredient	4 portions	10 portions
Butter or margarine	25 g	60 g
Flour	15 g	50 g
Milk	125 ml	310 ml
Egg yolks	3	8
Salt, cayenne pepper		
Cheese, grated	50 g	125 g
Egg whites	4	10

Energy	Cals	Fat	Sat fat	Carb	Sugar	Protein	Fibre
3,223 kJ	767 kcal	60.2 g	28.2 g	17.6 g	6.1 g	39.7 g	0.5 g

Using hard margarine.

1. Melt the butter in a thick-based pan.
2. Add the flour and mix with a kitchen spoon.
3. Cook out for a few seconds without colouring.
4. Gradually add the cold milk and mix to a smooth sauce.
5. Simmer for a few minutes.
6. Add 1 egg yolk, mix in quickly; immediately remove from the heat.
7. When cool, add the remaining yolks. Season with salt and cayenne.
8. Add the cheese.
9. Place the egg whites and a pinch of salt (a pinch of egg white powder will help strengthen the whites) in a scrupulously clean bowl and whisk until stiff.
10. Add one-eighth of the whites to the mixture and mix well.
11. Gently fold in the remaining seven-eighths of the mixture; mix as lightly as possible. Place into a buttered soufflé case.
12. Cook in a hot oven at 220 °C for 25–30 minutes for a large soufflé or approximately 10 minutes for individual soufflés.
13. Remove from the oven, place on a round flat dish and serve immediately.

Healthy eating tips
- Use sunflower margarine and semi-skimmed milk to make the sauce.
- No added salt is needed as the cheese has salt in it.

13 Bread and dough products

This chapter is relevant to the following units:

→ Prepare, cook and finish basic bread and dough products.

Recipes included in this chapter

Ingredients

The principal ingredients in bread and dough products are wheat flour and yeast. Bread and bread products form the basis of our diet and are staple products in our society. We eat bread at breakfast, lunch and dinner, as sandwiches, bread rolls, croissants, French sticks, and so on. Bread is also used as an ingredient for many other dishes, either as slices for sandwiches or toast, as fried bread or as breadcrumbs.

Dough consists of strong flour (flour with a high gluten and protein content), water, salt and yeast, which are kneaded together to the required consistency at a suitable temperature. It is then allowed to prove (to rise and increase in size), when the yeast produces carbon dioxide and water, which aerates the dough. When baked it produces a light, digestible product with flavour and colour.

Salted dough is more manageable than unsalted dough. Salt is usually added a few moments before the end of the kneading, since its function is to help expand the dough's volume.

Flour-based products provide energy and a variety of vitamins and minerals. Wholemeal bread products also provide roughage, an essential part of a healthy diet.

Dough

Fermentation

For dough to become leavened bread (bread that has risen, rather than flat bread) it must go through a fermentation process. This is brought about by the action of yeast, a living micro-organism rich in protein and vitamin B. The yeast reacts with enzymes in the dough, which converts sugar into alcohol, producing the characteristic flavour of bread. The action also produces carbon dioxide, which makes the bread rise.

Yeast requires ideal conditions for growth. These are:

- **warmth**: a good temperature for dough production is 22–30 °C
- **moisture**: the liquid should be added at approximately 37 °C – if it is cooler, the yeast may not activate; if it is any hotter it may kill the yeast
- **food**: this is obtained from the starch in the flour
- **time**: this is needed to allow the yeast to grow.

Dried yeast has been dehydrated and must be creamed with a little water before use. It will keep for several months in its dry state. Some types of dried yeast can be used straight from the packet.

Yeast will not survive in a high concentration of sugar or salt, and its growth will slow down in a very rich dough with a high fat and egg content.

When mixing yeast in water or milk, make sure that the liquid is at the correct temperature (37 °C), and disperse the yeast in the liquid (the word 'disperse' is used as living organisms cannot be dissolved).

Why does dough ferment?

It is interesting to understand why doughs ferment and what the effects are on the end product. In order to understand why yeast dough rises, it is important to note that the main ingredients of natural leavening are water, air and, most importantly, sugar, which is transformed into carbon dioxide and alcohol, and causes the leavening. The carbon dioxide forms bubbles inside the dough and makes it rise. Fermentation is a transformation undergone by organic matter (sugars).

Types of dough

Dough products come in a variety of forms and styles. The variety of flour alongside the additional ingredients incorporated, whether the dough is leavened or unleavened, provides dough products with their own unique qualities. The majority of doughs have some sort of leavening agent, usually yeast, or a starter, from which the natural yeast in flour is developed slowly over a long period of time and replaced with fresh flour and water as the required amount of the starter is used to produce the bread in question.

Some dough products do not require yeast as a raising agent. Soda bread, for example, uses bicarbonate of soda, an alkali which reacts with the acidic components within doughs and batters to release carbon dioxide. The carbon dioxide raises the product and helps with the development of texture. Other dough products, such as pitta bread and flatbreads, do not use a raising agent and are referred to as unleavened breads.

Enriched doughs

The basic bread dough of wheat flour, yeast and water may be enriched with fat, sugar, eggs, milk and numerous other ingredients. Some examples of enriched doughs are:

- **buns**: a rich dough enriched with eggs, butter and sugar, used for a wide variety of buns including Chelsea buns, Swiss buns and teacakes
- **savarin**: a rich yeast dough used for savarins, babas and marignans
- **brioche**: a rich yeast dough with a high butter (fat) content.

Laminated doughs

Croissants and Danish pastries are enriched doughs to which the fat is added by layering or lamination. This makes them softer to eat because the fat in the dough insulates the water molecules, keeping the moisture level higher during baking.

Danish pastries may be filled with frangipane, apple, custard, pastry cream, cherries and many other ingredients.

Speciality doughs

- **Blinis**: a type of savoury pancake traditionally made from buckwheat flour.
- **Naan bread**: a leavened Indian bread traditionally cooked in a tandoor (oven).
- **Pitta bread**: Middle Eastern and Greek unleavened bread.
- **Chapatti**: an Indian unleavened bread made from a fine ground wholemeal flour known as 'atta'.
- **Pizza dough**: this is traditionally made using '00 flour' – a fine flour produced from the central part of the wheat grain that produces light, crisp doughs. Pizza dough is often enriched with olive oil to provide moisture and flavour.

Convenience dough products

There are many different types of convenience dough product on the market.

- Fresh and frozen pre-proved dough products: for example, rolls, croissants, Danish pastries and French breads
- Bake-off products that are finished and ready for baking: these can be bought either frozen or fresh, or in modified atmosphere-packaged forms (in vacuum packs, for example). This process removes most of the oxygen around the product to slow down spoilage. Such products have to be kept refrigerated. They include garlic bread, bread rolls and Danish pastries.

Working with dough: quality points

- Fresh yeast should be removed from the refrigerator and used at room temperature.
- Check that all ingredients are weighed carefully.
- Work in a clean and tidy manner to avoid cross-contamination.
- Check all temperatures carefully.
- Note that wholemeal doughs absorb more water than white doughs; the volume of water absorbed by flour also varies according to its strength (the protein and bran content).

- When using machines, check that they are in good working order.
- Always remember the health and safety rules when using machinery.
- Divide the dough with a dough divider, hard scraper or hydraulic cutting machine. This is referred to as scaling the dough. This can be done by hand for smaller quantities.
- Check the divided dough pieces for weight. When weighing, remember that doughs lose up to 12.5 per cent of their water during baking.
- Keep the flour, bowl and liquid warm.
- Remember to knock the dough back (re-knead it) carefully once proved, as this will expel the gas and allow the yeast to be dispersed properly, coming back into direct contact with the dough.
- Proving allows the dough to ferment; the second prove is essential for giving dough products the necessary volume and a good flavour.
- Time and temperature are crucial when cooking dough products. Ensure the oven is at the correct temperature before placing the product in to bake.
- Always follow the manufacturer's instructions when using frozen dough products.
- Contamination can occur if doughs are defrosted incorrectly.

Faults in yeast doughs

If your dough has a close texture, this may be because:
- it was insufficiently proved
- it was insufficiently kneaded
- it contains insufficient yeast
- the oven was too hot
- too much water was added
- too little water was added.

If your dough has an uneven texture, this may be because:
- it was insufficiently kneaded
- it was over-proved
- the oven was too cool.

If your dough has a coarse texture, this may be because:
- it was over-proved, uncovered
- it was insufficiently kneaded
- too much water was added
- too much salt was added.

If your dough is wrinkled, this may be because it was over-proved.

If your dough is sour, this may be because:
- the yeast was stale
- too much yeast was used.

If the crust, is broken this may be because the dough was under-proved at the second stage.

If there are white spots on the crust, this may be because the dough was not covered before the second proving.

Storage of cooked dough products

Store dough products in clean, air-tight containers at room temperature or in a freezer for longer periods. Do not store in a refrigerator unless you want the bread to stale quickly for use as breadcrumbs. Staling will also occur quickly in products that contain a lot of fat and milk. Many commercial dough products contain anti-staling agents.

Crusty rolls and bread are affected by changes in storage conditions; they are softened by a damp environment and humid conditions, so should be stored in a dry environment to keep them crusty.

Bread

Today restaurants often offer a range of different flavoured breads. A wide variety is available internationally, with different nations and regions having their own speciality breads. Bread also plays an important part in many religious festivals, especially Christian and Jewish festivals.

Bulk fermentation

The traditional bread-making process is known as the bulk fermentation process. This was used by many bakers before the introduction of high-speed mixing and dough conditioners, which both eliminate the need for bulk fermentation time. However, this traditional method produces a fine flavour, which is evident in the final product.

Bulk fermentation time (BFT) is the term is used to describe the length of time that the dough is allowed to ferment in bulk. BFT is measured from the end of the mixing method to the beginning of the scaling (weighing) process. The length of BFT can be from one to six hours and is related to the level of salt and yeast in the recipe, as well as the dough temperature.

During the bulk fermentation process it is important that ideal conditions are adhered to:
- The dough must be kept covered to prevent the surface of the dough developing a skin.
- The appropriate temperature must be maintained and monitored to control the rate of fermentation.

Finishing and presentation

Depending of the type of product being made, there are a number of different finishes that can be applied to dough products. Certain breads, such as baguettes, are scored before they are baked, which helps to produce an appealing visual finish to the baked product.

Many breads are sprinkled with seeds, for example poppy, sesame and fennel, before they are baked. Others may have herbs added, such as the red onion and sage rolls that feature in this chapter, or are sprinkled with cheese, as seen with Parmesan rolls. A common but perhaps the most simple of finishes applied to breads is a light dusting of the same flour used to produce the bread. This is sieved over the bread once it has cooled and applies to many of the examples shown in this chapter.

Many dough products – including breads and laminated doughs, such as croissant and pain au chocolat – are brushed with egg wash before they are baked. This produces a light, golden-brown glaze during the baking process. Other products are glazed after baking, for example Swiss buns and Danish pastries, which are often finished with a fruit glaze and water icing. Other enriched doughs, such as Chelsea buns, are soaked with bun syrup while still hot after baking and sprinkled with nibbed sugar.

Video:
principles of
breadmaking
http://bit.ly/
17grKYK

Allergies

Gluten is the protein found in wheat, barley and rye, and to a lesser extent in yeast. An increasing number of people are intolerant to gluten, which results in damage to the lining of the small intestine. This is known as coeliac disease and people who are intolerant must avoid the consumption of wheat and flour-based products.

Although it is essential to clearly list all potential allergens when making fermented dough products, the allergens that are most likely to be used in their production include:

- gluten – flours and any products made from wheat, rye, barley and oats
- nuts – such as hazelnuts and nibbed almonds added to garnish Danish pastries, for example
- sesame seeds – often sprinkled on the surface of breads and rolls
- eggs – used in the production of enriched doughs
- lactose – for example, milk used in place of water in the production of dough; cheese used to glaze breads; yoghurt used in speciality doughs, such as naan.

Beyond the basic preparation of fermented doughs, attention is also required with regard to the additional ingredients that are used to complete the product. It is vitally important to assess any of the other potential allergens that are incorporated into fermented doughs, as well as the dough itself.

Test yourself

1 What is meant by fermentation?
2 Name two types of speciality bread.
3 Why is temperature so important when making bread dough using yeast?
4 What is the raising agent used in soda bread?
5 What is the difference between strong and soft flour?
6 State the nutritional benefits of wholemeal flour.
7 Give two examples, with descriptions, of dough products in the following categories:
   a enriched doughs
   b laminated doughs
   c speciality doughs.
8 Name three seeds that are often sprinkled on bread rolls before baking.
9 What is the difference between leavened and unleavened bread?
10 What is the meaning of the term 'scaling'?

Bread doughs

1 Wholemeal bread

Ingredient	Makes 2 loaves
Unsalted butter or oil	60 g
Honey	3 tbsp
Water, lukewarm	500 ml
Fresh yeast	25 g
or	
Dried yeast	18 g
Salt	1 tbsp
Flour, unbleached strong white	125 g
Flour, stoneground wholemeal	625 g

Energy	Cals	Fat	Sat fat	Carb	Sugar	Protein	Fibre
6,893 kJ	1,628 kcal	32.5 g	16.7 g	302.3 g	62.6 g	50.5 g	40.0 g

1 Melt the butter in a saucepan.

2 Mix together 1 tbsp of honey and 4 tbsp of the water in a bowl.

3 Disperse the yeast into the honey mixture.

4 In a basin, place the melted butter, remaining honey and water, the yeast mixture and salt.

5 Add the white flour and half the wholemeal flour. Mix well.

6 Add the remaining wholemeal flour gradually, mixing well between each addition.

7 The dough should pull away from the side of the bowl and form a ball. The resulting dough should be soft and slightly sticky.

8 Turn out on to a floured work surface. Sprinkle with white flour, knead well.

9 Brush a clean bowl with melted butter or oil. Place the dough in the bowl, cover with a damp cloth and allow to prove in a warm place. This will take approximately 1–1½ hours.

10 Knock back and further knead the dough. Cover again and rest for 10–15 minutes.

11 Divide the dough into two equal pieces.

12 Form each piece of dough into a cottage loaf or place in a suitable loaf tin.

13 Allow to prove in a warm place for approximately 45 minutes.

14 Place in a preheated oven, 220 °C and bake until well browned (approximately 40–45 minutes).

15 When baked, the bread should sound hollow and the sides should feel crisp when pressed.

16 Cool on a wire rack.

Variation

Alternatively, the bread may be divided into 50 g rolls, brushed with egg wash and baked at 200 °C for approximately 10 minutes.

Healthy eating tip

● Only a little salt is necessary to 'control' the yeast. Many customers will prefer less salty bread.

2 Seeded bread rolls

Ingredient	Makes 30 rolls
Strong flour	1 kg
Yeast	30 g
Water at 37 °C	600 ml
Salt	20 g
Caster sugar	10 g
Milk powder	20 g
Sunflower oil	50 g
Egg wash	
Poppy seeds	
Sesame seeds	

Energy	Cals	Fat	Sat fat	Carb	Sugar	Protein	Fibre	Sodium
633 kJ	150 kcal	3.4 g	0.5 g	26.0 g	1.2 g	5.3 g	1.4 g	0.3 g

Per roll.

1 Sieve the flour on to paper.

2 Dissolve the yeast in half the water.

3 Dissolve the salt, sugar and milk powder in the other half.

4 Add both liquids and the oil to the flour at once and mix on speed 1 for 5 minutes or knead by hand for 10 minutes.

5 Cover with cling film and leave to prove for 1 hour at 26 °C.

6 'Knock back' the dough and scale into 50 g pieces.

7 Shape and place in staggered rows on a silicone paper-covered baking sheet.

8 Prove until the rolls almost double in size.

9 Egg wash carefully and sprinkle with seeds.

10 Bake immediately at 230 °C with steam for 10–12 minutes.

11 Break one open to test if cooked.

12 Allow to cool on a wire rack.

Professional tip

Instead of weighing out each 50 g piece of dough, weigh out 100 g pieces and then halve them.

Placing bread rolls in staggered rows means they are less likely to 'prove' into each other. The spacing allows them to cook more evenly and more will fit on the baking sheet.

Variation

Try using other types of seed such as sunflower, linseed or pumpkin.

For a beer glaze mix, together 150 ml beer with 100 g rye flour and brush on before baking.

3 Parmesan rolls

1 Follow method for seeded rolls (recipe 2) up to step 5.
2 Lightly flour work surface and roll the dough into a rectangle until 3 cm thick.
3 Make sure the dough is not stuck to the surface.
4 Brush with water and cover with Parmesan.
5 Using a large knife, cut into squares 6 × 6 cm.
6 Place on a silicone paper-covered baking sheet and leave to prove until almost double in size.
7 Bake at 230 °C for 10–12 minutes with steam.
8 Cool on a wire rack.

Ingredient	Makes 30 rolls
Bread roll dough (see recipe 2 but omit the seeds)	
Parmesan cheese, grated	200 g

Energy	Cals	Fat	Sat fat	Carb	Sugar	Protein	Fibre	Sodium
2,169 kJ	512 kcal	9.9g	2.2g	94.3g	1.8g	17.5g	5.2g	1.0g

Professional tip

When making bread that requires rolling out as opposed to being individually shaped, it is helpful to decrease the liquid content by 10 per cent so it will be easier to process.

To ensure the squares are all the same size, mark a grid using the back of the knife before cutting.

4 Red onion and sage rolls

Ingredient	8 rolls	16 rolls
Red onion	½	1
Dried sage	¼ tsp	½ tsp
Bread roll dough (see recipe 2 but omit the seeds)		
Oil	1 tbsp	2 tbsp

Energy	Cals	Fat	Sat fat	Carb	Sugar	Protein	Fibre	Sodium
759 kJ	181 kcal	9.2g	1.7g	21.7g	2.8g	4.2g	1.2g	1.0g

1 Finely dice the red onion. Sweat it, then leave to cool.
2 Chop the sage and add it to the onion.
3 Pin out bread dough in a rectangle. Spread the onion and sage mixture over seven-eighths of the dough. Egg wash the exposed edge.
4 Roll the dough as you would for a Swiss roll, and seal the edge.
5 Cut into 50 g slices.
6 Place the slices on a prepared baking sheet and egg wash. Bake in a preheated oven at 220 °C for approximately 10 minutes. Cool on a wire rack.

5 Sundried tomato bread

Ingredient	2 × 450 g loaves
Sun-dried tomatoes, chopped	100 g
Water, warm	300 ml
Bread flour	500 g
Salt	10 g
Skimmed milk powder	12.5 g
Shortening	12.5 g
Yeast (fresh)	20 g
Sugar	12.5 g

Energy	Cals	Fat	Sat fat	Carb	Sugar	Protein	Fibre	Sodium
10,192 kJ	2,414 kcal	70.8 g	12.8 g	401.8 g	29.6 g	67.4 g	20.7 g	5.0 g

1 Soak the sun-dried tomatoes in boiling water for 30 minutes.

2 Sieve the flour, salt and skimmed milk powder.

3 Add the shortening and rub through the dry ingredients.

4 Disperse the yeast into warm water, approximately 37 °C. Add and dissolve the sugar. Add to the above ingredients.

5 Mix until a smooth dough is formed. Check for any extremes in consistency and adjust as necessary until a smooth elastic dough is formed.

6 Cover the dough, keep warm and allow to prove.

7 After approximately 30–40 minutes, knock back the dough and mix in the chopped sun-dried tomatoes (well drained).

8 Mould and prove again for another 30 minutes (covered).

9 Divide the dough into two and mould round.

10 Rest for 10 minutes. Keep covered.

11 Remould into ball shape.

12 Place the dough pieces into 15 cm diameter hoops laid out on a baking tray. The hoops must be warm and lightly greased.

13 With the back of the hand flatten the dough pieces.

14 Prove at 38–40 °C in humid conditions, preferably in a prover.

15 Bake at 225 °C for 25–30 minutes.

16 After baking, remove the bread from the tins immediately and place on a cooling wire.

6 Olive bread

Ingredient	4 loaves
Starter	
Yeast	40 g
Water at 37 °C	180 ml
Strong flour	225 g
Sugar	5 g
Dough	
Strong flour	855 g
Sugar	40 g
Salt	20 g
Water at 37 °C	450 ml
Olive oil	160 ml
Green olives, cut into quarters	100 g

Energy	Cals	Fat	Sat fat	Carb	Sugar	Protein	Fibre	Sodium
5,174 kJ	1,229 kcal	44.2g	6.5g	188.3g	3.5g	30.9g	15.9g	5.2g

1 For the starter, dissolve the yeast in the water, add the flour and sugar, mix well, cover and leave to ferment for 30 minutes.

2 For the dough, sieve the flour, sugar and salt into a mixing bowl, add the water followed by the starter and start mixing slowly.

3 Gradually add the oil and continue mixing to achieve a smooth dough.

4 Cover with cling film and prove for 1 hour or until double in size.

5 Knock back, add the olives and divide the dough into four.

6 Roll into long shapes and place on a baking sheet sprinkled with rice cones, return to the prover and leave until double in size.

7 Brush with olive oil and bake at 220 °C for 20–25 minutes.

8 When cooked, the bread should sound hollow when tapped on the base.

9 Leave to cool on a wire rack.

1 Make up the starter.

2 Starter ready for use after proving.

3 Start mixing in the ingredients for the main dough, tearing up the starter.

4 Continue mixing in the ingredients and working the dough.

5 Shape the dough.

6 Divide and roll into loaves.

7 Rye bread

Energy	Cals	Fat	Sat fat	Carb	Sugar	Protein	Fibre	Sodium
7,174 kJ	1,690 kcal	24.7g	2.9g	331.8g	12.5g	46.7g	46.2g	6.0g

Ingredient	1 loaf
Fresh yeast (or dried yeast may be used)	15g
Water, warm	60 ml
Black treacle	1 tbsp
Vegetable oil	1 tbsp
Caraway seeds (optional)	15g
Salt	15g
Lager	250 ml
Rye flour	250g
Unbleached bread flour	175g
Polenta	
Egg wash	

1 Disperse the yeast in the warm water (at approximately 37 °C).

2 In a basin mix the black treacle, oil, two-thirds of the caraway seeds (if required) and the salt. Add the lager. Add the yeast and mix in the sieved rye flour. Mix well.

3 Gradually add the bread flour. Continue to add the flour until the dough is formed and it is soft and slightly sticky.

4 Turn the dough on to a lightly floured surface and knead well.

5 Knead the dough until it is smooth and elastic.

6 Place the kneaded dough into a suitable bowl that has been brushed with oil.

7 Cover with a damp cloth and allow the dough to prove in a warm place until it is double in size. This will take about 1½–2 hours.

8 Turn the dough on to a lightly floured work surface, knock back the dough to original size. Cover and allow to rest for approximately 5–10 minutes.

9 Shape the dough into an oval approximately 25 cm long.

10 Place on to a baking sheet lightly sprinkled with polenta.

11 Allow the dough to prove in a warm place, preferably in a prover, until double in size (approximately 45 minutes to 1 hour).

12 Lightly brush the loaf with egg wash, sprinkle with the remaining caraway seeds (if required).

13 Using a small, sharp knife, make three diagonal slashes, approximately 5 mm deep into the top of the loaf.

14 Place in a preheated oven at 190 °C and bake for approximately 50–55 minutes.

15 When cooked, turn out. The bread should sound hollow when tapped and the sides should feel crisp.

16 Allow to cool.

Healthy eating tip
● Only a little salt is necessary to 'control' the yeast. Many customers will prefer less salty bread.

8 Soda bread

Ingredient	2 loaves
Flour, wholemeal	250 g
Flour (strong)	250 g
Bicarbonate of soda	1 tsp
Salt	1 tsp
Buttermilk	200 g
Water, warm	60 ml
Butter, melted	25 g

Energy	Cals	Fat	Sat fat	Carb	Sugar	Protein	Fibre	Sodium
8,341 kJ	1,970 kcal	39.8 g	20.9 g	357.8 g	18.5 g	67.9 g	20.9 g	3.6 g

1 Sift the flours, salt and bicarbonate of soda into a bowl.

2 Make a well and add the buttermilk, warm water and melted butter.

3 Work the dough for about 5 minutes.

4 Mould into 2 round loaves and mark the top with a cross.

5 Bake at 200 °C for about 25 minutes. When the bread is ready, it should make a hollow sound when tapped.

9 Bagels

Ingredient	10–12 bagels
Strong flour	450 g
Yeast	15 g
Water, warm	150 ml
Salt	10 g
Caster sugar	25 g
Oil	45 ml
Egg yolk	20 g
Milk	150 ml
Poppy seeds	

Energy	Cals	Fat	Sat fat	Carb	Sugar	Protein	Fibre	Sodium
670 kJ	158 kcal	2.1 g	0.5 g	32.7 g	5.0 g	6.2 g	1.6 g	0.8 g

1 Sieve the flour, place in a mixing bowl.

2 Make a well and add the yeast which has been dissolved in the water.

3 Mix a little of the flour into the yeast to form a batter, sprinkle over some of the flour from the sides and leave to ferment.

4 Mix together the salt, sugar, oil, egg yolk and milk.

5 When the batter has fermented add the rest of the ingredients and mix to achieve a smooth dough.

6 Cover and prove for 1 hour (BFT).

7 Knock back and scale at 50 g pieces, shape into rolls and make a hole in the centre using a small rolling pin.

8 Place on a floured board and prove for 10 minutes.

9 Carefully drop into boiling water and simmer until they rise to the surface.

10 Lift out and place on a silicone-covered baking sheet, egg wash, sprinkle or dip in poppy seeds and bake at 210 °C for 30 minutes.

Use a rolling pin to make a hole in the centre of each bagel

Poach the bagels in water

Egg wash the bagels and sprinkle with seeds before baking

10 Cholla bread

Ingredient	2 loaves
Butter or margarine	56 g
Flour (strong)	500 g
Caster sugar	18 g
Salt	1 tsp
Egg	1
Yeast	25 g

Energy	Cals	Fat	Sat fat	Carb	Sugar	Protein	Fibre	Sodium
4,876 kJ	1,154 kcal	30.1 g	16.1 g	198.1 g	13.1 g	35.0 g	10.3 g	1.2 g

1 Rub the butter or margarine into the sieved flour in a suitable basin.

2 Mix the sugar, salt and egg together.

3 Disperse the yeast in the water.

4 Add all these ingredients to the sieved flour and mix well to develop the dough. Cover with a damp cloth or plastic and allow to ferment for about 45 minutes.

5 Divide into 125–150 g strands and begin to plait as follows:

4–strand plait	5–strand plait
2 over 3	2 over 3
4 over 2	5 over 2
1 over 3	1 over 3

6 After moulding, place on a lightly greased baking sheet and egg wash lightly.

7 Prove in a little steam until double in size. Egg wash again lightly and decorate with maw seeds (poppy seeds).

8 Bake in a hot oven, at 220 °C for 25–30 minutes.

11 Focaccia

Ingredient	1 loaf
Active dry yeast	2 packets
Sugar	1 tsp
Lukewarm water (about blood temperature)	230 ml
Extra virgin olive oil, plus extra to drizzle on the bread	70 g
Salt	1½ tsp
Flour, unbleached all-purpose	725 g
Coarse salt	
Picked rosemary	

Energy	Cals	Fat	Sat fat	Carb	Sugar	Protein	Fibre	Sodium
12,915 kJ	3,052 kcal	78.7 g	11.5 g	553.6 g	14.7 g	66.7 g	30.0 g	5.6 g

1 Dissolve the yeast and sugar in half of the lukewarm water in a bowl; let sit until foamy. In another bowl, add the remaining water, the olive oil, and the salt.

2 Pour in the yeast mixture.

3 Blend in the flour, a quarter at a time, until the dough comes together. Knead on a floured board for 10 minutes, adding flour as needed to make it smooth and elastic. Put the dough in an oiled bowl, turn to coat well, and cover with a towel.

4 Let rise in a warm draught-free place for 1 hour, until doubled in size.

5 Knock back the dough, knead it for a further 5 minutes, and gently roll it out in to a large disc or sheet to approximately 2 cm thick.

6 Let rise for 15 minutes, covered. Oil your fingers and make impressions with them in the dough, 3 cm apart. Let prove for 1 hour.

7 Preheat the oven to 210 °C. Drizzle the dough with olive oil and sprinkle with coarse salt and picked rosemary.

8 Bake for 15–20 minutes in a very hot oven at 200 °C, until golden brown. Sprinkle with additional oil if desired. Cut into squares and serve warm.

12 Pizza

1 Sieve the flour and the salt. Rub in the margarine.

2 Disperse the yeast in the warm milk or water; add the caster sugar. Add this mixture to the flour.

3 Mix well, knead to a smooth dough, place in a basin covered with a damp cloth and allow to prove until doubled in size.

4 Knock back, divide into two and roll out into two 18 cm discs. Place on a lightly greased baking sheet.

5 Sweat the finely chopped onions and garlic in the oil until cooked.

6 Add the roughly chopped tomatoes, tomato purée, oregano, basil and sugar. Bring to the boil and simmer for 5 minutes.

7 Dilute the cornflour in a little water, stir into the tomato mixture and bring back to the boil.

8 Take the discs of pizza dough and spread 125 g of filling on each one.

9 Sprinkle with grated mozzarella cheese or lay the slices of cheese on top.

10 Bake in a moderately hot oven at 180 °C, for about 10 minutes.

The pizza dough may also be made into rectangles so that it can be sliced into fingers for buffet work.

Ingredient	2 × 18 cm
Flour, strong white	200 g
Pinch of salt	
Margarine	12 g
Yeast	5 g
Water or milk at 24 °C	125 ml
Caster sugar	5 g
Onions, finely chopped	100 g
Cloves of garlic, crushed	2
Sunflower oil	60 ml
Plum tomatoes, canned	200 g
Tomato purée	100 g
Oregano	3 g
Basil	3 g
Sugar	10 g
Cornflour	10 g
Mozzarella cheese	100 g

Energy	Cals	Fat	Sat fat	Carb	Sugar	Protein	Fibre
3,956 kJ	941 kcal	46.3 g	13 g	114.4 g	20.1 g	23.6 g	8.4 g

Using 100 per cent strong white flour.

Note

Pizza is a traditional dish originating from southern Italy. In simple terms it is a flat bread dough that can be topped with a wide variety of ingredients and baked quickly. The only rule is not to add wet ingredients, such as tomatoes, which are too juicy, otherwise the pizza will become soggy. Traditionally, pizzas are baked in a wood-fired brick oven, but they can be baked in any type of hot oven for 8–15 minutes depending on the ingredients. The recipe given here is a typical one.

Variation

Oregano is sprinkled on most pizzas before baking. This is a basic recipe and many variations exist. Some have the addition of olives, artichoke hearts, prawns, mortadella sausage, garlic sausage or anchovy fillets; other combinations include:
● mozzarella cheese, anchovies, capers and garlic
● mozzarella cheese, tomato and oregano
● ham, mushrooms, egg and parmesan cheese
● prawns, tuna, capers and garlic
● ham, mushrooms and olives.

13 Naan bread

Ingredient	6 portions
Flour (strong)	350 g
Caster sugar	1½ tsp
Salt	1 tsp
Baking powder	½ tsp
Fresh yeast	15 g
Warm milk (37 °C)	150 ml
Unsweetened plain yoghurt	150 ml
Butter, clarified	100 g
Poppy seeds	2 tbsp

Energy	Cals	Fat	Sat fat	Carb	Sugar	Protein	Fibre
1,619 kJ	386 kcal	20.5 g	12.0 g	48.3 g	5.0 g	10.1 g	1.8 g

With clarified butter – using ghee.

1 Sift the flour into a suitable bowl and add the sugar, salt and baking powder.
2 Mix the yeast into the warm milk and stir in the yoghurt. Mix thoroughly with the flour to form a dough.
3 Knead the dough until it is smooth. Cover with a clean cloth and leave to rise in a warm place for about 4 hours.
4 Divide the risen dough into 12 equal portions and, on a lightly floured surface, roll into balls.
5 Flatten the balls into oblong shapes, using both hands, and slapping the naan from one hand to the other.
6 Cook the naan bread on the sides of a tandoor oven or on a lightly greased griddle or heavy-bottomed frying pan.
7 Cook the naan on one side only. Brush the raw side with clarified butter and sprinkle with poppy seeds; turn over, cook the other side or brown under a salamander.

Note

This recipe comes from Punjab and goes well with tandoori meat dishes as well as vindaloos. Traditionally, naans are baked in clay ovens called a tandoor. They must be eaten fresh and hot, and served immediately.

Healthy eating tips
● Cook the bread without added fat.
● Naan bread is a useful accompaniment for fattier meat dishes.

Buns

14 Bun dough

1 Sieve the flour.

2 Dissolve the yeast in half the milk and add enough of the flour to make a thick batter, cover with cling film and place in the prover to ferment.

3 Rub the butter into the rest of the flour.

4 Beat the eggs and add the salt and sugar.

5 When the batter has fermented, add to the flour together with the liquid.

6 Mix slowly for 5 minutes to form a soft dough.

7 Place in a lightly oiled bowl, cover with cling film and prove for 1 hour at 26 °C.

8 Knock back the dough and knead on the table, rest for 10 minutes before processing.

Ingredient	12 buns	24 buns
Strong flour	500 g	1 kg
Yeast	25 g	50 g
Milk (scalded and cooled to 40 °C)	250 ml	500 ml
Butter	60 g	120 g
Eggs	2	4
Salt	5 g	10 g
Sugar	60 g	120 g

Bun wash

Bun wash is used for most bun recipes, including Bath and Chelsea buns, after baking.

Milk	250 ml
Caster sugar	100 g

1 Bring both ingredients to the boil and brush over liberally as soon the buns are removed from the oven. The heat from the buns will set the glaze and prevent it from soaking in, giving a characteristic sticky coat.

1 Sift the flour.

2 Rub in the fat.

3 Make a well in the flour and pour in the beaten egg.

4 Pour in the liquid.

5 Fold the ingredients together.

6 Knead the dough.

7 Before and after proving: the same amount of dough is twice the size after it has been left to prove.

15 Bath buns

Hot cross buns and Bath buns

Ingredient	12–14 buns
Basic bun dough (recipe 14)	1 kg
Bun spice	20 ml
Sultanas	200 g
Sugar nibs	360 g
Egg yolks	8

Energy	Cals	Fat	Sat fat	Carb	Sugar	Protein	Fibre	Sodium
827 kJ	196 kcal	6.5 g	3.6 g	31.9 g	13.4 g	4.5 g	1.4 g	0.1 g

1 Mix the bun spice into the basic dough and knead.
2 Add the sultanas, two-thirds of the sugar nibs and all the egg yolks.
3 Using a plastic scraper, cut in the ingredients (it is usual for the ingredients not to be fully mixed in).
4 Scale into 60 g pieces.
5 Place on a paper-lined baking sheet in rough shapes.
6 Sprinkle liberally with the rest of the nibbed sugar.
7 Allow to prove until double in size.
8 Bake at 200 °C for 15–20 minutes.
9 Brush with bun wash as soon as they come out of the oven.

16 Hot cross buns

Ingredient	12–14 buns	24 buns
Basic bun dough (recipe 14)	1 kg	2 kg
Currants	75 g	150 g
Sultanas	75 g	150 g
Mixed spice	5 g	10 g
Crossing paste		
Strong flour	125 g	250 g
Water	250 ml	500 ml
Oil	25 ml	50 ml

Energy	Cals	Fat	Sat fat	Carb	Sugar	Protein	Fibre	Sodium
744 kJ	177 kcal	6.7 g	3.6 g	26.8 g	8.3 g	4.6 g	1.2 g	0.1 g

1 Add the dried fruit and spice to the basic dough, mix well.
2 Scale into 60 g pieces and roll.
3 Place on a baking sheet lined with silicone paper in neat rows opposite each other and egg wash.
4 Mix together the ingredients for the crossing paste. Pipe it in continuous lines across the buns.
5 Allow to prove.
6 Bake at 220 °C for 15–20 minutes.
7 Brush with bun wash as soon as they come out of the oven.

Variation

To make fruit buns, proceed as for hot cross buns without the crosses.

17 Swiss buns

Ingredient	12–14 buns
Basic bun dough (recipe 14)	1 kg
Fondant	500 g
Lemon oil	5 ml

Energy	Cals	Fat	Sat fat	Carb	Sugar	Protein	Fibre	Sodium
697 kJ	165 kcal	5.6g	3.4g	27.0g	8.4g	3.4g	1.0g	0.0g

1 Scale the dough into 60g pieces.

2 Roll into balls then elongate to form oval shapes.

3 Place on a baking sheet lined with silicone paper, egg wash.

4 Allow to prove.

5 Bake at 220°C for 15–20 minutes.

6 Allow to cool then dip each bun in lemon-flavoured or plain white fondant.

18 Doughnuts

4 When proved, carefully place in a deep fat fryer at 180°C.

5 Turn over when coloured on one side and fully cook.

6 Drain well on absorbent paper.

7 Toss in caster sugar.

8 Make a small hole in one side and pipe in the jam.

Variation

The caster sugar can be mixed with ground cinnamon.

Ingredient	12 doughnuts
Basic bun dough (recipe 14)	1 kg
Caster sugar	500 g
Raspberry jam	250 g

Energy	Cals	Fat	Sat fat	Carb	Sugar	Protein	Fibre
918 kJ	218 kcal	13.3g	4.0g	22.6g	4.0g	3.6g	1.2g

Using hard margarine and peanut oil.

1 Scale the dough into 60g pieces.

2 Roll into balls and make a hole in the dough using a rolling pin.

3 Prove on an oiled paper-lined tray.

Health and safety !

As a fryer is not a regular piece of equipment found in a patisserie, a portable fryer is often used. Always make sure it is on a very secure surface in a suitable position. Never attempt to move it until it has completely cooled down. In addition, extreme care must be taken to avoid serious burns.

● Only use a deep fat fryer after proper training.
● Make sure the oil is clean and the fryer is filled to the correct level.
● Preheat before using but never leave unattended.
● Always carefully place the products into the fryer – never drop them in. Use a basket if appropriate.
● Never place wet products into the fryer.

19 Savarin dough

Ingredient	35 items
Strong flour	450 g
Yeast	1 g
Water at 40 °C	125 ml
Eggs	5
Caster sugar	60 g
Salt	Pinch
Melted butter	150 g

1 Sieve the flour and place in a bowl. Make a well.

2 Make a ferment by dissolving the yeast in the water and pour into the well.

3 Gradually mix the flour into the liquid, forming a thin batter. Sprinkle over a little of the flour to cover, then leave to ferment.

4 Whisk the eggs, sugar and salt.

5 When the ferment has erupted through the flour, add the eggs and mix to a smooth batter. Cover and leave to prove until double in size.

6 Add the melted butter and beat in.

7 Pipe the batter into prepared (buttered and floured) moulds one-third full.

8 Prove until the mixture reaches the top of the mould and bake at 220 °C for 12–20 minutes, depending on the size of the mould.

9 Unmould and leave to cool.

Professional tip

Savarin and savarin-based products are never served without first soaking in a flavoured syrup. They are literally dry sponges and should be:

● golden brown in colour with an even surface
● smooth, with no cracks, breaks or tears
● evenly soaked without any hard or dry areas
● sealed by brushing with apricot glaze after soaking.

Cooked products can be stored in the fridge overnight, but if left for too long they will dry out and cracks will appear. They are best wrapped in cling film, labelled and stored in the freezer.

Savarin syrup

Ingredient	3 litres
Oranges	2
Lemons	2
Water	2 litres
Sugar	1 kg
Bay leaf	2
Cloves	2
Cinnamon sticks	2

1 Peel the oranges and lemons and squeeze the juice.

2 Add all the ingredients into a large pan and bring to the boil, simmer for 2–3 minutes and pass through a conical strainer.

3 Allow to cool and measure the density (it should read 22° Baumé). Adjust if necessary. (More liquid will lower the density, more sugar will increase it.)

4 Reboil then dip the baked savarins into the hot syrup until they swell slightly. Check they are properly soaked before carefully removing and placing on to a wire rack with a tray underneath to drain.

5 When cooled, brush with boiling apricot glaze.

Note

It is important that savarin syrup is at the correct density. It should measure 22° Baumé on the saccharometer. If the syrup is too thin, the products are likely to disintegrate. If it is too dense it will not fully penetrate the product and leave a dry centre.

1 Cream the yeast in milk to make a ferment.

2 Add the dissolved yeast to the flour and sprinkle a little flour over it.

3 The mixture after fermentation.

4 Add beaten eggs, sugar and salt.

5 The dough after proving.

6 Add the butter.

7 After proving, pipe into moulds.

8 After proving for the final time.

20 Savarin with fruit

A savarin is baked in a ring mould, either large or individual.

Before glazing, sprinkle with kirsch and fill the centre with prepared fruit. Serve with a crème anglaise or raspberry coulis.

Energy	Cals	Fat	Sat fat	Carb	Sugar	Protein	Fibre	Sodium
1021 kJ	241 kcal	4.6g	2.5g	49.0g	40.0g	2.7g	0.7g	0.1g

Using 40g of fruit, 1 tsp of glaze and ¼ tsp of spirit per portion.

21 Marignans chantilly

A marignan is savarin dough baked in an individual boat-shaped mould or barquette.

Split the glazed marignans and fill with Chantilly cream. Once split, and before filling, they can be sprinkled with rum or orange-flavoured liqueur.

Energy	Cals	Fat	Sat fat	Carb	Sugar	Protein	Fibre	Sodium
1407 kJ	335 kcal	14.4g	8.7g	51.0g	41.0g	2.9g	0.5g	0.1g

Using 30g of Chantilly cream, 1 tsp of glaze and ¼ tsp of spirit per portion.

> **Professional tip**
>
> Savarin paste is notorious for sticking in the mould. Always butter moulds carefully and flour. After use do not wash the moulds but wipe clean with kitchen paper.

22 Blueberry baba

For a baba, currants are usually added to the basic savarin dough before baking.

As for marignans, split the glazed baba and fill with crème diplomate and blueberries or Chantilly cream.

Energy	Cals	Fat	Sat fat	Carb	Sugar	Protein	Fibre	Sodium
1439 kJ	342 kcal	14.4g	8.7g	54.0g	45.0g	3.0g	1.2g	0.1g

Using 15g blueberries, 30g of Chantilly cream, 1 tsp of glaze and ¼ tsp of spirit per portion.

This chapter is relevant to the following units:
→ Prepare, cook and finish basic pastry products.

Recipes included in this chapter

In addition to being one of the most important sections of the kitchen, pastry work can also be particularly enjoyable and rewarding. Although it is called 'pastry work', it actually includes making breads, desserts, sweets, and much more, not just goods made from pastry. Bakery products and desserts are explored in greater detail in Chapters 13, 15 and 16.

There is a range of pastes, all vital components of pastry work. Each type of paste is included in this chapter, along with several recipes that use it.

Ingredients for pastry work

This section provides information about the most commonly used ingredients in the production of pastry and bakery items.

The principal ingredients of pastry products are flour, fat, sugar, raising agents, eggs and cream. These ingredients form the basis of the various types of pastry products that are produced in this chapter. The type of pastry produced depends on the characteristics required. For example,

short pastry is crisp and savoury, whereas **puff pastry** is made from light layers of fine paste, separated by butter or a pastry fat that produces steam to push the layers apart during the baking process. The other types of pastry covered are forms of **sweet paste**, containing the crisp characteristics of short pastry but with a richer and sweeter flavour. **Choux paste** is used in the production of éclairs, profiteroles and choux buns, whereas **suet paste** is used to produce steamed puddings, rolls and dumplings that can be either sweet or savoury.

Flour

Flour is probably the most common commodity in daily use. It forms the foundation of bread, pastry and cakes, and is one of the most important ingredients in patisserie, if not *the* most important.

There is a great variety of high-quality flours made from cereals, nuts or legumes, such as chestnut flour, cornflour, and so on. They have been used in patisserie, baking, dessert cuisine and savoury cuisine in all countries throughout history. The most commonly used and most versatile flour, particularly in Western cuisine, is wheat flour.

Wheat flour

Wheat flour is composed of starch, gluten, sugar, fats, water and minerals.

- Starch is the main component.
- Gluten is also a significant element. Elastic and impermeable, it is the gluten that makes wheat flour the most common flour used in bread making.
- The quantity of sugar in wheat is very small but it plays a very important role in fermentation.
- Wheat contains a maximum of only 16 per cent water, but its presence is important.
- The mineral matter (ash), which is found mainly in the husk of the wheat grain and not in the kernel, determines the purity and quality of the flour.

Wheat goes through several distinct processes from the ear to the final product, flour. These are usually carried out in modern industrial plants, where wheat is subjected to the various treatments and phases necessary for the production of different types of flour. These arrive in perfect condition at our workplaces to be made into items such as sponge cakes, yeast dough, puff pastries, biscuits, pastries and much more.

The production of flour

White flour is made up almost entirely of the part of the wheat grain known as the endosperm, which contains starch and protein. When flour is mixed with water it is converted into a sticky dough. This characteristic is due to the gluten, which becomes sticky when moistened. The relative proportion of starch and gluten varies in different wheats; those with a low percentage of gluten (soft flour) are not suitable for bread making. For this reason, wheat is blended.

In milling, the whole grain is broken up, the parts separated, and then sifted, blended and ground into flour. Some of the outer coating of bran is removed, as is the wheatgerm, which contains oil and is therefore likely to become rancid and spoil the flour. For this reason wholemeal flour should not be stored for more than 14 days.

Types of flour

- White flour contains 72–85 per cent of the whole grain (the endosperm only).
- Wholemeal flour contains 100 per cent of the whole grain.
- Wheatmeal flour contains 85–95 per cent of the whole grain.
- High-ratio or patent flour contains 40 per cent of the whole grain.
- Self-raising flour is white flour that has had baking powder (usually bicarbonate of soda and tartaric acid) added to it.
- Semolina is granulated hard flour prepared from the central part of the wheat grain. White or wholemeal semolina is available.

Storing flour

Flour is a particularly delicate living material so it must be used and stored carefully. It must always be in the best condition, which is why storing large quantities is not recommended.

It must be kept in a clean, well-organised, disinfected and aerated storeroom. It must never be stored in warm and humid places.

Fats

Pastry goods may be made from various types of fat, either a single named fat or a combination. Examples of fats are butter, margarine, shortening and lard.

Butter

Butter brings smoothness, rich perfumes and aromas, and impeccable textures to pastry items. Butter is an emulsion – the perfect interaction of water and fat. It is composed of a minimum of 82 per cent fat, a maximum of 16 per cent water and 2 per cent dry extracts.

Here are some important facts about butter:
- Butter is the most complete fat.
- It is a very delicate ingredient that can quickly spoil if a series of basic rules are not followed in its use.
- It absorbs odours very easily, so it should be kept well covered and should always be stored far from anything that produces strong odours.
- When kept at 15 °C, butter is stable and retains all its properties: finesse, aroma and creaminess.
- It should not be kept too long: it is always better to work with fresh butter.
- Good-quality butter has a stable texture, pleasing taste, fresh odour, homogenous (even) colour and, most importantly, it melts perfectly in the mouth.
- It softens preparations such as cookies and petits fours, and keeps products like sponge cakes soft and moist.
- Butter enhances flavour – as in brioches, for example.
- The melting point of butter is between 30 °C and 35 °C.

Margarine

Margarine is often made from a blend of oils that have been hardened or hydrogenated (with the addition of hydrogen gas). Margarine may contain up to 10 per cent butterfat.

Cake margarine is a blend of hydrogenated oils to which an emulsifying agent is added that helps combine water and fat. Cake margarine may contain up to 10 per cent butterfat.

Pastry margarine is used for puff pastry. It is a hard plastic or waxy fat that is suitable for layering.

Shortening

Shortening is the term for some other fats used in pastry making. It is made from oils and is 100 per cent fat. Examples of shortening include hydrogenated lard and rendered pork fat.

Sugar

Sugar (or sucrose) is extracted from sugar beet or sugar cane. The juice is crystallised by a complicated manufacturing process and then refined and sieved into several grades, such as granulated, caster or icing sugars. Syrup and treacle are also produced as by-products during the production of refined sugar.

Loaf or cube sugar is obtained by pressing the crystals together while they are slightly wet, drying them in blocks, and then cutting the blocks into squares.

Fondant is a cooked mixture of sugar and glucose which, when heated, can be coloured and flavoured, and used for decorating cakes, buns, gâteaux and petits fours. Fondant is generally bought ready-made.

Inverted sugar

When sucrose is broken down with water, in a chemical process called hydrolysis, it separates into the two types of sugar that make it: fructose and glucose. Sugar that has been treated in this way is called inverted sugar and is, after sucrose, one of the most commonly used sugars in the catering profession, thanks to its sweetening properties.

Inverted sugar is used because:
- It improves the aroma of products.
- It improves the texture of doughs.
- It prevents the dehydration of frozen products.
- It reduces or stops crystallisation in ice cream making, improves smoothness and lowers its freezing point.

Glucose

Glucose takes on various forms:
- the characteristics of a viscous syrup, called crystal glucose
- its natural state, in fruit and honey
- a dehydrated white paste (used mainly in the commercial food industry, but also used in catering).

Glucose syrup:
- is a transparent, viscous paste
- prevents the crystallisation of boiled sugars, jams and preserves
- delays the drying of a product
- aids consistency and creaminess in ice cream and the fillings of chocolate bonbons
- prevents the crystallisation of ice cream.

Honey

Honey is the oldest known form of sugar. It is a very sweet, viscous syrup produced when bees extract nectar from flowers. It is 30 per cent sweeter than sucrose and generally has is light golden-brown appearance, although the colour varies depending on the species of bee, the flower from which the nectar is collected and the type of honey this produces.

Honey lowers the freezing point of ice cream. It can also be used like inverted sugar, but it is important to take into account that, unlike inverted sugar, honey will give its flavour to the preparation. Also, it is inadequate for preparations that require long storage, since honey recrystallises over time.

Isomalt

Isomalt is a sweetener that has been used by the food manufacturing industry for many years in the production of confectionery (sweets and gums). It has properties distinct from those of the sweeteners already mentioned. It is produced through the hydrolysis of sugar followed by hydrogenation (the addition of hydrogen). Produced through these industrial processes, this sugar is perfect for confectionery and chewing gum production, but it is now being used far more widely in the professional kitchen.

One of its most notable characteristics is that it can melt without the addition of water or another liquid. This is a very interesting property for making artistic decorations in cooked sugar. Its appearance is like that of confectioners' sugar: a glossy powder. Its sweetening strength is half that of sucrose and it is much less soluble than sugar, which means that it melts less easily in the mouth.

Isomalt's main advance in professional patisserie work over the past few years has been as a replacement for normal sugar or sucrose when making sugar decorations, blown sugar, pulled sugar or spun sugar. Isomalt is not affected by air humidity, so sugar pieces will keep for longer.

Raising agents

Raising agents are added to cake and bread mixtures to give lightness to the product, because they produce gases that expand when heated. The gases produced are air, carbon dioxide or water vapour. These gases are introduced before baking or are produced by substances added to the mixture before baking. When the product is cooked, the gases expand. These gases are trapped in the gluten of the wheat flour. The product rises and sets on further heating and cooking because of the pressure of the gluten.

Baking powder

Chemical raising agents cause a reaction between certain acidic and alkaline compounds, which produce carbon dioxide. The alkaline component is almost always sodium bicarbonate or sodium acid carbonate, commonly known as baking soda. It is ideal because it is cheap to produce, easily purified, non-toxic and naturally tasteless. Potassium bicarbonate is available for those on low-sodium diets, but this compound tends to absorb moisture, react prematurely and give a bitter flavour.

Baking powder may be used without the addition of acid if the dough or batter is already acidic enough to react with it to produce carbon dioxide. Yoghurt and sour milk contain lactic acid and often are used in place of water or milk in products such as scones, for example. Sour milk can also be added along with the baking soda as a separate 'natural' component of the leavening.

Baking powder contains baking soda and an acid in the form of salt crystals that dissolve in water. Ground dry starch is also added to prevent premature reactions in humid air by absorbing moisture, and to dilute the powder.

Most baking powders are 'double acting' – that is, they produce an initial set of gas bubbles when the powder is mixed into the batter and then a second set during the baking process. The first and smaller reaction is necessary to form many small gas bubbles in the batter or dough; the second is necessary to expand these bubbles to form the final light texture. This second reaction must happen late enough in the baking for the surrounding materials to have set, preventing the bubbles from escaping and the product from collapsing.

Baking powder is made from alkali (bicarbonate of soda) plus acid (cream of tartar – potassium hydrogen tartrate). Commercial baking powders differ mainly in their proportions of the acid salts. Cream of tartar is not normally used due to its high cost, so calcium phosphate and glucono delta-lactone are now commonly used in its place.

Water vapour

Water vapour is produced during the baking process from the liquid content used in the mixing. Water vapour has approximately 1,600 times the volume of the original water, but its raising power is slower than that of a gas. This method is used in the production of choux pastry, puff pastry, rough puff and flaky pastry, as well as batter products.

Using raising agents

- Always buy a reliable brand of baking powder.
- Store in a dry place in an airtight tin.
- Do not store for long periods of time: baking powder loses some of its residual carbon dioxide over time and therefore will not be as effective.
- Check the recipe carefully, making sure that the correct preparation for the type of mixture is used, otherwise, under- or over-rising may result.
- Sieve the raising agent with the flour and/or dry ingredients to give an even mix, and thus an even reaction.
- Distribute moisture evenly into the mixture to ensure even action of the raising agent.
- If a large proportion of raising agent has been added to a mixture, and is not to be cooked immediately, keep it in a cool place to avoid too much reaction before baking.

Too much raising agent causes:

- over-risen products that may collapse, giving a sunken effect
- a coarse texture
- poor colour and flavour
- fruit sinking to the bottom of the cake
- a bitter taste.

Insufficient raising agent causes:

- lack of volume
- insufficient lift
- close texture
- shrinkage.

Eggs

Eggs are an important and versatile ingredient in pastry work. Hens' eggs are graded in four sizes – small, medium, large and very large (see Chapter 6). For the recipes in this chapter, use medium-sized eggs (approximately 50 g), unless otherwise stated.

Eggs are used in pastry work because of their binding, emulsifying and coating properties. Eggs also add both protein and fat, thus improving the nutritional value and flavour of the product.

Milk

Full-cream, skimmed or semi-skimmed milk can be used for the desserts in this chapter.

Milk comes in many forms and is a basic element of the diet for many people throughout the world. Milk from cows is most commonly used in the production of patisserie products, although other types of milk are being used more frequently due to their nutritional properties and reduced allergenic risk (goat's milk ice cream, for example).

Milk consists of water, sugar and fat (with a minimum fat content of 3.5 per cent). It is essential in many products, from creams, ice creams, yeast doughs, mousses and custards to ganaches, cookies, tuiles and muffins. A yeast dough will change considerably in texture, taste and colour if it is made with milk instead of water.

Milk has a slightly sweet taste and little odour. Two distinct processes are used to conserve it:

- **Pasteurisation** – the milk is heated to between 73 °C and 85 °C for a few seconds, then cooled quickly to 4 °C.
- **Sterilisation (UHT)** – the milk is heated to between 140 °C and 150 °C for two seconds, then cooled quickly.

Milk is homogenised to disperse the fat evenly, since the fat has a tendency to rise to the surface (see 'Cream', below).

Here are some useful facts about milk.

- Pasteurised milk has a better taste and aroma than UHT milk.
- Milk is useful for developing flavour in sauces and creams, due to its lactic fermentation.
- Milk contributes to colour as well as to the development of texture and aroma in doughs.
- Because of its lactic ferments, it helps in the maturation of doughs and creams.
- Milk is much more fragile than cream. In recipes, adding it in certain proportions is advisable for a much more subtle and delicate final product.
- Other types of milk, such as sheep and goat's milk, can be very interesting to use in desserts.

Cream

Cream is the concentrated milk fat that is skimmed off the top of the milk when it has been left to sit. A film forms on the surface because of the difference in density between fat and liquid. This process is speeded up mechanically in large industries by heating and using centrifuges. Cream is used in many recipes because of its great versatility and capabilities.

Cream should contain at least 18 per cent butterfat. Cream for whipping must contain more than 30 per cent butterfat. Commercially frozen cream is available in slabs, typically ranging from 2 kg to 10 kg. Types, packaging, storage and uses of cream are listed in Table 14.1.

Whipping and double cream may be whipped to make them lighter and to increase volume. Cream will whip more easily if it is kept at refrigeration temperature. Indeed, all cream products must be kept in the refrigerator for health and safety reasons. They should be handled with care and, as they will absorb odour, they should never be stored near onions or other strong-smelling foods.

As with milk, there are two main methods for conserving cream:

- **Pasteurisation** – the cream is heated to between 85 °C and 90 °C for a few seconds then cooled quickly; this cream retains all its flavour properties.
- **Sterilisation (UHT)** – this consists of heating the cream to between 140 °C and 150 °C for two seconds; cream treated this way loses some of its flavour properties, but it keeps for longer.

Always use pasteurised cream when possible, for example in the restaurant when desserts are made for immediate consumption.

Here are some useful facts about cream.
- Cream whips with the addition of air, thanks to its fat content. This retains the air bubbles formed during beating.
- Understand how to use fresh cream; remember that it is easily over-whipped.

- Cream adds texture.
- Once cream is boiled and mixed or infused with other ingredients to add flavour, it will whip again if first left to cool completely (when preparing a chocolate Chantilly, for example).
- To whip cream well, it must be cold (around 4 °C).
- Cream can be infused with other flavours when it is hot or cold. The flavour of cream will develop if left to infuse prior to preparation.

Table 14.1 Types of cream

Type of cream	Legal minimum fat (%)	Processing and packaging	Storage	Characteristics and uses
Half cream	12	Homogenised; may be pasteurised or ultra-heat treated	2–3 days	Does not whip; used for pouring; suitable for low-fat diets
Cream (single cream)	18	Homogenised; pasteurised and packaged in bottles and cartons, sealed with foil caps; may be available in bulk	2–3 days in summer; 3–4 days in winter under refrigeration	A pouring cream suitable for coffee, cereals, soup or fruit; added to cooked dishes and sauces; does not whip
Whipping cream	35	Not homogenised; pasteurised and packaged like single cream	2–3 days in summer; 3–4 days in winter under refrigeration	Ideal for whipping; suitable for piping, cake and dessert decoration; used in ice cream, cake and pastry fillings
Double cream	48	Slightly homogenised; pasteurised and packaged like single cream	2–3 days in summer; 3–4 days in winter under refrigeration	A rich pouring cream; will whip; floats on coffee or soup
'Thick' double cream	48	Heavily homogenised; pasteurised and packaged like single cream; usually only sold in domestic quantities	2–3 days in summer; 3–4 days in winter under refrigeration	A rich, spoonable cream; cannot be poured
Clotted cream	55	Heated to 82 °C then cooled for 4½ hours; the cream crust is then skinned off; packed in cartons, usually by hand; may be available in bulk	2–3 days in summer; 3–4 days in winter under refrigeration	Very thick; has its own special flavour and colour; used with scones, fruit and fruit pies
Ultra-heat treated (UHT) cream	12 (half), 18 (single) or 35 (whipping)	Homogenised; heated to 132 °C for 1 second, then cooled immediately; aseptically packaged in polythene and foil-lined containers; available in catering-size packs	6 weeks if unopened; does not need refrigeration; usually date stamped	A pouring cream

Convenience products

Convenience mixes, such as short pastry, sponge mixes and choux pastry mixes, are increasingly used in a variety of establishments. These products have improved enormously over the last few years and give the chef the opportunity to save on time and labour; with skill, imagination and creativity, the finished products are not impaired.

Not surprisingly many caterers, including some luxury establishments, have turned to using frozen puff pastry. It is available in squares and rectangles, ready rolled, thereby avoiding the possibility of uneven thickness and the waste that can occur when rolling out yourself. The large food manufacturers dominate the frozen puff pastry market.

Manufactured puff pastry is available in three types, defined often by their fat content. The cheapest is made with the white hydrogenated fat, which gives the product a pale colour and a waxy taste. Puff pastry made with bakery margarine has a better colour and, often, a better flavour. The best-quality puff pastry is made with butter, giving a richer texture, colour and flavour.

Pastry bought in blocks is cheaper than pre-rolled separate sheets, but has to be rolled evenly to give an even bake. The sizes of sheets do vary with manufacturers and all are interleaved with greaseproof paper.

Filo pastry and *feuille de brick* are further examples of convenient pastry products. They are available in frozen sheets of various sizes. No rolling out is required and, once thawed, they can be used as required and moulded if necessary.

As well as convenience pastry mixes, there is a whole range of frozen products suitable to serve as sweets and afternoon tea pastries. These include fruit pies, flans, gâteaux and charlottes. The vast majority are ready to serve once defrosted, but very often they require a little more decorative finish. The availability of such products gives the caterer the advantage of further labour cost reductions, permitting the chef to concentrate on other areas of the menu.

Storage and food safety

- Store all goods according to the Food Safety and Hygiene Regulations 2013. Eggs should be stored in a refrigerator, flour in a bin with a tight-fitting lid, sugar and other dry ingredients in air-tight storage containers.
- Check all storage temperatures are correct.
- Make sure that storage containers are kept clean and returned ready for reuse. On their return they should be hygienically washed and stored.

- Handle all equipment carefully to avoid cross-contamination.
- Always work in a clean, tidy and organised way; clean all equipment after use.
- Take special care when using cream, and ensure that products containing cream are stored under refrigerated conditions.
- All piping bags must be sterilised after each use. Many kitchens use disposable plastic piping bags to avoid contamination and maximise freshness.
- Keep all small moulds clean and dry to prevent rusting.

Preparation and cooking techniques in pastry work

When handling ingredients for pastry work:
- check all weighing scales for accuracy
- follow recipes carefully.

Adding fat to flour

Fats act as a shortening agent. The fat has the effect of shortening the gluten strands in flour, which are easily broken when eaten, making the texture of the product more crumbly. However, the development of gluten in puff pastry is very important as long strands are needed to trap the expanding gases, and this is what makes the paste rise.

Fat can be added to flour by:
- **Rubbing in** by machine or by hand, for example, short pastry. When rubbing in it is much easier to produce a fine crumb if the fat is cold.
- **Creaming** by machine or by hand, for example, sweet pastry. This is easiest to do if the fat is 'plastic' (i.e. at room temperature). Always cream the fat and sugar well before adding the liquid.
- **The flour batter method**: for example, slab cakes.
- **Lamination**: for example, puff pastry.
- **Boiling**: for example, choux pastry.

Blending

Blending means mixing all the ingredients carefully by weight.

Handling pastry

Techniques used to work pastry include:
- **Folding**: for example, folding puff pastry to create its layers, as in *vol-au-vents* or *gâteau pithiviers*.
- **Kneading**: using a mixing machine or your hands to work dough or puff pastry in the first stage of making.

- **Relaxing**: keeping pastry covered with a damp cloth, cling film or plastic to prevent a skin forming on its surface. A period of resting allows the gluten in the pastry to relax and lose some of its resistance to rolling. It will also help to prevent the pastry from shrinking during the cooking process.
- **Shaping**: producing flans, tartlets, barquettes and other such goods with pastry. Shaping also refers to crimping with the back of a small knife using the thumb technique.
- **Docking**: piercing raw pastry with small holes to prevent it from rising during baking, as when cooking tartlets blind (without a filling).

Rolling

- Roll the pastry on a lightly floured surface; turn the pastry regularly to prevent it sticking. Keep the rolling pin lightly floured and free from the pastry.
- Always roll with care, treating the pastry lightly – never apply too much pressure.
- Always apply even pressure when using a rolling pin.

Cutting

- Always cut with a sharp, clean, damp knife.
- When using cutters, always flour them before use by dipping in flour. This will give a sharp, neat cut.
- Only use a lattice cutter on firm pastry; if the pastry is too soft, you will have difficulty lifting the lattice.

Glazing

A glaze is something that gives a product a smooth, shiny surface. Examples of glazes used for pastry dishes are as follows:

- A hot clear gel produced from a pectin source, obtainable commercially, for finishing flans and tartlets; always use while still hot. A cold gel is exactly the same except that it is used cold. The gel keeps a sheen on the goods and keeps out oxygen, which might otherwise cause discoloration.
- Apricot glaze, produced from apricot jam, acts in the same way as hot gels.
- Egg wash, applied prior to baking, produces a rich glaze during the cooking process.
- Icing sugar dusted on the surface of the product caramelises in the oven or under the grill.
- Fondant gives a rich sugar glaze, which may be flavoured and/or coloured.
- Water icing gives a transparent glaze, which may also be flavoured and/or coloured.

Cooking methods

The main cooking method used in the production of pastry products is baking. The time and temperature depend on the type of product being made. Pastry can also be steamed to make products such as fruit pudding or rolls, however, and certain pastes can also be deep-fried (samosa and filo pastes, for example).

Other considerations when preparing pastry items

- Ensure all cooked products are cooled before finishing.
- Always plan your time carefully.
- Understand why pastry products must be rested or relaxed and docked. This will prevent excessive shrinkage in the oven, while docking allows air to escape through the product, preventing any unevenness.
- Use silicone paper for baking in preference to greaseproof.

Finishing and presentation

It is essential that all products are finished according to the recipe requirements. Finishing and presentation is often a key stage in the process as failure at this point can affect the final appearance of the product. The way that goods are presented is an important part of the sales technique. Each product of the same type must be of the same shape, size, colour and finish. The decoration should be attractive, delicate and in keeping with the product range. All piping should be neat, clean and tidy.

Some methods of finishing and presentation are as follows:
- **Dusting**: a light sprinkling of icing sugar on a product using a fine sugar dredger or sieve.
- **Piping**: using fresh cream, chocolate or fondant, for example.
- **Filling**: with fruit, cream, pastry cream, etc. Avoid overfilling as this can give the product a clumsy appearance.

Piping fresh cream

- Piping fresh cream is a skill and, like all other skills, it takes practice to become proficient. The finished item should look attractive, simple, clean and tidy.
- All piping bags should be sterilised after each use, as these may well be a source of contamination; alternatively use a disposable piping bag.
- Make sure that all the equipment you need for piping is hygienically cleaned before and after use to avoid cross-contamination.

Test yourself

1 What is the ratio of fat to flour for:
   a short pastry
   b puff pastry
   c sugar pastry?
2 How is the fat added to the flour in the production of choux pastry?
3 What type of fat is required for the production of suet paste?
4 What is meant by the term 'lamination'?
5 Name five examples of products that can be produced using puff pastry.
6 Other than éclairs and profiteroles, name three products that are made using choux paste.
7 Name one pastry product, eaten as a dessert, which would be unsuitable for a vegetarian customer.
8 Name the faults associated with the production of short pastry.
9 What is the classic filling for a *gâteau pithiviers*?
10 Name three fillings that can be used in the production of sweet tarts.

Short pastry

1 Short paste (*pâte à foncer*)

Short pastry is used in fruit pies, Cornish pasties, etc.

Ingredient	400 g	850 g
Flour (soft)	250 g	500 g
Salt	Pinch	Large pinch
Butter or block/cake margarine	125 g	250 g
Water	40–50 ml	80–100 ml

1 Sieve the flour and salt. Add the butter in small pieces.

2 Start to rub the fat into the flour.

3 Continue to rub in.

4 Stop rubbing in once the mixture is crumbly and the lumps of butter are gone.

5 Make a well in the centre. Add water and start to mix it in.

6 Work into a firm dough.

7 Knead into a ball. Handle as little and as lightly as possible. Refrigerate until firm before rolling.

8 Roll out the paste for use.

Professional tip

The amount of water used varies according to:

- the type of flour (a very fine soft flour is more absorbent)
- the degree of heat (for example, prolonged contact with hot hands, or warm weather conditions).

Different fats have different shortening properties. For example, paste made with a high ratio of butter to other fat will be harder to handle.

Variation

For wholemeal short pastry, use wholemeal flour in place of half to three-quarters of the white flour.

Short pastry for sweet dishes such as baked jam roll may be made with self-raising flour.

Lard can be used in place of some or all of the fat (the butter or cake margarine). Lard has excellent shortening properties and would lend itself, in terms of flavour, to savoury products, particularly meat-based ones. However, many people view lard as an unhealthy product as it is very high in saturated fat. It is also unsuitable for anyone following a vegan or vegetarian diet as it is an animal product.

Faults

Possible reasons for faults in short pastry are detailed below.

Hard:
- too much water
- too little fat
- fat rubbed in insufficiently
- too much handling and rolling
- over-baking.

Soft–crumbly:
- too little water
- too much fat.

Blistered:
- too little water
- water added unevenly
- fat not rubbed in evenly.

Soggy:
- too much water
- too cool an oven
- baked for insufficient time.

Shrunken:
- too much handling and rolling
- pastry stretched while handling.

From left to right: correct, blistered and shrunken short paste

2 Quiche lorraine (cheese and ham savoury flan)

Ingredient	4 portions	10 portions
Short paste	100 g	250 g
Ham, chopped	75 g	150 g
Cheese, grated	50 g	125 g
Egg	1	2½
Milk	125 ml	300 ml
Cayenne pepper		
Sea-salt (e.g. Maldon)		

Energy	Cals	Fat	Sat fat	Carb	Sugar	Protein	Fibre
2,955 kJ	704 kcal	48.4 g	22.6 g	38.1 g	6.5 g	31.6 g	1.8 g

1 Lightly grease an appropriately sized flan ring or barquette, or tartlet moulds if making individual portions. Line thinly with pastry.

2 Prick the bottom of the pastry two or three times with a fork to dock.

3 Cook in a hot oven at 200 °C for 3–4 minutes or until the pastry is lightly set. Reduce the oven temperature to 160 °C.

4 Remove from the oven; press the pastry down if it has tended to rise.

5 Add the chopped ham and grated cheese.

6 Mix the egg, milk, salt and cayenne thoroughly. Strain over the ham and cheese.

7 Return to the oven at 160 °C and bake gently for approximately 20 minutes or until nicely browned and the egg custard mix has set.

Variation

The filling can be varied by using lightly fried lardons of bacon (in place of the ham), chopped cooked onions and chopped parsley.

A variety of savoury flans can be made by using imagination and experimenting with different combinations (for example, stilton and onion; salmon and dill; sliced sausage and tomato).

3 Fruit pie

Ingredient	4–6 portions	10–15 portions
Fruit (see note)	400 g	1.5 kg
Sugar	100 g	250 g
Water	2 tbsp	5 tbsp
Short paste	200 g	500 g
Egg wash		

Energy	Cals	Fat	Sat fat	Carb	Sugar	Protein	Fibre
6,808 kJ	1,621 kcal	65.0 g	26.6 g	260.0 g	144.1 g	15.3 g	15.0 g

For an apple pie.

1 Prepare the fruit, wash and place in a bowl.

2 Add the sugar and water, and mix gently. (Place a clove in an apple pie.)

3 Line an appropriately sized flan ring with two-thirds of the pastry, leaving a third for the top.

4 Fill the lined ring with the fruit mixture.

5 Dampen the edge of the pastry with a little water.

6 Roll out the reserved piece of pastry to cover the fruit.

7 Carefully lay the pastry on top of the fruit and firmly seal to the edge of the lined pastry. Cut off any surplus pastry. (This can be used to create a lattice effect by running strips of pastry in diagonal lines across the pie – see picture.)

8 Brush the top of the pie with egg wash and sprinkle with caster sugar.

9 Place the pie on a baking sheet and bake at 200 °C for 10 minutes; reduce the oven to 180 °C and continue to bake for another 25–30 minutes. If the pastry colours too quickly, cover it with a sheet of paper.

10 Once cooked, allow to cool slightly before removing the flan ring. Serve with custard, fresh cream or ice cream.

Preparation of fruit for pies

The pie may be filled with a single fruit or a combination such as blackberry and apple or damson and apple.

- apples – peeled, quartered, cored, washed, cut in slices
- cherries – stalks removed, stoned, washed
- blackberries – stalks removed, washed
- gooseberries – stalks and tails removed, washed
- damsons – picked, stoned and washed
- rhubarb – leaves and root removed, tough strings removed, cut into 2 cm pieces, washed.

4 Treacle tart

Ingredient	4 portions	10 portions
Short paste	125 g	300 g
Treacle	100 g	250 g
Water	1 tbsp	2½ tbsp
Lemon juice	3–4 drops	8–10 drops
Fresh white bread or cake crumbs	15 g	50 g

Energy	Cals	Fat	Sat fat	Carb	Sugar	Protein	Fibre
1,100 kJ	262 kcal	10.7 g	5.8 g	41.1 g	20.3 g	2.8 g	0.8 g

1 Lightly grease an appropriately sized flan ring, or barquette or tartlet moulds if making individual portions.

2 Line with pastry.

3 Warm the treacle, water and lemon juice; add the crumbs.

4 Place into the pastry ring and bake at 170 °C for about 20 minutes.

Variation

This tart can also be made in a shallow flan ring. Any pastry debris can be rolled and cut into 0.5 cm strips and used to decorate the top of the tart before baking.

Try sprinkling with vanilla salt as a garnish.

Sweet pastry

5 Sugar paste (sweet paste, *pâte à sucre*)

Sugar pastry is used for products such as flans, fruit tarts and tartlets.

Ingredient	400 g	1 kg
Sugar	50 g	125 g
Butter or block/cake margarine	125 g	300 g
Eggs	1	2–3
Flour (soft)	200 g	500 g
Salt	Pinch	Large pinch

Method 1 – sweet lining paste (rubbing in)

1 Sieve the flour and salt. Lightly rub in the margarine or butter to achieve a sandy texture.

2 Mix the sugar and egg until dissolved.

3 Make a well in the centre of the flour. Add the sugar and beaten egg.

4 Gradually incorporate the flour and margarine or butter and lightly mix to a smooth paste. Allow to rest before using.

Method 2 – traditional French sugar paste (creaming)

1 Taking care not to over-soften, cream the butter and sugar.

2 Add the beaten egg gradually and mix for a few seconds.

3 Gradually incorporate the sieved flour and salt. Mix lightly until smooth.

4 Allow to rest in a cool place before using.

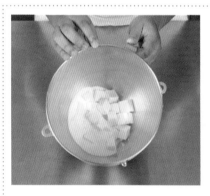

1 Measure out the sugar and cut the butter into small chunks.

2 Cream the butter and sugar together.

3 Add the beaten egg in stages, thoroughly mixing each time.

4 Incorporate the flour and salt.

5 Press into a tray and leave to chill.

6 The paste will need to be rolled out before use in any recipe.

The higher the percentage of butter, the shorter and richer the paste will become. However, as the butter will soften and melt during handling, the paste will become softer and more difficult to work with. Therefore chilling and light, quick handling are required when using a sweet paste with a high butter content.

This also applies to the working environment. For example, in a particularly warm kitchen, it will be more difficult to work with a paste of this structure than in a cooler kitchen.

The butter in this recipe could be reduced from 125 g to 100 g to make handling easier.

From left to right: short paste (recipe 1), rough puff paste (recipe 24) and sweet paste (recipe 5)

6 Flan cases

1 Allow 25 g flour per portion and prepare sugar pastry as per recipe 5.

2 Grease a flan ring and baking sheet.

3 Roll the pastry out so that the circumference is 2 cm larger than the flan ring. The pastry may be rolled between cling film or greaseproof or silicone paper.

4 Place the flan ring on the baking sheet.

5 Carefully place the pastry on the flan ring by rolling it loosely over the rolling pin, picking it up and unrolling it over the flan ring.

6 Press the pastry into shape without stretching it, being careful to exclude any air.

7 Allow a 0.5 cm ridge of pastry on top of the flan ring.

8 Cut off the surplus paste by rolling the rolling pin firmly across the top of the flan ring.

9 The rim can be left straight or moulded. Mould the edge with thumb and forefinger. Decorate either with pastry tweezers or with thumbs and forefingers, squeezing the pastry neatly to form a corrugated pattern.

Video: lining a flan
http://bit.ly/17grHMP

Baking blind

Some recipes call for the flan case to be baked blind, which means that it is baked before the filling is added. Line the pastry case with cling film and fill with baking beans (ceramic pie weights) or dried beans. Bake at 190 °C.

Place the pastry into the flan ring

Firm the pastry into the bottom of the ring

Bake blind, filled with beans, if the recipe requires

7 Egg custard tart

1 Roll out the pastry on a lightly floured surface, to 2 mm thickness. Use it to line a 20 cm flan ring, placed on a baking sheet.

2 Line the pastry with food-safe cling film or greaseproof paper and fill with baking beans. Bake blind in a preheated oven at 190 °C for about 10 minutes or until the pastry is turning golden brown. Remove the paper and beans, and allow to cool. Turn the oven down to 130 °C.

3 To make the custard filling, whisk together the egg yolks and sugar. Add the cream and mix well.

4 Pass the mixture through a fine sieve into a saucepan. Heat to 37 °C.

5 Fill the pastry case with the custard to 0.5 cm below the top. Place it carefully into the middle of the oven and bake for 30–40 minutes or until the custard appears to be set but not too firm.

6 Remove from the oven and cover liberally with grated nutmeg. Allow to cool to room temperature.

Ingredient	8 portions
Sweet paste	250 g
Egg yolks	9
Caster sugar	75 g
Whipping cream, gently warmed and infused with 2 sticks of cinnamon	500 ml
Nutmeg, freshly grated	

Energy	Cals	Fat	Sat fat	Carb	Sugar	Protein	Fibre	Sodium
1998 kJ	482 kcal	39.0 g	22.0 g	27.0 g	15.8 g	6.4 g	0.6 g	0.2 g

8 Fruit tart, tartlets or barquettes

Fruit tart

Ingredient	4 portions
Sweet paste	250 g
Fruit (e.g. strawberries, raspberries, grapes, blueberries)	500 g
Pastry cream	
Glaze	5 tbsp

1 Line a flan ring with paste and cook blind at 190 °C. Allow to cool.

2 Pick and wash the fruit, then drain well. Wash and slice/segment, etc. any larger fruit being used.

3 Pipe pastry cream into the flan case, filling it to the rim. Dress the fruit neatly over the top.

4 Coat with the glaze. Use a glaze suitable for the fruit chosen, for example, with a strawberry tart, use a red glaze.

Energy	Cals	Fat	Sat fat	Carb	Sugar	Protein	Fibre	Sodium
1907 kJ	454 kcal	18.7 g	10.7 g	68.0 g	39.0 g	6.8 g	3.6 g	0.3 g

Faults

Although this strawberry tart may appear to be fine at first glance, the husks of the strawberries are visible. It would be better to present the strawberries with their tops pointing upwards or sliced and overlapping.

There is also quite a wide gap between the rows of strawberries, showing the crème pâtissière underneath. This should be avoided.

The second photo shows the importance of ensuring that fillings are prepared and/or cooked properly. In this case, the crème pâtissière has not been cooked sufficiently or prepared accurately as the filling is not structured sufficiently to support the fruit once the tart has been cut.

Professional tip

Brush the inside of the pastry case with melted couverture before filling. This forms a barrier between the pastry and the moisture in the filling.

Tartlets

Energy	Cals	Fat	Sat fat	Carb	Sugar	Protein	Fibre	Sodium
690 kJ	165 kcal	8.7 g	2.7 g	21.1 g	6.3 g	2.0 g	1.2 g	0.1 g

1 Roll out pastry 3 mm thick.

2 Cut out rounds with a fluted cutter and place them neatly in greased tartlet moulds. If soft fruit (such as strawberries or raspberries) is being used, the pastry should be cooked blind first.

3 After baking and filling (or filling and baking) with pastry cream, dress neatly with fruit and glaze the top.

Certain fruits (such as strawberries and raspberries) are sometimes served in boat-shaped moulds (barquettes). The preparation is the same as for tartlets. Tartlets and barquettes should be glazed and served allowing one large or two small per portion.

9 Apple flan

Ingredient	4 portions	10 portions
Sweet paste	100g	250g
Pastry cream (crème pâtissière) (see recipe 36)	250ml	625ml
Cooking apples	400g	1kg
Sugar	50g	125g
Apricot glaze	2 tbsp	6 tbsp

Energy	Cals	Fat	Sat fat	Carb	Sugar	Protein	Fibre
1,428 kJ	340 kcal	13.8g	5.8g	53.8g	36g	3.5g	2.9g

1 Line a flan ring with sweet paste. Pierce the bottom several times with a fork.

2 Pipe a layer of pastry cream into the bottom of the flan.

3 Peel, quarter and wash the selected apple.

4 Cut into neat thin slices and lay carefully on the pastry cream, overlapping each slice. Ensure that each slice points to the centre of the flan then no difficulty should be encountered in joining up the pattern neatly.

5 Sprinkle a little sugar on the apple slices and bake the flan at 200–220°C for 30–40 minutes.

6 When the flan is almost cooked, remove the flan ring carefully, return to the oven to complete the cooking. Mask with hot apricot glaze or flan jelly.

Pipe the filling neatly into the flan case

Slice the apple very thinly for decoration

Arrange the apple slices on top of the flan

10 Lemon tart

1 Prepare 200 g of sweet paste, adding the zest of one lemon to the sugar.

2 Line a 20 cm flan ring with the paste.

3 Bake blind at 190 °C for approximately 15 minutes.

4 Prepare the filling: mix the eggs and sugar together until smooth, add the cream, lemon juice and zest. Whisk well.

5 Seal the pastry, so that the filling will not leak out. Pour the filling into the flan case and bake for 30–40 minutes at 150 °C until just set. (Take care when almost cooked as overcooking will cause the filling to rise and possibly crack.)

6 Remove from the oven and allow to cool.

7 Dust with icing sugar and glaze under the grill or with a blowtorch. Portion and serve.

Ingredient	8 portions
Sweet paste	200 g
Lemons	Juice of 3, zest from 4
Eggs	8
Caster sugar	300 g
Double cream	250 ml

Energy	Cals	Fat	Sat fat	Carb	Sugar	Protein	Fibre	Sodium
1907 kJ	456 kcal	25.0g	13.4g	53.0g	44.0g	8.5g	0.5g	0.2g

Note

The mixture will fill one 16 × 4 cm or two 16 × 2 cm flan rings. If using two flan rings, double the amount of pastry and reduce the baking time when the filling is added.

Professional tip

If possible, make the filling one day in advance. The flavour will develop as the mixture matures.

Variation

Limes may be used in place of lemons. If so, use the zest and juice of five limes or use a mixture of lemons and limes.

11 Lemon meringue pie

Ingredient	2 × 20 cm flan rings (16 portions)
Sweet paste flan cases	2
Granulated sugar	450 g
Lemons, grated zest	2
Fresh lemon juice	240 ml
Eggs, large	8
Large egg yolks	2
Unsalted butter, cut into small pieces	350 g
Meringue	
Egg whites	6
Caster sugar	600 g

Energy	Cals	Fat	Sat fat	Carb	Sugar	Protein	Fibre
12,138 kJ	2,895 kcal	147.4 g	84.8 g	379.4 g	305.0 g	36.4 g	4.2 g

1 Place the sugar into a bowl and grate the zest of lemon into it, rubbing together.

2 Strain the lemon juice into a non-reactive pan. Add the eggs, egg yolks, butter and zested sugar. Whisk to combine.

3 Place over a medium heat and whisk continuously for 3–5 minutes, until the mixture begins to thicken.

4 At the first sign of boiling, remove from the heat. Strain into a bowl and cool before filling the pastry cases.

5 Make the meringue (see page 528). Pipe it on top of the filled pie.

6 Colour in a hot oven at 220 °C.

12 Pear and almond tart

Ingredient	8 portions
Sweet paste	200 g
Apricot jam	25 g
Almond cream	350 g
Poached pears	4
Apricot glaze	
Flaked almonds	
Icing sugar	

Energy	Cals	Fat	Sat fat	Carb	Sugar	Protein	Fibre	Sodium
1500 kJ	359 kcal	23.0 g	10.3 g	34.0 g	24.0 g	5.7 g	3.6 g	0.3 g

1. Line a buttered 20 cm flan ring with sweet paste. Trim and dock.

2. Using the back of a spoon, spread a little apricot jam over the base.

3. Pipe in almond cream until the flan case is two-thirds full.

4. Dry the poached pears. Cut them in half and remove the cores and string.

5. Score across the pears and arrange on top of the flan.

6. Bake in the oven at 200°C for 25–30 minutes.

7. Allow to cool, then brush with apricot glaze.

8. Sprinkle flaked almonds around the edge and dust with icing sugar.

13 Bakewell tart

Ingredient	8 portions
Sweet paste	200 g
Raspberry jam	50 g
Egg wash	1 egg
Apricot glaze	50 g
Icing sugar	35 g
Frangipane (almond cream)	250 g

Energy	Cals	Fat	Sat fat	Carb	Sugar	Protein	Fibre	Sodium
1308 kJ	313 kcal	18.5g	8.6g	34.0g	24.0g	5.0g	1.5g	0.2g

1. Line a 20 cm flan ring using three-quarters of the paste, 2 mm thick.

2. Pierce the bottom with a fork.

3. Spread with jam and the frangipane.

4. Roll the remaining paste, cut into neat 0.5 cm strips and arrange neatly criss-crossed (lattice) on the frangipane; trim off surplus paste. Brush with egg wash.

5. Bake in a moderately hot oven at 200–210°C for 30–40 minutes. Brush with hot apricot glaze.

6. When cooled, brush over with very thin water icing. Sprinkle with flaked almonds.

14 Mince pies

Ingredient	12 small pies
Sweet paste	200g
Mincemeat (see below)	200g
Egg wash	1 egg
Icing sugar	

Energy	Cals	Fat	Sat fat	Carb	Sugar	Protein	Fibre	Sodium
2,009 kJ	479 kcal	23.4g	0.0g	66.6g	32.0g	4.6g	2.8g	0.3g

For a portion of two small pies.

1 Roll out the pastry 3mm thick.

2 Cut half the pastry into fluted rounds 6cm in diameter.

3 Place on a greased, dampened baking sheet. (Tartlet moulds may also be used.)

4 Moisten the edges. Place a little mincemeat in the centre of each.

5 Cut the remainder of the pastry into fluted rounds, 8cm in diameter.

6 Cover the mincemeat with pastry and seal the edges. Brush with egg wash.

7 Bake at 210°C for approximately 20 minutes.

8 Sprinkle with icing sugar and serve warm.

Accompany with a suitable sauce, such as custard, brandy sauce or brandy cream.

Mincemeat

Ingredient	
Suet, chopped	100g
Mixed peel, chopped	100g
Currants	100g
Sultanas	100g
Raisins	100g
Apples, chopped	100g
Barbados sugar	100g
Mixed spice	5g
Lemon, grated zest and juice of	1
Orange, grated zest and juice of	1
Rum	60ml
Brandy	60ml

1 Mix the ingredients together.

2 Seal in jars and use as required.

Variation

Short or puff pastry may also be used. Various toppings can also be added, such as crumble mixture or flaked almonds and an apricot glaze.

Choux pastry

15 Choux paste (*pâte à choux*)

Choux paste is used to make products such as éclairs, profiteroles and gâteau Paris-Brest.

Ingredient	750 g	1.5 kg
Water	250 ml	500 ml
Sugar	Pinch	Large pinch
Salt	Pinch	Large pinch
Butter or block/cake margarine	100 g	200 g
Flour (strong)	150 g	300 g
Eggs	4–5	8–10

1 Bring the water, sugar, salt and fat to the boil in a saucepan. Remove from the heat.

2 Add the sieved flour and mix in with a wooden spoon.

3 Return to a moderate heat and stir continuously until the mixture leaves the sides of the pan. (This is known as a panada.)

4 Remove from the heat and allow to cool.

5 Gradually add the beaten eggs, beating well. Do not add all the eggs at once – check the consistency as you go. The mixture should just flow back when moved in one direction (it may not take all the egg).

Variation

Wholemeal flour – 50 per cent, 70 per cent or 100 per cent – may be used to make choux paste.

Faults

Greasy and heavy paste:
● the basic mixture was over-cooked.

Soft paste, not aerated:
● flour insufficiently cooked
● eggs insufficiently beaten in the mixture
● oven too cool
● under-baked.

Split or separated mixture:
● egg added too quickly.

The choux buns on the left are light and well risen; those on the right are poorly aerated.

Video: making choux paste
http://bit.ly/
1Ldujdh

1 Cut the butter into cubes and melt them in the water.

2 Add the flour.

3 When the panada is ready, it will start to come away from the sides.

4 Add egg until the mixture is the right consistency – it should drop from a spoon under its own weight.

5 Pipe the paste into the shape required – these rings could be used for Paris-Brest (recipe 19).

6 A selection of shapes in raw choux paste.

16 Cream buns (*choux à la crème*)

Ingredient	Makes 10 buns
Choux paste	150 ml
Egg wash	
Chopped almonds and/or nib sugar	35 g
Whipped cream/Chantilly cream	300 ml
Icing sugar, to serve	

Energy	Cals	Fat	Sat fat	Carb	Sugar	Protein	Fibre	Sodium
752 kJ	182 kcal	16.4g	8.5g	6.7g	3.6g	2.2g	0.2g	0.0g

1 Place the choux paste into a piping bag with a 1 cm plain tube.

2 Pipe pieces the size of a walnut on to a lightly greased, dampened baking sheet.

3 Using a wet finger, gently press down any spikes or peaks of paste to make round bulbs of paste, then egg wash.

4 Bake at 200–220 °C for about 30 minutes.

5 Allow to cool. Make a hole in the base of each bun.

6 Fill with sweetened, vanilla-flavoured whipped cream (Chantilly cream) using a piping bag and small tube.

7 Sprinkle with icing sugar and serve with cream and fresh fruit such as strawberries or raspberries.

17 Profiteroles and chocolate sauce

Ingredient	10 portions
Choux paste	200 ml
Chocolate sauce (see page 560)	250 ml
Chantilly cream	250 ml
Icing sugar, to serve	

Energy	Cals	Fat	Sat fat	Carb	Sugar	Protein	Fibre
919 kJ	219 kcal	16.2 g	9.7 g	16.4 g	12.8 g	2.9 g	0.2 g

1 Spoon the choux paste into a piping bag with a plain nozzle (approx. 1.5 cm diameter).

2 Pipe walnut-sized balls of paste on to the greased baking sheet, spaced well apart. Level the peaked tops with the tip of a wet finger.

3 Bake for 18–20 minutes at 200 °C, until well risen and golden brown. Remove from the oven, transfer to a wire rack and allow to cool completely.

4 Make a hole in each and fill with Chantilly cream.

5 Dredge with icing sugar and serve with a sauceboat of cold chocolate sauce or coat the profiteroles with the sauce.

Variation

Coffee sauce may be served and the profiteroles filled with non-dairy cream. Profiteroles may also be filled with chocolate-, coffee- or rum-flavoured pastry cream.

18 Chocolate éclairs

Ingredient	12 portions
Choux paste	200 ml
Whipped cream/Chantilly cream	250 ml
Fondant	100 g
Chocolate couverture	25 g

Energy	Cals	Fat	Sat fat	Carb	Sugar	Protein	Fibre
516 kJ	123 kcal	9.5 g	5.7 g	8.8 g	7.3 g	1.1 g	0.1 g

Variations

For coffee éclairs (éclairs au café) add a few drops of coffee extract to the fondant instead of chocolate; coffee éclairs may also be filled with pastry cream (see page 476) flavoured with coffee.

1 Place the choux paste into a piping bag with a 1 cm plain tube.

2 Pipe into 8 cm lengths on to a lightly greased, dampened baking sheet.

3 Bake at 200–220 °C for about 30 minutes.

4 Allow to cool. Slit down one side, with a sharp knife.

5 Fill with Chantilly cream (or whipped cream) using a piping bag and small tube. The continental fashion is to fill with pastry cream.

6 Warm the fondant, add the finely cut chocolate, allow to melt slowly, adjusting the consistency with a little sugar and water syrup if necessary. Do not overheat or the fondant will lose its shine.

7 Glaze the éclairs by dipping them in the fondant; remove the surplus with the finger. Allow to set.

Traditionally, chocolate éclairs were filled with chocolate pastry cream.

Pierce the éclair

Pipe in the filling

Dip the éclair in fondant; wipe the edges to give a neat finish

19 Gâteau Paris-Brest

Ingredient	8 portions
Choux paste	
Crème diplomate (see page 476)	800 ml
For the praline	
Flaked almonds, hazelnuts and pecans (any combination)	375 g
Granulated sugar	500 g

Energy	Cals	Fat	Sat fat	Carb	Sugar	Protein	Fibre
3,180 kJ	761 kcal	47.4 g	14.7 g	74.1 g	69.9 g	14.1 g	0.2 g

Praline

1 Place the nuts on a baking sheet and toast until evenly coloured.

2 Place the sugar in a large, heavy, stainless steel saucepan. Set the pan over a low heat and allow the sugar to caramelise. Do not over-stir, but do not allow the sugar to burn.

3 When the sugar is lightly caramelised and reaches a temperature of 170 °C, remove from the heat and stir in the nuts.

4 Immediately deposit the mixture on a non-stick silicone mat. Place another mat over the top and roll as thin as possible.

5 Allow to cool completely. Break up and store in an airtight container.

Paris-Brest

1 Pipe choux paste (recipe 15) into rings and bake.

2 Slice each ring in half. Fill with a mixture of crème diplomate or pastry cream and praline.

20 Choux paste fritters (*beignets soufflés*)

Ingredient	Makes 8 portions
Choux paste	125 ml
Icing sugar or caster sugar, to serve	
Apricot sauce, to serve	125 ml

Energy	Cals	Fat	Sat fat	Carb	Sugar	Protein	Fibre
344 kJ	82 kcal	3.9g	1.3g	11.5g	8.8g	0.9g	0.2g

1 Using two spoons of the same size, shape the paste into quenelles.

2 Place on to strips of lightly greased, greaseproof paper.

3 Lower the pieces into moderately hot deep fat at 170 °C. Allow to cook gently for 10–15 minutes.

4 Drain well and roll in the caster sugar. The sugar can be flavoured at this point (ground cinnamon is often used at this stage).

5 Serve with a sauceboat of hot fruit-based sauce.

Shape the fritter with two spoons

Lower the fritters into hot oil on a strip of greaseproof paper

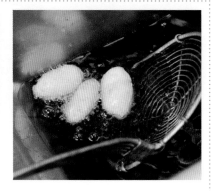

Lift them out with a spider

Suet pastry

21 Suet paste

Suet paste is used for steamed fruit puddings, steamed jam rolls, steamed meat puddings and dumplings.

1 Sieve the flour, baking powder and salt.

2 Mix in the suet. Make a well. Add the water.

3 Mix lightly to a fairly stiff paste.

Professional tip

Self-raising flour already contains baking powder so this element could be reduced in the recipe if using self-raising flour.

Vegetarian suet is also available to enable products to be meat-free.

Ingredient	400 g	1 kg
Flour (soft) or self-raising flour	200 g	500 g
Baking powder	10 g	25 g
Salt	Pinch	Large pinch
Prepared beef or vegetarian suet	100 g	250 g
Water	125 ml	300 ml

Faults

Heavy and soggy paste:
● cooking temperature may have been too low.

Tough paste:
● handled too much or over-cooked.

22 Steamed fruit puddings

	10 individual puddings or 1 large pudding
Suet paste (see recipe 21)	300 g
Fruit	1 kg
Sugar	200 g
Water	60 ml

Energy	Cals	Fat	Sat fat	Carb	Sugar	Protein	Fibre	Sodium
975 kJ	231 kcal	6.3 g	3.1 g	44.0 g	33.0 g	1.8 g	2.6 g	0.1 g

1 Grease a basin or individual moulds.

2 Line the moulds, using three-quarters of the paste.

3 Add the prepared and washed fruit and the sugar. (Add between one and two cloves in an apple pudding.)

5 Add water. Moisten the edge of the paste.

6 Cover with the remaining quarter of the paste and seal firmly.

7 Cover with greased greaseproof paper, a pudding cloth or foil.

8 Steam for about 1½ hours (large basin) or 40 minutes (individual moulds).

Serve with custard.

Variation

Steamed fruit puddings can be made with apple, apple and blackberry, rhubarb, rhubarb and apple, and so on.

Puff pastry

23 Puff paste (French method)

Ingredient	Makes approx. 1.5 kg
Flour (strong)	560 g
Salt	12 g
Pastry butter or pastry margarine	60 g
Water, ice-cold	325 ml
Lemon juice, ascorbic or tartaric acid, or white vinegar	A few drops
Pastry butter or pastry margarine	500 g

1 Sieve the flour and salt together.

2 Rub in the 60 g of pastry butter/pastry margarine.

3 Make a well in the centre.

4 Add the cold water and lemon juice or acid (to make the gluten more elastic), and knead well into a smooth dough in the shape of a ball.

5 Relax the dough in a cool place for 30 minutes.

6 Cut a cross halfway through the dough and pull out the corners to form a star shape.

7 Roll out the points of the star square, leaving the centre thick.

8 Knead the remaining butter/margarine to the same texture as the dough. This is most important – if the fat is too soft it will melt and ooze out, if it is too hard it will break through the paste when being rolled.

9 Place the butter or margarine on the centre square, which is four times thicker than the flaps.

10 Fold over the flaps.

11 Roll out to 30 cm × 15 cm, cover with a cloth or plastic and rest for 5–10 minutes in a cool place.

12 Roll out to 60 cm × 20 cm, fold both the ends to the centre, and fold in half again to form a square. This is one double turn.

13 Allow to rest in a cool place for 20 minutes.

14 Half-turn the paste to the right or the left.

15 Give one more double turn and allow to rest for 20 minutes.

16 Give two more double turns, allowing to rest between each.

17 Allow to rest before using.

Rub the first batch of butter into the flour

Mix in the water and lemon juice

Knead into a smooth dough

Roll the dough out into a cross shape

Knead the remaining butter in a plastic bag, then place it on the centre of the dough

Fold over each flap

Roll into a neat rectangle, then take each end and fold to meet in the centre

Fold again from the top end of the paste to the bottom

These photos have shown one double turn. When resting the turned and folded paste, leave an indented finger mark on the surface to show the number of turns completed

Professional tip

- Care must be taken when rolling out the paste to keep the ends and sides square.
- When rolling between each turn, always roll with the folded edge to the left.
- The addition of lemon juice (or other acid) helps to strengthen the gluten in the flour, thus helping to make a stronger dough, so that there is less likelihood of the fat oozing out.
- The rise is caused by the fat separating layers of paste and air during rolling. When heat is applied by the oven, steam is produced, causing the layers to rise and give the characteristic flaky formation. This is aeration by lamination.

Faults

The pastry on the left is unevenly laminated. Possible reasons for this:

- The paste was not folded equally.
- The paste was rolled too thinly.
- Reused scraps of paste were used, instead of making up a virgin paste.

24 Rough puff paste

Ingredient	475 g	1.2 kg
Flour (strong)	200 g	500 g
Salt	1 large pinch	2 large pinches
Butter or block/cake margarine (lightly chilled)	150 g	375 g
Water, ice-cold	125 ml	300 ml
Lemon juice, ascorbic or tartaric acid	10 ml	25 ml

1 Sieve the flour and salt.
2 Cut the fat into small pieces and lightly mix them into the flour without rubbing in.
3 Make a well in the centre.

4 Add the liquid and mix to a dough. The dough should be fairly tight at this stage.
5 Turn on to a floured table and roll into an oblong strip, about 30 × 10 cm, keeping the sides square.
6 Give one double turn (as for puff pastry).
7 Allow to rest in a cool place, covered with cloth or plastic for 30 minutes.
8 Give three more double turns, resting between each. (Alternatively, give six single turns.) Allow to rest before using.

Professional tip

Each time you leave the paste to rest, gently make finger indentations, one for each turn you have made.

Make a well in the centre of the flour and butter and add the liquid

Mix to a fairly stiff dough

Roll out and fold the ends to the middle

Keep rolling, folding and turning

The finished paste, ready to rest and then use

25 Puff pastry cases (*bouchées, vol-au-vents*)

Ingredient	Makes 12 bouchées/6 vol-au-vents
Puff paste	200 g
Egg wash	

1 Roll out the pastry to approximately 5 mm thick.

2 Cut out with a round, fluted cutter of the size required.

3 Place on a greased, dampened baking sheet; egg wash.

4 Dip a plain cutter of a slightly smaller diameter into hot fat or oil and make an incision 3 mm deep in the centre of each.

5 Allow to rest in a cool place.

6 Bake at 220 °C for about 20 minutes.

7 When cool, remove the caps or lids carefully and remove all the raw pastry from inside the cases.

Professional tip

Bouchées are filled with a variety of savoury fillings and are served hot or cold. They may also be filled with creams or curds as a pastry.

Larger versions are known as **vol-au-vents**. They may be produced in one-, two-, four- or six-portion sizes; a single-sized vol-au-vent would be approximately twice the size of a bouchée. When preparing one- and two-portion sized vol-au-vents, the method for bouchées may be followed. When preparing larger vol-au-vents, it is advisable to have two layers of puff pastry, each 5 mm thick, sealed together with egg wash. One layer should be a plain round, and the other of the same diameter with a circle cut out of the centre.

26 Cheese straws (*paillettes au fromage*)

Ingredient	8–10 portions	16–20 portions
Puff paste or rough puff paste	100 g	250 g
Cheese, grated	50 g	125 g
Cayenne pepper		

Energy	Cals	Fat	Sat fat	Carb	Sugar	Protein	Fibre
2,562 kJ	610 kcal	48.1 g	24.1 g	28.7 g	0.6 g	17.4 g	1.4 g

1 Roll out the pastry to 60 × 15 cm, 3 mm thick.
2 Sprinkle with the cheese and cayenne pepper.
3 Roll out lightly to embed the cheese.
4 Cut the paste into thin strips by length.
5 Twist each strip to form rolls in the strip.
6 Place on a silicone mat.
7 Bake in a hot oven at 230–250 °C for 10 minutes or until a golden brown. Cut into lengths as required.

27 Sausage rolls

Ingredient	Makes 12 × 8 cm rolls
Puff paste	200 g
Sausage meat	400 g
Egg wash	

1 Roll out the pastry to 3 mm thick into a strip 10 cm wide.
2 Shape the sausage meat into a roll 2 cm in diameter.
3 Place the sausage meat on to the pastry. Moisten the edges of the pastry.
4 Fold over and seal. Cut into 8 cm lengths.
5 Mark the edge with the back of a knife. Brush with egg wash.
6 Place on to a greased, dampened baking sheet.
7 Bake at 220 °C for approximately 20 minutes.

Energy	Cals	Fat	Sat fat	Carb	Sugar	Protein	Fibre
799 kJ	190 kcal	15.9 g	5.8 g	7.9 g	0.2 g	4.3 g	0.4 g

28 Gâteau pithiviers

Ingredient	2 × 22cm gâteaux
Puff paste	1 kg
Pastry cream	60 g
Frangipane	600 g
Egg wash (yolks only)	
Granulated sugar	

Energy	Cals	Fat	Sat fat	Carb	Sugar	Protein	Fibre	Sodium
1453 kJ	349 kcal	25.8g	9.4g	25.6g	10.4g	5.3g	1.7g	0.4g

For ¹⁄₁₀ of one gâteau.

1 Divide the paste into four equal pieces. Roll out each piece in a circle with a 22cm diameter, 4mm thick.

2 Rest in the fridge between sheets of cling film, preferably overnight.

3 Lightly butter two baking trays and splash with water. Lay one circle of paste on to each tray and dock them.

4 Mark a 16cm diameter circle in the centre of each.

5 Beat the pastry cream, if desired, and mix it with the frangipane.

6 Using a plain nozzle, pipe the cream over the inner circles, making them slightly domed.

7 Egg wash the outer edges of the paste. Lay one of the remaining pieces over the top of each one, smooth over and press down hard.

8 Mark the edges with a round cutter. Cut out a scallop pattern with a knife or use a cut piping nozzle as shown in the photo sequence.

9 Egg wash twice. Mark the top of both with a spiral pattern.

10 Bake at 220 °C for 10 minutes. Remove from the oven and sprinkle with granulated sugar. Turn the oven down to 190 °C and bake for a further 20 to 25 minutes.

11 Glaze under a salamander.

Adding the filling to the rolled base

Trimming the edge

Marking the top

29 Palmiers

Ingredient	
Puff paste (see page 465)	
Caster sugar	
Egg wash	

1 Roll out puff pastry into a square 3 mm thick.

2 Sprinkle liberally with caster sugar on both sides and roll into the pastry.

3 Fold into three from each end so as to meet in the middle; brush with egg wash and fold in two.

4 Cut into strips approximately 2 cm thick; dip one side in caster sugar.

5 Place on a greased baking sheet, sugared side down, leaving a space of at least 2 cm between each.

6 Bake in a very hot oven for about 10 minutes.

7 Turn with a palette knife, cook on the other side until brown and the sugar is caramelised.

Note

Palmiers are usually made from leftover or off-cuts of puff pastry. As a more biscuit-like property is sought, previously rolled pastry can be utilised because the rise required is not as much as in products such as bouchées and vol-au-vents.

Variation

Puff pastry trimmings are suitable for this recipe. Palmiers may be made in a wide variety of sizes. Two joined together with a little whipped cream may be served as a pastry or small ones for petits fours. They may be sandwiched together with soft fruit, whipped cream and/or ice cream and served as a sweet.

30 Pear jalousie

1 Roll out two-thirds of the pastry 3 mm thick into a strip 25 × 10 cm and place on a greased, dampened baking sheet.

2 Pierce with a docker. Moisten the edges.

3 Pipe on the frangipane, leaving 2 cm free all the way round. Place the pears on top.

4 Roll out the remaining one-third of the pastry to the same size. Chill before cutting.

5 Cut the dough with a trellis cutter to make a lattice.

6 Carefully open out this strip and neatly place on to the first strip.

7 Trim off any excess. Neaten and decorate the edge. Brush with egg wash.

8 Bake at 220 °C for 25–30 minutes.

9 Glaze with apricot glaze. Dust the edges with icing sugar and return to a very hot oven to glaze.

Ingredient	8–10 portions
Puff paste	200 g
Frangipane	200 g
Pears, poached or tinned (cored and cut in half lengthways)	5

Energy	Cals	Fat	Sat fat	Carb	Sugar	Protein	Fibre
1,178 kJ	282 kcal	17.8 g	5.1 g	27.2 g	17.5 g	3.8 g	0.8 g

31 Puff pastry slice (*mille-feuilles*)

1 Roll out the pastry 2 mm thick into an even-sided square.

2 Roll up carefully on a rolling pin and unroll on to a greased, dampened baking sheet.

3 Dock well.

4 Bake in a hot oven at 220 °C for 15–20 minutes; turn over after 10 minutes. Allow to cool.

5 Using a large knife, cut into three even-sized rectangles.

6 Keeping the best strip for the top, pipe the pastry cream on one strip.

7 Place the second strip on top and pipe with pastry cream.

8 Place the last strip on top, flat side up. Press gently. Brush with boiling apricot glaze to form a key.

Ingredient	10 portions
Puff pastry trimmings	600 g
Pastry cream	400 ml
Apricot glaze	
Fondant	350 g
Chocolate	100 g

Energy	Cals	Fat	Sat fat	Carb	Sugar	Protein	Fibre	Sodium
2013 kJ	479 kcal	22.0 g	8.2 g	69.0 g	49.0 g	5.8 g	1.1 g	0.4 g

Decorate by feather icing:

1 Warm the fondant to 37 °C (warm to the touch) and correct the consistency with sugar syrup if necessary.

2 Pour the fondant over the mille-feuilles in an even coat.

3 Immediately pipe the melted chocolate over the fondant in strips, 0.5 cm apart.

4 With the back of a small knife, wiping after each stroke, mark down the slice at 2 cm intervals.

5 Quickly turn the slice around and repeat in the same direction with strokes in between the previous ones.

6 Allow to set and trim the edges neatly.

7 Cut into even portions with a sharp, thin-bladed knife; dip into hot water and wipe clean after each cut.

8 For a traditional finish, crush the pastry trimmings and use them to coat the sides.

Variation

Whipped fresh cream may be used as an alternative to pastry cream.

The pastry cream or whipped cream may also be flavoured with an orange liqueur if desired.

Pipe cream between layers of pastry

Ice the top with fondant

Decorate with chocolate

32 Fruit slice (*bande aux fruits*)

Energy	Cals	Fat	Sat fat	Carb	Sugar	Protein	Fibre	Sodium
847 kJ	202 kcal	10.3g	3.5g	26.0g	14.3g	3.2g	1.6g	0.2g

Variation

Alternative methods are to use:
- short or sweet pastry for the base and puff pastry for the two side strips
- sweet pastry in a slice mould.

Ingredient	8–10 portions
Puff paste	250 g
Fruit (see note)	400 g
Pastry cream	250 ml (approximately)
Apricot glaze	2 tbsp

1 Roll out the pastry 2 mm thick in a strip 12 cm wide.

2 Place on a greased, dampened baking sheet.

3 Moisten two edges with egg wash; lay two 1.5 cm-wide strips along each edge.

4 Seal firmly and mark with the back of a knife. Prick the bottom of the slice.

5 Depending on the fruit used, either put the fruit (such as apple) on the slice and cook together, or cook the slice blind and afterwards place the pastry cream and fruit (such as tinned peaches) on the pastry. Glaze and serve as for flans.

Fruit slices may be prepared from any fruit suitable for flans/tarts.

33 Cream horns

Ingredient	Makes 16
Puff paste	250 g
Egg wash	
Icing sugar, to sprinkle	
Jam	50 g
Caster sugar	50 g
Vanilla pod/vanilla extract	Seeds from 1 pod/a few drops
Cream	500 ml

Energy	Cals	Fat	Sat fat	Carb	Sugar	Protein	Fibre
735 kJ	176 kcal	14.9 g	8.6 g	9.8 g	6.3 g	1.2 g	0.2 g

1 Roll out the pastry to 2 mm thick, 30 cm long.

2 Cut into 1.5 cm-wide strips. Moisten on one side.

3 Wind the strips carefully round lightly greased cream horn moulds, starting at the point and carefully overlapping each round slightly.

4 Brush with egg wash on one side and place on a greased baking sheet.

5 Bake at 220 °C for about 20 minutes.

6 Sprinkle with icing sugar and return to a hot oven for a few seconds to glaze.

7 Remove carefully from the moulds and allow to cool.

8 Place a little jam in the bottom of each.

9 Add the sugar and vanilla to the cream and whip until firm peaks form.

10 Place in a piping bag with a star tube and pipe a neat rose into each horn.

Variation

These may also be partially filled with pastry cream, to which various flavourings or fruit may be added. For example:
- praline
- chocolate
- coffee
- lemon
- raspberries
- strawberries
- mango
- orange segments.

34 Eccles cakes

Ingredient	12 cakes
Puff paste or rough puff paste	300 g
Egg white, to brush	
Caster sugar, to coat	
Filling	
Butter	50 g
Raisins	50 g
Demerara sugar	50 g
Currants	200 g
Mixed spice (optional)	pinch

Energy	Cals	Fat	Sat fat	Carb	Sugar	Protein	Fibre	Sodium
887 kJ	212 kcal	10.7 g	4.6 g	28.0 g	21.0 g	2.3 g	1.6 g	0.2 g

1 Roll out the pastry 2 mm thick.

2 Cut into rounds 10–12 cm diameter. Damp the edges.

3 Mix together all the ingredients for the filling and place 1 tbsp of the mixture in the centre of each round.

4 Fold the edges over to the centre and completely seal in the mixture.

5 Brush the top with egg white and dip into caster sugar.

6 Place on a greased baking sheet.

7 Cut two or three incisions with a knife so as to show the filling.

8 Bake at 220 °C for 15–20 minutes.

35 Apple turnovers (*chausson aux pommes*)

Ingredient	Makes 12
Puff paste	300 g
Dry, sweetened apple purée	250 g
Egg white, to brush	
Caster sugar, to coat	

Energy	Cals	Fat	Sat fat	Carb	Sugar	Protein	Fibre	Sodium
353 kJ	84 kcal	4.4 g	2.0 g	10.4 g	4.4 g	1.5 g	0.1 g	0.0 g

1 Roll out the pastry to 2 mm thick.

2 Cut into 8 cm diameter rounds.

3 Roll out slightly oval, to 12 × 10 cm.

4 Moisten the edges and place a little apple purée in the centre of each.

5 Fold over and seal firmly.

6 Brush with egg white and dip in caster sugar.

7 Place sugar-side up on a dampened baking sheet.

8 Bake in a hot oven, 220 °C, for 15–20 minutes.

Variation

Other types of fruit may be included in the turnovers, such as apple and mango; apple and blackberry; apple and passion fruit; and apple, pear and cinnamon.

Fillings

36 Pastry cream (*crème pâtissière*)

Left to right: pastry cream, crème diplomat and crème chiboust

Ingredient	Makes approximately 750 ml
Milk	500 ml
Vanilla pod	1
Egg yolks	4
Caster sugar	125 g
Soft flour	75 g
Custard powder	10 g

1 Heat the milk with the cut vanilla pod and leave to infuse.

2 Beat the sugar and egg yolks together until creamy white. Add the flour and custard powder.

3 Strain the hot milk, gradually blending it into the egg mixture.

4 Strain into a clean pan and bring back to the boil, stirring constantly.

5 When the mixture has boiled and thickened, pour into a plastic bowl, sprinkle with caster sugar and cover with cling film.

6 Chill over ice and refrigerate as soon as possible. Ideally, blast chill.

7 When required, knock back on a mixing machine with a little kirsch.

Variation

The recipes below are based on the recipe for pastry cream, with additional ingredients:

● **Crème mousseline**: beat in 100 g of soft butter. The butter content is usually about 20 per cent of the volume but this can be raised to 50 per cent depending on its intended use.

● **Crème diplomat**: when the pastry cream is chilled, fold in an equal quantity of whipped double cream.

● **Crème chiboust**: when the pastry cream mixture has cooled slightly, fold in an equal quantity of Italian meringue (recipe 42).

Additional flavourings can also be added to pastry cream, crème diplomat or crème chiboust.

Professional tip

At step 4, the microwave may be used effectively. Pour the mixture into a plastic bowl and cook in the microwave for 30-second periods, stirring in between, until the mixture boils and thickens.

37 Chantilly cream

Ingredient	Makes 500 ml
Whipping cream	500 ml
Caster sugar	100 g
Vanilla essence/fresh vanilla pod	A few drops to taste/seeds from 1 vanilla pod

1 Place all ingredients in a bowl. Whisk over ice until the mixture forms soft peaks. If using a mechanical mixer, stand and watch until the mixture is ready – do not leave it unattended as the mix will over-whip quickly, curdling the cream.

2 Cover and place in the fridge immediately.

38 Buttercream

Ingredient	350 g
Icing sugar	150 g
Butter	200 g

1 Sieve the icing sugar.

2 Cream the butter and icing sugar until light and creamy.

3 Flavour and colour as required.

Variation
- Rum buttercream – add rum to flavour and blend in.
- Chocolate buttercream – add melted chocolate, sweetened or unsweetened according to taste.

39 Boiled buttercream

Ingredient	750 ml
Eggs	2
Icing sugar	50 g
Granulated sugar or cube sugar	300 g
Water	100 g
Glucose	50 g
Unsalted butter	400 g

1 Beat the eggs and icing sugar until at ribbon stage (sponge).
2 Boil the granulated or cube sugar with water and glucose to 118 °C.
3 Gradually add the sugar at 118 °C to the eggs and icing sugar at ribbon stage, whisk continuously and allow to cool to 26 °C.
4 Gradually add the unsalted butter while continuing to whisk until a smooth cream is obtained.

Variation

Buttercream may be flavoured with numerous flavours and combinations of flavours, for example:
- chocolate and rum
- whisky and orange
- strawberry and vanilla
- lemon and lime
- apricot and passion fruit
- brandy and praline
- coffee and hazelnut.

1 Whisk the eggs.

2 Add the boiling sugar and water.

3 Add the butter.

40 Frangipane (almond cream)

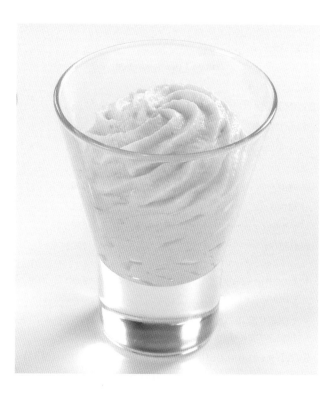

Ingredient	8 portions
Butter	100g
Caster sugar	100g
Eggs	2
Ground almonds	100g
Flour	10g

Energy	Cals	Fat	Sat fat	Carb	Sugar	Protein	Fibre	Sodium
997 kJ	240 kcal	18.5g	7.4g	15.0g	13.7g	4.4g	1.7g	0.2g

1 Cream the butter and sugar until aerated.

2 Gradually beat in the eggs.

3 Mix in the almonds and flour (mix lightly).

4 Use as required.

Variation

Try adding lemon zest or vanilla seeds to the recipe.

Cut the butter into small pieces and add to the sugar

Cream the butter and sugar together

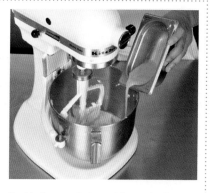

Beat in the eggs before adding to the flour

41 Ganache

Ingredient	Makes 750 g to 1 kg
Version 1 (for decoration)	
Double cream	300 ml
Couverture, cut into small pieces	350 g
Unsalted butter	85 g
Spirit or liqueur	20 ml
Version 2 (for a filling)	
Double cream	300 ml
Vanilla pod	½
Couverture, cut into small pieces	600 g
Unsalted butter	120 g

1 Boil the cream (and the vanilla for Version 2) in a heavy saucepan.

2 Pour the cream over the couverture. Whisk with a fine whisk until the chocolate has melted.

3 Whisk in the butter (and the liqueur for Version 1).

4 Stir over ice until the mixture has the required consistency.

The two versions have different textures. Version 1 is ideal for truffles; version 2 for tortes or fillings.

42 Italian meringue

Ingredient	Makes 250 g	Makes 625 g
Granulated or cube sugar	200 g	500 g
Water	60 ml	140 g
Cream of tartar	Pinch	Large pinch
Egg whites	4	10

1 Boil the sugar, water and cream of tartar to hard-ball stage of 121 °C. (To ensure the sugar is not heated beyond this point, it is advisable to remove from the heat at 115 °C as the sugar will continue to rise in temperature, and this will provide a little time to ensure the egg whites are whipped to the correct point.)

2 While the sugar is cooking, beat the egg whites to full peak and, while stiff, beating slowly, pour on the boiling sugar.

3 Use as required.

Boil the sugar

Combine with the beaten egg whites

The mixture will stand up in stiff peaks when it is ready

43 Swiss meringue

Ingredient	10 portions	15 portions
Egg whites, pasteurised	190 ml	300 ml
Caster sugar	230 ml	340 ml

Energy	Cals	Fat	Sat fat	Carb	Sugar	Protein	Fibre	Sodium
426 kJ	100 kcal	0.0g	0.0g	24.0g	24.0g	2.1g	0.0g	0.0g

1 Whisk the pasteurised egg whites and sugar over a bain-marie of simmering water until a light and aerated meringue is achieved.

44 Apple purée

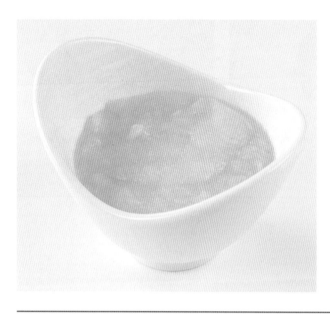

Ingredient	400 g	1 kg
Cooking apples	400 g	1 kg
Butter or margarine	10 g	25 g
Sugar	50 g	125 g

1 Peel, core and slice the apples.
2 Place the butter or margarine in a thick-bottomed pan; heat until melted.
3 Add the apples and sugar, cover with a lid and cook gently until soft.
4 Drain off any excess liquid and pass through a sieve or liquidise.

45 Stock syrup

Ingredient	750 ml	1.5 litres
Water	500 ml	1.25 litres
Granulated sugar	250 g	625 g
Glucose	50 g	125 g

1 Boil the water, sugar and glucose together.
2 Strain and cool.

Professional tip

The glucose helps to prevent crystallising.

15 Cakes, sponges, biscuits and scones

This chapter is relevant to the following units:
→ Prepare, cook and finish basic cakes, sponges, biscuits and scones.

Recipes included in this chapter

The base ingredients for making cakes, biscuits and scones are principally the same as those discussed in Chapter 14: flour, fat, sugar, raising agents, eggs and cream. However, there is an endless list of possibilities in terms of additional ingredients that could form part of the finished product, from chocolate, fondants, fruits and fruit products, through to nuts and pralines.

Cakes

Preparation methods for cakes

There are three basic methods of making cake mixtures, also known as cake batters. The working temperature of cake batter should ideally be around 21 °C.

Sugar batter method

For the sugar batter method, the fat (cake margarine, butter or shortening) is blended in a machine with caster sugar. This is the basic or principal stage; the other ingredients are usually then added in the order shown in the chart.

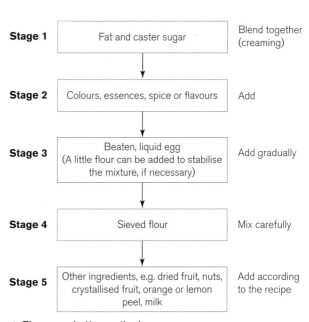

Stage 1	Fat and caster sugar	Blend together (creaming)
Stage 2	Colours, essences, spice or flavours	Add
Stage 3	Beaten, liquid egg (A little flour can be added to stabilise the mixture, if necessary)	Add gradually
Stage 4	Sieved flour	Mix carefully
Stage 5	Other ingredients, e.g. dried fruit, nuts, crystallised fruit, orange or lemon peel, milk	Add according to the recipe

▲ The sugar batter method

Flour batter method

For the flour batter method, the eggs and sugar are whisked to a half sponge; this is the basic or principal stage, which aims to foam the two ingredients together until half the maximum volume is achieved. Other ingredients are then added as shown in the chart.

A humectant, something which helps the product to stay moist, may also be added (for example, glycerine); if so, this is added at stage 2.

Stage 1 → Sieved flour (with cocoa powder, baking powder, if required)

Part added to

Stage 2 → Eggs and caster sugar whisked together to half volume (glycerine may be added)

Fold the eggs and sugar, in three or four stages, into the fat and flour, folding and blending carefully

Stage 3 → Equal quantities of cake margarine/fat and flour, creamed together

Stage 4 → Fold in the remaining flour

Stage 5 → Add other ingredients according to the recipe – e.g. nuts, fruit, milk

▲ The flour batter method

Blending method

The blending method is used for high-ratio cake mixtures. It uses high-ratio flour, specially produced so that it will absorb more liquid. It also uses a high-ratio fat, made from oil to which a quantity of emulsifying agent has been added, enabling the fat to take up a greater quantity of liquid.

High-ratio cakes contain more liquid and sugar, resulting in a fine, stable crumb, extended shelf life, good eating and excellent freezing qualities. The principal or basic stage is the mixing of the fat and flour to a crumbling texture. It is essential that each stage of the batter is blended into the next to produce a smooth batter, free from lumps. When using mixing machines, it is important to remember to:
- blend initially on a slow speed
- beat on a medium speed, using a paddle attachment.

When blending, always clear the mix from the bottom of the bowl to ensure that any first- or second-stage batter does not remain in the bowl.

Stage 1 Flour and dry ingredients (baking powder) — Sieve together

Stage 2 Fat and flour — Rub together to a crumbly texture

Stage 3 Sugar, dissolved in milk — Add slowly

Stage 4 Beaten eggs — Add

▲ The blending method

Baking powder in cakes

Baking powder may be made from one part sodium bicarbonate to two parts cream of tartar. In commercial baking the powdered cream of tartar may be replaced by another acid product, such as acidulated calcium phosphate.

When used under the right conditions, with the addition of liquid and heat, it produces carbon dioxide gas. As the acid has a delayed action, only a small amount of gas is given off when the liquid is added, and the majority is released when the mixture is heated. Therefore, when cakes are mixed they do not lose the property of the baking powder if they are not cooked right away.

Possible reasons for faults in cakes

If your cake has an uneven texture, this may be because:
- the fat was insufficiently rubbed in
- there was too little liquid
- there was too much liquid.

If your cake has a close texture, this may be because:
- there was too much fat
- your hands were too hot when rubbing in
- the fat to flour ratio was incorrect.

If your cake is dry, this may be because:
- there was too little liquid
- the oven was too hot.

If your cake has a bad shape, this may be because:
- there was too much liquid
- the oven was too cool
- there was too much baking powder.

If the fruit in the cake has sunk, this may be because:
- the fruit was wet
- there was too much liquid
- the oven was too cool.

If the cake has cracked, this may be because:
- there was too little liquid
- there was too much baking powder.

Batters and whisked sponges

Batters and sponges allow the production of a large assortment of desserts and cakes. Basically, they are a mix of eggs, sugar, flour and the air incorporated when these are beaten. Certain other raw materials can be combined – for example, almonds, hazelnuts, walnuts, chocolate, butter, fruit, ginger, anise, coffee and vanilla.

Sponge mixtures are produced from a foam of eggs and sugar. The eggs may be whole or separated. Examples of sponge products include gâteaux, sponge fingers and sponge cakes.

The egg white traps the air bubbles. When eggs and sugar are whisked together, they thicken until a maximum volume is reached; then flour is carefully folded in by a method known as cutting in. This is the most difficult operation, as the flour must not be allowed to sink to the bottom of the bowl, otherwise it becomes lumpy and difficult to clear. However, the mixture must not be stirred too much as this will disturb the aeration and cause the air to escape,

resulting in a much heavier sponge. If butter, margarine or oil is added, it is important that this is added at about 36°C, otherwise overheating will cause the fat or oil to act on the flour and create lumps, which are difficult – often impossible – to get rid of.

Stabilisers are often added to sponges to prevent them from collapsing. The most common are ethyl methyl cellulose and glycerol monostearate; these are added to the eggs and sugar at the beginning of the mixing.

Making sponge cakes

- You should never add flour or ground dry ingredients to a batter until the end because they impede the air absorption in the first beating stage.
- When making sponge cakes, always sift the dry ingredients (flour, cocoa powder, ground nuts, and so on) to avoid clumping.
- Mix the flour in as quickly and delicately as possible – rough addition of dry ingredients acts like a weight on the primary batter and can remove part of the air already absorbed.
- Flours used in sponge cakes are low in gluten content. In certain sponge cakes a proportion of the flour can be left out and substituted with cornstarch. This yields a softer and more aerated batter.
- The eggs used in sponge cake batters should be fresh and at room temperature so that they take in air faster.
- Adding separately beaten egg whites produces a lighter, fluffier sponge cake.
- Once sponge cake batters are beaten and poured into moulds or baking trays, they should be baked as soon as possible. Delays will cause the batter to lose volume.

Preparation methods

There are several methods of making sponge cake:
- **Foaming method** – whisking eggs and sugar together to the ribbon stage; folding in/cutting flour.
- **Melting method** – as with foaming, but adding melted butter, margarine or oil to the mixture at the final stage. The fat content enriches the sponge, improves the flavour, texture and crumb structure, and will extend shelf life.
- **Boiling method** – sponges made by this method have a stable crumb texture that is easier to handle and crumbles less when cut than the standard basic sponge containing fat (known as Genoise sponge). This method will produce a sponge that is suitable for dipping in fondant. The stages are shown in the chart.

- **Blending method** – this is used for high-ratio sponges, which follow the same principles as high-ratio cakes. As with cakes, high-ratio goods produce a fine, stable crumb, an even texture, excellent shelf life and good freezing qualities.
- **Creaming method** – this is the traditional method and is still used today for Victoria sandwich and light fruitcakes. The fat and sugar are creamed together, then beaten egg is added and, finally, the sieved flour is added with other dry ingredients as desired.
- **Separate yolk and white method** – this method is used for sponge fingers (recipe 20).

Stage 1	Eggs and sugar beaten together at 37°C to a thick sponge
Stage 2	Butter heated until near boiling point; flour and glycerine stirred in and beaten to a smooth paste
Stage 3	Use as required

Add to stage 2 in three or four parts, beating well to produce a smooth batter

▲ The boiling method

Possible reasons for faults in sponges

If your sponge has a close texture, this may be because:
- it was not beaten enough
- there was too much flour
- the oven was too cool or too hot.

If your sponge has a 'holey' texture, this may be because:
- the flour was insufficiently folded in
- the tin was unevenly filled.

If the sponge has a cracked crust, this may be because the oven was too hot.

If the sponge is sunken, this may be because:
- the oven was too hot
- the tin was removed during cooking.

White spots on the surface may indicate that it was not beaten enough.

Possible reasons for faults in Genoise sponges

If the sponge has a close texture, this may be because:
- the eggs and sugar were overheated
- the eggs and sugar were under-beaten
- there was too much flour
- the flour was insufficiently folded in
- the oven was too hot.

If the sponge is sunken, this may be because:
- there was too much sugar
- the oven was too hot
- the tin was removed during cooking.

If the sponge is heavy, this may be because:
- the butter was too hot
- the butter was insufficiently mixed in
- the flour was over-mixed.

The introduction of steam or moisture

Some cakes require an injection of steam, otherwise they become too dry while baking due to the dry atmosphere in the oven. Combination ovens are ideally suited for this purpose. The steam delays the formation of the crust until the cake batter has become fully aerated and the proteins have set. Alternatively, add a tray of water to the oven while baking. If the oven is too hot, the cake crust will form early and the cake batter will rise into a peak.

Points to remember when baking cakes and sponges

- Check all ingredients carefully.
- Make sure scales are accurate; weigh all ingredients carefully.
- Check ovens are at the right temperature and that the shelves are in the correct position.
- Check that all work surfaces and equipment are clean.
- Check that all other equipment required, such as cooling wires, is within easy reach.
- Always sieve flour to remove lumps and any foreign material.
- Make sure that eggs and fats are at room temperature.
- Check dried fruits carefully; wash, drain and dry if necessary.
- Always follow the recipe carefully.

- Always scrape down the sides of the mixing bowl when creaming mixtures.
- Always seek help if you are unsure.
- Try to fill the oven space when baking by planning production carefully; this saves time, labour and money.
- Never guess quantities. Time and temperature are important factors; they too should not be guessed.
- The shape and size of goods will determine the baking time and temperature: the wider and deeper the cake, the longer and more slowly it will need to bake.
- Where cake recipes contain a high proportion of sugar, this will caramelise the surface quickly before the centre is cooked. Therefore cover the cake with sheets of silicone or dampened greaseproof paper and continue to bake.
- When cake tops are sprinkled with almonds or sugar, the baking temperature needs to be lowered slightly to prevent over-colouring of the cake crust.
- When glycerine, glucose and inverted sugar, honey or treacle is added to cake mixtures, the oven temperature should be lowered as these caramelise at a lower temperature than sugar.
- Always work in a clean and hygienic way; remember the hygiene and safety rules, in particular the Food Safety and Hygiene Regulations, 2013.
- All cakes and sponges benefit from being allowed to cool in their tins as this makes handling easier. If sponges need to be cooled quickly, place a wire rack over the top of the tin and invert, then remove the lining paper and cool on a wire rack.

Biscuits

Preparation methods

Biscuits and cookies may be produced by the following methods:

Rubbing in

Rubbing in is probably the best-known method and is used to produce some of the most famous types of biscuits, such as shortbread. The method is exactly the same as that for producing short pastry.

- Rub the fat into the flour by hand or by machine. Dissolve the liquid and the sugar and mix into the flour to produce a smooth biscuit paste.

- Do not overwork the paste when mixing to combine. The consequence of overworking the paste at this stage is that the gluten in the flour will strengthen and result in the tightening of the paste. If this happens the paste will become very difficult to roll and is likely to shrink during the baking process.

Foaming

This is where a foam is produced from egg whites, egg yolks or both. Sponge fingers are an example of a two-foam mixture. Meringue is an example of a single-foam mixture using egg whites. Great care must be taken not to over-mix the product.

Sugar batter method

Fat and sugar are mixed together to produce a light, aerated cream. Beaten egg is added gradually. The dry ingredients are then carefully folded in. Cats' tongues and sablé biscuits are made in this way.

Flour batter method

Half the sieved flour is creamed with the fat. The eggs and sugar are beaten together before they are added to the fat and flour mixture. Finally, the remainder of the flour is folded in, together with any other dry ingredients. Some types of cookies are made using this method.

Blending method

This method requires the blending of all the ingredients together to produce a smooth paste. It is used to make almond biscuits using a basic commercial mixture.

Convenience cake, biscuit and sponge mixes

There is now a vast range of prepared mixes and frozen goods available on the market. Premixes enable the caterer to calculate costs more effectively, reduce labour costs (with less demand for highly skilled labour) and limit the range of stock items that need to be held.

Every year, more and more convenience products are introduced on to the market by food manufacturers. The caterer should be encouraged to investigate these products and to experiment in order to assess their quality.

Decorating and finishing for presentation

Fillings

Cakes, sponges and biscuits may be filled or sandwiched together with a variety of different types of filling. Some examples are presented below.

- Creams – buttercream (plain, flavoured and/or coloured), pastry cream (flavoured and/or coloured), whipped cream, clotted cream.
- Fruit – fresh fruit purée, jams, fruit mousses, preserves, fruit gels.
- Pastes and spreads – chocolate, praline, nut, curds.

Spreading and coating

The top and sides of smaller cakes and gâteaux are commonly covered with any of the following:

- fresh whipped cream
- fondant
- chocolate
- royal icing
- buttercream
- water icing
- meringue (French, Italian or Swiss)
- commercially manufactured preparations.

Piping

Piping is a skill that takes practice and there are many different types (plain or fluted) and sizes of piping tube available, producing a variety of presentations. The following may be used:

- royal icing
- meringue
- chocolate
- boiled sugar
- fondant
- fresh cream.

Dusting, dredging and sprinkling

These techniques are used to give products a final design or glaze during cooking, using sugar. Light dusting is usually performed with icing sugar or neige décor, an icing sugar product resistant to humidity but used in the same way, using a very fine sieve.

- **Dusting**: a light dusting, giving an even finish.
- **Dredging**: heavier dusting with sugar.
- **Sprinkling**: a very light sprinkle of sugar.

Caster or granulated white sugar, Demerara, Barbados or dark brown sugar can also be used, particularly if the product is returned to the oven for glazing, glazed under a salamander or glazed using a blow torch.

Other decorative media

Remember that decorating is an art form and there is a range of equipment and materials available to assist you in this work. Some examples of decorative media are as follows:

- Glacé and crystallised fruits – cherries, lemons, oranges, pineapple, figs.
- Crystallised flowers – rose petals, violets, mimosa, lilac.
- Crystallised stems such as angelica.
- Nuts – almonds (nibbed, flaked), coconut (fresh slices, desiccated), hazelnuts, brazil nuts, pistachio.
- Chocolate – rolls, vermicelli, flakes, piping chocolate, chips.

Piped biscuit pastes

Piped biscuits can be used for decoration. For example:

- cats' tongues (recipe 22)
- piped biscuits (recipe 25).

Storing cakes, sponges, biscuits and scones

Cakes, sponges, biscuits and scones are best eaten as fresh as possible to enjoy them at their prime. However, if storage is required, care must be taken to ensure that the commodities making up the product are taken into consideration. For example, a product containing a high-risk or fragile ingredient such as fresh cream must be kept chilled or frozen to prevent spoilage.

Other products, such as biscuits, will lose their short, crisp properties if not stored appropriately. Moisture in the atmosphere will become absorbed by such products and this will start to break down the structure of the biscuit.

Sponges, particularly low-fat or fatless sponges, will tend to dry out very quickly if they are left out in open air. Once a sponge is cut, the exposed sponge is extremely prone to drying, which is one reason why sponge products are often soaked with a flavoured syrup to prevent drying as well as adding flavour.

Steps to take when storing cakes, sponges, biscuits and scones to extend their shelf life are as follows:

- Store dry products such as biscuits and scones for short-term consumption in clean, air-tight plastic containers. Store the containers in a cool, dry, well-ventilated area that has been designated for such products.
- Store products such as fresh fruit and/or cream cakes or sponges for short-term consumption in refrigerators, ensuring that they are covered with cling film or stored in air-tight containers. This will help to prevent the products from drying during storage. It is important to note that sugars dissolve over time when stored and this can lead to sogginess in products and weeping of fruits.

- Cakes, sponges, biscuits and scones can be frozen very effectively. It is important that the product is cool before freezing. The product should be sealed to prevent contact with air, removing as much air as possible in the packaging itself. The product should then be labelled, dated and frozen, ensuring that stock is easily identifiable and stock rotation procedures are followed. A blast-freezer can be used to freeze rapidly before placing into a holding freezer. This can help to retain many of the quality points of such products, for example, moisture retention.

Test yourself

1 How much flour is required to produce a four-egg Genoise sponge?
2 Describe what is meant by the 'creaming' method.
3 Describe the production of sponge fingers (*biscuit à la cuillère*).
4 What is the ratio of fat to flour for shortbread biscuits?
5 Describe tuile biscuits and what they are used for.
6 Describe the preparation and baking of:

    a madeleines

    b *sablés à la poche* (piped biscuits).

7 List the ingredients and method for a traditional Victoria sandwich.
8 Give three possible reasons why a sponge might have a tight, close texture.
9 List the two components, and their ratios, that make up baking powder.
10 What is the benefit of the presence of steam when baking cakes and sponges?

Cakes and sponges

1 Victoria sandwich

Ingredient	2 × 18 cm cakes
Butter	250 g
Caster sugar	250 g
Soft flour	250 g
Baking powder	10 g
Eggs	5
Vanilla extract	½ tsp
Jam to fill	

Energy	Cals	Fat	Sat fat	Carb	Sugar	Protein	Fibre
6,866 kJ	1,635 kcal	94.3 g	39.3 g	184.7 g	106.6 g	23.3 g	3.6 g

Using hard margarine in place of butter.

This is a classic afternoon tea cake named after Queen Victoria. Although traditionally made in two halves, a slimmer version can be made by using a single sponge and splitting it.

1 Cream the butter and sugar until soft and light.

2 Sieve the flour and baking powder twice.

3 Mix together the eggs and vanilla extract.

4 Beat the eggs gradually into the butter and sugar mixture.

5 Fold in the flour.

6 Deposit into buttered and floured cake tins and level.

7 Bake at 180 °C for approximately 15–20 minutes.

8 Turn out on to a wire rack to cool.

9 Spread the bottom half with softened jam.

10 Place on the top sponge and dust with icing sugar.

1 Beat the sugar and butter together.

2 Place the mixture into buttered cake tins.

3 Flatten the top before baking.

Variation

In addition to jam, the sponge can be filled with either butter icing or Chantilly cream.

The official Women's Institute version specifies the cake is filled with jam only and dusted with caster not icing sugar.

2 Genoise sponge

Ingredient	Single sponge	Double sponge
Eggs	4	10
Caster sugar	100 g	250 g
Flour (soft)	100 g	250 g
Butter, margarine or oil	50 g	125 g

Energy	Cals	Fat	Sat fat	Carb	Sugar	Protein	Fibre
5,978 kJ	1,423 kcal	65.8 g	25.6 g	182.8 g	106.6 g	36.5 g	3.6 g

Using hard margarine (4 portions).

Video: making a genoise
http://bit.ly/1znWjDj

1 Whisk the eggs and sugar with a balloon whisk in a bowl over a pan of hot water.

2 Continue until the mixture is light and creamy and has doubled in bulk.

3 Remove from the heat and whisk until cold and thick (ribbon stage). Fold in the flour very gently.

4 Take a small amount of the mixture and combine it with the melted butter. Then return this to the rest of the mixture and fold through.

5 Place in a greased, floured genoise mould.

6 Bake in a moderately hot oven, at 200–220 °C, for about 30 minutes.

1 Ingredients for Genoise sponge and boiling water ready for use.

2 Add the sugar to the eggs.

3 Whisk them together over boiling water.

4 Carry on whisking as the mixture warms up.

5 When the mixture is ready, it will form ribbons and you can draw a figure eight with it.

6 Fold in the flour.

7 Add part of the flour mixture to the butter.

8 Place the mixture into greased cake tins.

9 After baking, turn the sponges out to cool on a rack.

3 Fresh cream and strawberry gâteau

Ingredient	8 portions
Genoise sponge made with vanilla	1
Stock syrup (see page 482)	100 ml
Raspberry jam	50 ml
Whipping or double cream	500 ml
Icing sugar	75 g
Strawberries, sliced	1 punnet

Energy	Cals	Fat	Sat fat	Carb	Sugar	Protein	Fibre
1,975 kJ	473 kcal	28.4 g	11.1 g	53.0 g	39.7 g	4.5 g	0.9 g

Based on 60 g of sponge per portion.

1 Carefully slice the sponge cake into three equal discs. Brush each with syrup.

2 Slowly whip the cream with the icing sugar to achieve the correct consistency.

3 Place the first piece of sponge on a cake board. Soak with syrup. Spread with a layer of jam, then a layer of cream. Scatter sliced strawberries on top.

4 Place the next piece of sponge on top. Repeat the layers of syrup, cream and strawberries. Top with additional cream.

5 Place the final piece of sponge on top.

6 Coat the top and sides with cream. Chill.

7 Comb scrape the sides of the gâteau. Pipe 12 rosettes on top. Decorate with strawberries and rounds of white chocolate.

4 Coffee gâteau

Ingredient	1 × 16 cm gâteau
Plain genoise sponge (recipe 2)	1 × 16 cm
Stock syrup flavoured with rum	50 ml
Coffee buttercream	750 g
Coffee marzipan	100 g
Fondant	500 g
Crystallised violets	
Chocolate squares	

Energy	Cals	Fat	Sat fat	Carb	Sugar	Protein	Fibre	Sodium
7881 kJ	1873 kcal	75.5g	41.3g	303.0g	282.0g	12.3g	1.8g	0.6g

For ¼ of the sponge.

1 Carefully split the sponge into three and line up the three pieces.

2 Place the sponge base on a cake card and moisten with rum syrup.

3 Pipe on an even layer of buttercream, no thicker than that of the sponge.

4 Place on the next layer of sponge, moisten with the syrup and repeat to give three layers of sponge and two of buttercream. Moisten the top with syrup.

5 Put in the fridge for 1–2 hours to firm up.

6 Work some coffee essence into the marzipan, roll out to 2 mm thick and lay over the gâteau, working the sides to prevent any creases.

7 Warm the fondant to blood heat, flavour with coffee essence and adjust the consistency with syrup.

8 Place the gâteau on a wire rack with a tray underneath to catch the fondant.

9 Starting in the centre and moving outwards, pour over the fondant to completely cover. Draw a palette knife across the top to remove the excess.

10 Add some melted chocolate to some of the fondant, adjust the consistency and squeeze through muslin. Decorate the gâteau by piping on a fine line design.

11 Finish the sides with squares of chocolate and the top with crystallised violets.

Professional tip

Mark the sponge by cutting a 'v' on the side before splitting horizontally; when reassembling, line up the marks so it goes back together exactly as it came apart.

Turn the sponge upside down before splitting so the base becomes the top; this is the flattest surface and will give the best finish.

It is best practice to use a genoise that was made the day before – fresh sponges do not cut well and are susceptible to falling apart.

Fondant should never be heated above 30 °C, as the shine will be lost.

Note

A good-quality coffee gâteau should have a moist sponge and a good balance between sponge and filling (as a guide, the thickness of the sponge and the depth of the buttercream should be equal). The coffee flavour should not be in question, and the decoration should reflect and complement the coffee theme. (It is sometimes easy to get carried away, so it is good to remember when decorating, 'less is definitely more'.)

Variation

Instead of enrobing with fondant, the top and sides can be covered with buttercream, the sides can be either comb-scraped or masked with toasted nibbed/flaked almonds or grated chocolate. The top can be piped with buttercream and/or decorated with coffee marzipan cut-out shapes.

To add another texture, place a disc of meringue or dacquoise on the bottom layer. Dacquoise is an Italian meringue with the addition of toasted ground hazelnuts, spread or piped on to a silicone mat and baked at 180 °C for 15–20 minutes. Cut out the desired shape half way through cooking.

5 Chocolate genoise sponge

Ingredient	2 × 16 cm sponges
Eggs	8
Caster sugar	225 g
Flour	175 g
Cocoa powder	50 g
Butter, melted	65 g

Energy	Cals	Fat	Sat fat	Carb	Sugar	Protein	Fibre	Sodium
1428 kJ	340 kcal	13.9 g	6.6 g	47.0 g	30.0 g	9.5 g	1.6 g	0.2 g

For ¼ of a sponge.

1 Whisk the eggs and sugar together to form a sabayon.

2 Slowly fold in the flour and cocoa powder.

3 Take a small amount of the mixture and combine it with the melted butter. Then return this to the rest of the mixture and fold through.

4 Place in a lined mould and bake at 180 °C for 15–20 minutes.

Make sure you have prepared all the equipment before you start.

Variation

For a lighter sponge, use 100 g of soft flour and 75 g of cornflour.

6 Chocolate gâteau

Ingredient	Single gâteau	Double gâteau
Chocolate genoise sponge (recipe 5)		
Eggs	4	10
Chocolate pieces	50 g	125 g
Stock syrup (see page 482), as required		
Chocolate glaze		
Buttercream		
Unsalted butter	200 g	500 g
Icing sugar	150 g	375 g
Block chocolate (melted in a basin in a bain-marie)	50 g	125 g

Energy	Cals	Fat	Sat fat	Carb	Sugar	Protein	Fibre
20,113 kJ	4,789 kcal	260.9 g	148.7 g	606.0 g	533.2 g	41.6 g	4.8 g

Using hard margarine and butter (4 portions).

1 Cut the genoise into three slices crosswise.

2 Prepare the buttercream and mix in the melted chocolate.

3 Lightly moisten each slice of genoise with stock syrup, which may be flavoured with kirsch, rum, etc.

4 Lightly spread each slice of genoise with buttercream and sandwich together.

5 Lightly coat the top and sides with chocolate glaze, then decorate with chocolate pieces.

7 Roulade sponge

You should be able to bend a roulade sponge

Ingredient	2 sheets	4 sheets
Eggs	8	16
Egg yolk	2	4
Caster sugar	260 g	520 g
Soft flour	170 g	340 g

1 Make sure the mixing bowl is clean, dry and free from grease.

2 Line the baking sheets with silicone paper cut to fit.

3 Set the oven at 230 °C.

4 Place the eggs and sugar in a mixing bowl, and stir over hot water until warm.

5 Whisk to the 'ribbon' stage and sieve the flour on to greaseproof paper.

6 Carefully fold in the flour.

7 Divide equally between the baking sheets and spread evenly with a drop blade palette knife. Place immediately in the oven for between 5 and 7 minutes.

8 As soon as the sponge is cooked, turn it out on to sugared paper, place a damp, clean cloth over it and lay the hot baking sheet back on top, then leave to cool. (This will help keep the sponge moist and flexible as it cools.)

Professional tip

Each sheet should be left on the paper on which it is cooked, individually wrapped, labelled, kept flat and stored in the freezer to stop it from drying out and losing flexibility.

Faults

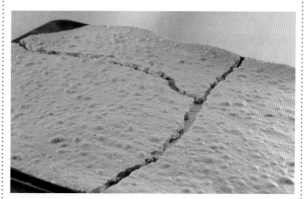

There are two reasons why a roulade sponge might become hard and crisp, instead of being pliable:
● baked at too low a temperature for too long
● mixture spread too thin.

Variation

A chocolate version can be made by substituting 30–40 per cent of the flour for cocoa powder. For a coffee sponge, add coffee extract to the eggs after whisking.

A roulade sponge may also be made using a 'split-egg' method, separating the eggs.

8 Swiss roll

Ingredient	4 portions	10 portions
Eggs	4	10
Caster sugar	100 g	250 g
Self-raising flour	100 g	250 g
Jam, as required		

Energy	Cals	Fat	Sat fat	Carb	Sugar	Protein	Fibre
4,445 kJ	1,058 kcal	25.3 g	8.0 g	182.7 g	106.5 g	36.5 g	3.6 g

1 Whisk the eggs and sugar with a balloon whisk in a bowl over a pan of hot water.

2 Continue until the mixture is light, creamy and double in bulk.

3 Remove from the heat and whisk until cold and thick (ribbon stage).

4 Fold in the flour very gently.

5 Grease a Swiss roll tin and line with greased greaseproof or silicone paper.

6 Pour in the mixture and bake at 220 °C for about 6 minutes.

7 Turn out on to a sheet of paper sprinkled with additional caster sugar.

8 Remove the paper from the Swiss roll, spread with warm jam.

9 Immediately roll up as tight as possible and leave to cool completely.

9 Cup cakes

Ingredient	20 portions
Flour (soft) or self-raising	200 g
Baking powder (if using plain flour)	1 level tsp
Salt (optional)	pinch
Margarine or butter	125 g
Caster sugar	125 g
Eggs	2–3

Energy	Cals	Fat	Sat fat	Carb	Sugar	Protein	Fibre
947 kJ	225 kcal	11.6 g	4.8 g	28.8 g	13.4 g	3.3 g	0.7 g

Using hard margarine.

Method 1: rubbing in

1 Sieve the flour, baking powder and salt (if using).

2 Rub in the butter or margarine to achieve a sandy texture. Add the sugar.

3 Gradually add the well-beaten eggs and mix as lightly as possible until combined.

Method 2: creaming

1 Cream the margarine and sugar in a bowl until soft and fluffy.

2 Slowly add the well-beaten eggs, mixing continuously and beating really well between each addition.

3 Lightly mix in the sieved flour, baking powder and salt (if using).

In both cases the consistency should be a light dropping one and, if necessary, it may be adjusted with the addition of a few drops of milk.

Variation

Cherry cakes: add 50 g glacé cherries cut in quarters and 3–4 drops vanilla essence to the basic mixture (method 2) and divide into 8–12 lightly greased cake tins or paper cases. Bake in a hot oven at 220 °C for 15–20 minutes.

Coconut cakes: in place of 50 g flour, use 50 g desiccated coconut and 3–4 drops vanilla essence to the basic mixture (method 2) and cook as for cherry cakes.

Raspberry buns: divide basic mixture (method 1) into 8 pieces. Roll into balls, flatten slightly, dip tops into milk then caster sugar. Place on a greased baking sheet, make a hole in the centre of each and add a little raspberry jam. Bake in a hot oven at 200 °C for 15–20 minutes.

Queen cakes: to the basic mixture (method 2) add 100 g washed and dried mixed fruit and cook as for cherry cakes.

10 Scones

1. Sieve the flour, baking powder and salt.
2. Cut the butter into small pieces and rub into the flour to achieve a sandy texture.
3. Dissolve the sugar in the cream.
4. Add the liquid to the dry ingredients and cut in with a plastic scraper, mix lightly and do not overwork. Wrap in cling film and chill for 1 hour.
5. Set the oven at 180 °C and line a baking sheet with silicone paper.
6. Roll out 2 cm thick on a floured surface, cut out with a plain or fluted cutter.
7. Brush with milk or egg wash and bake at 180 °C for approximately 15–20 minutes.
8. After 15 minutes, pull one apart to test if they are cooked.
9. Allow to cool and dust with icing sugar before serving.

Scones are traditionally served at afternoon tea with jam and butter or clotted cream, and are best served on the day they are made.

Ingredient	16 scones
Plain flour	450 g
Baking powder	25 g
Salt	pinch
Butter	225 g
Caster sugar	170 g
Sour cream	300 ml

Energy	Cals	Fat	Sat fat	Carb	Sugar	Protein	Fibre	Sodium
1196 kJ	291 kcal	16.6g	10.2g	34.0g	12.3g	3.2g	1.1g	0.4g

Per scone.

Variation

Fruit scones: add 50 g sultanas to the basic mix, or try adding dried cranberries or apricots as alternatives.

Professional tip

After cutting out the scones, turn upside down on the baking sheet. This will help them rise with straight sides.

11 Rock cakes

Energy	Cals	Fat	Sat fat	Carb	Sugar	Protein	Fibre
913 kJ	217 kcal	8.7 g	3.6 g	33.6 g	14.3 g	3.4 g	1.3 g

Using hard margarine.

Ingredient	Makes 16
Medium flour (50% soft and 50% strong flour)	500 g
Baking powder	30 g
Salt	3 g
Caster sugar	125 g
Egg	60 g
Butter	120 g
Currants	90 g
Citrus peel	30 g
Milk	180 g
Egg wash	
Caster sugar, to sprinkle	

1 Sieve the flour, baking powder and salt through a fine sieve.
2 Dissolve the sugar in the liquid egg.
3 Rub the butter into the flour to form a crumb mix.
4 Add the currants and citrus peel.
5 Blend in the milk to achieve a smooth mix.
6 Divide the mixture into small portions, approximately 70 g each, and place evenly on to a baking tray.
7 Egg wash and sprinkle with caster sugar.
8 Bake at 210 °C for 15–20 minutes, until light golden brown.

Variation

Add a small pinch of mixed spice.

12 Madeleines

Ingredient	Makes 45
Caster sugar	125 g
Eggs	3
Vanilla pod, seeds from	1
Flour	150 g
Baking powder	1 tsp
Beurre noisette	125 g

Energy	Cals	Fat	Sat fat	Carb	Sugar	Protein	Fibre	Sodium
392 kJ	94 kcal	5.2 g	3.0 g	10.8 g	5.8 g	0.7 g	0.2 g	0.1 g

For two madeleines.

1 Whisk the sugar, eggs and vanilla seeds to a hot sabayon.
2 Fold in the flour and the baking powder.
3 Fold in the *beurre noisette* and chill for up to 2 hours.
4 Pipe into well-buttered madeleine moulds and bake in a moderate oven.
5 Turn out and allow to cool.

13 Rich fruit cake

1 Cream the butter and sugar until soft and light.

2 Break up the eggs and beat in gradually.

3 Add the black treacle.

4 Sieve all the dry ingredients together and fold in.

5 Finally fold in the dried fruit and lemon zest.

6 Deposit into buttered cake tins lined with silicone paper.

7 Level the mix and make a well in the centre.

8 Check the cakes during baking, turn to make sure they are being cooked evenly.

9 Test to see if cooked with a metal skewer or needle.

10 Allow to cool completely before wrapping and storing in an airtight container.

In the UK fruit cakes are traditionally used as a base for celebration cakes such as Simnel and Christmas cakes, and for weddings.

Ingredient	16 cm diameter, 8 cm deep	21 cm diameter, 8 cm deep	26 cm diameter, 8 cm deep
Butter	150 g	200 g	300 g
Soft brown sugar	150 g	200 g	300 g
Eggs	4	6	8
Black treacle	2 tsp	3 tsp	1 tbsp
Soft flour	125 g	175 g	275 g
Salt	6 g	8 g	10 g
Nutmeg	3 g	4 g	5 g
Mixed spice	3 g	4 g	5 g
Ground cinnamon	3 g	4 g	5 g
Ground almonds	75 g	100 g	125 g
Currants	150 g	200 g	300 g
Sultanas	150 g	200 g	300 g
Raisins	125 g	150 g	225 g
Mixed peel	75 g	100 g	125 g
Glacé cherries	75 g	100 g	125 g
Lemons, grated zest of	½	¾	1
Oven temperatures			
	150 °C	140 °C	130 °C
Approximate cooking times			
	2 hours	3 hours	4½ hours

Energy	Cals	Fat	Sat fat	Carb	Sugar	Protein	Fibre	Sodium
2,367 kJ	563 kcal	24.8 g	11.3 g	81.9 g	69.4 g	8.8 g	2.8 g	0.6 g

Professional tip

This is a dense mixture. To prevent the outside becoming overcooked insulate the cake tins by standing on newspaper and tying several layers of newspaper around the sides.

The dried fruit can be pre-soaked in brandy or rum the day before, or, as the cake matures it can be given a 'drink' every so often.

Take a spoon and make a well in the centre of the mixture, this will help stop the cake doming as it bakes.

Unless filling the oven with cakes it is advisable to place a tray of water in the oven when baking. This will create steam and allow the cake to expand before the crust sets.

To test, insert a needle in the centre, when the cake is cooked the needle should come out clean and hot.

After cooling wrap in paper or foil and place in an airtight container and leave to mature for 3–4 weeks before covering with marzipan and decorating with icing.

Variations

If using square cake tins, increase the quantities by a quarter.

This cake can be made less rich by cutting down on the fruit and spices – these are all 'carried' ingredients and will not affect the cake as long as the basic ingredients (butter, sugar, eggs, flour) are not tampered with.

Faults

A	B	C	D

Cake A is domed ('cauliflower top'). This occurs if:
- the flour used is too strong
- the oven is too hot and/or too dry
- there is not enough fat
- the ingredients are over-mixed after adding flour.

Cake B has a sunken top ('M' fault). This is caused by adding too much baking powder and/or too much sugar.

Cake C has a sunken top and sides ('X' fault). This occurs if the mixture is too wet.

Cake D has a low volume. This occurs if:
- too much fat is added
- the mixture is too dry
- there is not enough aeration.

A good-quality fruit cake will:
- have straight sides, a flat top and good height
- have an even distribution of fruit
- be moist and dark.

14 Lemon drizzle cake

Energy	Cals	Fat	Sat fat	Carb	Sugar	Protein	Fibre	Sodium
1437 kJ	342 kcal	14.6g	8.6g	51.8g	67.0g	4.0g	0.9g	0.3g

For ⅛ of a cake, excluding icing.

Ingredient	2 × 16 cm cakes
Butter	250g
Caster sugar	400g
Lemons, grated zest of	3
Soft flour	380g
Baking powder	10g
Eggs	4
Vanilla extract	½ tsp
Milk	25 ml
Syrup	
Lemons, juice of	3
Caster sugar	100g

1 Cream the butter, sugar and zest until soft and light.

2 Sieve the flour and baking powder twice.

3 Mix together the eggs and vanilla extract.

4 Beat the eggs into the butter and sugar mixture.

5 Fold in the flour.

6 Add milk to achieve a dropping consistency.

7 Deposit into buttered and floured cake tins.

8 Bake at 165 °C for approximately 45 minutes.

9 Boil the lemon juice and sugar.

10 When the cake is cooked, stab with a skewer and pour over the syrup.

11 Leave to cool in the tin.

This cake can be finished with lemon icing and decorated with strips of crystallised lemon peel.

15 Apricot glaze

Ingredient	Makes 150 ml
Apricot jam	100 g
Stock syrup (see page 482) or water	50 ml

1 Boil the apricot jam with a little syrup or water.
2 Pass through a strainer. The glaze should be used hot.

Professional tip

A flan jelly (commercial pectin glaze) may be used as an alternative to apricot glaze. This is usually a clear glaze to which food colour may be added.

16 Water icing (glacé icing)

Ingredient	Makes 400 g
Icing sugar	400 g
Water, warm	60 ml

1 Sieve the icing sugar and start to add the warm water; add the water until the icing is thick enough to coat the back of a spoon.
2 If necessary, add more water or icing sugar to adjust the consistency.

Variation

Water may be replaced with other liquids to add flavour to the icing – for example, orange juice, mango juice, lemon juice, apple juice, lime juice, grape juice, passion fruit juice – or use a combination of juices with orange liqueur, kirsch, rum, calvados, etc.

17 Royal icing

Ingredient	Makes 400 g
Icing sugar	400g
Pasteurised egg whites	3
Lemon, juice of	1
Glycerine	2 tsp

1 Sift the icing sugar. Mix it well with the egg whites in a basin, using a wooden spoon.

2 Add a few drops of lemon juice and glycerine and beat until stiff.

Professional tip

Modern practice is to use egg white substitute or dried egg whites. Always follow the manufacturer's instructions for quantities.

Note

This amount of royal icing (400 g) is enough to cover a small (18 cm) cake.

18 Marzipan

1 Place the water and sugar in a pan and boil. Skim as necessary.

2 When the sugar reaches 116 °C, draw aside and mix in the ground almonds, then add the egg yolks and almond essence, and mix in quickly to avoid scrambling.

3 Knead well until smooth.

Ingredient	Makes 400 g
Water	250 ml
Caster sugar	1 kg
Ground almonds	400 g
Egg yolks	3
Almond essence	2–3 drops

Marzipan may be shaped into fruits, figures, etc.

19 Praline

Ingredient	Makes 1 kg
Granulated sugar	500 g
Water	200 ml
Glucose	100 g
Whole almonds	150 g
Hazelnuts	150 g

1 Boil the sugar, water and glucose to a light caramel.
2 Remove from the heat and immediately stir in the nuts.
3 Pour the mixture on a non-stick mat and cool until solid.
4 Break down to a fine powder using a food processor.

Biscuits

20 Sponge fingers (*biscuit à la cuillère*)

Ingredient	Approximately 60 × 8 cm fingers
Egg yolks	180 g
Caster sugar	125 g
Vanilla essence	Few drops
Soft flour	125 g
Cornflour	125 g
Egg whites	270 g
Caster sugar	125 g

Energy	Cals	Fat	Sat fat	Carb	Sugar	Protein	Fibre	Sodium
372 kJ	88 kcal	2.0g	0.6g	16.0g	8.8g	1.3g	0.2g	0.0g

For two biscuits.

1 Prepare a baking sheet by lining with silicone paper cut to fit and set the oven at 160 °C. Have ready a piping bag fitted with a medium plain tube. Scald two mixing bowls to ensure they are clean and free of grease.
2 Whisk the yolks, sugar and vanilla over a bain-marie until warm, then continue whisking off the heat until a thick, sabayon-like consistency is reached.
3 Sieve the flours on to paper.
4 In a second mixing bowl, whisk the whites with the sugar to a soft meringue.
5 Add the whisked yolks to the meringue and start folding in. Add the flour in 2 or 3 portions, working quickly but taking care not to overwork the mixture.
6 Using a plain piping tube, immediately pipe on to the prepared baking sheet in neat rows.
7 Dust evenly with icing sugar and immediately place in the oven for approximately 25 minutes.
8 When cooked, slide the paper (and biscuits) on to a cooling rack.
9 When cool, remove from the paper and store in an airtight container at room temperature, or leave on the paper and store in a dry cabinet.

Note

The literal translation of this is 'spoon biscuits', which comes from a time when the mixture would have been shaped between two spoons instead of being piped. They are traditionally used to line the mould for a Charlotte Russe, although the 'spooned' version would not lend itself to that.

Variation

Chocolate: instead of 125 g each of soft flour and cornflour, use 120 g soft flour, 60 g cornflour and 70 g cocoa powder.

Othellos: use the above recipe to make small, domed sponges. Hollow them out and fill with crème mousseline (see page 476). Sandwich pairs together and coat with coloured fondant.

Professional tip

It is easier to pipe the fingers all the same length if a template marked with parallel lines is placed under the silicone paper.

A common problem with this recipe is over-mixing and/or not working fast enough or being disorganised, which results in biscuits that collapse.

Sponge fingers should be pale in colour, very light in texture, be dusted with icing sugar and have a rounded shape. They should also be identical in length and width.

---

21 Tuiles

Ingredient	15–20 portions
Butter	100 g
Icing sugar	100 g
Flour	100 g
Egg whites	2

1 Mix all ingredients; allow to rest for 1 hour.
2 Spread to the required shape and size.
3 Bake at approx. 200–210 °C.
4 While hot, mould the biscuits to the required shape and leave to cool.

Energy	Cals	Fat	Sat fat	Carb	Sugar	Protein	Fibre	Sodium
417 kJ	100 kcal	5.5 g	3.4 g	12.1 g	7.0 g	1.1 g	0.3 g	0.1 g

22 Cats' tongues (*langues de chat*)

Pipe cats' tongues into their distinctive shape, thicker at the ends

Ingredient	Approximately 40
Icing sugar	125 g
Butter	100 g
Vanilla essence	3–4 drops
Egg whites	3–4
Flour (soft)	100 g

Energy	Cals	Fat	Sat fat	Carb	Sugar	Protein	Fibre	Sodium
676 kJ	161 kcal	8.3 g	5.2 g	20.7 g	13.2 g	2.1 g	0.4 g	0.1 g

Based on a portion of 4 biscuits.

1 Lightly cream the sugar and butter, add the vanilla essence.

2 Add the egg whites one by one, continually mixing and being careful not to allow the mixture to curdle.

3 Gently fold in the sifted flour and mix lightly.

4 Pipe on to a lightly greased baking sheet using a 3 mm plain tube, 2.5 cm apart.

5 Bake at 230–250 °C, for a few minutes.

6 The outside edges should be light brown and the centres yellow.

7 When cooked, remove on to a cooling rack using a palette knife.

23 Cigarette paste cornets

Ingredient	Approximately 30
Icing sugar	125g
Butter, melted	100g
Vanilla essence	3–4 drops
Egg whites	3–4
Soft flour	100g

Energy	Cals	Fat	Sat fat	Carb	Sugar	Protein	Fibre	Sodium
444 kJ	106 kcal	5.6g	3.6g	14.0g	8.8g	0.3g	0.2g	0.1g

For two biscuits.

1 Proceed as for steps 1–3 of recipe 22 (cats' tongues).

2 Using a plain tube, pipe out the mixture on to a lightly greased baking sheet into bulbs, spaced well apart. Place a template over each bulb and spread it with a palette knife.

3 Bake at 150°C, until evenly coloured.

4 Remove the tray from the oven. Turn the cornets over but keep them on the hot tray.

5 Work quickly while the cornets are hot and twist them into a cornet shape using the point of a cream horn mould. (For a tight cornet shape it is best to set the pieces tightly inside the cream horn moulds and leave them until set.) If the cornets set hard before you have shaped them all, warm them in the oven until they become flexible.

6 The same paste may also be used for cigarettes russes, coupeaux and other shapes.

24 Brandy snaps

Ingredient	Approximately 20 snaps
Strong flour	225 g
Ground ginger	10 g
Golden syrup	225 g
Butter	250 g
Caster sugar	450 g

Energy	Cals	Fat	Sat fat	Carb	Sugar	Protein	Fibre	Sodium
2146 kJ	510 kcal	21.0 g	13.1 g	82.0 g	66.0 g	1.5 g	1.0 g	0.4 g

For two snaps.

1 Combine the flour and ginger in a bowl on the scales. Make a well.

2 Pour in golden syrup until the correct weight is reached.

3 Cut the butter into small pieces. Add the butter and sugar.

4 Mix together at a slow speed.

5 Divide into 4 even pieces. Roll into sausage shapes, wrap each in cling film and chill, preferably overnight.

6 Slice each roll into rounds. Place on a baking tray, spaced well apart.

7 Flatten each round using a fork dipped in cold water, keeping a round shape.

8 Bake in a preheated oven at 200 °C until evenly coloured and bubbly.

9 Remove from oven. Allow to cool slightly, then lift off and shape over a dariole mould.

10 Stack the snaps, no more than 4 together, on a stainless steel tray and store.

25 Piped biscuits (*sablés à la poche*)

Ingredient	20–30 biscuits
Caster or unrefined sugar	75g
Butter or margarine	150g
Egg	1
Vanilla essence	3–4 drops
or	
Grated zest of one lemon	
Soft flour, white or wholemeal	200g
Ground almonds	35g

Energy	Cals	Fat	Sat fat	Carb	Sugar	Protein	Fibre	Sodium
993 kJ	237 kcal	15.2g	8.2g	23.3g	8.4g	3.4g	0.8g	0.2g

Based on 2 biscuits.

1 Cream the sugar and butter until light in colour and texture.

2 Add the egg gradually, beating continuously, add the vanilla essence or lemon zest.

3 Gently fold in the sifted flour and almonds, mix well until suitable for piping. If too stiff, add a little beaten egg.

4 Pipe on to a lightly greased and floured baking sheet using a medium-sized star tube (a variety of shapes can be used).

5 Some biscuits can be left plain, some decorated with half or whole almonds or neatly cut pieces of angelica and glacé cherries.

6 Bake in a moderate oven at 190 °C for about 10 minutes.

7 When cooked, remove on to a cooling rack using a palette knife.

26 Shortbread biscuits

Energy	Cals	Fat	Sat fat	Carb	Sugar	Protein	Fibre
507 kJ	121 kcal	7.0g	4.4g	14.1g	4.6g	1.2g	0.5g

Using butter.

Method 1

Ingredient	12 portions
Flour (soft)	150g
Salt	pinch
Butter or margarine	100g
Caster sugar	50g

1 Sift the flour and salt.
2 Mix in the butter or margarine and sugar with the flour.
3 Combine all the ingredients to a smooth paste.
4 Roll carefully on a floured table or board to the shape of a rectangle or round, 0.5cm thick. Place on a lightly greased baking sheet.
5 Mark into the desired size and shape. Prick with a fork.
6 Bake in a moderate oven at 180–200°C for 15–20 minutes.

Method 2

Ingredient	12 portions
Flour (soft), white or wholemeal	100g
Rice flour	100g
Butter or margarine	100g
Caster or unrefined sugar	100g
Egg, beaten	1

1 Sieve the flour and rice flour into a basin.
2 Rub in the butter until the texture of fine breadcrumbs. Mix in the sugar.
3 Bind the mixture to a stiff paste using the beaten egg.
4 Roll out to 3mm using caster sugar, prick well with a fork and cut into fancy shapes. Place the biscuits on a lightly greased baking sheet.
5 Bake in a moderate oven at 180–200°C for 15 minutes or until golden brown.
6 Remove with a palette knife on to a cooling rack.

Method 3

Ingredient	12 portions
Butter or margarine	100g
Icing sugar	100g
Egg	1
Flour (soft)	150g

1 Cream the butter or margarine and sugar thoroughly.
2 Add the egg and mix in. Mix in the flour.
3 Pipe on to lightly greased and floured baking sheets using a large star tube.
4 Bake at 200–220°C, for approximately 15 minutes.

16 Cold and hot desserts

This chapter is relevant to the following units:
→ Prepare, cook and finish basic cold and hot desserts.

Recipes included in this chapter

Ingredients commonly used in desserts

There are many important ingredients used in the production of desserts. Sugar provides the sweetness that is associated with desserts, but it also plays other roles that affect texture, aroma and, depending on its form, it can also help to reduce the risk of crystallisation in products such as ice cream and dehydration of frozen products such as sponges. Eggs and other dairy products, such as milk and cream, are also regular commodities found in desserts, as is salt, perhaps surprisingly, all of which are discussed below.

Sugar

For a detailed breakdown of the various forms of sugar and its uses, refer to the section 'Ingredients for Pastry Work' in Chapter 14.

Specific details on the way that sugar is used in the production of ice creams and sorbets is given later in this chapter.

Eggs

Eggs are one of the principal ingredients in cooking and essential for many desserts. Their great versatility and extraordinary properties as a thickener, emulsifier and stabiliser make their presence important in various creations in patisserie, including sauces, creams, sponge cakes, custards and ice creams. Although it is often not the main ingredient, it plays specific and determining roles in terms of texture, taste and aroma. Eggs are fundamental in products such as brioches, crème anglaise, sponge cakes and pastry cream. The extent to which eggs are used (or not) makes an enormous difference to the quality of the product.

A good custard cannot be made without eggs, as they cause the required coagulation and give it the desired consistency and finesse.

Eggs are also an important ingredient in ice cream where, due to the lecithin they contain, their yolks aid the emulsion of fats.

Eggs are used for several reasons:
- They act as a texture agent in, for example, pastry cream and ice cream.
- They intensify the aroma of pastries such as brioche.
- They enhance flavours.
- They give volume to whisked sponges and batters.
- They strengthen the structure of products such as sponge cakes.

- They act as a thickening agent, for example in crème anglaise.
- They act as an emulsifier in products such as mayonnaise and ice cream.

Quality and nutritional value

Important facts about eggs:
- A fresh egg (in shell) should have a small, shallow air pocket inside it.
- The yolk of a fresh egg should be bulbous, firm and bright.
- The fresher the egg, the more viscous (thick and not runny) the egg white.
- Eggs should be stored away from strong odours as their shells are porous and smells are easily absorbed.
- In a whole 60 g egg, the yolk weighs about 20 g, the white 30 g and the shell 10 g.

Egg yolk is high in saturated fat. The yolk is a good source of protein and also contains vitamins and iron. The egg white is made up of protein (albumen) and water. The egg yolk also contains lecithin, which acts as an emulsifier in dishes such as mayonnaise – it helps to keep the ingredients mixed, so that the oils and water do not separate.

Working with egg whites
- To avoid the danger of salmonella, if the egg white is not going to be cooked or will not reach a temperature of 70 °C, use pasteurised egg whites. Egg white is available chilled, frozen or dried.
- Equipment must be thoroughly clean and free from any traces of fat, as this prevents the whites from whipping; fat or grease prevents the albumen strands from bonding and trapping the air bubbles.
- Take care that there are no traces of yolk in the white, as yolk contains fat.
- A little acid (cream of tartar or lemon juice) strengthens the egg white, extends the foam and produces more meringue. The acid also has the effect of stabilising the meringue.
- If the foam is over-whipped the albumen strands, which hold the water molecules with the sugar suspended on the outside of the bubble, are overstretched. The water and sugar make contact and the sugar dissolves, making the meringue heavy and wet. This can sometimes be rescued by further whisking until it foams up, but very often the mixture has to be discarded and a new one produced.

Beaten egg white forms a foam that is used for aerating sweets and many other desserts, including meringues (see recipe 11). It is advisable to use Italian meringue in desserts that are not going to be cooked, such as bavarois.

Salt

Salt (chemical name 'sodium chloride') is a very important ingredient in all areas of cookery, including patisserie. Salt is a necessary part of the human diet and is present in small or large proportions in many natural foods. Salt considerably enhances many products, sweet or savoury. We generally associate it with seasoning foods to improve their flavour, but it is also necessary in the making of many sweet dishes.

It is a good idea to add a pinch of salt to all sweet preparations, nougats, chocolate bonbons and cakes to intensify flavours. Salt also softens sugar and butter, activates the taste buds and enhances all aromas. Salted caramel is an excellent example of how salt can benefit a sweet product.

What you need to know about salt

- Salt gives us the possibility of many combinations. At times these may seem normal (such as a terrine of foie gras and coarse salt), and, at others, surprising (such as praline with coarse salt).
- The addition of salt enhances the flavour of foods when its quantity is well adjusted; but if added in greater quantity than we are used to, it produces a very interesting, completely unknown result. Care needs to be taken when adding salt. There is a fine line between the enhancement of food with salt and spoiling it by adding too much.
- Excessive salt can cause high blood pressure, which could lead to strokes or heart attacks, so it should be used in moderation. For this reason, many chefs are looking for ways to reduce the amount of salt they use in their products and dishes.

Egg custard-based desserts

The essential ingredients for an egg custard are eggs and milk. Cream is often added to egg custard desserts to enrich them and to improve the feel in the mouth (mouth-feel) of the final product.

Egg custard mixture provides the chef with a versatile basic set of ingredients that covers a wide range of sweets. The mixture is often referred to as crème renversée. Some examples of sweets produced using this mixture are:

- crème caramel (recipe 3)
- bread and butter pudding (recipe 31)
- diplomat pudding
- cabinet pudding (recipe 33)
- queen of puddings
- baked egg custard.

Savoury egg custard is used to make:

- quiches
- tartlets
- flans.

When a starch, such as flour, is added to the ingredients for an egg custard mix, it changes the characteristic of the end product, as in pastry cream, for example.

- **Pastry cream** (also known as confectioner's custard or crème pâtissière) is a filling used for many sweets, gâteaux, flans and tartlets, and as a basis for soufflé mixes.
- **Sauce à l'anglaise** (crème anglaise) is used as a base for some ice creams. It is also used in its own right as a sauce to accompany a range of sweets.

Basic egg custard sets by coagulation of the egg protein. Egg white coagulates at approximately 60 °C, egg yolk at 70 °C. Whites and yolks mixed together will coagulate at 66 °C. If the egg protein is overheated or overcooked, it will shrink and water will be lost from the mixture, causing undesirable bubbles in the custard. This loss of water is called syneresis, commonly referred to as scrambling or curdling. This will occur at temperatures higher than 85 °C. Therefore, a sauce anglaise should be ideally cooked between 70 °C and 85 °C. The sauce will become thicker as it becomes closer to 85 °C, but is at risk of curdling beyond this temperature.

Traditional custard made from custard powder

Custard powder can be used to make custard sauce. It is made from vanilla-flavoured cornflour with yellow colouring added, and is a substitute for eggs. Sweetness is adjusted by adding sugar before mixing with milk and heating. The fat content can be reduced by making it with semi-skimmed milk rather than full-fat milk.

Points to remember when making egg custards

- Always work in a clean and tidy way, complying with food hygiene regulations.
- Check the temperature of refrigerators and freezers to ensure that they comply with the current regulations.
- Check all weighing scales for accuracy.
- Check all raw materials for correct use-by dates.
- Always wash your hands when handling fresh eggs or dairy products and other pastry ingredients.
- Prevent cross-contamination by not allowing any potentially harmful substances to come into contact with the mixture.

- Follow the recipe carefully.
- Always heat the egg yolks or eggs to 70 °C, or use pasteurised egg yolks or eggs.
- Ensure that all heating and cooling temperatures are followed.
- Always store the end product carefully at the right temperature.
- Never use cream to decorate a product that is still warm.

Ice creams and sorbets

Ice cream

Traditional ice cream is made from a basic egg custard sauce (sauce anglaise). The sauce is cooled and mixed with fresh cream. It is then frozen using a rotating machine (churn) where the water content forms ice crystals.

Ice cream should be served at around −13 °C; any colder and it will be too hard, any warmer and it will be too soft. Long-term storage should be at between −18 °C and −20 °C.

The traditional method of making ice cream uses only egg yolks, sugar and milk/cream in the form of a sauce anglaise base. Modern approaches to making ice cream use stabilisers (see page 515) and different sugars, and egg whites.

Ice cream regulations

The Dairy Products (Hygiene) Regulations 1995 apply to the handling of milk-based ice cream, while the Ice Cream (Heat Treatment) Regulations 1959 and 1963 apply to non-milk-based ice cream in any catering business or shop premises. The production process must also take into consideration the Food Hygiene Regulations 2006.

The regulations state that:

- Ice cream must be obtained from a mixture which has been heated to any of the temperatures in Table 16.1 for the times specified.
- The mix must be reduced to a temperature of not more than 7.2 °C within one and a half hours. This temperature must not be exceeded until freezing begins.
- If the ice cream becomes warm (above −2.2 °C) it cannot be sold/used until it has been heated again as described above.
- A complete cold mix that is reconstituted with water does not need to be pasteurised first to comply with these regulations.
- A complete cold mix reconstituted with water must be kept below −2.2 °C once it has been frozen.

Table 16.1 Time and temperature combinations set out by the Ice Cream (Heat Treatment) Regulations 1959

Temperature	Time (not less than)
65.5 °C	30 minutes
71.1 °C	10 minutes
79.4 °C	15 seconds

Ice cream needs this treatment to kill harmful bacteria. Freezing without the correct heat treatment does not kill bacteria; it allows them to remain dormant. The storage temperature for ice cream should not exceed −20 °C ideally, although standard freezers usually operate between −18 °C and −22 °C.

The rules for sterilised (UHT) ice cream are the same except that:

- The temperature for the heat treatment must not be less than 149.9 °C for at least two seconds.
- If the sterilised mix is kept in unopened, sterile and air-tight containers, there no requirement to refrigerate the mixture before it is frozen.
- In the case of non-milk based products, the temperature of opened containers must not exceed 7.2 °C, except where food mixtures are added that have a pH of 4.5 or less to make water ice or similar products and the combined product is frozen within one hour of combination.

Any ice cream sold must comply with the following compositional standards:

- It must contain not less than 5 per cent fat and not less than 2.5 per cent milk protein (not necessary in natural proportions).
- It must conform to the Dairy Product Regulations 1995.

For further information contact the Ice Cream Alliance (see www.ice-cream.org).

Ice cream making process

1 **Weighing**: ingredients should be weighed precisely in order to ensure the best results and regularity and consistency.
2 **Pasteurisation**: this is a vital stage in making ice cream. Its primary function is to minimise bacterial contamination by heating the mixture of ingredients to 85 °C, then quickly cooling it to 4 °C.
3 **Homogenisation**: high pressure is applied to cause the explosion of fats, which makes ice cream more homogenous, creamier, smoother and much lighter. It is not usually done for homemade ice cream.

4 **Ripening**: this basic but optional stage refines flavour, further develops aromas and improves texture. This occurs during a rest period (4 to 24 hours), which gives the stabilisers and proteins time to act, improving the overall structure of the ice cream. This has the same effect on a crème anglaise, which is much better the day after it is made than it is on the same day.

5 **Churning**: the mixture is frozen while air is incorporated at the same time. The ice cream is removed from the machine at about −10 °C.

Use of sugars

- **Sucrose** (common sugar) not only sweetens ice cream but also gives it body. An ice cream that contains only sucrose (not recommended) has a higher freezing point.
- The optimum sugar percentage of ice cream is between 15 and 20 per cent.
- Ice cream that contains **dextrose** (another type of sugar) has a lower freezing point, and better taste and texture.
- As much as 50 per cent of the sucrose can be substituted with other sweeteners, but the recommended amount is 25 per cent.
- **Glucose** (another type of sugar) improves smoothness and prevents the crystallisation of sucrose.
- The quantity of glucose used should be between 25 and 30 per cent of the sucrose by weight.
- **Atomised glucose** (glucose powder) is more water absorbent, so helps to reduce the formation of ice crystals.
- The quantity of dextrose used should be between 6 and 25 per cent of the substituted sucrose (by weight).
- **Inverted sugar** is a paste or liquid obtained from heating sucrose with water and an acid (for example, lemon juice). Using inverted sugar in ice cream lowers the freezing point.
- Inverted sugar also improves the texture of ice cream and delays crystallisation.
- The quantity of inverted sugar used should be a maximum of 33 per cent of the sucrose by weight. It is very efficient at sweetening and gives ice cream a low freezing point.
- **Honey** has very similar properties as those of inverted sugar.

Use of cream and egg yolks

- The purpose of **cream** in ice cream is to improve creaminess and taste.
- **Egg yolks** act as stabilisers in ice cream due to the lecithin they contain – they help to prevent the fats and water in the ice cream from separating.
- Egg yolks improve the texture and viscosity of ice cream.
- The purpose of stabilisers (for example, gum arabic, gelatine, pectin) is to prevent crystal formation by absorbing the water contained in ice cream and making a stable gel.

Use of stabilisers

Gelling substances, thickeners and emulsifiers are all stabilisers. They are products we use regularly, each with its own specific function, but their main purpose is to retain water to make a gel. The case of ice cream is the most obvious, in which they are used to prevent ice crystal formation. They are also used to stabilise the emulsion, increase the viscosity of the mix and give a smoother product that is more resistant to melting. There are many stabilising substances, both natural and artificial.

- The quantity of stabilisers in ice cream should be between 3 g and 5 g per kg of mix, with a maximum of 10 g.
- Stabilisers promote air absorption, making products lighter to eat and also less costly to produce, as air increases the volume of the product.

What you need to know about ice cream

- Hygienic conditions are essential while making ice cream – personal hygiene and high levels of cleanliness in the equipment and the kitchen environment must be maintained.
- An excess of stabilisers in ice cream will make it sticky.
- Stabilisers should always be mixed with sugar before adding, to avoid lumps.
- Stabilisers should be added at 45 °C, which is when they begin to act.
- Cold stabilisers have no effect on the mixture, so the temperature must be raised to 85 °C.
- Ice cream should be allowed to 'ripen' for 4 to 24 hours. This helps to improve its flavour properties.
- Ice cream should be cooled quickly to 4 °C, because micro-organisms reproduce rapidly, particularly between 20 °C and 55 °C.

Sorbets

Sorbets belong to the ice cream family; they are a mixture of water, sucrose, atomised glucose, stabiliser, fruit juice, fruit pulp and, sometimes, liqueurs.

- Sorbet is generally more refreshing and easier to digest than ice cream.
- Fruit for sorbets must always be of a high quality and ripe.
- The percentage of fruit used in sorbet varies according to the type of fruit, its acidity and the properties desired.
- The percentage of sugar will depend on the type of fruit used.
- The minimum sugar content in sorbet is about 13 per cent.
- As far as ripening is concerned, the syrup should be left to rest for 4 to 24 hours and never mixed with the fruit because its acidity would damage the stabiliser.
- Stabiliser is added in the same way as for ice cream.
- Sorbets are not to be confused with granitas, which are semi-solid.

Stabilisers and setting agents

Edible gelatine

Edible gelatine is extracted from animals' bones (for example, pork and veal) and, more recently, fish skin. Sold in sheets of 2 g, it is easy to precisely control the amount used and to manipulate it. Gelatine sheets must always be washed thoroughly with lots of cold water to remove impurities and any remaining odours. They must then be drained before use.

Gelatine sheets melt at 40 °C; they should be melted in a little of the liquid from the recipe before being added to the base preparation.

Pectin

Pectin is another commonly used gelling substance because of its great absorption capacity. It comes from citrus peel (for example, oranges, lemons), though all fruits contain some pectin in their peel.

It is a good idea to mix pectin with sugar before adding it to the rest of the ingredients.

Agar-agar

Agar-agar is a gelatinous marine algae found in Asia. It is sold in whole or powdered form and has a great absorption capacity. It dissolves very easily and, in addition to gelling, adds elasticity and resists heat (this is classified as a non-reversible gel). It is a vegetarian alternative to gelatine.

Carob gum

Carob gum comes from the seeds of the carob tree; it makes sorbets creamier and improves heat resistance.

Guar gum and carrageenan

Guar gum and carrageenan are natural products. Both of these gelling substances have similar properties to agar-agar, but they are not as commonly used.

Fruit-based and other desserts

Fruit is used as an ingredient in many desserts. It can be the main feature of a dessert, as in the case of a baked apple (*bonne femme*), peach Melba or pear belle Hélène, or in conjunction with other dessert bases and ingredients. Fruit can also form the main component of batter-based desserts, such as fritters and clafoutis, for example.

Fruit is used to contribute to sponge-based desserts, such as baked Alaska with cherries or caramelised banana (see Recipe 44), as a platform to support fruit mousses and/or bavarois, or as a component in steamed sponge puddings. Fruit is also regularly used in a variety of pastry-based desserts, such as tarte tatin, fruit tarts and barquettes.

Other dessert mediums include meringue (vacherins), egg custards (*crème renversée*) and purées (to flavour ice creams and sorbets). This provides just a few examples of the versatility of fruit and how it can be used alongside other mediums to produce an endless variety of desserts.

Quality and purchasing

Fresh fruit should be:

- whole and fresh looking (for maximum flavour the fruit must be ripe but not overripe)
- firm, according to type and variety
- clean, and free from traces of pesticides and fungicides
- free from external moisture
- free from any unpleasant foreign smell or taste
- free from pests or disease
- sufficiently mature; it must be capable of being handled and travelling without being damaged
- free from any defects characteristic of the variety in terms of their shape, size and colour
- free of bruising and any other damage.

Soft fruits deteriorate quickly, especially if they are not sound. Take care to see that they are not damaged or overripe when purchased. Soft fruits should look fresh; there should be no signs of wilting, shrinking or mould. The colour of certain soft fruits is an indication of their ripeness (for example, strawberries or dessert gooseberries).

Storing fruit

Hard fruits, such as apples, should be left in boxes and kept in a cool store. Soft fruits, such as raspberries and strawberries, should be left in their punnets or baskets in a cold room. Stone fruits, such as apricots and plums, are best placed in trays so that any damaged fruit can be seen and discarded. Peaches and citrus fruits are left in their delivery trays or boxes. Bananas should not be stored in chilled conditions because their skins will turn black.

Finishing and presentation

The finishing and presentation of desserts can lead to elaborate creations. With the use of ever-changing techniques, products and equipment, desserts offer chefs the opportunity to create mouth-watering dishes that are also also eye catching, impressive and imaginative.

Classically, some dessert products are finished by being filled, such as profiteroles and crêpes. Other desserts might include a chocolate cup filled with a mousse or cream, whereas others are glazed or gratinated, such as crème brûlée or bread and butter pudding.

Garnishing desserts offers endless opportunities and can be as simple as using some fresh fruit such as raspberries or other berries. Piping can also be used to enhance desserts: a cream or buttercream, for example, or a chocolate motif.

Other garnishes include items such as dried fruits and purées, fruit carpaccios and crisps, and even items such as popping 'space dust', intended to add the element of surprise by popping when it comes in contact with saliva in the mouth.

Healthy eating and desserts

Desserts and puddings remain popular with consumers today, but there is now a demand for products with reduced fat and sugar content, as many people are keen to eat a healthy diet. Chefs continue to respond to this demand by modifying recipes to reduce the fat and sugar content; they may also use alternative ingredients, such as low-calorie sweeteners where possible and unsaturated fats. Although salt is an essential part of our diet, too much of it can be unhealthy (see page 563), and this is something else that chefs should take into consideration.

Test yourself

1. Name three types of setting agent.
2. Describe what would happen to a crème caramel if it was cooked at 180 °C.
3. Name the three main types of meringues, and describe their production and use.
4. Describe the conditions that promote the foam of egg whites when making meringues.
5. Name two desserts that are finished with a glaze.
6. What is the difference between a cabinet and diplomat pudding?
7. Name five fruits suitable for stewing.
8. Describe the differences between the production of a 'pudding soufflé' and a 'fruit soufflé'.
9. Name four types of sugar, giving an example of their use in a dessert.
10. Explain why salt is sometimes used in the production of desserts.

Cold desserts

1 Fresh fruit salad

1 For the syrup, boil the sugar with the water and place in a bowl.

2 Allow to cool, then add the lemon juice.

3 Peel and cut the orange into segments.

4 Peel, quarter and core the apple and pear, then cut each quarter into two or three slices, place in the bowl with the syrup and mix in the orange segments.

5 Stone the cherries but leave them whole.

6 Cut the grapes in half, peel if required, and remove any pips. Add the cherries and grapes to the fruit and syrup mix.

7 Mix the fruit salad carefully and place in a glass bowl in the refrigerator to chill.

8 Just before serving, peel and slice the banana and mix in.

Variation

● Any of the following fruits may be used: dessert apples, pears, pineapple, oranges, grapes, melon, strawberries, peaches, raspberries, apricots, bananas, cherries, kiwi fruit, plums, mangoes, paw paws and lychees. Allow about 150g unprepared fruit per portion. All fruit must be ripe.

● Kirsch or an orange liqueur could be added to the syrup.

● Fruit juice (such as apple, orange, grape or passion fruit) can be used instead of syrup.

Ingredient	4 portions	10 portions
Stock syrup		
Caster sugar	50g	125g
Water	125ml	310ml
Lemon, juice of	½	1¼
Fruit		
Orange	1	2½
Dessert apple	1	2½
Dessert pear	1	2½
Cherries	50g	125g
Grapes	50g	125g
Banana	1	2½

Energy	Cals	Fat	Sat fat	Carb	Sugar	Protein	Fibre
493 kJ	117 kcal	0.0g	0.0g	30.3g	29.5g	0.9g	3.0g

2   Poached fruits or fruit compote

Poached rhubarb and pear

Ingredient	4 portions	10 portions
Stock syrup (see page 482)	250 ml	625 ml
Fruit	400 g	1 kg
Sugar	100 g	250 g
Lemon, juice of	½	1

Energy	Cals	Fat	Sat fat	Carb	Sugar	Protein	Fibre
531 kJ	126 kcal	0.0 g	0.0 g	33.5 g	33.5 g	0.2 g	2.2 g

Using pears.

Apples, pears

1   Boil the water and sugar.
2   Quarter the fruit, remove the core and peel.
3   Place in a shallow pan in sugar syrup.
4   Add a few drops of lemon juice.
5   Cover with greaseproof paper.
6   Allow to simmer slowly, preferably in the oven, cool and serve.

Soft fruits (raspberries, strawberries)

1   Pick and wash the fruit. Place in a glass bowl.
2   Pour on the hot syrup. Allow to cool and serve.

Stone fruits (plums, damsons, greengages, cherries)

1   Wash the fruit, barely cover with sugar syrup and cover with greaseproof paper or a lid.
2   Cook gently in a moderate oven until tender.

Rhubarb

1   Trim off the stalk and leaf and wash.
2   Cut into 5 cm lengths and cook as above, adding extra sugar if necessary. A little ground ginger may also be added.

Gooseberries, blackcurrants, redcurrants

1   Top and tail the gooseberries, wash and cook as for stone fruit, adding extra sugar if necessary.
2   The currants should be carefully removed from the stalks, washed and cooked as for stone fruits.

Dried fruits (prunes, apricots, apples, pears)

1   Dried fruits should be washed and soaked in cold water overnight.
2   Gently cook in the liquor with sufficient sugar to taste.

Variation

A piece of cinnamon stick and a few slices of lemon may be added to the prunes or pears, one or two cloves to the dried or fresh apples.

Any compote may be flavoured with lavender and/or mint.

Healthy eating tips
● Use fruit juice instead of stock syrup.
● If dried fruits are used, no added sugar is needed.

3 Crème caramel

Ingredient	4–6 portions	10–12 portions
Caramel		
Sugar, granulated or cube	100g	200g
Water	125ml	250ml
Cream		
Milk, whole or skimmed	0.5 litres	1 litre
Eggs	4	8
Sugar, caster or unrefined	50g	100g
Vanilla essence or a vanilla pod	3–4 drops	6–8 drops

Energy	Cals	Fat	Sat fat	Carb	Sugar	Protein	Fibre
868 kJ	207 kcal	7.2g	3.3g	30.2g	30.2g	7.3g	0.0g

Using whole milk.

1 Prepare the caramel by placing three-quarters of the water in a thick-based pan, adding the sugar and allowing to boil gently, without shaking or stirring the pan.

2 When the sugar has cooked to a golden-brown caramel colour, add the remaining quarter of the water, reboil until the sugar and water mix, then pour into the bottom of dariole moulds.

3 Prepare the cream by warming the milk and whisking on to the beaten eggs, sugar and essence (or vanilla pod).

4 Strain and pour into the prepared moulds.

5 Place in a roasting tin half full of water.

6 Cook in a moderate oven at 150–160°C for 30–40 minutes.

7 When thoroughly cold, loosen the edges of the crème caramel with the fingers, shake firmly to loosen and turn out on to a flat dish or plates.

8 Pour any caramel remaining in the mould around the creams.

Crème caramels may be served with whipped cream or a fruit sauce such as passion fruit, and accompanied by a sweet biscuit (e.g. shortbread, palmiers).

Professional tip

Adding a squeeze of lemon juice to the caramel will invert the sugar, thus preventing recrystallisation.

4 Crème brûlée

Ingredient	4 portions	10 portions
Milk	125 ml	310 ml
Double cream	125 ml	310 ml
Natural vanilla, essence or pod	3–4 drops	7–10 drops
Eggs	2	5
Egg yolk	1	2–3
Caster sugar	25 g	60 g
Demerara sugar		

Energy	Cals	Fat	Sat fat	Carb	Sugar	Protein	Fibre
1154 kJ	278 kcal	21.9 g	12.1 g	14.8 g	14.8 g	6.2 g	0.0 g

1 Warm the milk, cream and vanilla essence in a pan.

2 Mix the eggs, egg yolk and caster sugar in a basin and add the warm milk. Stir well and pass through a fine strainer.

3 Pour the cream into individual dishes and place them into a tray half-filled with warm water.

4 Place in the oven at approximately 160 °C for about 30–40 minutes, until set.

5 Sprinkle the tops with Demerara sugar and glaze under the salamander or by blowtorch to a golden brown.

6 Clean the dishes and serve.

Variation

Sliced strawberries, raspberries or other fruits (e.g. peaches, apricots) may be placed in the bottom of the dish before adding the cream mixture, or placed on top after the creams are caramelised.

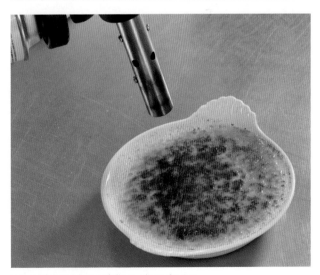

Use a blowtorch carefully to glaze the top

Video: making crème brûlée http://bit.ly/ 1vWYRwH

5 Zabaglione (sabayon with Marsala)

1 Whisk the egg yolks and sugar in a bowl until almost white.
2 Mix in the Marsala.
3 Place the bowl and its contents in a bain-marie of warm water.
4 Whisk the mixture continuously until it increases to four times its bulk and is firm and frothy.
5 Pour the mixture into glass goblets.
6 Accompany with a suitable biscuit (for example, sponge fingers).

Note

This is a traditional Italian dessert, which is sometimes prepared in the restaurant in a special zabaglione pan.

Variation

Use sherry, whisky or brandy instead of Marsala.

Ingredient	4 portions	10 portions
Egg yolks, pasteurised	8	20
Caster or unrefined sugar	200 g	500 g
Marsala	150 ml	375 ml

Energy	Cals	Fat	Sat fat	Carb	Sugar	Protein	Fibre
746 kJ	177 kcal	5.5g	1.6g	27.4g	27.4g	2.9g	0.0g

6 Fruit mousse

Ingredient	10 portions
Egg yolks	4
Sugar	50 g
Fruit purée	250 g
Gelatine	4 leaves
Lemon juice	
Lightly whipped cream	250 g
Italian meringue	
Sugar	112 g
Egg whites	2
Cream of tartar	pinch
Glaze topping	
Stock syrup	150 ml
Fruit purée	150 ml
Gelatine	3 leaves, soaked in cold water

Energy	Cals	Fat	Sat fat	Carb	Sugar	Protein	Fibre	Sodium
950 kJ	227 kcal	12.4 g	7.0 g	26.0 g	26.0 g	4.0 g	2.0 g	0.0 g

1 Mix the egg yolks and sugar together and slowly add the boiled fruit purée which has been flavoured with a squeeze of lemon juice.

2 Return to the stove and cook to 80 °C until slightly thickened. Do not boil.

3 Add the previously softened gelatine to the warm purée and mix until fully dissolved. Chill down.

4 Prepare the Italian meringue by placing the sugar in a pan and saturating in water.

5 Boil the sugar to 115 °C, then whisk the egg whites with a pinch of cream of tartar.

6 Once the egg whites are at full peak, gradually add the boiled sugar which now should have reached the temperature of 121 °C. Whisk until cold.

7 Once the purée is cold, but not set, incorporate the Italian meringue and whipped cream.

8 Place into piping bag and pipe into the desired ring mould, normally lined with a suitable sponge such as a jaconde.

9 Level the surface using a palette knife and refrigerate.

10 Once set, glace the surface, refrigerate.

11 To remove from the mould, warm the outside of the mould with a blow torch and remove the ring mould.

Glaze

1 Warm the syrup. Add the gelatine and stir until dissolved, then add the desired fruit purée.

2 Apply to the surface of the chilled mousse whilst in a liquid state, but not hot.

7 Bavarois

Ingredient	6–8 portions
Gelatine	10g
Eggs, pasteurised, separated	2
Caster sugar	50g
Milk (whole, semi-skimmed or skimmed)	250ml
Whipping or double cream (or non-dairy cream)	125ml

Energy	Cals	Fat	Sat fat	Carb	Sugar	Protein	Fibre
970 kJ	231 kcal	18.2g	10.9g	11.8g	11.8g	5.8g	0.0g

Using whole milk and whipping cream.

1 If using leaf gelatine, soak in cold water.

2 Cream the egg yolks and sugar in a bowl until almost white.

3 Bring the milk to the boil in a thick-based saucepan then whisk it into the egg yolk and sugar mixture; mix well.

4 Clean the milk saucepan and return the mixture to it.

5 Return to a low heat and stir continuously with a wooden spoon until the mixture coats the back of the spoon. The mixture must not boil.

6 Remove from the heat; add the gelatine and stir until dissolved.

7 Pass through a fine strainer into a clean bowl. Leave in a cool place, stirring occasionally until almost at setting point.

8 Fold in the lightly beaten cream.

9 Fold in the stiffly beaten whites.

10 Pour the mixture into a mould or individual moulds (which may be very lightly greased with almond oil).

11 Allow to set in the refrigerator.

12 Shake and turn out on to a flat dish or plates. Bavarois may be decorated with sweetened, flavoured whipped cream (crème Chantilly).

Flavours for bavarois

- **Raspberry or strawberry bavarois** (as shown): when the custard is almost cool, add 200g of picked, washed and sieved (puréed) raspberries or strawberries. Decorate with whole fruit and whipped cream.
- **Chocolate bavarois**: melt 50g chocolate couverture in the milk. Decorate with whipped cream and grated chocolate.
- **Coffee bavarois**: add coffee essence to the basic bavarois mixture, to taste.
- **Orange bavarois**: add the grated zest and juice of two oranges and one or two drops of orange colour to the mixture, and increase the gelatine by two leaves. Decorate with blanched, fine julienne of orange zest, orange segments and whipped cream.
- **Lemon or lime bavarois**: as for orange bavarois, but using lemons or limes in place of oranges.
- **Vanilla bavarois**: add a vanilla pod or a few drops of vanilla extract to the milk. Decorate with vanilla-flavoured sweetened cream (crème Chantilly).

Health and safety !

It is advisable to use pasteurised egg yolks and whites.

Healthy eating tips

Use semi-skimmed milk and whipping cream to reduce the overall fat content.

8 Chocolate mousse

Ingredient	8 portions	16 portions
Stock syrup at 30° Baumé (equal quantities of sugar and water will give 30° Baume)	125 ml	250 ml
Pasteurised egg yolks	80 ml	160 ml
Bitter couverture, melted	250 g	500 g
Gelatine (soaked)	2 leaves	4 leaves
Whipping cream, whipped	500 ml	1 litre

Energy	Cals	Fat	Sat fat	Carb	Sugar	Protein	Fibre	Sodium
1760 kJ	419 kcal	37.0 g	22.0 g	13.7 g	12.8 g	5.1 g	2.6 g	0.0 g

1 Boil the syrup.

2 Place the yolks into the bowl of a food mixer. Pour over the boiling syrup and whisk until thick (this is a *pâte à bombe*). Remove from the mixer.

3 Add all the melted couverture at once and fold it in quickly.

4 Drain the gelatine, melt it in the microwave and fold it into the chocolate sabayon mixture.

5 Add all the whipped cream at once and fold it in carefully.

6 Place the mixture into prepared moulds. Refrigerate or freeze immediately.

Faults

Possible causes of a heavy texture in chocolate mousse:
- The *pâte à bombe* is under-aerated.
- The cream is insufficiently whipped.
- The mix has been over-worked when folding in the cream and Italian meringue.

9 Vanilla panna cotta with stewed rhubarb

Ingredient	6 portions
Milk	125 ml
Double cream	375 ml
Aniseeds	2
Vanilla pod	½
Gelatine (soaked)	2 leaves
Caster sugar	50 g
Stewed rhubarb	
Rhubarb	500 g
Vanilla pod	1
Stock syrup	250 ml
Orange	1
Blueberries	75 g
Raspberries	50 g

Energy	Cals	Fat	Sat fat	Carb	Sugar	Protein	Fibre	Sodium
1808 kJ	436 kcal	34.0g	21.0g	31.0g	31.0g	3.0g	2.9g	0.0g

1 Prepare the rhubarb by finely peeling it.

2 Split the vanilla pod lengthways and scrape the seeds into a saucepan with the stock syrup and the zest and juice of the orange.

3 Bring the syrup to a gentle simmer and add the rhubarb. Stew until the rhubarb is cooked through but still holding its shape. Use a spider to remove the rhubarb and cut diagonally into strips.

4 For the panna cotta, boil the milk and cream, add aniseeds, infuse with the vanilla pod and remove after infusion.

5 Heat again and add the soaked gelatine and caster sugar. Strain through a fine strainer.

6 Place in a bowl set over ice and stir until it thickens slightly; this will allow the vanilla seeds to suspend throughout the mix instead of sinking to the bottom.

7 Fill individual dariole moulds.

8 Turn out the panna cotta and serve with the rhubarb. Decorate with a split, dried vanilla pod, a shortbread biscuit or a tuile.

10 Fruit fool

Method 2

Ingredient	4 portions	10 portions
Fruit purée (raspberry, strawberry, etc.)	400 g	1 kg
Caster sugar	100 g	250 g
Fresh whipped cream	250 ml	625 ml

Energy	Cals	Fat	Sat fat	Carb	Sugar	Protein	Fibre
1,540 kJ	370 kcal	25.3 g	15.8 g	35.7 g	35.7 g	2.0 g	1.2 g

For a strawberry fool.

Mix the ingredients and serve in coupes.

Method 3

Ingredient	4 portions	10 portions
Cornflour	35 g	85 g
Water	375 ml	940 ml
Sugar	100 g	250 g
Fruit purée (raspberry, strawberry, etc.)	400 g	1 kg
Cream	185 ml	460 ml

Energy	Cals	Fat	Sat fat	Carb	Sugar	Protein	Fibre
1,606 kJ	385 kcal	25.2 g	15.6 g	40.0 g	31.9 g	2.0 g	2.7 g

For a raspberry fool made with double cream.

1 Dilute the cornflour in a little of the water.

2 Boil the remainder of the water with the sugar and prepared fruit until soft.

3 Pass through a fine sieve.

4 Return to a clean pan and reboil.

5 Stir in the diluted cornflour and reboil. Allow to cool.

6 Lightly whisk the cream and fold into the mixture.

7 Serve as for method 1.

Professional tip

In methods 2 and 3 the fat content may be reduced by using equal quantities of cream and natural Greek-style yoghurt.

Method 1

Ingredient	4 portions	10 portions
Fruit (apple, gooseberry, rhubarb, etc.)	400 g	1 kg
Water	60 ml	150 ml
Granulated or unrefined sugar	100 g	250 g
Cornflour	25 g	60 g
Milk, whole or semi-skimmed	250 ml	625 ml
Caster or unrefined sugar	25 g	60 g

Energy	Cals	Fat	Sat fat	Carb	Sugar	Protein	Fibre
942 kJ	222 kcal	2.6 g	1.6 g	50.3 g	4.5 g	2.4 g	1.6 g

For an apple fool made with whole milk.

1 Cook the fruit to a purée in the water with the granulated sugar. Pass through a sieve.

2 Dilute the cornflour in a little of the milk and add the caster sugar.

3 Boil the remainder of the milk.

4 Pour on to the diluted cornflour and stir well.

5 Return to the pan on a low heat and stir to the boil.

6 Mix with the fruit purée. The quantity of mixture should not be less than 0.5 litres (for four portions).

7 Pour into glass coupes or suitable dishes and allow to set.

8 Decorate with sweetened whipped cream or non-dairy cream. The colour may need to be adjusted slightly with food colour.

11 Meringue

Ingredient	4 portions	10 portions
Lemon juice or cream of tartar		
Egg whites, pasteurised	4	10
Caster sugar	200 g	500 g

Energy	Cals	Fat	Sat fat	Carb	Sugar	Protein	Fibre	Sodium
913 kJ	214 kcal	0.1 g	0.0 g	52.0 g	52.0 g	4.0 g	0.0 g	0.1 g

1 Whip the egg whites stiffly with a squeeze of lemon juice or cream of tartar.

2 Sprinkle on the sugar and carefully mix in.

3 Place in a piping bag with a large plain tube and pipe on to silicone paper on a baking sheet.

4 Bake in the slowest oven possible or in a hot plate (110 °C). The aim is to dry out the meringues without any colour whatsoever.

Whipping egg whites

The reason egg whites increase in volume when whipped is because they contain so much protein (11 per cent). The protein forms tiny filaments, which stretch on beating, incorporate air in minute bubbles then set to form a fairly stable puffed-up structure expanding to seven times its bulk. To gain maximum efficiency when whipping egg whites, the following points should be observed.

Because of possible weakness in the egg-white protein, it is advisable to strengthen it by adding a pinch of cream of tartar and a pinch of dried egg-white powder. If all dried egg-white powder is used no additions are necessary.

Other points to note:
● Eggs should be fresh.
● When separating yolks from whites no speck of egg yolk must be allowed to remain in the white; egg yolk contains fat, the presence of which can prevent the white being correctly whipped.
● The bowl and whisk must be scrupulously clean, dry and free from any grease.
● When egg whites are whipped, the addition of a little sugar (15 g to 4 egg whites) will assist efficient beating and reduce the chances of over-beating.

12 Vacherin with strawberries and cream

Ingredient	4 portions	10 portions
Egg whites	4	10
Caster sugar	200 g	500 g
Cream (whipped and sweetened) or non-dairy cream	125 ml	300 ml
Strawberries, picked and washed)	100–300 g	250–750 g

Energy	Cals	Fat	Sat fat	Carb	Sugar	Protein	Fibre
1,436 kJ	341 kcal	12.6 g	7.9 g	56.3 g	56.3 g	3.9 g	0.6 g

1 Stiffly whip the egg whites. (Refer to the notes in recipe 11 for more guidance.)

2 Carefully fold in the sugar.

3 Place the mixture into a piping bag with a 1 cm plain tube.

4 Pipe on to silicone paper on a baking sheet.

5 Start from the centre and pipe round in a circular fashion to form a base of 16 cm then pipe around the edge 2–3 cm high.

6 Bake in a cool oven at 100 °C until the meringue case is completely dry. Do not allow to colour.

7 Allow the meringue case to cool then remove from the paper.

8 Spread a thin layer of cream on the base. Add the strawberries.

9 Decorate with the remainder of the cream.

Note

A vacherin is a round meringue shell piped into a suitable shape so that the centre may be filled with sufficient fruit (such as strawberries, stoned cherries, peaches and apricots) and whipped cream to form a rich sweet. The vacherin may be prepared in one-, two- or four-portion sizes, or larger.

Variation

Melba sauce may be used to coat the strawberries before decorating with cream.

Raspberries can be used instead of strawberries.

Healthy eating tips

● Try 'diluting' the fat in the cream with some low-fat fromage frais.

13 Lime soufflé frappe

Energy	Cals	Fat	Sat fat	Carb	Sugar	Protein	Fibre	Sodium
2,734 kJ	655 kcal	40.8 g	20.7 g	66.9 g	61.2 g	9.2 g	0.8 g	0.2 g

Ingredient	10 portions	15 portions
Couverture	150 g	200 g
Sponge, thin slices, cut into rounds	10	15
Lime syrup	100 ml	150 ml
Swiss meringue		
Sabayon		
Whipping cream	600 ml	900 ml
Lime zest, finely grated and blanched, and juice	8	12
Egg yolks	10	15
Caster sugar	170 g	250 g
Leaf gelatine, soaked in iced water	9½	14
To decorate		
Confit of lime segments		
Moulded chocolate		

1 Use individual stainless steel ring moulds. Cut a strip of acetate, 8 cm wide, to fit inside each ring. Cut a 6 cm strip to fit inside the first, spread it with tempered couverture and place inside the first strip, in the mould.

2 Place a round of sponge in the base of each mould and moisten with lime syrup.

3 Make the Swiss meringue (see page 481).

4 Whisk the cream until it is three-quarters whipped, then chill.

5 Whisk together the egg yolks, sugar and blanched lime zest. Boil the juice and pour it over

the mixture to make the sabayon. Whisk over a bain-marie until it reaches 75 °C, then continue whisking away from the heat until it is cold.

6 Drain and melt the gelatine. Fold it into the sabayon.

7 Fold in the Swiss meringue, and then the chilled whipped cream.

8 Fill the prepared moulds. Level the tops and chill until set.

9 To serve, carefully remove the mould, peel away the acetate, plate and decorate.

---

14 Trifle

Ingredient	6–8 portions
Sponge (made with 3 eggs)	1
Jam	25 g
Tinned fruit (pears, peaches, pineapple) in syrup	1
Sherry (optional)	
Custard	
Custard powder	35 g
Milk, whole or skimmed	375 ml
Caster sugar	50 g
Cream (¾ whipped) or non-dairy cream	125 ml
Whipped sweetened cream or non-dairy cream	250 ml
Angelica	25 g
Glacé cherries	25 g

Energy	Cals	Fat	Sat fat	Carb	Sugar	Protein	Fibre
2,280 kJ	543 kcal	29.1 g	17.1 g	66.2 g	51.3 g	8.2 g	1.9 g

1 Cut the sponge in half, sideways, and spread with jam.

2 Place in a glass bowl or individual dishes and soak with fruit syrup drained from the tinned fruit; a few drops of sherry may be added.

3 Cut the fruit into small pieces and add to the sponge.

4 Dilute the custard powder in a basin with some of the milk and add the sugar.

5 Boil the remainder of the milk, pour a little on the custard powder, mix well, return to the saucepan and over a low heat stir to the boil. Allow to cool, stirring occasionally to prevent a skin forming; fold in the three-quarters whipped cream.

6 Pour on to the sponge. Leave to cool.

7 Decorate with the whipped cream, angelica and cherries.

Variation

Other flavourings or liqueurs may be used in place of sherry (such as whisky, rum, brandy, coffee liqueur).

For raspberry or strawberry trifle use fully ripe fresh fruit in place of tinned and decorate with fresh fruit in place of angelica and glacé cherries.

A fresh egg custard may be used with fresh egg yolks (see page 558).

15 Lime and mascarpone cheesecake

Energy	Cals	Fat	Sat fat	Carb	Sugar	Protein	Fibre	Sodium
2,624 kJ	633 kcal	54.0g	32.3g	31.5g	24.3g	7.1g	0.0g	0.3g

Using cream cheese in place of mascarpone.

Ingredient	1 cheesecake
Ginger biscuits	200g
Butter, melted	200g
Egg yolks, pasteurised	125g
Caster sugar	75g
Cream cheese	250g
Mascarpone	250g
Gelatine, softened in cold water	15g
Limes, juice and grated zest of	2
Semi-whipped cream	275ml
White chocolate, melted	225g

1 Blitz the biscuits in a food processor. Mix in the melted butter. Line the cake ring with this mixture and chill until required.

2 Make a sabayon by whisking the egg yolks and sugar together over a pan of simmering water.

3 Stir the cream cheese and mascarpone into the sabayon until soft.

4 Meanwhile, warm the gelatine in the lime juice, and pass through a fine chinois. Whip the cream.

5 Pour the gelatine and melted white chocolate into the cheese mixture.

6 Remove from the food mixer and fold in the whipped cream with a spatula. Finally, whisk in the lime zest.

7 Pour over the prepared base. Chill for 4 hours.

16 Baked blueberry cheesecake

Ingredient	8–12 portions
Base	
Digestive biscuits	150g
Butter, melted	50g
Filling	
Full-fat cream cheese	350g
Caster sugar	150g
Eggs	4
Lemon, zest and juice of	1
Vanilla essence	1 tsp
Blueberries	125g
Soured cream	350ml

Energy	Cals	Fat	Sat fat	Carb	Sugar	Protein	Fibre
1,791 kJ	431 kcal	33.5g	19.5g	28.0g	19.7g	6.4g	0.4g

1 Blitz the biscuits in a food processor. Stir in the melted butter. Press the mixture into the bottom of a lightly greased cake tin with a removable collar.

2 Whisk together the cheese, sugar, eggs, vanilla and lemon zest and juice until smooth.

3 Stir in the blueberries, then pour the mixture over the biscuit base.

4 Bake at 160 °C for approximately 30 minutes.

5 Remove from the oven and leave to cool slightly for 10–15 minutes.

6 Spread soured cream over the top and return to the oven for 10 minutes.

7 Remove and allow to cool and set. Chill.

Iced desserts

17 Vanilla ice cream

1 Whisk the yolks and sugar in a bowl until almost white.

2 Boil the milk with the vanilla pod or essence in a thick-based pan.

3 Whisk on to the eggs and sugar; mix well.

4 Return to the cleaned saucepan, place on a low heat.

5 Stir continuously with a wooden spoon until the mixture coats the back of the spoon.

6 Pass through a fine strainer into a bowl.

7 Freeze in an ice cream machine, gradually adding the cream.

Ingredient	8–10 portions
Egg yolks	4
Caster or unrefined sugar	100 g
Milk, whole or skimmed	375 ml
Vanilla pod or essence	
Cream or non-dairy cream	125 ml

Energy	Cals	Fat	Sat fat	Carb	Sugar	Protein	Fibre
616 kJ	147 kcal	8.1 g	4.2 g	15.8 g	15.8 g	3.5 g	0.0 g

Using whole milk and single cream.

Variation

Coffee ice cream: add coffee essence, to taste, to the custard after it is cooked.

Chocolate ice cream: add 50–100 g of chopped couverture to the milk before boiling.

Strawberry ice cream: add 125 ml of strawberry pulp in place of 125 ml of milk. The pulp is added after the custard is cooked.

Rum and raisin ice cream: soak 50 g raisins in 2 tbsp rum for 3–4 hours. Add to mixture before freezing.

1 Whisk boiling milk into the egg yolks and sugar

2 Return the mixture to the hot pan used for the milk

3 Test the consistency on the back of a spoon

4 Pass through a fine strainer into a cold pot

5 The mixture will cool down; if it was left in the hot pan it would continue to cook

6 Gradually add cream to the mixture in the ice cream machine

18 Lemon curd ice cream

Ingredient	6–8 portions
Lemon curd	250 g
Crème fraiche	125 g
Greek yoghurt	250 g

Energy	Cals	Fat	Sat fat	Carb	Sugar	Protein	Fibre
774 kJ	185 kcal	8.9 g	5.2 g	24.8 g	16.7 g	2.8 g	0.0 g

1 Mix all ingredients together.

2 Churn in the ice cream machine.

19 Peach Melba

1 Poach the peaches. Allow to cool, then peel, halve and remove the stones.

2 Dress the fruit on a ball of the ice cream in an ice cream coupe or in a tuile basket.

3 Finish with the sauce.

The traditional presentation is to coat the peach in Melba sauce or coulis and decorate with whipped cream.

Professional tip

If using fresh peaches, dip them in boiling water for a few seconds, cool them by placing into cold water, then peel and halve.

Variation

Fruit Melba can also be made using pear or banana instead of peach. Fresh pears should be peeled, halved and poached. Bananas should be peeled at the last moment.

Ingredient	4 portions	10 portions
Peaches	2	5
Vanilla ice cream	125 ml	300 ml
Raspberry coulis	125 ml	300 ml

Energy	Cals	Fat	Sat fat	Carb	Sugar	Protein	Fibre
607 kJ	145 kcal	2.6g	1.3g	30.5g	30.2g	1.6g	1.3g

20 Pear belle Hélène

Traditional presentation

1 Serve a poached pear on a ball of vanilla ice cream in a coupe.

2 Decorate with whipped cream. Serve with a sauceboat of hot chocolate sauce.

Modern presentation

1 Coat a poached pear with chocolate sauce.

2 Dress on a plate with vanilla ice cream, more sauce and a tuile.

Energy	Cals	Fat	Sat fat	Carb	Sugar	Protein	Fibre	Sodium
1,888 kJ	453 kcal	29.7g	18.2g	44.5g	43.6g	4.5g	5.3g	0.0g

21 Apple sorbet

1 Cut the apples into 1 cm pieces and place into lemon juice.

2 Bring the water, sugar and glucose to the boil, then allow to cool.

3 Pour the water over the apples. Freeze overnight. Blitz in a food processor.

4 Pass through a conical strainer, then churn in an ice cream machine.

Professional tip

For best results, after freezing, process in a Pacojet.

Variation

Fruits of the forest sorbet: use a mixture of forest fruits instead of apples.

Ingredient	8–10 portions
Granny Smith apples, washed and cored	4
Lemon, juice of	1
Water	400 ml
Sugar	200 g
Glucose	50 g

Energy	Cals	Fat	Sat fat	Carb	Sugar	Protein	Fibre
673 kJ	158 kcal	0.1 g	0.0 g	41.5 g	38.7 g	0.4 g	2.4 g

22 Chocolate sorbet

Ingredient	8 portions
Water	400 ml
Skimmed milk	100 ml
Sugar	150 g
Ice cream stabiliser	40 g
Cocoa powder	30 g
Dark couverture	60 g

1 Combine the water, milk, sugar, stabiliser and cocoa powder. Bring to the boil slowly. Simmer for 5 minutes.

2 Add the couverture and allow to cool.

3 Pass and churn.

Energy	Cals	Fat	Sat fat	Carb	Sugar	Protein	Fibre
544 kJ	129 kcal	3.0 g	1.8 g	25.4 g	24.9 g	1.6 g	6.3 g

23 Raspberry parfait

Ingredient	6–8 portions
Italian meringue	
Caster sugar	150 g
Glucose	20 g
Water	80 ml
Egg whites	200 g
Additional ingredients	
Egg yolks, pasteurised	80 g
Caster sugar	60 g
Gelatine, soaked	1½ leaves
Raspberry liqueur	10 ml
Lemon juice	10 ml
Raspberry purée	120 g
Whipped cream	150 ml
Sponge	

Energy	Cals	Fat	Sat fat	Carb	Sugar	Protein	Fibre
981 kJ	234 kcal	10.7 g	5.6 g	31.3 g	30.2 g	4.7 g	0.5 g

1 Make up the Italian meringue (see page 480).

2 Combine the egg yolks and caster sugar in a stainless steel bowl. Whisk over a bain-marie to make a sabayon.

3 Drain the gelatine and dissolve it in the liqueur and lemon juice.

4 Fold the gelatine mixture into the sabayon, then fold in the raspberry purée.

5 Fold in the Italian meringue, then fold in the whipped cream.

6 Place into prepared moulds lined with sponge and freeze.

7 Once set, remove from the moulds.

8 In this presentation, the parfait has been lined with sponge only on the base. It is served with a raspberry coulis and fresh and dried raspberry garnishes.

24 Pancakes with apple

Ingredient	4 portions	10 portions
Cooked apple, thinly sliced	150 g	375 g
Flour, white or wholemeal	100 g	250 g
Salt	pinch	large pinch
Egg	1	2–3
Milk, whole, semi-skimmed or skimmed	250 ml	625 ml
Melted butter, margarine or oil	10 g	25 g
Oil for frying		
Caster sugar to serve		

1 Place a little cooked apple in a pan, add the pancake mixture and cook on both sides.
2 Turn out, sprinkle with caster sugar and roll up.

Energy	Cals	Fat	Sat fat	Carb	Sugar	Protein	Fibre
1,178 kJ	280 kcal	8.2 g	2.9 g	47.7 g	28.7 g	6.6 g	2.8 g

25 Baked apples (*pommes bonne femme*)

Ingredient	4 portions	10 portions
Medium-sized cooking apples	4	10
Sugar, white or unrefined	50 g	125 g
Cloves	4	10
Butter	20 g	50 g
Water	60 ml	150 ml

Energy	Cals	Fat	Sat fat	Carb	Sugar	Protein	Fibre	Sodium
663 kJ	156 kcal	5.1 g	2.2 g	29.7 g	29.5 g	0.4 g	2.7 g	

Using hard margarine.

1 Core the apples and make a 2 mm-deep incision round the centre of each. Wash well. Peel the apples for a modern presentation.
2 Place in a roasting tray or ovenproof dish.
3 Fill the centre with sugar and add a clove to each.
4 Place 5 g butter on each apple. Add the water.
5 Bake in a hot oven, at 200–220 °C, for 15–20 minutes.
6 Turn the apples over carefully.
7 Return to the oven until cooked, about 40 minutes in all.
8 Serve with a little cooking liquor and custard, cream or ice cream.

Professional tip

To protect the peeled apple, wrap it in lightly oiled greaseproof or silicone paper before putting it in the oven.

Cooking apples requires careful temperature control: some varieties will turn into purée very quickly. Check carefully at the end of step 5: some apples, baked without the skin, may be fully cooked by this point, in which case, skip steps 6 and 7.

Variation

● Traditional baked apples are cooked with the skin on.
● For stuffed baked apples, fill the centre of each apple with washed sultanas, raisins or chopped dates, or a combination of these.

26 Apple charlotte

Ingredient	8 individual or 2 small charlotte moulds
Dessert apples (Cox's)	1 kg
Butter	30 g
Caster sugar	100 g
Lemon, zest of	1
Breadcrumbs	
Large, thin-sliced loaf of bread	1
Clarified butter	250 g

Energy	Cals	Fat	Sat fat	Carb	Sugar	Protein	Fibre
2,163 kJ	515 kcal	22.3 g	9.3 g	74.5 g	23.4 g	9.4 g	6.1 g

Using hard margarine instead of butter.

1 Peel, core and cut the apples into thick slices.

2 Melt the butter in a pan, add the sugar and finely grated lemon zest.

3 Add the apples and simmer until barely cooked, stir in some breadcrumbs to absorb any liquid.

4 Cut out circles of bread for the top and base of the moulds.

5 Cut the crusts and the rest of the bread into fingers 2–3 cm wide, depending on whether you are making individual or larger charlottes.

6 Butter the moulds, dip half the circles in the clarified butter and place them butter-side down in the base of each mould.

7 Next, dip the bread fingers and line them around the outside of the moulds, slightly overlapping.

8 Fill the centre with the apple filling, pressing in carefully.

9 Dip the rest of the circles in the butter and place on top, pressing firmly.

10 Bake at 230 °C for 30–40 minutes until the bread is coloured and crisp.

11 Allow to cool slightly before unmoulding; serve with hot apricot sauce or crème anglaise.

> **Professional tip**
>
> As this dessert will most likely be plated and sent from the kitchen, it will more often than not be made in individual portions. Larger versions (such as that in the photograph) would be suitable for family or silver service, but could not be cut and made to look presentable if served from the kitchen.

Variation

Replace the apples with pears, or use a mixture of both.

Faults

A common fault is that the charlotte collapses when unmoulded (the larger versions are more prone to this). The main reasons for this are:

● The filling is too wet. To avoid this, ensure that cooking apples are never used, and do not overcook.
● The bread is not baked crisp enough to withstand the pressure of supporting the filling.

If making individual charlottes, make sure that the ratio of bread to filling is not compromised by using bread that is cut too thick or overlapping too much.

27 Apple fritters (*beignets aux pommes*)

Mixed fruit fritters

Ingredient	4 portions	10 portions
Cooking apples	400 g	1 kg
Flour, as needed		
Frying batter	150 g	375 g
Apricot sauce	125 ml	300 ml

Energy	Cals	Fat	Sat fat	Carb	Sugar	Protein	Fibre
1,034 kJ	246 kcal	10.2 g	1.9 g	38.9 g	25.0 g	2.1 g	3.0 g

Fried in peanut oil.

1 Peel and core the apples and cut into 0.5 cm rings.
2 Pass through flour, shake off the surplus.
3 Dip into the frying batter (see page 194).
4 Lift out with the fingers, into fairly hot deep fat: 185 °C.
5 Cook for about 5 minutes on each side.
6 Drain well on kitchen paper, dust with icing sugar and glaze under the salamander.

Serve with hot apricot sauce.

28 Griottines clafoutis

Ingredient	4 portions	10 portions
Eggs	2	5
Caster sugar	40 g	100 g
Flour	40 g	100 g
Milk	175 ml	440 ml
Kirsch	1 tsp	1 tbsp
Griottine cherries	28	70
Neige décor to dust		

Energy	Cals	Fat	Sat fat	Carb	Sugar	Protein	Fibre
790 kJ	187 kcal	4.3g	1.5g	28.8g	21.4g	6.7g	1.3g

This dish originates from the Limousin region of France and is traditionally made with black cherries.

1 Whisk the eggs and sugar together.

2 Add the flour and whisk until smooth.

3 Add the milk and kirsch; mix well and pass through a conical strainer.

4 Brush four (or ten) sur le plat dishes with soft butter.

5 Add seven cherries to each dish and pour over the batter.

6 Bake at 200 °C for 12–15 minutes until the batter has risen and set.

7 Serve warm, dusted with neige décor or icing sugar, and a kirsch sabayon.

Variation
- Griottines work particularly well in this dish but could be substituted for any other hard or fleshy fruit.
- Substitute 25 per cent of the flour with ground almonds or hazelnuts.
- To make a richer mixture, substitute up to half the milk with cream.

Professional tip
- Good-quality clafoutis should be golden brown and will rise around the edges but stay flatter in the centre. Check to make sure they are set; if not, bake for a little longer.
- Like most batters, this one benefits from resting before cooking and can be made the day before.
- Clafoutis can also be made in Yorkshire pudding tins and served unmoulded.

29 Rice pudding

4 Wash the rice and sprinkle into the boiling milk, stir, cover with a lid and allow to simmer until the rice is tender.

5 In a bowl whisk the eggs and sugar and drop in the butter.

6 Ladle a quarter of the boiling milk and rice on to the liaison, mix well and return all to the pan, carefully cook out until the mixture thickens, before removing from the heat (it must not be allowed to boil).

7 Place into suitable individual or large (usually china) dishes.

8 Grate with nutmeg and glaze under the salamander.

Serve with a warm seasonal fruit compote.

Variation

Place some good-quality jam in the base of the dish.

Place in a serving dish before piping meringue on top and baking in a hot oven until coloured.

Leftover rice pudding can be used as an alternative to crème pâtissière or frangipane as a filling for a baked flan.

Ingredient	10 portions
Milk	650 ml
Vanilla pod	1
Short grain rice	60 g
Liaison	
Pasteurised egg	60 g
Caster sugar	60 g
Butter (diced)	30 g

Energy	Cals	Fat	Sat fat	Carb	Sugar	Protein	Fibre	Sodium
455 kJ	108 kcal	4.5 g	2.5 g	14.5 g	9.4 g	3.5 g	0.1 g	0.1 g

1 Rinse a heavy pan with cold water and add the milk.

2 Split the vanilla pod, scrape out the seeds and add along with the pod.

3 Slowly bring to the boil.

Health and safety

As this recipe requires some ingredients that are not boiled, ensure all work surfaces and equipment are kept scrupulously clean.

It is recommended that pasteurised eggs are used.

Rice pudding can be held over service at a temperature of no less than 75 °C for 2 hours.

Any leftover rice pudding must be cooled to below 5 °C within 20 minutes, labelled and stored in a refrigerator.

Professional tip

Rinsing out the saucepan with cold water and adding the milk to the wet pan will help prevent the milk from catching on the bottom.

30 Baked rice pudding (*pouding de riz*)

Ingredient	4 portions	10 portions
Rice, short or whole grain	50 g	125 g
Sugar, caster or unrefined	50 g	125 g
Milk (whole, semi-skimmed or skimmed)	0.5 litres	1.25 litres
Butter or margarine	10 g	25 g
Vanilla essence	2–3 drops	6–8 drops
Grated nutmeg		

Energy	Cals	Fat	Sat fat	Carb	Sugar	Protein	Fibre
1,006 kJ	239 kcal	7.0 g	3.9 g	40.7 g	19.0 g	5.8 g	0.6 g

Using whole milk and hard margarine.

1 Wash the rice and place it in a pie dish or individual dishes.

2 Add the sugar and milk, and mix well.

3 Add the butter, vanilla essence and nutmeg.

4 Place on a baking sheet; clean the rim of the pie dish.

5 Bake at 180–200 °C, until the milk starts simmering.

6 Reduce the heat and allow the pudding to cook slowly, allowing 1½–2 hours in all (less time for individual dishes).

The pudding may be garnished with nuts, as shown.

31 Sticky toffee pudding

Ingredient	10 puddings
Dates	375 g
Water	625 ml
Butter	125 g
Caster sugar	375 g
Eggs	5
Soft flour	375 g
Baking powder	10 g
Vanilla compound	1 tsp

Energy	Cals	Fat	Sat fat	Carb	Sugar	Protein	Fibre
4,104 kJ	980 kcal	60.4 g	36.7 g	106.7 g	78.9 g	9.1 g	1.8 g

1 Remove stones and chop the dates, place in the water and simmer for about 5 minutes until soft, set aside to cool.

2 Butter and sugar individual dariole moulds.

3 Cream the butter and sugar until light in colour and aerated.

4 Gradually add the beaten eggs, beating continuously.

5 Sieve the flour and baking powder twice and fold in.

6 Finally add the dates and water and vanilla compound.

7 Fill the moulds three-quarters full and bake at 180 °C for 30–35 minutes.

> **Professional tip**
>
> Sticky toffee pudding can be steamed instead of baked. If steaming, remember to cover with a disc of silicone paper and seal with a pleated square of foil, as for steamed puddings (Recipe 38).

Sticky toffee sauce

Granulated sugar	600 g
Unsalted butter	300 g
Double cream	450 g
Brandy	30 ml

1 Make a dry caramel by carefully melting the sugar until a deep golden colour is achieved.

2 Cut the butter into small cubes, add to the cream and heat.

3 Gradually add the hot cream and butter to the caramel a little at a time.

4 Finally stir in the brandy.

To serve, coat the pudding with the sauce and serve with vanilla or milk ice cream.

---

32 Cabinet pudding

1 Cut the cake into 0.5 cm dice.

2 Mix with the lemon zest and fruits (which can be soaked in rum).

3 Place in a greased, sugared charlotte mould or 4 dariole moulds. Do not fill more than halfway.

4 Warm the milk and whisk on to the eggs, sugar and essence (or vanilla pod).

5 Strain on to the mould.

6 Place in a roasting tin, half full of water; allow to stand for 5–10 minutes.

7 Cook in a moderate oven at 150–160 °C for 30–45 minutes.

8 Leave to set for a few minutes before turning out.

Serve a fresh egg custard (page 558) or hot apricot sauce separately.

> **Variation**
>
> Diplomat pudding is made as for cabinet pudding, but served cold with either redcurrant, raspberry, apricot or vanilla sauce.

Ingredient	4 portions	10 portions
Plain sponge cake	100 g	250 g
Zest of unwaxed lemons, grated		
Currants and sultanas	25 g	60 g
Milk, whole or skimmed	0.5 litres	1.25 litres
Eggs	3–4	8–10
Caster or unrefined sugar	50 g	125 g
Vanilla essence or a vanilla pod	2–3 drops (1 pod)	7 drops (2 pods)

Energy	Cals	Fat	Sat fat	Carb	Sugar	Protein	Fibre
1,512 kJ	360 kcal	17.3 g	7.7 g	40.9 g	35.5 g	12.7 g	0.7 g

Using whole milk and 4 eggs.

33 Soufflé pudding

1 Boil the milk in a sauteuse.

2 Combine the flour, butter and sugar.

3 Whisk into the milk and reboil.

4 Remove from heat, add the egg yolks one at a time, whisking continuously.

5 Stiffly beat the whites and carefully fold into the mixture.

6 Three-quarters fill buttered and sugared dariole moulds.

7 Place in a roasting tin, half full of water.

8 Bring to the boil and place in a hot oven at 230–250 °C for 12–15 minutes.

9 Turn out on to a flat dish.

Serve with a suitable hot sauce, such as custard or sabayon sauce.

Ingredient	5 portions	10 portions
Milk, whole or skimmed	185 ml	375 ml
Flour, white or wholemeal	25 g	50 g
Butter or margarine	25 g	50 g
Caster or unrefined sugar	25 g	50 g
Eggs, separated	3	6

Variation

Orange or lemon soufflé pudding is made by flavouring the basic mixture with the grated zest of an orange or lemon and a little appropriate sauce. Use the juice in the accompanying sauce.

Energy	Cals	Fat	Sat fat	Carb	Sugar	Protein	Fibre
510 kJ	122 kcal	7.6g	3.2g	5.9g	4.8g	0.2g	0.0g

Using white flour and hard margarine.

34 Chocolate fondant

Ingredient	10 portions
Unsalted butter	260 g
Dark couverture	260 g
Eggs, pasteurised	120 g
Egg yolks, pasteurised	40 g
Caster sugar	150 g
Instant coffee	5 g
Plain flour	110 g
Baking powder	5 g
Cocoa powder	75 g
Salt	Pinch

Energy	Cals	Fat	Sat fat	Carb	Sugar	Protein	Fibre
2,830 kJ	675 kcal	46.8g	29.6g	55.9g	40.9g	11.0g	0.6g

1 Melt the butter and couverture together.

2 Warm the eggs, egg yolks, sugar and coffee and whisk to the ribbon stage.

3 Sieve all the dry ingredients twice.

4 Fold the chocolate and butter into the eggs.

5 Fold in the dry ingredients.

6 Pipe into individual stainless steel rings lined with silicone paper and placed on a silicone paper-lined baking sheet.

7 Bake at 190 °C for 5 minutes.

8 Carefully slide off the rings and serve with vanilla ice cream.

1 Melt the chocolate and butter in small pieces.

2 Fold the melted chocolate into the egg mixture.

3 Add the dry ingredients.

4 To make a contrasting centre, add white chocolate pieces on a base of the chocolate mixture.

5 Pipe in more of the chocolate mixture until the mould is full.

Professional tip

These fondants can be kept in the refrigerator and cooked to order. If they are chilled, then extend the cooking time by 2 minutes.

Chocolate fondant should have a liquid centre with a rich, buttery, chocolate taste. Because of the liquid centre, they are very delicate; if piped inside a ring they are much easier and quicker to serve, rather than trying to turn them out of a mould.

Precise timing is essential or the centre of the fondant will not be liquid.

Like most recipes, the quality of the finished product relies on the quality of the ingredients. Always use good-quality chocolate (couverture) which contains a high percentage of cocoa butter and solids.

Variation

Try adding salted caramel to the centre by making and freezing it in ice cube trays.

Serve with malt ice cream (just add malt powder instead of vanilla and mix in some crushed chocolates) or replace the cream with crème fraiche to give a less rich ice cream.

Prepare fondants in moulds lined with melted butter and roasted sesame seeds.

35 Bread and butter pudding

Ingredient	10 portions
Washed sultanas	100 g
Thin slices of white bread	Approximately 5
Butter, melted	200 g
Custard	
Vanilla pod	1
Milk	300 ml
Cream	300 ml
Eggs	5
Caster sugar	100 g
Nutmeg	
To finish	
Apricot jam	100 g

Energy	Cals	Fat	Sat fat	Carb	Sugar	Protein	Fibre	Sodium
1463 kJ	350 kcal	23.0 g	14.4 g	34.0 g	27.0 g	3.7 g	0.3 g	0.4 g

1 Butter an earthenware or other suitable dish and sprinkle with some of the sultanas.

2 Cut the crusts off the bread, dip in melted butter on both sides and cut in half diagonally.

3 Arrange overlapping bread slices neatly in the dish.

4 Sprinkle with more sultanas and cover with another layer of bread.

5 To make the custard, split the vanilla pod, add to the milk and cream and slowly bring to the boil.

6 Whisk the eggs and sugar together and add the boiling liquid, leave to infuse for 5 minutes before passing through a conical strainer.

7 Pour the custard over the bread and grate on some fresh nutmeg.

8 Place in a bain-marie and place in a moderate oven at 160 °C, pour hot water into the bain-marie until it comes half way up the dish.

9 Bake for around 45 minutes until the custard is just set.

10 Once removed from the oven sprinkle with sugar and place under the salamander to crisp up and colour the top.

11 Finally, brush with boiled apricot glaze and serve with pouring cream or crème fraiche.

Professional tip

Add the custard in two or three lots, allowing it to soak in before adding the next. This will prevent the bread floating to the top.

Variation

This pudding can be made in individual dishes or baked in a tray and cut and plated.

Try using alternatives to bread such as fruit loaf, brioche, baguette slices or panettone.

Soak the sultanas in rum the day before.

Try adding a layer of caramelised apple slices.

A chocolate version can be made by adding couverture (good-quality chocolate) to the custard.

Healthy eating tips
● Reduce the sugar content and add more dried fruit, apricots or cranberries.
● Try using milk only, semi-skimmed or skimmed.
● Dip the bread in the butter on just one side to reduce the fat content.

36 Apple crumble tartlets

Ingredient	10 tarts
Sweet paste	500 g
Dessert apples	5
Filling	
Soured cream	500 ml
Caster sugar	70 g
Plain flour	75 g
Egg	1
Vanilla extract	
Crumble	
Plain flour	80 g
Walnuts, chopped	60 g
Brown sugar	65 g
Ground cinnamon	Pinch
Salt	Pinch
Unsalted butter, melted	65 g
Icing sugar, to decorate	

1 Line individual tartlet moulds with the sweet paste.
2 Peel, core and finely slice the apples and divide between the tartlets.
3 Whisk together the soured cream, sugar, flour, egg and a few drops of vanilla, and pass through a conical strainer.
4 Pour over the apples and bake at 190 °C for 10 minutes.
5 Combine the dry crumble ingredients and mix with the melted butter.
6 Divide the crumble mixture between the tartlets and bake for a further 10 minutes.
7 Allow to cool slightly before unmoulding. Dust with icing sugar and serve with *sauce à l'anglaise*.

Variation

This dish could be made with pears or plums instead of apples.

Energy	Cals	Fat	Sat fat	Carb	Sugar	Protein	Fibre	Sodium
2200 kJ	541 kcal	36.0 g	19.3 g	51.0 g	20.0 g	7.3 g	2.6 g	0.3 g

37 Tarte tatin

Ingredient	10 portions
Granulated sugar	500g
Soft butter	120g
Caster sugar	120g
Dessert apples	5
Caramel, crushed	120g
Puff paste	150g

Energy	Cals	Fat	Sat fat	Carb	Sugar	Protein	Fibre	Sodium
1946 kJ	462 kcal	15.2g	7.2g	85.2g	79.9g	1.0g	1.3g	0.2g

Note

This is the name given to an apple tart that is cooked under a lid of pastry, but then served with the pastry underneath the fruit. This is a delicious dessert in which the taste of caramel is combined with the flavour of the fruit and finished with a crisp pastry base. It was the creation of the Tatin sisters, who ran a hotel-restaurant in Lamotte-Beuvron at the beginning of the last century. Having been made famous by the Tatin sisters the dish was first served at Maxim's in Paris as a house speciality. It is still served there to this day.

1 Make a dry caramel by placing the granulated sugar in a hot heavy-based saucepan. When the sugar reaches a deep amber colour, pour it out onto a silicone mat and leave to cool completely.

2 When cold, crush the caramel into small pieces.

3 Take a medium-sized sauteuse and spread the butter thickly around the base and sides. Sprinkle over the caster sugar and then sprinkle over the caramel. (Any spare caramel can be stored in an airtight container for later use.)

4 Peel, core and halve the apples (if large, cut into quarters) and pack into the sauteuse core-side up and with the cores running horizontally, not facing outside.

5 Roll out the pastry 2 mm thick and leave to rest.

6 Place the pan on a medium heat for 10–12 minutes to allow the caramel to melt and infuse.

7 Quickly lay over the pastry and trim, tucking the edges down the side of the pan.

8 Bake at 220 °C for 15 minutes until the pastry is crisp and the apples cooked through.

9 Invert onto a hot plate – please be aware this procedure can be tricky and requires two dry cloths and very careful handling.

10 Serve with cream, crème fraiche or ice cream.

38 Steamed sponge pudding

Ingredient	10 individual puddings
Butter	250 g
Caster sugar	250 g
Self-raising flour	250 g
Baking powder	15 g
Eggs	6
Milk	20–40 g

Energy	Cals	Fat	Sat fat	Carb	Sugar	Protein	Fibre	Sodium
1755 kJ	418 kcal	24.0 g	14.1 g	46.0 g	27.0 g	6.3 g	0.9 g	0.6 g

1 Cream the butter and sugar until lighter in colour and an increase in volume of approximately 30 per cent is achieved.

2 Sieve the flour and baking powder twice to ensure even dispersion.

3 Beat the eggs and gradually add to the butter and sugar, beating in each addition before adding the next.

4 Finally, fold in the dry ingredients.

5 Add enough milk to achieve a dropping consistency.

6 Fill buttered dariole moulds three-quarters full.

7 Place a disc of silicone paper on top and cover with foil; create a pleat to allow for expansion and crimp the edges around the lip of the mould to seal.

8 Steam for 45–50 minutes.

Flavours for sponge puddings

- **Vanilla**: scrape the seeds from a vanilla pod into the mixture at the creaming stage. Use the pod to flavour the accompanying crème anglaise.
- **Chocolate**: replace 50 g of the flour in the basic recipe with an equal amount of cocoa powder, and add 150 g ground almonds, a pinch of sea salt, a splash of coffee essence and two more eggs. Add extra butter to the base of the mould and cover with muscovado sugar before filling. Serve with hot chocolate sauce.
- **Lemon or orange**: add the grated zest of a large lemon or an orange to the mixture at the creaming stage. Serve with lemon or orange sauce as appropriate.
- **Sultana**: add 100 g of washed sultanas and a few drops of vanilla compound. Serve with crème anglaise. The sultanas may be replaced by any dried fruit.
- **Ginger**: add 10 g of ground ginger (sieved in with the dry ingredients) and 50 g of finely diced stem ginger folded in at the end. Serve with crème anglaise.
- **Golden syrup**: after buttering the mould pour a generous layer of warmed golden syrup into the base before adding the sponge mixture. Serve with crème anglaise sweetened with golden syrup.
- **Chocolate and fig/date**: add six diced figs or dates to the chocolate recipe above.

Note

A good-quality steamed sponge pudding will be light, moist and slightly spongy in texture. As steaming at 100 °C imparts no colour, it should be as light in colour as the ingredients allow.

39 Golden syrup pudding

Ingredient	5 portions	12 portions
Flour	150 g	300 g
Salt	pinch	large pinch
Baking powder	10 g	20 g
Suet, chopped	75 g	150 g
Caster or unrefined sugar	50 g	100 g
Lemon, zest of	1	2
Egg, beaten	1	2
Milk, whole or skimmed	125 ml	250 ml
Golden syrup	125 ml	250 ml

Energy	Cals	Fat	Sat fat	Carb	Sugar	Protein	Fibre
1315 kJ	313 kcal	13.0 g	5.9 g	47.8 g	26.6 g	4.3 g	0.9 g

1 Sieve the flour, salt and baking powder (or replace the flour and baking powder with self-raising flour) into a bowl.

2 Mix the suet, sugar and zest.

3 Add the beaten egg and milk and mix to a medium dough.

4 Pour the syrup in a well-greased basin or individual moulds (1 hour cooking time). Place the pudding mixture on top.

5 Cover securely; steam for 1½–2 hours.

Serve with a sauceboat of warm syrup containing the lemon juice, or with sauce anglaise or ice cream.

Variation

To make a treacle pudding, use a light treacle in place of the golden syrup. Vegetarian suet is available.

40 Christmas pudding

Ingredient	2 × 1 kg puddings
Currants	175 g
Sultanas	175 g
Raisins	350 g
Guinness	500 ml
Cognac	50 ml
Strong flour	175 g
Mixed spice	4 g
Nutmeg	4 g
Cinnamon	4 g
Breadcrumbs	175 g
Suet	350 g
Mixed peel	80 g
Ground almonds	80 g
Eggs	4
Soft dark brown sugar	175 g
Salt	3 g
Lemon, juice and zest of	1

Energy	Cals	Fat	Sat fat	Carb	Sugar	Protein	Fibre	Sodium
2077 kJ	495 kcal	23.9g	11.6g	64.9g	45.8g	6.3g	3.6g	0.2g

For ⅛ of a pudding.

1 Place all the dried fruit in a bowl, pour over the Guinness and cognac and leave to soak overnight.

2 Sieve the flour with the mixed spice, grate over the nutmeg and cinnamon and place in a large bowl.

3 Add the breadcrumbs, suet, peel and ground almonds and mix well.

4 Make a well in the centre.

5 Whisk the eggs, sugar and salt, add the lemon juice and zest.

6 Pour the wet ingredients into the well and add the soaked fruit.

7 Mix well.

8 Place mixture into two buttered pudding basins, cover with a disc of silicone paper and seal with foil, crimping around the edges.

9 Steam for 7 hours, cool and store in the fridge.

10 Reheat in the steamer for a couple of hours.
Serve with brandy or rum sauce and/or brandy butter.

Professional tip

Like a Christmas fruit cake, Christmas pudding is best made in September and allowed to mature.

41 Vanilla soufflé

Ingredient	10 individual soufflés
Base mixture	
Milk	500 ml
Vanilla pods	2
Butter	75 g
Strong flour	60 g
Egg yolks	10
Caster sugar	50 g
Additional ingredients for every 400 g of base mixture	
Egg whites	150 g
Caster sugar	60 g
Cornflour	12 g
Lemon juice	2–3 drops

Energy	Cals	Fat	Sat fat	Carb	Sugar	Protein	Fibre
932 kJ	223 kcal	13.7 g	6.7 g	19.5 g	13.9 g	6.6 g	0.2 g

1 Rinse a heavy saucepan with cold water and add the milk. Split the vanilla pod, scrape out the seeds, and add both to the milk. Put on the heat to boil.

2 Melt the butter in another heavy pan. Add the flour and cook out to form a white roux. Gradually add the boiling milk, mixing in each addition before adding the next.

3 When all the milk has been added, allow to simmer for a few minutes.

4 Whisk the egg yolks and sugar. Add to the mixture in the saucepan and keep stirring over the heat until the mixture starts to bubble around the edges. This forms the panada.

5 Pour on to a clean tray and cover with cling film to prevent a skin forming. Allow to cool. (This can be kept in the fridge until needed, as soufflés must be cooked to order.)

6 Take 400 g of the base and beat in a clean bowl until smooth.

7 Whisk the egg whites, sugar, cornflour and lemon juice to form firm peaks.

8 Add one-third of the whites to the base and mix in, then very carefully fold in the remaining whites.

9 Carefully fill prepared individual china ramekins (see below). Level the top and run your thumb around the edge, moving the mixture away from the lip of the mould.

10 Space well apart on a solid baking sheet (if they are close together they will not rise evenly and will bake stuck together).

11 Place immediately in the oven at 215 °C for 12–14 minutes.

12 The soufflés should rise out of the moulds by around 5–6 cm and have a flat top with no cracks.

13 Dust with icing sugar and serve immediately with fruit coulis and/or ice cream (chocolate or vanilla).

Preparing a soufflé mould

Mould preparation is very important. The rule is to butter the sides twice and the bottom once. Always use soft, not melted, butter, so that it stays where you put it. Give the moulds one coat all over to start with, then place in the fridge to set before giving a second coat only to the sides. (Giving the base two coats results in a puddle of butter in the bottom.)

After giving the sides a second coat of butter, the mould is usually coated with sugar.

Prepare the mould

Knock one-third of the meringue into the panada

Fold in the remaining meringue

Thumb the edge

Faults

Soufflé does not rise:
- under- or over-beaten whites
- wrong proportion of whites to base
- mixture left to stand before cooking
- moulds not buttered correctly.

Soufflé rises but drops back:
- too much egg white used.

Soufflé does not rise evenly:
- moulds not prepared correctly (mixture has stuck to the mould on one side)
- uneven heat in the oven.

Soufflé has a cracked top:
- too much egg white used
- egg white is overbeaten.

Professional tips

- Be organised with your timings. Make sure you have the moulds fully prepared and that the oven is up to heat well before the egg whites are whisked.
- Before whisking the egg whites, scald the bowl to remove any trace of fat.
- When the egg whites are whisked with the sugar, lemon juice and cornflour, they should be firm but creamy. Over-whisking will ruin them.
- The recipe uses more egg white than is needed – always take from the centre and leave behind the egg white on the edge of the bowl, which is never good.
- A soufflé should have flavour as well as an impressive 'rise'. Too much egg white can dilute the flavour.

Variation

This vanilla recipe is basic and can easily be adapted. For example, a **chocolate soufflé** can be made by adding melted chocolate and cocoa powder to the base. This will firm up the base mixture, so the whites mixture will need to be increased by 25–30 per cent to compensate.

Soufflés can be made in many different flavours and combinations. Recipes can vary considerably. For example, **fruit soufflés** can be made using a sabayon or a boiled sugar base.

As an alternative to coating the moulds with sugar, if compatible, dust them with cocoa powder, grated chocolate or try adding some cinnamon to the sugar.

42 Mango soufflé

Ingredient	4 portions	10 portions
Mango compote		
Mango	1	2½
Stock syrup	100–125 ml	250–300 ml
Mango soufflés		
Milk	100 ml	250 ml
Mango purée	150 ml	375 ml
Egg yolks	80 ml	200 ml
Caster sugar for liaison	60 g	150 g
Cornflour for liaison	15 g	40 g
Egg whites	150 ml	375 ml
Lemon juice	a few drops	a few drops
Caster sugar	30 g	75 g
Cornflour	5 g	12 g

Energy	Cals	Fat	Sat fat	Carb	Sugar	Protein	Fibre
1,116 kJ	264 kcal	6.8 g	2.1 g	45.0 g	34.6 g	8.5 g	4.8 g

To make the mango compote:

1 Remove the skin and stone from the mango and cut into small, neat dice.

2 Pour hot stock syrup over the mango dice and leave to cool.

To make the soufflés:

1 Bring the milk and mango purée to the boil.

2 Make the liaison by whisking the egg yolks with the caster sugar. Sieve in the cornflour and continue whisking until smooth.

3 Add one-third of the boiling liquid to the liaison.

4 Bring the rest of the liquid back to the boil. Whisk the liaison into it, then continue whisking until it returns to the boil. Simmer for 2–3 minutes. Cover and cool.

5 Whisk the egg whites, lemon juice, sugar and cornflour together to the consistency of shaving foam. Fold this into the cooled mango pastry cream mixture.

6 Place a spoonful of mango compote into the bottom of each prepared soufflé mould (see recipe 41 for soufflé mould preparation). Pour in the soufflé mixture and level it off with a palette knife.

7 Bake at 200 °C for approximately 12 minutes.

8 Remove carefully from the oven, dredge with icing sugar and serve immediately.

43 Lemon curd flourless soufflé

Ingredient	10 individual soufflés
Lemon curd	
Eggs	2
Caster sugar	100g
Lemons, juice of	5
Unsalted butter	60g
Cornflour	15g
Soufflés	
Eggs	9
Caster sugar	190g
Lemons, zest and juice of	5
Cream of tartar	Pinch
Egg-white powder	Pinch

Energy	Cals	Fat	Sat fat	Carb	Sugar	Protein	Fibre
1,179 kJ	280 kcal	13.3g	5.7g	31.7g	30.4g	10.1g	0.1g

To make the lemon curd:

1 Prepare by whisking all the ingredients over a pan of simmering water until the mixture thickens.

2 After preparing the soufflé moulds as described in recipe 41, divide the lemon curd mixture between them.

To make the soufflés:

1 Separate the eggs. Place together the yolks, sugar, lemon zest and juice, and whisk together well.

2 In a separate bowl, whisk the whites with the cream of tartar and egg-white powder until soft but in strong peaks.

3 Carefully fold the two mixtures together.

4 Fill the prepared moulds, level the top and run your thumb around the edge, moving the mixture away from the lip of the mould.

5 Place well apart on a heavy baking sheet and bake at 200 °C for 16–18 minutes.

6 Dust with icing sugar and serve immediately.

Note

As this dessert is gluten-free it would be suitable for coeliacs or those with a wheat intolerance.

44 Baked Alaska

1 Sit the ice cream or parfait on a base of sponge.

2 Cut more sponge to fit and completely cover.

3 Brush all over with the syrup.

4 Set on squares of silicone paper, coat with the meringue and decorate by piping on a design with a small plain tube.

5 Dust with icing sugar and place in a very hot oven at 230 °C for 2–3 minutes until the meringue is coloured.

Serve immediately with crème anglaise or a fruit coulis.

Ingredient	10 portions
Vanilla ice cream or parfait	10 × 5 cm diameter rings (500 g approx.)
Roulade sponge (see page 495)	1 sheet
Stock syrup flavoured with rum or kirsch	50 ml
Italian meringue	500 g

Energy	Cals	Fat	Sat fat	Carb	Sugar	Protein	Fibre
290 kJ	521 kcal	16.4g	7.3g	91.3g	81.2g	7.7g	0.6g

Variation

Classic variations are omelette soufflé milady, which contains poached sliced peaches with vanilla or raspberry ice cream, and omelette soufflé milord, which contains poached sliced pear with vanilla ice cream.

Professional tip

Baked Alaska is best made in advance and held in the freezer, then flashed through the oven just before serving. It is now common practice to colour the meringue with a blowtorch, but the meringue will have a much better texture and more even colouring if it is finished in the oven.

If making individual baked Alaskas, as in the photographs, take care not to upset the balance between filling and meringue – when scaled down it is easy to pipe on too much meringue.

Health and safety

Under no circumstances should this dessert be re-frozen once it has been removed from the freezer and baked. Ice cream is highly susceptible to contamination by bacteria, which can cause food poisoning.

Brush the sponge with syrup

Pipe meringue to cover

Pipe swirls of meringue to decorate

Sweet sauces

45 Sabayon sauce

Ingredient	8 portions (450–500 ml)
Egg yolks, pasteurised	6
Caster or unrefined sugar	100 g
Dry white wine	250 ml

1 Whisk the egg yolks and sugar in a 1-litre pan or basin until white.
2 Dilute with the wine.
3 Place the pan or basin in a bain-marie of boiling water.
4 Whisk the mixture continuously until it increases its bulk by four times and is firm and frothy.

Note

Sauce sabayon may be offered as an accompaniment to any suitable hot sweet (for example, soufflés or pudding soufflé).

Variation

A sauce sabayon may also be made using milk in place of wine, which can be flavoured according to taste (for example, with vanilla, nutmeg or cinnamon).

Energy	Cals	Fat	Sat fat	Carb	Sugar	Protein	Fibre
454 kJ	108 kcal	3.4 g	1.0 g	13.3 g	13.3 g	1.8 g	0.0 g

Using 5 egg yolks.

46 Fresh egg custard sauce (*sauce à l'anglaise*)

Ingredient	300 ml	700 ml
Egg yolks, pasteurised	40 ml	100 ml
Caster or unrefined sugar	25 g	60 g
Vanilla extract or vanilla pod (seeds)	2–3 drops/ ½ pod	5–7 drops/ 1 pod
Milk, whole or skimmed, boiled	250 ml	625 ml

Energy	Cals	Fat	Sat fat	Carb	Sugar	Protein	Fibre	Sodium
281 kJ	67 kcal	3.7 g	1.6 g	6.3 g	6.3 g	2.5 g	0.0 g	0.0 g

For 50 ml of sauce, using whole milk.

1 Mix the yolks, sugar and vanilla in a bowl.

2 Whisk in the boiled milk and return to a thick-bottomed pan.

3 Place on a low heat and stir with a wooden spoon until it coats the back of the spoon. Do not allow the mix to boil or the egg will scramble. A probe can be used to ensure the temperature does not go any higher than 85 °C.

4 Put through a fine sieve into a clean bowl. Set on ice to seize the cooking process and to chill rapidly.

Variation

Other flavours may be used in place of vanilla, for example:
- brandy
- cardamom seeds
- chocolate
- coffee or coffee liqueur
- kirsch
- orange flower water
- orange liqueur
- rum
- star anise
- whisky.

47 Custard sauce

Ingredient	Makes 250 ml
Custard powder	10 g
Milk, whole or semi-skimmed	250 ml
Caster or unrefined sugar	25 g

Energy	Cals	Fat	Sat fat	Carb	Sugar	Protein	Fibre
1,245 kJ	296 kcal	9.6g	6.0g	47.2g	38.0g	8.3g	0.3g

Using whole milk.

1 Dilute the custard powder with a little of the milk.
2 Boil the remainder of the milk.
3 Pour a little of the boiled milk on to the diluted custard powder.
4 Return to the saucepan.
5 Stir to the boil and mix in the sugar.

48 Fruit coulis

Ingredient	1.4 litres
Fruit purée	1 litre
Caster sugar	500 g
Lemon juice	10 g

1 Warm the purée.
2 Boil the sugar with a little water to soft-ball stage (121 °C).
3 Pour the soft-ball sugar into the warm fruit purée while whisking vigorously. Add the lemon juice. Bring back to the boil.
4 This will then be ready to store.

Professional tip

The reason the soft-ball stage needs to be achieved when the sugar is mixed with the purée is that this stabilises the fruit and prevents separation once the coulis is presented on the plate.

Adding lemon juice brings out the flavour of the fruit.

49 Strawberry sauce

Ingredient	Makes 225 ml	Makes 600 ml
Strawberries (fresh or puréed)	200 g	500 g
Icing sugar	50 g	125 g
Lemon juice	10 ml	25 ml

Blend all the ingredients together (using a liquidiser if using fresh fruit) and strain through a fine sieve.

Variation

Alternative fruits or purées that can be used include: peach, apricot, mango, paw paw, blackberry and raspberry. For peach sauce, for example, proceed as above, substituting peach purée for the strawberries.

50 Chocolate sauce

Method 1

Ingredient	300 ml	750 ml
Double cream	150 ml	375 ml
Butter	25 g	60 g
Milk or plain couverture callets	180 g	420 g

Energy	Cals	Fat	Sat fat	Carb	Sugar	Protein	Fibre	Sodium
1287 kJ	310 kcal	26.0 g	16.0 g	17.5 g	17.5 g	2.7 g	0.2 g	0.1 g

For 50 ml of sauce, using milk chocolate.

1 Place the cream and butter in a saucepan and gently bring to a simmer.

2 Add the chocolate and stir well until the chocolate has melted and the sauce is smooth.

Method 2

Ingredient	300 ml	750 ml
Caster sugar	40 g	100 g
Water	120 ml	300 ml
Dark chocolate couverture (75 per cent cocoa solids)	160 g	400 g
Unsalted butter	25 g	65 g
Single cream	80 ml	200 ml

1 Dissolve the sugar in the water over a low heat.
2 Remove from the heat. Stir in the chocolate and butter.
3 When everything has melted, stir in the cream and gently bring to the boil.

Energy	Cals	Fat	Sat fat	Carb	Sugar	Protein	Fibre	Sodium
1012 kJ	244 kcal	18.7 g	11.5 g	13.9 g	13.0 g	2.9 g	2.6 g	0.0 g

For 50 ml of sauce.

51 Butterscotch sauce

Ingredient	300 ml	750 ml
Double cream	250 ml	625 ml
Butter	62 g	155 g
Demerara sugar	100 g	250 g

Energy	Cals	Fat	Sat fat	Carb	Sugar	Protein	Fibre	Sodium
1454 kJ	351 kcal	31.0 g	19.4 g	18.3 g	18.3 g	0.8 g	0.0 g	0.2 g

For 50 ml of sauce.

1 Boil the cream, then whisk in the butter and sugar.
2 Simmer for 3 minutes.

52 Caramel sauce

1 In a large saucepan, dissolve the sugar with the water over a low heating and bring to boiling point.

2 Wash down the inside of the pan with a pastry brush dipped in cold water to prevent crystals from forming.

3 Cook until the sugar turns to a deep amber colour. Immediately turn off the heat and whisk in the cream.

4 Set the pan back over a high heat and stir the sauce with the whisk. Let it bubble for 2 minutes, then turn off the heat.

5 You can now strain the sauce and use it when cooled, or, for a richer, smoother sauce, pour a little caramel on to the egg yolks, then return the mixture to the pan and heat to 80 °C, taking care that it does not boil.

6 Pass the sauce through a conical strainer and keep in a cool place, stirring occasionally to prevent a skin from forming.

Ingredient	750 ml
Caster sugar	100 g
Water	80 ml
Double cream	500 ml
Egg yolks, lightly beaten (optional)	2

Energy	Cals	Fat	Sat fat	Carb	Sugar	Protein	Fibre	Sodium
883 kJ	213 kcal	19.9 g	12.1 g	8.1 g	8.1 g	1.0 g	0.0 g	0.0 g

For 50 ml of sauce.

53 Rum or brandy cream or butter

To make rum/brandy cream, flavour whipped, sweetened cream with rum or brandy to taste.

To make rum/brandy butter, cream equal quantities of butter and sieved icing sugar together and add rum or brandy to taste.

17 Healthy eating and special diets

This chapter is relevant to the following units:

→ Produce healthier dishes.
→ Prepare and cook food to meet requirements of allergy sufferers.

Healthy eating and producing healthier dishes

Why healthy eating is important

Obesity and its related health problems have increased dramatically in recent years. In the UK, for example, an estimated 24 million adults are classed as obese. Worldwide, it is estimated that half a billion adults are obese. There is also concern about the rising numbers of obese children.

Healthy eating is not just about reducing obesity, however. Research suggests that a third of all cancers are caused by poor diet. Diet can also be linked to high blood pressure, heart disease, diabetes, osteoporosis and tooth decay. Eating a balanced nutritious diet can help to protect us from these illnesses.

Increasing numbers of people now eat away from their own homes so those providing the food have a responsibility to be mindful of good nutrition.

Food, nutrition and exercise are crucial to our health and well-being. There is no doubt that making the right choices about what we eat and drink, combined with taking regular exercise, can protect against many diseases and poor health. There are also many immediate health and lifestyle benefits to be gained from healthy eating.

A balanced diet and good health

Foods are not 'good' or 'bad' – it is the overall balance of the diet that matters. This means having a variety of foods, basing meals on starchy foods and eating at least five portions of fruit and vegetables a day. The balance to strive for is illustrated in nationally agreed advice, the Eatwell plate (see next page).

The Eatwell plate focuses on the food groups that provide the basic nutrients. The advice given is that the diet should consist of:

- **more starchy foods** – such as cereals, breads, pasta, potatoes and rice; these provide energy and enable the body to function
- **more fruit and vegetables** – aim for five portions per day. Fruit and vegetables provide vitamins and fibre across the diet as well as antioxidants, which are thought to help prevent some cancers
- **moderate amounts of food from the milk and dairy, and meat, fish and alternative proteins groups** – as a guideline, two to three portions from each group per day; these provide protein and minerals that enable the body to maintain itself
- **very small amounts of foods containing fats and sugars, and drinks containing sugars** – selecting lower-fat options where possible; in addition, foods that are high in salt should be restricted. These foods are linked to heart disease, strokes, high blood pressure and obesity; by reducing our intake, we help to reduce the risk of these diseases.

Information on the portions of different types of foods that make up a healthy diet is given in the Eatwell plate from the UK government. For more information visit: www.dh.gov.uk/en/Publichealth/Nutrition/index.htm.

Media coverage and advice on nutrition can seem confusing but the most reliable advice remains the same and is outlined in Table 17.1 below.

The eatwell plate

FOOD
STANDARDS
AGENCY

food.gov.uk

Use the eatwell plate to help you get the balance right. It shows how
much of what you eat should come from each food group.

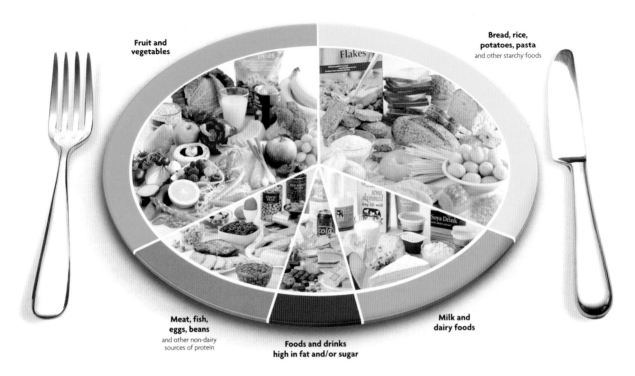

▲ The Eatwell plate

Table 17.1 Summing up healthy eating

What it is about	What it is not about	Immediate benefits
The bulk of the diet needs to come from starchy foods, preferably wholemeal bread, brown rice and pasta, and potatoes	Drastically cutting down on food	Better weight control
	Going hungry	Improved self-esteem
	Depriving yourself of treats	Looking and feeling better
Eating more fruit and vegetables	Spending more money on food	Feeling fitter, with more energy
Eating a little less of some food items	Not enjoying food	Enjoying a wide variety of foods
Enjoying good food and making wise food choices	'Brown and boring food'	Not buying expensive 'diet' products
	Just salads	Knowing that changes made today will have long-term benefits
Making small, gradual changes	Making major changes	
Feeling satisfied and good about food	Going on a 'special diet'	

Nutrients from food

Healthy eating is about selecting certain foods that provide the nutrients that are needed by the body in different amounts. If people choose foods in the advised proportions (mentioned above), they should obtain all the nutrients they need in the quantities that promote good health. Nutrients perform different functions in the body; Table 17.2 summarises some of the key nutritional terms you will encounter, plus the current guidance for health.

Table 17.2 Key nutritional terms and current guidance for health

Nutrient	Recommendations for a healthy diet
Fat is a very concentrated source of energy. The same weight of pure fat has over twice as much energy as sugar or starch. Fat is present in foods in two main types: saturated fat in foods from animal sources such as butter, cheese, meat and milk; unsaturated fat in foods from plants (e.g. oils, nuts and seeds) and oily fish (e.g. tuna, salmon, mackerel).	Cut down on fat intake, particularly the saturated types (usually from animal sources) that push up blood cholesterol. Switch to foods containing unsaturated fats. For example, use oils instead of butter and incorporate more oily fish, such as salmon, in menu planning.
Carbohydrate may be one of two types: sugars, which occur naturally in certain foods such as fruit and honey (but are added to many manufactured foods, particularly confectionery, cakes and biscuits); and starches, found naturally in satisfying foods such as bread, breakfast cereals, rice, pasta and potatoes.	We should aim for 50 per cent of our energy from starch, preferably unrefined starches, and cut back on sugars.
Fibre is found in plant foods and aids a healthy digestive system. Good sources include all wholegrain cereals, pulses, fruits, vegetables and nuts.	On current estimates we all eat around 20 g dietary fibre per day – the healthy goal is around 30 g per day.
Protein is the 'body-building' nutrient found in meat, fish, cheese and eggs, but also in vegetable sources such as cereals (e.g. pasta, breakfast cereals, bread), pulses and nuts.	Protein requirements are often overestimated. For example, adults only need between 35 g and 50 g of protein per day. This can be provided by a 100 g portion of chicken plus a carton of yoghurt and 200 g of baked beans.
Vitamins and minerals are needed in minute amounts for many bodily processes. Since the body cannot make these essential micronutrients, they have to be provided by the diet.	Recommended daily amounts for nine vitamins and 11 minerals are given in the government's report on Dietary Reference Values (see www.nutrition.org.uk/ nutritionscience/nutrients/nutrient-requirements).
Salt is sodium chloride, which is involved in maintaining the body's water balance. Sodium is a type of mineral; sodium chloride is added to many manufactured foods and in particularly high amounts in cured and snack foods.	There is now stronger evidence that our salt intakes are too high (estimated at about 8 g per day) and can lead to high blood pressure. The aim should be about 4 g of salt per day.
Energy comes from carbohydrates, fats, protein and alcohol. It is measured in calories, or joules, which are so tiny they are usually expressed in kilocalories (kcals) or kilojoules (kJ).	We need to balance energy intake through food with energy output through activity; this is needed for good health and control of body weight.

Preparing ingredients in a healthy way and cooking techniques to maximise nutritional value

Chefs have a vital role in making healthy eating an exciting reality for us all. Customer trends show that many people are looking for healthier eating options, particularly if they eat away from home every day. Interest in healthy eating is one of the major consumer trends to emerge in the last 20 years and represents an important and lasting commercial opportunity for chefs.

As well as escalating consumer demand, in some sectors, such as school catering, there are strict requirements relating to nutritional standards. Healthy options and nutritional information are now regularly included in contract catering menus.

Chefs can be highly influential in healthy eating. The ingredients and the proportions in which they are used, plus cooking and service methods chosen, can all influence the nutritional content of a dish or meal. The most effective approach to healthy catering is to make small changes to popular dishes, which may involve:

- Small changes in portion sizes – for example, adding a bread roll or jacket potato to a meal; this yields more starch in proportion to fat (effectively diluting the fat).
- Subtle modifications to recipes – for example, pizzas could be made with a thicker base, topped with mushrooms and roasted peppers, and with less mozzarella than usual but a sprinkling of Parmesan for flavour; omit the salt and rely on Parmesan, black pepper and chopped oregano to add flavour.

▲ A healthy portion size: baked hake with vegetables and mashed potato

▲ A traditional dish made healthier: Mexican bean pot and salad

Chefs are vital in developing healthier recipes that work. The skill is in deciding how dishes can be modified without losing quality. Some highly traditional dishes are best left alone, while subtle changes can be made to others with no loss in texture, appearance or flavour. See 'Healthy eating tips' throughout the recipe sections for ideas on how to prepare and cook food in a way that maximises nutritional values and how to present healthier dishes that are attractive to customers.

The key to healthier catering is to:
- **substitute healthier ingredients** – for example, use low-fat yoghurt or crème fraiche instead of cream, use wholemeal breadcrumbs
- **add extra vegetables** – for example, add a garnish to a dish; this could increase fibre, vitamins and minerals
- **reduce added fat** – for example, use olive oil or sunflower oil in place of butter or animal fats; trim fat from meats
- **change cooking method** – grill instead of frying, or steam vegetables instead of boiling to preserve vitamins

- **reduce sugar** – replace with a natural sweetener or alternative
- **reduce salt** – use herbs or spices to enhance flavour in place of salt; use of low-salt products.

Reading and interpreting food labelling

A number of outlets, such as restaurants, pubs, leisure attractions and cafes, have introduced nutritional information on their menus. This may include the use of recognised symbols that indicate a healthy choice or vegetarian choice, or where a specific item is included in the dish.

When using prepared commodities in the kitchen it is important to read the labels correctly. It is now common for any items on the allergen list to be written in bold as well as the use of symbols.

Many establishments have agreed to:
- display calorie information for most food and drink they serve
- print calorie information on menus
- provide recipe cards or information for each dish on the menu
- ensure the information is clear and easily visible at the point where people chose their food

Health and safety !

Take care when providing nutritional information on menus as there may be a danger of making misleading claims, which could break the law. If unsure, take advice.

Sauces, dressings, toppings and condiments

Where a variety of sauces, dressings and condiments are offered this will give the customer flexibility to make an informed decision with regard to healthier options. For example, offer butter, crème fraiche or cheese to accompany a baked potato.

Special diets

There will be occasions when caterers are asked to provide dishes or information on dishes to meet specific customer dietary requirements. Reasons for special diets generally fall into three categories:
- belief or ethical choice (for example, vegetarianism)
- religious choice
- medical reasons (for example, food intolerance or allergy).

Vegetarian/vegan and other ethical diets

Many people do not eat meat or fish for a variety of reasons, and some people do not eat any type of dish made with or containing the products of animals. You should be aware of the following diets:

- **semi-vegetarian or demi-vegetarian**: occasionally eat fish and/or meat
- **ovo-vegetarian**: do not eat milk and dairy products
- **lacto-vegetarian**: do not eat eggs
- **vegan**: do not eat any food of animal origin (including honey, dairy products and eggs); vegetables, fruits, grains, legumes, pasta made without eggs, soya products and other products of plants are acceptable
- **frutarian or fructarian**: eat only fruit, nuts and berries.

Religious diets

Adherents of the religions listed below have strict dietary requirements:

- **Hindu**: do not eat meat, fish or eggs. Orthodox Hindus are usually strict vegetarians; less-strict Hindus may eat lamb, poultry and fish, but definitely not beef as cattle have a deep religious meaning – milk, however, is highly regarded.
- **Jewish**: do not eat pork, pork products, shellfish and eels, meat and milk served at the same time or cooked together. Strict Jews eat only Kosher meat; milk and milk products are usually avoided at lunch and dinner (but are acceptable at breakfast).
- **Muslim**: do not eat pork, meat that is not halal (slaughtered according to custom), shellfish and alcohol (even when used in cooking).
- **Rastafarian**: do not eat processed food, pork, fish without fins (eels), alcohol, coffee or tea.
- **Sikh**: beef, pork, lamb, poultry and fish may be acceptable to Sikh men, but Sikh women tend to avoid all meat.

Medical diets

For medical reasons, the people on the special diets below do not eat the foods listed:

- **Dairy/milk-free**: milk, butter, cheese, yoghurt and any prepared foods that include milk products (check label).
- **Diabetics**: dishes that are high in sugar and/or fat (low-calorie sweeteners can be used to sweeten desserts).
- **Gluten-free**: wheat, wholemeal, wholewheat and wheatmeal flour, wheat bran, rye, barley and oats (some doctors say oats are permitted; the Coeliac Society advises against); and any dishes made with these including pasta, noodles, semolina, bread, pastries, some yoghurts, some cheese spreads, barley-based drinks, malted drinks, beer, some brands of mustard, and proprietary sauces made with flour (use cornflour to thicken; rice, potato, corn and sago are also acceptable).
- **Low-cholesterol and saturated fat**: liver, egg yolks and shellfish (which are high in cholesterol), beef, pork and lamb (which contain saturated fats), butter, cream, groundnut oil and margarine (use oils and margarines labelled high in polyunsaturated fats).
- **Low-fat**: any food that contains fat or has been fried or roasted.
- **Low-residue**: wholemeal bread, brown rice and pasta, fried and fatty foods.
- **Low-salt**: foods and dishes that have had salt added during cooking or processing (including smoked and cured fishes and meats, and hard cheeses) or contain monosodium glutamate.
- **Nut allergy**: nuts, blended cooking oils and margarine (since these may include nut oil; use pure oils or butter) and any dishes containing these (check label).

Food allergies and intolerances

For customers who have an intolerance or allergy to certain foods, these foods can be life threatening. In some cases people suffer anaphylactic shock (swelling of the face and mouth area, which restricts breathing); for others eating foods to which they are allergic or intolerant could cause severe stomach cramps, causing poor digestion and absorption of nutrients, which can lead to further health complications.

The 14 most-common food allergens include:

- cereals containing gluten (wheat, barley, rye and oats in some cases)
- crustaceans, for example prawns, crabs, lobster and crayfish
- eggs
- fish
- peanuts
- soybeans (as in tofu, TVP, soy sauce)
- milk (including yoghurts and cheese)
- nuts, such as almonds, hazelnuts, walnuts, pecan nuts, Brazil nuts, pistachio, cashew and macadamia (Queensland) nuts
- celery (and celeriac)
- mustard (including leaves and oil)

- sesame (oil and tahini)
- sulphur dioxide (a preservative found in some dried fruit)
- lupin (seeds and flour)
- molluscs, for example clams, mussels, whelks, oysters, snails and squid.

Regulations around food labelling and information for customers in relation to the major allergens state that these should be highlighted on food labels, within the ingredients list, or on information available for customers in a restaurant setting.

Food producers and businesses can choose which method they will use to emphasise these 14 allergens on their product labels, or how to indicate their use on menus. For example, this could be done by listing them in bold, contrasting colours or underlining. Some may also use an allergy advice statement on their products to explain this, for example: 'Allergy Advice: for allergens including cereals containing gluten, see ingredients in bold.' For restaurants this advice statement could be: 'Allergy Advice: please inform staff, who can provide a full list of allergens in our dishes.'

Anaphylaxis

This is the closing of the throat area in reaction to something eaten or ingested. It can cause swelling of the face and mouth area and can affect breathing. Those who suffer normally carry an EpiPen with them at all times – it contains adrenaline, which relaxes the muscles of the lungs and stimulates the heart, which can be injected should an anaphylactic reaction begin. Anaphylaxis may restrict the lifestyle of those who suffer from it – they may be more reluctant to eat out or travel due to concerns about the potential risk.

Minimising the risk of allergic reactions and preventing contamination

Food preparation staff need to be particularly careful to avoid cross-contamination; even very small traces of allergenic foods can trigger reactions for some people. As a caterer you can:

- be receptive to people with a food allergy, asking questions about the food on offer
- let the allergic person or carer check food labels and speak to the chef themselves
- not cater for the person if you are unable to do so safely
- train serving staff in relevant food allergy issues
- avoid the indiscriminate use of nuts, for example powdered nuts as a garnish, unless this is an essential part of the recipe
- ensure that ingredients of dishes are reflected in their name, for example 'nut and carrot salad'.

The five Cs

These are some of the safeguards that can be set in place in kitchens when providing dishes to meet specific dietary requirements:

- **Content**: read the ingredients lists for potential allergens; for example, malt vinegar contains barley and therefore should not be in dishes for coeliac (gluten-free) diets.
- **Contact**: even small traces of ingredients can cause an issue; wash hands after handling nuts or wear gloves. Segregate foods containing major allergens from other foods. If possible, keep certain preparation areas nut-free.
- **Contamination**: assess work practices to avoid cross-contamination of products. For example, if making dairy-free ice cream make it first and then store it separately; avoid frying with oils that have been used to cook other foods such as fish or nut cutlets.
- **Cleaning**: ensure that equipment is cleaned correctly; even better, use separate equipment. Soap and hot water followed by thorough rinsing have been shown to be effective in removing allergen traces.
- **Communication**: this should be into and out of the kitchen to ensure customers have sufficient confidence in the organisation to meet their requirements. Service staff should be able to pass information to customers about the contents of each dish, as well as explain to the kitchen staff the needs of each customer, ensuring that it is clear and recorded to enable it to be checked and confirmed as each dish is served.

There could also be a sixth C: common sense. If you are not clear about the ingredients or dishes being offered, then say so, and find out.

Test yourself

1 The components of food are divided into six main nutrient groups. What are they?

2 How could you increase dietary fibre in recipes with which you are familiar?

3 Which cooking methods do not require the addition of fat?

4 It is thought that there is too much fat in the average UK diet. Give three reasons why too much fat should be avoided.

5 List three groups that may request specific foods for dietary requirements.

6 Which food item should not be included in a dish for diabetic customers?

7 How many portions of fruit/vegetables is it recommended that we eat each day? Suggest what these could be; include portion sizes.

8 What is meant by 'an allergy'?

9 Which religious/cultural diets forbid the eating of pork and pork products?

10 Suggest three ways that chefs could make the food that they cook healthier.

18 Cold presentation

This chapter is relevant to the following units:
→ Prepare and present food for cold presentation.
→ Produce cold starters and salads.

Recipes included in this chapter

Cold presentation

'Cold presentation' means the preparation and presentation of raw and/or cooked foods into a wide variety of cold items.

Preparing and presenting cold dishes covers areas including salads, bread products, pies, pâtés, cured meats and fish. Cold food is popular in every kind of food service operation for at least three good reasons:

1 Visual appeal: when the food is attractively displayed, carefully arranged and neatly garnished, the customers can have their appetites stimulated by seeing exactly what is being offered.
2 Efficiency: cold food can be prepared in advance, allowing a large number of people to be served in a short space of time. Self-service is also economic in terms of staffing.
3 Adaptability: if cold food is being served from a buffet, the range of foods can be simple or complex and wide-ranging, depending on the type of operation.

Cold foods can either be pre-plated or served from large dishes and bowls. In both cases presentation is important: the food should appear fresh, neatly arranged and not over-garnished.

Quality points

Cold food must look clean and fresh. Its presentation should be appealing to the eye. Seasoning and flavour can be adjusted with accompaniments that enhance the eating experience – for example, lemon and Tabasco sauce may be offered with oysters.

For quality points for specific ingredients, refer to the sections below.

Preparation methods

Techniques used in cold preparation include:
- peeling, slicing, chopping and cutting
- carving or slicing to define portion or serving size
- seasoning: the light addition of salt, pepper and possibly other flavouring agents

- marinating: a richly spiced pickling liquid used to give flavour and to assist in tenderising meats such as venison. Simple marinades (for example, olive oil with herbs or soy sauce with herbs and/or spices) can be used with cuts of fish, chicken or meat.
- combining ingredients: be aware of the texture and flavour of many raw foods that can be mixed together or combined with cooked foods. Understand what combination of foods – for example, salads – is best suited to be served with other foods, such as cold meat or poultry.
- dressing: this can either mean an accompanying salad dressing, such as vinaigrette, or the arrangement of food for presentation on plates, dishes or buffets
- garnishing: the final addition to the dish, such as lettuce, quarters of tomato and sliced cucumber added to egg mayonnaise.

Equipment

Bowls, tongs, whisks, spoons, and so on, as well as food processors, mixing machines and blenders are used with cold preparations. The correct use of specialist equipment and tools enables the cold preparation chef to ensure consistency in dishes – for example, when grating or slicing vegetables for salads and so on.

Health and safety !

Where possible, use disposable plastic gloves when handling food.

Preparation for cold work

Well-planned organisation is essential to ensure adequate pre-preparation (*mise-en-place*), so that foods are assembled with a good work flow and are ready on time. Before, during and after assembling, and before final garnishing, foods must be kept in a cool place, cold room or refrigerator so as to minimise the risk of food contamination. Garnishing and final decoration should take place as close to the serving time as possible.

Develop simple artistic skills that require the minimum of time for preparation and assembly. Provide an attractive presentation of food at all times.

Whenever possible, the food on display to the public should be kept under refrigeration and the temperature should be checked to ensure that it is being maintained at a safe level.

Where customers are viewing closely, the food should ideally be displayed behind a sneeze screen.

Storage

Keep unprepared and prepared food under refrigeration at a temperature not exceeding 4–5 °C. Refrigeration will not kill the bacteria that are present in the foods, but it does help to prevent their growth.

Dishes prepared in advance should be covered with film and refrigerated at 1–3 °C to prevent them drying out.

Time and temperature

Because of the requirements of food safety, cold foods are often served straight from the refrigerator. This is an error because, at refrigerator temperature, food flavours are not at their best. Individual portions should be removed from refrigeration and allowed to stand at room temperature for 5–10 minutes before serving.

Food products for cold presentation
Hors d'oeuvres

The choice of a wide variety of foods, combination of foods and recipes is available for preparation and service as hors d'oeuvres and salads. Hors d'oeuvres can be divided into three categories:
1 single cold food items (smoked salmon, pâté, melon, etc.)
2 a selection of well-seasoned cold dishes
3 well-seasoned hot dishes.

Hors d'oeuvres may be served for lunch, dinner or supper, and the wide choice, colour appeal and versatility of the dishes make many items and combinations of items suitable for snacks and salads at any time of day.

Single-food hors d'oeuvres

Serve single-food hors d'oeuvres with bread or toast, butter separately, offered as a single portion or piece. Single-food hors d'oeuvres include meat, poultry, fish and vegetables, with an appropriate garnish or sauce.

Examples include smoked salmon, melon, avocado, potted meats or fish, oysters, pâtés and terrines.

Salads

Salads may be served as an accompaniment to hot and cold foods and as dishes in their own right. They can be served for lunch, tea, high tea, dinner, supper and snack meals. Salads may be divided in two types:
1 simple, using one ingredient
2 mixed, or composite, using more than one ingredient.

Some salads may form part of a composite hors d'oeuvre. Accompaniments include dressings and cold sauces.

Salad items should be fresh, cleaned correctly and, where cut, these should be of an even size and shape to enhance the presentation.

▲ Salads may be served as an accompaniment to hot and cold foods and as dishes in their own right

Terrines and pâtés

A slice of terrine served with a suitable garnish (for example, a small tossed salad dressed with vinaigrette and chopped fresh herbs) makes an ideal first course, or a small portion can form part of an hors d'oeuvres selection.

Pre-prepared pâtés or terrines are available in a wide variety of types and flavourings, which include liver (chicken, duck, and so on), poultry and game. Pâtés are usually cooked enclosed in a thin layer of bacon fat, or they may be enclosed in hot water pastry within a special mould.

Pâtés and terrines must be kept under refrigeration at all times and should never be allowed to stand in a warm kitchen or dining room because they are easily contaminated by food-poisoning bacteria.

Fish and vegetable pâtés and terrines are also available. When serving meat, poultry or game pâtés, a simple garnish of a fan of gherkin and a little salad is sufficient.

The use of plastic gloves and tools such as palate knives and slices will reduce the risk of contamination when cold foods are being handled.

Cooked and cured meats

The typical meats or poultry for cold presentation are roast beef, boiled or honey roast ham or gammon, roast chicken or turkey, and boiled ox tongue. These can be cooked and cooled, or leftover joints from previous hot meals can be used. Cold meats can also be bought in ready cooked or ready for service from suppliers. These include cured meats and salamis that can then be offered with a garnish and sauce.

The various ways to present and serve cold meats are:
- sliced from whole joints on the bone in front of the customer (in which case all bones that may hinder carving must be removed first)
- sliced from boned joints, which in some cases may be rolled and stuffed (also in front of the customer)
- pre-sliced in the kitchen, in which case the meat or poultry should be cut as close to service time as possible, otherwise it will start to dry and curl up; pre-sliced meats or poultry can be neatly cut, dressed with the slices overlapping each other, placed on to large dishes or individual plates, covered with cling film and kept under refrigeration; when large numbers of plated meals have to be prepared, plate rings can be used and the plates stacked in sensible-sized numbers.

When roast chickens are required for serving cold, ideally they should be cooked 1–2 hours before service, left to cool (preferably in a blast chiller) and then carved as required. In this way, the meat remains moist and succulent. Chickens can then be cut into eight pieces and the excess bones removed before serving.

Ham

Ham should not be confused with gammon. A gammon is the hind leg of a baconer weight pig and is cut from a side of bacon. A ham is the hind leg of a porker pig and is cut round from the side of pork with the aitch bone, and usually cured by dry salting. Ham is boiled and can be served hot or cold. Certain imported hams (Parma ham, Bayonne and Ardennes) are sliced thinly and eaten raw, generally as an hors d'oeuvre. In order to carve the ham efficiently it is necessary to remove the aitch bone after cooking. Traditional English hams include York and Bradenham.

Fish and shellfish

Whole fish or fillets can be prepared and served as cold dishes. These would be poached, cured or pickled, and could be purchased ready to serve or prepared in the kitchen.

Serving whole fish would be normal on a buffet table, as in whole salmon with a cucumber salad and dill mayonnaise. Whole shellfish might also be used, such as a dressed crab, or whole prawns as part of a cocktail.

Soused fish or ceviche can be served as an individual cold dish with a vegetable garnish and sauce.

Pies

Pies, such as game and pork pies, and flans, can be made in the kitchen or purchased pre-prepared ready for slicing and serving, which helps with ensuring consistency. They can be served as part of a cold buffet or as single portions.

Bread and pastry

Breads are used for sandwiches, canapés or as an accompaniment to many dishes to add texture. Consider types of bread that would add texture and flavour to the dish being served, for example toasted brioche with chicken parfait, wholemeal to accompany fish, and perhaps a focaccia crouton to accompany a tomato and basil salad.

Cold sauces and dressings
Salad dressings

These dressings may be varied by the addition of other ingredients. Salads should be lightly dressed or the dressing offered separately to give the customer the choice.

Chutneys and relishes

Chutneys are made from a variety of ingredients, usually fruit, preserved in sugar and acid after careful cooking. They are flavoured with a range of spices.

Chutneys may be served as an accompaniment to terrines and pâtés, salads, cold meats, poultry, game and cheese. They may also accompany a traditional curry (for example, mango chutney).

Relishes are similar to chutneys except they are generally smoother and do not always contain as much sugar.

Fruits and vegetables for use in relishes and chutneys must be unblemished and well washed. Good-quality vinegars with 5 per cent acetic acid must be used.

Pickles

Vegetables to be pickled are usually brined (unless they are to be used in a chutney or similar mixture, then it is not necessary). Brining removes the surplus water that would otherwise dilute the vinegar and make it too weak to act as a preservative.

Dry brining is used for watery vegetables such as cucumbers, marrows and tomatoes. Place the prepared vegetables in a deep bowl, sprinkle salt between the layers, allowing about half a teaspoon of salt per 500 g. Cover and leave overnight.

Wet brining is used for vegetables such as cauliflower and onions. Allow 50 g salt to 500 ml water (sufficient for about 500 g of vegetables); place the prepared vegetables in a deep bowl, cover with the brine and leave overnight. Root vegetables such as artichokes, and sometimes beetroot, are cooked in half-strength brine until tender. After brining, rinse and drain the vegetables.

Spiced vinegar is used to cover most simple pickles; the vinegar used for this – and for all pickles – must be of high quality, with an acetic acid content of not less than 6 per cent. Brewed malt vinegar is most commonly used but, for onions, cauliflower and other light-coloured vegetables, white vinegar may be used.

Test yourself

1. What is considered to be a safe temperature for storing sandwiches and canapés if they are not for immediate consumption?

2. Why is it advisable that foods taken from the fridge are allowed to stand at room temperature for five to ten minutes before being served?

3. What precautions should be taken into account when serving pre-prepared terrines and pâtés?

4. List three types of shellfish that may be served cold.

5. Presentation is considered to be an important indicator of quality, especially for cold buffet service. Name three other quality points you should look for.

6. When making mayonnaise and vinaigrette, which oils could be used to give a low-cholesterol product?

7. Describe the preparation of a crab cocktail.

8. When preparing cooked and cured food, why is the relationship of time and temperature important?

9. Describe how a joint of roast beef can be presented.

10. Suggest how the fat content of cold items could be reduced.

Vinaigrettes, dressings and cold sauces

1 Vinaigrette

Ingredient	4–6 portions
Olive oil, according to taste	3–6 tbsp
French mustard	1 tsp
Vinegar	1 tbsp
Salt and pepper, to taste	

Variation

Variations to vinaigrette include:
- English mustard in place of French mustard
- chopped herbs (chives, parsley, tarragon, etc.)
- chopped hard-boiled egg
- other good-quality oils, for example sesame seed or walnut
- different flavoured vinegars or lemon juice.

Energy	Cals	Fat	Sat fat	Carb	Sugar	Protein	Fibre
1,740 kJ	415 kcal	45.5g	6.3g	0.5g	0.1g	0.6g	0.0g

Using 3 tbsp oil for 4–6 portions. Using 6 tbsp oil for 4–6 portions this recipe provides: 3439 kJ/415 kcal energy, 90.5 g fat, 12.6 g saturated fat, 0.5 g carbohydrates, 0.1 g sugar, 0.6 g protein and 0.0 g fibre.

Combine all the ingredients together.

The number of portions yielded will depend on how the vinaigrette is used.

Video: making vinaigrette
http://bit.ly/
1DWIKjw

2 Balsamic vinegar and olive oil dressing

Ingredient	8 portions
Water	62 ml
Olive oil	250 ml
Balsamic vinegar	62 ml
Sherry vinegar	2 tbsp
Caster sugar	½ tsp
Seasoning	

Professional tip

The amount of balsamic vinegar needed will depend on its quality, age, etc. Add more or less as required.

This dressing works well because it is not an emulsion. The oil and vinegar provide a stark contrast and can be stirred just before serving.

1 Whisk all ingredients together and correct the seasoning.

3 Tomato vinaigrette

Ingredient	4 portions	10 portions
Tomatoes	200 g	500 g
Caster sugar	½ tsp	1¼ tbsp
White wine vinegar	1 tbsp	2½ tsp
Extra virgin olive oil	3 tbsp	8 tbsp
Seasoning		

Energy	Cals	Fat	Sat fat	Carb	Sugar	Protein	Fibre	Sodium
382 kJ	93 kcal	9.6g	1.4g	1.4g	1.3g	0.2g	0.3g	0.3g

1 Blanch and deseed the tomatoes; purée in a food processor.

2 Add the sugar, vinegar, olive oil and seasoning; whisk well to emulsify.

3 The vinaigrette should be smooth.

4 Mayonnaise

Ingredient	8 portions
Egg yolks, very fresh or pasteurised	3
Vinegar or lemon juice	2 tsp
Small pinch of salt	
English or continental mustard	½ tsp
A mild-flavoured oil such as corn oil or the lightest olive oil	250 ml
Water, boiling	1 tsp

Energy	Cals	Fat	Sat fat	Carb	Sugar	Protein	Fibre	Sodium
1248 kJ	303 kcal	33.0g	5.1g	0.1g	0.1g	1.1g	0.0g	0.1g

Health and safety

Because of the risk of salmonella food poisoning, it is strongly recommended that pasteurised egg yolks are used.

Faults

Mayonnaise may separate, turn or curdle for several reasons:
- you have added the oil too quickly
- the oil is too cold
- you have not whisked enough
- the egg yolks were stale and weak.

To reconstitute (bring it back together):
- Take a clean basin, pour 1 teaspoon of boiling water and gradually but vigorously whisk in the curdled sauce a little at a time.
- Alternatively, in a clean basin, whisk a fresh egg yolk with ½ teaspoon of cold water then gradually whisk in the curdled sauce.

Place yolks, vinegar, salt and mustard in the bowl of a food mixer

Whisk until thoroughly mixed

Continue to whisk vigorously and start to add the oil – this needs to be done slowly

Keep whisking until all the oil has been added

Whisk in the boiling water; taste and correct seasoning if necessary

Variation

Add:
- fresh chopped herbs
- garlic juice – peel a clove garlic and press it using a garlic press
- thick tomato juice.

Professional tip

If the mayonnaise becomes too thick while you are making it, whisk in a little of water or vinegar.

---

5 Andalusian sauce

Ingredient	Makes 250 ml
Mayonnaise	250 ml
Tomato juice or ketchup	2 tbsp
Red pepper, cut into julienne	1 tbsp

1 Combine all the ingredients.
May be served with cold salads.

Professional tip

For Andalusian sauce, Thousand Island dressing, green sauce and other similar recipes, use a blender to achieve the desired texture and flavour, but do not purée completely.

6 Green or herb sauce

Ingredient	4 portions	10 portions
Spinach, tarragon, chervil, chives, watercress	50 g	125 g
Mayonnaise	150 ml	375 ml

Energy	Cals	Fat	Sat fat	Carb	Sugar	Protein	Fibre	Sodium
1082 kJ	263 kcal	28.0 g	4.3 g	0.9 g	0.6 g	0.8 g	0.2 g	0.2 g

1 Pick, wash, blanch and refresh the green leaves.

2 Squeeze dry.

3 Pass through a very fine sieve.

4 Mix with the mayonnaise.

May be served with cold salmon or trout.

7 Tartare sauce

Ingredient	8 portions
Mayonnaise	250 ml
Capers, chopped	25 g
Gherkins, chopped	50 g
Sprig of parsley, chopped	

Energy	Cals	Fat	Sat fat	Carb	Sugar	Protein	Fibre	Sodium
911 kJ	221 kcal	24.0 g	3.6 g	0.8 g	0.6 g	0.6 g	0.1 g	0.2 g

1 Combine all the ingredients.

This sauce is usually served with deep-fried fish.

Professional tip

Finely chop the gherkins and capers and use a blender to give the desired texture and consistency, but do not purée completely.

Healthy eating tips

Proportionally reduce the fat by adding some low-fat yoghurt instead of some of the mayonnaise.

8 Remoulade sauce

1 Prepare as for tartare sauce (recipe 7), adding 1 teaspoon of anchovy essence and mixing thoroughly. Makes 8 portions.

This sauce may be served with fried fish. It can also be mixed with a fine julienne of celeriac to make an accompaniment to cold meats, terrines, etc.

Energy	Cals	Fat	Sat fat	Carb	Sugar	Protein	Fibre	Sodium
907 kJ	220 kcal	24.0g	3.6g	0.8g	0.6g	0.7g	0.1g	0.3g

9 Thousand Island dressing

Ingredient	8 portions
Mayonnaise	250 ml
Tomato ketchup	30 ml
White wine vinegar	1 tbsp
Caster sugar	1 tsp
Onion, finely chopped	15 g
Clove of garlic, finely chopped	1
Tabasco sauce	2 drops
Worcester sauce	½ tsp
Gherkins, finely chopped	2

Energy	Cals	Fat	Sat fat	Carb	Sugar	Protein	Fibre	Sodium
928 kJ	225 kcal	24.0g	3.6g	2.6g	2.3g	0.5g	0.1g	0.3g

1 Mix all ingredients together.

2 Use as a dressing for fish cocktails and salads.

Thousand Island dressing is an example of a dressing which has become a standard condiment.

10 Mint sauce

Ingredient	8 portions
Mint	2–3 tbsp
Caster sugar	1 tsp
Vinegar	125 ml

1 Chop the washed, picked mint and mix with the sugar.

2 Place in a china basin and add the vinegar.

3 If the vinegar is too sharp, dilute it with a little water. Serve with roast lamb.

Professional tip

A less acid sauce can be produced by dissolving the sugar in 125 ml boiling water and, when cold, adding the chopped mint and 1–2 tablespoon vinegar to taste.

Energy	Cals	Fat	Sat fat	Carb	Sugar	Protein	Fibre	Sodium
26 kJ	6 kcal	0.0g	0.0g	0.7g	0.6g	0.1g	0.0g	0.0g

11 Shellfish cocktail sauce

Method 1

Ingredient	4 portions	10 portions
Egg yolk, pasteurised	1	2½
Vinegar	1 tsp	2½ tsp
Salt, pepper, mustard		
Olive oil or sunflower oil	5 tbsp	12½ tbsp
Tomato juice or ketchup to taste		
Worcester sauce (optional)	2–3 drops	5–8 drops

1 Make the mayonnaise with the egg yolk, vinegar, seasonings and oil.

2 Combine with the tomato juice or ketchup to taste and Worcester sauce (if using).

Energy	Cals	Fat	Sat fat	Carb	Sugar	Protein	Fibre
889 kJ	216 kcal	22.7g	14.2g	1.9g	1.9g	1.2g	0.1g

Method 2

Ingredient	4 portions	10 portions
Lightly whipped cream or unsweetened non-dairy cream	5 tbsp	12½ tbsp
Tomato juice or ketchup	3 tbsp	8 tbsp
Salt, pepper		
Lemon juice	a few drops	a few drops

1 Mix all the ingredients together.

Healthy eating tips
● Keep added salt to a minimum.
● Extend the high-fat mayonnaise with low-fat yoghurt to proportionally reduce the fat content.

Note

Fresh or tinned tomato juice, or diluted tomato ketchup, may be used for both of these methods, but the use of tinned tomato purée gives an unpleasant flavour.

Flavoured oils

12 Herb oil

Ingredient	Makes 250 ml
Picked flat leaf parsley	25 g
Chives	10 g
Picked basil leaves	10 g
Picked spinach	100 g
Corn oil	250 ml

1 Blanch all the herbs and spinach for 1½ minutes.

2 Drain well, place with the oil in a liquidiser and blitz for 2½ minutes. Pass and decant when rested.

Uses include salads, salmon and other fish dishes.

13 Basil oil

Ingredient	Makes 200 ml
Fresh basil	25 g
Oil	200 ml
Salt, to taste	
Mill pepper	

1 Blanch and refresh the basil; purée with the oil.
2 Allow to settle overnight and decant.
3 Store in bottles with a sprig of blanched basil.

Variation

Basil extract can be used in place of fresh basil; 50 g of grated Parmesan or Gorgonzola cheese may also be added to the basil oil.

14 Lemon oil

Ingredient	Makes 250 ml
Lemons, rind (with no pith – the whitish layer between skin and fruit)	3
Lemongrass stick, cut lengthways and chopped into 2 cm strips	1
Grapeseed oil	250 ml
Olive oil	2 tbsp

1 Place all the ingredients into a food processor and pulse the mix until the lemon peel and lemongrass are approximately 3 mm thick.
2 Allow to stand for 2 days. Decant and store in the fridge until ready for use (or freeze for longer if you wish).

15 Mint oil

Ingredient	Makes 150 ml
Mint	100 g
Oil	150 ml
Salt	3 tbsp

1 Blanch the mint for 30 seconds.

2 Refresh and squeeze the water out.

3 Place in a blender and slowly add the oil.

4 Allow to settle overnight and decant into bottles.

Uses include lamb dishes, salads and fish dishes.

16 Vanilla oil

Ingredient	Makes 200 ml
Vegetable oil	200 ml
Vanilla pods, whole	6
Vanilla extract	50 ml

1 Warm the oil to around 60 °C; add the vanilla in its various forms and infuse, scraping all the seeds into the oil.

2 Store in a plastic bottle.

Uses include salads, salmon and other fish dishes.

17 Walnut oil

Ingredient	Makes 500 ml
Olive or walnut oil	500 ml
Walnuts, finely crushed	75 g
Parmesan cheese	75 g
Salt, to taste	50 ml
Mill pepper	

1 Mix all the ingredients together and bottle until required.

Chutneys, pickles and relishes

18 Tomato chutney

Ingredient	Makes 1 litre
Tomatoes, peeled	1.5 kg
Onions, finely chopped	450 g
Brown sugar	300 g
Malt vinegar	375 ml
Mustard powder	1½ tsp
Cayenne pepper	½ tsp
Coarse salt	2 tsp
Mild curry powder	1 tbsp

1 Peel and coarsely chop the tomatoes, then combine with the remaining ingredients in a large heavy-duty saucepan.

2 Stir over heat without boiling until the sugar dissolves. Simmer uncovered, stirring occasionally until the mixture thickens (about 1½ hours).

3 Place in hot, sterilised jars. Seal while hot.

Serve with cheese, cold meats or terrines.

19 Beetroot relish

Ingredient	Makes 1.75 litres
Beetroots, peeled and coarsely chopped	1 kg
Onions, finely chopped	800 g
Caster sugar	225 g
Coarse salt	1 tbsp
Ground allspice	1 tsp
Malt vinegar	500 ml
Plain flour	1 tbsp

1 Mix the chopped beetroot and onion together, add the sugar, salt, allspice and 375 ml of the vinegar to a large saucepan. Bring to the boil and simmer for 30 minutes.

2 Mix the flour with the remaining vinegar and whisk together well. (Make sure it is smooth and does not contain any lumps.) Add to the beetroot mixture. Stir until it is all well blended and thickens.

3 Place in hot sterilised jars. Seal while still hot.

20 Date and tamarind relish

Ingredient	Makes 625 ml
Dried tamarind	75 g
Boiling water	500 ml
Olive oil	2 tsp
Black mustard seeds	2 tsp
Cumin seeds	2 tsp
Fresh dates, stoned and chopped	500 g
Malt vinegar	60 ml

1 Place the dried tamarind into a suitable bowl and pour over the boiling water; allow to stand for 30 minutes.

2 Strain the liquid, pressing to extract all moisture, then discard the tamarind.

3 Heat the oil in a suitable saucepan. Cook the mustard seeds until they pop, then add the cumin seeds, dates, tamarind liquid and vinegar, and bring to the boil. Simmer for 5 minutes until almost dry.

4 Purée in a processor until smooth.

5 Place the hot relish into hot sterilised jars. Seal while hot.

21 Pickled red cabbage

1 Remove the outer leaves of the cabbage and shred the rest finely.

2 Place in a deep bowl, sprinkle each layer with dry salt and leave for 24 hours.

3 Rinse and drain, cover with spiced vinegar (see recipe 22 for mixed pickle) and leave for a further 24 hours, mixing occasionally. Pack and cover.

22 Mixed pickle

Ingredient	
Vegetables (cauliflower, cucumber, green tomatoes. onions, marrow)	
For the spiced vinegar	
Vinegar	1 litre
Blade mace	5 g
Allspice	5 g
Cloves	5 g
Stick cinnamon	5 g
Peppercorns	6
Root ginger (for hot pickle)	5 g

1 To make the spiced vinegar, tie the spices in muslin, place them in a covered pan with the vinegar and heat slowly to boiling point.

2 Remove from the heat and stand for 2 hours, then remove the bag.

3 Prepare the vegetables, with the exception of the marrow, and soak them in brine for 24 hours.

4 Peel the marrow, remove the seeds and cut into small squares, sprinkle and salt, and let it stand for 12 hours.

5 Drain the vegetables, pack them into jars, and cover with cold spiced vinegar.

6 Cover the jars and allow the pickle to mature for at least a month before use.

23 Pesto

Ingredient	Makes 250ml
Fresh basil leaves	100 ml
Pine nuts, lightly toasted	1 tbsp
Garlic, picked and crumbled	2 cloves
Parmesan cheese, grated	40 g
Pecorino cheese, grated	40 g
Olive oil	5 tbsp
Salt and pepper	

Variation

Use flat-leaved parsley in place of basil and walnuts in place of pine nuts.

Note

Pesto is traditionally served with large flat pasta called Trenetta.

Pesto is also used as a cordon in various fish and meat-plated dishes, e.g. grilled fish, medallions of veal.

1 Place all ingredients into a food processor and mix to a rough-textured sauce.

2 Transfer to a bowl and leave for at least 1 hour to enable the flavours to develop.

24 Tapenade

	4 portions	10 portions
Garlic cloves, crushed/chopped	1	3
Capers	45 g	110 g
Lemon juice	1 tbsp	2 tbsp
Anchovy fillets, chopped	6	15
Black olives, chopped	250 g	625 g
Parsley, chopped	1 tsp	2 tsp
Salt and pepper	Pinch	Pinch
Virgin olive oil	4 tbsp	10 tbsp
Roast cumin and chopped red chilli, to garnish		

Energy	Cals	Fat	Sat fat	Carb	Sugar	Protein	Fibre	Sodium
773 kJ	188 kcal	19.8g	2.9g	0.3g	0.1g	2.0g	2.7g	2.0g

1 Mix all the ingredients together, adding the olive oil to make a paste.

2 For a smoother texture, place garlic, lemon juice, capers and anchovies into a food processor and process until a smooth texture. Add the olives and parsley, and sufficient oil to form a smooth paste.

3 Season, if required.

4 Garnish with a sprinkle of roast cumin and chopped red chilli.

5 Serve chilled.

Note

Tapenade is a Provençale dish consisting of puréed or finely chopped black olives, capers, anchovies and olive oil. It may also contain garlic, herbs, tuna, lemon juice or brandy. Its name comes from the Provençale word for capers: *tapeno*. It is popular in the South of France, where it is generally eaten as an hors d'oeuvre, spread on toast.

25 Celeriac remoulade

Ingredient	4 portions	10 portions
Celeriac	200g	500g
Lemon	½	1¼
English or continental mustard	1 level tsp	2½ level tsp
Salt, pepper		
Mayonnaise, natural yoghurt or fromage frais	125ml	310ml

Energy	Cals	Fat	Sat fat	Carb	Sugar	Protein	Fibre
938 kJ	228 kcal	24.0g	3.9g	2.0g	1.6g	1.1g	1.9g

Note

Used as an accompaniment to pâtés or terrines, either by itself or mixed with remoulade sauce (recipe 7).

Healthy eating tips

Use natural yoghurt rather than mayonnaise/cream.

1 Wash and peel the celeriac. Cut into fine julienne.

2 Combine with the remoulade juice (lemon, mustard, seasoning) and the remainder of the ingredients.

26 Salad leaves

As these are eaten raw they may contain live food-poisoning bacteria; they must be thoroughly washed to remove any soil.

Lettuce (*laitue*) and iceberg lettuce

1 Trim off the root and remove the outside leaves.
2 Wash thoroughly and drain well.
3 The outer leaves can be pulled off and the hearts cut into quarters.

Cos lettuce (*laitue romaine*)

1 Trim off the root end and remove the outside leaves.
2 Wash thoroughly and drain well.
3 Cut into quarters.

Rocket

This is a small-leafed, sharp, peppery-tasting salad. Trim, wash well and drain.

Chicory (*endive belge*)

1 Trim off the root end.
2 Cut into 1 cm lengths; wash well and drain.

Curled chicory (*endive frisée*)

Thoroughly wash and trim off the stalk. Drain well.

Watercress (*cresson*)

Watercress, as the name suggests, is grown in water and, as there is always the danger that the water may have been polluted, it must be washed thoroughly in clean water.

Trim off the stalk ends, discard any discoloured leaves, wash thoroughly and drain.

Mustard and cress

1 Trim off the stalk ends of the cress.
2 Wash well and lift out of the water so as to leave the seed cases behind.
3 Drain well.

27 Mixed salad (*salade panachée*)

A typical mixed salad would consist of lettuce, tomato, cucumber, watercress, radishes, and so on – almost any kind of salad vegetable can be used.

Neatly arrange in a salad bowl; offer a vinaigrette separately.

28 Green salad (*salade verte*)

Any of the green salads – lettuce, cos lettuce, lamb's lettuce (also known as corn salad or mâche), curled chicory – or any combination of green salads may be used, and a few leaves of radicchio.
Neatly arrange in a salad bowl; serve with a vinaigrette separately.

29 French salad (*salade française*)

The usual ingredients are lettuce, tomato and cucumber, but these may be varied with other salad vegetables, and in some cases with quarters of egg.
A vinaigrette made with French mustard (French dressing) should be offered.

30 Radishes (*radis*)

Allow 3–5 radishes per portion.

1 Trim the green stems to about 2 cm long. Cut off the root end.

2 Wash well, drain. Cut into thin slices or serve whole. Dress neatly.

31 Cucumber

1 Peel the cucumber if desired.

2 Cut into thin slices and arrange neatly.

3 Lightly dress with vinaigrette or serve separately. Alternatively, cucumber may be sliced into 0.5 cm dice and bound with mayonnaise or yoghurt.

Note

This should not be served as a single hors d'oeuvre or main course.

Professional tip

To remove indigestible juices from the cucumber, slice and lightly sprinkle with salt. Allow the salt to draw out the water for approximately 1 hour, wash well under cold water and drain. This will make the cucumber limp.

Ingredient	4 portions	10 portions
Cucumber	½	1¼
Vinaigrette	1 tbsp	2½ tbsp

Energy	Cals	Fat	Sat fat	Carb	Sugar	Protein	Fibre	Sodium
80 kJ	20 kcal	1.7g	0.2g	0.7g	0.7g	0.3g	0.3g	0.0g

Healthy eating tips

● Vegetable-based salads are a healthy way to start a meal.
● Add the minimum amount of salt.

32 Tomatoes (*tomates*)

Allow 1 tomato per portion.

1 Wash the tomatoes. Remove the eyes and slice thinly or cut into segments.

2 Dress neatly.

33 Tomato salad (*salade de tomates*)

Ingredient	4 portions	10 portions
Tomatoes	200 g	500 g
Lettuce	¼	½
Vinaigrette	1 tbsp	2½ tbsp
Onion or chives (optional), chopped	10 g	25 g
Parsley or mixed fresh herbs, chopped		

1 Peel the tomatoes if required. Slice thinly and arrange neatly on the lettuce leaves.

2 Sprinkle with the vinaigrette, onion (blanched if required) and parsley.

Variation

Alternate slices of tomato and mozzarella with basic dressing.

Energy	Cals	Fat	Sat fat	Carb	Sugar	Protein	Fibre
99 kJ	24 kcal	1.7 g	0.3 g	1.7 g	1.7 g	0.9 g	1.0 g

34 Tomato and cucumber salad (*salade de tomates et concombres*)

Ingredient	4 portions	10 portions
Tomatoes	2	5
Cucumber	½	1¼
Vinaigrette	1 tbsp	2½ tbsp
Parsley or mixed fresh herbs, chopped		

1 Alternate slices of tomato and cucumber.
2 Sprinkle with the vinaigrette and parsley.

Professional tip

Blanch the tomatoes so that you can remove the skins, which are hard to digest.

Energy	Cals	Fat	Sat fat	Carb	Sugar	Protein	Fibre
112 kJ	27 kcal	2.0g	0.3g	1.9g	1.8g	0.5g	0.6g

35 Beetroot salad (*salade de betterave*)

Ingredient	4 portions	10 portions
Cooked beetroot, neatly cut or sliced	200 g	500 g
Onion or chives (optional), chopped	10 g	25 g
Vinaigrette	1 tbsp	2½ tbsp
Parsley, chopped		

Energy	Cals	Fat	Sat fat	Carb	Sugar	Protein	Fibre
134 kJ	32 kcal	2.0g	0.3g	3.2g	3.1g	0.7g	0.9g

Professional tip

- To cook the beetroot, blanch and then simmer it.
- Wear gloves when handling beetroot to avoid staining the skin.

Variation

Add 60–120 ml mayonnaise or natural yoghurt in place of vinaigrette (150–200 ml for 10 portions).

1 Combine all the ingredients, except the parsley, blanching the onion if required.
2 Dress neatly and sprinkle with the chopped parsley.

36 Coleslaw

Ingredient	4 portions	10 portions
White or Chinese cabbage	200 g	500 g
Carrot	50 g	125 g
Onion (optional)	25 g	60 g
Mayonnaise, natural yoghurt or fromage frais	125 ml	300 ml

Energy	Cals	Fat	Sat fat	Carb	Sugar	Protein	Fibre
629 kJ	150 kcal	14.8 g	2.2 g	2.9 g	2.9 g	1.5 g	1.8 g

Using mayonnaise.

1 Trim off the outside leaves of the cabbage.

2 Cut into quarters. Remove the centre stalk.

3 Wash the cabbage, shred finely and drain well.

4 Mix with a fine julienne of raw carrot and shredded raw onion. To lessen the harshness of raw onion, blanch and refresh.

5 Bind with mayonnaise, natural yoghurt or vinaigrette.

Healthy eating tips
Replace some or all of the mayonnaise with natural yoghurt and/or fromage frais.

Professional tip
Cut the cabbage into fine julienne to give the coleslaw a good, even texture.

37 French bean salad (*salade de haricots verts*)

Ingredient	4 portions	10 portions
French beans, cooked	200 g	500 g
Vinaigrette	1 tbsp	2½ tbsp
Salt, pepper		

Combine all the ingredients.

Professional tip
Cook the beans *al dente*, so that the salad will have a crunchy texture.

Energy	Cals	Fat	Sat fat	Carb	Sugar	Protein	Fibre
125 kJ	30 kcal	1.9 g	0.3 g	2.5 g	1.2 g	0.9 g	2.0 g

Healthy eating tips
Add salt sparingly.

38 Potato salad

1 Cut the potatoes into ½–1 cm dice; sprinkle with vinaigrette.

2 Mix with the onion or chive, add the mayonnaise and correct the seasoning. (The onion may be blanched to reduce its harshness.)

3 Dress neatly and sprinkle with chopped parsley or herbs.

This is not usually served as a single hors d'oeuvre or main course.

Professional tip

Mixing the potato, onion and mayonnaise gives a good flavour and texture, but be careful not to mix them too much or the potatoes will break up.

Variation

● Potato salad can also be made by dicing raw peeled or unpeeled potato, cooking them – preferably by steaming (to retain shape) – and mixing with vinaigrette while warm.

● Try adding two chopped hard-boiled eggs or 100 g of peeled dessert apple mixed with lemon juice, or a small bunch of picked watercress leaves.

● Potatoes may be cooked with mint and allowed to cool with the mint.

● Cooked small new potatoes can be tossed in vinaigrette with chopped fresh herbs (e.g. mint, parsley, chives).

Ingredient	4 portions	10 portions
Potatoes, cooked	200 g	500 g
Vinaigrette	1 tbsp	2½ tbsp
Onion or chive (optional), chopped	10 g	25 g
Mayonnaise or natural yoghurt	125 ml	300 ml
Salt, pepper		
Parsley or mixed fresh herbs, chopped		

Energy	Cals	Fat	Sat fat	Carb	Sugar	Protein	Fibre
503 kJ	120 kcal	8.7 g	1.3 g	10.0 g	0.3 g	1.0 g	0.7 g

Using mayonnaise.

39 Waldorf salad

Ingredient	4 portions	10 portions
Celery or celeriac	2 sticks/100 g	5 sticks/250 g
Russet apples	2	5
Walnuts, shelled and peeled	25 g	62 g
Mayonnaise		
Lettuce leaves, to serve		

Energy	Cals	Fat	Sat fat	Carb	Sugar	Protein	Fibre	Sodium
657 kJ	159 kcal	14.0 g	1.8 g	7.0 g	6.9 g	1.6 g	2.2 g	0.1 g

1 Dice celery or celeriac and crisp russet apples.

2 Mix with shelled and peeled walnuts and bind with mayonnaise.

3 Dress on quarters or leaves of lettuce (may also be served in hollowed-out apples).

When mixing in the mayonnaise, add just enough to give the right texture and flavour.

Healthy eating tips
Try using some yoghurt in place of the mayonnaise, which will proportionally reduce the fat.

---

40 Vegetable salad/Russian salad

Ingredient	4 portions	10 portions
Carrots	100 g	250 g
Turnips	50 g	125 g
French beans	50 g	125 g
Peas	50 g	125 g
Vinaigrette	1 tbsp	2–3 tbsp
Mayonnaise or natural yoghurt	125 ml	300 ml
Salt, pepper		

Energy	Cals	Fat	Sat fat	Carb	Sugar	Protein	Fibre
392 kJ	93 kcal	8.8 g	1.3 g	2.5 g	2.1 g	1.3 g	3.0 g

Using mayonnaise.

1 Peel and wash the carrots and turnips, cut into 0.5 cm dice or batons.

2 Cook separately in salted water, refresh and drain well.

3 Top and tail the beans, and cut into 0.5 cm dice; cook, refresh and drain well.

4 Cook the peas, refresh and drain well.

5 Mix all the well-drained vegetables with vinaigrette and then mayonnaise.

6 Correct the seasoning. Dress neatly.

Do not overcook the vegetables, and drain them well before adding the dressing – otherwise the salad will be too wet.

Healthy eating tips
● Try half mayonnaise and half natural yoghurt.
● Season with the minimum amount of salt.

41 Greek-style mushrooms

1 Combine all the ingredients except the mushrooms, to create a Greek-style cooking liquor.

2 Cook the mushrooms gently in the cooking liquor for 3 to 4 minutes.

3 Serve cold with the unstrained liquor.

Professional tip

Simmer the vegetables carefully so that they are correctly cooked and absorb the flavours.

Ingredient	4 portions	10 portions
Water	250 ml	625 ml
Olive oil	60 ml	150 ml
Lemon, juice of	1	1½
Bay leaf	½	1
Sprig of thyme		
Peppercorns	6	15
Coriander seeds	6	15
Salt		
Small white button mushrooms, cleaned	200 g	500 g

Energy	Cals	Fat	Sat fat	Carb	Sugar	Protein	Fibre
587 kJ	142 kcal	15.2 g	2.2 g	0.4 g	0.3 g	1.0 g	0.6 g

Variation

Other vegetables such as artichokes and cauliflower can also be cooked in this style, using the same liquor.

● For artichokes, peel and trim 6 artichokes for 4 portions (or 15 for 10); cut the leaves short and remove the chokes. Blanch the artichokes in water with a little lemon juice for 10 minutes, refresh, then simmer in the Greek-style liquor for 15–20 minutes.

● For cauliflower, trim and wash one medium cauliflower for 4 portions (2 for 10); break it into small sprigs about the size of cherries. Blanch the sprigs for about 5 minutes, refresh, then simmer in the Greek-style liquor for 5–10 minutes. Keep the cauliflower slightly undercooked and crisp.

42 Haricot bean salad

Ingredient	4 portions	10 portions
Haricot beans, cooked	200 g	500 g
Vinaigrette	1 tbsp	2½ tbsp
Parsley, chopped		
Onion, chopped and blanched if necessary	¼	½
Chives (optional)	15 g	40 g
Salt, pepper		

Energy	Cals	Fat	Sat fat	Carb	Sugar	Protein	Fibre
278 kJ	66 kcal	2.1 g	0.4 g	9.0 g	0.7 g	3.3 g	3.1 g

1 Combine all the ingredients.

This recipe can be used for any type of dried bean.

Healthy eating tips
● Lightly dress with vinaigrette.
● Add salt sparingly.

43 Three-bean salad

Use 200 g (500 g for 10 portions) of three different dried beans (for example, red kidney, black-eyed, flageolet). Proceed as for a haricot bean salad (recipe 42).

Energy	Cals	Fat	Sat fat	Carb	Sugar	Protein	Fibre
1,849 kJ	440 kcal	8.7g	1.1g	63.4g	6.3g	30.9g	36.0g

For 4 portions.

44 Lentil and goats' cheese salad

1 Rinse the lentils and place in a saucepan. Add the bay leaf and cover with water. Bring to the boil and simmer for 20–30 minutes until tender.

2 Drain and then place in a bowl. Add the spring onions, red pepper, parsley and cherry tomatoes; mix well.

3 For the dressing, whisk together in a bowl the oil, vinegar, honey and garlic, and stir into the lentils.

4 Serve on a bed of rocket, with the goats' cheese sprinkled over.

Ingredient	4 portions	10 portions
Puy lentils	100g	250g
Bay leaf	1	2½
Spring onions, finely chopped	4	10
Red pepper, finely chopped	1	2½ tbsp
Parsley, chopped	1 tbsp	2½ tbsp
Cherry tomatoes, sliced in half	400g	1 kg
Rocket leaves	200g	500g
Goats' cheese	100g	250g
Dressing		
Olive oil	1 tbsp	2½ tbsp
Balsamic vinegar	1 tbsp	2½ tbsp
Clear honey	2 tbsp	5 tbsp
Garlic clove, crushed and chopped	1	2½

Energy	Cals	Fat	Sat fat	Carb	Sugar	Protein	Fibre
907 kJ	216 kcal	9.2g	4.1g	22.8g	10.5g	11.9g	4.5g

Note

This dish provides a healthy, balanced starter.

45 Rice salad (*salade de riz*)

Ingredient	4 portions	10 portions
Tomatoes	100 g	250 g
Rice, cooked	100 g	250 g
Peas, cooked	50 g	125 g
Vinaigrette	1 tbsp	2½ tbsp
Salt, pepper		

Energy	Cals	Fat	Sat fat	Carb	Sugar	Protein	Fibre
906 kJ	216 kcal	6.9 g	1.1 g	34.6 g	3.3 g	5.9 g	8.3 g

For 4 portions.

1 Skin and deseed the tomatoes; cut into 0.5 cm dice.

2 Mix with the rice and peas.

3 Add the vinaigrette and correct the seasoning.

Healthy eating tips
- This dish is high in starchy carbohydrate and can be varied with different/additional vegetables.
- Lightly dress with vinaigrette and add salt sparingly.

Professional tip

Cook the rice so that it still has a bite, with the grains separate, not sticking together; it should not feel starchy in the mouth.

46 Brown rice salad

Ingredient	4 portions	10 portions
Brown rice	100 g	250 g
Salt		
Boiling water	175 g	440 g
Vinaigrette	1 tbsp	2½ tbsp
Tomatoes	100 g	250 g
Peas, cooked	50 g	125 g
Haricots verts, cooked and finely sliced	25 g	60 g
Cucumber, finely chopped	5 cm	12 cm
Spring onions, very finely chopped	3	7
Red dessert apple, chopped but not peeled	1	2½
Walnuts, finely chopped	25 g	60 g
Mixed peppers, deseeded, cut into fine dice	25 g	60 g

Energy	Cals	Fat	Sat fat	Carb	Sugar	Protein	Fibre	Sodium
1,127 kJ	270 kcal	16.3 g	2.3 g	28.1 g	6.9 g	4.2 g	3.5 g	0.3 g

1 Place the rice into a saucepan with a sprinkle of salt and cover with boiling water.

2 Bring the water back to the boil; stir once, put a lid on and simmer very gently for approximately 35–40 minutes, until all the liquid has been absorbed.

3 Empty the rice into a salad bowl, fluff it up with a fork and pour three-quarters of the vinaigrette over while it's still hot. Leave to cool.

4 While the rice is cooling, blanch the tomatoes, remove the skins and cut into quarters. Remove the seeds and cut in 0.5 cm dice.

5 Once the rice is cool, mix in the tomatoes and all the other ingredients, adding the remaining vinaigrette. Check the seasoning and keep in a cool place until needed.

47 Couscous salad with roasted vegetables and mixed herbs

Ingredient	4 portions	10 portions
Roasted vegetables (selection)	100 g	250 g
Couscous	250 g	625 g
Balsamic vinegar	1 tbsp	2½ tbsp
Olive oil	3 tbsp	8 tbsp
Lemon, juice of	¼	¾
Seasoning		
Fresh mint, chopped	½ tsp	1¼ tsp
Fresh coriander, chopped	½ tsp	1¼ tsp
Fresh thyme, chopped	½ tsp	1¼ tsp

Energy	Cals	Fat	Sat fat	Carb	Sugar	Protein	Fibre
1,248 kJ	300 kcal	12.5 g	1.7 g	42.2 g	8.6 g	6.6 g	3.8 g

1 Prepare the roasted vegetables.

2 Place the couscous in a suitable bowl and gently pour over 300 ml of boiling water (750 ml for 10 portions).

3 Stir well, cover and leave to stand for 5 minutes.

4 Separate the grains with a fork.

5 Add the balsamic vinegar, olive oil, lemon juice and seasoning.

6 Mix well, then stir in the chopped herbs.

7 Finish by adding the roasted vegetables.

8 Serve in a suitable bowl or use individual plates. For plated service, arrange the couscous neatly in the centre of the plate, arrange the roasted vegetables around, then garnish with fresh herbs.

Professional tip

When adding the vinegar and oil, add just enough to give the correct texture and flavour.

Healthy eating tips
- Use an unsaturated oil and lightly brush the vegetables when roasting.
- Use the minimum amount of salt.

48 Caesar salad

Energy	Cals	Fat	Sat fat	Carb	Sugar	Protein	Fibre
1,494 kJ	361 kcal	32.2g	7.9g	5.1g	2.0g	12.9g	1.2g

Using toast for croutons.

Ingredient	4 portions	10 portions
Cos lettuce (medium size)	2	5
Croutons, 2 cm square	16	40
Eggs, fresh	2	5
Dressing		
Garlic, finely chopped	1 tsp	2½ tsp
Anchovy fillets, mashed	4	10
Lemon juice	1 tsp	2½ tsp
Virgin olive oil	6 tbsp	15 tbsp
White wine vinegar	1 tbsp	2½ tbsp
Salt, black mill pepper		
To serve		
Parmesan, freshly grated	75 g	190 g

1 Separate the lettuce leaves, wash, dry thoroughly and refrigerate.

2 Lightly grill or fry (in good fresh oil) the croutons on all sides.

3 Plunge the eggs into boiling water for 1 minute, remove and set aside.

4 Break the lettuce into serving-sized pieces and place into a salad bowl.

5 Mix the dressing, break the eggs, spoon out the contents, mix with a fork, add to the dressing and mix into the salad.

6 Mix in the cheese, scatter the croutons on top and serve.

Professional tip

Because the eggs are only lightly cooked, they must be perfectly fresh, and the salad must be prepared and served immediately. In the interests of food safety, the eggs are sometimes hard boiled.

Alternatively, the salad may be garnished with hard-boiled gull's eggs.

Healthy eating tips
- No added salt is needed; anchovies and cheese are high in salt.
- Oven bake the croutons.
- Serve with fresh bread or rolls.

49 Niçoise salad

Ingredient	4 portions	10 portions
Tomatoes	100 g	250 g
French beans, cooked	200 g	500 g
Diced potatoes, cooked	100 g	250 g
Salt, pepper		
Vinaigrette	1 tbsp	2½ tbsp
Anchovy fillets	10 g	25 g
Capers	5 g	12 g
Stoned olives	10 g	25 g

Energy	Cals	Fat	Sat fat	Carb	Sugar	Protein	Fibre
217 kJ	52 kcal	2.4 g	0.4 g	6.3 g	1.2 g	1.7 g	2.5 g

1 Peel the tomatoes, deseed and cut into neat segments.
2 Dress the beans, tomatoes and potatoes neatly.
3 Season with salt and pepper. Add the vinaigrette.
4 Decorate with anchovies, capers and olives.

Healthy eating tips
- Lightly dress with vinaigrette.
- The anchovies are high in salt, so no added salt is necessary.

50 Avocado and bacon salad

Ingredient	4 portions	10 portions
Thin streaky bacon rashers, rind and excess fat trimmed	8	20
Fresh lemon juice	1 tbsp	2½ tbsp
Garlic clove, crushed finely	1	2½
Extra virgin olive oil	2 tbsp	5 tbsp
Salt and freshly ground black pepper		
Ripe avocados, medium	2	5
Snow pea sprouts, stems trimmed	50 g	125 g

Energy	Cals	Fat	Sat fat	Carb	Sugar	Protein	Fibre	Sodium
1,462 kJ	354 kcal	34.4 g	7.6 g	2.4 g	0.7 g	9.0 g	4.9 g	1.0 g

1 Grill the bacon rashers under a salamander until crisp. Transfer to a tray lined with kitchen paper and allow to cool.
2 Place the lemon juice and garlic in a mixing bowl and whisk in the olive oil. Season with salt and pepper.

3 Halve the avocados lengthways, remove the stones and peel the skin. Place the avocados on to a chopping board, cut side down, and cut in half lengthways, then crossways into slices 1 cm thick.
4 Layer the avocados, bacon and snow pea sprouts on serving plates, drizzling the dressing between the layers. Serve immediately.

Cold fish and shellfish dishes

51 Smoked salmon

Allow 35–50g per portion.

1 A side of smoked salmon must be carefully trimmed to remove the dry outside surface before service. Remove all bones (a pair of pliers is useful for this).

2 Carve the salmon on the slant, as thinly as possible.

3 Dress neatly, overlapping, on a plate or dish, decorated with sprigs of parsley Accompaniments include brown bread and butter, and lemon.

Note

Other smoked fish served as hors d'oeuvres include halibut, eel, conger eel, trout, mackerel, herring (buckling), cod's roe and sprats.

Healthy eating tips

Oily fish (such as salmon, trout, mackerel, rollmops and sprats) are high in omega-3 fatty acids, which are beneficial for health.

Energy	Cals	Fat	Sat fat	Carb	Sugar	Protein	Fibre
149 kJ	36 kcal	1.1g	0.3g	0.0g	0.0g	6.4g	0.0g

52 Oysters

Ingredient	4 portions
Rock or native oysters	24
Lemon	1
To accompany	
Brown bread and butter	
Tabasco or chilli sauce	

Note

Make sure the oysters have been grown in or fished from clean waters, and take note of the famous rule only to use them when there is an 'r' in the month, although rock oysters are available throughout the year.

Energy	Cals	Fat	Sat fat	Carb	Sugar	Protein	Fibre	Sodium
192 kJ	45 kcal	0.9g	0.2g	2.7g	1.0g	6.8g	0.4g	0.3g

Excluding accompaniments.

1 Select only those oysters that are tightly shut and have a fresh smell (category A is best, which means the waters they have grown in are clean).

2 To open an oyster, only the point of the oyster knife is used. Hold the oyster with a thick oven cloth to protect your hand.

3 With the oyster in the palm of your hand, push the point of the knife about 1 cm deep into the 'hinge' between the 'lid' and the body of the oyster.

4 Once the lid has been penetrated, push down. The lid should pop open. Lift up the top shell, cutting the muscle attached to it.

5 Remove any splintered shell from the flesh and solid shell.

6 Return each oyster to its shell and serve on a bed of crushed ice with chilli sauce, brown bread and lemon.

53 Dressed crab

Ingredient	1 portion
Whole crab, cooked	1 (200–300 g)
Salt, pepper	
Worcester sauce	
Mayonnaise	
Fresh white breadcrumbs	
Decoration as required, e.g. parsley and hard-boiled egg	

Energy	Cals	Fat	Sat fat	Carb	Sugar	Protein	Fibre	Sodium
1,974 kJ	474 kcal	28.6g	4.4g	0.8g	0.7g	53.1g	0.7g	1.2g

1 Remove large claws and sever at the joints.

2 Remove the flexible pincer from the claw.

3 Crack or saw carefully and remove all flesh.

4 Remove flesh from two remaining joints with the handle of spoon.

5 Carefully remove the soft undershell.

6 Discard the gills (dead man's fingers) and the sac behind the eyes.

7 Scrape out all the inside of the shell and pass through a sieve.

8 Season with salt, pepper, Worcester sauce and a little mayonnaise; thicken lightly with fresh white breadcrumbs.

9 Trim the shell by tapping carefully along the natural line.

10 Scrub the shell thoroughly and leave to dry.

11 Dress the brown meat down the centre of the shell.

12 Shred the white meat, taking care to remove any small pieces of shell.

13 Dress neatly on either side of the brown meat.

14 Decorate as desired, using any of the following: chopped parsley, hard-boiled white and yolk of egg, anchovies, capers, olives.

15 Serve the crab on a flat dish garnished with lettuce leaves, quarters of tomato and the crab's legs.

16 Serve a vinaigrette or mayonnaise sauce separately.

54 Cold salmon

Energy	Cals	Fat	Sat fat	Carb	Sugar	Protein	Fibre	Sodium
2,141 kJ	517 kcal	40.3g	6.5g	5.1g	4.5g	33.0g	1.8g	1.2g

Ingredient	2–3 portions	8–10 portions
Cooking liquid (court bouillon)		
Water	1 litre	2.5 litres
Salt	10g	25g
Carrots, sliced	50g	125g
Bay leaf	2–3	5–8
Parsley stalks		
Vinegar	60ml	150ml
Peppercorns	6	15
Onions, sliced	50g	125g
Sprig of thyme		
Salmon for service in darnes or portions		
Salmon, cleaned	500g	1.25kg
Court bouillon (see above)	400ml	1 litre
Cucumber	¼	½
Large lettuce	½	1
Tomatoes	80g	200g
Mayonnaise (recipe 4) or green sauce (recipe 6)	100ml	250ml

Salmon may be obtained in varying weights from 3.5–15kg: 0.5kg of uncleaned salmon yields 2–3 portions. Size is an important consideration, depending on whether the salmon is to be cooked whole or cut into darnes. A salmon of any size may be cooked whole. When required for darnes, a medium-sized salmon is more suitable.

For the court bouillon

1 Simmer all the ingredients for 30–40 minutes.
2 Pass through a strainer, use as required.

Cooking for service in darnes or portions

1 Cook the salmon in the court bouillon, either whole or cut into darnes.
2 Allow to cool thoroughly in the cooking liquid to keep it moist. Divide a whole salmon into eight even portions; for darnes, remove the centre bone and cut each darne in half, if required.
3 Except when whole, remove the centre bone, the skin and brown surface, and dress neatly on a flat dish.
4 Peel and slice the cucumber and neatly arrange a few slices on each portion.
5 Garnish with quarters of lettuce and quarters of tomatoes.
6 Serve the sauce or mayonnaise in a sauceboat separately.

Professional tip

Always allow the salmon to remain in the court bouillon until cold.

Cooking and presenting salmon whole

1 Scrape off all scales, from tail to head, using the back of a knife.

2 Remove all gills and clean out the head.

3 Remove the intestines and clear the blood from the backbone.

4 Trim off all fins. Wash well.

5 Place in a salmon kettle and cover with cold court bouillon.

6 Bring slowly to the boil, skim, then simmer very gently.

7 Allow the following approximate simmering times:
- 3.5 kg – 15 minutes
- 7 kg – 20 minutes
- 10.5 kg – 25 minutes
- 14 kg – 30 minutes.

8 Allow the cooked salmon to cool, then remove it from the liquid. Carefully remove the skin and the dark layer under the skin (which is cooked blood). The now bared salmon flesh should be perfectly smooth.

9 Make sure the salmon is well drained and place it on to the serving dish or board.

10 The salmon is now ready for decorating and garnishing. Keep this to the minimum and avoid over-covering the fish and the dish. Neatly overlapping thin slices of cucumber (the skin may be left on or removed), quartered tomatoes (which can be peeled and neatly cut), small pieces of hearts of lettuce can, if artistically set out, give a quick, neat-looking, appetising appearance. Remember though, time is money – there is no justification for spending a lot of time cutting fiddly little pieces of many different items to form patterns that often look untidy.

55 Fish salad (*salade de poisson*)

Ingredient	4 portions	10 portions
Cooked fish, free from skin and bone	200 g	500 g
Egg, hard-boiled	1	2–3
Cucumber (optional)	50 g	125 g
Lettuce	½	1
Parsley or fennel, chopped		
Salt, pepper		
Vinaigrette	1 tbsp	2–3 tbsp

Energy	Cals	Fat	Sat fat	Carb	Sugar	Protein	Fibre
978 kJ	233 kcal	13.5 g	3.0 g	1.5 g	1.4 g	26.4 g	1.3 g

For 4 portions.

1 Flake the fish.

2 Cut the egg and cucumber into 0.5 cm dice and finely shred the lettuce

3 Mix ingredients together and add the parsley.

4 Correct the seasoning and mix in the vinaigrette.

5 It may be decorated with lettuce, anchovies and capers.

Healthy eating tips
Use salt sparingly.

Note

Be careful not to overcook the fish.

56 Sea bass ceviche

Ingredient	4 portions	10 portions
Sea bass fillet, skinless, free of bone	400 g	1 kg
Large lime, juice only	1	2½
Yuzu juice	2 tbsp	5 tbsp
Coriander leaves, finely chopped	1 tbsp	2½ tbsp
Shallots, finely chopped	2	5
Ginger, shredded	1 tsp	2½ tsp
Red chilli, deseeded, finely chopped	1	2½
Sugar	1 tsp	2½ tsp
Light pomace oil or vegetable oil	1 tsp	2½ tsp
To serve		
Sea salt		
Crunchy raw salad of carrot, fennel and celeriac		

Energy	Cals	Fat	Sat fat	Carb	Sugar	Protein	Fibre	Sodium
540 kJ	128 kcal	3.8 g	0.6 g	3.8 g	3.5 g	19.8 g	0.5 g	0.3 g

1 In a shallow, non-metallic tray, combine all the ingredients except the fish.

2 Slice the fish at a 45 degree angle, 5 mm thick.

3 Place the fish into the curing liquid. Refrigerate for 20 minutes until the edges of the fish turn white (do not leave too long as the fish will cure through and resemble rollmops).

4 To finish, lay the fish neatly on a plate with a little of the curing garnish and juice.

5 Season with a little sea salt and serve with a crunchy salad.

Note

Yuzu is a citrus fruit grown in east Asia – the juice is available in bottles.

57 Soused herring or mackerel

Ingredient	4 portions	10 portions
Herrings or mackerel	2	5
Salt, pepper		
Button onions	25 g	60 g
Carrots, peeled and fluted	25 g	60 g
Bay leaf	½	1½
Peppercorns	6	15
Thyme	1 sprig	2 sprigs
Vinegar	60 ml	150 ml

Energy	Cals	Fat	Sat fat	Carb	Sugar	Protein	Fibre
605 kJ	144 kcal	11.1 g	2.4 g	0.8 g	0.8 g	10.3 g	0.3 g

1 Clean, scale and fillet the fish.

2 Wash the fillets well and season with salt and pepper.

3 Roll up with the skin outside. Place in an earthenware dish.

4 Peel and wash the onion. Cut the onion and carrots into neat, thin rings.

5 Blanch for 2–3 minutes.

6 Add to the fish with the remainder of the ingredients.

7 Cover with greaseproof paper and cook in a moderate oven for 15–20 minutes.

8 Allow to cool, place in a dish with the onion and carrot.

9 Garnish with picked parsley, dill or chives.

Healthy eating tips
● Serve with plenty of salad vegetables and bread or toast (optional butter or spread).
● Keep added salt to a minimum.

---

58 Crab, lobster, shrimp or prawn cocktail (*cocktail de crabe, homard, crevettes, crevettes roses*)

Energy	Cals	Fat	Sat fat	Carb	Sugar	Protein	Fibre
966 kJ	230 kcal	21.0 g	3.2 g	0.6 g	0.6 g	9.6 g	0.3 g

Professional tip

Portion control is important so that this dish does not cost too much to produce. The cocktail needs to be presented well.

Ingredient	4 portions	10 portions
Lettuce	½	1¼
Prepared shellfish	100–150 g	250–350 g
Shellfish cocktail sauce (see recipe 11)	125 ml	300 ml

1 Wash, drain well and finely shred the lettuce, avoiding long strands. Place about 2 cm deep in cocktail glasses or dishes.

2 Add the prepared shellfish: crab (shredded white meat only); lobster (cut into 2 cm dice); shrimps (peeled and washed); prawns (peeled, washed and, if large, cut into two or three pieces).

3 Coat with sauce.

4 Decorate with an appropriate piece of the content, such as a prawn, with the shell on the tail removed, placed on the edge of the glass of a prawn cocktail. A more modern presentation is to serve the cocktail plated.

59 Potted shrimps

Ingredient	4 portions	10 portions
Butter	100 g	250 g
Chives, chopped	2 tbsp	5 tbsp
Cayenne pepper, to taste		
Brown shrimps, peeled	600 g	1.5 kg
Clarified butter	6 tbsp	15 tbsp

Energy	Cals	Fat	Sat fat	Carb	Sugar	Protein	Fibre	Sodium
3,887 kJ	942 kcal	92.9 g	58.1 g	1.1 g	0.7 g	25.7 g	0.1 g	0.9 g

This is a real seaside dish, full of flavour and eaten with plenty of brown bread and butter. Lobster or langoustine can be used – although timings will need to be adapted accordingly. The traditional seasoning for potted shrimps is ground mace.

1 Put the butter, chives and cayenne pepper in a medium-sized pan and leave to melt over a gentle heat.

2 Add the peeled shrimps and stir over the heat for a couple of minutes until they have heated through, but don't let the mixture boil.

3 Divide the shrimps and butter between four small ramekins. Level the tops and then leave them to set in the refrigerator.

4 Spoon over a thin layer of clarified butter and leave to set once more. Serve with plenty of brown toast or crusty brown bread.

Professional tip

● Do not let the mixture boil (step 2) – if it does, the shrimps will become tough.
● Remove from the fridge and allow to warm slightly before serving, to bring out the flavour.

60 Fruits de mer

Ingredient	4 portions	10 portions
Lobster, cooked	1	2½
Crab, cooked	1	2½
Large prawns, cooked	12	30
Winkles, raw	100 g	250 g
Fresh clams	200 g	500 g
Fresh cockles	200 g	500 g
Mussels, live	200 g	500 g
Langoustines, live	6	10
White wine	75 ml	200 ml
Parsley stalks	4	10
Shallots, roughly chopped	2	5
Salt		
Oysters	12	30
For the sauces		
Mayonnaise (recipe 4)	250 ml	625 ml
Garlic cloves, finely chopped	2	5
Tomato ketchup	2 tsp	5 tsp
Brandy	1 tbsp	2½ tbsp
Tabasco sauce		
Red wine vinegar	100 ml	250 ml
Shallots, finely chopped	2	5
To serve		
Sprigs of parsley and lemon wedges, to garnish		
Chorizo sausage, warm, to garnish (optional)		

Energy	Cals	Fat	Sat fat	Carb	Sugar	Protein	Fibre	Sodium
3,440 kJ	828 kcal	56.5g	8.7g	6.8g	3.7g	65.6g	0.9g	2.3g

To prepare the seafood

1 Cut the lobster in half lengthways. Remove the stomach and give the claws a crack to break the shell.

2 Open the crab, remove the 'dead man's fingers' and cut the body into four. Give the claws a few cracks to break the shell – this will make getting the meat out at the table easier.

3 Put the prawns, winkles, clams, cockles, mussels and langoustines into a pan with the white wine, parsley stalks, shallots and salt. Bring to the boil, cover and steam for 4 minutes until the mussels, clams and cockles open. Remove from the water and put on a tray to cool.

4 Open the oysters with an oyster knife.

5 Place a generous portion of crushed ice on a tray. Arrange the lobster, crab, langoustines, clams, mussels, cockles, winkles, prawns and oysters on the ice, garnishing with lemon and parsley.

Note

Dead man's fingers are the crab's gills. You can see them inside the crab: they are grey and shaped like fingers.

To make the sauces

1 Divide the mayonnaise into thirds. Set one third to one side.

2 Mix the chopped garlic into another third of the mayonnaise.

3 To make seafood sauce, mix the tomato ketchup, the brandy and a dash of Tabasco into the remaining mayonnaise.

4 To make shallot vinegar, mix together the red wine vinegar and the shallots.

Serve the fruits de mer with the mayonnaise, aioli (garlic mayonnaise), seafood sauce, shallot vinegar, lemon wedges and Tabasco, and chorizo sausage if desired.

Cold meat dishes and pies

61 Chicken salad

Ingredient	4 portion	10 portion
Fresh chicken	1.5 kg	3.75 kg
Black peppercorns	10	25
Bay leaves	3	7
Cumin seeds, ground	2 tsp	5 tsp
Almonds, sliced	25 g	60 g
For the dressing		
Greek yoghurt	2 tbsp	5 tbsp
Mayonnaise	3 tbsp	7 tbsp
Lemons, juice and zest of	2	5
Cucumber, peeled and diced	1	2½
Fresh basil, picked and torn	25 g	60 g
To serve		
Mixed salad leaves	100 g	250 g
Vinaigrette	20 ml	50 ml

Energy	Cals	Fat	Sat fat	Carb	Sugar	Protein	Fibre	Sodium
4,752 kJ	1,148 kcal	95.2g	27.3g	3.6g	2.7g	70.0g	0.7g	0.4g

1 Place the chicken in a large saucepan and cover with water.

2 Add the peppercorns and bay leaves and bring to a gentle simmer. Poach gently for about 40 minutes and leave it to cool in the liquid.

3 Once cool, take the chicken out of the pan, remove the skin and shred the meat. Cover and place in a refrigerator.

4 Dry fry the cumin and almonds in a hot pan and leave to cool.

5 To make the dressing, mix the yoghurt, mayonnaise and lemon zest and juice in a large bowl.

6 Add the chicken, cucumber, cumin and almonds with the torn basil. Mix well and serve on a bed of the mixed salad leaves tossed lightly in vinaigrette.

62 Raised pork pie

Ingredient	4 portions	10 portions
Hot water paste		
Strong plain flour	250 g	500 g
Salt		
Lard or margarine (alternatively use 100 g lard and 25 g butter or margarine)	125 g	300 g
Water	125 ml	300 ml
Filling		
Shoulder of pork, without bone	300 g	1 kg
Bacon	100 g	250 g
Allspice (or mixed spice) and chopped sage	½ tsp	1½ tsp
Salt, pepper		
Bread, soaked in milk	50 g	125 g
Stock or water	2 tbsp	5 tbsp
Egg wash		
Stock, hot	125 ml	375 ml
Gelatine	5 g	12.5 g
Picked watercress and salad to serve		

Energy	Cals	Fat	Sat fat	Carb	Sugar	Protein	Fibre	Sodium
3,005 kJ	721 kcal	47.7 g	19.3 g	49.2 g	1.7 g	26.7 g	2.7 g	1.2 g

For the pastry:

1 Sift the flour and salt into a basin. Make a well in the centre.

2 Boil the fat with the water and pour immediately into the flour.

3 Mix with a wooden spoon until cool enough to handle.

4 Mix to a smooth paste and use while still warm.

For the filling:

1 Cut the pork and bacon into small even pieces and combine with the rest of the main ingredients.

2 Keep one-quarter of the paste warm and covered.

3 Roll out the remaining three-quarters and carefully line a well-greased raised pie mould. Ensure that there is a thick rim of pastry.

4 Add the filling and press down firmly.

5 Roll out the remaining pastry for the lid and egg wash the edges of the pie.

6 Add the lid, seal firmly, neaten the edges, cut off any surplus paste; decorate if desired.

7 Make a hole 1 cm in diameter in the centre of the pie; brush all over with egg wash.

8 Bake in a hot oven (230–250 °C) for approximately 20 minutes.

9 Reduce the heat to moderate (150–200 °C) and cook for 1½–2 hours in all.

10 If the pie colours too quickly, cover with greaseproof paper or foil. Remove from the oven and carefully remove tin. Egg wash the pie all over and return to the oven for a few minutes.

11 Remove from the oven and fill with approximately 125 ml of good hot stock in which 5 g of gelatine has been dissolved.

Serve when cold, garnished with picked watercress and offer a suitable salad.

63 Veal and ham pie

Ingredient	4 portions	10 portions
Hot water paste (see recipe 62)	125 ml	310 ml
Ham or bacon	150 g	375 g
Salt, pepper		
Egg, hard-boiled	1	2½
Lean veal	250 g	625 g
Parsley and thyme	½ tsp	1¼ tsp
Lemon, grated zest of	1	2½
Stock or water	2 tbsp	5 tbsp
Bread, soaked in milk	50 g	125 g
Gelatine	5 g	12.5 g

Energy	Cals	Fat	Sat fat	Carb	Sugar	Protein	Fibre
607 kJ	144 kcal	4.5 g	1.5 g	3.8 g	0.8 g	22.4 g	0.1 g

Proceed as for raised pork pie (recipe 62) but place the shelled egg in the centre of the mixture. Serve when cold, garnished with picked watercress and offer a suitable salad.

Partly fill the pie, then place egg(s) into the centre

Add the pastry lid and seal it firmly

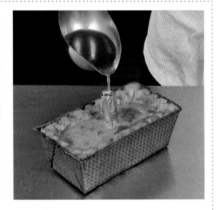

Pour gelatine dissolved in stock into the pie after baking

Pâtés and terrines

64 Liver pâté (*pâté de foie*)

Ingredient	4 portions	10 portions
Liver (chicken, pig, calf, lamb, etc.)	100 g	250 g
Butter or oil	25 g	60 g
Onion, chopped	10 g	25 g
Cloves of garlic	1	2½
Sprigs of parsley, thyme, chervil		
Fat pork	50 g	125 g
Salt, pepper		
Fat bacon	25 g	60 g

Energy	Cals	Fat	Sat fat	Carb	Sugar	Protein	Fibre
896 kJ	213 kcal	19.1 g	8.5 g	0.7 g	0.1 g	9.8 g	0.0 g

1 Cut the liver into 2 cm pieces.

2 Toss quickly in the butter or oil in a frying pan over a fierce heat for a few seconds with the onion, garlic and herbs.

3 Allow to cool.

4 Pass the liver and fat pork together through a mincer, twice. Season.

5 Line an earthenware terrine with wafer-thin slices of fat bacon.

6 Place the mixture into the terrine. Cover with fat bacon.

7 Stand in a tray half-full of water and bring to simmering point.

8 Cook in a moderate oven for 1 hour. Use a temperature probe to check that the centre reaches 70 °C.

9 Blast chill. When quite cold, cut into 0.5 cm slices and serve on lettuce leaves. Usually served accompanied with freshly made toast.

Note

This is a typical recipe for a homemade terrine, often seen on the menu as *pâté maison*.

Healthy eating tips
● Use an unsaturated oil (sunflower or olive). Lightly oil the pan and drain off any excess after the frying is complete.
● The bacon is high in salt so very little (or no) added salt is necessary.

65 Terrine of bacon, spinach and mushrooms

Ingredient	12 portions
Collar of bacon	1 kg
Carrot	1
Onion clouté	1
Bouquet garni	1
Celery	2 sticks
Peppercorns	8
Fresh spinach	500 g
Butter	50 g
Mushrooms (preferably morels)	200 g

Energy	Cals	Fat	Sat fat	Carb	Sugar	Protein	Fibre
1,436 kJ	347 kcal	30.4g	7.2g	1.2g	1.0g	17.0g	1.4g

Using common mushrooms.

1 If necessary soak the bacon overnight. Drain.

2 Place the bacon in cold water, bring to the boil, add the carrot, onion, bouquet garni, celery and peppercorns.

3 Simmer until tender.

4 Pick some large leaves of spinach to line the terrine dish. Blanch the leaves, refresh and drain.

5 Lightly cook the rest of the spinach gently; refresh, drain and shred.

6 Alternatively, shred the spinach raw, quickly cook in butter, drain and then blast chill.

7 Cook the mushrooms in a little butter, season and chill well.

8 When cool, remove the bacon from the cooking liquor and chop into small pieces.

9 Line the terrine with cling film, then the spinach leaves. Layer with bacon, mushrooms and spinach. Cover with spinach leaves and cling film. Wait for 12 hours or overnight.

10 When ready, turn out, slice and serve on plates, with leek and mushroom vinaigrette served separately.

Healthy eating tips
- Soaking the bacon overnight will remove some of the salt.
- Use only a little butter to cook the mushrooms.
- Use a minimum amount of salt to season the vinaigrette.
- Serve with warm bread rolls, butter optional.

Bread products

66 Sandwiches

For speed of production, sandwiches are made in bands by cutting the bread lengthways. Once filled, the crusts are removed and the sandwiches cut into fingers. Today, bakers will bake bread to your specification and slice it ready for use. The specification may also include speciality breads such as tomato, basil, walnut and olive bread.

Sandwiches may be made from every kind of bread, fresh or toasted, in a variety of shapes, and with an almost endless assortment of fillings. They may be garnished with potato or vegetable crisps and a little salad.

Sandwiches may also be cut into small cubes and a variety placed on a cocktail stick like a mini kebab.

Toasted sandwiches

These are made by inserting a variety of savoury fillings between two slices of hot, freshly buttered toast (for example, scrambled egg, bacon, fried egg, scrambled egg with chopped ham) or by inserting two slices of buttered bread with the required filling into a sandwich toaster.

Club sandwich

Energy	Cals	Fat	Sat fat	Carb	Sugar	Protein	Fibre	Sodium
3473 kJ	832 kcal	54.0g	18.3g	51.0g	4.5g	39.0g	3.1g	1.5g

Using 2 slices of bacon, 50 g chicken and 1 egg.

This is a filling of lettuce, grilled bacon, slices of hard-boiled egg, mayonnaise and slices of chicken layered between three slices of hot buttered toast.

Bookmaker sandwich

This is an underdone minute steak between two slices of hot buttered toast.

Double- and triple-decker sandwiches

Toasted and untoasted bread can be made into double-decker sandwiches, using three slices of bread with two separate fillings. Triple- and quadro-decker sandwiches may also be prepared. They may be served hot or cold.

Open sandwich or Scandinavian smorgasbord

These are prepared from a buttered slice of any bread, garnished with any type of meat, fish, eggs, vegetables or salad. Varieties of open sandwich include the following:

- smoked salmon, lettuce, potted shrimps, slice of lemon
- cold sliced beef, sliced tomato, fans of gherkins
- shredded lettuce, sliced hard-boiled egg, mayonnaise, cucumber
- pickled herring, chopped gherkin, capers (sieved), hard-boiled egg.

Bookmaker sandwich

A selection of open sandwiches

67 Wraps

Wraps are fillings wrapped in tortillas (plain or flavoured, for example, tomato or herb). A wide variety of fillings can be used, for example: chicken and roasted vegetables; beans and red pepper salad with guacamole (a well-flavoured avocado pulp).

Flat breads, such as pitta and ciabatta, can also be used with various fillings (for example, chicken tikka).

68 Bagels

Bagels are ring, doughnut-shaped rolls of leavened bread that are boiled before being baked, giving them a shiny finish and a soft middle (see page 426). They are traditionally filled with smoked salmon and cream cheese (a Jewish speciality) but other fillings can also be used.

Cut horizontally, bagels make a good base for open sandwiches.

69 Canapés

Canapés are usually offered with drinks before meals or at a drinks reception. They need to be small, attractive and well flavoured. A wide variety of cold canapés can be offered. Just a few examples are shown in the photo:

- *vichyssoise* (see page 76) with potato foam
- aubergine and pine nut fritters with chilli jam
- chive pancake, red onion confit and crème fraiche roulade
- buckwheat blini with fromage blanc, smoked salmon and avruga caviar
- sashimi beef with wasabi and toasted sesame seeds on a croûte
- rosemary shortbread with feta cheese, black olives and sun-roasted cherry tomato
- pumpernickel croûte with salmon tartare
- lemon and saffron chicken bruschetta
- Thai swordfish bonbon with samphire.

Some examples of hot canapés (not shown) are as follows:

- small Yorkshire puddings with a slice of beef topped with horseradish cream
- oyster beignets with garlic mayonnaise
- aubergine and goats' cheese tartlet
- monkfish spring rolls with remoulade sauce
- chicken and risotto croquettes
- small pizzas
- small pieces of chicken on skewers with bacon
- chicken satay
- angels on horseback (oysters wrapped with bacon)
- vegetable samosas (see page 241)
- latkes.

Dips for hot canapés may include:

- garlic mayonnaise
- yoghurt, cucumber and mint
- apricot chutney.

DYNAMIC LEARNING

Dynamic Learning is an online subscription solution that supports teachers and students with high quality content and unique tools. Dynamic Learning incorporates elements that all work together to give you the ultimate classroom and homework resource.

Teaching and Learning titles include interactive resources, lesson-planning tools, self-marking tests and assessments. Teachers can:
- Use the Lesson Builder to plan and deliver outstanding lessons
- Share lesson and resources with students and colleagues
- Track student progress with Tests and Assessments

Teachers can also combine their own trusted resources alongside those from **Practical Cookery for Level 2 NVQs and Apprenticeships**, which has a whole host of informative and interactive resources including:
- Schemes of work providing complete guidance on delivering all NVQ units
- Video demonstrations of key skills and techniques
- Interactive quizzes to practise and consolidate learning
- PowerPoint presentations to explain important concepts and generate discussion

Practical Cookery for Level 2 NVQs and Apprenticeships is available as a **Whiteboard eTextbook** an online interactive version of the printed textbook that enable teachers to:
- Display interactive pages to their class
- Add notes and highlight areas
- Add double page spreads into lesson plans

Additionally the **Student eTextbook** of **Practical Cookery for Level 2 NVQs and Apprenticeships** is a downloadable version of the printed textbook that teachers can assign to students so they can:
- Download and view on any device or browser
- Add, edit and synchronise notes across two devices
- Access their personal copy on the move

To find out more and sign up for free trials visit: **www.hoddereducation.co.uk/dynamiclearning**

Glossary

à la   In the style of

à la française   In the French style

à la minute   Cooked to order

à la carte   Dishes prepared to order and priced individually

Abatis de volaille   Poultry offal, giblets, etc.

Abats   Offal: heads, hearts, liver, kidney, etc.

Accompaniments   Items offered separately with a dish of food

Agar-agar   A vegetable gelling agent obtained from seaweed, used as a substitute for gelatine

Aile   A wing (of poultry or game birds)

Aloyau de boeuf   Sirloin of beef

Ambient   Room temperature, surrounding atmosphere

Amino acid   Organic acids found in proteins

Antibiotic   A drug used to destroy disease-producing germs within human or animal bodies

Antiseptic   A substance that prevents the growth of bacteria and moulds, specifically on or in the human body

Aromats   Fragrant herbs and spices

Arroser   To baste, for example during roasting

Ascorbic acid   Known as Vitamin C; found in citrus fruits and blackcurrants; necessary for growth and the maintenance of health

Aspic   A savoury jelly mainly used for decorative larder work

Assorti   An assortment

Au bleu   When applied to meat, this means very underdone

Au beurre   With butter

Au four   Baked in the oven

Au gratin   Sprinkled with cheese or breadcrumbs and then browned

Au vin blanc   With white wine

Bactericide   A substance that destroys bacteria

Bacterium (plural: bacteria)   Single-celled micro-organisms: some are harmful and cause food poisoning; others are useful, such as those used in cheese making

Bain-marie
- A container of water to keep foods hot without burning them
- A container of water for cooking foods without burning them
- A deep, narrow container for storing hot sauces, soups and gravies

Barding   Covering the breasts of birds with thin slices of bacon

Barquette   A boat-shaped pastry case

Basting   Spooning melted fat over food during cooking to keep it moist

Bat out   To flatten slices of raw meat with a cutlet bat

Bean curd   Also known as tofu (see below); a curdled, soft, cheese-like preparation made from soybean milk; a good source of protein

Beansprouts   Young shoots of dried beans, e.g. mung beans, alfalfa or soybeans

Beurre manié   Equal quantities of flour and butter used for thickening sauces

Blanc   A cooking liquor of water, lemon juice, flour and salt; also used to describe the white of chicken (breast and wings)

Blanch
- To make something white (referring to bones and meat)
- To cook but retain colour (referring to certain vegetables)
- To skin (referring to tomatoes)
- To make limp (referring to certain braised vegetables)
- To cook without colour, e.g. the first frying of fried potatoes (chips)

Blanquette   A white stew cooked in stock from which the sauce is made

Blitz   To rapidly purée or foam a light sauce, generally using an electric hand blender at the last moment before service

Bombay duck   Small, dried, salted fish; fried, it is used as an accompaniment to curry dishes

Bombe   An ice cream speciality of different flavours in a bomb shape

Bone out   To remove the bones

Botulism   A rare form of food poisoning

Bouchée   A small puff paste case, literally 'a mouthful'

Bouillon   Unclarified stock

Bouquet garni   A bundle of herbs (e.g. parsley stalks, thyme and bay leaf), tied in pieces of celery and leek

Brine   A preserving solution of water, salt, saltpetre and aromats, used for meats (e.g. silverside, brisket, tongue)

Brunoise   Small dice

Buttermilk   Liquid remaining from the churning of butter

Calcium   A mineral required for building bones and teeth, obtained from cheese and milk

Calorie   A unit of heat or energy, known as a kilocalorie

Canapé   Traditionally, a cushion of bread on which are served various foods, hot or cold; also used to describe small, attractive, well-flavoured dishes offered before a meal or at a drinks reception

Carbohydrate   A nutrient; there are three types of carbohydrate – sugar and starch, which provide the body with energy, and cellulose, which provides roughage (dietary fibre)

Carbon dioxide   A gas produced by all raising agents

Carrier   A person who harbours and may transmit pathogenic organisms without showing signs of illness

Carte du jour   Menu for the day

Casserole   An earthenware, fireproof dish with a lid

Cellulose   The coarse structure of fruit, vegetables and cereals that is not digested but is used as roughage (dietary fibre)

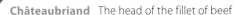

Châteaubriand The head of the fillet of beef

Chaud-froid A demi-glace or creamed velouté with gelatine or aspic added, used for masking cold dishes

Chiffonade Fine shreds, e.g. of spinach, lettuce

Chinois A conical strainer

Chlorophyll The green colour in vegetables

Ciseler To make slight incisions in the surface of a thick fillet of fish, on or off the bone, to allow even cooking

Civet A brown stew of game, usually hare

Clarification/to clarify To make something clear, such as stock, jelly or butter

Clostridium perfringens Food-poisoning bacterium found in the soil, vegetables and meat

Coagulation The solidification of protein; it is irreversible; examples occur when frying an egg or cooking meat

Cocotte Porcelain or earthenware fireproof dish

Collagen/elastin Proteins in connective tissue (e.g. gristle)

Compote Stewed (e.g. stewed fruit)

Concassé Coarsely chopped (e.g. parsley, tomatoes)

Confit Cooked meat, poultry or game preserved in good fat or oil

Consommé A simple, clear soup

Contamination The occurrence of any objectionable matter in food

Contrefilet Boned-out sirloin of beef

Cook out The process of cooking flour in a roux, soup or sauce

Cordon A thread or thin line of sauce

Correcting Adjusting the seasoning, consistency and colour

Côte A rib or chop

Côtelette A cutlet

Coulis Sauce made of fruit or vegetable puree (e.g. raspberry, tomato)

Coupe An individual serving bowl

Couper To cut

Court bouillon A well-flavoured cooking liquor for fish

Crème fraiche Whipping cream and buttermilk heated to 24–29 °C

Crêpes Pancakes

Credit note Issued when an invoice contains incorrect details; credit is therefore given

Croquettes Cooked foods moulded into a cylinder shape, coated in flour and egg, crumbed and deep-fried

Cross-contamination The transfer of micro-organisms from contaminated to uncontaminated hands, utensils or equipment

Croutons Cubes of fried or toasted bread served with soup; also triangular pieces served with spinach, and heart-shaped pieces with certain dishes

Crudités Small, neat pieces of raw vegetables served with a dip as an appetiser

Cuisse de poulet Chicken leg

Danger zone of bacterial growth The temperature range within which pathogenic bacteria are able to multiply; between 10 and 63 °C

Dariole A small mould, as used for crème caramel

Darne A slice of round fish (e.g. salmon) on the bone

Déglacer (to deglaze) To swill out a pan in which food has been roasted or fried, with wine, stock or water, in order to use the sediment for the accompanying sauce or gravy

Dégraisser To skim fat off liquid

Delivery note A form sent by a supplier with the delivery of goods

Demi-glace A brown stock reduced to a light consistency

Désosser To bone out meat

Detergent A substance that dissolves grease

Dilute To mix a powder (e.g. cornflour) with a liquid

Disinfectant A substance that reduces the risk of infection

Doily A fancy dish paper

Drain To place food in a colander, allowing liquid to seep out

Duxelle Finely chopped mushrooms cooked with chopped shallots

Eggwash Beaten egg with a little milk or water

Emulsion A mixture of liquid (e.g. vinegar) and oil, which does not separate when left to stand (e.g. mayonnaise, hollandaise)

Entrecôte A steak cut from a boned sirloin

Enzymes Chemical substances produced from living cells

Escalope A thin slice such as escalope of veal

Farce Stuffing

Fecule Fine potato flour

Feuilletage Puff pastry

Fines herbes Chopped fresh herbs (e.g. parsley, tarragon, chervil)

First aid materials Suitable and sufficient bandages and dressings, including waterproof dressings and antiseptic; all dressings must be individually wrapped

Flake To break something into natural segments (e.g. fish)

Flan An open tart

Fleurons Small, crescent-shaped pieces of puff pastry

Flute A 20 cm diameter French bread used for soup garnishes

Food-borne Bacteria carried on food

Food handling Any operation in the storage, preparation, production, processing, packaging, transportation, distribution and sale of food

Frappé Chilled (e.g. melon frappé)

Freezer burn Affects frozen items, which are spoiled due to being left unprotected for too long

Friandises Sweetmeats, petits fours

Fricassée   A white stew in which the meat, poultry or fish is cooked in the sauce

Friture   A pan that contains deep fat

Fumé   Smoked (e.g. *saumon fumé* is smoked salmon)

Garam masala   A combination of spices

Garnish   Served as part of the main item; trimmings

Gastroenteritis   Inflammation of the stomach and intestinal tract that normally results in diarrhoea

Gâteau   A cake of more than one portion

Ghee   The Indian name for clarified butter; ghee is pure butter fat

Gibier   Game

Glace   Ice or ice cream from which all milk solids have been removed

Glaze
- To colour a dish under the salamander (e.g. fillets of sole *bonne femme*)
- To finish a flan or tartlet (e.g. with apricot jam)
- To finish certain vegetables (e.g. glazed carrots)

Gluten This is formed from the protein in flour when mixed with water

Gratin   A thin coating of grated cheese and/or breadcrumbs on certain dishes, which is then browned under the grill or in an oven

Haché   Finely chopped or minced

Hazard   Something that could cause injury, ill health or harm

Hors d'oeuvre   Appetising first course dishes, hot or cold

Humidity   The amount of moisture in the air

Incubation period   The time between infection and the first signs of illness

Infestations   Pests breeding on the premises

Insecticide   A chemical used to kill insects

Invoice   A bill listing items delivered, with the costs of the items

Jardinière   Cut into batons

Julienne   Cut into fine strips

Jus-lié   Thickened gravy

Larding   Inserting strips of fat bacon into meat

Lardons   Batons of thick streaky bacon

Liaison   A thickening or binding

Macédoine
- A mixture of fruit or vegetables
- Cut into 0.5 cm dice

Magnetron   A device that generates microwaves in a microwave oven

Marinade   A richly spiced pickling liquid used to give flavour and assist in tenderising meats

Marmite   A stock pot

Mascarpone   An Italian cheese resembling clotted cream

Menu   A list of the dishes available

Micro-organisms   Very small living plants or animals (bacteria, yeasts, moulds)

Mignonette   Coarsely ground pepper

Mildew   A type of fungus, similar to mould

Mineral salts   Mineral elements, small quantities of which are essential for health

Mirepoix   Roughly cut vegetables (e.g. onions, leeks, celery and carrots), often with a sprig of thyme and a bay leaf, used as flavouring elements

Mise-en-place   Basic preparation before serving

Miso   Seasoning made from fermented soybeans

Monosodium glutamate (MSG)   A substance added to food products to increase flavour

Moulds   Microscopic plants (fungi) that may appear as woolly patches on food

Mousse   A dish of light consistency, hot or cold

Napper   To coat or mask with sauce

Natives   A menu term for English oysters

Navarin   Brown stew of lamb

Niacin   Part of Vitamin B; found in liver, kidney, meat extract, bacon

Noisette (nut)   A cut from a boned-out loin of lamb

Nutrients   The components of food required for health: protein, fats, carbohydrates, vitamins, mineral salts, water

Optimum   Best, most favourable

Palatable   Pleasant to taste

Pané   Floured, dipped in egg and crumbed

Panettone   A very light, traditional Italian Christmas cake

Parsley butter   Butter containing lemon juice and chopped parsley

Pass   To put through a sieve or strainer

Pathogen   A disease-producing organism

Paupiette   A stuffed and rolled strip of fish or meat

Paysanne   Cut in even, thin, triangular, round or square pieces

Persillé   Finished with chopped parsley

Pesticide   A chemical used to kill pests

Pests   Unwanted creatures that may enter food premises, e.g. cockroaches, flies, silverfish

Petits fours   Very small pastries, biscuits, sweets, sweetmeats

pH value   A scale indicating the acidity or alkalinity in food

Phosphorus   A mineral element found in fish; required for building bones and teeth

Piquant   Sharply flavoured

Piqué   Studded clove in an onion

Plat du jour   Special dish of the day

Poppadoms   Dried, thin, large, round wafers made from lentil flour, used as an accompaniment to Indian dishes

Printanier   A garnish of spring vegetables

Protein   The nutrient needed for growth and repair

Prove   To allow a yeast dough to rest in a warm place so that it can expand

Pulses   Vegetables grown in pods (peas and beans) and dried; a source of protein and roughage

Quark   A salt-free soft cheese made from semi-skimmed milk

Ragout   A stew, for example *ragout de boeuf* is brown beef stew

Rare   When applied to meat, it means underdone

Réchauffer   To reheat

Reduce   To concentrate a liquid by boiling

Refresh   To make cold under running cold water

Residual insecticide   An insecticide that remains active for a considerable period of time

Riboflavin   Vitamin B2; found in yeast, liver, eggs, cheese

Risk   The likelihood that a hazard will cause injury, ill health or harm

Rissoler   To fry to a golden brown

Rodents   Rats and mice

Roux   A thickening of cooked flour and fat

Sabayon   Egg yolks and a little water or wine, cooked until creamy

Saccharometer   An instrument for measuring the density of sugar

Salamander   A type of grill, heated from above

Salmonella   A food-poisoning bacterium found in meat and poultry

Sanitiser   A chemical agent used for cleaning and disinfecting surfaces and equipment

Sauté

- Toss in fat (e.g. *pommes sautées*)
- Cook quickly in a sauté pan or frying pan
- A brown stew of a specific type (e.g. veal sauté)

Seal   To place meat in a hot oven or pan to colour the surface and retain the juices

Seared   Cooked quickly on both sides in a little hot fat or oil

Seasoned flour   Flour seasoned with salt and pepper

Set

- To seal the outside surface
- To allow to become firm or firmer (e.g. jelly)

Shredded   Cut in fine strips (e.g. lettuce, onion)

Silicone paper   Non-stick paper (e.g. siliconised paper)

Singe   To brown or colour

Smetana   A low-fat product; a cross between soured cream and yoghurt

Sodium   Mineral element in the form of salt (sodium chloride); found in cheese, bacon, fish, meat

Soufflé   A very light dish, sweet or savoury, hot or cold

Soy sauce   Made from soybeans; used extensively in Chinese cookery

Spores   The resistant resting phase of bacteria, protecting them against adverse conditions such as high temperatures

Staphylococcus   A food-poisoning bacterium found in the human nose and throat, and also in septic cuts

Starch   A carbohydrate found in cereals, certain vegetables and farinaceous foods

Sterile   Free from all living organisms

Sterilisation   A process that destroys living organisms

Steriliser   A chemical used to destroy all living organisms

Stock rotation   The sequence of issuing goods, so that the first into store are the first to be issued

Strain   To separate the liquid from the solids by passing through a strainer

Sweat   To cook in fat under a lid without colour

Syneresis   The squeezing out of liquid from an overcooked protein and liquid mixture (e.g. scrambled egg, egg custard)

Table d'hôte   A meal at a fixed price; a set menu

Tahini   A strong-flavoured sesame seed paste

Tartlet   A small, round pastry case

Terrine   An earthenware dish used for cooking and serving pâté; also used as a name for certain products

Thiamine   Vitamin B1; it assists the nervous system; found in yeast, bacon, wholemeal bread

Timbale   A double serving dish

Tofu   Low-fat bean curd made from soybeans

Tourné   Turned, shaped in barrels or large olive shapes

Tranche   A slice

Trichinosis   A disease caused by hair-like worms in the muscles of meat (e.g. pork)

Tronçon   A slice of flat fish on the bone (e.g. turbot)

TVP   Texturised vegetable protein, derived from soybeans

Vegan   A person who does not eat fish, meat, poultry, game, dairy products, honey and eggs, and who does not use any animal products (e.g. leather)

Vegetarian   A person who does not eat meat, poultry or game

Velouté

- A basic sauce
- A soup of velvety or smooth consistency

Viruses   Microscopic pathogens that multiply in the living cells of their host

Vitamins   Chemical substances that assist the regulation of body processes

Vol-au-vent   A large puff pastry case

Wok   A round-bottomed pan used extensively in Chinese cooking

Yeast extract   A mixture of brewer's yeast and salt, high in flavour and protein

Yoghurt   An easily digested fermented milk product

Index of recipes

Index